FRANCIS J. MOLONEY SDB

THE JOHANNINE
SON OF MAN

WIPF & STOCK · Eugene, Oregon

Wipf and Stock Publishers
199 W 8th Ave, Suite 3
Eugene, OR 97401

The Johannine Son of Man
Second Edition
By Moloney, Francis J.
Copyright©1978 by Moloney, Francis J.
ISBN 13: 978-1-55635-583-7
ISBN 10: 1-55635-583-1
Publication date 8/20/2007
Previously published by Libreria Ateneo Salesiano, 1978

The Johannine Son of Man Revisited
previously published in *Theology and Christology in the Fourth Gospel:
Essays by the Members of the SNTS Johannine Writings Seminary,* Peeters, 2005

In
Gratitude
to my
Mother and Father

PREFACE

The following study was presented as a doctoral dissertation at the University of Oxford in the Trinity Term of 1975. It is published here without major alteration. Although I was tempted to remove some of the heavy documentation necessarily present in a dissertation, I have decided to leave it in the hope that the indications found there may be of service to some readers.

The work is simple in both its structure and purpose. Despite the never-ceasing interest in the Son of Man title, there is no work currently available which studies the christology involved in the use of the term in the Fourth Gospel. After an introductory chapter which surveys scholarly opinion, each occurrence of the title "the Son of Man" is studied in some detail. I have sought to discover John's theological point of view by firstly studying the structure and meaning of the context of each of the sayings.[1] Although the structure of the various sections is studied in some detail, I have not made great use of the principles of structuralism. I have deliberately chosen to follow the development of thought in a passage. There is, of course, the danger of subjectivism in such a method, and structuralism attempts to avoid that danger. However, it appears to me that a certain amount of subjectivism is still found in the work of the structuralists.[2] Once the structure and meaning of each particular context has been determined, then the various Son of Man sayings are studied in an attempt to find their theological significance within that context. A concluding chapter attempts to show, from the analysis which has preceded, that the Fourth Evangelist has a specific theological point to make when he uses the title "the Son of Man".

[1] I regard the Fourth Gospel as the result of considerable work in the combination of traditional sources and a more original Johannine contribution, resulting in a document with a unique theological point of view. In all that follows, 'John' and 'Johannine' are used without intention to imply anything about the precise identity of the author(s).

[2] For example, G. Gaeta, *Il dialogo con Nicodemo*, Studi Biblici 26, (Brescia, Paideia, 1974) is an excellent study of the synchronic structure of Jn. 2,23-3,21. However 3,31-36, a section which is so obviously parallel to 3,11-21, is dismissed in two pages as belonging to another context (pp. 20-21), and 2,1-22 is not considered at all. As Gaeta himself insists, we must allow the text to unfold according to its own logic and purpose (see p. 21). My attempt to do this led me to structure the material according to the development of the ideas in a passage.

Many people have been instrumental in the completion of the work which follows.

My chief debt is to Dr. M. D. Hooker, who has directed my research at the University of Oxford with great care. Her questioning of many of my assumptions and too rapid conclusions has been formative in more than the pages which follow. In her readiness to discuss my work and in the regular graduate seminars on christological texts she has, perhaps unwittingly, passed on her concern for "the problem of relating the givenness of the past with the exhilarating experience of the present".³ Gratitude must also be expressed to my teachers at the Salesian Pontifical University and the Pontifical Biblical Institute, Rome, especially to Fr. Ignace de la Potterie, S.J., who introduced me to Johannine studies, and Fr. Prosper Grech, O.S.A., who encouraged me to work in the field of New Testament Christology.

Thanks are due to the members of the Australian Province of the Salesian Society, who have not only financed my activities overseas, but have encouraged all my endeavours over ten long years during which they were prepared to allow one of their members pursue his studies, while they faced the ever increasing demands of their apostolate among the young. My own family has always been a source of great inspiration and encouragement. My gratitude to them all cannot be estimated.

I am also in debt to the Benedictine Sisters of St. Mary's Priory, Fernham, Oxfordshire, where a great deal of this work has been written in most congenial surroundings. In a particular way, I would like to thank Sister Mary Bernard, O.S.B., who has read and criticised every stage of my work. She has also typed the whole of the manuscript and prepared the indices. For her friendship, patience, and devotion to a very tedious task, I am more than grateful.

From all these people, and from many others not mentioned here, I have learnt most about Johannine Christianity: "No man has ever seen God; if we love one another, God abides in us and his love is perfected in us" (I Jn. 4,12).

Francis J. Moloney, S.D.B.

Salesian Pontifical University
Rome, 21st October, 1975

---

³ M. D. Hooker, "In his own Image?", in M. D. Hooker-C. Hickling (eds.), *What about the New Testament? Essays in Honour of Christopher Evans*, (London, SCM Press, 1975) p. 41.

PREFACE TO THE SECOND EDITION

It is a most encouraging experience, after only 18 months, to have to prepare a second edition of this book. After such a brief period of time it seemed hardly necessary to rework the whole of the original text, thus it is reproduced here in a corrected form. There are no additions or changes of position from the first edition. However, in the light of the reviews of the original work and the never-ending flow of literature on the Fourth Gospel, I have added an appendix in which I have attempted to present:

1. *A more extensive analysis of the background to the Johannine use of the title "the Son of Man".*

2. *A suggestion concerning the place and function of this particular christological point of view within the Johannine community.*

3. *A bibliography of the books and articles which have appeared since the original work was published.*

There is little need to add many personal notes to this second preface, as my gratitude is still due to the same people. However, I must thank the many scholars who have given time and effort to the reviewing of my book. A number of people have also communicated privately in a most stimulating and helpful fashion. Of these I am particularly grateful to the Rev. John G. Kelly of Parkes, N.S.W., Australia and Robert O'Brien, O.C.S.O., of Caldey Island, Wales.

Several reviewers have commented on the attractive presentation of the book.[1] This is entirely due to the thoughtfulness and professional skill of my confrere, Bro. Matthew Cavagnero, S.D.B., to whom I am most grateful. If it were possible to have a second dedication, it would have to be made to a "second family", who have always made my periods of exile in Rome much more than an academic exercise. To Egidio, Fausta, Claudio and Roberto Rea and to Tony Tombacco — grazie di cuore!

Francis J. Moloney, S.D.B.

Salesian Pontifical University
Rome, 24th May, 1978.

---

[1] For example, G. Menestrina in *BibOr* 19 (1977) 230; A. Segovia in *Archivo Teológico Granadino* 40 (1977) 274; J. Schlosser, "Chronique d'exégèse du Nouveau Testament", *RSR* 52 (1978) 40.

CONTENTS

ABBREVIATIONS

AGSU	Arbeiten zur Geschichte des Spätjudentums und Urchristentums
AssSeign	Assemblées du Seigneur
ATANT	Abhandlungen zur Theologie des Alten und Neuen Testaments
ATR	Anglican Theological Review
BibOr	Bibbia e Oriente
BibVChr	Bible et Vie Chrétienne
BJRL	The Bulletin of the John Rylands Library
BRes	Biblical Research
BTB	Biblical Theology Bulletin
BuL	Bibel und Leben
BZ	Biblische Zeitschrift
BZNW	Beihefte zur Zeitschrift für die Neutestamentliche Wissenschaft
CahRB	Cahiers Revue Biblique
CanadJT	Canadian Journal of Theology
CBQ	Catholic Biblical Quarterly
CollBrug	Collationes Brugenses
CollGand	Collationes Gandavenses
CuBíb	Cultura Bíblica
DBS	Dictionnaire de la Bible, Supplément
DivThom	Divus Thomas (Fribourg)
DThom	Divus Thomas (Piacenza)
EKK	Evangelisch-Katholisches Kommentar
EsprVie	Esprit et Vie
ET	Expository Times
EThRel	Etudes Théologiques et Religieuses
ETL	Ephemerides Theologicae Lovanienses
EvQu	Evangelical Quarterly
EvTh	Evangelische Theologie
FRLANT	Forschungen zur Religion und Literatur des Alten und Neuen Testaments
Greg	Gregorianum
HeyJ	Heythrop Journal
HTKNT	Herders Theologischer Kommentar zum Neuen Testament
HTR	Harvard Theological Review
HZNT	Handkommentar zum Neuen Testament
IB	The Interpreters' Bible
ICC	The International Critical Commentary
Interp	Interpretation
JBC	Jerome Biblical Commentary
JBL	Journal of Biblical Literature
JR	Journal of Religion
JTS	Journal of Theological Studies
KNT	Kommentar zum Neuen Testament
LumVie	Lumière et Vie
LXX	The Septuagint
MT	Masoretic Text
MüTZ	Münchener Theologische Zeitschrift
NCB	New Clarendon Bible
NEB	New English Bible
NedTTs	Nederlands Theologisch Tijdschrift

NRT	Nouveau Revue Théologique
NT	Novum Testamentum
NTD	Das Neue Testament Deutsch
NTS	New Testament Studies
RB	Revue Biblique
RBíCalz	Rivista Bíblica
RBibIt	Rivista Biblica Italiana
RecSR	Recherches de Science Religieuse
RHPR	Revue d'Histoire et de Philosophie Religieuses
RGG	Die Religion in Geschichte und Gegenwart
RNT	Regensburger Neues Testament
RSPT	Revue des Sciences Philosophiques et Théologiques
RSV	Revised Standard Version
RThom	Revue Thomiste
RThPh	Revue de Théologie et de Philosophie
SBT	Studies in Biblical Theology
ScEccl	Sciences Ecclésiastiques
Schol	Scholastik
ScotJT	Scottish Journal of Theology
Script	Scripture
SNT	Supplements to Novum Testamentum
SNTS	Society for New Testament Studies
StEv	Studia Evangelica
StPat	Studia Patavina
SymbOs	Symbolae Osloenses
TB	Theologische Blätter
TDNT	Theological Dictionary of the New Testament
THNT	Theologischer Handkommentar zum Neuen Testament
TLond	Theology
TLZ	Theologische Literaturzeitung
TR	Theologische Rundschau
TrTZ	Trierer Theologische Zeitschrift
TS	Theological Studies
TüTQ	Tübinger Theologische Quartalschrift
TynBull	Tyndale Bulletin
TZ	Theologische Zeitschrift
VD	Verbum Domini
ZKT	Zeitschrift für Katholische Theologie
ZNW	Zeitschrift für die Neutestamentliche Wissenschaft
ZSyTh	Zeitschrift für Systematische Theologie
ZTK	Zeitschrift für Theologie und Kirche

Abbreviated references to the biblical books are given in the usual way. The following literature is indicated with abbreviated titles:

Intertestamental Literature

Orac. Sibyll.	The Sibylline Oracles
Ps. Sol.	The Psalms of Solomon
Pseudo Jon.	The Pseudo Jonathan Targum
IQS	The Qumran Community Rule
Test. Abraham	The Testament of Abraham
Test. Judah	The Testament of Judah
Test. Levi	The Testament of Levi

Rabbinic Literature

Eccles. R.	Ecclesiasticus Rabbah
Gen. R.	Genesis Rabbah
Exod. R.	Exodus Rabbah
Mek. on Exod.	Mekilta on Exodus

Reference to tractates, e.g. Sanhedrin, Abboth, Sukka, without specification, indicates Mishnaic literature.

Philo

De Sac.	De Sacrificiis Abelis et Caini
Leg. All.	Legum Allegoriae
Mut.	De Mutatione Nominum

CHAPTER ONE

A JOHANNINE SON OF MAN CHRISTOLOGY ?
SURVEY OF OPINIONS

In the light of the never ceasing interest in the Son of Man problem,[1] it seems extraordinary that there has been so little written about the use of the term in the Fourth Gospel. Scholars often make this remark, but it remains true.[2] Perhaps there is no problem involved,[3] yet the Fourth Gospel uses "Son of Man" thirteen times[4] — only once less than Mark. It would appear that this term meant something to the author (or redactor) of the Gospel and that he was under the impression that it would mean something to his readers.

It would be false, however, to give the impression that nothing at all had been written. Several articles, a full length monograph and a survey of opinion from 1957 to 1969 have appeared in recent years.[5] There appears to be a

---

[1] The literature is immense. See I. H. Marshall, "The Synoptic Son of Man Sayings in Recent Discussion", *NTS* 12 (1965-66) 327-351. On the recent flurry of activity which produced four full-scale studies in one year, see Idem, "The Son of Man in Contemporary Debate", *EvQu* 42 (1970) 67-87.

[2] See H. Dieckmann, " 'Der Sohn des Menschen' im Johannesevangelium", *Schol* 2 (1927) 229; S. Schulz, *Untersuchungen zur Menschensohn-Christologie im Johannesevangelium. Zugleich ein Beitrag zur Methodengeschichte der Auslegung des 4. Evangeliums*, (Göttingen, Vandenhoeck und Ruprecht, 1957) pp. 37-38; S.S. Smalley, "The Johannine Son of Man Sayings", *NTS* 15 (1968-69) 278-281; B. Lindars, "The Son of Man in the Johannine Christology", in B. Lindars - S.S. Smalley (eds.), *Christ and Spirit in the New Testament: Studies in Honour of Charles Francis Digby Moule*, (Cambridge, CUP, 1973) p. 43; R. Maddox, "The Function of the Son of Man in the Gospel of John", in R.J. Banks (ed.), *Reconciliation and Hope: New Testament Essays on Atonement and Eschatology Presented to L.L. Morris on his 60th Birthday*, (Exeter, Paternoster Press, 1974) pp. 186-187.

[3] This could be reflected in the fact that three studies which have dealt with the subject were never published: P.D. Early, *The Conception of the Son of Man in the Fourth Gospel*, (Unpublished Dissertation, Southern Baptist Seminary, 1952); G. Iber, *Ueberlieferungsgeschichtliche Untersuchungen zum Begriff des Menschensohnes im Neuen Testament*, (Unpublished Dissertation, Heidelberg, 1953); J. Maldonado, *De Exaltatione Filii Hominis apud S. Joannem*, (Unpublished Dissertation, Studium Biblicum Franciscanum, Jerusalem, 1964).

[4] John 1,51; 3,13.14; 5,27; 6,27.53.62; 8,28; 9,35; 12,23.34 (twice); 13,31.

[5] As well as the literature mentioned in note 2, the following are concerned with the Johannine Son of Man: F.H. Borsch, *The Son of Man in Myth and History*, (London,

growing interest in the question.[6] As well as these studies which are directly concerned with the problem, it is often referred to passingly, but at times significantly, in studies of Johannine christology and eschatology. Many commentators on the Gospel also devote some space to a brief discussion of the term.

A study of all this, however, reveals that there is very little unanimity among scholars. W. Bousset has affirmed that the term in the Fourth Gospel is the "comprehensive designation of the preexistent and eternal glory of Jesus which surpasses everything earthly, in comparison with which the earthly sojourn of Jesus is only an episode",[7] while C. J. Wright thinks that it is not a theological title at all. For him it is used to express the real, though exceptional, humanity of Jesus.[8] Oscar Cullmann and A. J. B. Higgins understand the Son of Man christology in John as his fundamental and principal way of presenting

---

SCM Press, 1967) pp. 257-313; F.-M. Braun, "Messie, Logos et Fils de l'Homme", in E. Massaux (ed.), *La Venue du Messie. Messianisme et Eschatologie,* Recherches Bibliques VI, (Bruges, Desclée de Brouwer, 1962) pp. 133-147; C. Colpe, Art. ''υἱὸς τοῦ ἀνθρώπου'', *TDNT* VIII, pp. 464-470; H.-M. Dion, "Quelques traits originaux de la conception johannique de Fils de l'Homme", *ScEccl* 19 (1967) 49-65; C. de Beus, "Het gebruik en de betekenis van de uitdrukking 'De Zoon des Mensen' en het Evangelie van Johannes", *NedTTs* 10 (1955-56) 237-251; E. D. Freed, "The Son of Man in the Fourth Gospel", *JBL* 86 (1967) 402-409; A. J. B. Higgins, *Jesus and the Son of Man,* (London, Lutterworth, 1964) pp. 153-184; E. Kinniburgh, "The Johannine Son of Man", *StEv* 4 (1968) 64-71; F. W. Grosheide, ''υἱὸς τοῦ ἀνθρώπου en het Evangelium naar Johannes'', *Theologische Studiën* 35 (1917) 242-248; T. Preiss, "Le Fils de l'homme dans le IVe Évangile", *EThRel* 28 (1953) 7-61; R. Schnackenburg, "Der Menschensohn im Johannesevangelium", *NTS* 11 (1964-65) 123-137. This article is reproduced, with some modifications, as an excursus in his *The Gospel According to St. John,* (London, Herder, 1968) pp. 529-542 (English translation of *Das Johannesevangelium* I. Teil, HTKNT, [Freiburg, Herder, 1965]); E. M. Sidebottom, "The Ascent and Descent of the Son of Man", *ATR* 2 (1957) 115-122; Idem, "The Son of Man as Man in the Fourth Gospel", *ET* 68 (1956-57) 231-235. Both these articles and further consideration of the Johannine Son of Man are found in his book, *The Christ of the Fourth Gospel in the Light of First Century Thought,* (London, SPCK, 1961); Y. B. Tremel, "Le Fils de l'Homme selon Saint Jean", *LumVie* 12 (1963) 65-92. There has even been an article in Chinese: Hsia ch'i - Lung, "Lun Jowang fuyin chung ti 'jentzu' " (The Son of Man in John's Gospel), *Collectanea Theologica Universitatis Fuyen* 10 (1971) 467-502. A fine survey of much of this literature is found in E. Ruckstuhl, "Die Johanneische Menschensohnforschung 1957-1969", in J. Pfammatter-F. Furger (eds.), *Theologische Berichte* I, (Einsiedeln, Benziger, 1972) pp. 171-284.

    [6] Lindars, Smalley, Freed, Borsch, Ruckstuhl and Maddox have all written very recently.
    [7] W. Bousset, *Kyrios Christos. A History of the Belief in Christ from the Beginnings of Christianity to Irenaeus,* (New York, Abingdon, 1970) p. 213 (English translation of *Kyrios Christos: Geschichte des Christusglaubens von den Anfängen des Christentums bis Irenaeus,* FRLANT 4, [Göttingen, Vandenhoeck und Ruprecht, 1926]).
    [8] C. J. Wright, "Jesus the Revelation of God. His Mission and Message according to St. John", in H. D. A. Major - T. W. Manson - C. J. Wright, *The Mission and Message of Jesus. An Exposition of the Gospels in the Light of Modern Research,* (London, Ivor Nicholson and Watson, 1937) p. 683.

Christ,[9] while for E. D. Freed and H.-M. Dion, John has no specific Son of Man christology; the title is used merely to continue what is already involved in John's use of "Son of God" (Freed) and "Logos" (Dion).[10] These and other contrasting affirmations mark nearly all the work which has been done so far. There seems to be no Johannine Son of Man "discussion". Each author appears to proceed to his own conclusion without considering other suggestions, even though most note the work of some of their predecessors.[11]

The most comprehensive work on the Johannine Son of Man sayings is S. Schulz's monograph, *Untersuchungen zur Menschensohn-Christologie im Johannesevangelium*. This work is an important contribution to the study of the various traditional elements which possibly form the Fourth Gospel, but the title is misleading. The book is concerned with the historical and religious origin and development of the Johannine use of the title "the Son of Man". It is not concerned with the meaning of the title within the Johannine theological context. As Schulz himself says: "Die vorliegende Arbeit untersucht Ausprägung und Bedeutung der *Ueberlieferung* vom Menschensohn in der Gedankenwelt des Joh-Ev".[12] Perhaps the major contribution of the work is described by the sub-title: *Zugleich ein Beitrag zur Methodengeschichte der Auslegung des 4. Evangeliums.*

Schulz opens his work with a study of the various methods which have been used in the critical analysis of the Fourth Gospel from the Patristic era to the present. He maintains that most of the methods used are not designed to penetrate the depths of the Johannine material as they are merely recovery methods, or methods of reconstruction, which are but 'prolegomena' to a critical study of the Gospel itself (e.g. textual criticism, style criticism, vocabulary statistics, re-arrangement of the text, rhythm criticism, literary criticism etc.). Schulz is convinced that the only successful methods in a truly critical study of the Fourth Gospel are those which isolate and then examine small units of material, i.e. the so-called *Traditionsgeschichtliche* and *Religionsgeschichtliche Methoden.*[13]

By means of the study of the history of religion, one discovers the

---

[9] O. Cullmann, *The Christology of the New Testament*, (London, SCM Press, 1963) p. 187 (English translation of *Die Christologie des Neuen Testaments*, [Tübingen, J. C. B. Mohr, 1957]); A. J. B. Higgins, *Son of Man*, p. 155. See also T. Preiss, *Life in Christ*, SBT first series 13, (London, SCM Press, 1954) p. 24 (English translation of selected chapter from *La Vie en Christ*, [Neuchâtel, Delachaux et Niestlé, 1952]).

[10] E. D. Freed, "The Son of Man ...", p. 403; H.-M. Dion, "Quelques traits originaux ...", p. 64.

[11] See E. Ruckstuhl, "Die johanneische Menschensohnforschung...", p. 277: "Die meisten Gesprächsteilnehmer reden von der Sache und von ihrem Standort her, ohne dass man allzu aufmerksam aufeinander hört".

[12] S. Schulz, *Untersuchungen*, p. 37. Stress mine.

[13] S. Schulz, *ibid.*, p. 85.

multiplicity of religious and cultural influences behind a text, while through the study of the traditions one can come to identify the multiplicity and relative independence and brevity of various traditional segments. Is there any relation between the two methods? Is the smallness of the unit (*Traditionsgeschichte*) due in any way to the influence of the historical-cultural origins of that unit (*Religionsgeschichte*)? He answers this question positively. By a combination of these two methods, and with certain other methods playing contributive roles, Schulz believes that he will be able to identify the *Grundthemen* of the Fourth Gospel as isolable units of tradition and depositories of a multiplicity of identifiable elements from the history of religions. He is of the opinion that this new method, which he calls *Themageschichte*, could well be the form-criticism of the Fourth Gospel. As Dibelius affirmed that in the beginning of the Synoptic gospels there was the preaching,[14] Schulz holds that in the beginning of the Fourth Gospel there were the traditions in their multiplicity. This is a sharp departure from the widely accepted Bultmannian source theory.[15]

Having established his new method, Schulz turns to an examination of four "themes" to put it into practice.[16] He studies Son of Man passages (1,51; 3,13-15; 5,27-29; 6,27.53; 6,62; 12,23; 12,34; 13,31-32), Son passages (3,35-36; 5,19-23; 5,25-26; 3,16), Paraclete passages (14,14-17; 14,25-26; 15,26; 16,4b-11; 16,12-15) and Second Coming passages (14,1-3; 14,18-23; 14,27-28; 16,16.20-23a) asking the following questions:[17]

a) Do they rest on a tradition?

b) Can they be gathered around a single theme?

c) Is the original *Mutterboden* traditional late Jewish apocalyptic?

d) In which cultural-religious streams have they been re-interpreted and refashioned?

After a detailed study of these passages he concludes that the four "themes" all spring from the late Jewish apocalyptic Son of Man, especially as the figure is presented in the Book of Enoch. His overall conclusions are:[18]

---

[14] See M. Dibelius, *Die Formgeschichte des Evangeliums*, (Tübingen, J. C. B. Mohr, 1971⁶) pp. 8-34.

[15] For Bultmann, the title comes from Gnostic "Man" speculations. See R. Bultmann, "Die Bedeutung der neuerschlossenen mandäischen und manichäischen Quellen für das Verständnis des Johannesevangeliums", *ZNW* 24 (1925) 138-139. For a telling criticism of Schulz's work, from a Bultmannian point of view, see J. M. Robinson, "Recent Research in the Fourth Gospel", *JBL* 78 (1959) 247-252.

[16] S. Schulz, *op. cit.*, pp. 97-172.

[17] *ibid.*, pp. 97-98.

[18] *ibid.*, pp. 173-176.

a) Son of Man, Son, Paraclete and Second Coming themes are all traditional units in the Fourth Gospel.

b) They have their origin in the late Jewish presentation of the apocalyptic Son of Man.

c) They have all been re-interpreted in various circles before the Evangelist took them over. The main influences have been Hellenistic Gnosticism (mainly in the "Son" and "Second Coming" themes), Judaism and especially Jewish Christianity.

d) Christologically they are to be understood in the light of their origin — the late Jewish apocalyptic Son of Man.

After his analysis of the Son of Man sayings, Schulz concludes that they developed in the following fashion:[19]

a) The earliest sayings were 1,51; 3,13-15; 5,27-29; 6,27.53; 13,31-32. These sayings are directly dependent upon the apocalyptic Son of Man traditions.

b) Formed from these sayings, and linked by the use of "ascending and descending" or "lifting up and glorification" were 6,62; 8,28 and 12,23.34. These sayings are called "splinters" of the earlier Son of Man tradition (*Traditionssplitter*).

Not only does Schulz attempt to discover the history of the sayings, but he further classifies some of them according to their literary types:

a) Midrash: 1,51; 3,13-15; 5,27-29.

b) Homily: 6,27.53 [20]

c) Hymn: 13,31-32 [20]

Even if Schulz is correct in his isolation of various units of tradition, and in his tracing them back to their *religionsgeschichtliche Mutterboden*, he has not considered what *John* means when he uses the term. We do, however, question the validity of a great deal of his analysis.[21] His basic source for late Jewish apocalyptic Son of Man traditions is the Book of Enoch. He assumes that the Son of Man sections of this work were formative influences in the development of the Johannine tradition. There are serious doubts about this, voiced as early as 1953 by C. H. Dodd,[22] and more recently by Leivestad, Milik

---

[19] *ibid.*, pp. 122-123.
[20] He appears to be pushing his case a little too far when he attempts to classify into literary types such a limited quantity of material. See F. H. Borsch, *Son of Man*, p. 261, note 1; R. Schnackenburg, "Der Menschensohn im Johannesevangelium", pp. 123-124.
[21] For further critical remarks, see E. Ruckstuhl, "Die johanneische Menschensohnforschung ...", pp. 191-193.
[22] C. H. Dodd, *The Interpretation of the Fourth Gospel*, (Cambridge, CUP, 1953) pp. 241-242.

and others.[23] Schulz does not even refer to this problem.[24] Among the various
religious and cultural influences which he sees as formative in the Johannine
tradition, there is no space allowed for a possible re-interpretation of the Jewish
Son of Man by Jesus himself. The possibility of Jesus' using the term, and
thus influencing later Christian tradition, should have been considered.

One is left with the feeling that all this is too neat. Schulz moves through
a series of complex progressive and related stages, about which little or nothing
is known with any certainty. "Altogether it is so long a step from the Son
of Man with whom he begins to his view of the Fourth Gospel's versions of
this tradition that one must wonder if there are not more credible starting-
points".[25] The continued strict limitation of this term to words of Jesus,
even in the Fourth Gospel (12,34 is no exception), remains as the most press-
ing indication that the whole Son of Man question, both in the Synoptics and
in St. John, is in some way linked with the historical Jesus.[26]

These are serious difficulties, but our main objection lies in another
direction. In his concentration upon smaller units of tradition and their
development in Johannine circles, Schulz has not concerned himself with the
significance of the title for Johannine christology as a whole. The study of
the history of traditions is important, but we are more concerned here with
the theological point of view which unified the traditions. As J. Blank has
written:

> "Denn der Text selbst hat darüber hinaus noch etwas zu sagen, was in den
> 'Traditionen' noch nicht enthalten ist ... Die eigentliche Textauslegung beginnt
> doch erst, wenn die traditionsgeschichtlichen Bausteine beisammen sind".[27]

Schulz has not dealt with the fundamental problem of John's overall use of
the Son of Man title in contexts which seem, in most instances, to be a
long way from the original late Jewish apocalyptic birthplace which he gives

[23] R. Leivestad, "Der apokalyptische Menschensohn ein theologisches Phantom", in
Annual of the Swedish Theological Institute VI (1960) 49-105; Idem, "Exit the Apocalyptic
Son of Man", NTS 18 (1971-72) 234-267; J. T. Milik, "Problèmes de la littérature hénochique
à la lumière des fragments araméens de Qumran", HTR 64 (1971) 338-378; Idem, "Turfan
et Qumran: livre des géants juif et manichéen", in G. Jeremias-H. W. Kuhn-H. Stegemann
(eds.), *Tradition und Glaube. Das frühe Christentum in seiner Umwelt: Festgabe für Karl
Georg Kuhn zum 65. Geburtstag,* (Göttingen, Vandenhoeck und Ruprecht, 1971) pp. 117-
127; J. C. Hindley, "Towards a Date for the Similitudes of Enoch", NTS 14 (1967-68)
551-565.
[24] This is common to much German work. See, for example, H. E. Tödt, *The Son
of Man in the Synoptic Tradition*, (London, SCM Press, 1965) pp. 22-31 (English translation of *Der Menschensohn in der synoptischen Ueberlieferung,* [Gütersloh, Gerd Mohn,
1963]).
[25] F. H. Borsch, *Son of Man,* p. 261.
[26] See E. Ruckstuhl, "Die johanneische Menschensohnforschung..." p. 192.
[27] J. Blank, *Krisis. Untersuchungen zur johanneischen Christologie und Eschatologie,*
(Freiburg, Lambertus, 1964) p. 26.

them. He has shown us the historical and cultural influences which, in his opinion, produced the Johannine Son of Man sayings, but we are concerned with another problem — why John has used the term "the Son of Man" in a way which is peculiarly his.[28]

O. Cullmann claims that the term is a key to the Gospel of John. The Evangelist is reflecting and deliberately choosing his christological titles,[29] and his use of "the Son of Man" is more important than his limited use of "Logos". These two titles are used side by side to say the same thing. For Cullmann, the σάρξ of 1,14 should have been ἄνθρωπος but σάρξ had to be used, as the Word was already the pre-existent divine man (1,1).[30] John 1,14-18 is, then, a direct reference to the Son of Man.[31] It is close to Paul's presentation of Jesus as the "image of God" (II Cor. 4,4; Col. 1,15). Thus, John's Son of Man christology presents Jesus as the pre-existent divine man, and because "Jesus Christ is the image of God we are now able to know God himself".[32]

Despite Cullmann's claims for the importance of the Son of Man in the Fourth Gospel he has, in effect, denied any specifically Johannine Son of Man christology; there may be Logos and Son of God christologies, but the Son of Man appears to be used merely to say the same thing about Jesus: pre-existence, union with God and the revelation of God. John has developed to the stage where "the Son of Man is the Logos".[33]

Several scholars explicitly reject the possibility of a Johannine Son of Man christology. By this stage of the tradition it has been completely assimilated by the higher concepts of "Son (of God)" and "Logos". E. D. Freed,[34] basing himself on the premise that John's literary style is characterized by an ambiguous use of titles, claims that "the title Son of man is only a variation for at least two other titles, the Son of God and the Son".[35] There

---

[28] See the further remarks in this vein in J. Blank, *Krisis,* p. 27; G. B. Caird, "The Development of the Doctrine of Christ in the New Testament", in N. Pittenger (ed.), *Christ for Us Today.* Papers read at the Conference of Modern Churchmen, Somerville College, Oxford, July 1967, (London, SCM Press, 1968) pp. 69-70.

[29] O. Cullmann, *The Christology of the New Testament,* pp. 184-185.

[30] *ibid.,* p. 187.

[31] This is also tentatively suggested by C. Colpe, *TDNT* VIII, p. 470. Colpe's treatment of the Johannine Son of Man leads him to conclude that the Logos' becoming flesh and the Son of Man's descent both mean the same thing. This is true, but the Son of Man descended for a purpose, and this is explained by further sayings which are not applicable to the pre-existent Logos.

[32] O. Cullmann, *op. cit.,* p. 187.

[33] R. Otto, *The Kingdom of God and the Son of Man,* (London, Lutterworth, 1938) p. 298.

[34] E. D. Freed, "The Son of Man in the Fourth Gospel", pp. 402-409. See also J. Coutts, "The Messianic Secret in St. John's Gospel", *StEv* 3 (1964) 51-53. He claims that the Son of Man is "absorbed" by the Son of God title. See on this E. Ruckstuhl, "Die johanneische Menschensohnforschung ...", pp. 256-259.

[35] E. D. Freed, *art. cit.,* p. 403.

is no Son of Man christology, as the term is used as one variation among several of the names given for "Jesus".[36]

H.-M. Dion sees the Logos christology as the model for John's use of "the Son of Man".[37] The basic texts for Dion are 6,62 and 3,13. They have their roots in a Jewish-Wisdom "Word" theology.[38] The title "the Son of Man" adds the nuance of mission to the more ontological concept of the Logos. The stress in the Son of Man texts is on his ascent and descent — what Jesus does, rather than what he is. Nevertheless this mission ultimately depends upon his being the pre-existent Logos.[39] A similar line of thought is developed by A. Vergote[40] who claims that, despite Synoptic parallels,[41] the Johannine Son of Man christology is linked with John's dualistic world picture. The title is used to present Jesus as the descent of the divine into the world and his subsequent ascent to his place of origin.[42]

F.-M. Braun has argued that the messianic hope of Israel shifted from a prophetic hope in a royal line to a more speculative concept of eternal Wisdom, revealing the truth of God.[43] In the Fourth Gospel this was realised when the Logos became flesh to reveal the glory of the Father (see 1,14).[44] Although the term "Logos" is found only in the prologue, the same truth is proclaimed throughout the Gospel, especially in the use of the title "the Son of Man". John has taken it from Dan. 7 and I Enoch 48-49, as well as from Christian tradition. However, he has modified it for his own purposes, giving it themes which were current in Wisdom speculation and in Jewish apocalyptic.[45] John's use of "the Son of Man" was previous to his use of "Logos", which he devised at a later stage, "condensant en termes précis la pensée de l'apôtre".[46]

Along with Cullmann, Colpe, Dion and Vergote, Braun has highlighted the fact that in "the Son of Man" God has been revealed, as he is the Logos who has become flesh. There may well be a close link with the Wisdom traditions in this, but there are Son of Man sayings which indicate that John wants to say more than this in his use of the title. Braun has not mentioned

---

[36] *ibid.*, p. 409.

[37] H.-M. Dion, "Quelques traits originaux...", pp. 49-65.

[38] *ibid.*, p. 64.

[39] *ibid.*, pp. 64-65.

[40] A. Vergote, "L'exaltation du Christ en Croix selon le quatrième évangile", *ETL* 28 (1952) 5-23.

[41] *ibid.*, p. 8.

[42] *ibid.*, pp. 9-10.

[43] F.-M. Braun, "Messie, Logos et Fils de l'Homme", pp. 133-138.

[44] *ibid.*, pp. 139-141.

[45] *ibid.*, pp. 144-145. See also Idem, *Jean le théologien et les grandes traditions d'Israël et l'accord des Écritures d'après le quatrième Évangile*, (Paris, Gabalda, 1964) pp. 146-150; *Jean le théologien. Sa Théologie I: Le Mystère du Christ*, (Paris, Gabalda, 1966) pp. 60-61.

[46] F.-M. Braun, *art. cit.*, p. 145.

the crucifixion—elevation theme of 3,13-14; 8,28 and 12,34. Nor has he mentioned the judgment which the Son of Man is said to exercise in 5,27. These scholars who show that "the Son of Man" repeats throughout the Gospel what is said of "the Logos" in the prologue do not give the Johannine use of "the Son of Man" its full importance. It is true that "the Son of Man" continues, in the rest of the Gospel, what has been said of "the Logos" in the prologue, but the Johannine Son of Man presupposes and builds upon the key ideas of pre-existence and revelation. It does not merely repeat these ideas.

W. Bousset claims that Hellenistic thought has thoroughly divinised the Son of Man in John,[47] and C. de Beus has arrived at a similar conclusion along a different way. He first published an article in which he argued that the Synoptic Son of Man was primarily an eschatological figure.[48] In a subsequent article he shows how the Johannine Son of Man is a continuation of this eschatological theme which has been radically changed by the identification of Jesus, the Son of Man, with the Son of God.[49] In the Fourth Gospel, Jesus' being the Christ and the Son of God (see 20,31) is also what John means when he calls him "the Son of Man".[50]

Although J. Jeremias doubts that the Gnostic Son of Man had any influence on the Johannine Son of Man, he allows only 1,51 as a genuine Son of Man saying. The rest of the sayings are to be regarded as a Johannine elaboration in which there is no specific theological point being made. The only authentic saying continues what Jeremias has found in the Synoptic Gospels, that the oldest sayings refer to a future appearance of the Son of Man.[51]

It would appear from all this work that there is no specific Son of Man christology in the Fourth Gospel. The figure of Jesus has been so divinised by this stage of the tradition that he can only be understood as the pre-existent Logos and the Son (of God). Although present, the title "the Son of Man" has been absorbed by the highly developed understanding of Jesus as a presence of the divine among men.[52]

C. H. Dodd, however, sees in this a specific Son of Man christology.[53] John has taken the title from the Synoptic tradition, but he has entirely re-

---

[47] W. Bousset, *Kyrios Christos*, pp. 52-53. 211-213.

[48] C. de Beus, "Achtergrond de inhoud van de uitdrukking 'de Zoon des Mensen' in de synoptische evangeliën", *NedTTs* 9 (1954-55) 272-295.

[49] Idem, "Het gebruik en de betekenis van de uitdrukking 'de Zoon des Mensen' en het Evangelie van Johannes", *NedTTs* 10 (1955-56) 237-251.

[50] *ibid.*, pp. 250-251.

[51] J. Jeremias, "Die älteste Schicht der Menschensohnlogien", *ZNW* 58 (1967) 163-164. 170-171.

[52] See also G. P. Wetter, *"Der Sohn Gottes": eine Untersuchung über den Charakter und die Tendenz des Johannes-Evangeliums*, (Göttingen, Vandenhoeck und Ruprecht, 1916) p. 12. Wetter claims that all the titles have been levelled into a 'theios aner' christology.

[53] C. H. Dodd, *Interpretation*, pp. 241-249.

fashioned it. The term can be found "in a common and characteristic form" in the Hermetic literature, Hellenistic Judaism (Philo) and early Christian Gnosticism. This was an area of religious thought which was strongly under the influence of Platonism and speculative Judaism. Dodd therefore concludes that the idea is of an archetypal being, who is at the same time true humanity which is immanent in all individuals of the human species, because they, in turn, are offspring of God and are destined to be reunited with him.[54] The concept has been filtered through the Jewish Servant figure, who confusedly is both individual and corporate. The Johannine Son of Man embodies collec- tively the people of God, i.e. he embodies in himself redeemed humanity.[55] The startling newness of the Johannine presentation of this corporate ideal man is that it is tied to a historical figure. The Hellenistic "Anthropos" was a metaphysical abstraction. For John there is no doubt that it is a real person — a concrete historical individual of the human race — Jesus of Nazareth, the Son of Joseph.[56]

Most recently, R. G. Hamerton-Kelly has joined Dodd in seeing Alexandrian Judaism as being a factor in the development of the Johannine Son of Man idea.[57] John has taken over the traditional Son of Man christology which, according to Hamerton-Kelly, already contained hints of pre-existence in its use of the Wisdom myth[58] and, having identified Jesus as Wisdom with the Logos of Alexandrian Judaism, he was then able "to make the connection between Jesus, the Logos and the Son of Man, since the Logos was also the true heavenly man".[59]

Even before Dodd, R. H. Lightfoot had suggested that the term was directed to Hellenistic readers who would understand it as an "ideal humanity" which was manifested in the Lord.[60] E. M. Sidebottom understands John as presenting Jesus as a 'real man', but as a very special man who is linked with the image of God, the Servant and the Righteous One. For Sidebottom there is little or no need to search in Hellenistic circles for this 'ideal man'. The figure can already be found within the Jewish tradition, especially in Ezekiel's Son of Man, the Wisdom literature and the Isaian Suffering Servant.[61] Side-

---

[54] *ibid.*, pp. 243-244.
[55] *ibid.*, pp. 244-247. See also E. Schweizer, "Die Kirche als Leib Christi in den paulinischen Homologumena", *TLZ* 86 (1961) 168-169; Idem, "Der Menschensohn", *ZNW* 50 (1959) 204-205.
[56] C. H. Dodd, *op. cit.*, p. 249.
[57] R. G. Hamerton-Kelly, *Pre-Existence, Wisdom and the Son of Man, A Study of the Idea of Pre-Existence in the New Testament*, SNTS Monograph Series 21, (Cambridge, CUP, 1973) pp. 224-242.
[58] See *ibid.*, pp. 87-102.
[59] *ibid.*, p. 242.
[60] R. H. Lightfoot - C. F. Evans (ed.), *St. John's Gospel*, (Oxford, OUP, 1956) p. 104.
[61] E. M. Sidebottom, *The Christ of the Fourth Gospel*, pp. 75-136.

bottom claims every possible Old Testament reference as grist for his mill. He overstates his case, making the Johannine Son of Man the 'real man', the Judge and the Righteous Sufferer of the Old Testament, Wisdom and Jewish apocalyptic.   In his concentration on the 'real man' aspect he has no reference to the Son of Man's descent.   He concentrates on the ascent of the ideal man, but this is to ignore some of the evidence from the New Testament itself. Other English scholars have used the 'ideal man' concept to explain John's use of the title.   They see the origin of this usage in a heavenly man, referred to in Daniel, Enoch and Ezra.   This 'man' is Jesus, who becomes the unique mediator between heaven and earth.[62]

In a recent study devoted to Johannine eschatology, P. Ricca has also suggested that the Son of Man in the Fourth Gospel is the embodiment of 'new humanity'.[63]   He leads the whole community to union with God.   John has taken the title from Jewish apocalyptic and uses it for his special theology of the cross which is at once a theology of revelation, judgment and glory. The elevated Son of Man on the cross is the place where all men can make their final decision for or against God.

All of these studies which find traces of the 'ideal man', both corporate and individual, in the Johannine Son of Man may contain valuable insights concerning the background for the use of the title in John, but in looking to these more speculative sources an important aspect is generally minimised.   It is as the incarnate one that John refers to Jesus as the Son of Man.   The fact that the title appears on the lips of Jesus only during the public ministry also points to an interpretation which is closely linked with Jesus' public manifestation upon earth.   Dodd has pointed out that this is the extraordinary new twist which John has given to the Hellenistic concept, but it could equally be argued that the figure which was promised in Dan. 7 and applied to Jesus in the Synoptic tradition stands behind John's use of the title.

J. H. Bernard has defended a position which sees the Johannine Son of Man as basically in no way different from the Synoptic sayings.[64]   As in the Synoptic Gospels, the term remains an enigma, but to the believer it is the Son of Man who will be the future judge, who is the present deliverer, the founder of the Kingdom through his suffering, and who will give life through his death, in fulfilment of the servant role.[65]

---

[62] See C. K. Barrett, *The Gospel according to St. John,* (London, SPCK, 1954) p. 61 and passim.   Barrett insists on the relation of John's Son of Man with a primal, archetypal man; V. Taylor, *The Names of Jesus,* (London, Macmillan, 1953) p. 30; J. O. F. Murray, *Jesus according to St. John,* (London, Longmans, 1936) pp. 57-59.

[63] P. Ricca, *Die Eschatologie des vierten Evangeliums,* (Zürich, Gotthelf, 1966). pp. 92-105.

[64] J. H. Bernard, *A Critical and Exegetical Commentary on the Gospel of St. John,* ICC, (Edinburgh, T. and T. Clark, 1929).

[65] *ibid.,* pp. cxxxii-cxxxiii.   Bernard is followed, largely, by W. F. Howard, *Christ-*

Some scholars claim that John has used the Synoptic tradition, but has added further elements. M. Black sees the main additions as the "exaltation" and the "glorification" of the Son of Man, which have come to John from Isaian Servant language (see Is. 52,13). If this is the case then, for Black, John has not moved outside the original environment of the Synoptic Son of Man, which is closely linked with the Servant figure.[66] H. Dieckmann, T. Preiss and J. Héring see the main addition as the reference to pre-existence,[67] but they argue that this completes rather than distorts the Synoptic tradition.[68]

For B. Schwank there is no contact between the Synoptic and Johannine Son of Man traditions. Both, however, go back to equally ancient traditions and thus, taken side by side, the Synoptic Gospels and the Fourth Gospel can deepen our knowledge of the very early christological use of the title "the Son of Man".[69]

A recent attempt to connect the Johannine Son of Man tradition with the Synoptics (and even further back) has been made in an article by S. S. Smalley.[70] Dan. 7, I Enoch and IV Esdras are witnesses of a rounded theology of "honour through humiliation" which was possibly contemporaneous with John's traditions. They cannot be seen as formative elements in that tradition — they simply reflect contemporary religious thought. The Son of Man in this theology is not a superhuman figure with supernatural trappings.[71]

Smalley refuses to classify the sayings into groups, as they are, with the exception of 9,35, all consistent in form and meaning. After an analysis of these passages he finds that John:[72]

---

anity According to St. John, (London, Duckworth, 1943) pp. 110-112; J. N. Sanders - B. A. Mastin, *The Gospel According to St. John,* Black's New Testament Commentaries, (London, A. and C. Black, 1968) p. 106; L. Morris, *The Gospel according to John,* New International Commentary, (London, Marshall, Morgan, and Scott, 1971) pp. 172-173; E. K. Lee, *The Religious Thought of St. John,* (London, SPCK, 1962) pp. 138-145.

[66] M. Black, "The 'Son of Man' Passion Sayings in the Gospel Traditions", *ZNW* 60 (1969) 5-7. See also Idem, "The Son of Man Problem in Recent Research and Debate", *BJRL* 45 (1963) 305-318.

[67] H. Dieckmann, " 'Der Sohn des Menschen' im Johannesevangelium", pp. 229-247; T. Preiss, "Le Fils de l'Homme...", pp. 7-61. It should be noticed, however, that in a posthumous article, assembled from notes, Preiss shows a greater awareness of the newness of the Johannine Son of Man christology, resulting from the influence of Wisdom speculation. See T. Preiss, "Étude sur le ch. 6 de l'évangile de Jean", *EThRel* 46 (1971) 143-167; J. Héring, *Le Royaume de Dieu et sa Venue,* (Neuchâtel, Delachaux et Niestlé, 1959) pp. 254-257.

[68] See J. Héring, *op. cit.,* p. 257.

[69] B. Schwank, *Das Johannesevangelium,* Die Welt der Bibel, (Düsseldorf, Patmos, 1966-68) Vol. I, pp. 101-103.

[70] S. S. Smalley, "The Johannine Son of Man Sayings", pp. 278-301.

[71] *ibid.,* pp. 281-285. He is following M. D. Hooker, *The Son of Man in Mark,* (London, SPCK, 1967) pp. 11-74, against H. E. Tödt, *Son of Man,* pp. 22-31.

[72] S. S. Smalley, *art. cit.,* p. 299.

a) uses the imagery of Dan. 7, I Enoch and IV Esdras along with the Old Testament description of Israel as Son and Servant;

b) uses this imagery in a context of judgment, present suffering and future vindication of Israel, through its head — Jesus as the Son of Man;

c) has presented an Adam theology, based on Ps. 8 and Ezekiel, as well as Dan. 7. "Jesus concentrates into himself all that man was originally meant to be in relation to God".[73]

Although not very different from the Synoptic Son of Man, there are two new aspects:

a) Pre-existence (which is also found in I Enoch and IV Esdras).

b) The Synoptic present, suffering and future sayings are often found together in one Johannine phrase.

Despite the basic similarity between the Synoptic and Johannine Son of Man, we have completely different *logia* because John

> "is anxious for his readers to 'see' the real identity of Jesus as Christ and Son of God (20,31); and so it happens that all the Son of man sayings in the Fourth Gospel, including 9,35, have to do directly or indirectly with the question of the identity of Jesus and the 'witness' to him".[74]

Even here John is following a basically Marcan theme. It is John's version of the messianic secret. "The Son of Man" is used as a deliberately ambiguous term to unfold the mystery of Jesus' person, involving the issue of Jesus' authority, which is proclaimed (1,51), questioned (12,34) and vindicated (8,28), just as it was in Mark.[75]

Smalley sees all this as coming from a primitive paradosis. A. J. B. Higgins and H. E. Tödt have attempted to show that there are different strata of tradition involved in Son of Man *logia*. C. F. D. Moule has suggested that they are all different selections out of a single original collection.[76] How far back does this collection go? Smalley suggests that it is also the substratum for Rom. 5 and 8; Phil. 2; Col. 1; I Tim. 3 etc.,[77] and that it is a record of the earliest strata of christological interpretation. He argues that Jn. 3,14; 6,27.53.62; 8,28; 13,31-32 are "authentic".[78] They are Johannine in their form, but modified, not invented.[79]

---

[73] C. F. D. Moule, *The Phenomenon of the New Testament*, SBT Second Series 1, (London, SCM Press, 1967) p. 35.

[74] S. S. Smalley, *art. cit.*, p. 298.

[75] He again depends upon M. D. Hooker, *op. cit.*, pp. 189-198.

[76] C. F. D. Moule, *Phenomenon*, p. 34, note 21.

[77] S. S. Smalley, *art. cit.*, p. 300.

[78] Smalley is very optimistic about the historical value of the Fourth Gospel. See his "New Light on the Fourth Gospel", *TynBull* 17 (1966) 43-62.

[79] S. S. Smalley, "The Johannine ...", p. 301.

F. H. Borsch also traces the Johannine Son of Man back to primitive tradition.[80] He examines all the sayings showing how, in each case, they appear to have come from a very old traditional background which, in turn, is linked with a mythical "Man" figure, who is also King. He suggests that this Man-King was originally enthroned in a Babylonian New Year's feast. Borsch makes this link with his hypothetical background without telling us what all this would mean for Johannine christology. He is content to support the major thesis of his book — the "Kingly Man" as background for the whole of the Son of Man question — without concerning himself with John's particular use of this extraordinarily hypothetical tradition.[81]

Most recently, R. Maddox has argued, against Smalley, that one cannot hope to find a word for word report of Jesus' Son of Man sayings in the Fourth Gospel.[82] However, he is convinced that the Fourth Gospel "will show us how Jesus' teaching about himself as Son of Man looked from John's perspective".[83] Maddox does not concern himself greatly with historical questions, but attempts to see what connotations the term carries, and its link with the Synoptic use of the same term.[84] He subjects each saying to a brief analysis and finds that there is a basic theme throughout: Jesus the Son of Man brings a judgment which will give life to those who believe in him, i.e. those who belong to the Christian community and especially, as shown in chs. 3 and 6, those participating in the community's sacramental life. In all of his analysis, Maddox links the Johannine sayings with Synoptic parallels, and finds that, "in spite of considerable differences of vocabulary and imagery, the fundamental significance of the title 'the Son of Man' in John is not different from that which it has in the synoptic gospels".[85]

Barnabas Lindars considers the Fourth Gospel's use of the term as evidence for John's "unerring capacity to pierce through to the inner meaning of the primitive logia".[86] Lindars correctly insists that the use of the title is not accidental. It is used by John "because it provides him with the means to express the relationship of Jesus to God".[87] It appears in the contexts of judgment, the giving of life, the passion and the exaltation. Like the Synoptic Gospels, John received the title from Dan. 7,15-27, where the Son of Man

[80] F. H. Borsch, *The Son of Man in Myth and History*, pp. 257-313.

[81] See E. Ruckstuhl, "Die johanneische Menschensohnforschung..." pp. 251-252.

[82] R. Maddox, "The Function of the Son of Man in the Gospel of John", pp. 186-204. For his criticism of Smalley, see pp. 187-188 and p. 188, note 1. See also E. Ruckstuhl, "Die johanneische Menschensohnforschung..." pp. 272-273.

[83] R. Maddox, *art. cit.*, p. 189.

[84] See *ibid.*, pp. 286-290.

[85] *ibid.*, p. 203.

[86] B. Lindars, "The Son of Man in the Johannine Christology", pp. 43-60. For the quotation, p. 60.

[87] *ibid.*, p. 44.

is given royal power and honour, but there is also evidence that he was influenced by the exegesis of the early Church in his use of ὑψοῦν, which comes from Is. 52,13. Lindars refuses to see any contact with Gnosticism, Jewish Primal Man or Pauline Adam speculation. John has taken over and continued to develop the figure of "the Son of Man" already found in the Gospel tradition.

After this sound introduction to his study, Lindars' survey of the sayings suffers because of his "two edition" theory of the Gospel's formation.[88] He maintains that the title belongs to the first edition and this means that the threefold use of the title in John 6 is almost ignored; but it is more important to trace the Son of Man christology in the Gospel as we have it, rather than in a hypothetically reconstructed original Gospel. Lindars claims: "The christological argument of that chapter, and the special use of the Son-of-Man figure within it, interfere with the main argument of the rest of the book".[89] For Lindars, John's Son of Man christology is his way of presenting the relationship that existed between Jesus and God. What Lindars claims is true, but it is not enough, for out of the relationship flows the possibility that Jesus can reveal God with a unique authority, and thus the further possibility of life or death for those who accept or refuse the revelation of the Son of Man. This further aspect seems to be demanded by such sayings as 3,13-15; 6,27. 53 (!); 8,28; 9,35; 12,23.34.

In a monograph devoted to the Old Testament background of the Fourth Gospel, G. Reim has considered the Johannine Son of Man in a section of the work which is concerned with those aspects of Johannine christology which have come to John from earlier traditions.[90] The themes of judgment and the coming of the Son of Man are found in Dan. 7,10.13. The judgment by the Son of Man in 5,27-29, however, is foreign to John's overall theology of judgment because it has come to John through what Reim calls a Fourth Synoptic Gospel.[91] The sayings which speak of the coming Son of Man (3,13.14; 6,62; 8,28; 12,23.34; 13,31) use language which is foreign to Dan. 7,13 but which may have been influenced by Isaian Suffering Servant passages. Reim finds two elements which come to John directly from tradition:

a) The judgment theme, taken from the Fourth Synoptic Gospel (5, 27-29).

---

[88] See *ibid.*, pp. 44-45.
[89] *ibid.*, p. 44.
[90] G. Reim, *Studien zum alttestamentlichen Hintergrund des Johannesevangeliums*, SNTS Monograph Series 22 (Cambridge, CUP, 1974) pp. 252-256.
[91] See on this *ibid.*, pp. 206-216. Reim claims that there was a Fourth Synoptic Gospel, of which we have no knowledge, which supplied many of the more primitive elements in the Fourth Gospel, especially those which do not have parallels in the canonical Synoptic Gospels.

b) The ascension of the Son of Man, which probably comes from oral tradition (3,13a).

The rest of the sayings are developed by John: the Son of Man is Jesus who must be lifted up as the Servant was lifted up (see Is. 52,13); the Son of Man who has already been in heaven and who will ascend again (see 3,13-15) comes from Wisd. 9,9-10. To these speculations upon Old Testament themes, John adds the idea of the manna and the Eucharist (Jn. 6,27.53).

Both of the elements which Reim claims have come to John from tradition are based on speculation. We know nothing of a Fourth Synoptic Gospel, nor of an ascending Son of Man. The main purpose of Reim's work is to establish the traditional background for the use of the title and to see how John has reworked this tradition in order to support his theory of a signs source and a more reflective Jesus tradition which was influenced by the Wisdom books and the deuterocanonical literature.[92] He has not gone further than this, and he gives no indication that there is any aspect of Christ's person or mission involved in John's use of the title.

The most satisfactory recent study of the Johannine Son of Man comes from Rudolf Schnackenburg.[93] His work is an answer to three questions which he poses himself at the start of his investigation:

a) Is this term from tradition or from elsewhere?

b) Does John contain traditional elements, adding new ideas to form a new theological insight?

c) Is the Gnostic redeemer myth involved here?

He is opposed to any attempt to classify the sayings according to the Synoptic pattern, maintaining that all the sayings can be grouped around a single theme.[94] They are all united by the exaltation and glorification, which is also the "hour" of the ascension. The bread of life sayings presuppose ascent and descent, while 9,35 and 12,34b are questions about the Messiah who, for John, is the Son of Man. However, the questioners will only know this after the exaltation of Jesus.[95] Although the sayings may have had a variety of origins, the concept of "the Son of Man" is a unity.[96]

---

[92] See *ibid.*, p. 252: "Vor uns steht die Aufgabe, zu untersuchen, inwieweit der Evangelist den Titel ausserhalb des ihm in der Tradition vorliegenden Materials benutzt hat und warum". See also pp. 206-216. 233-261. See the review of R. E. Brown in *TS* 35 (1974) 558-561.

[93] R. Schnackenburg, "Der Menschensohn im Johannesevangelium", pp. 123-137. See also his *St. John* I, pp. 529-542. Reference will be made to this more recent excursus.

[94] R. Schnackenburg, *St. John*, I, p. 530.

[95] *ibid.*, p. 531.

[96] *ibid.*, p. 532.

Schnackenburg sees a close link between John and the Synoptics. There is no humiliation for John's Son of Man, but this happens because the cross is also the place of exaltation. The elevation and glorification of the Son of Man originate in the Synoptic passion predictions and Phil. 2,6-11. The language is also influenced by the Servant passage, Is. 52,13. John has his traditions through the Synoptics, but each tradition has gone its separate way.[97] "The fourth evangelist is aware of the traditional view, but his profounder theological contemplation has modified it for the benefit of his Christology".[98] Schnackenburg argues that the traditional Son of Man has been taken over and freely developed in the Johannine christology. There is an identification of the titles "Son" and "Son of Man" (see 17,4.5.24; 20,17) which would have been impossible in the Synoptic tradition. It appears to us that here Schnackenburg has failed to appreciate the difference between the Johannine use of "the Son (of God)" and "the Son of Man". The parallels between them should not be too closely drawn. While "the Son (of God)" is predicated of Jesus for all stages of his activity (see 17,1-5), "the Son of Man" refers only to the incarnate Logos. It refers to Jesus as a man. Even his being "lifted up" on the cross is only possible because of his human state.

Schnackenburg also considers the possibility of a Gnostic origin for the term in Johannine tradition. Depending upon the work of C. Colpe, H.-M. Schenke and G. Iber,[99] he refuses to see any link between John's Son of Man and the Gnostic redeemer myth. He finds that Gnosticism had the concept of a God "Man" at a very early date, but only took over the term "Son of Man" from Christianity, and interpreted it in the light of its own particular theories. There is a much closer parallel to the Johannine Son of Man in Wisdom speculation, where Wisdom is said to appear upon earth (see Bar. 3,37f.) to reveal heavenly things (see Wisd. 9,16f.). There is also the same movement between heaven and earth in order to bring a divine revelation which leads to salvation (see Bar. 3,29).[100]

G. Iber argues that there is a direct link between the traditional use of "the Son of Man" and the Johannine sayings.[101] He finds evidence for this in 1,51 and 5,27 which he regards as taken directly from traditional sayings about the apocalyptic Son of Man.[102] However, the rest of Johannine

---

[97] *ibid.*, pp. 534-537.

[98] *ibid.*, p. 535.

[99] C. Colpe, *Die religionsgeschichtliche Schule. Darstellung und Kritik ihres Bildes von gnostischen Erlösermythus*, FRLANT 78, (Göttingen, Vandenhoeck und Ruprecht, 1961); H.-M. Schenke, *Der Got "Mensch" in der Gnosis*, (Göttingen, Vandenhoeck und Ruprecht, 1962); G. Iber, *Untersuchungen*, pp. 11-17; 156-170.

[100] R. Schnackenburg, *op. cit.*, pp. 541-542.

[101] G. Iber, *Untersuchungen*, pp. 97-185. See esp. pp. 97-98; 147-148.

[102] As is common in German scholarship, I Enoch is accepted without question as a "source" for the Gospels' use of "the Son of Man". See above, pp. 5-6, note 24. Iber's

Son of Man logia have all been influenced by the idea of a Gnostic redeemer who has descended from heaven and who will return (3,13; 6,62), who is "lifted up" to glory (3,14; 8,28; 12,34) and who "will be lifted up" to glory (12,23; 13,31f.). The remaining sayings (6,27.53; 9,35) are products of the same background. Iber is concerned to show, however, that the title itself comes to John from the tradition, as it is not found in the Gnostic sources which may have influenced Johannine thought.[103]

A. J. B. Higgins has devoted a chapter of his study of the Son of Man to the use of the term in the Fourth Gospel.[104] While affirming at the start of the chapter that this is John's fundamental and principal christology, he then proceeds to show that John has no system in his use of the term! It is scattered haphazardly in the first thirteen chapters of the Gospel.[105] After an analysis of the sayings, Higgins concludes that they come from an extensive Son of Man source, probably liturgical, and that the Johannine sayings are but "fragmentary extracts" of that source.[106] Theologically John is bridging the gap in Jesus' own teaching between his reference to his passion and resurrection and his allusions to the Son of Man as the heavenly witness and the eschatological judge.[107]

Higgins' presentation is marred by his conviction that there are no "earthly" Son of Man sayings in John.[108] It could be argued that all the sayings are earthly.[109] In concluding that John's theological contribution to the understanding of the Son of Man is bridging the gap by having Jesus himself point to his exaltation as the Son of Man, Higgins seems to have forgotten that he refused to accept any of the Johannine sayings as "earthly". In bridging this gap, do we have to understand a missing step, where there is an earthly Johannine Son of Man? While some of Higgins' analysis of individual sayings is most helpful, his views on the wider issue of the christology of the Son of Man is too conditioned by what he has already decided about the Synoptic Son of Man, and spoilt by serious contradiction.

For E. Kinniburgh, the Johannine Son of Man is the place where God's dealings with men take place.[110] The use of the term always refers to a single event — the death of Christ. John is no longer concerned with the Synoptic

---

thesis, however, defended in 1953, was previous to the work of J. T. Milik and others, who have pointed to the important lack of evidence for the Similitudes at Qumran.

[103] *ibid.*, pp. 11-17; 156-170; 180-185.
[104] A. J. B. Higgins, *Son of Man*, pp. 153-184.
[105] The fact that it is used *only* in the first 13 chapters could be an indication that its use is far from haphazard.
[106] A. J. B. Higgins, *op. cit.*, pp. 181-182.
[107] *ibid.*, pp. 183-184.
[108] *ibid.*, pp. 154-155.
[109] As does F. H. Borsch, *Son of Man*, pp. 261-262.
[110] E. Kinniburgh, "The Johannine Son of Man", pp. 64-71.

future figure, "but now one who has been known, who has spoken to men and given them gifts, and whose glory is to be seen, not in the coming on the clouds of heaven, but in the death of a particular man at a particular time".[111]   Because of this event judgment has come into the world, as the crucified Jesus provokes either belief or disbelief.

J. L. Martyn sees the use of "the Son of Man" as a key to unlock the mystery of the Johannine problem.[112]   For Martyn, the Gospel as we have it is a "two level drama", which he describes in the following fashion:

> "The evangelist expands pieces of *einmalig* tradition into two level dramas, he produces what we may call a dynamic Christological *movement* portrayed in a story about (a) Jesus of Nazareth who (b) in John's own day identifies with flesh-and-blood Christian witnesses and yet claims solemnly to be the Son of God".[113]

Briefly, Martyn sees this christological movement as a first identification of Jesus as the Mosaic Messiah, because of Jesus' signs.   This can only be a first stage in the growth of faith.   The initiate must be led from this preliminary confession of Jesus to a more adequate acceptance of him.   For Martyn, this movement from belief in Jesus as the Mosaic Messiah to something more adequate was precisely what was happening in a Church-Synagogue conflict in the community which produced the Fourth Gospel.   From an affirmation about the Mosaic Messiah, the leaders of the Synagogue (the ἄρχοντες of 12,42; see also 3,1) are led through a midrashic discussion which inevitably ends in a decisive presentation of Jesus as the Son of Man.   This development may be seen in the following scheme:[114]

Jesus as Mosaic Prophet-King	*Midrashic Discussion*	*Jesus as the Son of Man*
3,2	3,4 (see 3,9)	3,13
3,14a		3,14b
6,14	6,30ff.	6,35.38.53; see 6,27
7,31.40	7,52; see 7,42; 8,13	8,12.28
9,17	9,28ff.; 9,34	9,35ff.

This Son of Man figure allows no midrashic discussion.   It calls for a decision. John insists that Jesus makes his presence unmistakably clear, not as a Mosaic Messiah, but as the Son of Man on earth.

---

[111] *ibid.,* p. 70.

[112] J. L. Martyn, *History and Theology in the Fourth Gospel,* (New York, Harper and Row, 1968).   What follows is a summary of his chapter: "To the Presence of the Son of Man" (pp. 120-142).

[113] *ibid.,* p. 121.   See also J. N. Sanders, *St. John,* p. 16.   For criticism of this, see E. Ruckstuhl, "Die johanneische Menschensohnforschung ...", pp. 266-267.

[114] J. L. Martyn, *op. cit.,* pp. 122-125.

Using Dan. 7 and I Enoch, Martyn defines this Son of Man as "not only a figure of heaven, but also a figure of judgment and of the future. His activity will mark the cosmic, catastrophic *krisis* which terminates the earthly course of events".[115]   Judgment is the essential note, and this judgment is already and always present in the Johannine vision of things. "In John's own time and place Jesus somehow makes effective his presence as the Son of Man".[116]   The sayings which link the Son of Man with the moment of "lifting up", glorification and the ascension are all to be understood in the light of 14,12. John's Son of Man will not always be on earth. The works of Jesus will be continued by his followers, and so will the call to decision before the Son of Man continue, precisely *because* he is going to the Father.

Throughout the Gospel of John is Jesus with the Father or on earth? He is both, because of the Paraclete "who creates the two-level drama".[117] Through the Paraclete the apparent variety of the Son of Man sayings can be explained. The Son of Man is the place of *krisis* — it is in the Son of Man that Jesus has his "suit with the world", and the Paraclete continues that suit. The Son of Man who ascends and descends, who is glorified, who judges etc., is to be understood in the light of the "two-level drama" created by the Paraclete.

> "The events to which John bears witness transpire on both the *einmalig* and the contemporary levels of the drama, or they do not transpire at all. In John's view, their transpiring on both levels of the drama is, to a large extent, the good news itself".[118]

This is a fascinating study, and does much to anchor the Johannine message in history, against Gnostic mysticising interpretations. Some of his basic presuppositions, however, remain hypothetical.[119]   It does not seem likely that the *Birkat ham-Minim* of Javneh, under Gamaliel, caused an immediate separation between Church and Synagogue. It was probably a much more gradual process than that supposed by Martyn, who sees the rift already clearly defined in the last decade of the first century. The identification which Martyn makes between the "rulers" and secret believers is little more than guesswork, and we have no proof, outside the reconstruction of Martyn himself, of the midrashic discussion which the Church used to lead the representatives of the Synagogue to accept or refuse Jesus as the Son of Man. It must again be pointed out that the figure of the Son of Man which Martyn reconstructs from

---

[115] *ibid.*, p. 130.
[116] *ibid.*, p. 133.
[117] *ibid.*, p. 140.
[118] *ibid.*, p. 142.
[119] See the review of Martyn's book by N. J. McEleney in *The Seminary Journal* 21 (1968) 38-39 and G. Stemberger, *La symbolique du bien et du mal selon Saint Jean*, (Paris, Le Seuil, 1970) p. 106, note 3.

I Enoch may have meant little to the Johannine Church,[120] although Martyn's case does not stand or fall by this interpretation.

W. A. Meeks has accepted Martyn's theory of the social alienation of John's Church, in a Synagogue-centred Jewish community, but he has another suggestion about the Johannine use of "the Son of Man".[121] The idea of the descending and ascending Son of Man was the product of the sociological situation of the community. They had to 'theologise' their particular situation which had come about because of their belief in Christ. They were living as "not of this world", rejected because of their belief. However, they alone had the key to the problem of union with God, so eagerly sought after by so many. Only the Johannine community could understand this mystery revealed to them by the Son of Man who had descended from heaven and who would ascend again, taking his faithful ones with him (see esp. 3,13-14).

> "In telling the story of the Son of Man who came down from heaven and then re-ascended after choosing a few of his own out of the world, the book defines and vindicates the existence of the community that evidently sees itself as unique, alien from its world, under attack, misunderstood, but living in unity with Christ and through him with God".[122]

This rapid survey of such a variety of opinions is, in many ways, confusing.[123] While there is a risk of doing violence to one or more of the interpretations, it appears that the various positions could be grouped in the following fashion:[124]

a) There is no explicit Son of Man christology, as the Son of Man means the same as the Logos, the Son or the Son of God (Freed, Cullmann, Colpe, Dion, Vergote, Braun, de Beus, Bousset, Jeremias).

b) The Johannine Son of Man is either the Hellenistic (Dodd, Lightfoot, Taylor, Murray, Hamerton-Kelly) or the Jewish (Sidebottom, Barrett, Ricca) ideal or perfect man.

c) John continues and perhaps adds to the Synoptic Son of Man idea (Bernard, Howard, Preiss, Héring, Morris, Sanders, Black, Maddox).

d) Perhaps John's Son of Man is even more traditional than the

---

[120] See above pp. 5-6 and notes 22-23.

[121] W. A. Meeks, "The Man from Heaven in Johannine Sectarianism", *JBL* 91 (1972) 44-72. See esp. pp. 66-72. See also his *The Prophet-King. Moses Traditions and the Johannine Christology*, SNT 14, (Leiden, E. J. Brill, 1967) pp. 292-295. 318-319.

[122] W. A. Meeks, *art. cit.*, pp. 69-70.

[123] There is little wonder that J. E. Davey, *The Jesus of St. John, Historical and Christological Studies in the Fourth Gospel,* (London, Lutterworth, 1958) p. 145 can write: " 'Son of Man' has for John a rather mysterious feel"!

[124] As the grouping here is a generalisation, there would sometimes be sharp differences in detail between scholars who are grouped together.

Synoptic figure. At least they go back to equally ancient roots (Smalley, Borsch, Schwank).

e) John knows the Synoptic tradition, but develops his own concept, within the context of his own christology (Lindars, Reim, Moule, Schnackenburg, Iber, Higgins).

f) The Johannine Son of Man presents a completely new concept (Kinniburgh, Martyn, Meeks).

In the face of this multiplicity of interpretations, it appears that the most satisfactory method to arrive at some sort of synthesis is to study each of the Johannine Son of Man sayings in its own immediate context. Far too often scholars — perhaps under the spell of the debate over the Synoptic Son of Man — delve into the origin and background of John's use of the term. This is a legitimate and necessary course of research, but it pays too little attention to the christology involved in the "putting together" of the various traditions. It would be opportune to examine the sayings as they stand in the overall context of the Gospel itself.[125] There are various tasks in New Testament research. As G. Macrae once put it: "It is one thing to attempt to distinguish the viewpoint of the 'Evangelist' from that of the final redactor; it is another to inquire into the intention of the Gospel as we have it".[126] It is to the latter task that we would like to turn, convinced that J. Blank was correct when he wrote: "Denn der Text selbst hat darüber ... etwas zu sagen, was in den Traditionen noch nicht enthalten ist".[127]

---

[125] This need is stressed by B. Lindars, "The Son of Man in the Johannine Christology", pp. 43-44. See also the important remarks of R. Maddox, "The Function of the Son of Man in the Gospel of John", pp. 186-190.

[126] G. Macrae, "The Fourth Gospel and *Religionsgeschichte*", CBQ 32 (1970) 17.

[127] J. Blank, *Krisis*, p. 26.

CHAPTER TWO

THE PROMISE OF THE SON OF MAN: John 1,51

As this work is concerned with the theological significance of the Son of Man title in the Fourth Gospel, the chapters which follow will devote considerable space to the structure and meaning of the immediate context of the various Son of Man sayings. This has not been done here, as there is universal agreement about the general structure of the first section of the Gospel. The origin and meaning of the various elements which make up the section are hotly disputed, especially as regards 1,1-18,[1] but the general structure of the section imposes itself as follows:

1, 1-18   The prologue
   19-34   Jesus and the Baptist
   35-51   The calling of the first disciples.

Some scholars subdivide further, but all follow this general division.[2] As this is the case, the meaning of the section will only be considered in its relationship to the discussion of 1,51.

[1] For an indication of the complexity of this discussion see E. Malatesta, *St. John's Gospel 1920-1965. A Cumulative and Classified Bibliography of Books and Periodical Literature on the Fourth Gospel*, Analecta Biblica 32 (Rome, Biblical Institute Press, 1967) pp. 69-78; H. Thyen, "Aus der Literatur zum Johannesevangelium", TR 39 (1974) 53-69. 222-252. See also F. Hahn, "Die Jüngerberufung Joh 1,35-51", in J. Gnilka (ed.), *Neues Testament und Kirche: Für Rudolf Schnackenburg*, (Freiburg, Herder, 1974) pp. 172-185.
[2] See the agreement between such different scholars as: R. Schnackenburg, *St. John*, I, pp. 221-332; R. E. Brown, *The Gospel according to John I-XII*, Anchor Bible 29, (New York, Doubleday, 1966) pp. cxxxviii-cxli; C. K. Barrett, *St. John*, pp. 125-156; A. Loisy, *Le quatrième Évangile*, (Paris, Emile Nourry, 1921) pp. 87-138; M.-J. Lagrange, *Évangile selon Saint Jean*, (Paris, Gabalda, 1936) pp. 1-53; E. C. Hoskyns, *The Fourth Gospel*, (London, Faber and Faber, 1947) pp. 136-184; H. van den Bussche, *Jean. Commentaire de l'Évangile spirituel*, (Bruges, Desclée de Brouwer, 1967) pp. 53-54; R. H. Lightfoot, *St. John*, pp. 77-105. Lightfoot follows this division, but adds 2,1-11 as a further introductory scene; R. Bultmann, *The Gospel of John. A Commentary*, (Oxford, Blackwells, 1971) pp. 13-108 (English translation of *Das Evangelium des Johannes*, [Göttingen, Vandenhoeck und Ruprecht, 1964] including the supplement of 1966). Bultmann retains these three divisions, although he re-arranges vv. 19-34; C. H. Dodd, *Interpretation*, pp. 292-296; A. Schlatter, *Der Evangelist Johannes. Wie er spricht, denkt und glaubt. Ein Kommentar zum 4. Evangelium*, (Stuttgart, Calwer, 1948) pp. 1-74. Like Lightfoot,

The calling of the first disciples closes with a strange saying: "And he said to him, 'Truly, truly I say to you (plural), you (plural) will see heaven opened and the angels of God ascending and descending upon the Son of Man' " (Jn 1,51).[3] This saying, coming as the last verse of the Johannine story of Jesus' first encounter with his disciples (vv. 35-51), begins a series of Son of Man sayings which continues till the end of Jesus' public ministry (12,23; 13,31). As it is the only title found on the lips of Jesus in the whole of this section of the Gospel — although it comes at the end of a series of christological titles applied to Jesus by others[4] — the verse is of considerable importance in the context of John 1, but scholars have come to little agreement concerning its interpretation.

It is questionable whether or not the saying originally belonged in its present context. It is generally admitted that 1,43-50 is homogeneous,[5] but many scholars see v. 51 as "a detached saying about the Son of Man".[6] There are, in fact, but few dissenting voices.[7] The saying is seen as difficult in its present context for the following reasons:

a) As Jesus has been talking to Nathanael in 1,50, the καὶ λέγει αὐτῷ in 1,51a appears to be an editorial join.

b) Although the saying is addressed to Nathanael alone, λέγω ὑμῖν and ὄψεσθε suggest that it was originally addressed to several persons, or a crowd.

Schlatter adds a fourth scene (2,1-12) in which the disciples are bound closer to Jesus; R. H. Strachan *The Fourth Gospel. Its Significance and Environment,* (London, SCM Press, 1941) pp. 99-121; W. Temple, *Readings in St. John's Gospel,* (London, Macmillan, 1945) pp. 3-32.
[3] All English Biblical quotations taken from the RSV, unless otherwise specified. This saying has been described as the more mysterious conclusion of a very mysterious passage. See F. Agnew, "Vocatio primorum discipulorum in traditione synoptica", *VD* 46 (1948) 138.
[4] See R. Schnackenburg, *St. John* I, pp. 507-514.
[5] But see B. Noack, *Zur johanneischen Tradition. Beiträge zur Kritik und der literarkritischen Analyse des vierten Evangeliums,* (Copenhagen, Rosenkilde, 1954) p. 154, and R. Bultmann, *John,* p. 98, who see vv. 50-51 as a separate unit.
[6] R. E. Brown, *John,* p. 88. See also R. Fortna, *The Gospel of Signs. A Reconstruction of the Narrative Source underlying the Fourth Gospel,* SNTS Monograph Series 11, (Cambridge, CUP, 1970) pp. 179-189; M.-E. Boismard, *Du Baptême à Cana (Jean 1,19-2,11),* (Paris, Cerf, 1956) p. 105; M. Goguel, *Jean-Baptiste,* (Paris, Payot, 1928) p. 189 speaks of 1,51 as "un débris d'une tradition plus complexe"; J. N. Sanders, *St. John,* p. 105; R. Schnackenburg, *St. John,* I, p. 320; S. Schulz, *Untersuchungen,* p. 98; Idem, *Das Evangelium nach Johannes,* NTD 4, (Göttingen, Vandenhoeck und Ruprecht, 1972) pp. 44-45; J. Wellhausen, *Das Evangelium Johannis,* (Berlin, Georg Reimer, 1908) p. 13; F. H. Borsch, *Son of Man,* p. 278; B. Lindars, "The Son of Man...", p. 46.
[7] Apart from the older commentators, who never pose the problem, the unity of the passage is seriously defended by W. Michaelis, "Joh 1,51, Gen 28,12 und das Menschensohn-Problem", *TLZ* 85 (1960) 564-566, and F. Spitta, *Das Johannes-Evangelium als Quelle der Geschichte Jesu,* (Göttingen, Vandenhoeck und Ruprecht, 1910) p. 63.

c) If one interprets the "you shall see greater things than these" of v. 50 as a reference to the Cana miracle (as do Lightfoot and Schlatter), then v. 51 seems to introduce an awkward second unfulfilled promise of "seeing".

d) Some suggest that the saying is related to Matt. 26,64 which, in turn, links it with Matt. 16,27-28 (Mk. 8,38b). These Synoptic sayings indicate Jesus' death, resurrection, ascension and returning in power, and it is suggested that this was the context which gave birth to Jn. 1,51.[8]

e) The open heaven and the ascending-descending movement of the angels have led others to trace the saying to various Synoptic scenes — Jesus' baptism, the transfiguration, the temptation, or one or other of the eschatological predictions of Synoptic Jesus.[9]

While the problems of *a*), *b*) and *c*) must not be ignored, not enough attention is paid to the very Johannine ἀμὴν ἀμὴν λέγω ὑμῖν.[10] A close scrutiny of the Old Testament parallels[11] and the Johannine texts themselves shows that this solemn introduction "never introduces a new saying unrelated to what precedes".[12] B. Lindars identifies a use of sources in which these double "amen" sayings ("sayings from the Jesus tradition"[13]) are used as "the groundwork of the grand Christological formulation".[14] Although 1,51 may have been added to the preceding verses at some stage of the tradition, John has used it in the final redaction as a saying which summarises the whole sequence of the chapter, and makes it relevant for the reader.[15] There

---

[8] R. E. Brown, *John*, p. 89; H. Windisch, "Joh 1,51 und die Auferstehung Jesu", *ZNW* 31 (1932) 199-204; N. A. Dahl, "The Johannine Church and History", in W. Klassen - G. F. Snyder (eds.), *Current Issues in New Testament Interpretation*, (London, SCM Press, 1962) p. 136; R. G. Hamerton-Kelly, *Pre-Existence*, pp. 229-230.

[9] E. Gaugler, "Das Christuszeugnis des Johannesevangeliums", in K. L. Schmidt (ed.), *Christus im Zeugnis der Heiligen Schrift und der Kirche*, Beihefte zur EvTh 2 (München, Kaiser, 1936) p. 45 sees it as originally referring to the parousia; M. Goguel, *Jean-Baptiste*, pp. 189-219 - Jesus' baptism; A. Loisy, *Le quatrième Évangile*, (Paris, Alphonse Picard et Fils, 1903) pp. 262-263 - a combination of material from the baptism and the temptation scenes; A. J. B. Higgins, *Son of Man*, pp. 159-160 - from sayings referring to the future glorification of Jesus; G. H. C. Macgregor, *The Gospel of John*, Moffatt Commentary, (London, Hodder and Stoughton, 1928) - from parousia sayings.

[10] The double "amen" is found *only* in John in the New Testament. It appears 24 times.

[11] Num. 5,22; Neh. 8,6; Pss. 41,14; 72,19. See also 1QS II,10,18; Mek. on Exod. 20,1.

[12] J. H. Bernard, *St. John*, p. 67. See also, K. Berger, *Die Amen Worte Jesu. Eine Untersuchung zum Problem der Legitimation in apokaliptische Rede*, BZNW 39, (Berlin W. de Gruyter, 1970) p. 28; W. Thüsing, *Die Erhöhung und Verherrlichung Jesu im Johannesevangelium*, Neutestamentliche Abhandlungen 21,1, (Münster, Aschendorff, 1970) p. 102. For a summary of recent discussion of the "amen" formulae, see J. Jeremias "Zum nicht-responsorischen Amen", *ZNW* 64 (1973) 122-123.

[13] B. Lindars, *Behind the Fourth Gospel*, Studies in Creative Criticism 3, (London, SPCK, 1971) pp. 44.52.

[14] *ibid.*, p. 52.

[15] *ibid.*, pp. 53-54.

are difficulties in the verse, but the main problem, the change from singular to plural in vv. 50-51 has a parallel in 3,7 where, however, most commentators let it pass. R. E. Brown, for example, writes of 3,7: "The pronoun in 'I told you' is singular; that in 'you must all be begotten' is plural. Nicodemus came speaking as 'we'; so through him Jesus addresses a wider audience".[16] Even though Nathanael did not come speaking as "we", perhaps the Evangelist is also speaking to a wider audience in the promise of 1,51. B. F. Westcott may well have been correct when he wrote of this verse: "The word is for Nathanael, but the blessing is for all believers".[17]

In the light of the typically Johannine "amen, amen I say to you" we may say that 1,51 says something important, which the Evangelist wanted to affirm with a certain amount of solemnity. Sanders has suggested that these "amen" formulae in the Fourth Gospel are "usually in passages of which the form and phraseology often suggest the prophetic activity of the evangelist himself or of his authority".[18] This could well be the case with 1,51, but what is more important here is to interpret what the prophecy is about — what the passage means in its present context in this particular Gospel — rather than trying to discover its original source and form. One could say that John 1,51 may have circulated outside the setting in which we now find it. What its precise setting was at that time can only be the subject of speculation, but in the Johannine tradition it can probably be placed here from the start. At least we can justly call it a Johannine saying, in the light of its introductory formula.[19] It made sense to someone where it now stands, or else it would not be there.[20] If one wishes to understand what the saying means in the Fourth Gospel, then one must interpret it in its present context.

While most scholars see a reference to Gen. 28,12,[21] some see the Old Testament passage as essential to the understanding of the saying, while others prefer to regard it as a casual reference.

H. Odeberg bases his interpretation upon two conclusions which he has drawn from Jewish speculation on Gen. 28,12.[22]

---

[16] R. E. Brown, *John,* p. 131.

[17] B.F. Westcott, *The Gospel According to St. John,* (London, John Murray, 1908) p. 28.

[18] J. N. Sanders, *St. John,* p. 105.

[19] See R. Schnackenburg, *St. John* I, p. 320.

[20] R. E. Brown, *John,* p. 89; B. Lindars, *The Gospel of John,* New Century Bible, (London, Oliphants, 1972) p. 122.

[21] The most serious exception to this is W. Michaelis, "Joh 1,51, Gen 28,12 und das Menschensohn-Problem". He sees the passage as a johannisation of Synoptic material, especially the temptation story, to produce a message of a "dauernden und vollkommen Gemeinschaft mit Gott" (col. 578). See on this, G. Reim, *Studien zum alttestamentlichen Hintergrund,* pp. 102-103.

[22] H. Odeberg, *The Fourth Gospel. Interpreted in Relation to Contemporaneous Religious Currents in Palestine and the Hellenistic-Oriental World,* (Uppsala, Almqvist, 1929) pp. 33-42.

a) From *Gen. R.* 68,12 he concludes that there have always been two interpretations of the *bô* found in the Hebrew text of Gen. 28,12. Upon what — or whom — did the angels descend? In the Rabbinic schools it was sometimes taken to refer to the ladder (a masculine *sullām* in Hebrew). This is reflected in the LXX's ἐπ' αὐτῆς referring to the Greek feminine κλίμαξ. [23] However, it was also interpreted as "upon him", meaning "upon Jacob". [24] For Odeberg, the latter interpretation stands behind John 1,51.

b) In the same midrash (68,12) Is. 49,3 is quoted: "I will be glorified in thee". The divine utterance does not, however, refer to Israel upon earth, as he is asleep and unaware of his real life. Here Odeberg introduces a Platonic-Gnostic type of interpretation. The one to be glorified is the *'êkônîn* of Israel, his "image" in heaven. The image is the true Israel, while the mere reflection of the ideal counterpart lies sleepingly unaware, in the person of Jacob.

In John 1,51, a connection is set up between the earthly man and his celestial counterpart. Others remain engulfed in sleep, but in the Son of Man this union is perfected by the communicating angels.

> "The disciples of Jesus will see the angels of God ascending and descending upon the Son of Man i.e. they will see the connexion being brought about by the celestial appearance, the Glory, δόξα of Christ, and his appearance in the flesh". [25]

Also important for Odeberg is an inclusive interpretation of the Son of Man: the man who believes in the Son of Man is brought into communion with that Son of Man. Seeing the glorification of the Son of Man implies that the "seer" partakes of the spiritual communion with the heavenly world. [26] Odeberg's interpretation means that:

a) There is only one revelation. Only the Son of Man reveals the "true image" of the δόξα.

b) All those who believe in the Son of Man will, in turn, reveal the δόξα and, like him, be one with the Father. [27]

---

[23] This interpretation is accredited to R. Hiyya.

[24] This interpretation is accredited to R. Jannai. See C. F. Burney, *The Aramaic Origin of the Fourth Gospel*, (Oxford, OUP, 1922) pp. 115-116 where he uses this confusion to show that Jn. 1,51 is based on a Semitic original.

[25] H. Odeberg, *op. cit.*, p. 36.

[26] *ibid.*, p. 40.

[27] This interpretation has been widely followed. See R. Bultmann, *John*, p. 105, note 3. Bultmann refuses to accept the inclusive sense of the Son of Man; N. A. Dahl, *art. cit.*, p. 136; R. H. Strachan, *Fourth Gospel*, pp. 10-11; F. H. Borsch, *Son of Man*, pp. 279-280, with reservations; R. G. Hamerton-Kelly, *Pre-Existence*, pp. 225-230. Hamerton-Kelly claims to be cautiously following Dodd, Bultmann and Schulz. He is, in effect, through Bultmann, very close to Odeberg. He has linked Odeberg's earthly man and

Joachim Jeremias has used some late Jewish speculation about the Bethel stone.[28] This stone is:

a) The holy stone which God created before the world, and from which the world spread out;

b) the place of the presence of God and

c) the place over which is found the gateway to heaven.

According·to Jeremias, Jn. 1,51 identifies the Son of Man with this stone, and thus Jesus is saying:

a) Where the Son of Man is — there is God's presence;

b) Where the Son of Man is — there is the gateway to heaven;

c) Where the Son of Man is — there stand the spirits of God in service, bringing down life, the living word of God.[29]

G. Quispel[30] sees Jn. 1,51 as a reflection of the *merkabah* mystique which Judaism developed from speculation on Ezek. 1,4ff.[31] According to this interpretation, Christ is presented as above, and not on the earth. God himself does not appear on the throne, but his *Offenbarungsgestalt*, his *kabod* (see also Is. 6,1 and Ezek. 1,26).[32] To satisfy this exegesis, Quispel understands the καταβαίνοντας as referring to a descent upon Nathanael, and the ἀναβαίνοντας as a movement upwards ἐπί the Son of Man. In this way the verse presents "God-in-Christ", rather than any heaven to earth communication or revelation. In the context of chapter one it is a promise of a future vision of the glorified Christ.[33]

M.-E. Boismard, again using the *Gen. R.* on Gen. 28,12-13, chooses the interpretation of R. Jose ben Simra, who puts himself in the place of Jacob

---

celestial counterpart to the Philonic Logos, as his main thesis is to show that the Johannine Son of Man is a pre-existent figure.

[28] J. Jeremias, "Die Berufung des Nathanael", *Angelos* 3 (1928) 2-5. He uses *Yalqut Gen.* 120; *Pirqe Rabbi Eli'ezer* 32,35 and the *Zohar on Gen.* 28,22.

[29] Jeremias is followed, with reservations, by I. Fritsch, " '... videbitis ... angelos Dei ascendentes et descendentes super Filium hominis' (Jo. 1,51)", *VD* 37 (1959) 1-11; W. D. Davies, *The Gospel and the Land. Early Christianity and Jewish Territorial Doctrine,* (Berkeley-Los Angeles-London, University of California Press, 1974) pp. 296-298; M. Balagué, *Jesucristo Vida y Luz. Estudio de los doce primeros capitulos del Evangelio de S. Juan,* (Madrid, Studium, 1963) pp. 119-120.

[30] G. Quispel, "Nathanael und der Menschensohn (Joh 1,51)", *ZNW* 47 (1956) 281-283.

[31] See G. G. Scholem, *Major Trends in Jewish Mysticism,* (London, Thames and Hudson, 1955) pp. 40-79.

[32] G. Quispel, *art. cit.,* p. 281.

[33] See also O. Michel, "Der Menschensohn", *TZ* 27 (1971) 102 and P. Borgen, "God's Agent in the Fourth Gospel" in J. Neusner (ed.), *Religions in Antiquity: Essays in Memory of Erwin Ramsdell Goodenough,* Studies in the History of Religions 14, (Leiden, E.J. Brill, 1968) pp. 145-146, for a similar use of the *merkabah* mystique.

and yearns for the contemplation of the Sanctuary — the power and the glory of the Lord (see *Gen. R.* 69,1).[34] Boismard then claims that, according to the Targums, Jacob sees this glory upon the ladder. In Jn. 1,51 Nathanael takes the place of Jacob who is "Israel", a term which, in popular etymology, means "seeing God". The idea of "seeing" appears to be very important in vv. 50-51, and thus Nathanael is the "true Israel" in the Johannine sense — the one who truly sees God in Jesus. The object of this "seeing" is the divine glory manifested in the cross and resurrection of Jesus which will, eventually, be seen by all the disciples.[35]

A major problem with any use of Rabbinic sources is dating. We can never be sure that these interpretations were popular at the time of Jesus, or at the end of the first century, when the Fourth Gospel was being finally redacted.[36] The *Genesis Rabbah* midrash is from fourth or fifth century Amoraim, while the *Yalqut* and the *Zohar* first made their appearance about 1300.

Odeberg takes for granted three points which we would question:

a) That this Jewish interpretation was current at the time of the composition of the Fourth Gospel;

b) that the use of the Platonic-Gnostic "image which is true reality" theory was also current at that time, and

c) that the Evangelist was so well versed in *both* of these streams of thought (and each represents a different line of mysticism), that he was able to produce Jn. 1,51 as a succinct and subtle combination of these two elements.[37]

Jeremias has based his interpretation in speculation on the Bethel stone which is not mentioned, or even alluded to, in Jn. 1,51. Some scholars doubt that Gen. 28,12 is referred to, and it seems far-fetched to abstract even further, basing one's interpretation upon an element which is not mentioned in the text.[38]

According to Quispel, the Son of Man is placed upon the throne as the revelation of God's Glory, towards which the angels move "ascending towards the Son of Man".[39] The descending angels, bearing this revelation, are moving towards Nathanael. If one could be sure that the *merkabah* speculations were

[34] M.-E. Boismard, *Du Baptême à Cana*, pp. 123-127.

[35] *ibid.*, pp. 126-127.

[36] See I. Fritsch, " '... videbitis angelos Dei...' ", p. 7.

[37] For further criticism of Odeberg, see H. Windisch, "Angelophanien um den Menschensohn auf Erden. Ein Kommentar zu Joh 1,51", ZNW 30 (1931) 221-223.

[38] See R. Bultmann, *John*, p. 105, note 3; H. Windisch, *art. cit.*, pp. 220-221.

[39] This part of his argument could be supported by the remarks of M. Black, *An Aramaic Approach to the Gospels and Acts*, (Oxford, OUP, 1954) p. 85 where he argues that ἐπί is a translation of *'al*, meaning "towards". However, Black has omitted these observations from the third edition of his book (Oxford, OUP, 1967).

current at the time of the composition of John, then this would be a very satisfactory solution, except for the fact that this cannot be read into the Greek of the text. There can be only one object upon which the angels descend, the Son of Man.

Boismard's use of the Targum on Gen. 28,13 has recently been described by R. Le Déaut as "deceiving and perilous".[40] Le Déaut is very much in favour of the use of the Targums for the interpretation of the New Testament, and this gives his criticism more weight. Boismard has used the Targum Onkelos, but is mistaken in his translation. The glory of Jahweh stands before him (Jacob) and not on the ladder. In this case "glory" (which is merely a substitute for Jahweh) is not the object of the celestial vision. At this same point the Neophiti Targum has: "The Lord stood beside him". The marginal reading of Neophiti has: "An angel of mercy from the Lord stood beside him". As Boismard's interpretation of the passage is entirely dependent upon his understanding of the Targum, these critical remarks from Le Déaut throw it very much into question.

None of these interpretations is wholly convincing. Many scholars see John 1,51 as a message of the communication which is now set up between Jesus, the Son of Man, and the heavenly world.[41] Some see this union in the light of Philo's commentary on Gen. 28,12 (*De Somniis* I, 140-141), where

---

[40] R. Le Déaut, "Targumic Literature and New Testament Interpretation", *BTB* 4 (1974) 273. See the detailed study of the various Targumic versions of Gen. 28,12 in F. Lentzen-Deis, *Die Taufe Jesu nach den Synoptikern. Literarkritische und Gattungs-geschichtliche Untersuchungen*, Theologische Studien 4, (Frankfurt, Josef Knecht, 1970) pp. 214-227.

[41] See F.-M. Braun, "Commentaire de l'Évangile selon Saint Jean", in L. Pirot-A. Clamer (eds.), *La Sainte Bible*, X (Paris, Letouzey et Ané, 1935) p. 327; R. Bultmann, *John*, pp. 105-106; H. Clavier, "Le problème du rite et du mythe dans le 4e évangile", *RHPhilRel* 31 (1951) 288-289; C. H. Dodd, *Interpretation*, pp. 293-294; U. Holzmeister, "Nathanael fuitne idem ac S. Bartholomaeus Apostolus?", *Biblica* 21 (1940) 29; G. Iber, *Untersuchungen*, pp. 108-110; M.-J. Lagrange, *S. Jean*, p. 52; F. Lentzen-Deis, "Das Motiv der Himmelsöffnung in verschiedenen Gattungen der Umweltliteratur des N.T.", *Biblica* 50 (1968) 321; Idem, *Die Taufe Jesu*, pp. 115-117; R. H. Lightfoot, *St. John*, p. 99; G. H. C. Macgregor, *John*, p. 44; J. Marsh, *Saint John*, Pelican New Testament Commentaries, (Harmondsworth, Penguin Books, 1968) p. 136; W. Michaelis, "Joh 1,51...", col 578; S. Schulz, *Untersuchungen*, pp. 102-103; H. Strathmann, *Das Evangelium des Johannes*, NTD 4, (Göttingen, Vandenhoeck und Ruprecht, 1963) p. 54; B. F. Westcott, *St. John*, p. 28; W. H. Cadman-G. Caird, *The Open Heaven*, (Oxford, Blackwells, 1969) p. 28; S. S. Smalley, "The Johannine Son of Man Sayings", p. 285; T. Zahn, *Das Evangelium des Johannes*, KNT, (Leipzig, A. Deichert, 1908) p. 140; B. Lindars, *John*, pp. 120-122; A. Loisy, *Quatrième Évangile*, (1921) p. 137; W. Bousset, *Kyrios Christos*, p. 53; O. Cullmann, *Salvation in History*, (London, SCM Press, 1967) p. 279 (English translation of *Heil als Geschichte: Heilsgeschichtliche Existenz im Neuen Testament*, [Tübingen, J. C. B. Mohr, 1965]); F. Spitta, *Johannes*, p. 63; E. M. Sidebottom, *The Christ of the Fourth Gospel*, pp. 123-124 et passim; L. Morris, *John*, pp. 169-172; P. Ricca, *Die Eschatologie des vierten Evangeliums*, p. 95; E. Käsemann, *The Testament of*

the angels (and the logoi) are seen as ministers of God. In Jesus' life of difficulty, and in his miraculous activity, angels are the communicating and the assisting link between the Father and the Son (Holzmeister, Lagrange, Loisy [1921], Zahn). Arriving at much the same conclusion but along a different way is Windisch.[42] He sees Jn. 1,51 as a fragment of an older theology which spoke of the Son of Man in a way which was lost as the Gospels were formed. Windisch finds evidence in the Gospels for two basic Son of Man christologies:

a) The traditional one, speaking of the Son of Man who would come at the end of time and

b) a second, now lost, christology which spoke of the Son of Man as a weak and humble figure upon earth, who needed God's support. The angels were used in this christology to speak mythologically of the support which God gave to this humble man.

It is the latter christology which is reflected in Jn. 1,51.[43] It dies out in the Synoptic tradition because of the growing importance of the eschatological Son of Man, and in the Johannine tradition because of the dominant "Logos" christology.

Some stress the important newness of this union between heaven and earth (Bousset, Clavier, Cadman, Smalley, Dodd). Cullmann sees the Son of Man as the replacement of the Temple, the place where God was present to his people.[44] Others see the important stress on the future involvement of the disciples in this union, which they will see in faith (Bultmann, Lentzen-Deis, Lightfoot, Westcott). Schulz interprets the saying as having meanings at two levels: there is already a certain union established, but at the same time it is the promise of a future, more perfect union at the parousia.[45]

Because of the communication established between heaven and earth, the Son of Man is promised as the place *par excellence* of God's revelation.[46] While

---

Jesus (London, SCM Press, 1968) p. 70 (English translation of *Jesu letzter Wille nach Johannes 17,* [Tübingen, J.C.B. Mohr, 1966]); C.H. de Beus, "Het gebruik en de betekenis ...", pp. 248-249.

[42] H. Windisch, "Angelophanien um den Menschensohn auf Erden ...", pp. 215-233.

[43] G. Iber's treatment of this saying (*Untersuchungen,* pp. 100-111) is largely concerned with a refutation of this suggestion.

[44] W. D. Davies, *The Gospel and the Land,* pp. 296-298 argues that it is the Bethel sanctuary which is replaced by the Son of Man.

[45] S. Schulz, *Untersuchungen,* p. 103; Idem, *Johannes,* p. 44.

[46] See E. C. Hoskyns, *Fourth Gospel,* p. 183; W. F. Howard-A. J. Gossip, "The Gospel according to St. John", in *The Interpreter's Bible,* (New York-Nashville, Abingdon, 1952) Vol. VIII, p. 290; R. E. Brown, *John,* p. 91; R. Schnackenburg, *St. John,* I, p. 320; O. Cullmann, *The Christology of the New Testament,* p. 186; B. Vawter, "The Gospel according to John", in *The Jerome Biblical Commentary,* (London, Geoffrey Chapman, 1969) p. 427; A. Loisy, *Quatrième Évangile,* (1903) p. 263; J. N. Sanders, *St. John,* p. 106; A. Schlatter, *Johannes,* p. 64; F. Hahn, *Christologische Hoheitstitel. Ihre Geschichte*

some use Jewish sources to arrive at this conclusion (Hoskyns, Howard, Iber, Davies), others find no need for it (Brown, Schnackenburg, Cullmann, Vawter, Sanders, Schlatter, Hahn, Higgins, Loisy [1903], Fritsch). Cullmann's interpretation of the Son of Man's taking over the role of the Temple makes him both a place of communication and a place of revelation. For A. Serra, who uses the targums to show that there was a link in Jewish thought between the Bethel and the Sinai theophanies, Christ is not only the new Jacob and the new means of communication, but also the new Sinai.[47] G. Reim, using the *Genesis Rabbah*, Dan. 7 and Philo's use of Wisd. 9,9-10 (*De Somniis I*, 142), argues that the revelation in question is the teaching of God, which can be learnt from the Son of Man.[48]

All of these scholars, despite differences in important details, correctly understand the saying as a reference to the revelation which is to be found in the Son of Man. As one commentator has put it:

> "Jesus himself is the link between heaven and earth (3,13). He is the means by which the realities of heaven are brought down to earth. ... The expression then is a figurative way of saying that Jesus will reveal heavenly things to men, a thought which is developed throughout the Gospel".[49]

E. C. Hoskyns explains the meaning of Jn. 1,51 by citing Col. 2,9: "For in him the whole fulness of deity dwells bodily".[50]

There are, however, some who see the saying as a promise to the disciples that they would see the future glory of the Son of Man, especially in the cross and resurrection. Boismard has defended this position,[51] but a similar line is taken by Dahl and Van den Bussche.[52] Van den Bussche firmly refuses any idea of a communication between heaven and earth:

> "Bien qu'inspiré par la vision de l'échelle de Jacob (Gen. 28, 10-17) le *logion* n'annonce pas des rapports continus entre le ciel et la terre, depuis Cana jusqu'au terme de la vie publique: les termes employés sont trop solennels pour viser toute la vie publique: ils visent une théophanie extra-ordinaire".[53]

This is to undervalue the importance of the incarnation for John. There is no need for an extraordinary theophany for John to use solemn language, as

---

im frühen Christentum, FRLANT 83, (Göttingen, Vandenhoeck und Ruprecht, 1966) p. 39, note 6; A. J. B. Higgins, *Son of Man*, pp. 158-159; W. D. Davies, *The Gospel and the Land*, pp. 296-298; I. Fritsch, " ' ... videbitis angelos Dei ...' ", pp. 8-11.

[47] A. Serra, "Le tradizioni della teofania Sinaitica nel Targum del pseudo-Jonathan Es. 19,24 e in Giov. 1,19-2-12", *Marianum* 32 (1971) 1-39.

[48] G. Reim, *Studien zur alttestamentlichen Hintergrund*, pp. 101.104. See also, pp. 97-98

[49] L. Morris, *John*, p. 171.

[50] E. C. Hoskyns, *Fourth Gospel*, p. 212.

[51] See above, pp. 28-30.

[52] N. A. Dahl, "The Johannine Church and History", pp. 136-137; H. van den Bussche, "L'attente de la grande révélation dans le 4ᵉ évangile", NRT 75 (1953) 1012; Idem, *Jean*, pp. 128-129.

[53] H. van den Bussche, *Jean*, p. 128.

the presence of God's glory in the words and works of Jesus (see 1,14) throughout the Fourth Gospel merits such solemn language.[54]

A great deal of this literature centres its attention on the reference to Gen. 28,12, the open heaven, the ascending and descending angels and the vision which the disciples will have. Too little attention seems to have been paid to the use of the term "the Son of Man" in the passage. Here we have a title which appears thirteen times in the Fourth Gospel. Presuming the author (or the redactor) knew what he was saying as he wrote down his Gospel, it seems logical to suppose that "the Son of Man" meant something to him, and that he used the title with this meaning in mind. One of the problems which arise from modern methods of critical analysis is that material tends to be divided into smaller and smaller units.[55] It is possible that these methods obscure rather than clarify,[56] as one can often find patterns in the material — particularly the Johannine material — which will only be noticed if considered as a whole. Following the lead of a suggestion made by J. H. Bernard, one can discover a pattern in some of the Synoptic Son of Man sayings which seems to be reflected in Jn. 1,51, if it is read in conjunction with its immediate context.[57]

The verse comes at the end of a long series of titles, given to Jesus by the Evangelist or by other people. Nathanael's reaction to Jesus' statement that he saw him under the fig tree (v. 48) is to make a full confession of faith: "Rabbi, you are the Son of God! You are the King of Israel!" (v. 49). Jesus' reply is a saying about the Son of Man.[58] When one turns to the Petrine confession in the three Synoptic Gospels, one finds a similar pattern, where titles of messianic dignity are answered by the use of "the Son of Man":

Mk. 8,29:   "Peter answered him, 'You are the Christ'".

Matt. 16,16:   "Simon Peter replied, 'You are the Christ, the Son of the living God'".

Lk. 9,20:   "And Peter answered 'The Christ of God'".

The immediate reply to this confession of what was, in the tradition, an original

---

[54] See C. H. Dodd, "Eternal Life", in *New Testament Studies*, (Manchester, MUP, 1953) pp. 161-173; I. Fritsch, " ' ... videbitis angelos Dei ...'", p. 11.

[55] See S. Schulz, *Untersuchungen*, pp. 82-85. Schulz, however, sees this tendency as a wholly positive development, as it helps us to come more precisely to the historical and religious origin of each small unit.

[56] For the complexity of the Johannine material, where there is an interweaving of various themes and patterns see E. D. Freed, "The Son of Man in the Fourth Gospel", pp. 402-403; E. Kinniburgh, "The Johannine 'Son of Man' ", pp. 64-65; B. Lindars, "The Son of Man in the Johannine Christology", pp. 43-44.

[57] J. H. Bernard, *John*, p. 69.

[58] See also H. Conzelmann, *An Outline of the Theology of the New Testament*, (London, SCM Press, 1969) p. 337; L. Morris, *John*, pp. 171-172; R. Schnackenburg, *St. John*, pp. 507-514; E. M. Sidebottom, *The Christ of the Fourth Gospel*, p. 163.

"You are the Christ", is given in terms of the suffering Son of Man (see Mk. 8,31; Matt. 16,21; Lk. 9,22). It should also be noticed that as Jesus goes on to explain the role of the Son of Man he speaks in terms of the Son of Man who will come in glory, accompanied by angels (see Mk. 8,38; ·Matt. 16,27; Lk. 9,26).

Another parallel to this pattern can be found in Mk. 14,61-62 (Matt. 26,63-64; Lk. 22,67-71). Here the context is different, but we are still dealing with formulae closely connected with a confession of faith. The High Priest accuses Jesus with the question: "Are you the Christ, the Son of Blessed?" (Matthew has "the Son of God"). Jesus replies: "I am, and you will see the Son of Man sitting at the right hand of power, and coming with the clouds of heaven" (Mk. 14,62). When asked of his messiahship, in terms of "the Christ", Jesus replies in terms of "the Son of Man". Whatever one makes of the historicity of these scenes, we are dealing with something that was firmly embedded in the Gospel tradition.

It may have been the recognition of this pattern which led scribes in the early Church to add ἀπ' ἄρτι to Jn. 1,51, taking it from Matt. 26,64. A temporal determination ἀπ' ἄρτι is added before the verb ὄψεσθε in ˙the Alexandrinus, the majority of minuscules, two old Latin witnesses, the Peshitta and Harclean Syriac versions. On the other hand, it is omitted by all the older witnesses: P⁶⁶, P⁷⁵, Vaticanus, Sinaiticus, most of the old Latin versions, the Vulgate and the Coptic versions. Some important commentators show an inclination to accept this reading, as it reflects Johannine realised eschatology.[59] It seems, however, that the weight of external evidence from the "neutral" and "Western" texts is overwhelming. One can better explain the addition of the ἀπ' ἄρτι from Matt. 26,64 than its omission from the earlier texts.[60]

In the Synoptic accounts of the trial scene one can see a progression, moving towards an almost Johannine realised eschatology. Mark simply has: "And you will see the Son of Man" (Mk. 14,62), while Matthew reports: '·From this time onward you will see the Son of Man" (Matt. 26,64). Luke, reworking the passage, has: "But from now on the Son of Man shall be seated at the right hand of the power of God" (Lk. 22,69). One can understand why the scribes were tempted to add "from now on" to the Johannine text, if they too had recognised a pattern. Jesus replied to an explicit messianic confession with the enigmatic figure of the Son of Man, whose authority could already be seen "from now on": It is in the Fourth Gospel that one would

---

[59] C. K. Barrett, *St. John*, p. 155; A. Schlatter, *Johannes*, p. 63; H. Windisch, "Angelophanien um den Menschensohn auf Erden ...", p. 218; T. Zahn, *Johannes*, p. 139; A. Loisy, *Quatrième Évangile*, (1903) p. 264, note 1.

[60] The koiné textual tradition tends to smooth out texts in this fashion. See H. Zimmermann, *Neutestamentliche Methodenlehre. Darstellung der historisch-kritischen Methode*, (Stuttgart, Katholisches Bibelwerk, 1968) p. 46.

expect to find this type of eschatology, but John uses the title in his own way. While he appears to follow a traditional pattern in using "the Son of Man" to reply to the titles scattered through the preceding reactions to Jesus, he has his own insight into what the title means. In Jn. 1,51 we have a saying which is programmatic. Jesus makes a promise that something *will* be seen. What will be seen is the revelation of the glory of God in the Son of Man.

John's use of the title must be understood in the light of the series of titles which have been used from 1,18 onward.[61] The entire passage is clearly centred on the question of Jewish messianic expectations. The Baptist turns people away from himself; he refuses the titles of "Christ" (v. 20), "Elijah" (v. 21a) and "the Prophet" (v. 21b) and points to Jesus saying: "Behold the Lamb of God" (v. 29). Explaining his own role he says: "I have seen and have borne witness that this is the Son of God" (v. 34).

John's disciples turn to this new figure and understand him from the start in the light of Jewish messianic expectations. The Evangelist has the first disciples speak of Jesus as "the Messiah" (v. 41), "him of whom Moses in the law and also the prophets wrote" (v. 45), "Rabbi", "Son of God" and "King of Israel" (v. 49).[62] In v. 51 Jesus replies, starting with the solemn double "amen". Westcott comments on the double "amen": "The words by their emphasis generally presuppose some difficulty or misunderstanding to be overcome; and at the same time mark the introduction of a new thought carrying the divine teaching further".[63] Westcott is correct, at least in this case, when he speaks of "a misunderstanding to be overcome". In Jn. 1,19-49 the belief of the early Church is reflected, but John indicates another point of view which is particularly his in the reply of v. 51.[64] He may also be correcting the beliefs of the Church which he knew, as they did not go far enough in their confessions of faith. In the Johannine Gospel the most important thing about Jesus is that he came from heaven.[65]

---

[61] B. Lindars, "The Son of Man...", pp. 45-46 sees the importance of the series of titles, but fails to appreciate the importance of the relationship between "the Son of Man" and the rest of the titles. As the "original" conclusion came in v. 49, v. 51 is but a "further climax". In fact, v. 51 is the only climax of this section of the Gospel as it has come down to us.

[62] See R. Schnackenburg, *St. John*, I, pp. 507-508; Idem, "Die Messiasfrage im Johannesevangelium", in J. Blinzler-O. Kuss-F. Mussner (eds.), *Neutestamentliche Aufsätze: Festschrift J. Schmid zum 70. Geburtstag*, (Regensburg, Pustet, 1963) pp. 246-247; J.T. Forestell, *The Word of the Cross. Salvation as Revelation in the Fourth Gospel*, Analecta Biblica 57, (Rome, Biblical Institute Press, 1974) p. 25.

[63] B.F. Westcott, *St. John*, p. 48.

[64] See R. Schnackenburg, "Die Messiasfrage ...", p. 243: "Der Evangelist will nicht einen völlig anderen 'Christus'-Gedanken an ihre Stelle setzen, sondern sie in Jesus als erfüllt aufweisen, freilich in einem ungeahnten, viel höheren Sinn".

[65] See E. Käsemann, "The Prologue to John's Gospel", in *New Testament Questions of Today*, (London, SCM Press, 1969) p. 155 (English translation of *Exegetische Versuche*

This has not been explained, as yet, in the narrative of the Gospel. John's readers have been told the full truth in the prologue (1,1-18, see esp. vv. 1-2. 14. 18). They have been given the key which can unlock the whole mystery of the chapters which follow,[66] but the disciples, as actors in the Johannine drama of the life of Jesus, do not have this key. To them it will be unfolded in the signs and discourses which are to follow. This is a part of Johannine technique. We know the truth because we have read about it in the prologue. However, we still have to see it worked out in the life and works of Jesus. In Jn. 1,51 Jesus speaks of something that those who believe in him will see. They will see the opening of heaven: a way of saying that they will see the revelation of the heavenly — that which is "from heaven".[67] There will be angels ascending and descending upon the Son of Man, just as there were heavenly hosts at the birth of the Messiah (Lk. 2,13-14) and heavenly figures at the transfiguration scene (Matt. 9,4 parr.), scenes which were understood by the Evangelists as the revelation of the heavenly origin and the heavenly commerce of Jesus.[68] There is an allusion to Gen. 28,12 where the *bô* was taken to mean "upon him". Thus the message is one of continual communion between the heavenly and the earthly, taking place in Jesus, the Son of Man.

Jn. 1 can be divided into two sections, each concluding with an important christological statement. The prologue leads to v. 18: "the only Son", while vv. 19-51 lead to "the Son of Man" in v. 51. Both of these conclusions are concerned with the revelation of God through Jesus who, coming from the

---

und Besinnungen II, [Göttingen, Vandenhoeck und Ruprecht, 1965]); R. Schnackenburg, "Die Messiasfrage ...", pp. 250-252; T. E. Pollard, *Johannine Christology and the Early Church*, SNTS Monograph Series 13, (Cambridge, CUP, 1970) pp. 6-16, esp. 13-15.

[66] M. D. Hooker has recently argued this case most convincingly. See "The Johannine Prologue and the Messianic Secret", *NTS* 21 (1974-75) 40-58. She has taken up Lightfoot's suggestion that Mark has a prologue which explains the Messianic secret right from the start of the Gospel, and argues that John is doing exactly the same thing, but in a very different form. See also R. H. Lightfoot, *St. John*, p. 11: "1,1-18, usually called the prologue, is designed to enable the reader to understand the doctrines of the book"; see also C. K. Barrett, "The Prologue of St. John's Gospel", in *New Testament Essays*, (London, SPCK, 1972) pp. 27-29; E. K. Lee, *The Religious Thought of St. John*, pp. 56-59; E. Käsemann, *art. cit.*, p. 167. Although differing very much in his understanding of the prologue from Hooker, Lightfoot and Barrett, Käsemann concludes his study by claiming that it is "an indication of direction for the Gospel and the readers for whom it is meant, which really anticipates the conclusion: 'It is with the story of the Son of God that we have to do' (20,31)".

[67] See E. Lentzen-Deis, "Das Motif der Himmelsöffnung", pp. 315-327. The theme of the opening of the heavens and a subsequent revelation of the truth is frequent in the apocalyptic literature. See, for example, Rev. 4,1; 19,11; *Test. Levi*, 18,1-14; *Test. Judah*, 29,1-6.

[68] See G. Iber, *Untersuchungen*, pp. 100-102.

Father, has made him known (see v. 18). Jesus is "the only Son" [69] and "the Son of Man": the revelation of the heavenly among men.

> "The self-revelation of Jesus — or God's revelation of himself in Jesus — is far more than any human knowledge, no matter how striking (cf. v. 48); it is a proclamation of salvation which has been brought from heaven and is disclosed in the words and works of the Son of Man on earth, something 'greater' than can be achieved by human insight and religious expectation".[70]

But all of this still lies ahead of his newly called disciples. It is still to be seen by those who believe in him, and for this reason we do not find "from now on" here. What they are to see is yet to come; it will slowly unfold, starting with the miracle at Cana (see 2,11). It is important to notice that this revelation will be granted only to believers. The use of the verb ὁράω (see 3,36; 11,40; 16,16; I Jn. 3,2), the reference to the "true Israelite" and the whole tone of v. 50 make it clear that v. 51 is a promise to believers ... "this you will see — if you believe".[71]

The whole Gospel will be a gradual unfolding of the promise of 1,51.[72] The title "the Son of Man" is used to point to something greater (v. 50) than titles of honour. Rabbi, Son of God, King of Israel are not denied by the reply of Jesus, but something more is indicated:[73] the Son of Man is the one

---

[69] This may be "the only God", which does not alter our argument. For this reading see B. M. Metzger, *A Textual Commentary on the Greek New Testament,* (London-New York, United Bible Society, 1971) p. 198. See, however. W. H. Cadman, *The Open Heaven,* pp. 15-18 for a convincing contrary opinion.

[70] R. Schnackenburg, *St. John* I, pp. 511-512. See also M. Baron, "La progression des confessions de foi dans les dialogues de S. Jean", *BibVChr* 82 (1968) 33-34; J. R. Michaels, "Nathanael under the Fig Tree", *ET* 78 (1966) 183.

[71] See O. Cullmann, "Εἶδεν καὶ ἐπίστευσεν. La vie de Jésus, objet de la 'vue' et la 'foi' d'après le quatrième évangile", in *Aux Sources de la Tradition chretienne: Mélanges Goguel,* (Neuchâtel, Delachaux et Niestlé, 1950) pp. 52-61; C. Traets, *Voir Jésus et le Père en lui selon l'Évangile de Saint Jean,* Analecta Gregoriana 159, (Rome, Editrice Gregoriana, 1967) pp. 73. 125-128; F. Hahn, "Sehen und Glauben im Johannesevangelium", in H. Baltensweiler-Bo Reicke (eds.), *Neues Testament und Geschichte. Historisches Geschehen und Deutung im Neuen Testament: Oscar Cullmann zum 70. Geburtstag,* (Tübingen, J. C. B. Mohr, 1972) pp. 125-141.

[72] W. H. Cadman, *The Open Heaven,* pp. 28. 60-62; E. Käsemann, *The Testament of Jesus,* pp. 6-7; J. T. Forestell, *The Word of the Cross,* p. 67; W. F. Howard, *Christianity According to St. John,* pp. 162-164.

[73] See M. de Jonge, "Jewish Expectations about the 'Messiah' according to the Fourth Gospel", *NTS* 19 (1972-73) 250: "Titles like 'prophet', 'teacher sent by God', 'king' or even 'Messiah' do not correspond completely with the real status and authority of Him to whom they point. The terms are not wrong but insufficient; they may be used in a wrong context and are, therefore, in need of further definition". See also W. H. Cadman, *The Open Heaven,* p. 28. The use of "Son of God" on the lips of Nathanael is not the correct Johannine sense of the term. Along with 'Rabbi' and 'King of Israel', it is to be understood in a more secular, messianic sense (see II Sam. 7,14; Ps. 2,7). See, on this, M.-J. Lagrange, *St. Jean,* p. clv; J. T. Forestell, *The Word of the Cross,* p. 23.

"by whom God becomes manifest to men".[74]

> "It is not quite certain to what extent Nathanael is portrayed as living up to John's standards, but in any case the deeper meaning is hinted at in Jesus' reply, which emphasizes that Nathanael's faith should not be based on astonishment about Jesus' superior knowledge but on 'greater things' which he will see. These 'greater things' are not specified but it is clear that the evangelist connects them with Jesus' reference to the 'Son of Man' who will be in permanent contact with God in heaven. John 1 starts in heaven and ends in heaven, God's unique link with man being Jesus, the Son of God and the Son of Man".[75]

Those who believe in Jesus will see the revelation of God. While on the one hand this discussion is centred around popular messianic expectation in the Johannine Church, on the other hand, John has used this to develop his christological argument. At this stage of the Gospel we are merely told that Jesus, as the Son of Man, is God's revelation among men; the next time we encounter this title we will be told that all who believe in the Son of Man, the revelation of God who must be lifted up on the cross, will have eternal life in him (3,13-15).

The saying does not seem to point to any particular historical fulfilment. There is no scene in the life of the Johannine Jesus where angels ascend and descend upon him.[76] The whole of the ministry of Jesus is the manifestation of God's truth and a revelation of God to men (see 1,14.17; 3,11-21.31-36; 8,31-32; 14,6; 16,7; 18,37-38) and this passage is a promise that this will take place and be seen by those who believe. There is, however, a supreme moment of glory and revelation in the life of Jesus — the elevation on the cross. J. Duncan M. Derrett has recently attempted to show that for the oriental mind, the cross would have been suggested by the reference to the ladder and to Jacob, who "was seen as a method by which angels, messengers, passed between God and man, and was himself the cause of their exaltation or depression".[77] Derrett claims that the simple ladders of the Middle East,

[74] W.H. Cadman, *op. cit.,* p. 28. This very important fact is seldom noticed by scholars. V. 51 and its use of "the Son of Man" is taken in association with the titles applied to Jesus in vv. 19-50. The fact that in v. 51 "greater things" are promised, and that Jesus is replying to Nathanael's confession go unobserved.

[75] M. de Jonge, "Jesus as Prophet and King in the Fourth Gospel", *ETL* 49 (1973) 168-169.

[76] This saying is often included among the "ascending and descending" Son of Man sayings found elsewhere in the Gospel (see 3,13; 6,62). This must be avoided, as it is the angels who ascend and descend, not the Son of Man. See for an example of this J.H. Charlesworth, "A Critical Comparison of the Dualism in IQS 3,13-4,26 and the 'Dualism' Contained in the Gospel of John", in J.H. Charlesworth, (ed.), *John and Qumran,* (London, Geoffrey Chapman, 1972) p. 98.

[77] J.D.M. Derrett, *Law in the New Testament,* (London, DLT, 1970) p. 416. See also Idem, "Figtrees in the New Testament", *HeyJ* 14 (1973) 263-264.

Iran, the Himalayan regions and further Asia would immediately recall a cross. This saying, then, is addressed to those who are prepared to accept the paradox of a Son of God and King of Israel who goes to a cross. B. Lindars has argued that there could be a symbolic description of the Synoptic baptismal scenes (see Matt. 3,16; Lk. 3,21). In John, however, the glorious theophany will take place in the future, in the passion, when the Son of Man is glorified.[78]

While Derrett's claims remain quite unproven,[79] and those of Lindars remain somewhat speculative, the attempt to link 1,51 with the cross may well be a valuable suggestion. Other scholars, as we have already noted, in searching for Synoptic traces in this strange saying, have looked to Mk. 13,26; 14,62; Matt. 26,64 and Lk. 17,22.[80] They suggest parallels where "the Son of Man" is used with the verb ὁράω. Perhaps a further parallel could be found in the peculiarly Matthean passage, where the Son of Man is again found in the company of angels, although the verb is not present:

"When the Son of Man comes in his glory, and the angels with him, then he will sit on his glorious throne" (Matt. 25,31).[81]

The scene which follows this saying (vv. 32-46) is Matthew's description of the criteria which will be used in the judgment of mankind. It may be that Jn. 1,51 also refers to an enthronement, but, for John, the enthronement will not be some timeless future moment of judgment, as in Matthew. John may have drawn this moment back into history, as judgment takes place in the moment when the Son of Man is "lifted up" on the cross (see 3,14; 8,28; 12,31-33). John announces the link between the enthronement on the cross and his version of the judgment of the world in chapter 12:

"Now is the judgment of this world, now shall the ruler of this world be cast out; and I, when I am lifted up from the earth, will draw all men to myself" (12,31-32).

The promises concerning the Son of Man who would be "lifted up" (3,14; 8,28) are clarified in the "I saying" of 12,31-33, as Jesus' public life comes to its conclusion.

---

[78] B. Lindars, "The Son of Man in the Johannine Christology", p. 46. See also E. C. Hoskyns, *Fourth Gospel*, p. 183.

[79] The claim that the eastern mind would immediately see the connection between the ladder and the cross remains unproven, and the paradox involved in John's passion narrative does not seem to be the point at issue in 1,51.

[80] See above, p. 25, note 9. See also J. T. Forestell, *The Word of the Cross*, pp. 23-24.

[81] See on this verse, S. E. Johnson, "King Parables in the Synoptic Gospels", *JBL* 74 (1955) 37-39; W. Grundmann, *Das Evangelium nach Matthäus*, THNT, (Berlin, Evangelische Verlagsanstalt, 1971) pp. 524-526. Both Grundmann and Bultmann (*The History of the Synoptic Tradition*, (Oxford, Blackwells, 1968) pp. 123-124 (English translation of *Die Geschichte der synoptischen Tradition*, [Göttingen, Vandenhoeck und Ruprecht, 1931]) argue that the whole passage is pre-Matthean. John may well have had contact with the idea at a very early stage.

The main point of Jn. 1,51 is to assert that Jesus, the Son of Man, will be the place of heavenly revelation. However, the reaction of the world to this revelation will be its judgment. The supreme moment of that revelation and judgment is found in the cross. For the moment, the disciples are told that they will see God's revelation in the Son of Man, but it could be suggested that they are told this in terms which recall a traditional scene of Jesus as the judge, enthroned and in the company of his angels (Matt. 25,31). It is only on the cross that the "greater things" will finally be seen, when the high point of God's revelation to the world and its consequent judgment is fulfilled (see 19,30.35-37).

It must be admitted, however, that, apart from the presence of "the Son of Man" and the reference to angels, the evidence in Jn. 1,51 for an enthronement scene similar to Matt. 25,32 is tenuous. At this stage of our study such a link cannot be shown, although a closer examination of the other Johannine Son of Man sayings may help us towards a fuller understanding of the present passage's manifold implications.[82]

It does appear, however, that we can affirm with reasonable confidence that the Johannine Jesus, like the Jesus of the Synoptic tradition uses "the Son of Man" title over against other titles given to him by his listeners. It is not simply a title of honour, but seems to be linked with the dominant theme of revelation. Jesus may be Rabbi, Son of God and King of Israel, but he is more; he is the Son of Man, in whom God is revealed to man. This first use of "the Son of Man" promises a future revelation which believers will see. It may also hint at the revelation and judgment which will take place on the cross, although this is not yet clear. In conclusion, we have found that:

a) John 1,51 is not just a "débris d'une tradition plus complexe" (Goguel), which is meaningless in its present context.

b) We seem to be dealing with the johannisation of a traditional pattern, where "the Son of Man" is used by Jesus to reply to other titles of honour which are referred to him.

c) The saying speaks of the Son of Man's close and continual intercourse with heaven and, through this, his being the revelation of God. The promise —that the disciples will see all this in the context of faith — is to be slowly unfolded as the Gospel itself unfolds. It will be worked out during the whole of the public life of Jesus.[83]

---

[82] W.D. Davies, *The Gospel and the Land,* p. 296 argues that "the verse is kaleidoscopic".

[83] See E. Schwartz, "Aporien im vierten Evangelium", in *Nachrichten von der königlichen Gesellschaft der Wissenschaften zu Göttingen,* (1908) p. 517. Schwartz points out that the saying has the form of a solemn prophecy. It comes at the beginning of the book and demands some fulfilment in the subsequent narrative. See also B. Lindars, "Son of Man", p. 46; J. T. Forestell, *The Word of the Cross,* p. 24.

his first Son of Man saying in the Fourth Gospel clearly has a special
e, and plays an important role, both in its immediate context and in
ospel as a whole. There is no explicit mention of the "exaltation" or
ication", so typical of many of the later sayings; for the moment, we
 promise of greater things which will be seen, coming at the end of
s of titles and concluding the first scene from the life of the Johannine
  It emphasises the Son of Man's close and continual contact with heaven,
; at his origin and goal, admirably introducing the reader to the Johannine
f Man, the unique revealer.[84]

Against G. Iber, *Untersuchungen*, pp. 110-11, who sees the use of the title as in
 Johannine. He accepts that there is a current apocalyptic "Son of Man" idea
'ohn has merely drawn back into history. See instead, R. Schnackenburg, *St. John*,
2; C. Colpe, *TDNT* VIII, pp. 468-469; J. T. Forestell, *The Word of the Cross*, p. 23.

CHAPTER THREE

THE UNIQUE REVEALER WHO MUST BE 'LIFTED UP':
John 3,13-14

I - General Structure and Meaning of John 2,23-3,36

The literary phenomena of John 3 have been a perennial 'crux interpretum'. The difficulties are immediately evident:

a) The dialogue between Jesus and Nicodemus (vv. 1-10) changes into an almost impersonal reflection after the double 'amen' of v. 11a. In vv. 11b-12 Jesus speaks to "you" in the plural, referring to himself as "we". From v. 13 onward he continues in the third person singular. A similar phenomenon takes place in the second part of the chapter. After the dialogue of John the Baptist with the Jews (vv. 25-30), there is another monologue written entirely in the impersonal third person singular.

b) The themes which are dealt with in vv. 11-21 and 31-36 seem to go well beyond anything called for by the discussion between Nicodemus and Jesus or the Baptist and his interlocutors. They could be described as a synopsis of Johannine theology. As Paul announced his "Gospel" to his readers in Rom. 1,16-17, so does John appear to do in 3,11-21.31-36.[1]

Thus, on the one hand we have two reasonably credible narratives, while on the other we have fully developed Johannine theology, magisterially pronounced. There have been various attempts to explain away these difficulties by rearranging the text. R. Bultmann, J. H. Bernard and C. J. Cadoux have suggested that 3,31-36 originally followed after 3,21,[2] as it was all part of an original theme of "the coming of the revealer as the *Krisis* of the world".[3] G. H. C. Macgregor thinks that vv. 14-21 should be transposed to follow 12,32. In this way 3,13-15 would take the place of 12,33 (which is a gloss). 3,16-21 should then be inserted between 12,34 and 12,35-36.[4]

---

[1] J. Blank, *Krisis*, p. 53 entitles a chapter of his work: "Joh 3: Das johanneische Kerygma".
[2] R. Bultmann, *John*, pp. 131-133; J.H. Bernard, *St. John*, pp. xxiii-xxiv; C.J. Cadoux, "The Johannine Account of the Early Ministry of Jesus", *JTS* 20 (1919) 316-317.
[3] R. Bultmann, *John*, p. 131.
[4] G.H.C. Macgregor, *John*, p. 77.

J. G. Gourbillon has also solved the problems of chapter 12 by patching it up with parts of chapter 3.[5] He sees the whole episode (2,23-25; 3,1-3; 3,31-36; 3,22-30, in that order) as filling a gap in the second part of chapter 12. S. Mendner suggests that the final redaction of this passage took place in the second century, between A.D. 125-175.[7] The scene originally came after the events described in 7,45-52, and was told in 3,2.3a.7b.9.10.12b.13a and excerpts from vv. 31-35,[8] but the dialogue was later shifted to the present position because of its connection with the story of the cleansing of the Temple, another scene which was historically late in the life of Jesus, as reported in the Synoptic Gospels, but was transferred to chapter 2 to suit John's theological purpose.[9]

R. Schnackenburg sees 3,13-21 and 31-36 as primitively belonging to a kerygmatic sermon or homily composed by the Evangelist.[10] This homily is a compendium of the 'good news' of Jesus (eine Zusammenfassung der 'Botschaft' Jesu), originally occasioned by the discourse with Nicodemus, which is to be taken as historical; however 3,31-36 came first.[11] The present order of the text was due to later disciples of John who redacted the passage in its present fashion because:

a) the use of "heaven" in v. 13 recalled the "heavenly things" of v. 12, and thus vv. 13-21 were inserted after v. 12, and

b) the "he who is of the earth" from v. 31 was understood as referring to John the Baptist, and thus vv. 31-36 followed vv. 22-30, which are about the activity of the Baptist.[12]

While most of the reconstructed texts which these scholars produce read very logically, any suggestion of this nature is highly speculative, as Schnackenburg admits,[13] and the variety of the suggestions outlined above is a clear indication of the subjective nature of this speculation. Mendner has suggested chapter 7 as the correct location for chapter 3, while Macgregor and Gourbillon suggest chapter 12; John Bligh has argued for its belonging to the end of chapter 9.[14] C. H. Dodd has rightly pointed out that v. 31 does not

---

[5] J. G. Gourbillon, "La parabole du serpent d'airain et la 'lacune' de ch. III de l'Évangile selon S. Jean", *Vivre et Penser* 2 (1942) 213-226.

[6] For the reconstruction of ch. 12, see pp. 223-226.

[7] S. Mendner, "Nikodemus", *JBL* 77 (1958) 293-333.

[8] *ibid.*, pp. 314-316.

[9] *ibid.*, pp. 316-319.

[10] R. Schnackenburg, *St. John* I, p. 361; Idem, "Die situationsgelösten Redestücke in Joh 3", *ZNW* 49 (1958) 88-99. See, however, E. Ruckstuhl, "Die johanneische Menschensohnforschung ...", pp. 235-236.

[11] J. Blank, *Krisis*, p. 56 follows Schnackenburg in this.

[12] R. Schnackenburg, *St. John* I, p. 362; Idem., "Die situationgelösten Redestücke ...", pp. 97-99.

[13] R. Schnackenburg, *St. John* I, pp. 54-55.363.

[14] J. Bligh, "Four Studies in John II: Nicodemus", *HeyJ* 8 (1967) 40-51.

follow smoothly after v. 21.   If our manuscripts had given that sequence, he claims, modern critics would have discovered that there was an obvious break at v. 21.[15]

Is it impossible to understand the text as it now stands?   C. H. Dodd has indicated an important methodological principle:

> "I conceive it to be the duty of an interpreter at least to see what can be done with the document as it has come down to us before attempting to improve upon it ... I shall assume as a provisional working hypothesis that the present order is not fortuitous, but deliberately devised by somebody — even if he were only a scribe doing his best — and that the person in question (whether the author or another) had some design in mind, and was not necessarily irresponsible or unintelligent".[16]

In rearranging the text, scholars fail to recognise and appreciate what E. C. Hoskyns has called John's "self-contained allusiveness".[17]   One of the striking characteristics of this Gospel is its method of elucidating themes by means of progressive reflection.[18]   To try to smooth out these apparently irregular passages is to force the text into the logic of the modern interpreter, and to rob it of the considerable dramatic effect which the Evangelist builds up by the interplay of narrative, dialogue, monologue and meditative reflection of the Evangelist himself.[19]   John 3 is an example of this Johannine method and, as such, should not be arbitrarily rearranged.

It is our task to see what can be done with this text as it has come down to us.[20]   There certainly appears to be a close link between vv. 11-21 and 31-36,

---

[15] C. H. Dodd, *Interpretation*, p. 309.

[16] *ibid.*, p. 290.   E. C. Hoskyns also makes this point: "We must not rise from the first discourse with the feeling that though Nicodemus was a sensible person, the Evangelist is not" (*Fourth Gospel*, p. 201).

[17] E. C. Hoskyns, *op. cit.*, p. 67.

[18] See W. A. Meeks, "The Man from Heaven in Johannine Sectarianism", pp. 55-56. Meeks criticises Bultmann's "obsessive attempts to discover a *rational* sequence in the Johannine discourses and narratives by the incredibly complex rearrangement-hypothesis in his commentary".   He remarks further: "We have not yet learned to let the symbolic language of Johannine literature speak in its own way" (p. 47).   See also J. T. Forestell, *The Word of the Cross*, pp. 13-14; D. Deeks, "The Structure of the Fourth Gospel", *NTS* 15 (1968-69) 107-129.

[19] See H. Windisch, "Der johanneische Erzählungsstil", in *EUCHARISTERION: Studien zur Religion und Literatur des Alten und Neuen Testaments Hermann Gunkel zum 60. Geburtstag dargebracht von seinen Schülern und Freunden*, FRLANT 19, (Göttingen, Vandenhoeck und Ruprecht, 1923) Vol. II, pp. 174-213.

[20] In our attempt to do this we have been largely guided by I. de la Potterie, "Structura Primae Partis Evangelii Johannis (Capita III et IV)", *VD* 47 (1969) 130-140; Idem, "Ad Dialogum Jesu cum Nicodemo (Jo. 2,23-3,21)", *VD* 47 (1969) 141-150; Idem, "Nascere dall'acqua e nascere dallo Spirito", in I. de la Potterie-S. Lyonnet, *La Vita secondo lo Spirito*, (Rome, AVE, 1967) pp. 53-56.   See also the useful criticism of de la Potterie, and the further suggestions of L. J. Topel, "A Note on the Methodology of Structural Analysis in Jn. 2,23-3,21", *CBQ* 33 (1971) 211-220.   See also M. de Jonge, "Nicodemus and Jesus: Some Observations on Misunderstanding and Understanding in the Fourth Gospel", *BJRL* 53 (1970) 337-359; G. Gaeta, *Il dialogo con Nicodemo*.

but do they have to be made into one discourse? Perhaps what we have here
is John's way of giving his readers two variations on fundamental themes of
this theology. These themes are presented in vv. 11-21 and taken up again
in vv. 31-36 in the following manner:

vv. 11-21		*vv. 31-36*
v. 11	=	v. 32
v. 12	=	v. 31a
v. 13	=	v. 31b
vv. 15-16	=	vv. 35-36a
v. 17	=	v. 34
vv. 18-19	=	v. 36b

Two closely linked themes stand out: the revelation brought by Jesus (see
vv. 11-15 = vv. 31-34) and the consequent judgment which flows from man's
response to this revelation (see vv. 16-21 = vv. 35-36).[21]

It is difficult to determine where Jesus' discourse starts and finishes and
where Johannine reflection begins. However, it is important to understand
that the whole chapter is a Johannine reflection. The Evangelist has used
different techniques, and probably different sources, as he winds his way through
a rich theological presentation. After the discourse with Nicodemus, he has
Jesus annouce himself as "the Son of Man" and "the Son of God", revealer
and judge, while after the encounter between John the Baptist and the Jews,
the Evangelist himself presents Jesus — again as the revealer and consequently
as the place of judgment.[22] Thus, John has moved through dialogue, monologue
and narrative to a final reflection of his own. There is a variety of literary
forms, and possibly of sources, but using these variations John has given us a
unit which could well be called a miniature Gospel of St. John.[23]

Our division of the chapter follows the indications of the text itself.
Where John changes key by a change of form, he is most likely moving to

[21] See R. E. Brown, *John*, pp. 159-160; M.-J. Lagrange, *St. Jean*, p. 96; J. H. Bernard,
St. John, p. 123; J. Graf, "Nikodemus (Joh 3,1-21)", *TüTQ* 132 (1952) 84-86.

[22] See R. E. Brown, *John*, p. 149: "All Jesus' words come to us through the channels
of the evangelist's understanding and rethinking, but the Gospel presents Jesus as speaking
and not the evangelist". See also R. Schnackenburg, *Das erste Wunder Jesu (Joh 2,1-11)*,
(Freiburg, Herder, 1951) p. 34: "Das Johannesevangelium will kein besonderes Jesusbild,
aber ein Christusbild bieten, dass ein vertieften Christusglaube schaut."; W. F. Howard,
Christianity according to St. John, p. 128.

[23] The question of sources arises. Is John using a revelation discourse along with
some sign or narrative source, which he welds together with his own material? This may
well be the case, although the details of the various sources can only be the subject of
speculation. While prepared to admit that there are sources behind the Fourth Gospel,
our concern is not to trace these sources, but to see what the author is trying to say
in the final product. See the important remarks in this regard in J. T. Forestell, *The
Word of the Cross*, p. 11-16, and the concluding chapter of G. Gaeta, *op. cit.*, pp. 133-168.

another stage in his argument. As this is the case, then we can start our division at 2,23 and divide chapter 3 in the following manner:

I - *Introduction*: 2,23-25: *The theme is stated.*

While most scholars see 2,23-25 as an introduction to the Nicodemus scene,[24] it seems likely that these verses indicate the theme of a series of "types of faith" running from 2,1 to 4,54.[25] The central thought is indicated by the two-fold use of πιστεύειν in v. 23 to refer to those who "believed in his name" because of the signs which they saw and in v. 24 to tell us that Jesus does "not trust himself to them".[26] The theme of correct belief in Jesus and its results (the revelation of the new order, which leads to life) is to be central in the two 'kerygmatic' sections which follow (see vv. 12.15.16.18.36). The chapter deals with a critical assessment of faith in Jesus. The faith of the "many who believed in his name" is not blameworthy, but it is not sufficient to merit Jesus' trusting himself to them.[27] What is to follow will be a spelling out of this fact. V. 25 provides the link with 3,1: he knew all *men*, he needed no one to bear witness of *man*, and he himself knew what was in *man* (v. 25), but there was a *man* of the Pharisees named Nicodemus, who is about to serve as John's first example of the faith demanded by Jesus.[28]

---

[24] R. Schnackenburg, *St. John* I, p. 360; B. Lindars, *John*, pp. 135-137; W. Bauer, *Das Johannesevangelium erklärt*, HZNT 6, (Tübingen, J. C. B. Mohr, 1935), p. 49; F.-M. Braun, "St. Jean", p. 333; R. E. Brown, *John*, pp. 126-127; M. de Jonge, "Nicodemus and Jesus ...", p. 341; E. C. Hoskyns, *Fourth Gospel*, pp. 202-203; W. F. Howard, "St. John", p. 502; M.-J. Lagrange, *St. Jean*, pp. 70-71; A. Loisy, *Quatrième Évangile*, pp. 153-155; G. H. C. Macgregor, *John*, p. 65; J. Wellhausen, *Johannis*, p. 16; F. Spitta, *Johannes*, p. 78; H. Strathmann, *Johannes*, p. 65; A. Wikenhauser, *Johannes*, pp. 68-69; T. Zahn, *Johannes*, pp. 176-178.

[25] See I. de la Potterie, "Structura Primae Partis Evangelii Johannis", p. 132.

[26] Scholars are baffled by this reference to "signs". As yet Jesus has worked no signs in Jerusalem. Which signs could have led them to their belief? Perhaps this problem is less urgent if we see 2,23-25, not as a logical temporal continuation of what has preceded, but more as a statement of a theological theme, present in 2,1-4,54. C. H. Dodd has probably come closest to the mind of John when he suggested that the events of Cana and the Temple cleansing are the "signs" which signify that Christ has come to inaugurate a new theological order (*Interpretation*, p. 303). A similar suggestion is made by H. van den Bussche, *Jean*, p. 160. G. Gaeta, *Il dialogo con Nicodemo*, pp. 35-44 misses this point, as he has omitted 2,1-22 from his considerations. We see 2,23-25 as the statement of a theological theme in the midst of a series of "examples of faith", but Gaeta links these verses with 3,1-2a as a part of the introduction to Nicodemus.

[27] See J. McPolin, *The "Name" of the Father and of the Son in the Johannine Writings*, (Rome, Biblical Institute Dissertation, 1972) pp. 53-62.

[28] Some scholars refuse to admit this link. See W. Bauer, *Johannesevangelium*, p. 50; M.-J. Lagrange, *St. Jean*, p. 72; A. Loisy, *Quatrième Évangile*, p. 155; B. F. Westcott, *St. John*, p. 49. They maintain that the ἄνθρωπος of 3,1 is used in the sense of τις. See

II - 3,1-10: *The dialogue with Nicodemus.*

The first example, Nicodemus, fails because he cannot reach beyond the limitations of his traditional Jewish faith.[29] Nicodemus, as "a man of the Pharisees" and "a ruler of the Jews", represents Judaism.[30] Jesus and Judaism are the two parties in the discussion, but it is not to be regarded as a Johannine anti-Jewish polemic. As Jesus is completely open with his interlocutor, and will later reveal himself completely to him (vv. 11-21), the basic point of the discussion is not so much to show how Judaism is wrong but, more positively, to tell Judaism what is necessary for salvation.[31] Nicodemus, within his limitations, is prepared to see Jesus as a Rabbi, a teacher, "from God", a prophet, and even as having God with him, a dignity reserved for the great men of Israel (see LXX Exod. 3,12 where the title is applied to Moses, and Jer. 1,8 where the prophet is told that Jahweh is "with him"),[32] but he cannot or will not understand the message of rebirth from above in the spirit.[33] V. 10 indicates that Nicodemus, as "a teacher of Israel" should have understood this. All of this is ἐπίγεια, and has been a part of Israel's heritage (see Wisd. 9,16-18; Job 34,14; Exod. 15,8; Pss. 18,15; 51,10; Is. 40,7; 44,3; 59,21; Ezek. 11,19-20; 36,26-27; Joel 2,28-29. See also 1QS III, 13-IV,26, especially 1QS IV, 20-22). Then Nicodemus drops out of the picture, as from now on Jesus speaks of the only one who can reveal the ἐπουράνια, the Son of Man who "speaks of what he knows", nevertheless John wants us to see Nicodemus, who has failed because of his incomplete faith (vv. 1-10), listening to the discourse which follows.[34] It is in answer to Nicodemus' incomplete faith that Jesus replies in terms of "the Son of Man".

F. Blass-R.Debrunner-R. W. Funk, *A Greek Grammar of the New Testament and Other Early Christian Literature*, (Chicago, University of Chicago Press, 1967) para. 301,2. It seems improbable, however, that the original writer of these words, with the regular succession of ἄνθρωπος did not intend them to be linked. Why did the author not use τις in this case, where ambiguity would clearly arise? W. A. Meeks, "Man from Heaven ...", pp. 54-55 argues that Nicodemus is a "type" of the people referred to in 2,23-25. See also G. Gaeta, *op. cit.*, pp. 42-44.

[29] See the detailed studies of I. de la Potterie, "Jesus et Nicodemus: de necessitate generationis ex Spiritu (Jo. 3,1-10)", *VD* 47 (1969) 194-214, and G. Gaeta, *op. cit.*, pp. 44-69

[30] I. de la Potterie, *art. cit.*, p. 194; C. K. Barrett, *St. John*, p. 170; M. de Jonge, "Jesus and Nicodemus...", p. 338; J. Marsh, *St. John*, p. 173; U. Holzmeister, "Grundgedanke und Gedankengang im Gespräche des Herrn mit Nikodemus", *ZKT* 45 (1921) 531; J. N. Sanders, *St. John*, pp. 122-123; W. A. Meeks, "Man from Heaven..", p. 55.

[31] See R. Schnackenburg, *St. John*, I, p. 364.

[32] J. H. Bernard, *St. John*, p. 101 points out that, surprising though it may sound to us, this phrase "expressed the general belief of Judaism" about great Israelites.

[33] See H. Leroy, *Rätsel und Missverständnis. Ein Beitrag zur Formgeschichte des Johannesevangeliums*, Bonner Biblischer Beiträge 30, (Bonn, Haustein, 1968) pp. 124-136; G. Gaeta, *op. cit.*, pp. 42-46.

[34] This is probably why Nicodemus later appears in such a favourable light (see 7,50-52; 19,38-42).

III - *3,11-21: Jesus' monologue arising out of his encounter with Nicodemus.*[35]

Although · Jesus has used "amen, amen I say to you" twice before in his conversation with Nicodemus (vv. 3 and 5) here his use of it represents a new beginning.[36] In vv. 11b-12 Jesus addresses "you" in the plural, referring to himself as "we". As the monologue continues, its tone becomes even more meditative and impersonal as Jesus speaks of the Son of Man, God and the work of the only Son of God (vv. 13-21).[37] Yet this section is not to be divorced from the preceding conversation. The "amen, amen I say to you" always has reference to something that has been said already, which is expanded or set in a new light.[38]

Jesus has spoken to Nicodemus of the ἐπίγεια of the "new generation" which had already been promised in the tradition of Israel, and which happened to man while still on earth.[39] All that has been said so far is real; it can come about, but there is a further mystery which cannot be called ἐπίγεια. It is ἐπουράνια and can only be fully understood and spoken of by one who has seen it and knows it, Jesus himself.[40] It is Jesus who reveals the truth about the establishment of the new order. By sending him to the "lifting up" on the cross, God has given man the possibility of eternal life (see v. 15). God's only Son has come into the world to bring life, but with it he brings judgment. He does not condemn (v. 17), but man condemns himself, by refusing the life which is offered by the revelation of Jesus.

IV - *3,22-30: John the Baptist and the Jews.*

We are clearly dealing with a different section here and the main difficulty is to understand what it has to do with the argument of the rest of the

---

[35] See the detailed studies of I. de la Potterie, "Jesus et Nicodemus: de revelatione Jesu et vera fide in eum (Jo. 3,11-21)", *VD* 47 (1969) 257-283, and G. Gaeta, *op. cit.*, pp. 69-105.

[36] L. Brun, "Jesus als Zeuge von irdischen und himmlischen Dingen, Jo 3,12-13", *SymbOs* 8 (1929) 58: "3,11 hat dem vorgehenden Gespräch gegenüber eine gewisse Selbständigkeit".

[37] A. Schlatter, *Johannes*, p. 85 gives examples from Jewish literature to show that this change of persons is a common practice.

[38] See J. H. Bernard, *St. John*, pp. 66-67. See above, pp. 25-26.

[39] See R. Schnackenburg, *St. John* I, pp. 377-380; W. Bauer, *Johannesevangelium*, p. 55; L. Brun, "Jesus als Zeuge ...", p. 65; E. C. Hoskyns, *The Fourth Gospel*, p. 205; W. F. Howard, "St. John", pp. 507-508. W. Thüsing, *Erhöhung*, pp. 255-257 argues, in line with his overall thesis, that "the heavenly things" are the works that the glorified Christ will perform from his place beside the Father. However, there is no suggestion in v. 12 of "doing works". The "heavenly things" and "earthly things" are not "performed", but "told" in v. 12. The context is concerned with relevation.

[40] W. Thüsing, *op. cit.*, p. 254: "V. 11 konstatiert — von dem Tadel an Nikodemus aus — die Situation des Offenbarerwirkens Jesu den Juden gegenüber".

chapter. The point at issue in these verses, as in all the Johannine John the Baptist passages, is not the figure of the Baptist himself, but his role in relation to Jesus.[41] After an introductory passage (vv. 22-24), which has its own problems,[42] we are told that a discussion arose between a disciple of John and a Jew, over purifying. We are not told what the exact nature of the discussion was, but they come to see John, asking him about baptism and the success of Jesus. The Evangelist, who may well be using a source here,[43] probably understands the "purification" as baptism. The Baptist's reply places the whole discussion in the context of revelation. That which John the Baptist has is "from heaven" (v. 27). The Baptist is now, as all men should be, "the one who stands and hears him" (v. 29). He has understood what the Johannine Jesus demands from man and as such, in this context he is a foil to the misunderstanding of Nicodemus. He understands that what Jesus brings is "from heaven", just as his own role as "the one sent before him" (v. 28) was given to him "from heaven". He is not the Christ, but he has pointed to him (see 1,29-34) and now he must listen to, and rejoice in, the revelation brought by "the voice of the bridegroom" (see v. 29; 5,25; 10,3; 16,27; 18,37).[44] Vv. 27-29 make it clear that no one, not even the Baptist, can lay claim to the unique position of Jesus described in v. 13.[45] Because the Baptist has *rightly* understood the mystery of Jesus, he can say: "He must increase, but I must decrease (v. 30)".[46] The Baptist is open to the revelation of the "heavenly things", which are again summarised for the reader in the Evangelist's reflection of vv. 31-36.[47]

[41] See I. de la Potterie, "Giovanni Battista e Gesù testimoni della verità nel quarto vangelo", in *Gesù Verità*, (Torino, Marietti, 1973) pp. 167-178; M. D. Hooker, "John the Baptist and the Johannine Prologue", *NTS* 16 (1970) 354-358; C. K. Barrett, "The Prologue of St. John's Gospel", pp. 39-45; J. M. Boice, *Witness and Revelation in the Gospel of John*, (Grand Rapids, Eerdmans, 1970) pp. 80-88; R. Schnackenburg, "Die Messiasfrage ...", pp. 244-246; B. Lindars, "Two Parables in John", *NTS* 16 (1969-70) 324-329; J. T. Forestell, *The Word of the Cross*, pp. 19-23.

[42] It is outside our scope to investigate the archeological-geographical discussion about "Aenon near Salim", or the historicity of the baptism of Jesus (see the contradiction between 3,22 and 4,2). See R. E. Brown, *John*, pp. 150-152 for a summary of this. For some interesting suggestions on both the topology and theology involved here, see M.-E. Boismard, "Aenon, près de Salem (Jean 3,23)", *RB* 24 (1973) 218-229.

[43] See R. Fortna, *The Gospel of Signs*, pp. 179-180 for this possibility.

[44] See R. Bultmann, *John*, p. 254: "Jesus does not 'show' us any particular thing (10,32; 14,8f.) in the sense of displaying an object or state of affairs to our view. His 'showing' consists in his speaking to us and challenging us to believe". See also J. Blank, *Krisis*, p. 141, note 76.

[45] See B. Lindars, *John*, p. 169.

[46] See W. A. Meeks, "Man from Heaven ...", p. 57.

[47] See W. H. Cadman, *The Open Heaven*, pp. 71-73.

V - 3,31-36: *The Evangelist's reflection, arising out of the discussion between the Baptist and the Jews.*

There is a sharp break between v. 30 and v. 31. Many scholars neglect this, and are led to identify the Baptist with the one "who is of the earth".[48] W. Bauer and C.K. Barrett believe that the Baptist is still speaking,[49] while those who identify Jesus as the speaker (e.g. Schnackenburg, Bernard, Bultmann, Gourbillon)[50] have to rearrange the text to make this possible. Leaving the text as it has come down to us, one feels compelled to understand the Evangelist as the speaker, commenting on the Baptist scene by recalling once again the basic elements of Johannine christology which he had already pronounced, in the words of Jesus, in vv. 11-21.[51]

Jesus is "he who comes from heaven" (v. 31) to tell man what he has seen and heard. The authority of his revelation lies in his having come from heaven. It is Jesus who "utters the words of God" (v. 34), and belief in the revelation brought by Jesus will gain eternal life (v. 36); he who does not obey, and turns away, will experience the wrath of God.

The Evangelist appears to have formed John 3 by working with sources, uniting various traditional elements, to produce a unity. There is every possibility that the Nicodemus and the Baptist scenes have a historical origin. 3,31-36 could well be made up of a pre-Johannine tradition which was already connected with the story of the Baptist.[52] Jn. 3,34b may be an echo of 1,33; Matt. 3,12; Mk. 1,18 and Lk. 3,16, all of which could have originally belonged to a John the Baptist source. In v. 36c we find ἡ ὀργή. This word is not found anywhere else in the Johannine literature, but it is found in the Synoptic tradition (Matt. 3,7; Lk. 3,7) in the preaching of the Baptist. Other interesting points of contact can be found: it is possible that the introduction of the light theme in vv. 19-21 is the subtle introduction to the Baptist. In 1,6-8 it is the Baptist who came "to bear witness to the light" and this is precisely what he is doing in 3,27-30. One could conclude then, that the whole chapter is

---

[48] See C. K. Barrett, *St. John*, p. 187; W. Bauer, *Johannesevangelium*, p. 64; R. E. Brown, *John*, pp. 160-161; R. H. Lightfoot, *St. John*, p. 120; J. N. Sanders, *St. John*, p. 135. M. Black, *An Aramaic Approach*, pp. 146-149 argues that the Baptist is the speaker throughout, as he suggest that a "Greek sayings-group, translated from Aramaic sayings of the Baptist was used by St. John" (p. 149).

[49] See above, note 48.

[50] See above, pp. 42-43.

[51] See M.-J. Lagrange, *St. Jean*, p. 96; C. H. Dodd, *Interpretation*, pp. 308-311; R. Bultmann, *John*, p. 162, note 2.

[52] See C. H. Dodd, *Historical Tradition in the Fourth Gospel*, (Cambridge, CUP, 1963) pp. 281-287. This could also be concluded from the suggestion of M. Black (see above, note 48); Black may well be right in his identification of a traditional Aramaic unit. It is not necessary, however, to claim that it comes from a collection of Aramaic sayings of John the Baptist. It may simply be a piece of traditional material, as argued above.

assembled by the Evangelist, using blocks of traditional material, but subjecting all his sources to his own theological point of view. This is especially noticeable in vv. 11-21 where the vocabulary, style and thought are completely Johannine. The rest of the material, although it may have come to John, is heavily reworked, especially vv. 31-36, as it is the Evangelist who is speaking to his readers throughout. It is his point of view which must concern us.

The following structure seems to emerge from the analysis of John 3:

I   - 2,23-25: The question of the correct type of faith.

II   - 3,1-10: The first example, Nicodemus, fails to go beyond the limitations of his traditional Jewish faith. He has not correctly understood nor believed in Jesus.

III - 3,11-21: Jesus reflects on this in a monologue:

  vv. 11-15: Jesus, the Son of Man, the revealer of the "heavenly things".

  vv. 16-21: The salvation-condemnation brought by this revelation which has come into the world.

IV - 3,22-30: The second example, John the Baptist, understands the role of Jesus as the revealer from heaven, and sees his own role in the light of that understanding.

V   - 3,31-36: The Evangelist reflects upon this:

  vv. 31-34: Jesus, "he who comes from heaven" is the revealer of "the words of God".

  vv. 35-36: The salvation-condemnation brought by this revelation which has come into the world.

II - The Son of Man in John 3,13-14

By means of this interplay of dialogue, monologue, narrative and reflection, John has given his readers a compendium of his own christology.[53] During the course of all this he has applied to Jesus the titles which are most frequent in his Gospel: the Son, the Son of God and the Son of Man. The titles "the Son" or "the Son of God", as explained in v. 31a: "He who comes from above", v. 31b: "He who comes from heaven" and v. 34: "He whom God has sent", make sense to a reader who accepts John's theological point of view. But what does he mean by his use of "the Son of Man" in vv. 13-14? Can

---

[53] The parallel between the meaning and structure of vv. 11-21 and vv. 31-36 can be carried into 12,46-48. There John is again summarising, as he brings the story of the public life and preaching of Jesus to a close. Note the relationship of thought, structure and language in 3,15-16 (19) = 12,46; 3,17-18 = 12,47-48; 3,19 = 12,46.48.

this title simply be equated with the titles denoting Jesus' Sonship? [54]   Does it have a meaning and a function of its own?

Nicodemus, as "a man of the Pharisees" and "a ruler of the Jews" represents a group of people in the Johannine audience.[55]   In 12,42 we are told that there were many ἄρχοντες who believed, but were afraid.   John is critical of this fear (see 12,43: "They loved the praise of men more than the praise of God").   They had not come to a correct belief in the   σημεῖα (see v. 37), while the true disciples of Jesus will see the same "signs", believe and thus gain eternal life (see 20,30-31).   This weak and faulty faith is precisely what John is describing in 2,23-25, a passage stating the theme behind the events of chapter 3.   They are believers, and Nicodemus is a believer, but they seem to stand on the wrong side of a dividing line.   There are believers who live in communion with him whom God has sent into the world, and there are believers to whom Jesus does not trust himself.[56]

Nicodemus, as a representative of the Jewish authorities, and an example of the people named in 2,23-25, does not merely ask questions in an evening discussion.   He confesses his faith in Jesus as "Rabbi", a teacher come from God, a doer of signs and he believes that God is with him.[57]   It is in answer to this confession of faith that the rest of the discourse unfolds.   A true rebirth, as told already in the Old Testament and the tradition of Israel, must be a first step in the correct understanding of Jesus, but Nicodemus cannot even grasp this (see v. 9b).[58]   Nevertheless, Jesus proceeds, and reaches the high point of his reply in vv. 11-15, which is then further elucidated in vv. 16-21.

In vv. 11-15 the Evangelist makes it clear in what respects the faith of the group represented by Nicodemus, the group of 2,23-25 and 12,37-43, falls short of true Johannine faith.   In reply to the titles given to Jesus by Nicodemus, Jesus himself replies in terms of "the Son of Man".[59]

Jesus is everything that Nicodemus has called him: he has God with him (see 8,29; 16,32) and he is a teacher *par excellence* (see 7,16-17; 7,28-29), but

---

[54] As E. D. Freed, "The Son of Man in the Fourth Gospel", pp. 403-404 would maintain.   He holds that in 3,13-14 the Son of Man is identical in its function with the titles of Son and Son of God in vv. 16-18.

[55] J. L. Martyn, *History and Theology in the Fourth Gospel*, pp. 74-76 argues that Nicodemus represents members of the Sanhedrin at the time of John, who secretly believed. This can hardly be claimed with any certainty.

[56] See M. de Jonge, "Nicodemus and Jesus ...", pp. 338-341.

[57] See above, p. 47, note 32.   See also G. Reim, *Studien zum alttestamentlichen Hintergrund*, pp. 119-120.   Reim sees this as a reference to Deut. 18,15 ff.

[58] Note the use of γινώσκω in v. 10.   The use of this verb in John generally refers to the knowledge which arises from an observable fact.   See I. de la Potterie, "Οἶδα et γινώσκω.   Les deux modes de la connaissance dans le quatrième évangile", *Biblica* 40 (1959) 709-725.

[59] See U. Holzmeister, "Grundgedanke und Gedankengang ...", p. 531: "Jesus will den Ratsherren von der falschen Messiaserwartung abbringen".

this is not enough.   To confess this, without previously understanding that Jesus is the Son of Man, in the sense of vv. 13-14, is not to confess enough. Jesus gives witness to what he has seen — this is the revelation of the truth, but it is not accepted (v. 11).   Jesus is the one who possesses the information, and who can decide what he will reveal (v. 12),[60] but this demands a knowledge of the "heavenly things", and a descent of the one who knows these things. John describes this in the event of the descent of the Son of Man.[61]   What follows in vv. 13-15 is not so much a description of the "heavenly things", but more a statement that Jesus is the revealer of the "heavenly things" and that, consequently, all who believe may have eternal life in him.[62]   As Nicodemus has confessed to a belief in Jesus which is insufficient, Jesus now replies to this incomplete faith in terms of the Son of Man and his function.   It is faith in the Son of Man which is true Johannine faith (see 9,35).

V. 13 however, presents many difficulties.   The general sense of the verse is that the Son of Man is the one who has come down from heaven.   But v. 13a speaks of an "ascension" in the perfect tense — ἀναβέβηκεν.   The RSV translates the verse: "No one has ascended into heaven but he who descended from heaven, the Son of Man".   This translation drops the first word of the Greek (καί), and makes the Son of Man the only one who has ever ascended into heaven, but the verse should be more closely united to what has gone before (vv. 11-12), concerning the revelation of the "heavenly things".[63]   It is in the light of a current discussion about the revelation of these heavenly things that the ἀναβέβηκεν can be correctly understood.

Loisy, Bauer, Brown, Bultmann, Barrett, Wikenhauser, Cullmann, van den Bussche, Mollat and Segalla interpret the perfect of ἀναβαίνειν as a reference to the historical ascension of Jesus,[64] claiming that this statement is to be

---

[60] See W. A. Meeks, "Man from Heaven ...", p. 54: "The point of v. 12 is not at all the contrast between heavenly and earthly information, but the contrast between the questioner and the one who possesses the information".

[61] See I. de la Potterie, "La notion de témoignage dans saint Jean", in J. Coppens et alii (eds.), *Sacra Pagina*, II, Miscellanea Biblica Congressus Internationalis Catholicus de Re Biblica, (Gembloux, Duculot, 1959) p. 195.   He comments on 3,11: "Si donc Jésus déclare qu'il parle de ce qu'il sait et qu'il témoigne de ce qu'il a vu auprès du Père, on voit déjà que le thème johannique du témoignage sera, lui aussi, un thème de révélation".

[62] See L. Brun, "Jesus als Zeuge ...", p. 69: "Der Spruch handelt vom Menschensohn als Mittler der Offenbarung, als Verkündiger himmlischer Dinge"; J. T. Forestell, *The Word of the Cross*, pp. 42-43.

[63] See J. Blank, *Krisis*, p. 76, note 76: " καί ist in diesem Fall weiterführende Konjunktion; 'auch' "; L. Brun, "Jesus als Zeuge ...", p. 69.   The importance of this link has been expertly examined by G. Gaeta, *Il dialogo con Nicodemo*, pp. 72-78.

[64] A. Loisy, *Quatrième Évangile*, p. 165; W. Bauer, *Johannesevangelium*, p. 56; R. E. Brown, *John*, p. 145; R. Bultmann, *John*, pp. 149-151; C. K. Barrett, *St. John*, p. 177; A. Wilkenhauser, *Das Evangelium nach Johannes*, RNT, (Regensburg, Pustet, 1948) p. 73; O. Cullmann, *Christology*, p. 185; H. van den Bussche, *Jean*, pp. 168-169; G. Segalla, "Preesistenza, Incarnazione e Divinità di Cristo in Giovanni", *RivBIt* 22 (1974) 162; Idem, "Cinque schemi cristologici in Giovanni", *StPat* 20 (1973) 17-19.

understood as the reflection of the later church, placed anachronistically upon the lips of Jesus, making his ascension a past but still efficacious event.[65]

This solution presents difficulties. After speaking of the ascension as a past event, Jesus then speaks of the cross as still in the future (v. 14). In fact, Jesus' going to heaven is always spoken of in a future tense (see 20,17; 14,2; 12,8.28; 16,28; 17,5).[66] Such a clumsy anachronism, so out of tune with the rest of the Gospel, can hardly be the meaning of ἀναβαίνειν here. There is no description of an ascension in the Fourth Gospel.[67] Jesus goes to the Father and pours out the Spirit, as he promised (see 14,2.16.26; 16,7.28; 17,5), but for John all this is one event — the moment of his glorification, which is at once the "lifting up" upon the cross, the pouring out of the Spirit and the birth of true faith which comes from beholding the glorified Jesus (see 19,28-37).

A more satisfactory solution is suggested by Bernard, Westcott and Lagrange.[68] Jesus does not say that *he* has ascended, but that no one (οὐδείς) has ascended. In making this affirmation John is merely using a stock phrase from Jewish tradition (see Dt. 30,12; Prov. 30,4; Bar. 3,29; Wisd. 9,16-18; IV Esdras 4,8) which appears to be directed against any suggestion that man could ascend to heaven to learn the secrets of God, and then descend again to reveal them. The other side of the polemic — an affirmation that this did, in fact, happen — is well attested in Jewish literature (see, for example, Onkelos, Pseudo Jon. and Fragment Targums on Deut. 30,11-14; Targum on Ps. 68,19; Martyrdom of Isaiah 2,9; 3,7-10;[69] I Enoch 71; II Baruch 2,1-8; III Baruch; Life of Adam and Eve 25-28; II Enoch 1; Test. of Abraham, Recension A: 10-15, Recension B: 8-12). The first part of John 3,13, then, is a denial of the possibility of any human agent for the revelation of the things from above. To act as a revealer a human would have to ascend to heaven to learn these things.[70] This possibility, in accordance with orthodox tradition, is denied.[71]

---

[65] C. K. Barrett, *St. John,* p. 177.

[66] See L. Brun, "Jesus als Zeuge ...", p. 70; R. Schnackenburg, *St. John* I, p. 393.

[67] Recently W. J. P. Boyd, "Ascension according to John", *TLond* 70 (1967) 207-211 has suggested that sections of the last discourse (14,1-29; 15; 16,1-16 and 17) belong after the crucifixion. Ch. 17 was spoken as the ascension was taking place.

[68] J. H. Bernard, *St. John,* p. 111; B. F. Westcott, *St. John,* p. 53; M.-J. Lagrange, *St. Jean,* pp. 80-81.

[69] See A. Young, "A Study of the Relation of Isaiah to the Fourth Gospel", *ZNW* 46 (1955) 216-218. 232.

[70] See H. Odeberg, *Fourth Gospel,* pp. 72-94 for copious references to literature which speaks of the ascension of a revealer (from Jewish, Hermetic and Mandaean sources). See especially pp. 88-89, where he claims that Jn. 3,13 "can scarcely be interpreted otherwise than as a strong refutation of some current and prominent doctrine or belief of the time concerning the possibility of ascent into heaven". Odeberg (pp. 94-95) concludes that the polemic was against Jewish *Merkabah* mysticism. See also the material examined by M. Smith, "Observations on *Hekkalot Rabbati*", in A. Altmann (ed.), *Biblical and Other Studies,* Studies and Texts 1, (Harvard, Harvard University Press, 1963) pp. 142-160.

[71] That this discussion was current in some circles in the early Church could be

There is one exception to this — the Son of Man. The point made is not that the Son of Man has ascended (which he has done, and this is duly noted by an early commentator who adds: "he who is in heaven") but that he descended. What Jesus is saying is that he can speak of the heavenly things, not because he has gone up, but because he has come down. The exception involved in the εἰ μή refers to the impossibility of a human's revealing the things of God. The Son of Man has done this because he is the one who has come down in the incarnation. Of course, for the early Church, Jesus had ascended, and the early gloss "he who is in heaven" tells us, in parenthesis, that even though Jesus did not have to ascend to receive the revelation which he gives to men, he has nevertheless ascended. This gloss, however, would be out of place in the mouth of the Johannine Jesus, who would hardly speak of his being on earth and in heaven at the same time.

The above interpretation hinges on the understanding of the εἰ μή as a restriction which does not correspond to what has preceded.[72] There is a continuation in the development of an idea, with a new element being introduced, in contrast with what has gone before. A similar use of εἰ μή is found again in v. 27, but v. 13 is stronger, having the sense and force of ἀλλά This usage is found in Rev. 21,27: "Nothing unclean shall enter it, nor anyone who practises abomination or falshood, but (εἰ μή) only those who are written in the Lamb's book of life" (see also Matt. 12,4; Lk. 4,27; Acts 27,22). There is no doubt that those who are written in the Lamb's book of life are not unclean, nor the practisers of abomination or falsehood. In Jn. 3,13 the εἰ μή is used in a similar fashion: There is no one who has ascended, but, contrary to the fact of the protasis, one has descended, the Son of Man.[73]

This usage reflects the common Hebrew exception, expressed by the use of *kî 'im* (see Gen. 32,39; 15,4; Deut. 7,5; I Sam. 2,15; 8,19; Ps. 1,2). P. Joüon paraphrases its sense as: "La chose n'est pas ainsi, mais ...".[74] Although the saying in Jn. 3,13 does not immediately appear open to this understanding, the author has deliberately constructed a sentence which balances around the εἰ μή. In a well balanced sentence, the descent of the Son of Man is set in

indicated by Rom. 10,6-7. The use of ἀναβαίνειν here, as in Jn. 3,13 has nothing to do with the ascension of Jesus, but with man's efforts to reach him. Paul points out in v. 8 that such efforts are not necessary.

[72] See M.-J. Lagrange, *St. Jean*, pp. 80-81.

[73] See F. Blass-A. Debrunner-R. W. Funk, *A Greek Grammar*, para. 428; M. Zerwick, *Biblical Greek*, (Rome, Biblical Institute Press, 1963) para. 471. W. Bauer-W. F. Arndt-F. W. Gingrich, *A Greek-English Lexicon of the New Testament and Other Early Christian Literature*, (Chicago, University of Chicago Press, 1957) s.v. εἰ VI, 7b and J. H. Moulton-G. Milligan, *The vocabulary of the Greek Testament*, p. 182 s.v. εἰ give examples of this usage in classical literature and the papyri.

[74] P. Joüon, *Grammaire de l'Hébreu Biblique*, (Rome, Pontifical Biblical Institute, 1923) para. 172c.

direct opposition to any claims of a revealer who had ascended to heaven to receive the truth:[75]

καὶ

A	οὐδεὶς	A1	ὁ υἱὸς τοῦ ἀνθρώπου
B	ἀναβέβηκεν	B1	καταβάς
C	εἰς τὸν οὐρανὸν	C1	ὁ ἐκ τοῦ οὐρανοῦ

εἰ μὴ

He has placed "the Son of Man" at the end of the phrase to balance the "no one" which opened it. This may appear to be grammatically clumsy, but once the structure of the sentence is recognised, the opposition between the οὐδεὶς and ὁ υἱὸς τοῦ ἀνθρώπου is seen as the point at issue: there is only one who can reveal the truth with ultimate authority, the one who descended, the Son of Man.[76]

In a study which generally leads to convincing arguments for the Philonic, Rabbinic and Samaritan background for many major themes in the Gospel, W. A. Meeks grudgingly comments on 3,13:

> "As in the gnostic myths, the *ascent* of Jesus in the Fourth Gospel cannot be separated from his prior *descent...* This pattern of descent/ascent of a heavenly messenger has no direct parallel in the Moses traditions (except for an isolated statement by Philo[77]); it has been and remains the strongest support for the hypothesis that the Johannine christology is connected with gnostic mythology".[78]

---

[75] See I. de la Potterie, "Jesus et Nicodemus ...", p. 262; J. Bligh, "Four Studies in John II ...", p. 48; G. Gaeta, *Il discorso con Nicodemo*, pp. 76-78. 91-92.

[76] In adopting the above interpretation of 3,13, we reject any suggestion of a Gnostic revealer who descends and ascends. For this case, see R. Bultmann, *John*, pp. 146-153; Idem, "Die Bedeutung der neuerschlossenen mandäischen und manichäischen Quellen ...", pp. 138-139; S. Schulz, *Untersuchungen*, pp. 105-106; Idem, *Johannes*, pp. 58-59; G. Iber, *Untersuchungen*, pp. 156-170. He argues that the title "the Son of Man" comes from the tradition and not from Gnosticism. However, 3,13 and 6,62 are about "die Rückkehr' des Erlösers in seine himmlische Heimat". (p. 157). There may well have been Gnostic influences in the streams of Jewish thought that John is combatting, and this may determine his use of the idea of a descent to speak of the incarnation, but John is certainly not Gnostic at this point. See also F. Mussner, *ZΩH. Die Anschauung vom "Leben" im vierten Evangelium unter Berücksichtigung der Johannesbriefe*, Münchener Theologische Studien. Historische Abteilung 5, (München, Zink, 1952) pp. 123-127. J. P. Miranda, *Der Vater der mich gesandt hat: Religionsgeschichtliche Untersuchungen zu den johanneischen Sendungsformeln, zugleich ein Beitrag zur johanneischen Christologie und Ekklesiologie*, European University Papers 23/7, (Bern, Herbert Lang, 1972) pp. 66-82 has shown, in considerable detail, that John's use of ἀναβαίνειν comes from the Jewish traditions of the ascension of Moses, Elias and others. It has no connection with the return of the Gnostic redeemer to his homeland.

[77] *De Sac.*, 8-10. See W. A. Meeks, *The Prophet-King*, pp. 104-105.

[78] *ibid.*, p. 297.

This is a disappointing conclusion, as Meeks has shown in his work that there was a tradition about the "ascent" of Moses.[79] It was because Moses had ascended that he could become God's agent on earth "as prophet, his unique messenger, conveying divine secrets; as king, his vice-regent".[80] It appears that Meeks has found further evidence in support of the case which we have argued above. Among other things, John is opposed to this Moses mysticism, which honours Moses as God's agent among men because he has ascended to the heavens to have direct contact with God himself.[81] No one, not even Moses, has ascended to bring back the divine secrets. The only one who is capable of such a revelation is the Son of Man, who has descended in the incarnation. Meeks has difficulty because he holds that the ascension referred to in v. 13a is the ascension of Jesus, so he reluctantly falls back on Gnostic parallels to explain this. Yet, he correctly understands the passage as part of a polemic against a "Moses-centred piety",[82] and shows that this polemic is found, not only in 3,13, but in the theme of "no-one has ever seen God" which is general throughout the Gospel (see 1,17-18; 6,46; I John 4,12. See especially 5,37 in the light of Deut. 4,12).

In the context of vv. 11-13 Jesus tells us: "I am telling you what I have seen. You cannot understand these things, for not one of you has ascended to heaven to discover them; but the Son of Man has come down from heaven and, as such, can speak with unique authority".[83]

R. Schnackenburg refuses to accept this interpretation, but his own suggestions are determined by his rearrangement of the text; v. 13 is seen as

[79] For his survey of the material, see *ibid.*, pp. 110-111 (Philo); 192-195 (Samaritan sources); 235-236 (later Rabbinics).

[80] *ibid.*, p. 295.

[81] See, on this, P. Borgen, "God's Agent in the Fourth Gospel", p. 146: "John's ideas in 3,3-13 seem to be a polemic against the very idea expressed by Philo. John says that the vision of God's kingdom and the second birth from above are not brought about by ascent into heaven to the Son of Man. It is rather the heavenly man's descent which brings about the second birth". G. Reim, *Studien zum alttestamentlichen Hintergrund*, pp. 110-155, esp. 130-144 has argued that there is a close link between the Fourth Gospel and Moses speculation. He does not, however, see any conflict between Jesus and Moses, as we do. He holds that the God-Moses relationship was a model for the God-Jesus relationship in Johannine theology. See also, G. Gaeta, *op. cit.*, pp. 92-93.

[82] W. A. Meeks, *op. cit.*, pp. 298-301.

[83] This interpretation is followed, with various nuances, by J. Bligh, "Four Studies in John ...", p. 48; I. de la Potterie, "Jesus et Nicodemus ...", pp. 262-264; B. Lindars, *John*, p. 156; Idem, "The Son of Man ...", p. 48; E. C. Hoskyns, *Fourth Gospel*, p. 217; B. Schwank, *Johannesevangelium*, Vol. I, pp. 144-147; P. Guichou, *Evangile de Jean*, (Paris, Lethielleux, 1962) p. 60; E. M. Sidebottom, *The Christ*, pp. 120-123; J. Graf, "Nikodemus ...", pp. 67-68. 73-74; A. Feuillet, *Études Johanniques*, (Paris, Desclée, 1962) pp. 77-78; W. F. Howard, "St. John", p. 508; L. Morris, *St. John*, pp. 222-223; G. Gaeta, *op. cit.*, pp. 76-78. 91-92.

the conclusion of vv. 31-36.[84]   This separates it from v. 14, where the Son of Man title is repeated, in direct reference to what has been said in v. 13.   He admits that the use of ἀναβέβηκεν is not a "general statement", and that the Johannine Jesus does not speak anachronistically, as a rule.   However, in this case, the explanation must be that of an anachronism.[85]   Thus he can claim:

> "It is the earthly Jesus seen in the light of his future power of salvation. This 'heavenly man', who merely ascends 'where he was before' (6,62), is enabled by his ascent to lead to salvation those who have joined themselves to him in faith".[86]

There is no need for this solution which is, as Schnackenburg himself admits, out of character with the rest of the Gospel's presentation of Jesus.   The text can be logically explained by following the traditional order, understanding v. 13 as a statement about Jesus as the unique revealer here on earth, without anachronistically placing him in heaven.

H. Odeberg paraphrases the verse as: "No one has ever entered or can ever enter the Kingdom of God, nor ascend to the highest realm of the celestial world, without being united (through faith) with the Son of Man".[87]   He interprets the verse as a polemic against Jewish schools which held that great saints and prophets of Israel had ascended to heaven to attain the knowledge of divine things.   John is pointing out that no one can do this, except in and through faith in the Son of Man.   Odeberg has missed the importance of the elevation of the Son of Man in the context of vv. 11-15.   It is true that the believer comes to have 'life', but not through some sort of mystical union. The believer must believe in the revelation which will be made fully public when the Son of Man is lifted up on the cross (see v. 14).

L. Brun, R. H. Strachan and W. H. Rigg have argued from the use of the Son of Man in 1,51 that the meaning in 3,13 is again one of continual contact between the earthly and the heavenly.[88]   The ἀναβέβηκεν and the textually doubtful "he who is in heaven" both refer to the inner continual union of Jesus with the Father.   "Living under our earthly conditions, Christ is still in heaven, since he is not alone because of his uninterrupted communion with the Father (8,16; 16,32)".[89]   This interpretation makes the use of "ascension" in v. 13a a reference to some sort of spiritual experience.   While the union of the Son with the Father is in line with the thought of the Evangelist, it does not seem to be the issue here.   The use of "the Son of Man" in 1,51 is

---

[84] See above, p. 43.

[85] R. Schnackenburg, *St. John* I, p. 393. See also p. 392, note 22.

[86] *ibid.*, p. 393.

[87] H. Odeberg, *Fourth Gospel*, p. 97. See also pp. 96-98.

[88] L. Brun, "Jesus als Zeuge ..."; R.H. Strachan, *Fourth Gospel*, pp. 137-138; W.H. Rigg, "St. John 3,13", *TLond* 20 (1930) 98-99.

[89] W.H. Rigg, *art. cit.*, p. 98.

not primarily a question of the personal communion between the Father and the Son, but of the revelation which is a consequence of that union. In 1,50 Nathanael is told that he will see greater things. Jesus tells Nathanael of the Son of Man's close and continual intercourse with heaven and, through this, of his being the revelation of God. The promise of 1,50-51, that the disciples would see "greater things", is now being further clarified by 3,13 and specified by the further use of the Son of Man in 3,13-15.[90]

An important textual question shows that the ascension of v. 13a was understood to refer to the ascension of Jesus. There is a wide attestation for the addition of "he who is in heaven". The exclusion of these words is supported by almost uniquely Egyptian witnesses (P[66 75], Sinaiticus, Vaticanus, Regius, Freer Gospels, some uncials and the Coptic and Ethiopic versions). As well as its wide attestation, there are considerable variations in the readings of those manuscripts which retain it, especially in the Syriac version. This could indicate that it was objectionable or difficult for the early translators. Nevertheless, it is excluded by our best witnesses, and should probably be omitted as a later christological addition.[91] The Johannine Jesus does not speak of himself as being in heaven, but a later editor, in the light of the ἀναβέβηκεν of v. 13a, could well have been tempted to tell us that the Son of Man was now in heaven. This was, for the early Church, a very important objective fact, but its inclusion in v. 13c confuses the issue, as the verse is not concerned with the ascension of Jesus, but with the descent of the Son of Man as the revealer of heavenly things.[92]

John 3,14-15 is the specification of the fact proclaimed in 3,13. Jesus, and only Jesus, can reveal the heavenly things. The verses which follow (vv. 14-15), telling of the method and purpose of the revelation of the Son of Man, are tightly linked with v. 13 by καί. This καί is best understood as a co-ordinating "and so ...".[93] Paradoxically, the high point of the revelation

---

[90] F. H. Borsch, *Son of Man*, pp. 270-277 traces the saying back to a mythological Son of Man who is both in heaven, as a reality, and on earth as a man designated to eventually become the real Son of Man. His arguments are extremely speculative, and depend upon a great number of late, and possibly Christian, sources. S. Schulz, *Untersuchungen*, pp. 105-106 and *Johannes*, pp. 59-60, has traced the ascent and descent of the Son of Man back to Jewish apocalytic (see I Enoch 70-71). This theme has then been reinterpreted in Gnostic and Christian sources. Schulz is concerned with the background to the saying, and adds little to clarify its meaning in its present context.

[91] This is difficult to decide. Opinions are divided. Among the editors of the Greek text, it is included by Tischendorf, Weiss, Vogels, Bover, but excluded by Westcott and Hort, von Soden, Merk, Aland and *The Greek New Testament*.

[92] See B. M. Metzger, *A Textual Commentary*, pp. 203-204; M. Mees, "Lectio brevior im Johannesevangelium und ihre Beziehung zum Urtext", *BZ* 12 (1968) 115; Idem, "Erhöhung und Verherrlichung Jesu im Johannesevangelium nach dem Zeugnis neutestamentlicher Papyri", *BZ* 18 (1974) 34.

[93] See F. Blass-A. Debrunner-R. W. Funk, *A Greek Grammar*, par. 442; T. Zahn, *Johannes*, p. 198. See especially, G. Gaeta, *Il discorso con Nicodemo*, pp. 78-79.

will not take place in some glorious theophany, but ...

And so,
As Moses lifted up the snake in the desert
So must the Son of Man be lifted up
So that all who believe may have eternal life in him.

The Son of Man who is the unique revealer (v. 13) must be lifted up so that all may have eternal life in him (vv. 14-15). In the 'lifting up' the unique revealer, the only place on earth where heavenly things may be found, is placed on high so that all may look upon him. Just as it was essential for God's plan that Moses lifted up the snake to restore life to the chosen people, so it is an essential part of God's plan (δεῖ) that the Son of Man, where God reveals himself, be lifted up, so that all who look upon him may have eternal life. The logical link between v. 13 and v. 14 is tight. It is *because* Jesus, the Son of Man, is the unique revelation of God, that he must be lifted up. If the unique importance of the Son of Man had not been clearly stated in v. 13, then there would be no point in what is said in vv. 14-15.

W. A. Meeks has shown that a Mosaic tradition stands behind vv. 14-15. The Mosaic "gift" which gave life in the desert has now been replaced by the superior "gift" of Jesus.[94] Misled by his understanding of the ascension in v. 13a, Meeks has failed to identify the same close link with Mosaic traditions in that passage. It does appear possible, however, that among the great saints of Israel who were supposed to have ascended to heaven, Moses was of great importance. John 3,13 is, therefore, denying that Moses ascended to receive the revelation of God as there is only one who brings that revelation, the Son of Man. The whole passage (vv. 13-15) is further unified by its unique background,[95] and it should not be split apart by rearrangement theories.[96]

In Num. 21,8-9 the serpent is fixed to a stake (*nēs* LXX: σημεῖον) by God's command. The Israelites who gazed upon this elevated serpent were able to survive in spite of their being bitten. John's points of comparison are the 'lifting up', the 'gazing upon' and the 'gaining of life'.[97] The placing of the serpent upon the stake and the consequent salvation is all an activity of God in

---

[94] See W. A. Meeks, *The Prophet-King*, pp. 287-292.

[95] See also G. Reim, *Studien zum alttestamentlichen Hintergrund*, pp. 135-136.

[96] See above, pp. 42-44.

[97] C. K. Barrett, *St. John*, p. 178; R. G. Hamerton-Kelly, *Pre-Existence*, p. 232; W. Thüsing, *Erhöhung*, p. 7 rightly point out that John is in no way interested in the Jewish speculation on this OT passage (see especially II Kings 18,4; Wisd. 16,6-7; *Rosh Hashanah* 3,8) which has an apologetic approach to this Mosaic use of a "graven image". T. W. Manson, "The Argument from Prophecy", *JTS* 46 (1945) 130-132 claims that John's use of Num. 21 is in polemics with Jewish interpretation. See also T. F. Glasson, *Moses in the Fourth Gospel*, SBT 40, (London, SCM Press, 1963) pp. 33-39; G. Reim, *op. cit.*, pp. 197-198. 266.

the Old Testament passage. Similarly, the plan of God is behind the 'lifting up' of the Son of Man, and this is indicated by the use of δεῖ, taken from the tradition of the early Church,[98] and extended here to apply to the life-giving consequences of the 'lifting up', for all who believe.[99]

There are various interpretations of the Johannine theme of 'lifting up' Bultmann, Wikenhauser, Vergote and Müller go back to the use of ὑψωθῆναι in other parts of the New Testament (Acts 2,33; 5,31; Phil. 2,9) where it refers to the ascension-exaltation of Jesus. From this they argue that John is referring to the ascension, and that the cross is merely a symbol of Jesus' being raised up to heaven.[100] These scholars point to the reference to Jesus' ascension in v. 13a as support for their claim, but, as we have already seen, the ascension is not mentioned there. In the only other place where John may speak of the ascension (20,17) there is no reference to 'exaltation'. On the other hand, the four texts which do mention 'exaltation' (3,14; 8,28; 12, 32.34) all point to the cross.[101] W. Thüsing has argued that the Johannine use of ὑψωθῆναι is to be understood as an expression of the regality of Christ, exercised from the cross.[102] While one may have reserves regarding the

---

[98] This use of δεῖ is generally admitted as a connection between this saying and the Synoptic passion predictions. See H. Schelkle, *Die Passion Jesu in der Verkündigung des Neuen Testaments,* (Heidelberg, Kerle, 1949) pp. 109-111; W. Grundmann, Art. "δεῖ" *TDNT* II, p. 24; E. Fascher, "Theologische Beobachtungen zu δεῖ ", in *Neutestamentliche Studien für Rudolf Bultmann,* BZNW 21, (Berlin, Töpelmann, 1957) pp. 228-254; H. E. Tödt, *Son of Man,* p. 164. S. Schulz, *Untersuchungen,* p. 108 claims that the term belongs to apocalyptic rather than Christian sources. F. H. Borsch, *Son of Man,* p. 90 goes further than most scholars in seeing a link between resurrection, elevation, 'handing over' and glorification as a logical growth from the Synoptic tradition to its Johannine expression here.

[99] See R. Schnackenburg, *St. John* I, pp. 395-396.

[100] R. Bultmann, *John,* pp. 152-153. See note 4; A. Wikenhauser, *Johannes,* p. 73; A. Vergote, "L'exaltation du Christ ..." pp. 5-23; H. van den Bussche, *Jean,* pp. 169-171; Th. Müller, *Das Heilsgeschehen im Johannesevangelium,* (Zürich, Gotthelf, n.d.) pp. 49-50.

[101] See W. Thüsing, *Erhöhung,* pp. 1-12.

[102] There has been considerable discussion concerning the possible Aramaic background to ὑψωθῆναι. A. Schlatter, *Johannes,* p. 96 suggested that the two meanings: "to raise up" and "to crucify" could be given to the verb zᵉqaph, found in a North Syrian dialect which could have been used in Jerusalem in the first century. E. Hirsch, *Studien zum vierten Evangelium,* in Beiträge zur historische Theologie 11, (Tübingen, J. C. B. Mohr, 1936) p. 51 argues from this point that an Aramaic Johannine *Grundschrift* was written in Antioch. G. Kittel, "'izdᵉqēph = ὑψωθῆναι = Gekreuzigtwerden", ZNW 35 (1936) 282-285 argues against Hirsch that this play on words, as a pun, was possible in any Aramaic dialect. J. H. Bernard, *St. John,* pp. 114-115 and F. C. Burkitt, "On 'lifting up' and 'exalting' ", in *JTS* 20 (1918-19) 336-338 refuse to accept any Aramaic influence. M. McNamara, "The Ascension and Exaltation of Christ in the Fourth Gospel", *Script* 19 (1967) 65-73 has discovered that the Neophiti Targum uses sᵉlēq to mean "to be taken up" and "to die". He suggests that this stands behind John's play on words. M. Black, *An Aramaic Approach,* p. 141, G. Bertram, Art. "ὑψόω", *TDNT* VIII, p. 610, note 38 and G. Iber, *Untersuchungen,* pp. 151-152 accept an Aramaic play on words. It should be noted, however, that this play on words is equally possible in Greek. See W. Bauer-

exclusive role which Thüsing wants to give to the moment of the cross in Johannine theology, it is clear that this moment is uppermost in John's mind when he uses ὑψωθῆναι, as the redactional note in 12,33 clarifies: "He said this to show *by what manner of death he was to die*".[103]

The parallel used in 3,14 excludes any possible reference to the ascension. In the story of Num. 21, Moses, obedient to God's command, placed a bronze serpent upon a stake for the people to gaze upon. In this way they were saved. There is no suggestion that the snake moved off from its position on the stake to ascend into heaven! If it had, then it would have defeated the purpose of its erection, as the people could no longer look at it.[104]   When Jesus says that just as Moses lifted up (ὕψωσεν) the snake, so must the Son of Man be lifted up (ὑψωθῆναι) he means just that. The Son of Man will also be lifted up on a stake. There is no hint of an ascension in the lifting up, although by using ὑψόω the meaning of 'exaltation' is certainly involved, but in John there is no separation between the cross, the resurrection and the glorification.[105]

John anticipates the regality of the ascended Christ by speaking of the elevated Son of Man on the cross, and this anticipation of Jesus' kingship gives

---

W. F. Arndt-F. W. Gingrich, *A Greek-English Lexicon,* p. 858.   It is not necessary to establish an Aramaic *Grundschrift* to give meaning to the double sense implied by John. This double meaning of the Greek root can be found in secular Greek writing. See Artemidorus Daldianus, *Onirocriticon* I, 76; IV, 49. See D. W. Wead, *The Literary Devices in John's Gospel,* Theologische Dissertationen IV, (Basel, Kommissionsverlag F. Reinhart, 1970) pp. 35.101, note 29.

[103] Thüsing is followed, at least in the insistence that the primary concern of these passages is the cross, by R. Schnackenburg, *St. John* I, pp. 396-397; J. Blank, *Krisis,* pp. 80-85. Both of these scholars, however, reject Thüsing's thesis that the cross is the only reference involved in the 'lifting up'. They see it rather as the "Anfang und Beginn der Erhöhung" (J. Blank, *Krisis,* p. 84). A similar position is taken by R. E. Brown, *John,* p. 146; C. H. Dodd, *Interpretation,* p. 306; T. Zahn, *Johannes,* pp. 200-201; M.-E. Boismard, "La Royauté du Christ dans le quatrième évangile", *LumVie* 57 (1963) 43-63; I. de la Potterie, "L'exaltation du Fils de l'homme (Jn. 12,31-36)", *Greg* 49 (1968) 460-478; J. Riaud, "La gloire et la royauté de Jésus dans la passion selon saint Jean", *BibVChr* 56 (1964) 28-44; M.-J. Lagrange, *St. Jean,* p. 81; A. Loisy, *Quatrième Évangile,* p. 166. For H. Odeberg, *Fourth Gospel,* pp. 99-100.111, there is no reference to the cross. He understands it as a spiritual experience in which the believer is elevated to the glory of salvation through a mystic union with the Son of Man. S. Schulz, *Untersuchungen,* pp. 105-106 maintains that originally there was only a reference to an apocalyptic enthronement, which has been reinterpreted in a Gnostic and Christian sense.

[104] The original text makes no such suggestion; nor does later speculation on this text. See above p. 60, note 97. Gnostic reflection does have the snake ascend, but this is a fantastic speculation upon the Johannine text. See Hippolytus, *Ref.* V, 12,1-17,13. See especially V,12,6-12; 16,4-16. These texts are found in W. Foerster-R. McL. Wilson (eds.), *Gnosis. A Selection of Gnostic Texts,* Vol I: Patristic Evidence, (Oxford, OUP, 1972) pp. 284-292.

[105] See J. T. Forestell, *The Word of the Cross,* pp. 61-65.

a special character to the whole of the Johannine passion narrative.[106] The regality of Jesus is not of this world (18,36), but one which must be accepted in faith (18,35-38). Jesus is a king who has come into the world "to bear witness to the truth" (18,37), and the cross is the high point of this revelation. John tells of man's reply of faith to Jesus' revelation in his solemn conclusion to the crucifixion: "They shall look upon him whom they have pierced" (19,37).[107] The shift from the ascended Christ to the crucified Jesus as the place of 'elevation' is an extraordinary and peculiarly Johannine step. In earlier christologies the cross marked the lowest point of humiliation, which was then followed by the exaltation, leading to Jesus' installation as Lord at the right hand of the Father (Acts 2,33-36; 5,30-31; Phil. 2,8-11),[108] but for John the cross is not a moment of humiliation which has to be overcome by the resurrection and the saving power of Christ as Lord; for John, this saving power is in the cross itself.

The background for this extraordinary point of view may well have included Is. 52,13. There it is said that the Servant of the Lord ὑψωθήσεται καὶ δοξασθήσεται σφόδρα.[109] This text is possibly behind Phil. 2,9 and it is possible that the Johannine view of the cross did have its starting point in the more traditional pattern. The particularly Johannine step is the identification of the cross with the moment of exaltation, subtly presented in the double meaning of ὑψόω. The identification of the exaltation with the glorification

---

[106] See W. A. Meeks, *The Prophet-King*, pp. 61-81; E. Haenchen, "Historie und Geschichte in den johanneischen Passionsberichten", in *Die Bibel und Wir. Gesammelte Aufsätze II*, (Tübingen, J. C. B. Mohr, 1968) pp. 182-207; F. Hahn, "Der Prozess Jesu nach dem Johannesevangelium", *EKK* 2 (1970) 23-96; A. Dauer, *Die Passionsgeschichte im Johannesevangelium. Eine traditionsgeschichtliche und theologische Untersuchung zu Joh 18,1-19,30*, Studien zum Alten und Neuen Testament, (München, Kösel, 1972).

[107] See W. Thüsing, *Erhöhung*, pp. 20-21.

[108] The use of the title "the Son of Man" with the theme of exaltation is also typically Johannine. The early Church used Ps. 110,1 for its exaltation christology. There is considerable discussion about the connection between the christology based on Ps. 110,1 and the Son of Man christology. See O. Cullmann, *Christology*, pp. 179-188; S. Schulz, *Untersuchungen*, pp. 104-109. E. Schweizer, *Erniedrigung und Erhöhung bei Jesus und seinen Nachoflgern*, ATANT 28 (Zürich, Zwingli, 1955) pp. 33-38 links the two through the Righteous Sufferer in Wisdom, but F. Hahn, *Christologische Hoheitstitel*, pp. 112-125, denies all contact. N. Perrin, *Rediscovering the Teaching of Jesus*, (London, SCM Press, 1967) pp. 164-198, argues that the New Testament Son of Man figure is the result of speculation on Dan. 7 in the light of Ps. 110. W. O. Walker, "The Origin of the Son of Man Concept as Applied to Jesus", *JBL* 91 (1972) 482-490 holds that it was Ps. 8 which caused Dan. 7 and Ps. 110 to be linked. For M. Black, "The Son of Man Problem in Recent Research and Debate", pp. 314-317; F. H. Borsch, *Son of Man*, pp. 285-291 and S. S. Smalley, "The Johannine Son of Man Sayings", p. 292, the Johannine point of view may well be the oldest.

[109] See, among others, C. H. Dodd, *Interpretation*, p. 247; R. E. Brown, *John*, p. 146; G. Reim, *Studien zum alttestamentlichen Hintergrund*, pp. 174-176; J. T. Forestell, *The Word of the Cross*, pp. 64-65.

is easily understood in the light of the Old Testament (as well as Is. 52,13, see Pss. 22,28; 50,15; 21,1-6; 3,3).[110] The step from glorification to revelation is again well within the Old Testament tradition, where *kābôd* is so often the term used for the revelation of the presence and power of God among his people (see Exod. 16, 6-7; 33,17-23; Is. 3,8; 4,2; Ezek. 1,26-28; 3,23; 43,2-5; Ps. 24,7-10; Ps. 29 etc.).[111] Once the lifting up on the cross has been understood as something more than a material lifting up, and made into a moment of exaltation, then the process of Cross = Exaltation = Glory = Revelation can be fully understood within a traditional pattern of thought.[112] We suggest that this is the way John eventually arrived at his very personal view of the cross as the supreme moment in the revelation of God, in the elevated Son of Man (see as well as 3,14; 8,28; 12,32.34; 13,31; 19,37).

While v. 14 indicates the manner in which this will take place, the clause of v. 15 tells of its purpose. John is still dependent upon Num. 21:

Num. 21,8 (LXX)	*Jn. 3,15*
πᾶς ὁ δεδηγμένος	πᾶς ὁ
ἰδὼν αὐτὸν	πιστεύων
ζήσεται	ἔχῃ ζωὴν αἰώνιον

The point of comparison between the raised serpent and the elevated Christ is that all who believe may have eternal life in him.[113] The Son of Man lifted up on the cross is the place of salvation and life for the believers, on the condition that their faith is true faith in the Son of Man. V. 16 which is closely linked with what precedes by γάρ and which repeats and enlarges upon v. 15 describes true believers in the usual Johannine way: πᾶς ὁ πιστεύων εἰς αὐτόν. The rest of Jesus' monologue (vv. 16-21) presents the soteriological consequence of Jesus' elevation on the cross. The exalted Jesus becomes the king of believers because he reveals the love of the Father,

---

[110] See M. D. Hooker, *Jesus and the Servant*, (London, SPCK, 1959) pp. 105-106. See p. 192 for note 1 of p. 106.

[111] See R. E. Brown, *John*, pp. 34. 503-504; J. T. Forestell, *The Word of the Cross*, p. 66; T. Worden, "The Glory of God", *The Clergy Review*, 60 (1975) 85-94.

[112] B. Lindars, "The Son of Man...", p. 48 suggests that the Johannine reason for placing the glorification of Jesus in the cross lies in the fact "that the glory of Jesus as the Son of Man consists in his union with the Father, and the cross most fully reveals this because it is the ultimate expression of the union of his will with the Father's". It is not as "the Son of Man" that John speaks of Jesus' union with the Father, but as "the Son (of God)".

[113] The majority of commentators link ἐν αὐτῷ with ἔχῃ rather than with πιστεύων See, for example, C. K. Barrett, *St. John*, p. 179; R. Schnackenburg, *St. John* I, p. 379; R. E. Brown, *John*, p. 133; J. Blank, *Krisis*, p. 85; J. H. Bernard, *St. John*, p. 116; I. de la Potterie, "Jesus et Nicodemus ...", pp. 266-268.

and communicates life to those who look upon him in faith.[114] Those who look upon the crucified Christ have already judged themselves, in refusing the light of God's revelation which has come into the world.[115] Thüsing has rightly affirmed:

"Wenn wir den joh ὑψωθῆναι-Begriff auf eine kurze Formel bringen wollen, können wir sagen: *die joh Erhöhung ist die Erhebung Jesu auf den Thron des Kreuzes - bzw. seine Erhebung zum offenbarenden Heilszeichen*".[116]

In this way Jesus has corrected the confession of Nicodemus. He believes in Jesus as a Rabbi, a teacher from God, and a man of God. But he has not understood what that means, and thus his faith falls short of the mark. The essential thing to believe is that Jesus, the Son of Man, has come down from heaven (v. 13), that he is the Son sent by the Father (vv. 16-18, v. 36). In the whole of the Fourth Gospel, Jesus is presented as "from God" (see 1,1-18; 3,2; 3,13; 9,16.33; 16,27; 1,6; 6,31-58 passim; 8,42; 16,28), and thus his teaching is also "from God" (see 7,17) and can only be understood by those who are "from God" (see 8,47). This is what Nicodemus has failed to understand, despite his confession in 3,2, and what John the Baptist has properly understood. The monologue of Jesus and the commentary of the Evangelist (vv. 11-21; 31-36) have pointed this out by, among other things, the titles which are given to Jesus: Son of Man, Son and Son of God, he who comes from above, he who comes from heaven and he whom God has sent.

The meanings of the two basic titles — "the Son" and "the Son of Man" are not, however, identical.[117] The structure of the two discourses, as outlined above,[118] shows that the titles are used in slightly different contexts.

v. 13	The Son of Man
v. 14	The Son of Man
v. 16	The only Son of God
v. 17	The Son
v. 18	The only Son of God

In the second summary (vv. 31-36), these passages, and the implications of the titles used, are repeated in a different form:

---

[114] See the comments of R. Bultmann, *John*, pp. 153-160, especially p. 154.

[115] See W. Thüsing, *Erhöhung*, pp. 14-15.

[116] *ibid.*, p. 33. See also J. Blank, *Krisis*, p. 85; J. Marsh, *St. John*, p. 182; A. Schlatter, *Johannes*, p. 96.

[117] See B. Lindars, "The Son of Man ...", pp. 43-44. Against E. D. Freed, "The Son of Man in the Fourth Gospel", pp. 403-404.

[118] See above, pp. 46-51.

v. 31a	(parallel to vv. 11-13)[119]	He who comes from above
v. 31b	(parallel to vv. 11-13)[119]	He who comes from heaven
v. 34	(parallel to v. 17)[119]	He whom God has sent
v. 35		The Son
v. 36a		The Son
v. 36b		The Son

The Son of Man is indeed, like the Son, "from above", and both reveal the truth, but a further clarification of the meaning of "the Son of Man" in v. 13 may be had by turning to the parallel vv. 31-32. No mention is made of a relationship with the Father; we are merely told of his origin. The parallel to v. 17 informs us that the Son is sent by God. "The Son" is not found in vv. 13-14 nor in vv. 31-32, while it occurs frequently elsewhere in the passage. On the other hand, "the Son of Man" is not found in vv. 31-32, which we have used to explain that title. It could be suggested that the Evangelist, remaining faithful to the tradition, could not use the title in a reflection which did not come from the mouth of Jesus himself. Thus, while in vv. 31-32 the concepts of vv. 11-13 are repeated and explained, "The Son of Man" could not possibly appear. In vv. 31-32 the one from above comes and speaks what he has seen and heard, and this is clearly a reference to the revelatory role of the "one from above", but there is no mention made of his being sent by God until v. 34 which, we maintain, is parallel to v. 17. There appears to be an important difference between the two titles, if we are correct in looking to these parallels for an explanation of what they mean. The place of origin for "the Son of Man" and "the Son" is the same: both come from above, but when the role of Jesus is explained in terms of the relationship between him and the Father, "the Son" is used (vv. 16.17.18. 35. 36). "The Son of Man" only appears in one context — that of Jesus as the unique revealer who is "lifted up". The functions are, of course, very close. Sonship is also closely related to Jesus' role as revealer, but only in so far as he is sent by the Father, to do the will of the Father (doing the works with which the Father has charged him: see 4,34; 5,36; 9,4; 17,4; fulfilling the will or the command of the Father: see 6,38, 10,18; 12,49; 14,31; 15,10).[120] The Son of Man is never spoken of in this way; the title seems to point to the place among men where revelation occurs, but the Son of Man lifted up on a cross (3,14) is the authentic revelation of God (3,13). When John speaks of the human event of the cross he speaks of the Son of Man (3,14; 8,28; 12,23; see 19,5), never of the Son (of God).

---

[119] See above, p. 45.

[120] See R. Bultmann, *John*, p. 145, note 5.

What has been promised by the first use of the title in 1,51 — the future revelation of God in the Son of Man — has now been further specified:[121] the Son of Man is the unique revealer and his revelation will save all those who believe in him. In answer to the series of titles which Nicodemus has confessed, Jesus has replied, correcting his misunderstanding, by using the title "the Son of Man". Jesus' statement is still cryptic, but it will become clearer as the Gospel continues to develop. This is a part of the tension created by the Evangelist; like "the hour" with which the elevation of the Son of Man is closely linked, one waits for the final revelation of all that is promised by this term.[122]

[121] See R. H. Lightfoot, *St. John,* pp. 117-118 on this link between 1,51 and 3,13-14. See also B. Lindars, "The Son of Man ...", p. 47: "To those who have pondered the implications of 1,51 this should occasion no surprise. For if there is a link between earth and heaven through the earthly ministry of him who is to be glorified as Son of Man, then it is through Jesus that the divine knowledge is mediated to men". See also, G. Gaeta, *Il discorso con Nicodemo,* pp. 90-94.

[122] See C. H. Dodd, *Interpretation,* p. 306. 375-376; G. Ferraro, *L' "ora" di Cristo nel Quarto Vangelo,* Aloisiana 10, (Rome, Herder, 1974) pp. 292-294.

CHAPTER FOUR

THE SON OF MAN AS JUDGE:
John 5,27

I - General Structure and Meaning of John 5,1-30

It has been argued above that Jn. 2,1-4,54 is to be seen as a unit dealing with various "types of faith".[1] Jn. 4,46-54 has been used to close that section, showing the faith of the royal official, but also to introduce the theme of chapter 5, where John uses Jesus' healing activity as the departure point for the important discourse which follows (vv. 19-47).[2] There is a major break, however, at the beginning of ch. 5, where John announces: "After this there was a feast of the Jews, and Jesus went up to Jerusalem" (5,1). There is little agreement among scholars regarding the feast referred to,[3] but it is probably of little importance for a correct understanding of the miracle, controversy and discourse which follow in ch. 5. The feast in question there is clearly the Sabbath (see vv. 9, 10, 16 and the Jewish traditions behind vv. 17-18). Yet 5,1 has its place in the overall structure of the Gospel. The following chapters of the Gospel are an encounter between Jesus and the traditional feasts of Judaism (ch. 5: Sabbath; ch. 6: Passover;[4] chs. 7-8: Tabernacles; chs. 9-10: aftermath of Tabernacles; 10,22-39: Dedication).[5] The

---

[1] See above, pp. 46-51.

[2] C. H. Dodd, *Interpretation*, pp. 318-319.

[3] Some have suggested Tabernacles, while others have argued for Passover. Pentecost has been suggested, following some early Patristic traditions. See F.-M. Braun, "In Spiritu et Veritate", *RThom* 52 (1952) 263-265. J. Bowman, "The Identity and Date of the Unnamed Feast of John 5,1", in H. Goedicke (ed.), *Near Eastern Studies in Honor of William Foxwell Albright*, (Baltimore-London, Routledge and Kegan Paul, 1971) pp. 43-46 goes to some length and detail to show, rather unconvincingly, that the feast referred to is Purim. A. Guilding, *The Fourth Gospel and Jewish Worship, A Study of the Relation of St. John's Gospel to the Ancient Jewish Lectionary System*, (Oxford, OUP, 1960) pp. 85-86 and M. J. Moreton, "Feast, Sign and Discourse in John 5", *StEv* 4 (1968) 209-213 suggest Rosh Hashanah.

[4] This plan of Jewish feasts could be a reason why Jn. 6 is "out of place". There are geographical and literary difficulties, but once we admit that John was using sources to suit his theological plan, then these difficulties are given only a secondary importance.

[5] See R. E. Brown, *John*, pp. 201-204; B. Lindars, *John*, p. 207.

first verse of ch. 5 opens a whole section and as such is more an introduction to a general theme, rather than a reference to a specific feast.

Vv. 2-9a tell the story of the curing of a paralytic at Bethesda.[6] After setting the scene (vv. 2-5) John comes to the miracle by means of terse questions and answers (vv. 6-7), concluding with Jesus' command: "Rise, take up your pallet, and walk" (v. 8). The story concludes in v. 9 when we are told that this is exactly what the man did.[7] There are similarities between this miracle and that of Mk. 2,1-12 (see par. Matt. 9,1-8, where it takes place after the healing of the centurion's servant), but there is probably no dependence.[8] There are good arguments in defence of the basic historicity of the event, despite the fact that John is the only Evangelist who reports it.[9]

The miracle, as is usual in the Fourth Gospel, serves as a springboard for a Johannine discourse.[10] We are introduced immediately to the point at issue: "now that day was the Sabbath" (v. 9b), and after a somewhat roundabout process, where Jesus has to find the cured man to reveal himself so that his identity can be made known to the Jews, we are told: "And this is why the Jews persecuted Jesus, because he did this on the Sabbath" (v. 16). Jesus' reply to the persecution, and the Jews' *correct* understanding of that reply, which they refuse to accept, give sense to the discourse which follows from vv. 19-47.[11] The reply: "My Father is working still, and I am working" (v. 17) presupposes a thesis of Rabbinic theology.[12]

It was clear to the Jews that God could not rest on the Sabbath, but this caused them serious theological difficulties. On the one hand the Torah

---

[6] We are not told that the man is a paralytic. This is generally assumed, as he could not move quickly.

[7] See R. Fortna, *The Gospel of Signs*, pp. 48-54 for the reconstruction of this passage as a "miracle story" which John used as a source. Despite the usefulness of these suggestions, they remain hypothetical.

[8] See R. E. Brown, *John*, pp. 208-209; C. H. Dodd, *Tradition*, p. 175; E. Haenchen, "Johanneische Probleme", ZTK 56 (1959) 46-50; R. Schnackenburg, *Das Johannesevangelium* II. Teil, HTKNT, (Freiburg, Herder, 1971) pp. 121-122; A. Duprez, *Jésus et les dieux guérisseurs. A propos de Jean V*, CahRB 12, (Paris, Gabalda, 1970) pp. 138-143.

[9] The geographical detail, obtuseness of the man, betrayal to the Jews etc. do not seem to serve a theological purpose. See, R. E. Brown, *John*, p. 209; A. Duprez, *Jésus et les dieux guérisseurs*, pp. 170-172.

[10] See E. Lohse, "Miracles in the Fourth Gospel", in M. D. Hooker-C. Hickling (eds.), *What about the New Testament? Essays in Honour of Christopher Evans*, (London, SCM Press) pp. 64-75. On Jn. 5, see p. 69; R. H. Strachan, *Fourth Gospel*, p. 166; R. Fortna, *op. cit.*, p. 49.

[11] C. K. Barrett, *St. John*, p. 213: "This very important verse is the seed out of which the discourse which fills the rest of the chapter grows".

[12] See *Gen. R.* 11,10; *Exod. R.* 30,6.9. The same discussion is found in Philo. See *De Cherubim* 86-90; *Leg. All.* 1,5-6. For further examples see esp. A. Schlatter, *Johannes*, pp. 146-151; C. H. Dodd, *Interpretation*, p. 321; R. Schnackenburg, *Johannesevangelium* II, pp. 126-128.

taught clearly that God rested on the Sabbath (see Gen. 2,2; Exod. 20,11; 31,17), yet on the other hand the faith of Israel preserved the belief that God never left the world to follow its own destiny. God always directed history, and especially the history of his chosen people. Life goes on: children are born on the Sabbath; people die on the Sabbath; God must be always giving life and judging; he could not possibly cease to be active on the Sabbath, or else history would come to an end. He must, therefore, be "working still" on the Sabbath, but only God could be allowed this prerogative.[13] Yet Jesus has included himself under the rubric of his Father who works on the Sabbath. The claim of Jesus is a blasphemy of the highest order (see Gen. 3,5; Is. 14,14; Ezek. 28; Dan. 11,31-36; II Macc. 9,12; see also II Thess. 2,4) to those who refuse to accept Jesus as the "Word made flesh, dwelling among us, full of grace and truth" (1,14).[14] The shocked refusal of the Jews to accept these claims can be understood in the light of Jewish tradition. Jesus has not arrogantly contradicted this tradition. He has claimed that the Father works on the Sabbath, and his own working on the Sabbath must be understood in the light of his relationship with the Father. The discourse which follows is a theological exposition of the relationship which exists between the Father and the Son, a relationship which vindicates Jesus' authority to break the Sabbath Law.[15]

There is some hesitation among scholars as to where the material should be divided. Some would like to place a division before v. 16, as this is where John starts to speak of the refusal of the Jews to accept Jesus' claims to have power over the law of the Sabbath,[16] while others see a division coming between v. 16 and v. 17: a new start is made with "But Jesus answered them ...", thus making v. 16 the conclusion of all that has gone before.[17]

Using literary criteria we see the first part of the lengthy discourse in vv. 19-30. From vv. 9b-18 we have comments of the Evangelist (vv. 9b, 16, 18), words of Jesus in direct speech (vv. 14, 17) and a report of the proceed-

[13] See *Aboth* 4,22.
[14] Again one can see the importance of the prologue as the key which the reader has to understand the claims of Jesus. See above, p. 36, note 66.
[15] See J. Marsh, *St. John*, p. 245. It is generally accepted that the chapter does not need internal rearrangements. However, A. C. Sundberg, "*Isos To Theo* Christology in John 5,17-30" *RibRes* 15 (1970) 19-31 has argued that the discourse should be rearranged as vv. 17-20, 26, 21; 22 and 27 are couplets; 23-24; 25 is a couplet with 28-29; 30. This rearrangement eliminates any subordination of Jesus, making him equal to God. Apart from the lack of any objective proof for such a rearrangement, the passage must be understood in the light of the rest of the Gospel, where Jesus is subject to the will of the Father (see 6,38; 10,18; 12,49; 14,31; 15,10 etc.).
[16] See R. Schnackenburg, *Johannesevangelium* II, p. 124; C.K. Barrett, *St. John*, p. 214; B. Vawter, "John", p. 434.
[17] See G.H.C. Macgregor, *John*, p. 181; R.H. Strachan, *Fourth Gospel*, p. 166; J. Wellhausen, *Johannis*, p. 26.

ings between the cured man and the Jews, once again in direct speech (vv. 10-13, 15). V. 19 starts with a solemn: "Jesus said to them, 'Truly, truly I say to you' ". The typically Johannine use of οὖν tells us that something important is about to follow which is, nevertheless, connected to what has gone before.[18] Vv. 16-18 conclude the narrative and, at the same time, give rise to the following discourse.[19]

Where does the discourse end? There is a break at v. 29 or at v. 30, as the argument changes at that point, and Jesus begins to speak of μαρτυρία. The noun or verb appears five times in vv. 31-32, while it has not appeared at all in vv. 19-30. The dominant themes of the first part of the discourse are the giving of life and judgment. As v. 30 still concerns itself with the question of the judgment brought by Jesus, it probably belongs to the discourse which precedes it.[20] This is confirmed by the fact that there is a deliberate inclusion between vv. 19 and 30:

v. 19	*v. 30*
οὐ δύναται ὁ υἱὸς	οὐ δύναμαι ἐγὼ
ποιεῖν ἀφ' ἑαυτοῦ οὐδέν	ποιεῖν ἀπ' ἐμαυτοῦ οὐδέν

The first part of the discourse in Jn. 5 appears to be contained within the limits of two verses which speak of Jesus' absolute dependence upon the Father. The discourse shows how Jesus' relationship with the Father works itself out in Jesus' role of life-giver and judge.[21]

---

[18] See F. Blass-A. Debrunner-R. W. Funk, *A Greek Grammar*, para. 451,1 and especially, E. A. Abbott, *Johannine Grammar*, (London, A. and C. Black, 1906) Nos. 2191-2200; F. Zorell, *Lexicon Graecum Novi Testamenti*, (Paris, Lethielleux, 1961) Col. 957, No. 2a.

[19] H. van den Bussche, *Jean*, p. 223 calls the section vv. 16-18 "le dossier" and remarks: "Et Jean de conclure: Jésus est l'égal de Dieu, il est le Fils de Dieu. Telles sont les grandes lignes du raisonnement sur lequel s'appuie la première partie du discours christologique en Jean 5". The link between the words and idea of vv. 16-18 and 19-30 is well shown by P. Gächter, "Zur Form von Joh 5,19-30", in J. Blinzler-O. Kuss-F. Mussner (eds.), *Neutestamentliche Aufsätze*, p. 65.

[20] See J. Blank, *Krisis*, pp. 181-182. For a detailed analysis of the linguistic links between vv. 19-29 and v. 30, see A. Vanhoye, "La composition de Jean 5,19-30", in A. Descamps-A. Halleux (eds.), *Mélanges Bibliques en hommage au R. P. Béda Rigaux*, (Gembloux, Duculot, 1970) pp. 260-262.

[21] Most scholars see the discourse as running from v. 19 to v. 30. See J. Blank, *Krisis*, p. 109, note 1; M.-J. Lagrange, *St. Jean*, pp. 142-143; C. H. Dodd, *Interpretation*, p. 320; E. C. Hoskyns, *Fourth Gospel*, p. 267; B. Lindars, *John*, pp. 221-227; S. Schulz, *Untersuchungen*, pp. 109-110; R. H. Lightfoot, *St. John*, pp. 141-145; R. Bultmann, *John*, p. 247; J. N. Sanders, *The Gospel according to St. John*, p. 166; T. Zahn, *Johannes*, p. 288; J. C. Fenton, *The Gospel according to John*, NCB (Oxford, Clarendon Press, 1970) p. 67; A. Wikenhauser, *Johannes*, pp. 116-119; J. Bligh, "Jesus in Jerusalem", *HeyJ* 4 (1963) 115-134; F.-M. Braun, "St. Jean", p. 354; P. Gächer, "Zur Form ...", pp. 65-68; W. F.

The internal structure of the discourse itself has been the source of yet further discussion. Jesus tells his accusers that he is not claiming anything which places him beyond Israel's God. He is not a rebel, setting himself against God, as everything he does and says is from this God, who is his Father. Throughout the Fourth Gospel Jesus points to the Father as the origin of his deeds (see 7,28; 8,42) and of his words (see 3,34; 8,26; 12,49), and vv. 19-20a show all the marks of Johannine theologising.[22] However, C. H. Dodd and P. Gächter have claimed, independently, that a traditional parable stands behind vv. 19-20a. The parable takes the form of a negative statement: a son can do nothing by himself, but only what he sees his father doing; followed by a positive statement: whatever the father does, the son does likewise; and concluding with the reason why the latter is true: because the father loves his son and shows him everything he is doing.[23] This suggestion has met with approval from R. E. Brown and B. Lindars,[24] but the absolute use of ὁ υἱός has caused R. Schnackenburg to regard the theory as "improbable", as the title, used theologically here, is too far removed from a traditional background.[25] Gächter, Brown and Lindars link v. 30 with the parable. The change from the parabolic third person in vv. 19-20a to the first person in v. 30 shows that v. 30 is the application of the parable, made by Jesus himself, before those who accused him of breaking the Sabbath.[26] Thus the *Sitz im Leben Jesu* given in the Fourth Gospel, a polemic over the Sabbath Law, is the correct one.

The problem of the eschatology of vv. 21-29 has caused further suggestions concerning the structure and the redaction of the discourse. The simplest and

Howard, "St. John", pp. 546-549; J. Jeremias, *Johannes,* pp. 132-133; X. Léon-Dufour, "Trois chiasmes johanniques", *NTS* 7 (1960-61) 253-255; A. Loisy, *Quatrième Évangile,* p. 209; H. Strathmann, *Johannes,* p. 100; H. van den Bussche, *Jean,* pp. 223-224; A. Vanhoye, "La composition ...", pp. 259-274; A. Duprez, *Jésus et les dieux guérisseurs,* pp. 148-149; A. Beel, "Sermo Jesu post paralytici sanationem (Jo. 5,19-30)", *CollBrug* 39 (1939) 434; G. Ferraro, *L'"ora" di Cristo,* pp. 138-140.

[22] Contrary to the opinion of B. Lindars who, in an unpublished paper, "Midrashic Methods in the Discourses of John", given at the SNTS Conference at Southampton in 1973, claims "there is a complete absence of theologising" in vv. 19-20a (p. 2). See also his "The Son of Man ...", pp. 50-51.

[23] C. H. Dodd, "A Hidden Parable in the Fourth Gospel", in *More New Testament Studies,* (Manchester, MUP, 1968) pp. 30-40; P. Gächter, "Zur Form ...", pp. 67-68.

[24] R. E. Brown, *John,* pp. 218-219; B. Lindars, *John,* pp. 221-222; Idem, "Two Parables in John", pp. 318-324. In his unpublished paper, "Midrashic Methods ...", Lindars claims that this traditional parable which stands behind vv. 19-30 is further proof for his theory that the double "amen" phrases introduce "sayings from the Jesus tradition". See above, p. 25.

[25] R. Schnackenburg, *Johannesevangelium* II, pp. 129-130.

[26] See P. Gächter, "Zur Form ...", p. 67. J. Jeremias has seen this same parable behind Matt. 11,27. See *New Testament Theology,* Vol. I: "The Proclamation of Jesus", (London, SCM Press, 1971) pp. 56-61 (English translation of *Neutestamentliche Theologie* I. Teil: Die Verkündigung Jesu, [Gütersloh, Gerd Mohn, 1971]).

most radical suggestion is that vv. 28-29 reflect a later "final eschatology", foreign to John and, as such, should be regarded as an insertion.[27]   For Bultmann, these verses are the result of the efforts of an ecclesiastical redactor who has tried to bring John's "realised eschatology" within the bounds of the traditional eschatology of the end time.   Although not all the scholars who see vv. 28-29 as an insertion would point to an ecclesiastical redactor, they are one in seeing the passage as non-Johannine.

An unwillingness to accept this radical dissecting of the text has led to various suggestions concerning the literary growth of the passage.   M.-E. Boismard has suggested that it was composed in two stages, of which vv. 26-30 is the earlier.[28]   He compares the two stages of growth in the following fashion:

a) In vv. 26-30

— there is no contact with I John

— Jesus is presented as the Danielic Son of Man (see Dan. 7,13.14.21; 12,2) as in the Synoptic tradition.

— vv. 28-29 clearly refer to a physical resurrection, with no indication of time.

b) In vv. 19-25

— the contact with I John is strong

— Jesus is presented in terms of the Johannine Father-Son relationship

— v. 25 speaks of a spiritual resurrection, taking place here and now.

From this Boismard concluded that vv. 19-25 are a "relecture" of vv. 26-30, representing a later stage in the development of the tradition.   The stage reflected in vv. 19-25 is also reflected in I John.[29]   Boismard makes this relationship with I John an important issue.   One wonders how he would explain such "future" sayings as I John 2,28; 3,2 and 4,17.

R. E. Brown has followed this suggestion, without committing himself to a judgment concerning the earlier or later development of the two different eschatological motifs.[30]   He calls vv. 19-25: "The twofold Sabbath work of Jesus, namely, to give life and to judge — realised eschatology",[31] while vv. 26-

---

[27] See R. Bultmann, *John*, pp. 237-239. 261; H. Becker, *Die Reden des Johannesevangeliums und der Stil der gnostischen Offenbarungsreden*, (Göttingen, Vandenhoeck und Ruprecht, 1956) p. 72; S. Schulz, *Untersuchungen*, pp. 109-111; Idem, *Johannes*, pp. 89-90; A. J. B. Higgins, *Son of Man*, pp. 167-168; A. Loisy, *Quatrième Évangile*, pp. 213-214; R. Schnackenburg, *Johannesevangelium* II, pp. 145-150; J. Wellhausen, *Johannis*, p. 26.

[28] M.-E. Boismard, "L'évolution du thème eschatologique dans les traditions johanniques", *RB* 68 (1961) 507-524.   On n. 5,19-30, see pp. 514-518.

[29] *ibid.*, p. 518.

[30] R. E. Brown, *John*, pp. 218-220.

[31] *ibid.*, p. 218.

30 are given the sub-title: "Duplicate of division 1. The same themes in terms of final eschatology".[32] For Brown, the Johannine tradition has preserved two forms of the discourse, as reflected in vv. 21-25 and vv. 26-29. The introduction to the discourse is formed by the parable of vv. 19-20,[33] and it is concluded by what was originally the application of the parable, in v. 30.[34]

Gächter argues that John's original discourse was vv. 19-20, 24, 30. As we have already seen, he argues that the parable and its application in vv. 19-20, 30 were traditional, and John added the clearly Johannine v. 24. The rest of the discourse has been gathered from various sources by the Evangelist, notably vv. 28-29 from a traditional apocalyptic source. Gächter has insisted that behind the various elements of the discourse stands the figure of the Evangelist. This is indicated by the fact that the final structure of the discourse is chiastic, with v. 24 as the central statement.[35]

This suggestion has also been made, with variations, by X. Léon-Dufour and A. Vanhoye.[36] Both Léon-Dufour and Gächter make v. 24 the centre of the chiasm, but this leads them into difficulty, as they then have v. 25 and v. 28 on the same side of the chiasm, but this is hardly correct. Vanhoye avoids this by making vv. 24-25 the central statement.[37] However, the importance of Vanhoye's work lies not only in his attempt to find a chiasm in the discourse, but more especially in his detailed linguistic and stylistic analysis of the passage, to show that the discourse cannot be dissected into old and more recent sections, nor accredited to various hands; for Vanhoye, the passage is a whole and must be interpreted as such.[38] The great variety of suggestions which scholars make to prove the contrary once again leads to scepticism, and one must return to Dodd's attempt "to see what can be done with the document as it has come down to us before attempting to improve upon it".[39]

There may well be a parable behind vv. 19-20, but it must be admitted that Schnackenburg is correct when he points to the important addition of a

---

[32] *ibid.*, p. 219.

[33] See above, p. 72.

[34] R. E. Brown, *John*, pp. 220-221. The final redaction has taken place, according to Brown, in the last stage of his reconstructed "5 stage" theory. See pp. xxiv-xxxix.

[35] P. Gächter, "Zur Form ...", p. 65.

[36] X. Léon-Dufour, "Trois chiasmes johanniques", pp. 253-255; A. Vanhoye, "La composition de Jn. 5,19-30", pp. 268-272.

[37] A. Vanhoye, *art. cit.*, pp. 271-272. Vanhoye is followed in this by G. Ferraro, *L' "ora" di Cristo*, pp. 139-141.

[38] *ibid.*, pp. 262-268. See p. 268: "L'auteur se rattache à la tradition biblique, telle qu'on la trouve en particulier dans les psaumes et les livres sapientiaux. Il utilise inlassablement le parallélisme synonymique et antithétique et les divers genres de dispositions symétriques".

[39] C. H. Dodd, *Interpretation*, p. 290.

Johannine "Son" christology in these verses.[40]   There is obviously a change of tone in vv. 28-29, where traditional apocalyptic language appears to be used, but does this mean that these verses are to be excluded because they are foreign to Johannine theology?   An equally valid presupposition is to admit that they belong to the Gospel and that they must be there for some purpose, and to try to understand what that purpose is.[41]

The giving of life and judging were a prerogative of God alone.   The Father is the source of all life and judgment, but he has given these functions over to the Son.   As the Father gives life, so does the Son (v. 21); the Father could judge, but he has given his authority to the Son (v. 22) and he has done this so that both the Father and the Son would be honoured.   The honour which is to be given to the Son, however, is not a product of the new power which the Son has been given, but rather the necessary consequence of the fact which is affirmed from vv. 19-23: the Father and the Son are one in their activity.[42]   Having stated that the authority to give life and to judge has been given to the Son, a sort of summing up of what this means follows in the central section of the discourse, vv. 24-25.   Introduced by solemn "amen" phrases, the discourse pauses as it announces that he who hears Jesus' word has life and will not be judged, but has passed from the death which sin has brought,[43] into the life which comes from faith in Jesus and his word.   This is a high point in Johannine realised eschatology.   John's readers are told that the hour of the giving of life is coming — and now is!   The event of Jesus Christ is the source of that life and judgment.[44]   It is important to notice that while judgment is always present as a sub-theme, vv. 24-25 are mainly concerned with the authority of the Son as the life-giver.

From v. 26 to v. 27 we have a repetition of the themes of vv. 21-23, but there is a subtle change in each case.   In v. 21 we were told of the Son's life-giving activity, because of his dependence upon the Father; now in v. 26 we discover the basis of that life-giving power: the Father, who has life in

---

[40] See J. T. Forestell, *The Word of the Cross*, pp. 51-52. It is interesting that D. F. Strauss, who was among the first to point to a specifically Johannine Gospel, sees Jn. 5,20 as one of John's "favorite ideas and phrases". See D. F. Strauss, *The Life of Jesus Critically Examined*. Translated from the German *Das Leben Jesu kritisch bearbeitet*, under the editorship of P. C. Hodgson, (London, SCM Press, 1973) pp. 372-373. See W. G. Kümmel, *The New Testament. The History of the Investigation of its Problems*, (London, SCM Press, 1973) pp. 124-126 (English translation of *Das Neue Testament: Geschichte der Erforschung seiner Probleme*, [Freiburg, Karl Alber, 1970]) for a survey of Strauss' work on John.

[41] See, among others, J. H. Bernard, *St. John*, p. 239.

[42] See A. Beel, "Sermo Jesu post paralytici sanationem", p. 437.

[43] See J. Blank, *Krisis*, p. 142: "Alle Toten = alle Menschen, die sich auf Grund ihrer Unheilssituation 'im Tode' befinden". See on this pp. 143-158.

[44] See J. Blank, *Krisis*, pp. 134-140; G. Ferraro, *L' "ora" di Cristo*, pp. 143-150.

himself has granted to the Son that he also may have life in himself. In v. 27 the interplay between what the Son does and the basis of that activity is reversed. In v. 22 we learnt that all judgment had been given to the Son by the Father. This is the basis of the Son's judging activity, it is not a description of the activity itself; but in v. 27 we are told of the exercising of this authority (κρίσιν ποιεῖν)   and Jesus is spoken of as "Son of Man".

As there is so much interplay of themes and repetition of ideas, Gächter, Léon-Dufour and Vanhoye understandably search for some sort of chiastic structure. All of these scholars, however, have difficulty in forming a chiasm, and their results are often complicated or artificial. Perhaps it is wiser not to look for a chiasm, but simply to notice John's "self-contained allusiveness" in his movement from theme to theme and back again. The discourse appears to move in the following fashion:

vv. 19-20: Theological introduction: the absolute dependence of the Son upon the Father.

v. 21: The *exercising* of the Son's authority to give life (ζῳοποιεῖν).

v. 22: The *basis* of the Son's authority to judge (ὁ πατὴρ ... δέδωκεν).

v. 23: Theological reflection: the honour due to the Son because of his relationship with the Father.

vv. 24-25: The Son as the life-giver, with judgment as a sub-theme (ἔρχεται ὥρα... ἀκούσουσιν τῆς φωνῆς).

v. 26: The *basis* of the Son's authority to give life (ὁ πατὴρ ... ἔδωκεν).

v. 27: The *exercising* of the Son's authority to judge — as Son of Man (κρίσιν ποιεῖν).

vv. 28-29: The Son as judge, with life-giving as a sub-theme (ἔρχεται ὥρα... ἀκούσουσιν τῆς φωνῆς).

v. 30: Theological conclusion: the absolute dependence of Jesus upon the Father.

The troublesome vv. 28-29 are a repetition, in traditional apocalytic language, of what has already been said in vv. 24-25 in 'realised' terms. All the dead will hear his voice and come forth to life if they have done well — or to judgment if they have done badly. In vv. 24-25 the readers of the Fourth Gospel learnt that if they listened to Jesus' word, they already possessed eternal life (v. 24). There were also those who had already died, or those who would soon die, who would also hear Jesus' word and come to eternal life. In both of these passages, vv. 24-25 and vv. 28-29, so often contraposed,

John is saying the same thing, but in vv. 28-29 judgment has become the key theme, while Jesus' life-giving role is present as a sub-theme.[45]

The first part of the discourse concludes with the inclusion of v. 30. The judgment theme of v. 29 is continued and it is again said that the role of Jesus as judge, as also his life-giving role, although not mentioned here, is the result of his total dependence upon the Father who sent him.

II - The Son of Man in John 5,27

As we have seen, the discourse is tightly structured, with the themes of Jesus as life-giver and judge being balanced against one another throughout. Even when the discourse is mainly concerned with Jesus' life-giving authority (vv. 24-25), his role as judge is in the background, while when the judicial function of the Son is described (vv. 28-29) his life-giving authority is not neglected. Within this structure, vv. 21 and 26 along with vv. 22 and 27 seem to play a central role:[46]

	Jesus as Life-giver	*Jesus as Judge*
Basis of authority	v. 26: "For as the Father has life in himself, so he has granted to the Son also to have life in himself"	v. 22: "The Father judges no one but has given all judgment to the Son"
Exercising of authority[47]	v. 21: "For as the Father raises the dead and gives them life, so also the Son gives life to whom he will."	v. 27: "And has given him authority to execute judgment, because he is the Son of Man."

We must now turn to examine v. 27 within this context. It is apparent that the Son of Man saying is not without importance within the general structure of the section of the discourse which runs from vv. 19-30.

---

[45] See J. Blank, *Krisis*, pp. 174-176. Blank shows that the literary and theological link between these two passages cannot be ignored. He maintains that Bultmann has eliminated vv. 28-29 for reasons of *Sachkritik* although claiming that it is for literary reasons. Blank shows that not only are vv. 28-29 literarily united to the whole discourse, but also that the *Sache* is Johannine. See also M.-J. Lagrange, *St. Jean*, p. 149; F. Hahn, *Christologische Hoheitstitel*, pp. 40-41, note 6; T. Zahn, *Johannes*, p. 301.

[46] See F. Hahn, *Christologische Hoheitstitel*, pp. 40-41, note 6. Hahn speaks of the interplay of the "Dass" and the "Wie". See also G. Iber, *Untersuchungen*, pp. 141-142. The relationship is also brought out by H. Odeberg, *Fourth Gospel*, p. 191.

[47] R. Bultmann, *John*, p. 450: "He is the Revealer who has the ἐξουσία of κρίνειν and of ζῳοποιεῖν (5,21.27)".

In Jn. 5,27 Jesus claims that all power of judging has been given over
to the Son, because he is the Son of Man. The verses which follow (vv. 28-
29) immediately take up apocalyptic language and eschatological concepts,
apparently in sharp contrast to what has gone before, especially in v. 25. We
see v. 22 as closely linked with v. 27. In v. 22 Jesus tells his accusers that
all judgment has been given to the Son, and we could add in parenthesis —
because he is the Son of the Father. Turning to v. 27 one finds that Jesus
goes further — the Son also *exercises* judgment, "because he is Son of Man".

Vv. 26-27 come between two statements which deal with life and judgment,
one present — a giving of life, with its sub-theme of judgment, taking place
here and now (vv. 24-25) and the other future — a judgment, with its sub-theme
of life, which will take place at some non-specified time in the future (vv. 28-
29). It has already been mentioned that some scholars insist that vv. 28-29
do not belong to this context.[48] These verses are either the work of an
ecclesiastical redactor (Wellhausen and Bultmann), or a non-Johannine passage
added during the later redaction of the Gospel (Schulz, Higgins, Loisy, Hirsch).
R. Schnackenburg's recent commentary takes up a middle position by concluding that the passage belongs to a later redaction which added these traditional
apocalyptic elements, but which has not betrayed the eschatological thought
of John — "aber für seine theologische Zeilsetzung in den Hintergrund gedrängt
hat". Schnackenburg claims that people very close to Johannine thought,
probably those responsible for I John, also made these redactional additions
to the Gospel.[49]

Against this opinion, the vast majority of scholars have argued for the
inclusion of vv. 28-29 in ch. 5.[50] Several have pointed to the link with vv. 24-

---

[48] See above, p. 73, note 27. See also E. Hirsch, *Studien zum vierten Evangelium*,
p. 57.

[49] R. Schnackenburg, *Johannesevangelium* II, pp. 144-150. See also his excursus,
"Das eschatologische Denken im Johannesevangelium", on pp. 530-544.

[50] See C. K. Barrett, *St. John*, pp. 217.219; W. Bauer, *Johannesevangelium*, p. 87;
J. H. Bernard, *St. John*, pp. 244-245; J. Blank, *Krisis*, pp. 164-172; M.-J. Lagrange, *St.
Jean*, p. 149; R. H. Lightfoot, *St. John*, pp. 144-145; B. Lindars, *John*, pp. 226-227; H.
Pribnow, *Die johanneische Anschauung vom "Leben". Eine biblische-theologische Unter-
suchung in religionsgeschichtlicher Beleuchtung*, Greifswalder theologische Forschungen 4,
(Greifswald, Bamberg, 1934) pp. 132-135; E. C. Hoskyns, *Fourth Gospel*, p. 271; A.
Corell, *Consummatum Est. Eschatology and Church in the Gospel of St. John*, (London,
SPCK, 1958) pp. 162-164 (English translation of *Consummatum est. Eskatologi och Kyrka
i Johannesevangeliet*, [Stockholm, Svenska Kyrkans Diakonistryrelses Bokforlag, 1950]);
C. H. Dodd, *Interpretation*, pp. 147-148; P. Ricca, *Die Eschatologie des vierten Evangeliums*,
pp. 147-149; A. Schlatter, *Johannes*, p. 169; H. Strathmann, *Johannes*, p. 104; H.-D.
Wendland, *Die Eschatologie des Reiches Gottes bei Jesus. Eine Studie über den Zusammen-
hang von Eschatologie, Ethik und Kirchenproblem*, (Gütersloh, Bertelsmann, 1931) pp. 80-
88; B. F. Westcott, *St. John*, p. 87; A. Wikenhauser, *Johannes*, p. 301; F. Mussner, ZΩH.
Die Anschauung vom "Leben", pp. 140-144; H. Odeberg, *The Fourth Gospel*, pp. 208-209.
See the important remarks of E. Käsemann, *The Testament of Jesus*, pp. 70-73.

25,[51] while others have looked into the rest of the Gospel, seeing vv. 28-29 fulfilled in the Lazarus scene, where a dead man does hear the voice of Jesus and comes forth from the tomb.[52] The presence of a teaching about the final judgment is a fact in the Fourth Gospel (see 4,36; 5,29; 6,27; 6,39-54; 11,24; 12,25.48; 13,19; 14,1.27.29; 16,1-4.33; the confirmation of what is said in 11,23-24 by Jesus' reply in vv. 25-26).[53] These elements cannot be lightly brushed away, without taking a great deal from the Gospel.[54] Before leaving this question, two further considerations might be mentioned which militate against the elimination of a future eschatology from the Fourth Gospel.

a) John has not revolutionised the Synoptic tradition by introducing his realised eschatology. While apocalyptic elements are certainly strong in the Synoptic tradition, both present and future elements are found intermingled throughout the tradition (see Mk. 1,15; Matt. 11,6 par. Lk. 7,23; the crisis parables of Lk. 12,16-20. 54-56; Mk. 8,38; Matt. 25,31-46).[55]

b) The work of J. L. Martyn has made us more conscious that the Fourth Gospel was not written in a vacuum.[56] The author was bound by space and time, grappling seriously with the problems of his community. Written at the end of the first century, when death was surely one of the church's most serious problems (not only the problem of violent death, but especially the gradual loss of contact, through death, with the original witnesses to Jesus) is it possible that John would compose a theology with complete disgregard for "the other side of death"? People from John's community believed in Jesus, but they were still dying a physical death. John must have had a word to say to this problem, to counterbalance such statements as: "He

---

[51] See J. Blank, *Krisis*, pp. 174-176; M.-J. Lagrange, *St. Jean*, p. 149; B..F Westcott, *St. John*, p. 87; T. Zahn, *Johannes*, p. 301; F. Hahn, *Christologische Hoheitstitel*, pp. 40-41, note 6.

[52] See C. H. Dodd, *Interpretation*, pp. 147-148; J. C. Fenton, *John*, p. 72; R. H. Lightfoot, *St. John*, pp. 144-145; W. Reiser, "The Case of the Tidy Tomb: The Place of the Napkins of John 11,44 and 20,7", *HeyJ* 14 (1973) 52-53; J. T. Forestell, *The Word of the Cross*, pp. 32-33.

[53] H. Pribnow, *Die johanneische Anschauung vom "Leben"*, pp. 102-121.

[54] Although he has overstated his case, L. van Hartingsveld, *Die Eschatologie des Johannesevangeliums. Eine Auseinandersetzung mit Rudolf Bultmann*, (Assen, Van Gorcum, 1962) has argued that John's basic eschatology is the traditional "future eschatology". See on this book, J. Blank, *Krisis*, pp. 350-353.

[55] See J. Blank, *Krisis*, pp. 164-172; H.-D. Wendland, *Die Eschatologie des Reiches Gottes*, p. 88; W. H. Cadman, *The Open Heaven*, pp. 46-49; C. F. D. Moule, *The Birth of the New Testament*, Black's New Testament Commentaries, Companion Volume I, (London, A. and C. Black, 1966) p. 102.

[56] J. L. Martyn, *History and Theology in the Fourth Gospel;* See also S. S. Smalley, "Diversity and Development in John", *NTS* 17 (1970-71) 276-292; D. M. Smith, "Johannine Christianity: Some Reflections on its Character and Delineation", *NTS* 21 (1974-75) 222-248, esp. 238-244.

who hears my word and believes him who sent me, has eternal life" (5,24). It will not do to arrive, through the elimination of the parts added by later redaction, to a Jesus figure preaching a Heideggerian authentic and inauthentic man. Some members of the Johannine community may not have been greatly helped by such a figure. In the face of this problem, it appears that John balanced his teaching of a realised eschatology by using the more traditional idea of an end time.[57]

It is important to recognise that the eschatology of Jn. 5,28-29 is a part of Johannine thought, and that these verses can be understood in their present context.

> "Alongside and interwoven are the 'already now' and the 'not yet'. The life
> in the 'now' and the life 'looked forward to' in the future belong together.
> This is the basis not only of Johannine devotion but of the New Testament
> as a whole".[58]

Jesus, as Son of Man, stands between the 'already now' and the 'not yet' in Jn. 5,27. Some scholars have claimed that the anarthrous use of "Son of Man" in 5,27 is John's way of saying that all power of judgment has been given over to him because he is "man".[59] As he is one of us, he has been given authority to judge: "Jesus is qualified and authorised to judge because he has shared the experiences of men as one of themselves".[60] The power which

---

[57] See J. Blank, *Krisis*, pp. 178-181; W. F. Howard, *Christianity According to St. John*, pp. 106-128. 201-204; A. Corell, *Consummatum Est*, pp. 107-109; D. Mollat, Art. "Jugement", *DBS* IV, cols. 1382-1385; G. Stählin, "Zum Problem der johanneischen Eschatologie", *ZNW* 33 (1934) 225-259; W. G. Kümmel, "Die Eschatologie der Evangelien", *TB* 15 (1936) 235-239; P.-H. Menoud, "L'originalité de la pensée johannique", *RThPh* 28 (1940) 245-253; C. F. D. Moule, "A Neglected Factor in the Interpretation of Johannine Eschatology", in *Studies in John: Presented to Professor Dr. J. N. Sevenster on the Occasion of his Seventieth Birthday*, SNT 24, (Leiden, E. J. Brill, 1970) pp. 155-160.

[58] G. Stählin, "Zum Problem ...", p. 258, as translated in A. Corell, *Consummatum Est*, p. 81. See also the remarks of A. Loisy in his 1903 edition of *Le Quatrième Évangile*, p. 410: "Les critiques ... méconnaissent le véritable esprit du quatrième Évangile; ils veulent faire de l'auteur un logicien scolastique, au lieu de la prendre pour ce qu'il est, un profond mystique qui voit ensemble la 'réalité, l'image symbolique, l'idée, qui n'oublie jamais tout à fait l'une quand il paraît s'occuper de l'autre, et qui fonde l'unité de sa doctrine sur une conception de la vie assez large pour embrasser la destinée complète de l'homme". He joined these critics when he wrote his revised edition in 1921. See also J. Gnilka, "Der historische Jesus als der gegenwärtige Christus im Johannesevangelium", in J. Sint (ed.), *Bibel und Zeitgemässer Glaube II: Neues Testament*, (Klosterneuberg, Klosterneuburger Verlagsanstalt, 1967) pp. 159-171; C. F. D. Moule, *The Birth of the New Testament*, p. 98; G. Ferraro, *L' "ora" di Cristo*, pp. 142-148.

[59] E. M. Sidebottom, *The Christ of the Fourth Gospel*, p. 93; M.-J. Lagrange, *St. Jean*, p. 148; R. Leivestad, "Exit the Apocalyptic Son of Man", p. 252; G. H. C. Macgregor, *John*, p. 179; A. Schlatter, *Johannes*, p. 152; W. Temple, *Readings*, p. 114; T. Zahn, *Johannes* p. 299; A. Beel, "Sermo Jesu...", p. 438; H. Odeberg, *Fourth Gospel*, p. 199.

[60] C. K. Barrett, *St. John*, p. 218.

is given to Jesus is that of judging, and the whole passage has been concerned with judgment. In the verses which follow, Jesus speaks of the final eschatological judgment. The themes of judgment and an appearance at the end of time are traditionally attributed to the Son of Man (see Mk. 8,38 parr.; 13,26 parr.; 14,62 parr.; Matt. 19,28; 24,29-30.39; Lk. 12,8; 17,30; 18,8; 21,36), and it seems hardly possible that John would have used υἱὸς ἀνθρώπου in such a context without intending the phrase to be understood as titular.[61] This does not exclude the possibility that Jesus' humanity is referred to, and that there is a 'qualitative' element in the use of the term, as John's choice of language is often aimed at various nuances in meaning.[62]

In Jn. 5,27 we may have one of the earliest witnesses to the Son of Man traditions, as here, more than anywhere else, there seems to be a direct dependence upon the Greek text of Dan. 7,13. Both the LXX and Theodotion have the anarthrous ὡς υἱὸς ἀνθρώπου:

John 5,27	LXX Dan. 7,13-14	Theodotion Dan. 7,13-14
v. 27b: ὅτι υἱὸς ἀνθρώπου ἐστιν	v. 13: ὡς υἱὸς ἀνθρώπου ἤρχετο	v. 13: ὡς υἱὸς ἀνθρώπου ἐρχόμενος
v. 27a: καὶ ἐξουσίαν ἔδωκεν αὐτῷ	v. 14: καὶ ἐδόθη αὐτῷ ἐξουσία	v. 14: καὶ αὐτῷ ἐδόθη ἡ ἀρχὴ

The Danielic background for the whole context is further shown by the close similarity between Jn. 5,28b-29 and LXX Dan. 12,2.[63] The saying has been used, however, in the light of Christian tradition. The Son of Man in Dan. 7,13-14 is not established as a judge, although judgment is given to the Saints of the Most High in 7,22. The Son of Man is judge in I Enoch (see 69,27), and in the Synoptic tradition this attribute of the Son of Man is more fully exploited than in Daniel (see, for example, Mk. 14,62; Matt. 26,64; Lk. 21,27). It seems probable that the use of the title in Jn. 5,27 has come to the

---

[61] See C. K. Barrett, *St. John*, p. 218; J. Blank, *Krisis*, p. 163; R. E. Brown, *John*, p. 220; R. G. Hamerton-Kelly, *Pre-Existence*, p. 235; J. L. Martyn, *History and Theology*, pp. 130-131; A. J. B. Higgins, *Son of Man*, pp. 167-168.

[62] See D. W. Wead, *The Literary Devices in John's Gospel*, pp. 30-46.

[63] Against A. J. B. Higgins, *Son of Man*, pp. 165-166; F. H. Borsch, *Son of Man*, p. 294, who hold that there is no reference to Dan. 7. The close relationship between Daniel and Jn. 5 has recently been discussed at considerable length by G. Ferraro, *L' "ora" di Cristo*, pp. 71-81. See also G. Iber, *Untersuchungen*, pp. 112-118; J. L. Martyn, *History and Theology*, pp. 129-131; S. Schulz, *Untersuchungen*, pp. 111-113; R. G. Hamerton Kelly, *Pre-Existence*, pp. 235-236; C. F. D. Moule, *Phenomenon*, p. 92; B. Lindars, "The Son of Man ...:, pp. 51-52; G. Segalla, "Cinque schemi cristologici ...", pp. 14-15. See also B. Vawter, "Ezekiel and John", *CBQ* 26 (1964) 450-458 who explains it in terms of Ezekiel, rather than Daniel.

Evangelist directly from Dan. 7, but understood in the light of very early Christian interpretation.[64]

As well as these arguments from the context and the background for a titular understanding of the term, E. C. Colwell claimed, on purely grammatical grounds, that a predicative nominative noun which precedes the verb should be understood in a definite sense.[65]   Recently, P. B. Harner has argued that the question of a noun's being definite or indefinite has probably been correctly defined by Colwell, but that its being qualitative or not is a question which must be examined on its own.[66]   His concluding remarks could be pertinent to our consideration of Jn. 5,27:

> "The categories of qualitativeness and definiteness ... are not mutually exclusive, and frequently it is a delicate exegetical issue for the interpreter to decide which emphasis a Greek writer had in mind".[67]

It appears that "Son of Man" in its present context is definite, i.e. titular, but it may well retain a "qualitative" sense.

The judgment which is to be exercised has already been made clear.   The Father has sent the Son into the world to 'speak' to men.   He has revealed the possibility of life or of judgment in the person of Jesus.   He who hears the voice of that revelation "here and now" has already passed into life, while he who has refused to hear the voice has come into judgment.   The promise of life and judgment is not limited, however, to those who were privileged to hear the Johannine discourses.   There were many who were "in the tombs" and there would be an encounter for these people also.   They would hear the word, even though they were already "on the other side of death".   The figure of the Son of Man stands between these two statements, and it is as Son of Man that Jesus will judge, both now and in the future.[68]   The Son of Man who is both a present and future judge is close to the Synoptic presentation of the same figure, as in several places in the Synoptic tradition it is made clear that one's future judgment is determined by how one reacts to the Son of Man here and now (see esp. Mk. 8,38; Lk. 12,8-9).

---

[64] See J. Blank, *Krisis*, pp. 162-163; C. H. Dodd, "The Portrait of Jesus in John and the Synoptics" in W. R. Farmer-C. F. D. Moule-R. R. Niebuhr (eds.), *Christian History and Interpretation: Studies Presented to John Knox*, (Cambridge, CUP, 1967) pp. 183-198; G. Reim, *Studien zum alttestamentlichen Hintergrund*, p. 186.

[65] E. C. Colwell, "A Definite Rule for the Use of the Article in the Greek New Testament", *JBL* 52 (1933) 12-31. On Jn. 5,27 see p. 14. C. F. D. Moule, *An Idiom Book of New Testament Greek*, (Cambridge, CUP, 1959) p. 177 is often cited in support of the "qualitative" interpretation, but it should be noticed that Moule leaves the question open, mentioning Colwell's article with approval.

[66] P. B. Harner, "Qualitative Anarthrous Predicate Nouns: Mark 15,39 and John 1,1", *JBL* 92 (1973) 75-87. See esp. pp. 76. 85-86.

[67] *ibid.*, p. 87.

[68] See F. Mussner, *ΖΩΗ. Die johanneische Anschauung vom "Leben"*, pp. 140-144.

Why does John use the title "Son of Man" in v. 27? All through the discourse Jesus has been referred to as "the Son" (vv. 19,20,21,22,23,25,26), and with the appearance of the term "Son of Man" in v. 27 the former title disappears, although the person being referred to is always Jesus. If the term merely refers to Jesus' humanity, then we have no sudden change of titles, but if, as we have argued, the title is implied here, even though the form is anarthrous, there seem to be two possible solutions to our question:

a) The title "Son of Man" is to be regarded as synonymous with "the Son".[69] The use of "Son of Man" could have come about through a natural tendency to use this apocalyptic term in the context of vv. 28-29,[70] or it could simply be a linguistic game played by the author.[71]

b) The Evangelist has used this title for a purpose, having some specifically theological point to make. There are many who hold that "Son of Man" must be maintained,[72] even though some of them would insist that it is redactional.[73] These scholars generally understand the title here in the light of its traditional use, and thus tie it closely to the apocalyptic judgment scene which follows in vv. 28-29.

It is true that the title is used in its traditional sense in relation to vv. 28-29, and this is an important indication that John took this title from the tradition, but it seems possible that it may have meant something more for John. His use of it in such an emphatic position indicates that the title applies to Jesus' role as life-giver and judge, as it has been presented in the whole discourse. If the Evangelist has used these words accidentally, then he has merited the criticism of Bultmann, who regards the title here as "another, and indeed unnecessary and clumsy repetition".[74] This does not, however, appear to be the case. In 5,27 John is speaking of the judging activity of the incarnate Son. If one turns to the rest of the Gospel, one will find that the Son did not come into the world to judge (see 3,17; 5,24; 8,15; 12,47), but it is also obvious that the incarnation has brought judgment into the world (see 3,19-21; 5,22; 8,24; 9,39; 12,31). Perhaps it is in the light of this apparent contradiction that we are to understand John's use of the title "Son of Man" in our present context. We are told in v. 22 that

---

[69] See A. Schlatter, *Johannes*, p. 152; J. Blank, *Krisis*, pp. 163-164; R. Bultmann, *John*, pp. 260-261; C. Colpe, *TDNT* VIII, p. 465; E. D. Freed, "The Son of Man ...", p. 404; H. van den Bussche, *Jean*, p. 233; B. Lindars, "The Son of Man ...", p. 51.

[70] See esp. R. Bultmann, *John*, pp. 260-261. Also C. K. Barrett, *St. John*, p. 218.

[71] See esp. E. D. Freed, "The Son of Man...", p. 404.

[72] J. H. Bernard, *St. John*, p. 244; R. E. Brown, *John*, p. 220; O. Cullmann, *Christology*, p. 186; J. C. Fenton, *John*, p. 72; R. G. Hamerton-Kelly, *Pre-Existence*, p. 235; J. Marsh, *St. John*, p. 264; Y. B. Tremel, "Le Fils de l'Homme ...", pp. 85-86.

[73] See the reference to Higgins, Schnackenburg and Schulz in note 27 of p. 73.

[74] R. Bultmann, *John*, p. 260.

all judgment has been given to the Son, but the point that John is making in v. 22 is not the exercising of judgment by the Son, but rather the relationship that exists between the Father and the Son.[75] The context makes this clear. The Son is totally dependent upon the Father, but the Father has passed on to the Son his traditional authority to give life and to judge, even on the Sabbath. That the relationship between the Father and the Son is the point at issue here is made clear by v. 23: all this has been done for the Son so that honour may be given to both Father and Son. This is not an honour which is inspired by the Son's authority to judge, but rather an honour which depends upon the fact that the Father and the Son are so closely united in the Father's giving of all things to the Son.

In v. 27 we are told that not only does the Son *have* all judgment, given to him by the Father, but that he also *exercises* this judgment (κρίσιν ποιεῖν), because he is the Son of Man. It is as Son of Man that Jesus is the present and future judge, not as Son. Jesus is presented as "the Son" in the Fourth Gospel when the Evangelist wishes to speak of him in his relationship with the Father.[76] V. 26, for example, tells us that the Son has life in himself, because this has been granted to him by the Father. To this same Son is added another authority: he not only *has* all judgment, given to him by the Father (v. 22), but he *exercises* that judgment because he is the Son of Man (v. 27). In other words, the Son has to be further specified by yet another title — the Son of Man — when his exercising of judgment is in question. The title has not slipped into this context by accident, but it is clearly a deliberate addition to what has been claimed for Jesus as "the Son". As such, it is a vital clue to our understanding of what John means by the title "the Son of Man".[77]

Judgment, in the Fourth Gospel, is intimately linked with revelation (see 3,19; 8,16; 12,31; 16,8; 16,11), and the judgment spoken of in vv. 24-25 refers to this self-judgment of men in their reaction to the revelation of Jesus Christ. This is continued in v. 27: judgment *takes place* in the Son of Man. All of this is peculiarly Johannine, but v. 27 also belongs to what follows in vv. 28-29, and in this John shows that he is still in contact with the traditional beliefs of the early Church.[78] Precisely because we know the

---

[75] See H. van den Bussche, *Jean,* p. 230.

[76] See R. Schnackenburg, *Johannesevangelium* II, pp. 150-168. This is a fine excursus: " 'Der Sohn' als Selbstbezeichnung Jesu im Joh Ev".

[77] See M. de Jonge, "Jesus as Prophet and King...", p. 171: "5,27 *specifies* that the Son executes judgment as Son of Man, and in this whole passage it is clear that man s attitude towards Jesus *now* is a matter of eternal life and death". Stress of "specifies" mine. See also W. Temple, *Readings,* p. 84. Against these G. Iber, *Untersuchungen,* pp. 128-142 claims that John is entirely dependent upon the meaning which the term had in apocalyptic traditions.

[78] See above pp. 79-81.

traditional picture of the Son of Man as a figure who will come at the end of time to judge all men, we are able to appreciate, in this context, what is peculiarly Johannine in the Son of Man of v. 27. The Johannine Son of Man is "where judgment takes place" in the manner described in vv. 24-25.

Seen in this way, the apparent contradiction between 5,22.27 and 8,15 etc. is resolved. Jesus' claim to judge no one (8,15) is true. This was not the purpose of his coming into the world (3,17), nor was it his practice (8,1-11).[79] However, judgment resulted from his presence (5,22.27; 3,19-21).[80] He does judge, but this is merely a consequence of the truth which he reveals to the world. The judgment which he exercises is a necessary part of his being the revealer.[81]

In Jn. 1,51 we found that Jesus promised those who believed in him that they would see God's revelation in him, the Son of Man, and we also detected hints of some future moment of judgment in that revelation. In Jn. 3,13-14 we again saw the Johannine Jesus presented as the unique revealer — the only one who had come down from heaven in the incarnation. All those who accept this revelation will have eternal life, while those who refuse it will be condemned (3,16-21). Here, in Jn. 5,27 we have the reason behind this: Jesus, as the Son of Man who reveals the truth, also brings judgment.

The Son is sent to do the Father's will (see 4,34; 5,36; 9,4; 6,38; 10,18; 12,49; 14,31; 15,10) and in this is the Father revealed. The function of Jesus as "the Son" is the active role of bringing to the world what the Father has entrusted to him.[82] John uses the term "the Son of Man", on the other hand, to speak of the place, among men, where all this will occur. He is the elevated Son of Man upon whom all will look (see 3,14; 8,28; 12,31-33; 19,37). It is in this elevated Son of Man that one can find life by believing in him (3,13-15). "The Son of Man", then, appears to be a title used almost in a passive sense of a "locus revelationis". Those scholars who wish to see the anarthrous "Son of Man" in 5,27 as qualitative certainly have a point, as the Son of Man, revealer and judge, is present among men.[83] We are never

---

[79] The "Pericopa de Adultera", added on the basis of the claim made by Jesus in 8,15, is an eloquent testimony to this belief of the Johannine Church.

[80] See W. Temple, *Readings*, p. 135; E. M. Sidebottom, *The Christ of the Fourth Gospel*, p. 162: "The idea is of an impartial order of truth set up in which judgment comes to light."

[81] See J. Blank, *Krisis*, pp. 158-164.

[82] See W. H. Cadman, *The Open Heaven*, pp. 3-14.

[83] The "qualitative" use of the phrase, however, must not be understood as the whole answer. It does not eliminate the possibility of its also being a title. See F. Tillmann, "Jesus, der Menschensohn", *Biblische Zeitfragen* 1 (1908) 7; E. C. Hoskyns, *Fourth Gospel*, pp. 270-271; C. F. D. Moule, "Neglected Features in the Problem of 'the Son of Man' ", in J. Gnilka (ed.), *Neues Testament und Kirche: Für Rudolf Schnackenburg*, (Freiburg, Herder, 1974) p. 420.

told that the Son of Man is sent by the Father, nor that the Son of Man is doing the Father's will, as this is reserved for contexts which speak of Jesus as "the Son". The Son of Man is where revelation and judgment take place (see 1,51) among the men who will 'lift up' the unique revealer on a cross (3,13-14). The Son of Man is the one who, consequently, will exercise all judgment (5,27). It is as Son of Man that Jesus appears upon the scene, a man among men.

> "There is no question of a pre-existent Son of Man: He is the human figure, to whom God has imparted the authority to be revealer and therefore also judge of those who repudiate the revelation".[54]

What has been announced in 1,51 and 3,13-14 is clarified still further in 5,27: Jesus, the Son of Man, is the revealer and, because of this, he is the judge.

---

[54]   W.H. Cadman, *The Open Heaven*, p. 34. See also pp. 41-42.

CHAPTER FIVE

THE SON OF MAN AS THE GIVER OF LIFE:
John 6,27.53.62

I - General Structure and Meaning of John 6

John 6 must stand as a testing ground for every endeavour to explain the Fourth Gospel in a coherent fashion. Any scholar who turns to the Fourth Gospel finds himself faced with the immense problems which arise from this chapter. Is ch. 6 to be read before ch. 5? What is the relationship between the miracle stories of Jn. 6,1-21 and those of Mk. 6,32-52 (Matt. 14,13-33; Lk. 9,10b-17)? Is a literary link to be found, rather, in Mark's second multiplication of bread, in Mk. 8,1-10, with its consequent demand for a sign and discussion over the leaven of Herod and the Pharisees (Mk. 8,11-21)? Even if these problems are satisfactorily answered, there are further difficulties, posed by the discourse itself. How is the discourse to be divided? Is it about the Eucharist or about a more sapiential theme?[1] Did the section vv. 51c-58 belong to the original discourse, or is it a later interpolation? What is the relationship of vv. 60-65 to vv. 51c-58? The general structure and meaning of John 6 pose problems which could fill several monographs,[2] and we cannot handle them in detail here.

If one uses strictly geographical and historical criteria for establishing the order of chapters 5 and 6, it is immediately obvious that they must be reversed. At the end of ch. 4 Jesus is in Cana of Galilee and in ch. 6 he is still in Galilee, on the shore of the lake. In ch. 5, however, he goes up

---

[1] We will use the term "sapiential" in opposition to "Eucharistic", following R. E. Brown, *John*, pp. 272-275, for want of a better term. It is used to describe an interpretation of the discourse as a call to belief in the revelation brought by and in Jesus, in order to come to eternal life.

[2] See, for example, a recent monograph on the discourse: P. Borgen, *Bread from Heaven. An Exegetical Study of the Conception of Manna in the Gospel of John and in the Writings of Philo*, SNT 10, (Leiden, E. J. Brill, 1965). Another recent monograph has been concerned only with the textual problems of Jn. 6,52-71. See R. Kieffer, *Au delà des recensions? L'évolution textuelle dans Jean VI, 52-71*, Coniectanea Biblica. New Testament Series 3, (Lund, Gleerup, 1968).

to Jerusalem and meets opposition there, while at the start of ch. 7 he is
going about in Galilee because he can no longer travel freely in Judea (see
7,1). These facts have led many scholars to rearrange the chapters at this
point.[3] This reorganisation, however, has its own difficulties. Even though
Jesus is still in Galilee, there remains a sharp break between 4,46-54 and 6,1-2.
This is especially clear if one compares this passage with other more satisfactory
transitions (see 2,12-13).[4] One is always perplexed by these rearrangements,
as they are not based on any external evidence. Such a multitude of hypotheses
leads one to conclude that this approach is too subjective. As we are dealing
with the dislocation of a whole block of material, Bultmann's theory of the
mixing up of the pages in a codex could help, although Schnackenburg, who
hesitatingly opts for rearrangement,[5] is sceptical about such a possibility.[6]
However, Bultmann's rearrangement calls for the reorganisation of verses and
half verses inside the chapter itself, and this strains the imagination considerably.[7]

Are the criteria used by those who advocate a rearrangement valid? Bultmann himself notes:

> "John gives his portrayal in a series of large detailed pictures. And even if
> he fits these pictures into a chronological scheme, the individual sections
> are still not intended as particular historical scenes, but as representative
> pictures of the revelation-event".[8]

This is the criterion which must be used. While admitting that the Fourth
Gospel is in every way a "gospel" in form, it is at the same time a theological
presentation of Jesus, the Son of God, as the revealer, so that those who
believe in him may have eternal life (see 20,31). What has been said concerning the relationship that exists between the Father and the Son in ch. 5 must
come before what is said about the Bread of Life (see esp. vv. 34-46). C. H.
Dodd has pointed out the vital importance of ch. 5 for the correct understanding

[3] Scholars of differing points of view have agreed on this. Some rearrange on a
large scale: See R. Bultmann, *John*, pp. 209-210; J. H. Bernard, *St. John*, pp. xvii. 171;
G. H. C. Macgregor, *John*, pp. 124-126. On the other hand, there are others who are
more conservative in their approach: See R. Schnackenburg, *Johannesevangelium* II,
pp. 6-11; A. Guilding, *The Fourth Gospel and Jewish Worship*, pp. 45-46; H. Strathmann,
Johannes, pp. 96-98; A. Wikenhauser, *Johannes*, p. 97; F.-M. Braun, "L'eucharistie selon
S. Jean", *RThom* 70 (1970) 5; W. Temple, *Readings*, pp. xxxiii. 73. M. Shorter, "The
Position of Chapter VI in the Fourth Gospel", *ET* 84 (1973) 181-183 suggests that ch. 6
originally preceded 10,22.
[4] See R. E. Brown, *John*, pp. 235-236 for further difficulties which arise from rearrangement. See also G. Reim, *Studien zum alttestamentlichen Hintergrund*, p. 236.
[5] R. Schnackenburg, *Johannesevangelium* II, p. 11: "Letzte Sicherheit erhalten wir
nicht".
[6] *ibid.*, pp. 6-7. See also W. G. Wilson, "The Original Text of the Fourth Gospel.
Some Objective Evidence against the Theory of Page Displacements", *JTS* 50 (1949) 59-60.
[7] See R. Bultmann, *John*, 218-237.
[8] *ibid.*, p. 210.

of ch. 6. It is in ch. 5 that the reader learns of Jesus' radical dependence upon the Father.

> "It is by virtue of an unbroken identity of will and purpose, resting upon unqualified dependence of the Son on the Father, that Christ 'works the works of God' ".[9]

In this we are in full agreement with R. E. Brown:

> "No rearrangement can solve all the geographical and chronological problems in John, and to rearrange on the basis of geography and chronology is to give undue emphasis to something that does not seem to have been of major importance to the evangelist".[10]

The discussion concerning the relationship between John and the Synoptics has always turned to the miracle stories of Jn. 6,1-21, as these miracles are the only ones common to all the Gospels.[11] The question is not of great importance for our immediate discussion, although the wider possibility of contact between the Johannine and the Synoptic traditions could certainly have serious implications for our enquiry. As far as the miracles in Jn. 6 are concerned, however, the work of C. H. Dodd and ·R. E. Brown in this regard seems to leave little doubt that behind these accounts there is a common tradition which has grown independently.[12]

The division and structure of the discourse on the Bread of Life is so strongly influenced by each scholar's stance on the content of the discourse that there are nearly as many theories as there are interpreters. It is extremely difficult to give a satisfactory indication of the various positions which have been adopted by recent scholarship.[13]

---

[9] C. H. Dodd, *Interpretation*, p. 340.

[10] R. E. Brown, *John*, p. 236. See also C. K. Barrett, *St. John*, p. 227; H. Schlier, "Joh 6 und das joh Verständnis der Eucharistie", in J. Sint (ed.), *Bibel und Zeitgemässer Glaube* II, pp. 71-74; N. Uricchio, "Le teorie delle trasposizioni nel Vangelo di S. Giovanni", *Biblica* 31 (1950) 129-163. See esp. 161: "Ci lascia profondamente diffidenti sia per il pronunziato soggettivismo ... sia per i dissensi".

[11] Only some recent work is mentioned here. An excellent survey of the whole discussion is found in J. Blinzler, *Giovanni e i Sinottici. Rassegna informativa*, (Brescia, Paideia, 1969). This is a translation, brought up to date, of *Johannes und die Synoptiker. Ein Forschungsbericht*, (Stuttgart, Katholisches Bibelwerk, 1965). See, on John 6, S. Mendner, "Zum Problem Johannes und die Synoptiker", *NTS* 4 (1957-58) 282-307; E. Haenchen, "Johanneische Probleme", *ZTK* 56 (1959) 19-55. See esp. pp. 31-34; W. Wilkens, "Evangelist und Tradition im Johannesevangelium", *TZ* 16 (1960) 81-90; E. D. Johnston, "The Johannine Version of the Feeding of the Five Thousand — an Independent Tradition?", *NTS* 8 (1961-62) 151-154; E. K. Lee, "St. Mark and the Fourth Gospel", *NTS* 3 (1956-57) 51-55; C. K. Barrett, "John and the Synoptic Gospels", *ET* 85 (1973-74) 228-233.

[12] R. E. Brown, *John*, pp. 236-250. See esp. the very helpful chart on pp. 240-243; C. H. Dodd, *Tradition*, pp. 196-222. See also R. Fortna, *A Gospel of Signs*, pp. 62-63.

[13] For a survey of earlier work, see P. Gächter, "Die Form der eucharistischen Rede Jesu", *ZTK* 59 (1935) 438. Gächter himself sees the whole discourse as Eucharistic and

F. J. Leenhardt, who sees Eucharistic teaching throughout the whole discourse, attempts to show that it is based on the second Marcan miracle of the multiplication (Mk. 8,1-21). According to Leenhardt, the Marcan story makes three points:

a) Jesus multiplies the bread and feeds the multitude (Mk. 8,1-10).

b) By asking for a sign, the Pharisees demand a Messiah of the Davidic order (vv. 11-13).

c) The dialogue on the sea points to the spiritual understanding of the episode (vv. 14-21).

The same threefold pattern is carried into John 6,1-21 and then repeated in the discourse and thus the chapter is divided in the following fashion:[14]

a) Multiplication of the loaves: vv. 1-13
   = vv. 26-35: The nature of the bread

b) Attempts to make Jesus King: vv. 14-15
   = vv. 36-47: The Father must bring men to Jesus

c) The crossing of the sea: vv. 16-21
   = vv. 48-70: The necessity for a spiritual understanding.

J. Schneider endeavours to show that the discourse is to be divided into three sections: *a*) vv. 27-40; *b*) vv. 41-51; *c*) vv. 52-58.[15] These sections are unified by the fact that they all reflect upon several central themes: Moses, Christ and the Father, faith and faithful believers, earthly manna and heavenly bread. Each section contains the statement "I am the bread", as well as a reference to the fathers in the desert.[16] Although vv. 51b-58 may have originally grown in a cultic setting, they are not to be separated from the rest of the discourse.[17] The discourse must be understood as a unit, a threefold meditation upon the same truths: Jesus as the giver of life, and the necessity of faith, which will be given by the Father.[18]

S. Temple has divided the discourse into three strands.[19] He finds a core of oral tradition which is a "simple account of a discussion between Jesus and

divides it into two sections: a) vv. 35-47, b) 48-58. (see pp. 422-444). For what follows, see R. E. Brown, *John*, pp. 293-294, which we have adapted and supplemented.

[14] F. J. Leenhardt, "La structure du chapitre 6 de l'évangile de Jean", *RHPR* 39 (1959) 1-13.

[15] J. Schneider, "Zur Frage der Komposition von Joh 6, 27-58 (59) — (Die Himmels-brotrede)", in W. Schmauch (ed.), *In Memoriam Ernst Lohmeyer*, (Stuttgart, Evangelisches Verlagswerk, 1951) pp. 132-142; C. K. Barrett, *St. John*, pp. 234-236, also divides the discourse in this way.

[16] *ibid.*, pp. 136-139.

[17] *ibid.*, pp. 140-142. See esp. p. 141 on the cultic background.

[18] *ibid.*, p. 142.

the people who follow him across the lake, concluding with an exchange between Jesus and the Twelve".[20]   This core is made up of vv. 24-35; 41-43; 45; 47; 60; 66-70.   Secondly he finds Johannine expansions of this core, which he regards as a "rabbinising" or "targumising" of the original story, but still along the lines of the belief of the earliest Church.[21]   This strand is made up of vv. 36-40, 44; 46; 61-65.   The purpose of these additions was to bring the original story into line with his purpose as expressed in 20,31: to convince his readers that Jesus was the Son of God.   Finally, a Eucharistic homily has been added (vv. 48-59).   Here the author of ch. 21 has used doublets of the earlier strands to present Jesus in the light of the accepted doctrine of the Eucharist.[22]

J. Bligh has a twofold division: *a*) vv. 26-47; *b*) vv. 48-65.[23]   In each of these sections Bligh finds a threefold pattern, twice repeated: Christ making an offer — incredulity — faith as a gift of God.[24]   He sees vv. 51-58 as a later addition, originally having no relation with vv. 61-63.   However, this addition has changed the whole discourse into a Eucharistic reflection, and it is in the light of vv. 51-58 that one should interpret the whole chapter.[25]

T. Worden, having started his investigation of John 6 by discussing the doctrinal significance of the chapter,[26] examines, in a second article, his presuppositions that:

a) The whole discourse is about the Eucharist.

b) The discourse is written for the Christians of John's Church.

He finds that the text is composite, being made up of:

Text A: vv. 26, 30-35, 37-39, 41-44, 48-50, 58-59.

Text B: vv. 27-29, 36, 40, 45-47, 51-57.[27]

Both of these texts come from Jesus himself, although A is sapiential and B is clearly Eucharistic.   Following B. Gärtner,[28] Worden claims that Text A

[19] S. Temple, "A Key to the Composition of the Fourth Gospel", *JBL* 80 (1961) 220-232. See the typographically divided text on pp. 222-223.

[20] *ibid.*, p. 224.

[21] *ibid.*, pp. 229-230.

[22] *ibid.*, p. 232.

[23] J. Bligh, "Jesus in Galilee", *HeyJ* 5 (1964) 3-21.

[24] *ibid.*, p. 17. He also finds that this division is chiastically structured, following X. Léon-Dufour, "Trois chiasmes johanniques", pp. 251-253.

[25] J. Bligh, *art. cit.*, pp. 19-21.

[26] T. Worden, "The Holy Eucharist in St. John", *Script* 15 (1963) 97-106.

[27] Idem, "The Holy Eucharist in St. John", *Script* 16 (1964) 10-14.

[28] B. Gärtner, *John 6 and the Jewish Passover*, Coniectanea Neotestamentica 17, (Lund, Gleerup, 1959).

was spoken by Jesus at one of the Passovers, when he described himself as the Bread of Life, the true Wisdom; while Text B comes from Jesus' institution of the Eucharist.[29]

H. Schürmann, who has claimed that v. 51c refers to the death of Jesus and, as such, is closely linked to vv. 27 and 34, has divided the discourse into two sections: *a*) vv. 26-52; *b*) vv. 53-58.[30] For Schürmann, vv. 53-58 are the Eucharistic re-presentation of what has already been said in vv. 26-52, given in language taken from the Eucharistic practice of the Johannine Church.[31]

X. Léon-Dufour opens the discourse at v. 34, as vv. 26-34 are described as "the question".[32] The question is asked, and then the discourse unfolds in two stages: *a*) vv. 35-47: the Bread from Heaven; *b*) vv. 48-58: the living Bread, given to eat. The conclusion to the discourse, vv. 59-65, is called "the option". The two sections of the discourse proper begin with "I am" statements, and the second part is marked by the themes of giving and eating. D. Mollat and A. Feuillet have also followed this division.[33] Feuillet has shown that the discourse can be explained in its entirety by reference to the Wisdom literature:

vv. 35-47: Jesus as Bread = Jesus as the revealer from God

vv. 48-58: Jesus as the bread for nourishment.[34]

H. van den Bussche suggests another threefold division: *a*) vv. 26-31 refer to the Bread as the work of God accomplished by the Son of Man; *b*) vv. 32-46 tell the reader that the real bread is he who has descended from heaven; *c*) vv. 47-59 conclude the discussion by stating categorically that this real bread gives eternal life.[35]

Most scholars, and especially commentators, divide the discourse from vv. 22-34, where the discussion which Jesus has with the Galileans introduces the theme of the bread from heaven (v. 32). The discourse proper starts in v. 35 and proceeds until v. 51. It is here that scholars differ most in their

---

[29] T. Worden, *art. cit.*, pp. 15-16.

[30] H. Schürmann, "Joh 6,51c — ein Schlüssel zur grossen johanneischen Brotrede", *BZ* 2 (1958) 244-262.

[31] *ibid.*, pp. 261-262. See also Idem, "Die Eucharistie als Representation und Applikation des Heilsgeschehens nach Jo 6,53-58", *TrierTZ* 68 (1959) 30-45. 108-118.

[32] X. Léon-Dufour, "Le mystère du Pain de Vie (Jean VI)", *RecSR* 46 (1958) 481-523.

[33] D. Mollat, "Le chapitre VIe de Saint Jean", *LumVie* 31 (1957) 107-119; A. Feuillet, "Les thèmes bibliques majeurs du discours sur le pain de vie", in *Études Johanniques*, (Paris, Desclée, 1962) pp. 47-129. For his division, see pp. 48-49.

[34] See also M. Conti, *Il discorso del pane di vita nella tradizione sapienziale*, (Levanto, 1967). Most recently, J.-N. Aletti, "Le discours sur le pain de vie. Le fonction des citations de l'Ancien Testament", *RecSR* 62 (1974) 169-181 has arrived at the same division by using structuralism.

[35] H. van den Bussche, *Jean*, pp. 247-252. See also pp. 252-274.

divisions. The majority of scholars, understanding v. 51c as Eucharistic,[36] divide the discourse at v. 51b.[37] Others would start the more Eucharistic section of the discourse after v. 50, regarding the whole of v. 51 as Eucharistic,[38] while others, especially after the work of H. Schürmann, who has attempted to show that v. 51c is not so much Eucharistic as a reference to the passion,[39] start the Eucharistic section with the "murmuring" of v. 52.[40] This discussion rests entirely upon the interpretation of vv. 51-58. The Eucharistic insinuations can hardly be denied, but to what extent can these verses be called a "Eucharistic homily"? The conviction that they are entirely Eucharistic has led to the discussion concerning the originality of this section of the discourse. Many scholars see it as a later addition.[41] Some claim that they were added by an ecclesiastical redactor, anxious to add sacramental references to a Gospel which originally contained none,[42] while others would see the editing hand of the people who were responsible for Jn. 21 and I Jn.[43] For some, the Evangelist himself added these verses, in order to make clear the secondary references to the Eucharist which were already present in the

---

[36] Reflecting I Cor. 11,24 and Mk. 14,24.

[37] See W. Bauer, *Johannesevangelium*, p. 99; J. H. Bernard, *St. John*, pp. clxx. 207; G. Bornkamm, "Die eucharistische Rede im Johannesevangelium", *ZNW* 47 (1956) 161-162; R. Bultmann, *John*, pp. 218-220; F. Hahn, "Die alttestamentliche Motive der urchristlichen Abendmahls-Ueberlieferung", *EvTh* 27 (1967) 343-344; J. Jeremias, "Joh 6,51c-58 — redaktionell?", *ZNW* 44 (1952-53), 256-257; E. Lohse, "Wort und Sakrament im Johannes-evangelium", *NTS* 7 (1960-61) 116-117; J. Racette, "L'unité de discours sur le pain de vie", *ScEccl* 9 (1957) 83-84; G. Richter, "Zur Formgeschichte und literarischen Einheit von Joh 6, 31-58", *ZNW* 60 (1969) 33-34 and passim; J. N. Sanders, *St. John*, pp. 195-196; A. Wikenhauser, *Johannes*, pp. 105-106; W. Wilkens, "Das Abendmahlzeugnis im vierten Evangelium", *EvTh* 18 (1958) 354-356.

[38] See F.-M. Braun, "St. Jean", p. 361; R. E. Brown, *John*, pp. 284-294; C. H. Dodd, *Interpretation*, pp. 337-338; M.-J. Lagrange, *St. Jean*, pp. 182-183; H. Odeberg, *Fourth Gospel*, pp. 259-260 makes the division here, but does not regard what follows as Eucharistic; E. Schweizer, "Das johanneische Zeugnis vom Herrenmahl", *EvTh* 12 (1952-53) 353-363; R. H. Strachan, *Fourth Gospel*, p. 185; B. Vawter, "John", p. 437; G. Ghiberti, "Il c. 6 di Giovanni e la presenza dell'Eucaristia nel 4° Vangelo", *Parole di Vita* 14 (1969) 105-106.

[39] See above, p. 92.

[40] See C. K. Barrett, *St. John*, p. 235; J. D. G. Dunn, "John VI — A Eucharistic Discourse?", *NTS* 17 (1970-71) 329; E. C. Hoskyns, *Fourth Gospel* pp. 278-281; B. Lindars, *John*, p. 253; G. H. C. Macgregor, *John*, p. 153; J. Marsh, *St. John*, p. 293; L. Morris, *John*, pp. 376-377; R. Schnackenburg, *Johannesevangelium* II, pp. 84-89; B. F. Westcott, *St. John*, p. 99.

[41] As we will be mentioning these scholars under various headings, for a general bibliography on this, see P. Borgen, *Bread from Heaven*, p. 25, note 1.

[42] R. Bultmann, *John*, pp. 218-220; E. Lohse, "Wort und Sakrament ...", pp. 110-111; E. Käsemann, *The Testament of Jesus*, p. 32.

[43] F. Hahn, "Die alttestamentlichen Motive ...", p. 341. pp. 343-344; J. Jeremias, "Johanneische Literarkritik", *TB* 20 (1941) 44; S. Temple, "A Key to the Composition of the Fourth Gospel", p. 232.

miracle stories and the first part of the discourse.[44]   R. E. Brown, in particular, has been convinced by G. Bornkamm that vv. 60-63 cannot refer back to vv. 51c-58.   They must refer back to the earlier part of the discourse, and thus vv. 51c-58 have broken the logical link between vv. 35-50 and vv. 60-65.[45]

H. Schürmann, however, is convinced that v. 51c belongs to vv. 35-50, as its primary reference is to the redemptive death of Jesus.[46]   Schürmann has pointed out that to speak of an "either-or" decision regarding v. 51 is a mistake.   Although he claims that v. 51c points back to vv. 27 and 34, referring to the death of Jesus, he also shows that this does not "seal off" v. 51 from any contact with vv. 52-58.   The Eucharist and the giving of life would not be totally separate concepts for John.[47]   Schürmann's study, although directly concerned only with v. 51, adds strength to the claim that the discourse cannot be broken down into original and redactional sections.

From the point of view of style-criticism, E. Ruckstuhl has shown that it is impossible to separate vv. 51-58 from the rest of the discourse.[48]   E. Schweizer, another specialist in Johannine style-criticism, holds that it is difficult to decide either way,[49] and J. Jeremias has decided, in the light of the evidence marshalled by Ruckstuhl, that the redactional passage must come from the hand of the Evangelist himself.[50]

Those who argue for the unity of the discourse find difficulty in explaining the clearly Eucharistic language of vv. 51-58.   Yet those who argue for various redactional theories are generally prompted by criteria which are far from objective.[51]   P. Borgen seems to have found a background to the whole discourse which overcomes these difficulties.[52]

---

[44] W. Wilkens, "Das Abendmahlzeugnis ...", p. 354; R. E. Brown, *John*, pp. 284-291.

[45] See R. E. Brown, *John*, pp. 299-300; G. Bornkamm, "Die eucharistische Rede im Johannesevangelium", pp. 161-169.

[46] H. Schürmann, "Joh 6,51c — ein Schlüssel zur grossen johanneischen Brotrede", esp. pp. 249-254. See also R. Schnackenburg, *Johannesevangelium* II, p. 83. This has recently been denied by U. Wilckens, "Der eucharistische Abschnitt der johanneischen Rede vom Lebensbrot (Joh 6,51c-58)", in *Neues Testament und Kirche*, pp. 226-227. He insists that v 51c is *only* Eucharistic.

[47] H. Schürmann, *art. cit.*, pp. 249-250.

[48] E. Ruckstuhl, *Die literarische Einheit des Johannesevangeliums, der gegenwärtige Stand der einschlägigen Forschungen*, Studia Friburgensia, n.f. 3 (Freiburg in der Schweiz, S. Paul, 1951) pp. 220-271. See also Idem, "Literarkritik am Johannesevangelium und eucharistische Rede (Jo 6,51c-58)", *DivThom* 23 (1945) 153-190. 301-333.

[49] E. Schweizer, "Das johanneische Zeugnis ...", pp. 353-355.

[50] J. Jeremias, "Joh 51c-58 — Redaktionell?", pp. 256-257. G. Richter, "Zur Formgeschichte ...", pp. 52-53 attempts to show that there are literary differences, but his attempt is slight. G. Bornkamm, "Vorjohanneische Tradition oder nachjohanneische Bearbeitung in der eucharistische Rede Johannes 6", in *Geschichte und Glaube* II, BEvTh 53, (München, Kaiser, 1971) pp. 52-54 refuses to accept these studies as an indication of the unity of the passage.

[51] Bultmann's arbitrary exclusion of all possible sacramental references is the clearest example of this.

[52] P. Borgen, *Bread from Heaven*.

Borgen shows that Philo's language and method of paraphrase, weaving fragments of a haggadic tradition together with words of the Old Testament, is also reflected in later Rabbinic exegesis.[53] Using Philo's *Mut.* 253-263 and *Leg. All.* III, 162-168 as examples, he finds patterns which are reflected in such Rabbinic literature as *Mekilta on Exodus* 16,4 and *Exodus Rabbah* 25,2. He has chosen these passages because the same haggadic fragments which are common to these documents (especially "bread" — "descending from heaven") are also found throughout the discourse in John 6 (see vv. 33, 38, 41, 42, 50, 51, 58).[54] Although Philo lacks the "descending" motif, it is present in the Rabbinic literature. A tradition common to both Philo and the Rabbis is that of the fathers of Israel eating manna in the desert. Again this can be found in the "eating" references of the discourse (see vv. 31a, 49, 53, 54, 56, 57, 58).[55] "These suggest the strong probability that the fragments listed from John 6, 31. 49. 53. 54. 55. 56. 57. 58. are taken from summaries of events at the Exodus".[56] When one adds to this the repetition of the quotation from the Old Testament, first used in 6,31b and then taken up in vv. 32-35, 38, 41, 42, 48-51, 52-58 one might conclude that "the words in the quotation from the Old Testament in John 6,31b are paraphrased together with fragments from haggadic traditions in John 6,31-58".[57]

B. Gärtner and A. Guilding have also tried to show that there is a direct link with Jewish popular exegesis in John 6.[58] Both of these scholars fail to achieve any kind of certitude. It is impossible to make detailed links with either a Jewish-Christian Passover (Gärtner) or with the Synagogue Lectionary (Guilding) because we do not have enough evidence for such background.[59] However, the work of these scholars does confirm that John 6 can be very easily set into the context of Jewish Passover speculation.[60]

---

[53] P. Borgen, *op. cit.*, pp. 14-20.

[54] *ibid.*, pp. 20-21.

[55] *ibid.*, p. 21.

[56] *ibid.*, p. 22.

[57] *ibid.*, p. 23. For this practice at Qumran, see pp. 24-25, note 2.

[58] B. Gärtner, *John 6 and the Jewish Passover;* A. Guilding, *The Fourth Gospel and Jewish Worship*, esp. pp. 58-67. See also, E. J. Kilmartin, "The Formation of the Bread of Life Discourse (John 6)", *Script* 12 (1960) 75-78; Idem, "Liturgical Influence on John 6", *CBQ* 22 (1960) 183-191; D. Daube, *The New Testament and Rabbinic Judaism*, (London, Athlone, 1956) pp. 36-51. 158-169.

[59] See esp. L. Morris, *The New Testament and the Jewish Lectionaries*, (London, Tyndale Press, 1964) for a thorough criticism of Guilding's work. See also B. Malina, *The Palestinian Manna Tradition*, (Leiden, E. J. Brill, 1968) pp. 102-104.

[60] See G. Ziener, "Johannesevangelium und urchristliche Passafeier", *BZ* 2 (1958) 263-274 has attempted to show that the whole of the Gospel reflects a Jewish-Christian Passover tradition. His theory also denies proof. See R. E. Brown, "The Eucharist and Baptism in John", in *New Testament Essays*, (London, G. Chapman, 1967) p. 80, n. 11.

Having established that John is using a haggadic tradition in ch. 6, Borgen then sets out to show that Philo's *Mut.* 253-263, *Leg. All.* III, 162-168 and John 6 all follow the same homiletic pattern.[61] The texts from Philo both have a "master text" from the Pentateuch which is continually cited and paraphrased.[62] In Jn. 6,31-58 Borgen finds the same pattern:

v. 31	*Old Testament quotation:* [63]
	a) He gave them bread from heaven
	b) to eat
vv. 32-48	*paraphrase part a) of the quotation:*
v. 32	bread from heaven ... gives
v. 33	bread ... from heaven
v. 34	give ... bread
v. 35	bread
v. 38	from heaven
v. 41	murmured ... the bread ... from heaven
v. 42	from heaven
v. 43	murmur

[61] P. Borgen, *op. cit.*, pp. 28-57. See also his earlier articles: "The Unity of the Discourse in John 6", *ZNW* 50 (1959) 277-278; "Observations on the Midrashic Character of John 6", *ZNW* 54 (1963) 232-240.

[62] *ibid.*, pp. 29-33.

[63] This text is not a direct quotation. Borgen maintains that it reflects a whole pericope from Exodus. Exod. 16,4 and 16,15 are in the quotation and the paraphrase, while Exod. 16,2 is used in the paraphrase (see *op. cit.*, pp. 40-42). E. D. Freed, *Old Testament Quotations in the Gospel of John*, SNT 11, (Leiden, E. J. Brill, 1965) pp. 11-16 and J.-N. Aletti, "Le discours sur le pain de vie..", pp. 190-191 independently establish the same Old Testament background for Jn. 6,31. These suggestions, however, have been seriously questioned by G. Richter, "Die alttestamentliche Zitate in der Rede vom Himmelsbrot, Joh 6,26-51a", in J. Ernst (ed.), *Schriftauslesung: Beiträge zur Hermeneutik des Neuen Testaments und im Neuen Testament*, (Münster, Schöninghaus, 1972) pp. 194-251. This thorough study attempts to show that, rather than a quotation from the Old Testament, v. 31b is a reflection of a traditional Jewish haggadah on the manna. Despite the exhaustive nature of the work, Richter has failed to discuss the significance of the καθώς έστιν γεγραμμένον of v. 31a. He regards these words as belonging to the pre-Johannine haggadah which John has taken over (p. 221). But what do these words mean, even if Richter is correct? W. A. Meeks, "Man from Heaven ...", p. 58, note 50 has criticised Borgen's "fixation on the Scripture text so loosely cited in vs. 31". Meeks accepts, however, that the discourse unfolds in the way described by Borgen, claiming that v. 31 is "a saying of Jesus rather than a scripture text that provides the starting point of the 'midrash' ". Whatever the solution to the question of the text in v. 31, it seems to us that Borgen has discovered a pattern which may use as its starting point an Old Testament quotation (and this still appears the most likely suggestion), a Jewish haggadic tradition or a saying of Jesus. Recently, J.-N. Aletti, "Le discours sur le pain de vie..", pp. 190-197, has argued that the whole discourse can be understood as a contrast of "last events and eschatological fulfilment", but only if one understands vv. 31 and 45 as a deliberate use of the Old Testament.

| v. 45 | Quotation from prophecy |
| v. 48 | bread |

vv. 49-58   *paraphrase part b) of the quotation*:

v. 49	ate
v. 50	bread ... from heaven ... eat
v. 51	bread ... from heaven ... eats ... bread ... bread which ... shall give
v. 52	give ... to eat
v. 53	eat
v. 58	bread from heaven ... ate ... eats ... bread.

Thus, the first part of the quotation cited in v. 31: "He gave them bread from heaven", is paraphrased and discussed in vv. 32-48. The second part: "to eat", is then paraphrased and interpreted in vv. 49-58. The paraphrase of part *a)* of the quotation is, however, also carried into the paraphrase of "to eat".[64]

Borgen identifies further common elements in this midrashic treatment of an Old Testament text in Philo and in John 6. Not only is there a major text followed by a paraphrase, but also an inclusion between the opening and closing sections of the discourse (vv. 31-33 have all the key words of v. 58);[65] all three examples studied by Borgen have a key text and a secondary text (*Leg. All.* III, 165 = Exod. 12,4; *Mut.* 263 = Gen. 17,20-21; Jn. 6,45 = Is. 54,13). While Philo has all his sub-texts from the Torah, John has his text from a Prophet.[66]

Further parallels from Philo, the Jewish midrashim and also from Paul show certain common characteristics:[67]

a) There is a correspondence between the opening and closing parts of the homily.

b) In addition to the main quotation from the Old Testament, there is at least one other subordinate quotation, also from the Old Testament.

---

[64] This twofold division, centred upon the use of "from heaven" and "to eat" was used by E. Galbiati, "Il Pane della Vita", *BibOr* 5 (1963) 102-105. See also G. Segalla, "La struttura circolare-chiasmatica di Gv. 6, 26-58 e il suo significato teologico" *BibOr* 13 (1971) 191-198.

[65] P. Borgen, *op. cit.,* pp. 35-38.

[66] *ibid.,* pp. 38-39. Although beyond proof, the fact that John uses Is. 54 for his sub-text may indicate that this homiletic process has been worked out in the context of a Jewish Christian Passover. See B. Lindars, *John,* pp. 250-253. G. Richter, "Die alttestamentliche Zitate ...", pp. 251-271 again denies that there is a direct use of the Old Testament. For him, it comes from a Jewish haggadah based on Is. 54,13. The "it is written in the prophets" is not a Johannine introduction to the quotation, but comes to John in the haggadah.

[67] P. Borgen, *op. cit.,* pp. 46-51.

c) Words from the major text are paraphrased and quoted in the homily.

This pattern occurs, with remarkable consistency, in Jn. 6,31-58. Borgen appears to have shown that the discourse is a unit, based upon a Jewish homiletic pattern. He has added weight to the style-critical considerations of Ruckstuhl and Schweizer.[68] Although tentative, further support has been indirectly given to Borgen's argument by suggestions from R. Le Déaut and G. Vermes.[69] Le Déaut suggests a reading for the Targum Neophiti on Num. 11,6-7 which could illustrate the attitude of contestation which greeted the announcement of the Bread from heaven. Vermes suggests a reading for the Targum Neophiti on Exod. 16,15 as: "He (Moses) is the bread which the Lord has given you to eat". Both of these suggestions show that Jewish exegesis is a possible background for the themes of John 6.

For Borgen, some of the discourse, and especially vv. 51-58, has Eucharistic overtones, where the midrash has been influenced by early Christian Eucharistic traditions.[70] When Jesus spoke of his "flesh" as the bread which is given for the life of the world (v. 51c) and demanded that his hearers eat the flesh of the Son of Man and drink his blood (v. 53), it appears certain that some reference is being made to the Eucharist. However, opinions vary greatly when scholars come to discuss to what extent the discourse, or part thereof, is directly Eucharistic.[71]

H. Odeberg, A. Schlatter, H. Strathmann, W. H. Cadman, E. C. Hoskyns, B. F. Westcott and J. H. Bernard[72] have argued that the whole discourse (vv. 35-58) refers to the revelation by and in Jesus. Odeberg has claimed that the realism of vv. 51-53 has nothing to do with the Eucharist, but that it refers to the reality of Jesus: "the acquisition of the heavenly bread, the

---

[68] See above, p. 94, notes 48-50. Borgen's work has been widely accepted, although frequently with reservations. See, B. Lindars, *John*, pp. 249-253; R. Schnackenburg, "Zur Rede vom Brot aus dem Himmel: eine Beobachtung zu Joh 6,52", *BZ* 12 (1968) 248-252; Idem, "Das Brot des Lebens", in *Tradition und Glaube*, pp. 328-342; B. J. Malina, *The Palestinian Manna-Tradition*, pp. 102-106. It is interesting to note that before Borgen a similar suggestion had been made by A. Finkel, *The Pharisees and the Teacher of Nazareth. A Study of their Background, their Halachic and Midrashic Teachings, the Similarities and Differences*, AGSU 4, (Leiden, E. J. Brill, 1964) pp. 158-159.
[69] R. Le Déaut, "Une aggadah targumique et les murmures de Jean 6", *Biblica* 51 (1970) 80-83; G. Vermes, "He is the Bread: Targum Neofiti Exodus 16,15", in E. E. Ellis-M. Wilcox, (eds.), *Neotestamentica et Semitica. Studies in Honour of Matthew Black*, (Edinburgh, T. and T. Clark, 1969) pp. 256-263.
[70] P. Borgen, *op. cit.*, pp. 89-96, esp. pp. 91-94.
[71] A summary of the various positions, which we have enlarged upon, is given in R. E. Brown, *John*, p. 272.
[72] H. Odeberg, *Fourth Gospel*, pp. 235-269; A. Schlatter, *Johannes*, pp. 170-180; H. Strathmann, *Johannes*, pp. 115-130; W. H. Cadman, *The Open Heaven*, pp. 78-88; E. C. Hoskyns, *Fourth Gospel*, pp. 284-298; B. F. Westcott, *St. John*, pp. 99-108; J. H. Bernard, *St. John*, pp. 190-213. See also pp. clxvii-clxix.

'imperishable food', was no mere allegory".[73] To take the "flesh and blood" reference in its material sense is to miss the whole point of the discourse, and to make the same mistake as Nicodemus made earlier in the Gospel — understanding that "J's realistic expressions refer to objects of the terrestrial world instead of to objects of the celestial world".[74] O. S. Brooks and J. D. G. Dunn have also questioned the Eucharistic application of the discourse, claiming that its main purpose is to emphasise the incarnate Jesus, given up to death, as the bread of life.[75] In this they are close to Hoskyns, who contends that the most important point of the discourse is to affirm the humanity of Jesus.[76] L. Morris has claimed that while the discourse is primarily sapiential, there may be hints of the Eucharist in it.[77]

A larger group of scholars divide the discourse into two sections. Vv. 35-50 (51) speak in purely sapiential terms about the revelation of God in and by Jesus, while vv. 51-58 refer to the Eucharistic flesh of Jesus. C. H. Dodd, C. K. Barrett, M.-J. Lagrange, E. Schweizer, P.-H. Menoud, H. Klos, R. H. Strachan, J. Wellhausen, U. Wilckens, A. Wikenhauser and W. Wilkens have argued this case, although they refuse to accept that vv. 51-58 are redactional.[78] R. Bultmann and G. Bornkamm also claim that there is a sharp break between what is said in vv. 35-51b and vv. 51c-58. For Bultmann, vv. 51c-58 are fully Eucharistic, and are to be excised as the addition of an ecclesiastical redactor.[79] Bornkamm has concluded that vv. 51c-58 are secondary by showing that vv. 60-65 contradict what is said in vv. 51c-58, while they form an excellent conclusion for vv. 35-51b.[80]

---

[73] H. Odeberg, *op. cit.*, p. 239.

[74] *ibid.*, p. 239. See, however, the remarks of Hoskyns (*Fourth Gospel*, p. 286) on the importance of created reality in this discourse.

[75] O. S. Brooks, "The Johannine Eucharist", *JBL* 82 (1963) 293-300; J. D. G. Dunn, "John VI — A Eucharistic Discourse?", pp. 328-338.

[76] E. C. Hoskyns, *Fourth Gospel*, pp. 284-298.

[77] L. Morris, *John*, pp. 354-381.

[78] C. H. Dodd, *Interpretation*, pp. 337-340; C. K. Barrett, *St. John*, pp. 237-247; M.-J. Lagrange, *St. Jean*, pp. 169-186; E. Schweizer, "Das johanneische Zeugnis ...", pp. 341-343; H. Klos, *Die Sakramente im Johannesevangelium*, (Stuttgart, Katholisches Bibelwerk, 1970) pp. 68-69; R. H. Strachan, *Fourth Gospel*, pp. 183-185; J. Wellhausen, *Johannis*, pp. 30-32; A. Wikenhauser, *Johannes*, pp. 101-110; W. Wilkens, "Das Abendmahlzeugnis ...", pp. 354-370; P.-H. Menoud, "L'originalité de la pensée johannique", pp. 254-255; U. Wilckens, "Der eucharistische Abschnitt der johanneischen Rede vom Lebensbrot ...", pp. 220-248.

[79] R. Bultmann, *John*, pp. 218-236.

[80] G. Bornkamm, "Die eucharistische Rede im Johannes-Evangelium", pp. 161-169. Although R. E. Brown sees Eucharistic references in other parts of the discourse, and in this differs from Bornkamm, he sees vv. 52-58 as secondary because they contradict vv. 60-65, especially vv. 62-63. In the light of Borgen's work, however, Bornkamm has changed his thesis considerably. He now suggests that an originally Johannine sapiential discourse has been rendered Eucharistic (vv. 49-58) by a later anti-docetic redactor. See "Vorjohanneische oder nachjohanneische Bearbeitung ...", pp. 59-64.

Some hold that the whole of the discourse is Eucharistic. This view is defended, in various ways, by A. Loisy, O. Cullmann, W. Bauer, M.-F. Berrouard, J. Bligh, F. J. Leenhardt, J. Marsh, R. H. Lightfoot, A. Guilding, W. Temple, J. Racette, A. Richardson, J. L. Lilly, and B. Vawter.[81]   Braun, Leenhardt and Marsh suggest a gradual build up to the final revelation in vv. 51-58, while Cullmann finds Eucharistic references in almost every verse.

There are some who see the discourse as referring to both revelation and the Eucharist. The main proponent of this "two-level" theory has been X. Léon-Dufour, and he has been followed by H. van den Bussche.[82]   A variation of this point of view is offered by A. Feuillet, R. E. Brown and B. Lindars.[83] For them the two themes are present throughout the first part of the discourse (vv. 35-50), where revelation is the main idea and the Eucharist plays a secondary role.   In the second part (vv. 51-58), only the Eucharist is referred to, although Lindars shows how this is closely linked to Christ's death.

Despite the wealth of discussion, no single line of thought imposes itself, with the exception of Borgen's work on the background and structure of the discourse.[84]   However, we are convinced that this chapter was coherent to the

---

[81] A. Loisy, *Quatrième Évangile*, p. 233.   Loisy claims that the whole discourse was originally a Eucharistic hymn, made up of vv. 26-27, 32-33, 47-48, 51, 53-58.   The rest of the discourse is "remplissage"; O. Cullmann, *Early Christian Worship*, SBT 10, (London, SCM Press, 1953) pp. 93-102 (English translation of *Urchristentum und Gottesdienst*, [Zürich, Zwingli-Verlag, 1950] and *Les Sacrements dans l'Évangile johannique*, [Paris, Presses Universitaires de France, 1951]); W. Bauer, *Johannesevangelium*, pp. 96-106; M.-F. Berrouard, "La multiplication des pains et le discours du pain de vie (Jean 6)", *LumVie* 18 (1969) 63-75; J. Bligh, "Jesus in Galilee", pp. 3-21; F.-M. Braun, "St. Jean", pp. 361-367; Idem, "L'eucharistie selon S. Jean", pp. 5-29; F. J. Leenhardt, "La structure du chapitre 6 ...", pp. 1-13; J. Marsh, *St. John*, pp. 293-308; R. H. Lightfoot, *St. John*, pp. 155-162; A. Guilding, *The Fourth Gospel and Jewish Worship*, pp. 58-59; W. Temple, *Readings*, p. 80; J. Racette, "L'unité du discours ...", pp. 82-85; A. Richardson, *St. John*, Torch Commentaries, (London, SCM Press, 1959) pp. 102-105; B. Vawter, "John", pp. 436-438; Idem, "The Johannine Sacramentary", *TS* 17 (1956) 151-166; G. H. C. Macgregor, "The Eucharist in the Fourth Gospel", *NTS* 9 (1962-63) 111-119; J. L. Lilly, "The Eucharistic Discourse of John 6", *CBQ* 12 (1950) 48-51.   Lilly argues that the whole discourse, as it stands, was delivered by Jesus!

[82] X Léon-Dufour, "Le mystère du pain de vie ...", pp. 481-523; H. van den Bussche, *Jean*, pp. 247-252.

[83] A. Feuillet, "Les thèmes bibliques majeurs ...", pp. 53-128; R. E. Brown, *John*, pp. 272-275, 284-285; B. Lindars, *John*, pp. 250-253.

[84] Although some of his points are well made, we do not think that G. Richter, "Zur Formgeschichte ...", pp. 21-55 has summoned sufficient evidence against Borgen. He is prepared to accept Borgen's midrashic method as far as v. 51b, and thus uses Borgen's arguments to prove that vv. 51c-58 are not a part of the original discourse. For Richter, the midrashic development of "to eat" runs only from vv. 48-51b (pp. 23-24). It is true that the theme is not so frequently repeated in vv. 51c-58, but the use of it in vv. 52,53 and 58 still has to be explained.   For further criticism of Richter's arguments see, U. Wilckens, "Der eucharistische Abschnitt ...", pp. 227-228.

person who wrote (or redacted) it, and also to the early Church which received it. That the latter was the case is evident from the lack of major variants in the text which has come down to us,[85] but many questions about the theme (or themes) of vv. 22-71 are still far from being solved. Is the discourse sapiential, Eucharistic — or both? If it is both, which theme predominates in the various sections of the discourse which obviously unfolds as it proceeds?

John sets the scene for the discourse in vv. 22-33 and triggers it off with the misunderstanding of v. 34. In this preparatory section, v. 27 introduces the theme for the whole discussion: "Do not labour for the food which perishes, but for the food which endures to eternal life, which the Son of Man will give you; for on him has God the Father set his seal".[86] The discourse is concerned with the gift which the Son of Man, who has been authorised by the Father, will give: a gift which will "endure to eternal life". To receive this gift, Jesus explains, one must "believe in him whom he (ὁ θεός) has sent" (v. 29). We are concerned with very Johannine terms:

a) Son of Man (see 1,51; 3,13-14; 5,27; 6,27. 53. 62; 8,28; 9,35; 12,23. 34; 13,31).

b) Belief in (πιστεύειν εἰς) Jesus (see 1,12; 2,11.23; 3,16.18.36; 4,39; 6,29.35.40; 7,5.31.38.39.48; 8,30; 8,35.36; 10,42; 11,25; 11,26.45.48; 12,11.36.37.42.44.46; 14,1.12; 16,9; 17,20).

c) Eternal life (see 3,15.16.36; 4,14.36; 5,24.39; 6,27.40.47.54.68; 10,28; 11,25.50; 17,2.3).

d) Jesus as the one sent by the Father (see 3,17.34; 5,36.38; 6,29.57; 7,29; 8,42; 10,36; 11,42; 17,3.8.18.21.23.25; 20,21).

What we have in these few verses is a summary of one of the major concerns of Johannine christology: a belief in Jesus, the revealer of the Father, which leads to eternal life.

John now starts his midrashic method by introducing the Old Testament quotation in v. 31. What is to follow is an explanation — using the words of the Old Testament quotation — of the basic tenet of Johannine christology which has been stated in vv. 27-33. This is wholly sapiential. There is nothing startlingly new in what is claimed by Jesus in vv. 35-51. Speaking in terms of himself as the Bread of life, which recalls many Old Testament references

---

[85] See on this, R. Kieffer, *Au delà des Recensions? L'évolution textuelle dans Jean VI, 52-71;* V. Salmon, *Quatrième Évangile. Histoire de la tradition textuelle de l'original grec,* (Paris, Letouzey, 1969); M. Mees, "Sinn und Bedeutung westlicher Textvarianten in Jo 6,31-58", *BZ* 13 (1969) 244-255.

[86] See C. K. Barrett, *St. John,* p. 235: "The whole discourse is summarized here". See also J. Schneider, "Zur Frage ...", p. 133; F. J. Leenhardt, "La structure du chapitre 6 ...", pp. 4-5; B. Vawter, "John", p. 436; J. Wellhausen, *Johannis,* p. 33.

(see Amos, 8,11-13; Is. 55, 1-3; Sir. 14,9; 24,21; 15,3; Wisd. 16,20-26; Prov. 9,5),[87] Jesus states that belief in him whom the Father has sent will bring the believer to eternal life (see especially v. 40). The complaint of the Jews about the origin of Jesus in vv. 41-42 introduces a most important question.[88] Their main objection is to his claim to have "come down from heaven". It is precisely because the Jews can never come to understand this fact that they can never have correct Johannine faith in Jesus. Why is it important that Jesus' claim to have "come down from heaven" be accepted? This is explained in vv. 44-51, especially in vv. 46-48:

> "Not that anyone has seen the Father except him who is from God; he has seen the Father. Truly, truly I say to you, he who believes has eternal life. I am the bread of life".

In terms that recall the prologue (see 1,18), Jesus affirms his unique role as the revealer of God and consequently as the only place where the world can find eternal life. Failure to understand this means failure to understand the Johannine Jesus. Yet the Jews continue to make the same mistake as Nicodemus (see 3,1-10), unable to go beyond the "manna" which their fathers ate in the desert. The bread which Jesus offers is of a different order. At this stage of the discourse, the crucial "Eucharistic" passage starts. The critics who want to see this as a completely different line of thought are making the author, or the final redactor, into someone who is "necessarily irresponsible or unintelligent".[89] If this passage has been added by a redactor or by John at a later stage in the Gospel's growth, how well he has worked! He has not only succeeded in catching many nuances of Johannine style in his addition, but he has been able to knit in his redactional passage by continuing the discourse where it originally ended for a few words (v. 51c). He then adds v. 52 in the same vein as vv. 25-34, 41-42 and v. 60, taking up the discourse again

---

[87] On the Wisdom background for this imagery, see A. Feuillet, "Les thèmes majeurs ...", pp. 61-88; F.-M. Braun, "Messie, Logos et Fils de l'homme", p. 142; J. Blank, "Die johanneische Brotrede", *BuL* 7 (1966) 201-202; T. Preiss, "Étude sur le ch. 6 de l'Évangile de Jean", pp. 155-157; E. Galbiati, "Il Pane della Vita", pp. 105-108. For a detailed study of this possible background, see M. Conti, *Il discorso del pane di vita nella tradizione sàpienziale*.

[88] See M. de Jonge, "Jesus as Prophet and King ...", pp. 167-168: "It is clear ... that the unique relationship between Jesus and God is underlined by means of the expression 'my Father' (vss 32,37,40,44 and especially vs 46) and the notion of 'descent from heaven' (vss 33,41,42,50,51); consequently ... the fact that the Jews regard Jesus as the Son of Joseph and think they know his father and mother (vs 42), shows that they do not understand the real secret of his coming into the world; he is not simply a prophet like Moses as a second Moses, but the Son of God who came to do God's will (vs 38), that is: to give eternal life to all who believe (vss 39-40 and passim)". The importance of this Father-Son relationship for ch. 6 presupposes what the author has already established in ch. 5.

[89] C. H. Dodd, *Interpretation*, p. 290.

in v. 53. A redactor who was capable of working like this would hardly add a passage which contradicted what immediately preceded and succeeded his addition. Whatever the solution concerning the stage at which these verses were written, they are to be read as a continuation of what has already been said.

H. Schürmann has shown that v. 51c belongs to the context which we have just outlined.[90] Σάρξ is not a Eucharistic word in the Fourth Gospel,[91] despite the possible links which this verse may appear to have with Marcan and Pauline traditions.[92] It is used to speak of the incarnation in 1,14 and in the rest of the Gospel, outside ch. 6, it is a negative element in man which resists Jesus and his revelation (see esp. 8,15).[93] The use of ὑπέρ and διδόναι can also be traced to traditional passion language, rather than to the Eucharist (see, for example, Mk. 10,45. See also the δώσει of Jn. 6,27).[94] We suggest that the discourse is not broken at v. 51, but continued by the addition of another essentially Johannine theme: the cross.[95] Jesus' unique role as the revealer is often linked with the cross in the Fourth Gospel. In 3,13 Jesus was presented as the unique revealer, while in 3,14 there was an immediate reference to the cross. In 12,31-33 Jesus speaks of the supreme revelation in which all men will be drawn to him — when he is lifted up on a cross.[96] The same process is taking place here. What is said from vv. 52-58 is the continuation — admittedly in different language — of what has already been said. The same truths are repeated, first negatively (v. 53) and then positively (v. 54). All this is true because Jesus and his word is the real bread (v. 55) which bring about a true union between the believer and the object of that belief (v. 56),[97] because, as we have heard earlier (see vv. 39-40), Jesus is the one sent by the Father (v. 57), the perfect fulfilment of all that has been promised and pre-figured in Moses and the manna in the desert (v. 58).

If one is searching for proof of a Eucharistic celebration in the Johannine Church, it is to be found in Jn. 6,51-58. Although the theme and theology

---

[90] H. Schürmann, "Joh 6,51c — ein Schlüssel zur grossen johanneischen Brotrede", pp. 244-262.

[91] See *ibid.*, pp. 250-255.

[92] See Mk. 14,24; I Cor. 11,24.

[93] See E. Schweizer, Art. "σάρξ", *TDNT* VII, pp. 138-140; S. de Ausejo, "El concepto de 'carne' aplicado a Cristo en el IV Evangelio", in J. Coppens-A. Descamps-E. Massaux (eds.), *Sacra Pagina*, Miscellanea Biblica Congressus Internationalis Catholici de Re Biblica, (Gembloux, Duculot, 1959), Vol. II, pp. 219-234.

[94] See H. Schlier, "Joh 6 und das joh Verständnis der Eucharistie", pp. 79-82.

[95] See J. D. G. Dunn, "John VI — A Eucharistic Discourse?", pp. 328-338. See esp. pp. 337-338. See also C. H. Dodd, *Interpretation*, p. 353.

[96] See also 8,28; 12,23-24; 13,31.

[97] This theme is mentioned here for the first time in the Gospel. Like so many themes in John, it will grow in importance. It reaches its zenith in ch. 17.

of vv. 26-50 are continued, they are clearly phrased in language which recalls the Eucharist. Odeberg is probably correct when he insists that to understand this passage as the Johannine teaching on the Eucharistic body and blood of our Lord is to fall into the same mistake as Nicodemus in ch. 3 and the Jews throughout this present chapter, who keep straining to bring the discourse into categories which they can accept.[98] However, Odeberg exaggerates in his spiritualisation of the discourse. It appears inevitable that the Eucharistic references would be seen and understood by John's readers. R. E. Brown, among others, has argued convincingly for hints of Eucharistic themes throughout the discourse,[99] but John appears to be developing a very important, sapiential line of thought, without interruption, from vv. 26-58. To do this he has used a current midrashic method, into which he has introduced language which comes directly from the Eucharistic celebrations which he knew. John is not primarily concerned with the Eucharist, or Jesus' Eucharistic presence, but with the unique revelation of God in and by Jesus, a revelation which will reach its high point in the piercing of the body and the spilling of the blood of Jesus at Calvary (see 19,34-37). It is amply clear from the rest of the New Testament that the event of Calvary was commemorated in the Eucharistic celebrations of the early Church (see Mk. 14,22-31; Matt. 26,15-30; Lk. 22,14-23; I Cor. 11, 23-25).[100] John has also used the language of this commemoration in his midrashic exposition of the true bread from heaven.[101] The whole discourse is about the gaining of eternal life through belief in Jesus. John's use of Eucharistic language would certainly remind his readers of the importance of their Eucharistic celebrations.[102] Yet, the main point of the discourse must be understood in the sense which Jesus himself explains

[98] See H. Odeberg, *Fourth Gospel*, p. 289.

[99] R. E. Brown, *John*, p. 247. See also E. Galbiati, "Il Pane della Vita", pp. 101-110; H. Schlier, "Joh 6 und das joh Verständnis der Eucharistie", pp. 69-95; E. Janot, "Le Pain de Vie", *Greg* 11 (1930) 161-170; F.-M. Braun, "L'eucharistie selon S. Jean", pp. 11-17; E. Springer, "Die Einheit der Rede von Kapharnaum (Jo 6)", *BZ* 15 (1918-21) 319-334; G. Ghiberti, "Il c. 6 di Giovanni e la presenza dell'eucaristia nel 4° Vangelo", pp. 106-119.

[100] E. Ruckstuhl, "Wesen und Kraft der Eucharistie in der Sicht des Johannesevangeliums", in *Das Opfer der Kirche. Exegetische, dogmatische und pastoraltheologische Studien zum Verständnis der Messe*, Luzerner theologische Studien 1, (Luzern, Rex-Verlag, 1954) pp. 52-58; J. Skrinjar, "De terminologia sacrificali in Joh. 6,51-56", *DThom* 74 (1971)᾽ 189-197; F.-M. Braun, "L'eucharistie selon S. Jean", pp. 6-8.

[101] It is important to recognise that the Johannine Church celebrated the Eucharist. While maintaining the position outlined above, that the whole discourse is sapiential, one could still argue with Brown (*John*, pp. 287-291) that the "backbone of vss. 51-58 is made up of material from the Johannine narrative of the institution of the Eucharist" (p. 287). This is very different, however, from claiming that vv. 51-58 are merely the Johannine teaching about the Eucharistic presence of Jesus.

[102] The passover setting of ch. 6 is probably also important in this regard. See L. Morris, *The New Testament and the Jewish Lectionaries*, pp. 64-72; J. K. Howard, "Passover and Eucharist in the Fourth Gospel", *ScotJT* 20 (1967) 329-337.

in vv. 40, 47, 54 and 58.[103]   In vv. 40 and 47, where the language is less Eucharistic, we find: "Everyone who sees the Son and believes in him should have eternal life" (v. 40) and "He who believes has eternal life" (v. 47).   In vv. 54 and 58, although expressed in more Eucharistic terms, the same thing is being said: "He who eats my flesh and drinks my blood has eternal life" (v. 54) and "Who eats this bread will live for ever" (v. 58).   Even in v. 56 where the extremely realistic τρώγειν is used, it is counterbalanced by the use of μένειν ἐν, which John uses frequently to speak of the inward, enduring personal union which exists between Jesus and the Father (14,10), Christians and Christ (15,4.5.7; I Jn. 2,6.24), Christ and Christians (15,4.5), Christians and God (I Jn. 2,24.27; 3,6.24; 4,13) God and Christians (I Jn. 3,24, 4,12-13.15).   Thus in this one verse we have the simultaneous presence of a Eucharistic practice (eating) and a sapiential consequence (remaining in Christ and Christ in them).[104]   Although the whole exposition of the "bread from heaven" has drawn hints of Eucharistic language from the author, it is not until he comes to the second section of the Old Testament quotation — "to eat" — that he draws almost uniquely on Eucharistic language, applying what has been said so far to a message of faith in the encounter with Jesus in the Eucharist.[105]

The use of Eucharistic language must have served as an immediate recall of their celebrations for the readers of the Gospel.   While John is not primarily concerned with the presence of Jesus in the celebration of the Eucharist, the immediate application of the basic sapiential message for John's audience is obvious: it is in the Eucharist where one can encounter the flesh and blood of Christ.   John is working at two levels here, but the main thrust of his argument is to continue the sapiential theme of the whole discourse.   The recalling of the Eucharist plays a secondary but important role in so far as it was the concretising in the community practice of the Eucharist of what John has proclaimed throughout the discourse.[106]

---

[103] See S. S. Smalley, "Liturgy and Sacrament in the Fourth Gospel", *EvQ* 29 (1957) 159-170.   See esp. pp. 166-167.

[104] See E. Ruckstuhl, "Wesen und Kraft ...", pp. 58-78; F.-M. Braun, "L'eucharistie selon S. Jean", pp. 22-23; G. Percorara, "De verbo 'manere' apud Joannem", *DThom* 14 (1937) 157-171; F. Hauck, Art. "μένω", *TDNT* IV, p. 576; W. F. Howard, *Christianity According to St. John*, p. 205.

[105] See P. Borgen, *op. cit.*, pp. 33-42.

[106] Against the exaggerated interpretations of those who see the "life" imparted in v. 57 as the gift one receives by frequenting the Eucharist.   See, for example, G. Crocetti, "Le linee fondamentali del concetto di vita in Jo. 6,57", *RBibIt* 19 (1971) 375-394.   See, on this, H. Schürmann, "Die Eucharistie als Representation und Applikation des Heils-geschehens nach Joh 6,53-58", pp. 30-45, 108-118; F.-M. Braun, "L'eucharistie selon S. Jean", pp. 17-22; U. Wilckens, "Der eucharistische Abschnitt ...", pp. 220-248.   Wilckens has insisted that the passage is entirely Eucharistic, but that it is the application of the sapiential message to the concrete existence of the faithful.   The passage comes from a

This appears to be a logical solution to the complicated discussions which have been aroused by John 6. Given that the discourse is a unit, we must suppose that there is a certain unity of idea. The language is Eucharistic at times, but the dominating themes are not those of the Eucharist and the presence of Jesus in the Eucharistic celebrations. The discourse is concerned, rather, with belief in Jesus and eternal life. This suggestion also explains away the difficulty raised by Bornkamm and Brown, who claim that v. 63 contradicts vv. 51-58.[107] They see vv. 26-50 as sapiential,[108] and the discussion of vv. 60-65 has no sacramental reference, which suggests that it presupposes vv. 26-50. This is especially true of v. 63, where, recalling 3,6, the distinction between πνεῦμα and σάρξ is made. It is clearly stated that the revelation brought by Jesus — "the words" — are πνεῦμα and ζωή. As vv. 51-58 are not sapiential, but Eucharistic, then they have been inserted between v. 50 and v. 60, interrupting what was once a purely sapiential line of thought. If, however, vv. 51-58 continue the discussion of vv. 26-50 in more Eucharistic language, as we have argued, then v. 63 follows vv. 51-58 quite logically.[109] John simply continues to clarify his main point, which he has been making in vv. 51-58, just as he has made it in vv. 26-50. This is not to deny sacramentalism in John. The use of Eucharistic language in ch. 6 indicates that this sacrament played an important role in his community. There are, of course, other sacramental references in the Fourth Gospel and there is no need to resort to forced interpretations to find them.[110]

In conclusion to this lengthy, but nevertheless sketchy, presentation of the current discussion concerning John 6, we would claim that Jn. 6,26-58 is a unit, a midrashic homiletic paraphrase upon the Old Testament text in v. 31, as far as its form is concerned. Its content is primarily sapiential, repeating the great themes of Johannine christology: Jesus is at once the revealer and the revelation of God and through belief in him men may come to eternal life. This message is couched in the Eucharistic language of the Christian community in which John lived, and traces of this language are to be found throughout the whole of the discourse. However, the high point of the Eucharistic language comes in vv. 49-58, when the author turns to his midrashic paraphrase of the words "to eat". The Eucharistic references are the concret-

completely different (Eucharistic) source, but belongs to the discourse as it stands and must not be eliminated from it. See especially his remarks on pp. 237-238.

[107] G. Bornkamm, "Die eucharistische Rede ...", pp. 161-169; R. E. Brown, *John,* pp. 299-300. See also, S. Schulz, *Johannes,* pp. 101-103.

[108] For Bornkamm there is no sacramental reference in vv. 26-50, while for Brown the Eucharist is already a subtheme in these verses.

[109] See E. Schweizer, "Das johanneische Zeugnis ...", p. 356. He sees v. 63 as the key to the understanding of the whole passage as a unit. It renders vv. 51-58 sapiential.

[110] See on this, R. Schnackenburg, "Die Sakramente im Johannesevangelium", in *Sacra Pagina* II, pp. 235-254; R. E. Brown, "The Johannine Sacramentary", in *New Testament Essays,* pp. 51-76; H. Klos, *Die Sakramente im Johannesevangelium.*

isation in the life of the community of the encounter with the life-giving Son of Man.[111] The proof of both the literary and thematic unity of the discourse is found in vv. 60-65 where, in spite of the failure of his own disciples to accept this σκληρὸς λόγος, he reaffirms that it is the *words* which he has spoken which are spirit and life (see v. 63).[112]

II - The Son of Man in John 6,27.53.62

Apart from the use of "bread from heaven" (vv. 31, 32, 33, 41, 50, 58), "bread of life" (vv. 35, 48) and "living bread" (v. 51), there are few titles applied to Jesus throughout the discourse of John 6. John's major christological title "the Son" appears only once (v. 40) while "the Son of Man" appears three times (vv. 27, 53, 62). Because "the Son of Man" appears in such varied contexts — v. 27 is in the dialogue which prepares for the discourse proper, v. 53 is one of the major statements of the so-called Eucharistic section and v. 62 is found in the concluding reaction of Jesus' disciples — some scholars claim that the title points to a unity of theme throughout the discourse, as it would mean the same throughout.[113] Others, however, hold that its use in such a variety of contexts shows that it has no meaning of its own; its use in v. 53 has come about merely because it was used in Eucharistic celebrations.[114] A. J. B. Higgins has maintained that while the Son of Man in v. 62 is closely linked with other Johannine Son of Man sayings, vv. 27 and 53 come from a very special Johannine source which expressed the main articles of the Johannine

[111] See P.-H. Menoud, "L'originalité de la pensée johannique", pp. 253-261.

[112] G. Boccali, "Un 'mashal' evangelico e la sua applicazione: Gv. 6,63", *BibOr* 10 (1968) 53-58 has attempted to show that v. 63 contains a proverb in which "spirit" is in no way opposed to "flesh". This is somewhat contrived, and not necessary to save the unity of the discourse. See, instead, W. G. Kümmel, *The Theology of the New Testament According to its Major Witnesses: Jesus - Paul - John*, (London, SCM Press, 1974) (English translation of *Die Theologie des Neuen Testaments nach seinen Hauptzeugen*, [Göttingen, Vandenhoeck und Ruprecht, 1972]) p. 312: "It is evident ... that eating the Lord's supper mediates the same salvation as does faith, because the believer receives the divine Spirit even in the Lord's supper"; H. Schürmann, "Die Eucharistie als Repräsentation ...", pp. 108-118; J. Giblet, "L'Eucharistie dans l'évangile de Jean", *Concilium* 40 (1969) 60-62; E. Ruckstuhl, "Wesen und Kraft ...", pp. 78-84; D. Mollat, "Le chapitre VIᵉ de Saint Jean", pp. 107-119; A. Vanneste, "Le pain de vie descendu du ciel", *AssSeign* 54 (1966) 41-53; J. T. Forestell, *The Word of the Cross*, pp. 141-145; W. F. Howard, *Christianity According to St. John*, pp. 204-205; F. J. Moloney, "John 6 and the Celebration of the Eucharist", *The Downside Review* 93 (1975) 243-251.

[113] See R. Schnackenburg, *Johannesevangelium* II, pp. 48-51. 90-92. 104-105. See also Idem, *St. John* I, pp. 530-532.

[114] R. Bultmann, *John*, p. 235; S. Schulz, *Untersuchungen*, pp. 116-117; C. Colpe, *TNDT* VIII, p. 469.

kerygma in terms of the Son of Man.[115]   B. Lindars sees ch. 6 as belonging to the second edition of the Gospel and claims that the Johannine Son of Man christology "is complete, and stands out more clearly, when attention is confined to the sections which belong to the first edition".[116]   He makes little of these sayings, seeing them as "consistent" with the other sayings, but in no way contributing to an understanding of what John means when he uses "the Son of Man".[117]

Turning from our general discussion of the structure and meaning of the chapter to a more detailed study of each of these sayings in their context, we should be able to determine whether or not John has a specific theological point to make in his use of "the Son of Man".[118]

1. *The Son of Man in John 6,27*

Throughout the discourse, Jesus is identified with the manna. P. Borgen, among others, has shown that this is based on a midrashic tradition, common to both diaspora and Palestinian Judaism, in which the bread from heaven was identified with Wisdom and the Torah.[119]   Closely linked with this theme is the suggestion of vv. 14-15 that Jesus was being hailed as the second Moses, "the Prophet", who would come to give the manna which would usher in the end time (see II Baruch 29,8; Mekilta on Exodus 16,25; Eccles. R. I,9).[120] Yet it is clear that John is not prepared to accept this identification, as Jesus refuses to accept the acclamation of vv. 14-15: he "withdrew again to the hills by himself" (v. 15).[121]   When evening came his disciples set out across the lake by themselves.   It is difficult to explain the present position of the miracle story which follows. Perhaps it comes here because it depends upon traditional material, but what is its relation to the acclamation of vv. 14-15? We would suggest that the point of this traditional story in the Fourth Gospel is the ἐγώ εἰμι of v. 20 (see Mk. 6,50). Jesus has refused the

[115] A. J. B. Higgins, *The Son of Man,* p. 175.
[116] B. Lindars, "The Son of Man ...", p. 45.
[117] See *ibid.,* pp. 58-59.
[118] See J. Blank, "Die johanneische Brotrede", p. 197: "Die Brotrede ist in ihrer Christologischen Thematik grundlegend durch die johanneische Menschensohn-Christologie bestimmt"; see also C. H. Dodd, *Interpretation,* p. 248; D. Mollat, "Le chapitre VIᵉ de Saint Jean", pp. 116-117.
[119] P. Borgen, *op. cit.,* pp. 148-164; see also C. H. Dodd, *Interpretation,* pp. 336-337; E. M. Sidebottom, *The Christ of the Fourth Gospel,* pp. 131-132. For Rabbinic references, see H. L. Strack-P. Billerbeck, *Kommentar zum Neuen Testament aus Talmud und Midrasch,* (München, C. H. Beck, 1922-61) Vol. II, pp. 482-485.
[120] See T. F. Glasson, *Moses in the Fourth Gospel,* p. 45. E. C. Hoskyns, *Fourth Gospel,* pp. 293-294; W. A. Meeks, *The Prophet-King,* pp. 87-99.
[121] See R. Schnackenburg, "Die Messiasfrage im Johannesevangelium", pp. 252-253.

acclamation of vv. 14-15, yet he comes to his disciples using the language of an Old Testament theophany.[122]

Not knowing where he has gone, the crowd rush from place to place in search of him (vv. 22-24) and when they eventually find him, they again give him a title — "Rabbi" (v. 25, see 1,49) — but Jesus points to the limitations of their desire to find him. They are still "earth bound", seeking wonderful signs and food to eat; they are limited by their "fleshly" interpretation of who Jesus is (see 3,6). Jesus refuses this by pointing to a "bread" which cannot be understood in these categories: a bread which will be given by the Son of Man, which will endure to eternal life (vv. 26-27). This bread is, then, contrasted with the manna brought by Moses, which was a less "fleshly", but still limited, notion that would come to the mind of the faithful Jew (see vv. 31-33).[123] In this there is a similar pattern in the use of "the Son of Man" to that found in 1,51 and 3,13-14: "the Son of Man" is a title used by Jesus himself to correct an insufficient acclamation of him by onlookers.[124] The fact that this contrast is not understood by the Jews (v. 34) gives John the chance to unfold the rest of the discourse moving, as he so often does, from a misunderstanding to a further explanation of the truth.[125]

After the solemn "amen" phrase of v. 26, Jesus proclaims that the true food which will endure into eternal life, unlike the manna offered by Moses,

---

[122] See R. E. Brown, *John*, pp. 533-538, esp. pp. 533-534; C. H. Dodd, *Interpretation*, pp. 344-345.

[123] J. L. Martyn, *History and Theology*, pp. 112-119 maintains that this is an example of a practice which actually happened in the Johannine Church. In the debate between the Church and Synagogue discussion started with Moses and then moved, by means of further midrashic discussion, to a final and decisive presentation of the Son of Man. See his chapter, "From the Expectation of the Prophet-Messiah like Moses ...to the Presence of the Son of Man" (pp. 91-142). See also R. G. Hamerton-Kelly, *Pre-Existence*, p. 240; E. M. Sidebottom, *The Christ of the Fourth Gospel*, pp. 71-73.

[124] See J. Blank, "Die johanneische Brotrede", pp. 205-206; M.-F. Berrouard, "La multiplication des pains ...", pp. 65-66; J. Giblet, "L'eucharistie dans l'évangile de Jean", pp. 56-57. It is possible that the use of "the Son of Man" in v. 27 is correcting the title "Rabbi" in v. 25. See R. E. Brown, *John*, p. 261; M.-J. Lagrange, *St. Jean*, p. 172.

[125] See G. Macrae, "Theology and Irony in the Fourth Gospel", in R. J. Clifford-G. W. Macrae (eds.), *The Word in the World: Essays in Honour of Frederick L. Moriarty, S.J.*, (Cambridge, Mass., Weston College Press, 1973) pp. 83-96; H. Leroy, *Rätsel und Missverständnis*, pp. 100-107; Idem, "Das johanneische Missverständnis als literarische Form", *BuL* 9 (1968) 196-207; J. H. Bernard, *St. John*, pp. cxi-cxii; R. Bultmann, *John*, p. 135, note 1: "The ambiguity of Johannine concepts and statements which lead to misunderstandings does not consist in one word having two meanings, so that the misunderstanding comes as a result of choosing the wrong one; it is rather that there are concepts and statements which at first sight refer to earthly matters, but properly refer to divine matters. The misunderstanding comes when someone sees the right meaning of the word, but mistakenly imagines that its meaning is exhausted by the reference to earthly matters".

which perished,[126] is that which the Son of Man will give.[127]   W. Bauer has gone to some length to show that Greek pagan mythology had these ideas,[128] but there is ample Old Testament and Rabbinic evidence for a Jewish back-ground to the concept of a bread which provides spiritual nourishment (see esp. Exod. 16,12; Is. 55,2).[129]   The use of ἐργάζομαι does not mean that one can gain this bread by one's own efforts, as this would be to contradict the statement that it is a gift of the Son of Man.   The verb has, rather, the meaning of "striving for".   W. Bauer has suggested that it could mean "digest" or "assimilate",[130] but this suggestion is hard to fit in with the continual use of ἐργάζομαι and ἔργα in vv. 28-30.[131]

Those who see the whole discourse as Eucharistic refer immediately to the Eucharistic bread, showing the close similarity between v. 27 and vv. 51 and 53.[132]   What is meant, however, is found closer at hand.   Asked for an explanation in v. 28, Jesus replies in v. 29: "This is the work of God, that you believe in him whom he has sent".[133]   It is belief in Jesus whom the Father has sent that will lead to eternal life (see 3,15.16.36; 5,24; 10,10.28; 11,25; 12,50; 17,2; 20,31).   This is the message of the whole discourse, and it is repeated like an antiphon throughout both the more sapiential and the Eucharistic sections of it (vv. 33, 35, 40, 47, 48, 51, 53 [negatively], 54).   It is again stated by both Jesus and Peter in the crisis which follows the discourse (vv. 63,68).   R. Schnackenburg properly understands John's mind when he interprets 6,27 by referring to 4,14: "Whoever drinks of the water that I shall give him will never thirst; the water that I shall give him will become in him a spring of water welling up to eternal life".[134]   In both of these sayings, the nourishment which Jesus will give is clearly the revelation of God in his word and person, as only this nourishment can lead to eternal life.   Yet, in 6,27, to speak of Jesus in his role as the revelation of God John

---

[126] Taking the references here to be closely connected with the whole context of Moses and the manna.

[127] Reading the future, with P[75], Vaticanus, Alexandrinus etc. See, on this, R. Schnackenburg, *Johannesevangelium* II, p. 48.

[128] W. Bauer, *Johannesevangelium*, p. 95.

[129] See A. Feuillet, "Les thèmes majeurs ...", pp. 52-61; M. Conti, *Il discorso del pane di vita*, pp. 19-61; G. Reim, *Studien zum alttestamentlichen Hintergrund*, pp. 150-151. 192-193; A. Young, "A Study of the Relation of Isaiah to the Fourth Gospel", pp. 228-230; F.-M. Braun, "Messie, Logos et Fils de l'Homme", p. 142; T. Preiss, "Étude sur le ch. 6 ...", pp. 155-157. B. Lindars, *John*, p. 255, following Guilding, suggests that ch. 55 of Isaiah was a part of Passover *haphtarot* in the Jewish lectionary. While this is very attractive, it remains hypothetical.

[130] W. Bauer, *A Greek-English Lexicon*, p. 307.

[131] See G. Richter, "Die alttestamentliche Zitate...", p. 195, note 11.

[132] See A. Feuillet, *art. cit.*, pp. 61-64; X. Léon-Dufour, "Le mystère du pain ...", p. 564, note 2; A. Wikenhauser, *Johannes*, p. 105.

[133] See H. Strathmann, *Johannes*, p. 118.

[134] R. Schnackenburg, *Johannesevangelium* II, pp. 49-51.

uses the title "the Son of Man". It is the Son of Man who will give this bread of life.[135]

Some scholars have attempted to explain the use of a traditional title in this context by claiming that the "food" of v. 27 refers to eschatological food, thus retaining what they consider the basic idea of the traditional Son of Man figure.[136] F. H. Borsch has also attempted to show that the use of the title is traditional, reflecting Mk. 14,25 = Matt. 26,29 = Lk. 22, 15-18 and Enoch 62, 14, resulting in the figure of a Royal Man who dispenses food to his people.[137] None of these suggestions is very convincing because of the context of vv. 26-33. While the validity of these efforts to find a traditional background for the saying is not questioned, it is our concern to find what the saying, in its present form, means in its present context. It could well be true that the Johannine Son of Man sayings have their roots in the traditional sayings, but we are largely concerned with what John is saying when he uses the title in his own very individual fashion.

The difficulty is entirely avoided by Bultmann, Schulz and Richter, who regard the title as a redactional addition.[138] For Bultmann and Richter it is the addition of an editor, while Schulz sees it as an addition made before the Evangelist, as an interpretation of v. 27a in the light of vv. 51 and 53. He claims that the title was used in Eucharistic celebrations and thus has come to be used here, and especially in v. 53. There is, however, no indication of the Eucharistic use of "the Son of Man" anywhere, not even in Ignatius, who does have the title in a Eucharistic context, but not directly linked to the Sacrament (see Eph. 20,2).

C. K. Barrett and R. H. Strachan understand the title in the light of "heavenly man" speculation,[139] while M.-J. Lagrange, G. H. C. Macgregor, W.

---

[135] See G. Reim, *Studien zum alttestamentlichen Hintergrund*, pp. 133-134. 255. John has not used "the Son of Man" in ch. 4, where it could have been expected if our understanding of the title is correct. This is probably caused by his sources, and by the fact that the whole of the chapter is to be understood in the light of Samaritan messianic expectations (see esp. 4,19. 22. 25. 26. 29. 39. 42).

[136] H. van den Bussche, *Jean*, p. 253; R. E. Brown, *John*, p. 264. B. Lindars, "The Son of Man ...", pp. 58-59 understands the verse in the light of Jewish eschatological hopes. This does not fit his thesis, but he discounts the verse as foreign, claiming that it "belongs to an artificial dialogue" (p. 59). See the posthumous study of T. Preiss, "Étude sur le ch. 6 ...", pp. 143-167 where he looks to traditions concerning the eschatological celebration of Wisdom.

[137] F. H. Borsch, *The Son of Man*, p. 296. S. S. Smalley, "The Johannine Son of Man Sayings", pp. 293-294 argues that behind this saying lies the traditional motif of the rejection of the Son of Man.

[138] R. Bultmann, *John*, p. 225, note 1; G. Richter, "Zur Formgeschichte ...", p. 39, note 1; S. Schulz, *Untersuchungen*, p. 115.

[139] C. K. Barrett, *St. John*, p. 238; R. H. Strachan, *Fourth Gospel*, pp. 185-186.

Temple and B. F. Westcott suggest that Jesus is here presenting the perfect man who, because of his authority among men, is able to dispense the food which will remain for eternal life.[140]

> "It is from Him in whom our human nature is perfectly fulfilled that we receive the satisfaction of our souls; for this function His perfect humanity qualifies Him, as also for Judgement, of which this is one possible form — cf. 5,27".[141]

More attention must be given to the immediate context of the saying where there are several hints that the Son of Man saying is closely linked with other such sayings in the Fourth Gospel. The Son of Man will give the food — yet he *is* the food (v. 35), the bread which is "come down from heaven" (v. 33). In the rest of the Gospel the use of καταβαίνειν is applied to Jesus only in 3,13, another Son of Man saying: it is as the Son of Man that Jesus speaks of himself as the one coming down from heaven.[142] In Jn. 6 the theme of "descending" is very important (see vv. 33, 38, 41, 42, 50, 51, 58), as it is the midrashic repetition of the ἐκ τοῦ οὐρανοῦ from the Old Testament quotation in v. 31.[143] The Son of Man will give the bread ... yet the Son of Man *is* the bread which comes down from heaven.[144] It is as "the Son of Man" that Jesus provides the food that will remain until eternal life; there is no other, as is made clear in the controversy with Jesus' interlocutors who are prepared to accept him as the Prophet like Moses. In v. 32 there is a clear contrast between the two "breads" which are offered. After the solemn "amen" statement, Jesus says that his Father will give the ἄρτος ἀληθινός, and this bread is that which is coming down from heaven, to give life to the world (v. 33). Life can only be had, however, by those who work for the bread which endures (v. 27) and Jesus has made it clear what that "work" is in v. 29: "This is the work of God, that you believe in him whom he has sent".

The Son of Man *will* give the food — the revelation of the truth. The use of the future tense in δώσει points to another central issue in Johannine christology which seems to be continually connected with "the Son of Man": Jesus' unique role as the revealer of God is often linked with the cross.[145] This was particularly clear in 3,13-14 and appears to be repeated again in 8,28a;

---

[140] M.-J. Lagrange, *St. Jean*, p. 173; G. H. C. Macgregor, *John*, p. 138; W. Temple, *Readings*, p. 84; B. F. Westcott, *St. John*, p. 100.

[141] W. Temple, *Readings*, p. 84.

[142] See R. Schnackenburg, *Johannesevangelium* II, p. 48: " 'Der Menschensohn' ist nicht etwa eine einfache, verhüllende Selbstbezeichnung Jesu, sondern ruft im Joh-Ev den ganzen Vorstellunskomplex des vom Himmel herabgestiegenen und dorthin wider aufsteigenden Menschensohnes hervor".

[143] *ibid.*, p. 49.

[144] See R. Bultmann, *John*, pp. 226-228. 343-344.

[145] See above, p. 103.

12,23-34; 13,31. There may also be a hint of the cross as a place of revelation and judgment in 1,51.[146]

> "Whenever John uses the title Son of man he is making a reference, sometimes more, sometimes less direct to the self-offering on the cross, and the glory that it brings. So here. Already Jesus is preparing his Galilean hearers for the profound truth that it will be by his death and resurrection that they will be able to attain eternal life".[147]

The Son of Man is the giver of the revelation which will have its supreme moment at Calvary. Why is this so? There appear to be two reasons given here, and they are mutually dependent. Firstly, the Son of Man has authority to reveal God because he is ὁ καταβαίνων ἐκ τοῦ οὐρανοῦ. Meeks has shown that there was a tradition concerning the ascent and descent of Moses,[148] while Odeberg has gathered copious proof that there was a myth of the ascension of a revealer in Jewish, Hermetic and Mandean circles.[149] There also seems to have been a debate about the possibility of the great saints of Israel having ascended to heaven to receive knowledge of God, so that they could descend again in order to reveal that knowledge (see Onkelos, Pseudo Jon. and Fragment Targums on Deut. 30,11-14; Targum on Ps. 68,19; Deut. 30,12; Prov. 30,4; Bar. 3,29; Wisd. 9,16-18; IV Esdras 4,8).[150] As we have already seen, Jn. 3,13-14 has cut across this discussion by claiming that no one has ever ascended to heaven to receive knowledge of God, but there is one who has descended from being πρὸς τὸν θεόν (1,1) — the Son of Man.[151] Using a combination of Wisdom and perhaps Philonic terms, John has spoken of this great revelation of God as ὁ λόγος in referring to his state πρὸς τὸν θεόν (1,1), while in his historic, fully human existence among men as the place where God is revealed, John speaks of him as "the Son of Man".[152]

This authority is further spelt out by v. 27c: τοῦτον γὰρ ὁ πατὴρ ἐσφράγισεν ὁ θεός. The use of οὗτος makes the statement emphatic: "For *this* is the one whom God the Father has sealed". What is meant by the use of the verb σφραγίζειν is debated. It is clearly an important statement in the context and does, in fact, supply the second reason why the Son of Man is the place where God is revealed.

H. van den Bussche, referring to Old Testament uses of "to seal" (Hagg. 2,23; Is. 29,11; Jer. 22,24) concludes that the verb is juridical and eschatologi-

---

[146] See above, pp. 38-40.
[147] J. Marsh, *St. John*, p. 295. See also E. C. Hoskyns, *Fourth Gospel*, p. 292. On the other hand, C. K. Barrett, *St. John*, p. 238, speaks of a time after the glorification, when his gifts would be fully available to men.
[148] W. A. Meeks, *The Prophet-King*, pp. 110-111. 192-196. 235-236.
[149] H. Odeberg, *Fourth Gospel*, pp. 72-89.
[150] See above, pp. 54-55.
[151] See above, pp. 54-57.
[152] In this we agree with those scholars who see the title as referring to Jesus' humanity. See above, p. 112, note 140.

cal.[153]   B. F. Westcott has suggested that it refers to Jesus' consecration unto death by the Father,[154] and a similar argument is pursued by J. Marsh, who sees the aorist as a "prophetic perfect", referring to the future glory of the cross and resurrection.[155] For B. Lindars and F. H. Borsch it is a reference to Jesus, being chosen or marked out,[156] while for M.-J. Lagrange and G. H. C. Macgregor it is the authority of his miracle-working power that is referred to, including the miracle of the incarnation itself.[157]

The majority of scholars, however, would agree with C. K. Barrett that the "sealing" means that it is "God the Father who attests the authority and truth of Jesus".[158] There are various ways in which one can understand the attestation of God to the authority of the Son of Man. It is better, perhaps, to speak not only of the authority, but also of the authenticity of the Son of Man as revealer. What is being said here is: "You must work for the bread which endures for eternity; that bread will be given to you in the revelation of the Son of Man. It is to the Son of Man, and to him alone, that God has given such authority; what he reveals is the authentic revelation of God". This is what the discourse will later call the ἄρτος ἀληθινός (see v. 32). Scholars generally refer to 3,33 to prove that what we have claimed is true. The parallel is not as close as some would suggest, as in ch. 3 it is "he who comes from above" who sets the seal, whereas in 6,27 it is God who sets the seal upon the Son of Man who comes from above. Nevertheless, what is said in 3,31-36 about Jesus as the revealer is an excellent explanation of 6,27.[159] It would appear that in 6,27 it means: "to attest, certify, acknowledge (as a seal does on a document)".[160] As an author puts his own seal on his missive to show its authenticity and to give it his authority,[161] so has God the Father done with the Son of Man, his unique revelation. "He is the Son of Man, who has come down from heaven (1,51; 3,13), bearing the credentials (seal) of God the Father".[162] The aorist refers back

---

[153] H. van den Bussche, *Jean*, pp. 253-254.
[154] B. F. Westcott, *St. John*, p. 100.
[155] J. Marsh, *St. John*, p. 295.
[156] B. Lindars, *John*, p. 255; F. H. Borsch, *Son of Man*, p. 298.
[157] M.-J. Lagrange, *St. Jean*, p. 173; G. H. C. Macgregor, *John*, pp. 138-139.
[158] C. K. Barrett, *St. John*, p. 238. See also E. C. Hoskyns, *Fourth Gospel*, p. 292; J. H. Bernard, *St. John*, p. 191; W. H. Cadman, *The Open Heaven*, pp. 85-86; J. L. Martyn, *History and Theology*, p. 115; L. Morris, *John*, p. 359; J. Blank, "Die johanneische Brotrede", p. 257. R. H. Strachan, *Fourth Gospel*, pp. 185-186 speaks in terms of a sovereign giving his approval to his ambassador.
[159] W. Bauer, *Johannesevangelium*, p. 95 refuses any link with 3,33 and claims that 6,27 doubtless means: "eine Begabung mit göttlichen Kräften, die den Sohn befähigen den Gläubigen die Himmelsnahrung zu spenden".
[160] W. Bauer, *Greek-English Lexicon*, p. 804.
[161] See H. G. Liddell-R. Scott, *Greek-English Lexicon*, (Oxford, OUP, 1940) p. 1742.
[162] W. F. Howard, "St. John", p. 563.

to the moment in history when the Word became flesh, when the λόγος πρὸς τὸν θεόν became the revelation of God among men (see 1,1.14.18).[163]

The discourse upon the bread from heaven starts by announcing its theme, the perfect fulfilment of the hopes of Israel. They, however, had their own ideas of how the second Moses and the eschatological manna would appear. Jesus cuts across these expectations and announces in 6,27 that their hopes are in vain, pinned upon the false hope of a Mosaic Prophet whose manna would perish. Jesus offers a revelation which will endure — which will produce eternal life — and he offers it to men in his role as the Son of Man.[164]

2. The Son of Man in John 6,53

While we insist that the whole discourse is concerned primarily with the revelation of God by and in the Son of Man, v. 53 seems to point to the Eucharist. In concluding the previous section of the discourse (vv. 35-51) Jesus has announced that the supreme moment in the revelation that the Son of Man had come to bring was to be in his death: "The bread which I shall give is my own flesh for the life of the world (v. 51c). The use of σάρξ here is to be interpreted in the light of 1,14.[165] It is as the incarnate logos that Jesus is able to give his "flesh" for the life of the world. This is the only way in which the claims of v. 51c can make sense: because of Jesus' origin πρὸς τὸν θεόν his death at Calvary is a revelation of God's glory and salvation for those who believe. Thus "flesh" in v. 51c purposely recalls that "the Word became flesh". How else could mere "flesh" give life to the world? If the discourse at this stage was concerned *only* with the Eucharist, v. 63 would make little sense,[166] and H. Schürmann is correct when he points out that it is not a case of "either-or".[167] While v. 51c is not in itself Eucharistic, in its present context it is an introduction to the sub-theme of the Eucharist which is more clearly announced in v. 53. Considerations of the death of Jesus could never have been far removed from a reflection upon the ἀνάμνησις of that event in the Eucharistic celebrations of the early Church (see I Cor. 11, 23-26). The Eucharistic overtones of what follows are but a logical consequence of the reference to Jesus' death in v. 51c.[168]

---

[163] Against those who find, from other NT references, that "to seal" must be baptismal. See, for example, J. H. Bernard, *St. John*, p. 191.

[164] See J. Blank, "Die johanneische Brotrede", pp. 197-201; 257-258. Blank has shown that the theme of revelation dominates John's use of "the Son of Man" in ch. 6.

[165] See E. Schweizer, *TDNT* VII, p. 140, note 309; H. Odeberg, *Fourth Gospel*, p. 260; G. H. C. Macgregor, "The Eucharist in the Fourth Gospel", pp. 116-117.

[166] See H. Schürmann, "Joh 6,51c — ein Schlüssel ...", pp. 251-260.

[167] *ibid.*, pp. 249-250.

[168] See H. van den Bussche, *Jean*, p. 270.

The misunderstanding of the crowd leads the discourse to another solemn "amen" statement. We are again, as in v. 27, dealing with something of particular significance in v. 53. There are three points made by Jesus in this verse:

a) The necessity to eat the flesh and drink the blood

b) of the Son of Man

c) in order to have life.

The negative conditional sentence — "Unless you eat the flesh ... and drink his blood ... you have no life" — is the clearest reference to the Eucharist in the whole discourse. Yet, is it primarily an invitation to participate in the Eucharistic celebration? Several scholars have pointed out that this negative conditional formula hints at a polemic against docetic elements in the community, who rejected the value of the humanity of Jesus.[169] Jesus announces that to eat his flesh and drink his blood is none other than to accept his true humanity. "Flesh" and "blood" represent vividly and realistically that Jesus, the mediator of eternal life, has expressed his function in the role of a human being.[170] However, following a line of thought which is now becoming regular in the Gospel, Jesus speaks of this true human being as sacrificed. The reference to the eating of the flesh is the continuation of what Jesus has been saying since v. 27, but the addition of a demand that one drink the blood of the Son of Man necessarily implies that this blood be spilt.[171] In all of this, the new element introduced into the discourse is the explicit reference to the death of Jesus — a death which would give eternal life to those who believed in him. Yet, even this is not entirely new, as it has already been alluded to in the δώσει of v. 27.

In the context of the whole discourse, this appears to be the main point which is made by the negative command to eat the flesh and drink the blood of the Son of Man. However, there is certainly a Eucharistic sense in which these words must have been understood in the early Church, and in which they are to be understood today. The immediate reference to the participation, in faith, which one must have with the crucified Christ in order to come to eternal life is certainly the main point, but this never remained at a purely noetic level in the early Church. They had their Eucharistic celebrations where

---

[169] See R. Schnackenburg, *Johannesevangelium* II, p. 91; O. S. Brooks, "The Johannine Eucharist ...", pp. 293-300; W. H. Cadman, *The Open Heaven*, pp. 87-88; R. H. Strachan, *Fourth Gospel*, p. 191; W. Temple, *Readings*, p. 94; W. Wilkens, "Das Abendmahlzeugnis ...", pp. 356-358.

[170] O. S. Brooks, "The Johannine Eucharist ...", pp. 297-298. See also T. Preiss, "Étude sur le ch. 6 ...", pp. 163-165.

[171] See esp. A. Schlatter, *Johannes*, p. 178; R. H. Lightfoot, *St. John*, p. 162; B. F. Westcott, *St. John*, p. 107; B. Lindars, *John*, p. 268; L. Morris, *John*,, p. 379; C. H. Dodd, *Interpretation*, p. 339; S. S. Smalley, "The Johannine Son of Man Sayings", p. 293; H. Strathmann, *Johannes*, p. 125; E. Ruckstuhl, "Wesen und Kraft ...", pp. 54-58.

this union with the crucified Christ was proclaimed and celebrated: "For as often as you eat this bread and drink this cup you proclaim the Lord's death until he comes" (I Cor. 11,26; see Lk. 22,19-20).[172] The reference to "eating" and "drinking" would not be missed. It is quite possible that behind this verse stands the Johannine version of the institution of the Eucharist as Brown, among others, has recently argued.[173] Both levels of understanding must be maintained — a primary reference to a reception, in faith, of the revelation of the crucified Jesus, and a secondary, but important, reference to the continuing possibility of that encounter with the sacrificed redeemer in the Eucharist.[174]

If our interpretation is correct, then we find here another typically Johannine technique. In the question of v. 52, the Jews ask how (πῶς) this man can give his flesh to eat. The reply which Jesus gives, starting with the solemn "amen" saying, is not a direct answer to the question; in fact, it shows how far they are from a true understanding of him.[175] He has not been sent by the Father in order to give his "flesh" in the way in which the Jews have tried to understand it, but to give a food that will produce life (see v. 57). He is able to do this because he is from the Father, because he has "come down from heaven" (v. 58) to reveal to men the truth which is food that will not perish, as the food of their fathers and the hopes of the old dispensation, pinned on a second Moses, have failed. He is the living bread (v. 35), and whoever eats him — believes in him — will have eternal life (v. 58). The continual recalling of these basic "facts" for Johannine christology make it clear that the πῶς of the Jews in v. 52 is already a sign of a failure to comprehend, just as the repeated πῶς of Nicodemus in ch. 3 is never answered, but is shown to be a misunderstanding of the origin and mission of the Johannine Jesus (see Jn. 3,4.9).[176] The same technique is used with the Samaritan woman (4,9), the Jews at the Feast of Tabernacles (7,15; 8,33), the Pharisees who wonder about the cure of the man born blind (9,16b), the Jews who fail to understand the significance to the Son of Man who must be "lifted up" (12,34) and with the doubting Thomas who fails to see that Jesus is the way (14,5).[177]

---

[172] See on this, J. Jeremias, *The Eucharistic Words of Jesus*, (London, SCM Press, 1966) (English translation of *Die Abendmahlsworte Jesu*, [Göttingen, Vandenhoeck und Ruprecht, 1960]) pp. 89-125. On the Lucan text, see pp. 139-160.

[173] R. E. Brown, *John*, pp. 287-291.

[174] J. Marsh, *St. John*, p. 305 has argued that the addition of the reference to the blood is the touch which makes the verse clearly Eucharistic. This is true if it does not detract from the importance of the "blood" for the idea of sacrifice which is also involved here. See also C. K. Barrett, *St. John*, p. 246.

[175] See H. Leroy, *Rätsel und Missverständnis*, pp. 109-124.

[176] See above, pp. 47-48.

[177] See I. de la Potterie, "Jesus et Nicodemus ...", p. 201; J.-B. Bauer, "πῶς in der griechischen Bibel", *NT* 2 (1958) 81-91.

Leaving, for the moment, the reference to the Son of Man, we find further confirmation for the sapiential understanding of v. 53 in the punishment for those who do not eat the flesh and drink the blood of the Son of Man — "You have no life in you". This is but the negative restatement of one of the key ideas of the whole discourse (see vv. 27, 33, 35, 47, 48, 51, 54, 63, 68). The discourse is not broken by v. 53, but it is continued and the same points are being made here as have been made throughout the rest of the words which Jesus has addressed ,to the Jews.[178] Now that the development of the author's thought has arrived at the point where he announces that the revelation of the Son of Man will take place in the cross, his use of Eucharistic language comes to the fore, but the demand that is always being made by Jesus is that they believe in him. Whether this is stated in principle (vv. 35-58) or with an important reference to the practical application of that belief in the Eucharist, (vv. 51-58), the effect of the belief is the same — to have life (v. 58).

In this context, and in the light of the use of "the Son of Man" throughout the rest of the Gospel, the title in v. 53 becomes more readily understandable.

The appearance of the title here has caused difficulty for the commentators. Various suggestions have been made to explain its presence. Bultmann, Schulz, Higgins, Colpe, Sanders and Reim, convinced that v. 53 is wholly Eucharistic, make various suggestions to show that it is an editorial addition. For Bultmann, Schulz and Colpe it has come into this context because of its presence in the Eucharistic celebrations of the community.[179] This is an assumption which cannot find support anywhere in the New Testament or, for that matter, from the Eucharistic references of the earliest Church.[180] Sanders suggests that it comes from another source,[181] while Higgins goes further by identifying the source: it is a Johannine special source in which the main articles of the kerygma — in this case the Eucharist — were expressed in terms of the Son of Man.[182] Reim suggests that the original discourse was to do with the Son of Man giving the manna for eternal life. When the Eucharistic thought was added to this, the title was retained.[183]

S. S. Smalley stands at the other end of the scale, claiming that this saying reflects a traditional theme about the rejection of the Son of Man,[184] and F. H. Borsch, pursuing his theme of a "Royal Man" figure also claims that the saying

[178] See R. Schnackenburg, *Johannesevangelium* II, pp. 90-91.

[179] R. Bultmann, *John*, p. 235; S. Schulz, *Untersuchungen*, pp. 116-117; C. Colpe, *TDNT* VIII, pp. 465-466.

[180] See above, p. 111. See also R. Schnackenburg, *Johannesevangelium* II, pp. 91-92 and esp. p. 91, note 2.

[181] J. N. Sanders, *St. John*, pp. 195-196.

[182] A. J. B. Higgins, *Son of Man*, p. 175.

[183] G. Reim, *Studien zum alttestamentlichen Hintergrund*, p. 256.

[184] S. S. Smalley, "The Johannine Son of Man Sayings", p. 293.

is traditional.[185]   He finds difficulty in the fact that there is no tradition of the Man who gives himself to be eaten, but Borsch suggests that behind this saying is a tradition of the Royal Man who gives to eat, and this has been coloured by Eucharistic practice.   Even if the claims of Smalley and Borsch could be conclusively substantiated, there is such a long distance between their suggested background for v. 53 and what is actually found there that this hypothetical traditional background is of little assistance in our attempt to understand the specifically Johannine use of the title "the Son of Man".

C. K. Barrett, O. Cullmann and R. Schnackenburg all suggest that the Son of Man points to the heavenly man who has descended to give life to the world.[186]   M.-J. Lagrange, A. Schlatter, R. H. Strachan, W. Temple and B. F. Westcott have argued that the title here, as elsewhere, refers to the perfect humanity of Jesus.[187]   "Weil er der Menschensohn ist, hat er Fleisch, und deshalb ist Sterben die Weise, wie er zum Geber des Lebens wird".[188]

A combination of these last two suggestions seems best to catch the point that John is making when he uses "the Son of Man" here.   In complete accord with the rest of the discourse, Jesus claims that in the total assimilation of him — eating his flesh and drinking his blood — the believer will have eternal life.   It is as a man among men that· Jesus is able to offer himself as the revelation of God which must be accepted.   However, this revelation has its validity (see v. 55) from the fact that he has been sent by the Father (v. 57), that he has come down from heaven (v. 58).   What is being claimed by Jesus here is a repetition of what has already been said in v. 27.[189]   Now the "food" is specified: it is the body and blood of the Son of Man.   The hint given by the future tense of δώσει is also made clearer as the spilling of the blood is a reference to the cross.   Once again, the Son of Man is the title chosen by John to speak of Jesus as the place where God is revealed.   The Son of Man is revelation itself, which must be consumed.

There is an important reference to the Eucharist here,[190] but the choice of the title "the Son of Man" warns us against a fully Eucharistic interpretation. The attempts of Bultmann and Schulz to show that "the Son of Man" comes from a Eucharistic background are not convincing, and there is no further indication that the Fourth Gospel — or the Synoptic tradition — ever used the title in a Eucharistic context.   There are, however, many references to

---

[185] F.H. Borsch, *Son of Man*, p. 299.
[186] C.K. Barrett, *St. John*, p. 246; O. Cullmann, *Christology*, p. 186; R. Schnackenburg, *Johannesevangelium* II, pp. 91-92.
[187] M.-J. Lagrange, *St. Jean*, p. 184; A. Schlatter, *Johannes*, pp. 178-179; R. H. Strachan, *Fourth Gospel*, p. 190; W. Temple, *Readings*, pp. 94-95; B. F. Westcott, *St. John*, p. 107.
[188] A. Schlatter, *Johannes*, p. 178.
[189] See J. H. Bernard, *St. John*, p. 209.
[190] See above, pp. 116-117.

the Son of Man who must suffer and die (see Mk. 8,31 = Lk. 9,22; Mk. 9,12 = Matt. 17,12b; Mk. 9,31 = Matt. 17,22 = Lk. 9,44; Mk. 10,33 = Matt. 20,18 = Lk. 18,31; Mk. 10,45 = Matt. 20,28; Matt. 26,2; Lk. 17,25; Lk. 24,6-7) and to the Son of Man who, in suffering and dying, would be lifted up to draw all men to himself and, in giving glory to the Father, be himself glorified (see Jn. 3,13-15; 8,28; 12,20-26; 12,27-34; 13,31). By combining these two traditions,[191] it would appear that John has continued to develop his own christology of the Son of Man, as the place where God shows his glory. Only the Son of Man will give the food which remains forever (v. 27) and this is to be had in the full acceptance, in faith, of the revelation of God by and in the Son of Man, which will reach its climax on Calvary (v. 53). "It is Christ, who lived and died and rose again, who is to be received as the revelation of the Father".[192]

3. The Son of Man in John 6,62

The reaction to the discourse is one of complaint and dissatisfaction. Because of the difficult demands made by what they have just heard, even the disciples of Jesus take offence (v. 60). We have reached, with vv. 60-71, a major crisis in John's story of the life of Jesus. This indicates the importance of the discourse which has preceded the reaction of Jesus' listeners. It is going to divide them into two groups: those who refuse to believe (vv. 64 and 67) and those who, believing, confess that Jesus is the one chosen and consecrated by God — "You are the holy one of God" (v. 69).[193] As this is the case, it is most probable that the discourse would be a statement about the person and message of Jesus — a teaching which is now accepted or rejected.[194] We have attempted to show that this is the case, and that vv. 51-58 are not to be regarded as uniquely Eucharistic or secondary, but as a continuation of basic Johannine christological themes found in vv. 35-50.

The reply of Jesus to the dissatisfaction of his listeners is found in vv. 62-63. Interpreters have difficulty with v. 62 because it is an aposiopesis, that is, a conditional clause which has the protasis, but lacks the apodosis. Most

---

[191] We are not suggesting that John consciously "reworked" these Synoptic Son of Man sayings. He was, however, almost certainly aware of a tradition of a suffering Son of Man.

[192] B. Lindars, *John*, p. 268.

[193] See S. Cipriani, "La confessione di Pietro in Giov. 6,69-71 e i suoi rapporti con quella dei sinottici (Mc. 8,27-33 e paralleli)", in *San Pietro*. Atti della XIX settimana biblica, (Brescia, Paideia, 1967) pp. 93-111; M. Baron, "La progression des confessions de foi dans les dialogues de S. Jean", pp. 35-37.

[194] Bultmann has seen the importance of this scene. However, it is so important that it cannot originally have belonged to the end of ch. 6 as it comes too early in the story. See *John*, pp. 285-287.

commentators accept that the ἀναβαίνοντα refers to the ascension of Jesus,[195] and consequently suggest two possible apodoses:

a) If they were to see the Son of Man ascending to where he was before, their difficulties would be even greater. Can they not accept his word?[196]

b) If they were to see the Son of Man ascending to where he was before, then the offence of these words would be diminished or removed, as they would know that he had authority to make such statements.[197]

A third possibility, originally suggested by B. F. Westcott, contrives to combine both a positive and a negative reaction to the protasis. "The offence must be faced as the costly decision of faith made before man can eat and drink the flesh and blood of Christ and, being united with him in death, receive the gift of eternal life".[198] Thus the ascension of Jesus will prove to be the testing ground for true and false faith in Jesus.[199]

None of this discussion gives complete satisfaction. Why should John introduce the ascension at this crucial point for his readers? The ascension of Jesus, in the Lucan fashion demanded by these interpretations, plays no further role in the Fourth Gospel. Even the difficult 20,17 need not be interpreted in this sense.[200] Yet these scholars put all the weight of their argument on the event of the ascension. Some of them, seeing the difficulty, claim that ἀναβαίνειν is closely linked with ὑψωθῆναι which is also often applied to the Son of Man (3,14; 8,28). They claim that the ascension spoken of here is the cross, as it is the cross which will be the supreme testing ground for faith.[201] While this is certainly closer to Johannine thought, it is hard to under-

---

[195] R. Bultmann, *John*, p. 445; R. E. Brown, *John*, p. 296; S. S. Smalley, "The Johannine Son of Man Sayings", pp. 294-295. For Smalley this saying reflects traditional ascension motifs which must be understood as the vindication of the rejected Son of Man.

[196] R. Bultmann, *John*, p. 445; J. H. Bernard, *St. John*, pp. 216-217; A. Loisy, *Quatrième Évangile*, p. 246; S. Schulz, *Untersuchungen*, pp. 117-118; E. Schweizer, "Das johanneische Zeugnis ...", p. 357.

[197] W. Bauer, *Johannesevangelium*, p. 101; E. C. Hoskyns, *Fourth Gospel*, p. 300; R. H. Lightfoot, *St. John*, p. 169; M.-J. Lagrange, *St. Jean*, p. 187; H. Strathmann, *Johannes*, p. 127; A. Schlatter, *Johannes*, p. 179.

[198] C. K. Barrett, *St. John*, p. 250.

[199] Thus, with varying nuances, C. K. Barrett, *St. John*, p. 250; J. C. Fenton, *John*, p. 81; R. G. Hamerton-Kelly, *Pre-Existence*, p. 231; B. F. Westcott, *St. John*, p. 109; H. van den Bussche, *Jean*, pp. 276-277; T. Zahn, *Johannes*, p. 358. W. Thüsing, *Erhöhung*, pp. 261-262 links the condition with the discourse — when you "look upon" the ascension of the Son of Man, then you will understand my discourse upon the bread of life.

[200] See, for this discussion, R. E. Brown, *John*, pp. 1011-1017; W. Thüsing, *Erhöhung*, pp. 263-276.

[201] See W. H. Cadman, *The Open Heaven*, p. 90; W. F. Howard, "St. John", p. 575; B. Lindars, *John*, p. 273. It is also suggested as a possibility by C. K. Barrett, *St. John*, p. 250; R. Bultmann, *John*, p. 445; R. Schnackenburg, *Johannesevangelium* II, p. 104.

stand why John, if he wanted to speak of the cross, did not use ὑψωθῆναι. Another difficulty which this explanation must solve is the meaning of ὅπου ἦν τὸ πρότερον. This is generally explained by seeing both the ascension and the 'lifting up' as taking place at Calvary, with the last part of the verse referring to the ascension motif. This is rather clumsy, as the τὸ πρότερον is clearly a reference to some sort of pre-existence.

It is from the hint of pre-existence that we should start our attempt to understand this difficult saying. We have argued that throughout the discourse "the Son of Man" has been used of Jesus to speak of him as the one who has come down from heaven to bring and to give the true bread: the revelation of God among men. If this was the case in vv. 27 and 53, it should be borne in mind in our interpretation of v. 62. The purpose of the saying in v. 62 is not to drive away his disciples who find it difficult to accept what their master has said. On the contrary, it should be understood as an effort on Jesus' part to press the validity of his claims. This is precisely what he is doing. The ὅπου ἦν τὸ πρότερον recalls the fact that the Son of Man has come down from heaven (see 3,13) and this is what gives his claims authority. It is because of his origin πρὸς τὸν θεόν (1,1) that what Jesus had said in the discourse is valid.[202]

In the Son of Man saying of 3,13-14 we learnt that there is only one who has descended from heaven, Jesus, the Son of Man. The use of the title in vv. 27 and 53 has further strengthened Jesus' claim to be the unique revealer; yet he is doubted. What must he do to be able to make full claim on his listeners — ascend to where he was before? "Then what if you were to see the Son of Man ascending to where he was before?" (v. 62) — would you still take offence? John is again entering into controversy with the popular idea that the great patriarchs, prophets and especially Moses, had ascended on high to receive the revelation of God, so that they could bring it down to men.[203] John refuses to accept this, as he shows throughout his Gospel that the unique revealer is not one who has "ascended" so that he might "descend" again, bringing the revelation of God with him. The unique revealer is the one who has "come down" from where he was τὸ πρότερον. In the beginning he was πρὸς τὸν θεόν (1,1). He became flesh (1,14) and thus became the promise of the revelation of God to men (1,18.51). The "descent" of Jesus is his incarnation. In his pre-existent state he is called the Logos, but as man he is sometimes referred to as "the Son" and sometimes as "the Son of Man". When John speaks of Jesus' relationship with his Father, he uses "the Son", but when he wishes to point out to his readers that in this "man" God is revealed, he uses "the Son of Man". In 6,60-65 the claims of the Son of Man in vv. 27 and 53 are being doubted and questioned, so Jesus

---

[202] See G. Reim, *Studien zum alttestamentlichen Hintergrund*, p. 255.
[203] See above, pp. 54-55.

asks his audience what sort of proof they require. Do they want "to see" the Son of Man ascend into heaven for a short while, like Moses, Isaiah, Enoch etc., so that he might return and tell them what he saw? There is no need for Jesus to "ascend" — he has been there τὸ πρότερον. To ask that he ascend is completely to misunderstand his origin. It is because of his origin "with God" that his revelation is true; he has no need to ascend.

If we understand v. 62 in this sense, then v. 63 loses its enigmatic character. John has asked a rhetorical question and a typically Johannine answer is found in v. 63. It is not an answer, but an accusation: "You are still seeking after the things of the flesh". The word "flesh" here is to be understood in the light of its usual theological sense throughout the Gospel: the negative element which holds the Jews back from a true understanding of Jesus (see esp. 3,6; 8,15). It is certainly not a contradiction of vv. 51-58. The Jews still want to measure Jesus by their wordly standards, but Jesus refuses this. Recalling his discussion with Nicodemus, Jesus chastises them for their obtuseness in his regard. They are still behaving as men "born of the flesh", judging in a fleshly way and making fleshly demands (see 3,6). This is of no avail, as it is the Spirit which gives life. They must be as men born of the spirit (see 3,6), and then they will come to understand that in the revelation of the unique Son of Man who has come down from heaven they can find life. "The words that I have spoken to you are spirit and life" (v. 63b). There will be no ascension to where he was before — that would be to succumb to their petty demands, similar to the ones they have already made in vv. 30-31. There is only one life-giving principle: the words of Jesus, i.e. the revelation of God which is to be found in the Son of Man.

Understood in this way, the many difficulties presented by vv. 62-63 appear to lessen: "The Son of Man" is again the place where God reveals himself; a Johannine rhetorical question which is not really answered is used; the discourse and vv. 60-65 seem to follow upon one another coherently, and the "ascent" of v. 62 is not seen as referring to some almost Lucan ascension event which cannot be found elsewhere in the Fourth Gospel.

Jesus, as the Son of Man, is the man from heaven. He is the only one who has pre-existed in heaven by the Father.[204] Now, as the Son of Man, he is fully human; he is the place among men where man can come "to hear", "to see", "to touch" and "to look upon" the manifestation of the Father to us (see I Jn. 1,1-2). Commenting on 6,62, C. H. Dodd has rightly said: "As Son of Man ... He is ἐκ τῶν ἄνω. Yet in Him the eternal Logos ...was made σάρξ, and in and through the σάρξ He established communication with men".[205]

---

[204] See H.-M. Dion, "Quelques traits originaux ...", pp. 60-64; H. Dieckmann, " 'Der Sohn des Menschen' im Johannesevangelium", p. 237.
[205] C. H. Dodd, *Interpretation*, p. 341.

CHAPTER SIX

THE CROSS: THE REVELATION OF THE SON OF MAN AS 'EGO EIMI '
John 8,28

I - General Structure and Meaning of John 8,12-30

The conflict between Jesus and his opponents develops as John 8 unfolds. Within the context of the Feast of Tabernacles,[1] and continuing the discourse which has run from 7,14, where "Jesus went up into the temple and taught" (see 18,20; 6,59; 7,28; 8,20), John brings the opposition between Jesus and the Jews to an open conflict.[2]

Although the majority of scholars see this logical development, R. Bultmann, H. Becker and G. H. C. Macgregor find that the present state of the text is the result of a series of dislocations. Bultmann detaches v. 12 from the discourse and places it before 12,44-50. This is followed by 8, 21-29 and 12,34-36. Bultmann entitles this regrouped material "The Light of the World". However, even in this reconstruction, vv. 26-27 are to be regarded as a misplaced fragment, inserted here incorrectly by the redactor, who has been misled by the occurrence of ταῦτα λαλῶ in vv. 26 and 28.[3] The section vv. 13-20 is also foreign to its present context. It belongs to another division of the original Gospel which Bultmann calls "The Judge" (5,19-47; 7,15-24; 8,13-20). Thus, ch. 8 as it stands in the traditional Gospel is the result of confusing editorial work and cannot be properly understood in its present order.[4] H. Becker follows Bultmann in his rearrangement of the text, attempting to reconstruct a Gnostic source for the whole discourse.[5] G. H. C. Macgregor

---

[1] It is generally held that the πάλιν of 8,12 is a continuation of what has preceded in ch. 7. It is universally admitted that 7,53-8,11 did not belong to the original text.

[2] See H. Strathmann, *Johannes*, pp. 143-144; C. H. Dodd, *Interpretation*, p. 347.

[3] R. Bultmann, *John*, pp. 350-351. For criticism of this suggestion see G. Bornkamm, "Der Paraklet im Johannesevangelium", in *Festschrift Rudolf Bultmann zum 65. Geburtstag überreicht*, (Stuttgart, W. Kohlhammer, 1949) pp. 34-35; D.M. Smith, *Composition and Order*, p. 159.

[4] R. Bultmann, *John*, pp. 342-347. See on this, D. M. Smith, *op. cit.*, pp. 155-163 and the reconstructed text on pp. 189-195.

[5] H. Becker, *Die Reden des Johannesevangeliums*, pp. 114-116 and the reconstructed *Quelle* on pp. 132-133.

is less radical in his approach, but attempts to integrate ch. 8 more closely with ch. 7, resulting in the sequence: 7,15-24; 8,12-20; 7,1-14; 7,25-52; 8,21-59.[6]

Apart from the very important consideration that these rearrangements are not based on objective criteria, there seem to be theological reasons, rising from the material itself, which argue for the retention of the traditional order. V. 12 is not "out of place" merely because "light" is not mentioned again until 9,5. The whole of the first section of ch. 8 is concerned with Jesus' revelation of the Father, and there is every possibility that "light" is used here in this sense. The chapter is held together by the three-fold repetition of ἐγώ εἰμι (vv. 12, 24, 28. See also v. 18). The shift in the opponents of Jesus from the ὄχλος (7,12.20.31-32.40.43.49) to the Pharisees (8,13) and "the Jews" (8,22) does not necessarily indicate that we are dealing with a different discourse in each case.[7] As the opposition becomes sharper and Jesus' reply becomes more and more explicit, so the personality of the opposition becomes clearer. No longer is it the amorphous "crowd", but the Pharisees and the Jews — terms which are almost synonymous in the Fourth Gospel.[8] It appears quite unnecessary to rearrange ch. 8 in order to make sense out of it.[9]

The literary structure of the chapter also points to its unity. It is possible that the whole of the narrative and discourse which is tied to the Feast of the Tabernacles is included between the ἐν κρυπτῷ of 7,10 and the ἐκρύβη of 8,59. There are close links between chapters 7 and 8: Jesus, origin and destiny (7,27-28; 8,14); judgment by external, human standards (7,24; 8,15); knowledge of Jesus and the one who sent him (7,28; 8,19); inability to take Jesus because his hour had not yet come (7,30; 8,20); Jesus' going away (7,33b; 8,21a); their search for him (7,34a; 8,21c); misunderstanding of this fact (7,35; 8,22); the repetition by the Jews of Jesus' statement (7,36; 8,22).[10] This seems to indicate a careful composition in which important themes are stated and restated. It is hardly the haphazard result of the careless work of a redactor. W. Kern has arranged an elaborate analysis of the poetic structure of 8,12-58, in which he finds five divisions, each with a definite strophic pattern.[11] The divisions are: A — 12-19; B — 21-30; centre of the chiasm — 31b-41a; B[1] — 41b-47; A[1] — 49-58. While these suggestions are interesting, and should warn us against rearranging the material, Kern's structure seems

---

[6] G. H. C. Macgregor, *John,* pp. 192-224.

[7] See H. Strathmann, *Johannes,* p. 143.

[8] See R. E. Brown, *John,* pp. lxx-lxxiii; E. Grässer, "Die antijüdische Polemik im Johannesevangelium", *NTS* 11 (1964-65) 74-90; J. Jocz, "Die Juden im Johannesevangelium", *Judaica,* 9 (1953) 129-142; E. K. Lee, *The Religious Thought of St. John,* pp. 121-123.

[9] For further criticism of these rearrangement theories, see J. Blank, *Krisis,* pp. 183-184; R. Schnackenburg, *Johannesevangelium* II, pp. 238-239.

[10] See R. E. Brown, *John,* pp. 343. 349.

[11] W. Kern, "Die symmetrische Gesamtaufbau von Joh 8,12-58", *ZKT* 78 (1956) 451-454.

forced. He sees A and B as mainly concerned with the truth of Jesus' judgment, while A¹ and B¹ balance this by a presentation of the untruthfulness of Jesus' opponents. While these ideas are certainly present, they appear to be subordinated to other more important themes. They should not be exaggerated merely to suit a division of the material.

Perhaps it is better to follow the indications of the text itself. There seems to be a clear break at v. 20, where the Evangelist concludes his first section by telling his readers where the discussion of vv. 12-20 took place.[12] The second section of the discourse starts with v. 21, where we again find πάλιν.   However, it is not clear whether it should finish after or before the editorial comment in v. 30.[13]

Several factors point to the choice of v. 30 as the end of the division. The ταῦτα of v. 30 should be closely connected to the discussion which immediately preceded it. We are also told that after these words, "many believed in him" (v. 30). This is a positive evaluation of their faith. In v. 31 Jesus speaks again, but "to the Jews who had believed in him".[14] The "many" of v. 30 appear to fade out of the picture, as "the Jews" of v. 31 will not demonstrate true faith in Jesus as the encounter proceeds. In v. 31 Jesus speaks to some who have believed, but have not come to the full commitment that is demanded from them. This can be seen from the harsh words which follow (see vv. 37, 39-47, 50, 55) and their final reaction to him in v. 59: "So they took up stones to throw at him".[15]   There is still hope for Jesus' interlocutors in 8,12-30 and some of them, in fact, do come to correct faith. From 8,31 onwards this glimmer of hope is gone. Jesus and the Jews are at

---

[12] M.-J. Lagrange, *St. Jean*, p. 231 points to the inclusion between the two uses of ἐλάλησεν (vv. 12 and 20) as a further indication that the Evangelist himself divided his material in this fashion.

[13] The following, among others, divide the material at v. 29: J. Blank, *Krisis*, pp. 183. 231; J. Jeremias, *Johannes*, pp. 180-183; A. Loisy, *Quatrième Évangile* (1903), pp. 550-559; R. Schnackenburg, *Johannesevangelium* II, p. 238; H. Strathmann, *Johannes*, p. 144; J. Wellhausen, *Johannis*, pp. 39-45; A. Wikenhauser, *Johannes*, pp. 138-141; W. F. Howard, "St. John", pp. 594-598; S. Schulz, *Johannes*, p. 131. The following prefer to close the section after v. 30: J. H. Bernard, *St. John*, pp. 291-304; F.-M. Braun, "St. Jean", pp. 380-389; C. H. Dodd, *Interpretation*, p. 346; E. C. Hoskyns, *Fourth Gospel*, pp. 328-330; M.-J. Lagrange, *St. Jean*, pp. 231-240; B. Lindars, *John*, pp. 312-323; J. Marsh, *St. John*, p. 357; L. Morris, *John*, pp. 435-476; R. H. Strachan, *Fourth Gospel*, p. 205; W. Temple, *Readings*, pp. 133-140; B. Vawter, "St. John", pp. 441-443; B. F. Westcott, *St. John*, pp, 127-133; *The Greek New Testament*.

[14] In v. 30 the verb πιστεύειν is used with εἰς, while in v. 31 it is followed by a dative. This could be an indication of the two different types of faith. The second type (v. 31) is insufficient. See W. F. Howard, *Christianity According to St. John*, pp. 87-88. 155-158; J. H. Moulton, *Grammar of New Testament Greek* I (Edinburgh, T. and T. Clark, 1908) p. 67; R. E. Brown, *John*, pp. 513-515 and the bibliography mentioned there. Against this distinction is R. Bultmann, Art. "πιστεύω", *TDNT* VI, pp. 222-223.

[15] See J. H. Bernard, *St. John*, p. 304; B. F. Westcott, *St. John*, p. 133.

complete cross-purposes, and the section concludes with a violent rejection of all that Jesus has claimed (v. 59).

Our division makes 8,12-30 clearly distinct from vv. 31-59.[16] This is important for our interpretation of vv. 12-30, which we see as a last effort on the part of Jesus to give witness to the truth before an unbelieving audience, in the hope that the discussion will bear fruit. John's use of πιστεύειν εἰς in v. 30 could be an indication that he is, at least in part, successful.[17] This suggestion is further supported by the use of the conditional in the crucial statement of v. 24.[18] All is not lost: they will not die in their sins if they believe that Jesus is ἐγώ εἰμι. There are similar conditionals in vv. 31 and 51, where the possibility of life is again offered, but on both occasions this possibility is immediately refused by the angry retort of the Jews in vv. 33 and 52. The "if" of v. 31 is the test which is applied to their limited faith. The reply of v. 33 is the first sign of their failure. In v. 25 the question asked is to be understood as one of puzzlement: "Who are you who claim to be the ἐγώ εἰμι?" There is none of this in vv. 31-59, where the decision against Jesus has already been made, culminating in his public rejection in v. 59.

The discussion in vv. 12-30 is best understood if it is seen as an explanation of the claims of v. 12.[19] "By calling himself the 'light of the world' Jesus describes himself as the Revealer".[20] What is to follow is concerned with the witness which Jesus, the revealer, has come to bring. To speak of himself as "the light of the world" in this context is certainly not "out of place".[21]

---

[16] M.-J. Lagrange, *St. Jean*, pp. 235-240. 240-256 has caught this distinction. He entitles vv. 21-30: "Péril pour les Juifs à méconnaître l'envoyé de Dieu" (p. 235) and vv. 31-56: "Les fils charnels d'Abraham, fils du diable plutôt qu'enfants de Dieu, refusent de reconnaître le Fils de Dieu" (p. 240).

[17] Not all share this view. R. E. Brown, *John*, p. 348 suggests that v. 30 is an editorial addition to split up the discourse. C. H. Dodd, "A L'arrière-plan d'un discours johannique", *RHPR* 37 (1957) 6 sees no significance in the variation and R. Schnackenburg, *Johannesevangelium* II, pp. 259-260 cites Dodd with approval. See also E. C. Hoskyns, *Fourth Gospel*, p. 338. However, J. H. Bernard, *St. John*, pp. 304-305 does see the difference. See esp. p. 304: "Those who 'believed in Him' were fewer in number than those who 'believed Him' — a larger body who are addressed in the next verse, and of whom some, as the sequel shows, soon began to cavil at His teaching". See also B. F. Westcott, *St. John*, p. 133; J. Marsh, *St. John*, pp. 361-362.

[18] See B. F. Westcott, *St. John*, p. 131.

[19] Against Bultmann and Becker, who would detach v. 12 from the rest of the discourse, claiming that it does not fit this context. See above, pp. 124-125. See also R. E. Brown, *John*, p. 343, who argues that the theme of light is not picked up again until 9,5. B. Lindars, *John*, pp. 313-314 sees v. 12 as a theme which belongs to ch. 9 but which has been placed here deliberately. Although somewhat foreign, it serves an important purpose, as "light" refers to witness and judgment. See also J. N. Sanders, *St. John*, pp. 221-222.

[20] R. Bultmann, *John*, p. 342.

[21] See F. Mussner, *ZΩH*, pp. 164-171.

Some have attempted to show that the idea of Jesus' being the light originates in Greek or other pagan myths,[22] but it is now generally held that this claim finds its roots in Jewish tradition,[23] and the Qumran discoveries have given further support to this opinion.[24] The theme is not foreign to primitive Christian tradition (see Acts 13,47; Phil. 2,15; Col. 1,12-13; Eph. 5,8; I Pet. 2,9) and John may well have been drawing from his Christian as well as his Jewish heritage.[25] However, it is primarily the Fourth Gospel itself which must furnish the interpreter with the reasons for Jesus' claims.

Throughout the Gospel Jesus is identified with the light which is here and now present among men (see 9,5). However, this presence of the light is almost invariably a call to decision.[26] The prologue shows that there is a double possibility: the true light has come into the world, but the reaction to the light is two-fold — those who "receive him not" and those who "receive him" (1,11-12).[27] This theme of the true light which can be accepted or refused is continued throughout the rest of the account of the public life of Jesus (see 3,19-21; 11,9-10; 12,35-36; 12,46-50). The light is the truth which Jesus has come to bring. In 1,9 the light is specified as τὸ ἀληθινόν and in 3,21 we are told that ὁ δὲ ποιῶν τὴν ἀλήθειαν comes to the light. This is to claim that what the light has to offer is the revelation of the only valid truth — the revelation of the Father himself. The double possibility is presented in 8,12b, where the chance of an escape from darkness to light is offered to those who "follow" Jesus.[28]

---

[22] See W. Bauer, *Johannesevangelium*, pp. 119-121; R. Bultmann, *John*, p. 342, note 5; A. Loisy, *Quatrième Évangile*, pp. 286-287. Loisy suggests that John is in a polemic with the Attis cult.

[23] See C. K. Barrett, *St. John*, pp. 276-278; H. Odeberg, *Fourth Gospel*, pp. 286-290; A. Schlatter, *Johannes*, pp. 205-206; R. H. Strachan, *Fourth Gospel*, pp. 205-207; R. Schnackenburg, *Johannesevangelium* II, pp. 240-243; H. Strathmann, *Johannes*, pp. 144-145; G. Reim, *Studien zum alttestamentlichen Hintergrund*, pp. 164-166; H. Preisker, "Jüdische Apokalyptik und hellenistischer Synkretismus im Johannes-Evangelium, dargelegt an dem Begriff 'Licht'", *TLZ* 77 (1952) 673-678; E. K. Lee, *The Religious Thought of St. John*, pp. 36-38.

[24] For a summary of the Qumran evidence, see H. Braun, *Qumran und das Neue Testament*, (Tübingen, J. C. B. Mohr, 1966) Vol. I, pp. 122-124; R. E. Brown, *John*, p. 340.

[25] See esp. C. K. Barrett, *St. John*, pp. 276. 278-279; E. C. Hoskyns, *Fourth Gospel*, pp. 330-331.

[26] See D. Mollat, Art. "Jugement", *DBS* IV, cols. 1380-1381; J. T. Forestell, *The Word of the Cross*, pp. 31-32; H. Preisker, "Jüdische Apokalyptik ...", col. 676.

[27] See F. M. Braun, "St. Jean", p. 381; W. H. Cadman, *The Open Heaven*, pp. 107-108; B. Lindars, *John*, p. 314; L. Morris, *John*, pp. 438-439; A. Loisy, *Quatrième Évangile* (1903) pp. 551-552.

[28] The word ἀκολουθέω is used throughout the New Testament to speak of commitment to Jesus. See G. Kittel, Art. "ἀκολουθέω", *TDNT* I, pp. 213-215; J. Blank, *Krisis*, pp. 184-185; R. Schnackenburg, *Johannesevangelium* II, p. 241; J. Dupont, *Essais sur la*

That v. 12 is concerned with the witness which Jesus has come to bring in his word and person is confirmed by the fact that this is the theme of the discussion which follows immediately. The Pharisees are not prepared to accept this witness, as they quibble over the legal demands of Num. 35,30 and Deut. 17,6. Jesus' reply takes the discussion beyond these demands. Although it is Jesus' witness which is in question, he does not argue with them on a legal point. Efforts to show that his reply is an explanation of how, in fact, he does fulfil the Law are misguided. In fact, he does not, because one of the witnesses cited in v. 18 is the witness which he bears to himself, and this is not valid.[29] Jesus' reply is concerned with his origin and his mission, as these are the factors which give authenticity to his claims.[30] In v. 14 it is his origin which makes his testimony true and in v. 15 the Pharisees are unable to grasp the validity of the revelation of Jesus because they judge κατὰ τὴν σάρκα. Many scholars see this as a repetition of the κατ' ὄψιν of 7,24[31] and this may certainly be involved. However, there is probably a further reference to the σάρξ of Jesus himself (see 1,14). They are unable to go beyond mere external experience because they stop at the "fleshly" Jesus.[32] They refuse to go further than this, to seek the ultimate reason for the validity of his claims: the one who sent him (see vv. 16, 18). If this is the case, then we are still dealing with the question of Jesus' origins in v. 15.[33]

Any discussion concerning Jesus' witness and his judgment must take due account of his origin "with the Father" (see 1,1-2). To stop short at the appearance of the historical Jesus is to miss John's point: "For the Law was given through Moses, grace and truth through Jesus Christ" (1,17). The Law has been superseded by this completely new reality — the presence of God in the person and message of Jesus Christ.

As this is the case, perhaps more significance can be given to the ἐγώ εἰμι ὁ μαρτυρῶν of v. 18. Although not an absolute use of the "I am", it could well be a claim on the part of Jesus to be the authentic revelation of God,

---

Christologie de Saint Jean, (Bruges, Editions de l'Abbaye de Saint André, 1951) p. 72: "Suivre Jésus, c'est essentiellement croire en lui, recevoir son témoignage".

[29] See the later prohibition of such witness in *Rosh Hashanah* 3,1 and *Ketuboth* 2,9.

[30] C. K. Barrett, *St. John,* p. 275: "These questions turn upon one that has already been under discussion, namely the Whence and Whither which determine the nature and work of Jesus". See also R. H. Lightfoot, *St. John,* p. 189.

[31] See, for example, J. H. Bernard, *St. John,* p. 294; C. H. Dodd, *Interpretation,* p. 352; M.-J. Lagrange, *St. Jean,* p. 233.

[32] See C. K. Barrett, *St. John,* p. 279; F.-M. Braun, "St. Jean", p. 382; M.-J. Lagrange, *St. Jean,* p. 233; A. Loisy, *Quatrième Évangile* (1903) p. 554; A. Schlatter, *Johannes,* p. 206; H. Strathmann, *Johannes,* p. 145. For W. Bauer, *Johannesevangelium,* p. 121, the phrase is Gnostic and means "being absorbed by matter".

[33] See J.-P. Charlier, "L'exégèse johannique d'un précepte légal: Jean 8,17", *RB* 67 (1960) 512-513; R. Schnackenburg, *Johannesevangelium* II, pp. 245-246.

with a reference to the *"nî hû'* of Is. 43,10.[34] Jesus judges no one in the way that the Pharisees judge — or in the way that anyone from "below" would judge, for that matter. His judgment is one that flows from his being sent into the world by the Father, as the light of the world (see vv. 15-16). The demands of the Law are rendered useless. The witness and consequent judgment which have taken the place of the Law are those brought from "above" — the witness and judgment of the Father and the one whom he has sent.[35] The light is almost invariably a call to decision. Although not explicit in vv. 12-20, this is the judgment which Jesus will bring. His judgment is a consequence of his being sent by the Father to witness to the Father among men. Men will judge themselves by their decision for or against the witness which the light brings into the world (see esp. 12,44-50).[36] The validity of this judgment is unquestionable, because it is based in the unity which exists between the Father and the Son (v. 19).

> "Alles vermeintliche 'Wissen' um Gott und das Heil wird zu einem erschüttern-
> den Nichtwissen, wenn man dem nicht glaubt, der das wahre Wissen von Gott
> besitzt und den Weg zum Heil offenbart".[37]

The point at issue here is not so much the vindication of the testimony of Jesus before his questioners, but rather the aggressive affirmation of the origin of Jesus which, in turn, puts the validity of his witness outside the reach of the questioning of the Law.[38] It is the affirmation of the truth about his origins which renders the questions of the Pharisees pointless, and leaves them gasping with puzzlement in the question of v. 19, a further indication of their inability to go beyond their own categories.[39] The Rabbis spoke of the Law as a lamp or a light, basing themselves on Ps. 119,105 and Prov. 6,23.[40] Jesus' claim to be the light of the world has fulfilled these hopes, but his origin and union with the Father demand that his listeners go beyond what

---

[34] See J.-P. Charlier, *art. cit.*, pp. 513-514. This suggestion is refused by C. K. Barrett, *St. John*, p. 242 and R. Bultmann, *John*, pp. 225-226, note 3. It is proposed, with hesitation, by J. H. Bernard, *St. John*, p. cxviii and p. 296 and accepted by B. Lindars, *John*, p. 318, and G. Ferraro, *L'« ora » di Cristo*, p. 171. Although Barrett refuses to give great importance to the "I am" part of the saying, he argues that the use of the article is important, and that it alludes to Is. 43,10.

[35] See I. de la Potterie, "La notion de témoignage dans saint Jean", in *Sacra Pagina*, Vol. II, p. 196; D. Mollat, Art. "Jugement", *DBS* IV, col. 1380.

[36] See J. Blank, *Krisis*, pp. 216-226; E. C. Hoskyns, *Fourth Gospel*, p. 333: "The purpose of His witness is to evoke faith; its rejection involves ultimate condemnation".

[37] R. Schnackenburg, *Johannesevangelium* II, p. 248. See also pp. 247-248.

[38] See A. Schlatter, *Johannes*, p. 207; J. T. Forestell, *The Word of the Cross*, pp. 38-39.

[39] See C. K. Barrett, *St. John*, p. 279: "The ensuing discourse traces their complete ignorance of the origin, destiny and significance of Christ, and of their own".

[40] See *Test. Levi* 14,4; *Exod. Rabb.* 36,3. Strack-Billerbeck, *Kommentar*, Vol. II, pp. 521-522. 552-553.

they learnt from their Jewish traditions.[41]   John concludes this section (vv. 12-20) not only with a reference to the place where the discussion occurred, but also by announcing that the hour had not yet come.   In this way he heightens the tension of the narrative, as his readers know the inevitable conclusion to these controversies will arrive when that "hour" does come (see 12,23; 13,1).   In that moment the judgment of the world will come.   It is ironically in the moment when the light appears to be vanquished that the supreme revelation of God's glory will take place, and the elevated Son of Man will draw all men to himself (see 12,31-33).

The discussion is resumed in v. 21 with another πάλιν.   Now the question of Jesus' origin and destiny is openly the point at issue.   He is going to a destiny which he alone knows, and if his listeners try to find him without a change of heart, they will never succeed (v. 21).   They must make their decisions now, while they can see and hear the revelation of God.   The key to their misunderstanding (v. 22) is again explained in terms of Jesus' origin. Recalling his discussion with Nicodemus (3,12-15), he tells them that they fail to understand because they are ἐκ τῶν κάτω while he is ἐκ τῶν ἄνω (v. 23).[42]   This gulf must be overcome if they wish to be saved from their sins. It is still a possibility, and Jesus tells them clearly that the gulf can be bridged if they will believe in him: "You will die in your sins unless you believe that I am he" (v. 24).[43]

There has been a great deal of discussion concerning the origin of the "I am" formulae,[44] but there is now a general agreement that it is Jesus' most striking claim to a unique relationship with God.   There may be hints of Exod. 3,14 in the use of the formula, but it seems more likely that it comes

---

[41] This is the thesis of J. L. Martyn, *History and Theology*, who sets the development of the Gospel in the context of the struggle between the Johannine Church and the Synagogue.   See also C. K. Barrett, *St. John*, p. 276; A. Richardson, *St. John*, p. 117.

[42] For some, this reference to "above" and "below" is more a reference to the moral causes of separation from Jesus.   See J. H. Bernard, *St. John*, pp. 299-300; A. Schlatter, *Johannes*, p. 209; M.-J. Lagrange, *St. Jean*, p. 236.   The question of "origins" is by far the more important issue here.

[43] See R. Bultmann, *John*, p. 348: "The division between what is above and what is below need not be absolute.   For the Revealer who comes down from above enables man to ascend into the heights.   The division is only made final by unbelief".   See also J. C. Fenton, *John*, pp. 99-100.

[44] See, above all, E. Schweizer, *Ego Eimi ... Die religionsgeschichtliche Herkunft und theologische Bedeutung der johanneischen Bildreden, zugleich ein Beitrag zur Quellenfrage des vierten Evangeliums*, FRLANT 38, (Göttingen, Vandenhoeck und Ruprecht, 1939).   See also, the more recent work of H. Zimmermann, "Das absolute Ἐγώ εἰμι als neu-testamentliche Offenbarungsformel", *BZ* 4 (1960) 54-69. 266.276.   A. Feuillet, "Les *Ego Eimi* christologiques due quatrième évangile", *RecSR* 54 (1966) 5-22. 213-240; J. B. Harner, *The "I am" of the Fourth Gospel*, Facet Books, Biblical Series 26, (Philadelphia, Fortress Press, 1970); R. E. Brown, *John*, pp. 533-538; D. Daube, "The 'I am' of the Messianic Presence", in *The New Testament and Rabbinic Judaism*, pp. 325-329.

from the prophetic literature, and especially Deutero-Isaiah.[45] H. Zimmermann
has shown that the use of a formula of divine revelation has progressed from
such sayings as Is. 43,10:

> " 'You are my witnesses' says the Lord 'and my servant whom I have chosen,
> that you may know and believe me and understand that I am He' "
> (*ki 'ªnî hû'*).

and Is. 45,18:

> "I am the Lord (*'ªnî YHWH*)
> and there is no other",

through the LXX, where both of these formulae are translated by ἐγώ εἰμι
to the use of ἐγώ εἰμι as a revelation formula in the New Testament.[46] There
is a constant in this development. Both for Deutero-Isaiah and for John, the
formula is used to reveal the one and only God. In Deutero-Isaiah the
formula is used in contexts which assert the unique God Jahweh over against
the claims of "other gods". Jahweh *reveals* himself in these formulae. So
it is in John: Jesus reveals his unique claim to divinity, his union with the
Father, by the use of this formula. "Wie Jahwe viele Male innerhalb des AT
durch die Offenbarungsformel sein Wesen und seinen Willen kundtut, so
offenbart er sich im NT durch seinen Christus. Wenn also Jesus das ἐγώ εἰμι
ausspricht, offenbart er zunächst nicht sich, sondern den Vater (s. Joh 8,24f)".[47]
The use of the formula in 8,24 (as in 8,28) is John's way of affirming the
union of the Father and the Son.[48] In Jesus the Father is revealed, and to be
freed from their sins, the Jews must have faith in that revelation, found uniquely
in Jesus.[49]

The astonishment which greets this claim is understandable. The "Who
are you?" (v. 25a) is not polemical, but an honest question which shows,
however, that Jesus' audience has still not understood anything that has been
said to them. They have not been able to go beyond their judgments,
κατὰ τὴν σάρκα, for which they were reprimanded in v. 15. This may be
understood from John's summary of the situation in v. 27: "They did not

---

[45] See P. B. Harner, *op. cit.*, pp. 6-15; H. Zimmermann, *art. cit.*, pp. 60-69; G. Reim,
Studien zum alttestamentlichen Hintergrund, pp. 166-173. Insufficient attention is paid to
the "I am" formulae of the Pentateuch. See, for example, Exod. 14,4.18; 20,2.5; 29,46;
Lev. 19; 11,45; 20,7. On these sayings and their link with Deutero-Isaiah, see W. Zimmerli,
"Ich bin Jahwe", in *Geschichte und Altes Testament: Albrecht Alt zum 70. Geburtstag*,
Beiträge zur historischen Theologie 16, (Tübingen, J. C. B. Mohr, 1953) pp. 179-209.

[46] H. Zimmermann, *art. cit.*, pp. 60-69. See also Is. 41,4; 43,13; 46,4; 48,12; Deut.
32,39. See also R. E. Brown, *John*, pp. 536-537.

[47] H. Zimmermann, *art. cit.*, p. 270. See also R. E. Brown, *John*, p. 537.

[48] P. B. Harner, *op. cit.*, pp. 43-45; C. K. Barrett, *St. John*, pp. 282-283; J. Blank,
Krisis, p. 227; M.-E. Boismard, "La royauté du Christ ...", p. 58; B. Lindars, *John*,
pp. 320-321; A. Loisy, *Quatrième Évangile*, p. 291; W. Bauer, *Johannesevangelium*, p. 123;
J. H. Bernard, *St. John*, pp. 300-301.

[49] See R. Schnackenburg, *Johannesevangelium* II, pp. 253-254.

understand that he spoke to them of the Father".[50]   This complete lack of understanding is the cause of the very difficult words of v. 25b.

Are we dealing with a question or a statement?   It is clear that τὴν ἀρχήν may be used adverbially.[51]   It is almost impossible to make sense out of the phrase if τὴν ἀρχήν is taken as an accusative noun, unless one adds something further.   If it is a question, then τὴν ἀρχήν is translated as "at all" and ὅτι is simply "why".   This leaves us with a translation: "Why am I speaking to you at all?"[52]   There are variations on the exact form of the question, but the grammarians and many commentators find this the most satisfactory solution.[53]   In translating the phrase as a statement, several words have to be supplied.   It is generally translated as an affirmation about the nature of Jesus, so an ἐγώ εἰμι is added, ἀπό is understood as governing τὴν ἀρχήν and the ὅτι as a relative ὅ τι "that which".   These additions again give various possibilities: "I am from the beginning what I tell you" or "I am what I tell you from the beginning".[54]   Another suggestion is that the τὴν ἀρχήν remain adverbial, giving the translation: "Primarily (I am) what I am telling you".[55]   These suggestions see v. 25b as a continuation of the discussion concerning the nature of Jesus.   The main argument for this interpretation is that it fits the context better than a question.[56]   R. E. Brown, tentatively followed by B. Lindars and L. Morris, uses the evidence of P[66] which has: "I told you at the beginning what I am also telling you now", to

---

[50] See J. H. Bernard, *St. John*, p. 303; J. C. Fenton, *John*, p. 100: "The Jews ask the right question, since everything hinges on the person of Jesus".

[51] This adverbial use is quite frequent.   See H. G. Liddell-R. Scott, *A Greek-English Lexicon*, p. 252, s.v. ἀρχή I, i b.c.

[52] Very close to the question is the exasperated remark, which translates the ὅτι as "that": "That I speak to you at all!".

[53] M. Zerwick, *Biblical Greek*, (Rome, Pontifical Biblical Institute, 1963) para. 222; J. H. Moulton-G. Milligan, *The Vocabulary of the Greek Testament*, p. 81, s.v. ἀρχή W. Bauer-W. F. Arndt-F. W. Gingrich, *A Greek-English Lexicon*, p. 111, s.v. ἀρχή I, b.; W. Bauer, *Johannesevangelium*, p. 123; J. Blank, *Krisis*, p. 228; F.-M. Braun, "St. Jean", p. 383; R. Bultmann, *John*, p. 353; M.-J. Lagrange, *St. Jean*, p. 238; A. Loisy, *Quatrième Évangile*, p. 292; G. H. C. Macgregor, *John*, p. 215; A. Schlatter, *Johannes*, p. 210; R. Schnackenburg, *Johannesevangelium* II, pp. 254-255; R. H. Strachan, *Fourth Gospel*, p. 209; H. Strathmann, *Johannes*, pp. 141; 157; W. Temple, *Readings*, p. 139; J. Wellhausen, *Johannis*, pp. 40-41; B. F. Westcott, *St. John*, pp. 131; 142-143; G. Bornkamm, "Der Paraklet im Johannesevangelium", pp. 34-35; C. H. Dodd, *Tradition*, p. 230, note 1; S. Schulz, *Johannes*, p. 131; NEB text; RSV margin.

[54] See C. K. Barrett, *St. John*, p. 283.

[55] J. H. Bernard, *St. John*, pp. 301-302.

[56] See C. K. Barrett, *St. John*, pp. 283-284; W. F. Howard, "St. John", p. 598; J. Marsh, *St. John*, p. 360.   Marsh rules the interpretation of the phrase as a question as "quite unacceptable" on account of the context.   However, A. Schlatter, *Johannes*, p. 210 argues for the question because, he claims, a question better suits the context!

translate the phrase as: "What I have been telling you from the beginning".[57]

While the argument for the interpretation of v. 25b as a statement has some very important advocates,[58] the necessary additions appear too demanding. Perhaps the ἐγώ εἰμι could be carried over from v. 24, although this is a little forced. The accusative (ἀπὸ) τὴν ἀρχήν would be extraordinary in the Fourth Gospel, where one finds ἀπ' (ἐξ) ἀρχῆς to express from the beginning" (see 8,44; 15,27; 16,4; I Jn. 1,1; 2,7.13-14; 3,8.11). Finally the present tense of λαλῶ is handled violently when one translates it as "what I am saying from the beginning".[59] A perfect should be used to convey this meaning. Although this translation may appear to suit the context better than the question, it runs the risk of being a *tour de force* on the part of the interpreter to make it do so.[60]

It appears that v. 25b should be understood as a rhetorical question, as a gesture of "a mood of yearning impatience".[61] In vv. 23-24 Jesus has described the gap which must be bridged if the Jews are to be saved from their sins, and he has told them how this is possible. Yet, in their inability to go beyond what they can see and touch, they fail to understand. Their puzzled question of v. 25a reveals this. In the face of this obtuseness after the clarity of vv. 23-24 Jesus asks: "What is the point of talking to you?" There are so many dire judgments that Jesus could bring against them on account of their hard-headedness (v. 26a) but this must not be his way.[62] He has not come to do his own will, but that of the one who sent him (see 4,54; 5,30; 6,38; 8,29; 9,4; 12,49), and the one who sent him is true. He will not be swayed by the failure of the audience to understand, because he is ἀληθής, which involves a never-changing fidelity.[63] This is why Jesus must

---

[57] R. E. Brown, *John*, pp. 347-348; B. Lindars, *John*, p. 321; L. Morris, *John*, pp. 448-450. Morris is aware of the difficulties involved in the scant value of the P[66] reading taken on its own.

[58] See also E. C. Hoskyns, *Fourth Gospel*, pp. 335-336 (This section is, in fact, the work of F. N. Davey); R. H. Lightfoot, *St. John*, p. 191; L. Morris, *John*, pp. 448-449; H. Odeberg, *Fourth Gospel*, pp. 294-295; RSV text; NEB margin.

[59] See R. Schnackenburg, *Johannesevangelium* II, p. 255.

[60] The Latin Fathers have generally understood it as a statement, while the Greeks have almost universally read it as a question. For summaries of the Patristic evidence, see R. Bultmann, *John*, pp. 351-353 and notes; M.-J. Lagrange, *St. Jean*, pp. 236-238; R. E. Brown, *John*, pp. 347-348.

[61] R. H. Strachan, *Fourth Gospel*, p. 209. See also H. van den Bussche, *Jean*, p. 310: "Une formule de rhétorique et la phrase est une exclamation de fatigue".

[62] This sense of contrast between v. 26a and 26b exists because of the ἀλλά. See F. Blass-A. Debrunner-R. W. Funk, *A Greek Grammar*, para. 447,1; C. K. Barrett, *St. John*, p. 284. This is often lost in attempts to link v. 26a and b. See, for example, B. F. Westcott, *St. John*, p. 351. R. Bultmann, *John*, p. 351 sees the importance of the contrast, but omits the verse as an un-Johannine fragment!

[63] See G. Quell, Art. "ἀλήθεια", *TDNT* I, pp. 232-237; R. E. Brown, *John*, pp. 499-501; R. Bultmann, Art. "ἀλήθεια", *TDNT* I, 248-249.

continue to speak to the world, performing not his own will, but that which he has learnt from the one who sent him (v. 26b). Only when Jesus is met by open refusal will he accuse them of their sin (8,31-59, see esp. vv. 44-47).

The comment that John makes in v. 27 is in complete agreement with this interpretation. The one who sent Jesus stands behind the whole discussion. Ultimately Jesus is concerned, not with the Jews' reaction to himself, but to the Father who sent him. He has been speaking of his Father throughout.[64] They have not understood this, so Jesus makes a last attempt to convince his audience, in vv. 28-29, which, in the context appear to be the promise of an authentic revelation which will take place in the elevated Son of Man (v. 28a). This elevated Son of Man will reveal the Father, the one who sent him, the one who never leaves him, the one whom Jesus always seeks to please (vv. 28b-29). After this second attempt to speak clearly (the first attempt of vv. 23-24 having failed) a slight ray of hope breaks through. Many believe in him (v. 30). However, John moves on towards the "hour" by allowing that section of Jesus' listeners to fade from the scene, as he continues the discussion in v. 31, with some who do not fully commit themselves to Jesus.[65]

II - The Son of Man in John 8,28

Despite his discouragement (vv. 25-26), Jesus continues to "speak to them of the Father" (v. 27). The revelation of the Father seems to reach a high point in v. 28. The use of οὖν connects the verse logically with what has gone before. His listeners have not understood him up to this point. Now he utters a more solemn statement: "When you have lifted up the Son of Man, then you will know that I am he".

At first glance this appears to be a relatively obvious statement. Even though the Jews cannot, as yet, understand that Jesus is the revealer of the Father, they will come to this knowledge when they have "lifted up" the Son of Man. From 3,14 the reader is already aware that this "lifting up"

---

[64] See R. E. Brown, *John*, p. 350: "The editorial remark in vs. 27 assures us that we have been interpreting Jesus' words correctly, and that their burden concerns his unique association with divinity, so unique that God is his Father". Our interpretation attempts to overcome the difficulties which the text is said to cause for v. 25b, when read as a question. The thought moves in the following fashion: i. a clear statement of the truth (vv. 23-24); ii. total lack of comprehension (v. 25a); iii. frustration on the part of Jesus (v. 25b); iv. a continued resolve, despite the difficulties, to do the will of the Father (v. 26). This fits our conviction that vv. 12-30 are basically positive in tone, leading to the correct faith of some in v. 30.

[65] See above, pp. 126-127.

refers to Jesus' death on the cross, and this will be made even clearer in 12,27-36.[66] When Jesus is raised up on the cross, then the Jews will know that he is "I am" — that he reveals the Father because of a unique relationship which exists between Jesus and his Father, who is none other than God.[67] "After the crucifixion and exaltation of Jesus, men will realize who he is by perceiving his unity with the Father".[68]

However, there are several problems involved in this apparently clear statement of fact. The verb ὑψώσητε is active. In other places where the Son of Man's "lifting up" is mentioned (3,14; 12,34) the verb is passive and closely linked with δεῖ expressing a divine necessity somewhat like the passion predictions of the Synoptic Gospels (see Mk. 8,31; 9,31; 10,33 parrs.). Here, it is almost an accusation: "When *you* have lifted up the Son of Man". The reference is clearly to the activity of the Jews in crucifying Jesus. It is the Jews, Jesus' interlocutors throughout the discussion, who will come to the knowledge that Jesus is the authentic revelation of the Father.

Will this knowledge be for their condemnation or for their salvation? In v. 21 Jesus told the Jews that he was going away, that they would seek him, but that they would not find him. They would die in their sins. In v. 28 another verb is used to speak of his going away, as the Jews are told that they will "lift him up". Is the result of this lifting up to be as negative as his "going away" in v. 21? Is their knowledge "too late" for any hope of salvation? [69] According to this interpretation, the Jews have condemned themselves by daring to refuse and condemn the revealer of the truth. Now there is no longer any hope. "At the very moment when they think they are passing judgment on him, he becomes their judge".[70] This conclusion is forced upon us if we look for some subsequent event which fulfils the prophecy when, after the crucifixion, the Jews come to know that Jesus is the revelation of the Father and accept him. It would have been obvious to John's readers that they had *not* come to know and understand Jesus when they nailed him on a cross.[71] For some scholars, the evidence that the saying speaks of the condemnation of the Jews is found in the tragedy of their subsequent history.[72]

---

[66] See above, pp. 61-64 for a discussion of John's use of ὑψόω. This passage again makes it clear that the ascension is not involved, as the Jews are the subject of the verb, and they were not instrumental in Jesus' ascension. See J.H. Bernard, *St. John*, p. 303.

[67] See above, pp. 131-132.

[68] P.B. Harner, *The "I am" of the Fourth Gospel*, p. 44.

[69] Thus R. Bultmann, *John*, p. 350; W. Bauer, *Johannesevangelium*, pp. 123-124; J.H. Bernard, *St. John*, p. 303; M.-J. Lagrange, *St. Jean*, pp. 238-240; H. Strathmann, *Johannes*, p. 148; B. Vawter, "John", p. 441; S. Schulz, *Johannes*, p. 132.

[70] R. Bultmann, *John*, p. 350.

[71] C.K. Barrett, *St. John*, p. 284.

[72] M.-J. Lagrange, *St. Jean*, p. 239: "Il faudra bien qu'ils le comprennent lorsqu'ils se verront anéantis comme peuple, dispersés parmi des gentils, empressés à croire en Jésus".

This interpretation, however, has some serious difficulties. The word γινώσκειν in the Fourth Gospel is never a negative word (see 7,17.26; 8,37; 10,38; 14,31; 17,23). In fact, it is continually linked with the Johannine idea of correct faith (see 6,69; 8,31-32; 10,38; 16,30; 17,7-8; I John 4,16).[73] The only other place where the activity of men in the death of Jesus is mentioned is in 19,37: "They shall look upon him whom they have pierced". This is not a negative condemnation, but, by quoting Zech. 12,10, John refers to the saving power of the cross of Christ.[74] The very similar passage in 12,32 is also positive: "And I, when I am lifted up from the earth, will draw all men to myself". It would appear that 8,28 may also have to be understood in a more positive light.[75] That this is the case is further indicated by the result of the discussion, as reported in v. 30: "Many believed in him". What is promised in v. 28a is not condemnation, but hope.

C. K. Barrett has argued that v. 28a is written for John's audience, as it was obvious that Jesus' crucifixion had not brought about any change of heart on the part of the Jews. The "you" referred to are the people of John's time.[76] While the crucifixion did not lead to the conversion of the Jews, it still remains true that the earliest Church was composed of people who were very conscious of their Jewish roots and that the earliest missionary activity was carried out exclusively among Jews.[77] The Fourth Gospel sounds very like a discussion between the Johannine Church and the hostile Synagogue, which has expelled the members of this new sect,[78] and v. 28a can be understood very well in this context. The Jews were responsible for Jesus' death but, for the Fourth Gospel, the death was a proof that Jesus was "I am".[79] This is why John has used the double meaning ὑψόω. In the activity of crucifying Jesus the Jews have been accessories to the glorification of Jesus. If they wish to be saved from their sins, they can still find that salvation in the cross of Christ whom they themselves have crucified.

---

[73] See R. Bultmann, Art. "γινώσκω", *TDNT* I, pp. 711-713; E. K. Lee, *The Religious Thought of St. John*, pp. 220-225.

[74] See on this, W. Thüsing, *Erhöhung*, pp. 19-22; A. Vergote, "L'exaltation du Christ en croix ...", pp. 13-23; R. Schnackenburg, "Das Schriftzitat in Joh 19,37", in J. Schreiner (ed.), *Wort, Lied und Gottespruch: Beiträge zu Psalmen und Propheten: Festschrift für Joseph Ziegler*, Forschung zur Bibel 2, (Würzburg, Echter, 1972) pp. 244-245; J. T. Forestell, *The Word of the Cross*, pp. 88-92.

[75] See R. Schnackenburg, *Johannesevangelium* II, p. 257.

[76] See C. K. Barrett, *St. John*, p. 284.

[77] See J. Jeremias, *Jesus' Promise to the Nations*, SBT 24 (London, SCM Press, 1967) (English translation of *Jesu Verheissung für die Völker*, [Stuttgart, Kohlhammer, 1959]); F. Hahn, *Mission in the New Testament*, SBT 47, (London, SCM Press, 1965) pp. 47-59 (English translation of *Das Verständnis der Mission im neuen Testament*, [Neukirchen-Vluyn, Neukirchener-Verlag, 1963]).

[78] See J. L. Martyn, *History and Theology*.

[79] See C. K. Barrett, *St. John*, p. 284; R. E. Brown, *John*, p. 350; W. F. Howard, "St. John", p. 192; G. H. C. Macgregor, *John*, p. 216; J. Marsh, *St. John*, pp. 359-360.

R. Bultmann has attempted to base the authority of Jesus' claims in
v. 28a in his being the Son of Man. To do this, he makes "the Son of Man"
the predicate of the otherwise absolute "I am". It is at the moment of the
elevation of Jesus upon the cross that the Jews will understand that he is
the Son of Man.[80]   While this would be linguistically possible, it seems hardly
probable. The Son of Man in the Fourth Gospel is linked with the theme
of "lifting up" (see 3,14; 12,34) and not with the "I am" statements. The
absolute "I am" of v. 28a seems to catch up and repeat what has already
been said in v. 24. To make "the Son of Man" the predicate of v. 28a would
cause the loss of the obviously intended repetition.[81]

According to v. 28a, when Jesus, the Son of Man, is raised up on the
cross, then the Jews will see and know that there is a oneness between Jesus
and the Father. Then they will know that everything he teaches and does
comes from the Father (v. 28b). In a word, they will know that Jesus, the
Son of Man, is the revealer and the revelation of God.[82]   His revelation is, in
itself, neither salvation nor condemnation — it is the possibility of both. The
Evangelist preaches a message of Christ glorified on the cross and Jews of
John's day, as in the day of Jesus himself, could find life or death in that
cross. It is the decision of the Jews for or against the revelation of the
Son of Man, lifted up on the cross, which will bring them salvation or
condemnation. Thus, the promise of v. 28a is about neither salvation nor
condemnation, but rather the possibility of both, offered to the Jews in the
time of Jesus and in the time of the Johannine Church.[83]

> "Wenn sie den Menschensohn am Kreuze erhöht haben werden, stehen sie
> wie einst ihre Vorfahren in der Wüste vor einem von Gott gesetzten Zeichen,
> vor dem sie sich entscheiden müssen zwischen Heil und Unheil".[84]

Once again we find John using the title "the Son of Man" in a context
of revelation, and consequently, of judgment. When Jesus goes on after v. 28a
and says: "I do nothing on my own, but speak thus as the Father taught me"
(v. 28b), John is making it amply clear that v. 28a is concerned with the
revelation of the Father which Jesus has come to bring. This revelation has
its claim to authority because it is totally dependent upon the Father. What

---

[80] R. Bultmann, *John*, p. 349. See also A. Wikenhauser, *Johannes*, p. 140; E. D.
Freed, "The Son of Man ...", p. 405.

[81] See R. Schnackenburg, *Johannesevangelium* II, p. 256.

[82] See T. Müller, *Das Heilsgeschehen im Johannesevangelium*, pp. 33-36; J. T.
Forestell, *The Word of the Cross*, p. 64.

[83] See E. C. Hoskyns, *Fourth Gospel*, p. 336; A. Loisy, *Quatrième Évangile*, pp. 292-
293; T. Zahn, *Johannes*, pp. 408-409; R. H. Strachan, *Fourth Gospel*, p. 209; W. Temple,
Readings, pp. 139-140. This interpretation, modifying the positive interpretation of W.
Thüsing, *Erhöhung*, pp. 15-19, insists that whether the knowledge is *zum Heil* or *zum
Unheil* depends upon the Jews' reaction, not upon the event itself of Jesus' elevation.

[84] M. Mees, "Erhöhung und Verherrlichung Jesu...", p. 38.

Jesus says is, ultimately, the word of the Father; it is authentic revelation, and whoever accepts or refuses this revelation will come to life or death accordingly (see 3,16-21; 3,31-36; 5,19-29; 12,46-50).[85] This is but a further explanation of what Jesus has claimed in v. 12, when he presented himself as the light of the world, who could bring light and life to those who followed him.[86]

V. 29 continues with the assertion of the validity of Jesus' revelation. The revelation of the Son of Man lifted up on the cross is valid, not only because Jesus has spoken what he has heard from the Father (v. 28b), but because the Father remains continually with him and has not left him alone. After the present tense of μετ' ἐμοῦ ἐστιν, one expects a perfect tense which would logically claim that the Father has never left Jesus alone. He was with him before all things, and remains with him. Instead, we find the aorist ἀφῆκεν. This could refer to the incarnation. When the pre-existent Logos, who had been "with" God (1,1-2) entered the world of flesh (1,14), the Father did not abandon him but was, even then with him. It could also be John's way of telling his readers that even in the apparent solitude of the cross, the Father was with Jesus (see Mk. 15,34). It is because of this continual presence of the Father "with" Jesus that he can claim to be "I am".

The ὅτι of v. 29c may explain why the Father never left Jesus: "because I always do what is pleasing to him"; it is better understood, however, as the introduction to a clause of consequence.[87] The logic of the passage is then as follows: when the Jews lift up the Son of Man on the cross, then they will be able to understand that he is the authentic revelation of God (v. 28a), for Jesus, the Son of Man, has revealed what he has learnt from the Father, and his revelation is uniquely valid (v. 28b). But there is more to it than this; there is a unity between the Son and the Father which extends to their very presence "with" one another. The Father did not leave him to work out his task alone; the Father is with him (v. 29ab). *Because of this,* all that the Son does is pleasing to the Father, as it is in perfect concurrence with his will (v. 29c).[88] At last, finally understanding this, many believed in him (v. 30).

Jesus is presented as the uniquely authentic place of revelation, and the title given to him is "the Son of Man". As in other Son of Man sayings, one

---

[85] Against M.-J. Lagrange, *St. Jean,* p. 191, who sees v. 28b as a transition to v. 29. See on this, R. Bultmann, *John,* p. 353.

[86] See above, pp. 127-128.

[87] See W. Bauer-W. F. Arndt-F. W. Gingrich, *A Greek English Lexicon,* p. 593, s.v. ὅτι 1, dγ.

[88] C. H. Dodd, *Interpretation,* pp. 93-96; 349-350 suggests that Jesus' being sent by the Father is involved in his being "I am" which the Rabbis sometimes rendered as *'ᵃnî wᵉhû'* meaning "I and the one who sent me".

can trace a gradual development in the discussion of who Jesus is, reaching a climax in the presentation of Jesus as the Son of Man, the unique revealer who must be believed in if one hopes to walk in the light of life (v. 12).[89] During the earlier part of the discourse Jesus is presented as a Mosaic prophet: "Yet many people believed in him; they said, 'When the Christ appears, will he do more signs than this man has done?... This is really the prophet'" (7,31. 40). However, not all are happy with this identification, so they begin to ask questions about his origins: "Are you from Galilee too? Search and you will see that no prophet is to rise from Galilee" (7,52, see also 7,40-43). Now the discussion has come to face the vital question about Jesus — where he comes from. However, his questioners are judging κατὰ τὴν σάρκα in their questions about Galilee (see 8,15), so Jesus steers the discussion in the correct direction in 8,12-30. Throughout this passage Jesus is concerned with his origin "from above" and his being sent by the Father (see v. 14, 16, 18, 19, 21, 23, 26, 27, 28, 29). Because this is true, he is the one who can authentically reveal the Father. Unless the Jews believe this, they will die in their sins (v. 24) but despite their obtuseness (vv. 25-27), they will be able to look upon the Son of Man whom they have lifted up on the cross (see also 19,37) and there they will find God's revelation to men (v. 28). This will not be limited to any historical moment, as for the Evangelist the glory of God will always shine forth from Christ crucified. As such, the cross will always be the place where man can find God's revelation to men, and either accept it or refuse it.[90] As in other Johannine Son of Man sayings, the question which stands behind the discussion is "Who is Jesus?". Several answers are given, none of them entirely satisfactory, until Jesus himself gives the answer in terms of "the Son of Man", revealer and judge.[91] What will happen as a consequence of the knowledge which comes from the elevated Son of Man is their own responsibility (see 3,16-21.31-36; 5,19-29; 12,46-48).

The title appears to be deliberately chosen by John for use in this context of revelation and judgment. It is Jesus, the man who lived, preached and was lifted up upon a cross, who is the unique revelation of God among men,[92] because he alone can claim to be "from above".

---

[89] See J. L. Martyn, *History and Theology*, pp. 124-125; G. Reim, *Studien zum alt-testamentlichen Hintergrund*, pp. 122-124.

[90] See R. Bultmann, *John*, pp. 349-350.

[91] See F. H. Borsch, *Son of Man*, p. 304, note 1. Borsch has noticed the pattern in 8,28a and remarks: "If John 8,28a once did stand in some relationship to a question like 'Who are you?' in v. 25, there is then a certain progression of thought not unlike that found in the synoptic narratives of the *confession* at Caesarea Philippi and in the trial scene. In all of these cases a 'Who is Jesus?' question leads to a statement about the Son of Man". See also our remarks above, pp. 47-50.

[92] See W. G. Kümmel, *The Theology of the New Testament*, pp. 275-277. When referring to the use of the "I am" with "the Son of Man" in 8,28 Kümmel comments: "When, with the introduction of this Old Testament-Jewish predicate of God for Jesus,

Although revelation and judgment are major themes throughout the Gospel, when John uses "the Son of Man" he appears to be consistently pointing to Jesus as the man who, because he has come from above (see 3,13-14; 6,62), reveals the Father with unique authority (1,51; 3,13-14; 6,27.53; 8,28). The revelation brought by the Son of Man subsequently leads to judgment (5,27; 8,28). As yet, we have only been given hints concerning the supreme moment of this revelation and judgment (1,51; 3,14; 6,51-58; 8,28), but we know that it will take place when the Son of Man is "lifted up" (3,14; 8,28). Subsequent sayings (see 12,20-26.34; 13,31; 19,5) will indicate further that this moment is Jesus' exaltation upon the cross.

John makes the claim that God himself appears in the man Jesus, still even in this context he has not forgotten that God is making himself perfectly visible in the man Jesus, and therefore even here he has not simply equated Jesus with God or presented him as a divine being" (p. 277).

CHAPTER SEVEN

BELIEF IN THE SON OF MAN:
John 9,35

I - General Structure and Meaning of John 9

While most scholars see John 9 as an example of the dramatic skill of
the author,[1] some have sought to identify sources and various hands in its
composition. H. Becker finds fragments of a Gnostic discourse in vv. 4, 5
and 35[2] and J. Wellhausen with F. Spitta sees the change from "Pharisees"
(vv. 13 and 16) to "the Jews" (v. 18) as an indication that vv. 17-23 (or
vv. 18-23) have been added by the Evangelist.[3] Spitta sees further additions
to the *Grundschrift* in vv. 5 and 29-34a; vv. 35-41 have also been added
later as a theological and allegorical conclusion to the whole section. In fact,
according to Spitta, the purpose of these additions was to make what was
originally a simple miracle story and a subsequent encounter with the authorities
into an allegory.[4]

For R. Bultmann, the miracle and subsequent encounter is the beginning
of a section in his reconstructed Gospel which he entitles "The Light of the
World". The whole section is made up of 9,1-41; 8,12; 12,44-50; 8,21-29;
12,34-36; 10,19-21. Chapter 9 is basically a unit which comes from the Signs
Source. There are embellishments from the Evangelist in vv. 4-5; 22-23;
29-30 and 39-41. The editor has shown his hand in vv. 16-17 and 35-38.[5]

---

[1] See R. Schnackenburg, *Johannesevangelium* II, p. 303: "Es ist eine meisterhafte
Darstellung, die mit dramatischer Erzählkunst zugleich theologische und zeitgeschichtliche
Tendenzen verfolgt"; R. E. Brown, *John*, p. 376: "We have here Johannine dramatic skill
at its best". See the presentation of J. M. Thomson, "An Experiment in Translation",
The Expositor, 8th Series, Vol. 16 (1918) 119-123. He arranges the chapter into a series
of dramatic scenes.

[2] H. Becker, *Die Reden des Johannesevangeliums*, pp. 83-84. See p. 132 for the
reconstructed text.

[3] J. Wellhausen, *Johannis*, pp. 45-47; F. Spitta, *Johannes-Evangelium*, pp. 202-203.

[4] F. Spitta, *op. cit.*, pp. 199-209. For criticism of Spitta, see R. Bultmann, *John*,
p. 329, note 3.

[5] R. Bultmann, *John*, p. 329. See pp. 312-315 for his reconstruction of chapters 8-10.

Because of the difficult passage from 8,59 to 9,1, F. Tillmann has placed the whole of ch. 9 after 7,27.[6]

The problem of sources arises from the account of the healing miracle (vv. 1-7). While some scholars would see Mk. 8,22-26 as the source for John's account,[7] most would claim that John is working with traditional material, which may have Synoptic contacts, but which is independent of the Synoptic tradition.[8]

Here, as throughout the Gospel, John has worked with traditions older than the Gospel itself to construct his version of the healing of a blind man. The chapter must be understood as a unit:

> "Whatever may have been the history of composition, it does not appear that we could at present improve upon the existing order without disintegrating the work which has come down to us, and relying upon mere speculation".[9]

Many scholars merely give a general division:

vv.   1-12:   The miracle and its immediate consequences
vv. 13-34:   The discussion before the Pharisees
vv. 35-41:   Theological conclusion,[10]

but J. L. Martyn uses a criterion for further division which does not atomise the passage, but rather serves to heighten the tension, throwing into greater relief the skill of the author-redactor. He recalls "the ancient maxim that no more than two active characters shall normally appear on stage at one time, and that scenes are often divided by adherence to this rule".[11] Applying this to John 9, Martyn produces the following division:[12]

vv.   1-7 :   Jesus, his disciples and the blind man
vv.   8-12:   The blind man and his neighbours
vv. 13-17:   The blind man and the Pharisees
vv. 18-23:   The Pharisees and the blind man's parents
vv. 24-34:   The Pharisees and the blind man

---

[6] F. Tillmann, *Das Johannesevangelium übersetzt und erklärt*, (Berlin, Hermann Walther, 1914) pp. 127-128. 149-150.

[7] J. Wellhausen, *op. cit.*, pp. 46-47; J. C. Fenton, *John*, pp. 104-105; J. Jeremias, *Johannes*, p. 199.

[8] See C. H. Dodd, *Tradition*, pp. 181-188. See the very useful chart on p. 182; R. Fortna, *The Gospel of Signs*, pp. 70-74; R. E. Brown, *John*, pp. 378-379; J. L. Martyn, *History and Theology*, pp. 3-5.

[9] C. H. Dodd, *Interpretation*, p. 355.

[10] This division is followed, with slight variations, by C. H. Dodd, *Interpretation*, pp. 354-362; C. K. Barrett, *St. John*, pp. 292-304; J.H. Bernard, *St. John*, pp. 323-341; E. C. Hoskyns, *Fourth Gospel*, pp. 350-360; W. Bauer, *Johannesevangelium*, pp. 133-138; B. F. Westcott, *St. John*, p. 143; J. Blank, *Krisis*, p. 252; M.-J. Lagrange, *St. Jean*, p. 258.

[11] J. L. Martyn, *History and Theology*, p. 6. See also S. Schulz, *Johannes*, p. 144.

[12] J. L. Martyn, *op. cit.*, p. 6.

vv. 35-38:   Jesus and the blind man
vv. 39-41:   Jesus and the Pharisees.

This division puts the stress where it is needed: in the encounter which both the blind man and the Pharisees have with Jesus. Throughout, Jesus and the reactions of others to him are the centre of interest. It is important to notice, in this division, the subtle movement from Jesus to the blind man to the Pharisees, back to the blind man and finally to Jesus again. Then there is a final confrontation, up till now avoided, between Jesus and the Pharisees.[13] Because of the unity of purpose which the author displays throughout the whole of the chapter, most scholars would agree with Lagrange: "Le morceau a une unité parfaite".[14]

Before any analysis of the meaning of John 9, one must decide on the role of the chapter within the wider context of Jn. 8-10. Is this encounter with the light a conclusion to the bitter polemic of ch. 8, where Jesus was questioned because of his claim to be the light of the world (8,12-13),[15] or is it a preparation for ch. 10, in which the Pharisees, who should have been the shepherds of Israel, are condemned as thieves and robbers who have come to destroy (see 10, 7-10 and Ezek. 34)?[16] Some see 9,39-41 as distinct from the rest of the chapter, as the two verses serve to introduce ch. 10.[17]

While the passage from 8,59 to 9,1 is certainly difficult, there are too many continuing themes to see this chapter as totally unrelated to what has preceded it. As historical links are not of major importance to John, in his assembling of the material, too much should not be made of these difficulties.

---

[13] Recent commentators have tended to follow the more detailed division. Although not identical in every detail, the following divide the chapter into scenes, depending on the people involved: R. E. Brown, *John*, p. 204; B. Lindars, *John*, pp. 341-352; B. Noack, *Zur johanneischen Tradition*, p. 115; R. Schnackenburg, *Johannesevangelium* II, p. 303; H. Strathmann, *Johannes*, pp. 156-157; A. Wikenhauser, *Johannes*, pp. 151-157; G. Bornkamm, "Die Heilung des Blindgeborenen, Johannes 9", in *Geschichte und Glaube II*, Beiträge zur EvTh 53 (München, Kaiser, 1971) pp. 65-72. Among the older commentators, see E. Hirsch, *Studien zum vierten Evangelium*, p. 81; W. Temple, *Readings*, p. 153; J. Wellhausen, *Johannis*, pp. 45-47; J. M. Thomson, "An Experiment in Translation", pp. 119-123.

[14] M.-J. Lagrange, *St. Jean*, p. 257.

[15] See C. K. Barrett, *St. John*, p. 293; F.-M. Braun, "St. Jean", p. 389; E. C. Hoskyns, *Fourth Gospel*, p. 352; M.-J. Lagrange, *St. Jean*, pp. 256-257; R. H. Lightfoot, *St. John*, p. 199.

[16] See R. E. Brown, *John*, pp. 203. 388-390; C. H. Dodd, *Interpretation*, pp. 345-362; J. H. Bernard, *St. John*, pp. 323. 341. In Bernard's reconstruction, ch. 9 is followed by 10, 19-22 (see p. xxiv); B. Lindars, *John*, pp. 337-339; W. Temple, *Readings*, p. 153; B. Vawter, "John", p. 443; B. F. Westcott, *St. John*, p. 143.

[17] See R. Bultmann, *John*, p. 339. For Bultmann, vv. 39-41 are the addition of the Evangelist. They are added to bring out the symbolic meaning of what has gone before and to introduce the discourse which follows. See also G. H. C. Macgregor, *John*, p. 2; H. Strathmann, *Johannes*, p. 163.

They are, of course, clear evidence that the Gospel is the product of earlier traditions, but that is not our present concern. The whole of ch. 8 considered the identity of Jesus as a consequence of his having claimed to be the light of the world (8,12; see vv. 19, 25, 27, 33, 48, 53, 58). This theme is continued into ch. 9, where Jesus again claims to be the light of the world (9,5) and gives a man sight, as a symbolic proof of the fact. Once again the question of Jesus' identity arises (see 9,10-12, 16, 17, 24, 29, 33, 35-37). Throughout chapters 8-9 the Jews or Pharisees have asked questions about Jesus' identity, but have failed to see the truth because they do not wish to see it (see 9,39-41). The condemnation of the Jewish leaders which follows in ch. 10, alongside the proclamation of Jesus as the Good Shepherd (10,11), is not something new and unprepared for, but is very closely linked with what has gone before in Jesus' encounter with these leaders in both chapters 8 and 9. Attempts to separate ch. 9 from either ch. 8 or ch. 10 lose sight of this fact.[18] Jn. 9,39-41 are indeed an introduction to ch. 10, but they are also a conclusion to ch. 9. The theme of blindness in these verses cannot be separated from what has gone before.[19] This chapter is the mid-point in the development of the Gospel from chapters 7 to 11. Ch. 7 is also concerned with the identity of Jesus (see 7,12. 15-18. 27-29. 35-36. 40-44), while ch. 11 again proclaims Jesus as the light of the world (11,9-10). Naturally, there are new themes, and older themes are further developed within this complex, but the 'self-contained allusiveness' of the Gospel is lost by attempts to seal off one section from another.[20]

In the miracle and its ensuing discussion in ch. 9, Jesus is presented as the light of the world who can be accepted (the man born blind) or refused (the Pharisees). This is the judgment which he came to bring (9,39) as the Son of Man (v. 35), an object of faith who speaks and who can be seen (v. 37).

The miracle story is introduced by a dialogue which sets the theme for the whole chapter.[21] After seeing the man who has been blind ἐκ γενετῆς,[22] the disciples ask who is responsible for this ailment. Their question reflects Jewish belief that a child born with an ailment suffered either because of the sins of his parents or because of a sin which he himself committed while still

---

[18] See R. Schnackenburg, *Johannesevangelium* II, pp. 302-303; R. H. Lightfoot, *St. John*, p. 201; H. van den Bussche, *Jean*, p. 322.

[19] See J. Blank, *Krisis*, pp. 252-253.

[20] See S. Sabugal, *'Christos'. Investigación exegética sobre la cristología joannea*, (Barcelona, Herder, 1972) pp. 235-255 for a detailed analysis of the structure and unity of 7,1 to 11,54. See also D. Mollat, "La guérison de l'aveugle-né", *BibVChr* 23 (1958) 22-23.

[21] See J. Blank, *Krisis*, pp. 252-254.

[22] This is the only occurrence of this construction in the New Testament, and it is clearly theological. The miracle which is to follow is not the restoration of something which has been lost, but a new creation. See C. K. Barrett, *St. John*, p. 243; E. C. Hoskyns, *Fourth Gospel*, p. 352; B. Lindars, *John*, p. 341; A. Schlatter, *Johannes*, p. 222.

in the womb.[23] As happens so often in the Fourth Gospel, Jesus' reply cuts across the question, saying that the situation exists ἵνα φανερωθῇ τὰ ἔργα τοῦ θεοῦ ἐν αὐτῷ (v. 3). This is an important remark; God is to reveal his works in what follows:

> "Ce n'est point en punition de ses péchés personels que l'homme est aveugle, ni par la faute de ses ancêtres immédiats; il est tel par une sorte de nécessité providentielle, pour fournir matière à la révélation de Dieu".[24]

This is made clearer in vv. 4-5. The task entrusted to Jesus and which he in turn entrusts to his followers, is to work the works of the one who sent him. Jesus, for John, is the fulness of the revelation of God among men. However, his being the light of the world is conditioned by the arrival of "the night" and by his presence in the world. This is often taken to mean that vv. 4-5 refer to the historical Jesus. This was the interpretation of the early scribes who in v. 4 wrote "I must work the works of him who sent me".[25] The better manuscript tradition, however, shows that the disciples were involved in the task: "We must work the works of him who sent me".[26] The presence of the light in the world, doing the works of the Father, will not be limited to his historical life, but will continue into his presence in the church:[27]

> "The work of Jesus appears not to be terminated in the time of his earthly life. On the contrary, his going to the Father inaugurates a time in which

[23] See Exod. 20,5; 34,7; Num. 14,18; Deut. 5,9; Jer. 31,29-30; Ezek. 18,2; Tob. 3,4; Lk. 13,2. For the possibility of pre-natal sin, see Strack-Billerbeck, *Kommentar*, II, pp. 527-529. W. Bauer, *Johannesevangelium*, p. 133 has some interesting Gnostic and Hellenistic parallels. See also R. Bultmann, *John*, p. 330, note 8; A. Schlatter, *Johannes*. pp. 222-223.
[24] A. Loisy, *Quatrième Évangile*, (1903) p. 588. See also E. Lohse, "Miracles in the Fourth Gospel", pp. 69-70.
[25] ἐμὲ δεῖ is the reading of the majority of the Mss: corrected version of Sinaiticus, Alexandrinus, Ephraim rescript, Koridethi, K, X, majority of the minuscules, Vulgate, Syriac, Tatian, Chrysostom.
[26] ἡμᾶς δεῖ is found in P⁶⁶, P⁷⁵, the first hand of Sinaiticus, Vaticanus, L, Freer Gospels, Palestinian Syriac, Bohairic Coptic, Ethiopic, Georgian, Origen, Jerome, Nonnus and Cyril. This latter reading appears to be preferable (a) because of its somewhat superior external support, and (b) because it is more probable that copyists would have altered ἡμᾶς to ἐμὲ than vice-versa. See B. Metzger, *A Textual Commentary on the Greek New Testament*, p. 227. The reading ἐμὲ δεῖ is preferred by D. Mollat, "St. Jean", p. 112; H. van den Bussche, *Jean*, p. 323. A. Wikenhauser, *Johannes*, p. 152 sees this reading as "sachlich richtiger" even though "we" is better attested.
[27] Against H. Strathmann, *Johannes*, p. 157, who sees vv. 4-5a as a promise of the passion. For J. L. Martyn, *History and Theology*, pp. 7-10, this presence in the Johannine Church is so real that John can speak of Jesus' being doubled with an early Christian preacher. See also R. Schnackenburg, *Johannesevangelium* II, pp. 306-307; C. K. Barrett, *St. John*, pp. 295-296; J. H. Bernard, *St. John*, p. 327; E. C. Hoskyns, *Fourth Gospel*. pp. 353-354.

his followers do his works. Indeed 9,4a leads us to see this continuation of Jesus' works as an activity of the Risen Lord in the deeds of Christian witnesses".[28]

The day and night referred to in v. 4 must be understood in their relationship to Jesus as the light. In Jesus alone does the world have its day, in which men may walk safely (see 12,35). In his absence comes the darkness of the night.[29] "As long as I am in the world" means, for John, as long as the revelation brought by Jesus is proclaimed, then the true light of the world will be present among men.

In vv. 1-5 John has given the theological introduction to the sign.[30] What follows shows what all this means in practice:[31]

"Le miracle de l'aveugle n'est pas fait pour démontrer que Jésus est la lumière du monde, mais pour représenter dans un fait matériel, sous une forme plus sensible encore, la vérité signifiée par cette métaphore".[32]

The miracle story itself is told very briefly (vv. 6-7) as John's major interest lies in the ensuing interrogations, during which the man born blind shows a steady growth in his understanding and knowledge of Jesus.[33] Questioned by his neighbours (vv. 8-12) he can only say that his benefactor was "the man called Jesus" (v. 11). His first encounter with the Pharisees (vv. 13-17) leads to a confession that Jesus is "a prophet" (v. 17).[34] After his parents have rid themselves of all responsibility (vv. 18-23) he is again questioned by the Pharisees (vv. 24-34) and this time he makes a most important Johannine confession: Jesus is "from God" (v. 33).[35] He is now well on the way to a

---

[28] J. L. Martyn, *History and Theology*, p. 8.
[29] See C. K. Barrett, *St. John*, p. 296.
[30] J. Bligh, "Four Studies in John I: The Man Born Blind", *HeyJ* (1966) 132-133 argues that vv. 4-5 were an independent logion, originally chiastic, which John has inserted for theological motives. Despite their clumsiness in the context, they are essential for a correct understanding of John's message.
[31] For what follows, see R. E. Brown, *John*, p. 377.
[32] A. Loisy, *Quatrième Évangile* (1903) p. 590. See also the 1921 edition, pp. 309-310.
[33] See D. Mollat, "La guérison de l'aveugle-né", pp. 27-30; M. Baron, "La progression des confessions de foi dans les dialogues de S. Jean", pp. 37-39; C. K. Barrett, *St. John*, p. 297; J. Blank, *Krisis*, p. 257; R. E. Brown, *John*, p. 377; E. C. Hoskyns, *Fourth Gospel*, pp. 355-356; R. H. Lightfoot, *St. John*, p. 199; A. Loisy, *Quatrième Évangile*, (1903) p. 592; B. F. Westcott, *St. John*, p. 146; J. Marsh, *St. John*, pp. 380-381. J. L. Martyn, *History and Theology*, p. 12, note 30, does not see this as a progression in the identification of Jesus, but prefers to link it with the historical situation of the Johannine Church in its conflict with the Synagogue. It is "rather a progression from identification to confrontation". See also, pp. 119. 141-142.
[34] Against A. Richardson, *John*, p. 126; F. Hahn, *Christologische Hoheitstitel*, p. 397, we do not see this title as messianic here. It is given to an unusual and holy man. See C. K. Barrett, *St. John*, p. 298; W. Bauer, *Johannesevangelium*, p. 135; B. Lindars, *John*, p. 346; G. Reim, *Studien zum alttestamentlichen Hintergrund*, p. 124.
[35] See especially, J. Blank, *Krisis*, p. 257.

proper understanding of Jesus. At this point, Jesus re-enters the action which he has continued to dominate even in his absence,[36] and in this encounter with the person of Jesus, the man born blind sees and confesses belief in him as "the Son of Man" (vv. 35-37).

While the interrogation of the man born blind has led to his progressive growth in the knowledge and understanding of Jesus, the Pharisees or "the Jews" go further and further away from the light. In the first interrogation they accept the fact of the miracle (v. 15) and while some object to the making of clay on the Sabbath, others seem open to a more positive evaluation of Jesus (v. 16). In the second interrogation the latter group seems to have disappeared. Now they doubt the very fact of the miracle. They call upon the man's parents in an attempt to prove that he was never blind (vv. 18-23). When this fails they return to the man himself, and they show little interest in finding out the truth about Jesus. They try to trap him by asking him to repeat again the details of the miracle (v. 27). Their final refusal of Jesus is found in v. 29, where they refuse to acknowledge his heavenly origin, and because of this will never be able to come to a proper understanding of Jesus. In the end they are reduced to heaping abuse upon the man who has persisted in telling the truth and giving witness to the light in their presence (v. 34).

As the man born blind's coming to the light has led to a confession of faith in Jesus as the Son of Man, so the Pharisees' growth in hardness of heart is also terminated by an encounter with Jesus, and a condemnation.[37] Jesus has come for a special kind of judgment: those who do not see will now be able to see. This is clearly a reference to the man born blind, who has thrice admitted that he did not know what was asked of him (vv. 12, 25, 36). Because he was open to the possibility of further knowledge, he was open to the light, and he finally comes to see that light in the Son of Man. Those who see will become blind: a judgment on the Pharisees, who arrogantly asserted on three occasions that they had no need of Jesus because they knew all that was to be known (vv. 24, 29, 31. See also v. 16).[38] What they know is that God has spoken to Moses and with this they are content. In their self-sufficiency they refuse the Word of God himself, not acknowledging his heavenly origin. They are content with an inferior mediator — Moses

---

[36] See J. Blank, *Krisis*, p. 255; C. H. Dodd, *Interpretation*, p. 357: "The defendant proper is Jesus Himself, judged *in absentia*".

[37] Again one should notice how carefully this passage has been constructed. Jesus meets and cures the blind man. This sets off a reaction in which the various actors take their stance vis-à-vis Jesus, even though he is not present. At the conclusion of this, Jesus returns to the scene and issues a final statement on each reaction: acceptance of the man born blind's confession, and condemnation for the Pharisees.

[38] John has brought out this contrast by having the man born blind admit οὐκ οἶδα (vv. 25, 36), while the Pharisees insist οἴδαμεν (vv. 24, 29, 31). See C. K. Barrett, *St. John*, p. 304.

(v. 29). For this reason, their sin remains (v. 41). What Jesus says here is a repetition of what he has said earlier: "I told you that you would die in your sins, for you will die in your sins unless you believe that I am he" (8,24, see 8,28). This is precisely what they refuse to believe. What has been promised in 8,12: "I am the light of the world; he who follows me will not walk in darkness, but will have the light of life", has been acted out in the experience of the man born blind, while what was threatened in 8,24 has also been acted out in the experience of the Pharisees.[39]

II - The Son of Man in John 9,35

Many manuscripts read "the Son of God" in place of "the Son of Man" in 9,35. It is almost universally accepted, however, that "the Son of Man" is the correct reading. In view of the external evidence of P[66], P[75], Sinaiticus, Vaticanus, Bezae, Freer Gospels, Sinaitic Syriac, and Bohairic Coptic versions, added to the extreme improbability of θεοῦ being altered to ἀνθρώπου in the context of a confession,[40] the reading "Do you believe in the Son of Man?" can be regarded as virtually certain.[41]

Precisely because the man born blind is asked to confess his faith in the Son of Man, commentators have varied greatly in their understanding of the title in this context. The interrogation of the man has led to his expulsion from the Synagogue,[42] but he has not yet come to understand fully what has happened to him, or why it has happened (see v. 36).

---

[39] See M.-J. Lagrange, *St. Jean*, p. 271: "Le péché sur ce point ne commence que lorsqu'on prétend n'avoir besoin de lumière ... c'est ainsi que le péché d'aveuglement volontaire a pénétré en eux et qu'il demeure, parce qu'il détruit la racine même du salut, le désir d'être instruit et corrigé, de recevoir la lumière et d'en user". See also R. Schnackenburg, *Johannesevangelium* II, p. 321.

[40] This is the only passage in the New Testament where someone is asked to "believe in" the Son of Man. Despite the textual evidence, which he does not consider, J. Bligh, "The Man Born Blind...", pp. 141-142, decides that "the reading 'Son of God' seems preferable, for the man born blind is the only person in St. John's narrative who adores Christ during the public ministry".

[41] See B. Metzger, *A Textual Commentary on the Greek New Testament*, pp. 228-229.

[42] Despite the claims of J. H. Bernard, *St. John*, pp. 343. 347 and W. F. Howard, "St. John", p. 617, who tend to minimise the seriousness of the expulsion, and F.-M. Braun, "St. Jean", p. 392; M.-J. Lagrange, *St. Jean*, p. 266; L. Morris, *John*, pp. 488-489; J. N. Sanders, *St. John*, p. 242 and J. Bligh, *art. cit.*, p. 139, who claim that this expulsion could well have taken place during the life of Jesus, it appears that J. L. Martyn, *History and Theology*, pp. 17-40, has shown that the expulsion is evidence for the rift between the Johannine Church and the Synagogue. As B. Lindars, *John*, p. 347 has said: "John speaks of the cost of discipleship in terms of the conditions with which his readers were familiar". Martyn overstates his case in trying to identify this breach with the *Birkat*

At the beginning of the chapter (v. 5) the theme of the light was taken up (see 8,12) and further explained. In the miracle and the discussion which followed it has continued to shine and to cause division.[43] The man born blind initiated his life of "seeing" by a decision for the light, but he has not yet fully understood what has happened. Jesus, therefore, takes the initiative, as he must (see 1,18; 3,13; 6,44.65; 14,6; 15,5),[44] and seeks out the man. John has deliberately made it clear that Jesus has sought out the man to present himself to him as the Son of Man (see esp. 5,14. See also 1,43.45; 7,34-36)[45] as a decisive final test of the faith of the now "seeing" man born blind. It is clear that the confession is vital to a correct understanding of the whole chapter, as it forms the climax of the man born blind's gradual progress to true faith.

In this context one would normally expect a confession of belief in Jesus as "Lord" (see I Cor. 12,3; Rom. 10,9; Phil. 2,11) or "Son of God" (see Acts 8,37), and this has probably caused the variant reading. Some scholars play down the difference between "the Son of Man" and "the Son of God", claiming that it makes little difference which title is used, as they both point to the divine sonship of Jesus.[46] This is hardly a satisfactory solution, as it leaves one still wondering, if "the difference is not in this context very important",[47] why "the Son of Man" is used at all. If John really meant to say "the Son of God", then why did he not say it? B. Lindars has suggested that "John is probably saving up 'Son of God' for the climax in 10,36".[48] John uses his titles carefully, and this suggestion may be valid, but the choice

---

ham-Minim of Javneh, which he tries to date more precisely than is possible. However, his main point remains valid. For further comments and criticism, see R. Schnackenburg, "Zur Herkunft des Johannesevangeliums", *BZ* 14 (1970) 7-10; B. Vawter, "Some recent developments in Johannine Theology", *BTB* 1 (1971) 33-40; G. Stemberger, *La symbolique du bien et du mal*, p. 106, note 3. For an exhaustive bibliography of this discussion, see S. Sabugal, *'Christos'*, pp. 310-313. See the earlier suggestions along the line followed by Martyn, from E. C. Hoskyns, *Fourth Gospel*, pp. 360-363; K. L. Carroll, "The Fourth Gospel and the Expulsion of Christians from the Synagogues", *BJRL* 40 (1957) 19-32.

[43] See above, pp. 127-128.

[44] See R. Schnackenburg, *Johannesevangelium* II, p. 320.

[45] Against W. Bauer, *Johannesevangelium*, p. 137 and A. Loisy, *Quatrième Évangile*, p. 317, who see the meeting as fortuitous. See, instead, E. C. Hoskyns, *Fourth Gospel*, p. 359; R. Schnackenburg, *Johannesevangelium* II, p. 320.

[46] See F.-M. Braun, "St. Jean", p. 394; E. D. Freed, "The Son of Man ...", p. 406; A. Richardson, *St. John*, p. 128. See also J. Marsh, *St. John*, pp. 388-389.

[47] A. Richardson, *St. John*, p. 128.

[48] B. Lindars, *John*, p. 350. While 9,35 is clearly a climax, it could be asked whether 10,36 is such. In many ways it is only "reported speech" (although where it is reported from remains a mystery. Jesus has not called himself "Son of God" in the immediate context). The climax of the passage really comes in 10,37-38. See also B. Lindars, "The Son of Man ...", p. 55.

of "the Son of Man" here, in order to save the main christological title for the climax still has to be explained.[49]

Others avoid the difficulty of this strange title in a confessional context by claiming that, to the man born blind and the Johannine community, the Son of Man was the Christ.[50] J. Jeremias, who makes little of the title in this context, sees it as a reflection of the practice of the Johannine community: a convert had to confess his belief in the name of Christ before he could be accepted into the community. Once again the question must be asked — if John meant to have the man confess his faith in Jesus as the Christ, then why did he not use the title?

As this title is so often found in eschatological contexts in the Synoptic tradition, some see 9,35 as a typical johannisation of a traditional title. The man born blind is asked to believe that in the person of Jesus eschatological hopes have been made present.[51] Bultmann's existential interpretation of the "present eschatological moment" merits particular consideration. The difficulty of the man born blind has arisen because "He does not know that, if he wants to see Jesus as he really is, he must leave the old sphere completely behind him".[52] Any good man could have come to the confessions of vv. 17 and 33. Jesus' question demands that he go beyond this to see in the Son of Man the Word of God. He does so and "this is why the healed man can confess 'Lord I believe!' and worship the Revealer".[53] While openness to revelation is certainly involved in 9,35 Bultmann has typically avoided any relation of the revelation to the figure of the Son of Man, Jesus. This would be to give relevance to the 'Christ according to the flesh', which Bultmann will not admit.[54] The demands being made on the man are that he commit himself totally to the risk of the Word, without the help of the human figure who reveals that Word.[55] It is in the decision which is made here and now that the eschatological moment takes place. According to Bultmann, this is how John has rendered present the traditional future eschatology.[56]

---

[49] W. Bauer, *Johannesevangelium*, p. 137 does not think so: "Auf welche Weise er ihn erkannt hat, sollte man bei Jo gar nicht fragen". Others point to the difficulty, but do not seek to resolve it. See S. S. Smalley, "The Johannine Son of Man Sayings", pp. 296-297.

[50] See E. C. Hoskyns, *Fourth Gospel*, p. 359; A. Loisy, *Quatrième Évangile*, p. 317; J. Jeremias, *Johannes*, p. 207; L. Morris, *John*, p. 494: "Whichever text we adopt, faith in Christ is meant".

[51] See R. Bultmann, *John*, p. 338; R. G. Hamerton-Kelly, *Pre-Existence*, p. 241; W. F. Howard, "St. John", p. 619; H. Strathmann, *Johannes*, p. 160; A. Wikenhauser, *Johannes*, p. 156, C. Colpe, *TDNT* VIII, p. 465.

[52] R. Bultmann, *John*, p. 338.

[53] *ibid.*, p. 339.

[54] See R. Bultmann, *Glauben und Verstehen* I, (Tübingen, J. C. B. Mohr, 1954) p. 101.

[55] R. Bultmann, *John*, p. 339.

[56] Not all the scholars mentioned in note 51 would agree with Bultmann's interpretation.

It is true that John has used a traditional title, rendering present what was once future.[57] However, in the light of vv. 39-41, the aspect of the 'end time' which John has rendered present still appears to be judgment. Jesus has presented himself as the light (v. 5) and this has been accepted in full by the man born blind (vv. 35-38) but refused by the Pharisees (vv. 24-34). Out of this situation flows the judgment which Jesus has come to bring (v. 39). Bultmann's suggestions read modern existentialism into a first century situation.[58]

C. K. Barrett admits that the question of Johannine realised eschatology is present, but sees the main point being made by the choice of a title which, throughout the Fourth Gospel, refers to the archetypal man.[59] For John, the Son of Man is the heavenly man — "the sole means of union between heaven and earth".[60] The man born blind knows this and asks that this Son of Man be indicated to him. In his profession of faith "the sign and interpretation are now both complete: the blind man has received physical sight, and has also, through Jesus the light of the world, seen the truth and believed in Jesus as the Son of man".[61]

Recent scholarship has questioned the influence of heavenly man speculation upon the Son of Man figure in the New Testament.[62] Within the context of Jn. 9, Barrett's theory of seeing God in Jesus, the primal man,[63] only goes half way to explain why "the Son of Man" was used. Barrett has mentioned that light and judgment are involved. These concepts are, in fact, far more important to our understanding of the use of the title than possible speculation about the heavenly man. Jesus, the Son of Man, is a heavenly man in so far as he has come down from heaven (see 3,13; 6,62), but John does not wish to affirm this merely as a fact. His having come down from heaven gives him a unique authority as the light, the revealer of the Father who sent him (see 3,13-14; 6,27; 8,28), and consequently as the place where men will judge themselves as they accept or refuse this revelation (see 3,13-21; 5,26-29; 8,21-30; 9,35-41; 12,27-36).

---

[57] It must be noted that there are Synoptic sayings which call for a decision 'here and now' (see Mk. 1,15; Matt. 11,6; Lk. 12,16-20; 12,54-56; Mk. 8,38; Matt. 25, 31-46).

[58] To do this, he has resorted to his rearrangements and sources. See W. A. Meeks, *The Prophet-King*, pp. 1-17.

[59] C. K. Barrett, *St. John*, pp. 302-303. See also J. Marsh, *St. John*, pp. 387-388.

[60] C. K. Barrett, *St. John*, p. 302.

[61] *ibid.*, p. 303.

[62] See especially C. Colpe, *TDNT* VIII, pp. 410-415; Idem, *Die Religionsgeschichtliche Schule*; H.-M. Schenke, *Der Gott "Mensch" in der Gnosis*. Both of these studies are a detailed criticism of the use of the gnostic "Man" for the idea of "redeemed redeemer". The material which they survey, however, shows that the concept of a "heavenly man", both Gnostic and Jewish, is not the background for the Johannine Son of Man. See on this, C. Colpe, *TDNT* VIII, p. 415; E. Ruckstuhl, "Die johanneische Menschensohnforschung", pp. 182-183.

[63] C. K. Barrett, *St. John*, p. 302.

Although the title is not found in New Testament confessions J. H. Bernard and W. Bousset have argued that the question posed by Jesus is the "criterion of Christian discipleship" which was put to the man born blind.[64] Bernard claims that at the time of Jesus "Son of Man" was not a messianic title, but it referred to the role of Jesus as the deliverer of humanity at large.[65]

A. J. B. Higgins, against H. Conzelmann, argues that the saying is evidence for "the Son of Man" as a *Bekenntnis-Titel*.[66] He admits that 9,35 stands alone among all the Johannine sayings, but claims that it shows the title as "the evangelist's fundamental and principal Christology".[67] F. H. Borsch, after showing that the title was in no way confessional in the early Church,[68] also suspects that the Son of Man was once crucial to much of the tradition, and that the Church's faith in Jesus as the Christ has hidden this from us.[69] These suspicions may be well-founded, but they can never be more than suspicions, because of the lack of evidence. However, restricting ourselves to the Johannine community, we may find that a confession of faith in Jesus as the Son of Man, as they understood the title, is perfectly coherent, despite the fact that this type of confession is not found in the rest of the New Testament.

Other scholars see John's use of "the Son of Man" here as his way of indicating the humanity of Jesus. In this man God is communicated to all men;[70] the Son of Man is the Son of God among men.[71] For Westcott, Jesus the man is a new object of faith. In him we have the foundation of a new human society which is distinct from the society of Judaism, represented by the Pharisees who have rejected the light.[72]

Finally, there is a group of scholars who see the title in this context as closely linked with the theme of judgment, which follows in vv. 39-41.[73]

---

[64] J. H. Bernard, *St. John*, p. 338; W. Bousset, *Kyrios Christos*, p. 213: "The faith of the Christian community is summarised in contrast to the Synagogue".

[65] J. H. Bernard, *St. John*, pp. cxxx- cxxxi.

[66] A. J. B. Higgins, *Son of Man*, p. 155. See H. Conzelmann, Art. "Jesus Christus", *RGG* III, (Tübingen, J. C. B. Mohr, 1959) col. 631.

[67] A. J. B. Higgins, *op. cit.*, p. 155. See also O. Cullmann, *Christology*, p. 186.

[68] F. H. Borsch, *Son of Man*, p. 304.

[69] *ibid.*, p. 305. See also S. S. Smalley, "The Johannine Son of Man Sayings", p. 295.

[70] W. H. Cadman, *The Open Heaven*, p. 35; B. Lindars, *John*, p. 350: "Thus the reading Son of man here places the confession of faith in the larger frame of the special Johannine theology of the manifestation of the divine glory in the incarnate life of Jesus". See also his "The Son of Man ...", pp. 55-56.

[71] M.-J. Lagrange, *St. Jean*, p. 269. See also A. Schlatter, *Johannes*, p. 231; W. Temple, *Readings*, p. 160.

[72] B. F. Westcott, *St. John*, pp. 149-151.

[73] R. E. Brown, *John*, p. 375. Brown also sees a link between Jn. 9,35, Lk. 18,8 and Matt. 8,30 where "the Son of Man" is used in a context of faith and discipleship; R. H. Lightfoot, *St. John*, p. 203; J. N. Sanders, *St. John*, p. 244; H. van den Bussche, *Jean*, p. 326.

Taking the title from tradition, John has used it here to show that judgment is now taking place in the Son of Man, already present as judge. In seeing the link with the traditional Son of Man, these scholars are closer to the context in their understanding of John's realised eschatology than was Bultmann in his existential interpretation, but they have not seen the Johannine idea of revelation which leads to judgment, which is also involved in the use of the title here, as elsewhere in the Gospel.

A great deal of the complexity of 9,35 can be resolved by studying the saying within the wider context of the whole of ch. 9, and by relating it to other Johannine Son of Man sayings. Vv. 1-5 are essential to a correct understanding of the chapter as a whole, as here John tells us that the encounter which Jesus has with the man born blind and the Pharisees is "that the works of God might be made manifest in him" (v. 3). Jesus presents himself as the light of the world (v. 5) and thus sets the tone for the whole episode.[74]

When one turns to vv. 35-41, one finds what could well be seen as a theological spelling out of the consequences of the encounter which Jesus has had with those who do not see (see vv. 12, 25, 26), but are willing to receive sight, and those who, in the arrogance of their "seeing" and knowing (see vv. 16, 24, 29, 31) are not willing to stand in the new light which Jesus brings.[75]

The contrast with the Pharisees is immediately indicated by the fact that Jesus "seeks out" the one whom the Pharisees have "cast out" (v. 35a).[76] The question which Jesus poses is indeed a demand for a profession of faith. The solemn πιστεύειν εἰς calls for a total commitment, in faith, to the Son of Man. What is meant by "the Son of Man" must be found in the answer which Jesus gave to the very question that we are asking. The man born blind also asked: "Who is he?" (v. 36). There are two elements in the answer which Jesus gave: sight and hearing. Jesus presents himself before the man as one to be seen and heard.

The verb ὁράω is used almost invariably in contexts of revelation. It is impossible for "the world" to *see* God or to come to the knowledge of God (1,18; 5,37), but Jesus reveals what he has *seen* (1,34; 3,11; 3,22; 8,38). He *speaks* what he has *seen with his Father* (8,38; 6,46; 14,7; 14,9). Those

[74] See C. H. Dodd, *Interpretation*, p. 358: "It appears then that the dominant theme of this episode is not the coming of light as such, but its effect in judgment. The fact that the coming of Christ brings light into the world is stated symbolically with the utmost brevity, and the weight is laid upon the elaborate dialogue which dramatically exhibits judgment in action".
[75] See C. K. Barrett, *St. John*, p. 302. Barrett suggests that Is. 6 is behind this. See also p. 303 where Barrett comments on v. 39: "The narrative being now completed Jesus sums up its meaning". See also J. H. Bernard, *St. John*, p. 339.
[76] See R. Schnackenburg, *Johannesevangelium* II, p. 320.

who believe in Jesus, will *see* (1,50-51; 11,47; 16,16-22), while those who *refuse to see* are condemned (3,36; 5,37-38; 6,36; 15,24). The supreme revelation of God will take place when they "look upon" the elevated Son of Man (3,13-15; 19,35-37). Jn. 9,37 the first positive act of the man who has just been given his sight is to *see* Jesus, the Son of Man. The solemnity of Jesus' reply and the general Johannine idea of "seeing" indicate that here we are dealing with the man's encounter with the revelation of the truth. As yet no decision has been made but, in truly Johannine fashion, the man who has regained his sight is confronted with the Son of Man, whom he *sees*. A decision must be made, and it is, in v. 38.

Similarly, when Jesus speaks he reveals his Father. The use of the verb λαλέω in the mouth of Jesus carries with it the assurance of being the revelation of God.[77] The discourses often begin or end with λαλέω (see 8,12.20; 10,6; 12,36; 17,1). Jesus *speaks* of what he knows from the Father (3,11.34; 8,25-26.38; 12,49-50; 14,10; 16,25) and he *speaks* with a unique authority (7,17. 18. 26. 46; 18,20). This word gives life, peace and joy (6,63; 15,3. 11; 16,33; 17,13). Yet, the word judges (12,48) and will condemn those who refuse to listen (8,40; 12,48; 15,22). Because of all this, Jesus can say to the Samaritan woman that the one who reveals the Father in a unique way, the ἐγώ εἰμι, *speaks* to her (see 4,26; and Is. 52,6).[78]

Jesus' identification of himself, in v. 37, as the Son of Man who is seen and who is heard must mean that in Jesus, the Son of Man, the man born blind can see and hear the revelation of God among men.[79] Jesus asks him to put all his faith in this revelation of God which he has come to bring. The other Johannine Son of Man sayings (1,51; 3,13-14; 5,27; 6,27.53.62; 8,28) have shown that John understood and used the title to refer to Jesus as the revealer and as revelation itself. Now the Gospel has reached the stage where John can use the title in a formula which could well be a confession of faith.[80]

---

[77] On both "seeing" and "speaking" as Johannine expressions for revelation, see R. Schnackenburg, "Offenbarung und Glaube im Johannesevangelium", *BuL* 7 (1966) 172-175; J. Gnilka, "Zur Theologie des Hörens nach den Aussagen des Neuen Testaments", *BuL* 2 (1961) 77-79; G. Segalla, "L'esperienza cristiana in Giovanni", *StPat* 18 (1971) 300-309; I. de la Potterie, "La notion de témoignage dans Saint Jean", pp. 193-208.

[78] See J. T. Forestell, *The Word of the Cross*, p. 27.

[79] R. Schnackenburg, *Johannesevangelium* II, p. 321 sees this scene as "einer dialogischen Begegnung von Glaubenden mit dem Offenbarer". S. Schulz, who did not examine 9,35 in his study of the Johannine Son of Man sayings, points out in his commentary (*Johannes*, p. 146) that John places this title in the context of his "Revealer-Christology": "Jesu Antwort ist nichts anderes als die Selbstoffenbarung Gottes".

[80] The reaction of the man born blind (vv. 38-39a) is regarded by some as a later addition to the text. See R. E. Brown, *John*, p. 375; C. L. Porter, "John 9,38,39a: A Liturgical Addition to the Text", *NTS* 13 (1966-67) 387-394; B. Lindars, *John*, p. 351 This is based on some manuscript evidence and on the fact that only here in the Fourth

However, the use of the title is not only to present Jesus as the place of revelation. The revelation brought by and in the Son of Man is a rendering present of the traditionally eschatological moment of judgment,[81] but what is meant by "judgment" in this context is fully Johannine. It is not the judgment that forms part of the Synoptic Son of Man tradition (see Matt. 25,31-46; Lk. 9,26; 12,27-28),[82] where the Son of Man is an active judge. Here we are told that the Son of Man has come into the world "for judgment" (v. 39), but this is not to deny what has been said in 3,17; 5,24; 8,15 and what will be said in 12,47; that Jesus did not come to judge. To say that Jesus has come into the world εἰς κρίμα does not necessarily mean that he has come as a judge, but for "the judicial decision which consists in the separation of those who are willing to believe from those who are unwilling to do so".[83]

This is Jesus' role as the Son of Man. He is the revelation of God among men, the light of the world (v. 5), who manifests God to men (v. 3) because he is seen and heard (v. 37) by people who are prepared to see and hear him (v. 39). In their decision they judge themselves, according to their choice of the light or the darkness.[84] V. 41 tells us that the Pharisees have already judged themselves. In answer to their haughty question of v. 40 [85] Jesus tells them that because of their inability to accept the light of the world, their guilt remains. They have already been threatened with this possibility in 8,21.24. In ch. 9 this threat comes closer to being a reality. In 8,28 the possibility of life or death was offered to the Jews, in the revelation brought by the Son of Man.[86] In ch. 9 they have made a choice against the

---

Gospel is προσκυνεῖν used, and that ἔφη is extremely rare (only at 1,23 and, in some witnesses, at 9,36). We see these verses as entirely in accord with the context, where a positive reaction from the man born blind is demanded. See B. Metzger, *A Textual Commentary*, p. 229; R. Schnackenburg, *Johannesevangelium* II, p. 322, note 5. On the early liturgical use of John 9, see E. C. Hoskyns, *Fourth Gospel*, pp. 363-365; R. Schnackenburg, *op. cit.*, pp. 325-328.

[81] See above, pp. 151 and 153-154.

[82] See J. Blank, *Krisis*, pp. 262-263.

[83] W. Bauer, *A Greek English Lexicon*, p. 452. See also C. K. Barrett, *St. John*, p. 303; R. Bultmann, *John*, pp. 341-342; E. C. Hoskyns, *Fourth Gospel*, p. 360; M.-J. Lagrange, *St. Jean*, pp. 270-271; G. H. C. Macgregor, *John*, pp. 230-231; R. Schnackenburg, *Johannesevangelium* II, p. 323; H. van den Bussche, *Jean*, p. 326; B. F. Westcott, *St. John*, p. 150. This is contrary to the opinion of J. H. Bernard, *St. John*, p. 339, who speaks of an act of distiguishing between good and bad, and so of judging. It must be noticed, also, that in the Synoptic tradition men, in effect, judge themselves by their response to the Son of Man (see esp. Mk. 8,38).

[84] See C. K. Barrett, *St. John*, pp. 303-304; R. Schnackenburg, *Johannesevangelium* II, p. 323; J. Blank, *Krisis*, pp. 262-263.

[85] C. K. Barrett, *St. John*, p. 304. The answer "no" is obviously expected.

[86] See above, chapter 6, pp. 135-141.

Son of Man and the revelation which he has brought.[87]   For this reason, their guilt remains (9,41) and they are well on the way to dying in their sins (8,21.24).[88]

Thus, the Son of Man saying in 9,35 is a confession of faith, but a Johannine confession of faith.   It matters little that this title is not found in other New Testament confessions; it is the Johannine understanding of the title which makes such a confession possible.   Again John has shown how he can take a traditional theme and remodel it for his own theological purpose. John would probably have been aware that the early Church called for a confession of faith from her initiates.   However, the confession of faith which John asks for is to be made in the Son of Man, the revelation of God among men.[89]

As in so many other sayings, we again see a gradual progression in the movement towards the Son of Man title (see vv. 11, 17, 33).   J. L. Martyn argued that this was the way the Johannine community carried on its dialogue with the Synagogue:[90] starting from a discussion about the Mosaic Messiah (v. 29), the initiate was led through a midrashic discussion to a final confession in Jesus as the Son of Man.   While it is demanding too much of the evidence to make such a precise description of this process in the Johannine community, he has certainly shown that there is a gradual movement to faith in almost every instance of John's use of "the Son of Man".[91]

The hint given in 9,29 has led W. A. Meeks to a suggestion concerning the conflict which produced the reference to Moses.   He argues that Jn. 5 and 9 reflect the same situation, and these conflicts provide glimpses of at least one segment of the environment which produced the Johannine traditions.[92] The Johannine community was in conflict with a Jewish community which "put its trust in Moses as the supreme prophet, God's emissary and revealer, and defender in the heavenly court of the true Israelites who trusted him".[93]   There may be some truth in this, but the main point of the discussion is Jesus-

---

[87] R. Bultmann, *John*, p. 341: " 'Blindness' is no longer simply a wandering in the dark, which can always become aware that it is lost, and so have the possibility of receiving sight; for now it has forfeited this possibility".

[88] What is involved here is far more than the moral failure suggested by J. H. Bernard, *St. John*, pp. 340-341 and B. Lindars, *John*, p. 352.

[89] See G. Bornkamm, "Die Heilung des Blindgeborenen..", p. 71: "Das Bekenntnis wird dem Glaubenden nicht als ein absurdum aufgenötigt, es ist vielmehr die Antwort, die schlicht und dankbar das geschehene Wunder der Offenbarung annimmt und vor dem Offenbarer sich beugt".

[90] J. L. Martyn, *History and Theology*, pp. 120-142, esp. 122-125.

[91] See also above, pp. 33-37 (on 1,51); 51-53 (on 3,13-14); 108-109 (on 6,27); 139-140 (on 8,28).

[92] W. A. Meeks, *The Prophet-King*, pp. 38. 293-295.

[93] *ibid.*, p. 295.

centred, not Moses-centred.[94]   The chapter has been concerned with the question of who Jesus is:

a) vv. 1-7 describe a miracle which Jesus performs so that God's works may be displayed.   In vv. 3b-4 Jesus declared that "We must carry out the works of him who sent me as long as it is day".   In v. 5 Jesus calls himself "the light of the world", and in v. 7 the title ἀπεσταλμένος also seems to refer to Jesus.[95]

b) In the gradual progress of the man born blind to full faith we see a reaction to the miracle.   His growth in true faith leads him from a belief in Jesus as "the man called Jesus" (v. 11) to a declaration that "he is a prophet" (v. 17) to the crucial statement concerning Jesus' origins: "If this man were not from God ..." (v. 33).   Having arrived at this point in his confession of Jesus, it is but a short step to accept Jesus' disclosure of himself as the Son of Man in v. 35.

c) The reaction of the Jews fails because it stops short of the mark. Meeks is right when he sees v. 29 as evidence for a discussion concerning a Mosaic prophet.   However, it is only one element in the discussion; it is the stumbling block for the learned Pharisees.   Deut. 13,1-5 and 18,15-22 ask that a prophet be tested by seeing that his prophecies become true.[96]   This is, in fact, what is done in vv. 13-17, but it leads to a σχίσμα among the Pharisees (v. 16) while the man born blind concludes logically: "He is a prophet" (v. 17).

What is it that prevents the Pharisees from seeing Jesus for what he is? They do not know πόθεν ἐστίν (v. 29).   This, ultimately, is what separates them from the man born blind (vv. 33-34) and from Jesus.   Unless they are able to understand his origins, they will never understand his being the Son of Man, who reveals τὰ ἐπουράνια (see 3,12-14) with authority, because he is ἐκ τῶν ἄνω (8,23).   The Pharisees are unable to go beyond the revelation brought by Moses which, as we have seen in 3,13-14, John opposes by presenting Jesus as the unique emissary of God and as his unique revealer.[97]

The traditional pattern of a gradual progression, through a series of confessions to arrive at "the Son of Man" seems to come into play once again, but John's link with traditional ideas could be further reflected by the close similarity in theme which ch. 9 has with the cure of the blind man in Mk. 8, 22-26.   This miracle, in Mark, follows immediately after a passage

---

[94]   See M. de Jonge, "Jesus as Prophet and King ...", pp. 170-172.
[95]   K. Müller, "Joh 9,7 und das jüdische Verständnis des Siloh-Spruches", *BZ* 13 (1969) 251-256.
[96]   See also Strack-Billerbeck, *Kommentar* II, p. 480.
[97]   See above, pp. 54-57. See also M. de Jonge, "Nicodemus and Jesus: Some observations on Misunderstanding in the Fourth Gospel", pp. 349-351.

which dealt with the blindness of the disciples (see 8,14-21, esp. vv. 15, 18, 21)[98] and precedes the Petrine confession (8,29) which Jesus corrects in terms of "the Son of Man" (8,31). R. H. Lightfoot has shown that there is a remarkable parallel "which can hardly be fortuitous" between Mk. 8,22-26 and 8,27-29.[99] Jesus takes Peter and his companions, whom we know from 8,14-21 to be "blind", away from the crowd (see 8,23a) and he brings them to see the truth in stages (vv. 27-28 and v. 29. See vv. 23 and 25). When the disciples come to the truth, they are told to be silent (v. 30. See v. 26). This should be carried further, however, as it is not until v. 31 that the whole truth is revealed, when Jesus speaks to them of the Son of Man. This process of growth is what we have found in Jn. 9 and, as in the Marcan version, it is faith in the Son of Man which is understood as "true sight".[100]

The use of "the Son of Man" in the confessional passage of 9,35 is a continuation of the same themes that we have found linked with the title in the first eight chapters of the Fourth Gospel: [101] Jesus is presented as the unique revealer of God, and consequently as the place of judgment. It is not necessary to find other New Testament passages where "the Son of Man" is made the object of a confession of faith; it is sufficient to recognise what this title meant in the Johannine Church: Jesus as the place where God's revelation is to be found and consequently, as the place where men will judge themselves. As this is the case, it is not strange to find the Johannine Jesus asking: "Do you believe in the Son of Man?".[102]

---

[98] See W. Grundmann, *Das Evangelium nach Markus*, THNT 2, (Berlin, Evangelische Verlagsanstalt, 1973) pp. 164-165; E. Schweizer, *The Good News according to Mark*, (London, SPCK, 1971) pp. 160-164 (English translation of *Das Evangelium nach Markus*, [Göttingen, Vandenhoeck und Ruprecht, 1967]).

[99] R. H. Lightfoot, *History and Interpretation in the Gospel*, (London, Hodder and Stoughton, ·1935) pp. 90-91. See also M.-J. Lagrange, *Evangile selon Saint Marc*, (Paris, Gabalda, 1920) pp. 202-203; D. E. Nineham, *Saint Mark*, The Pelican Gospel Commentaries, (Harmondsworth, Penguin, 1963) pp. 218-219; S. E. Johnson, *A Commentary on the Gospel According to St. Mark*, Black's New Testament Commentaries, (London, A. and C. Black, 1972) pp. 144-145.

[100] C. H. Dodd, *Tradition*, pp. 181-188 has shown that, apart from vv. 5 and 7, the Johannine miracle "is cast in a traditional mould" (p. 184). The parallel could be carried further, as Mark proceeds beyond the revelation of Jesus as the Son of Man to the transfiguration, and the proclamation that Jesus is the Son of God (Mk. 9,7). Jn. 10 is also concerned with Jesus' Sonship, highlighted by the climax of 10,30: "I and the Father are one".

[101] See R. Schnackenburg, *Johannesevangelium* II, p. 322.

[102] See G. Iber, *Untersuchungen*, p. 185.

CHAPTER EIGHT

THE CROSS AND THE GLORIFICATION OF THE SON OF MAN:
John 12,23.34

I - General Structure and Meaning of John 12

John 12, in its present order, is made up of various elements. Some appear to be based upon traditional material. The anointing at Bethany, vv. 1-8 (see Mk. 14,3-9; Matt. 26,6-13; Lk. 7,36-50) and the triumphant entry into Jerusalem, vv. 12-19 (see Mk. 11,1-11; Matt. 21,1-11; Lk. 19,28-40) both appear to have connections with the Synoptic tradition. The encounter with the Greeks (vv. 20-36) also has close parallels in the Synoptic Gethsemane scenes and in other isolated Synoptic sayings (see Mk. 8,35; 10,45; 8,34; 14,34-36; 9,7; 1,11; Matt. 16,25; 10,39; 20,28; 16,24; 26, 38-39; 17,5; 3, 17; Lk. 9,23-24; 17,33; 22,41-43; 9,35; 3,22b; 10,18). Throughout, however, there are also passages found only in John (see vv. 9-11; 16-19; 20-24; 28-36; 42-43; 44-50).

Various difficulties are found in the logical sequence of the passage. There seem to be three crowds involved. There is a crowd, mentioned in vv. 17 and 18, who have seen Lazarus raised and who now believe in Jesus. Another is mentioned in v. 9. They have heard about the miracle and have arrived at Bethany before Jesus left for Jerusalem. Finally, a large crowd is mentioned in v. 12. This crowd goes out to meet Jesus on his way to Jerusalem. The arrival of the Greeks (v. 20) and their desire to "see" Jesus seem to be forgotten, as Jesus starts a discourse in v. 23 and they are not mentioned again. In v. 34 the crowd speaks as if Jesus has referred to himself as the Son of Man, but there is no mention of this in the immediate context. After what appears to be a redactional Johannine reflection on the unbelief of the Jews (vv. 37-43), which could well have concluded the section, Jesus is again introduced, and he "cries out" a short discourse which has little connection with what has immediately preceded (vv. 44-50).

Attempts have been made to reconstruct the chapter, or to place its various units in more logical sequences throughout the rest of the Gospel. Wellhausen suggests that the whole chapter is redactional: none of it belongs to the *Grundschrift*, but it has been assembled from a variety of sources and loosely put together by an editor.[1]   F. Spitta, who also attempts to find a *Grundschrift,* is not so pessimistic, and allows vv. 12-15 and 19 to his *Grundschrift,* seeing the rest of the chapter as redactional.[2]

H. Becker, in his attempt to reconstruct the Gnostic discourse which he surmises stands behind the Fourth Gospel, finds that some of chapter 12 originally belonged to a discourse on the light of the world (11,9; 9,4; 9,39; 9,41; 8,12; 12,44; 12,47-48; 12,49-50; 8,21-23; 8, 28b-29; 12,35-36).[3]   He sees 12,31 as the opening of what was originally a farewell speech (12,31; 16,5; 16,12 etc.).[4]

These suggestions, however, are not attempts to solve the difficulties which the chapter presents.   They are efforts to reconstruct the origins of the Gospel, but they do not answer the question why the Gospel has been given the form in which it has come down to us.   Other scholars have gone further by suggesting that chapter 12 is made up of passages which have been somehow displaced.

Bernard has placed vv. 44-50 between v. 36a and v. 36b.[5]   Macgregor has followed him in this, but has added parts of John 3 to resolve the problem raised by the question about the Son of Man in v. 34.   His reconstruction of the latter part of the chapter is: 12,32; (12,33 is a gloss [6]); 3,14-15; 12,34; 3,16-21; 12,35-36a; 12,44-50; 12,36b-43.[7]   J. G. Gourbillon has taken the suggestion further by reconstructing the whole of the discourse in the following fashion: [8]

12, 20-22:	Prologue and the occasion of the discourse
23-26:	First part of the discourse
27-30:	A first intermediary section, with the interruption of the voice from heaven
12,31; 3,14-21; 12,32-33:	The second part of the discourse, the parable of the bronze serpent
12,34:	Second intermediary section, with the reaction of the crowd

[1] J. Wellhausen, *Johannis,* pp. 55-58.
[2] F. Spitta, *Johannes,* pp. 260-272.
[3] H. Becker, *Die Reden des Johannesevangeliums,* p. 132.
[4] *ibid.,* p. 93. See p. 135 for the reconstructed text.
[5] J. H. Bernard, *St. John,* p. 445. See also p. xxv.
[6] See also H. J. Flowers, "Interpolations in the Fourth Gospel", *JBL* 40 (1921) 155-156.
[7] G. H. C. Macgregor, *John,* p. 268-270. See also his article "A suggested Rearrangement of the Johannine Text (Ioh. 3,14-36; 12,30-36)", *ET* 35 (1923-24) 476-477. See also B. Noack, *Zur johanneischen Tradition,* p. 146; W. C. van Unnik, "The Quotation from the Old Testament in John 12,34", *NT* 3 (1959) 174.
[8] J. G. Gourbillon, "La parabole du serpent d'airain...", pp. 213-226. See especially pp. 217-218:   He is followed by A. Wikenhauser, *Johannes,* pp. 197-198.

12,35-36a; 12,44-50:	Third part of the discourse
12, 36b-43:	Conclusion.

According to Gourbillon we have our traditional text because of a misplacement of the pages in an early codex.[9] While his reconstructed text reads very well,[10] the theory of misplaced pages is far-fetched. Is it possible that all the codices of the Fourth Gospel misplaced the same pages? It is very unlikely they would be *inadvertently* misplaced at the hypothetical stage when there was only one such codex. We have no ancient textual tradition which gives us a hint of the sequence suggested by Bernard, Macgregor and Gourbillon.

A more radical rearrangement is suggested by Rudolf Bultmann. The majority of chapter 12 is placed in the final section of the first half of the Gospel, which Bultmann calls "The Way of the Cross". This section is made up of 11,55-12,33; 8,30-40; 6,60-71.[11] The aim of this section is to "teach us to understand the passion of Jesus as the completion of his work and as his glorification".[12] The rest of the chapter, as we have it now, was originally scattered through the "Light of the World" discourse; 9,1-41; 8,12; 12,44-50; 8,21-29; 12,34-36; 10,19-21.[13] The remaining section, 12,37-43, stands apart from the rest of the chapter. It is a retrospective glance over the public activity of Jesus, serving as a conclusion to the account of that activity.[14]

Behind any rearrangement theory stands a premise that the Gospel in its traditional order does not make sense, and that we must reorganise it to find its correct meaning. The dangers of subjectivism in any such attempt are obvious. D. M. Smith, criticising Bultmann's reorganisation of chapter 12, has shown that his reconstruction makes no more sense than the traditional order. Smith maintains, rightly, that Bultmann's section of "The Way of the Cross", coming at the end of the first half of the Gospel, is "the inevitable consequence of his treatment of chapters 6 and 8 and his reconstruction of the Lichtrede".[15] He has some passages left over, and he reconstructs his last section with these remnants which do not, in fact, follow very logically.[16]

---

[9] J. G. Gourbillon, *art. cit.*, p. 222.

[10] See *ibid.*, pp. 223-226.

[11] R. Bultmann, *John*, pp. 412-433.

[12] *ibid.*, p. 392. On this section, see D. M. Smith, *The Composition and Order of the Fourth Gospel*, pp. 166.168. For the reconstructed text, see pp. 198-201.

[13] R. Bultmann, *John*, pp. 354-358. See in this D. M. Smith, *op. cit.*, pp. 155-163. For the reconstructed text, see pp. 192-195.

[14] R. Bultmann, *John*, pp. 452-454.

[15] D. M. Smith, *op. cit.*, p. 167.

[16] See D. M. Smith, *op. cit.*, pp. 167-168 for a more detailed criticism of Bultmann's "Way of the Cross" section. See also pp. 160-163 for a criticism of his "Light of the World" discourse.

D. Mollat, in the *Bible de Jérusalem,* has suggested that 12,44-50 were not originally a part of the chapter.[17] There is no indication of time and place, and this short discourse seems to have very little logical link with what has gone before. These verses may have been an insertion, in a very Johannine style, of a summary of Jesus' public life, added by an editor for the publication of the Gospel.[18] M.-E. Boismard has carried this suggestion further in a series of articles devoted to the problem.[19] He finds that the passage has three peculiarities:

1. Certain stylistic features which show the trace of a strange hand;[20]

2. An earlier eschatological point of view, which is not yet "realised";[21]

3. Christological features which also show an earlier stage. Jesus does not speak of the Father-Son relationship; he is presented as the Sent One.[22] Boismard suggests that this latter feature depends upon Deut. 18,15-18, where Moses is presented as God's Sent One, who speaks the words which he is commanded to speak. Boismard sees this as a reflection of a targumic reading of Deut. 18,15-18, found especially in v. 49.[23]

While this passage has certain stylistic traits which are unique, these may be the result of redactional touches. We need not regard the whole passage as secondary because of them. We have already argued that a "future" eschatology is not foreign to John,[24] and while the Father-Son relationship is not apparent, it is abundantly clear that the Father stands behind Jesus' being the Sent One.

The passage is certainly very loosely attached to what has gone before. It is a summary of all that has happened in the first twelve chapters. As such, it finds its rightful place at the conclusion of chapter 12. It is clear that the Fourth Gospel has come to us after several stages of rethinking and reworking. We must allow for this in the many literary difficulties which are

---

[17] D. Mollat, "St. Jean", p. 148.

[18] I. de la Potterie, "L'exaltation du Fils de l'homme...", pp. 460-461 follows Mollat in this.

[19] M.-E. Boismard, "Le caractère adventice de Jo. 12,45-50", in *Sacra Pagina,* II, pp. 189-192; "Les citations targumiques dans le quatrième Évangile", *RB* 66 (1959) 374-378; "L'évolution du thème eschatologique...", pp. 507-514.

[20] M.-E. Boismard, "Le caractère adventice...", pp. 190-191.

[21] M.-E. Boismard, "L'évolution du thème eschatologique...", pp. 510-511.

[22] *ibid.*

[23] M.-E. Boismard, "Les citations targumiques...", pp. 376-378. "L'évolution du thème eschatologique...", pp. 510-511.

[24] See above, on John 5, pp. 78-81.

found throughout the Gospel. But the theological point which John is making is of primary importance and the literary difficulties must not be allowed to distract the reader from this theological point of view, expressed by the Gospel in the form in which we find it in the oldest manuscripts — the form in which it has come down to us.[25]

John 12,9-19 is clearly made up of various elements. Verses 9-11 and 16-19 stand out immediately as a Johannine "frame" around the traditional story of the triumphal entry.[26] John has given three "crowds" a place in the story, two of which are found in the "frame" (vv. 9,17-18), while the third is in the traditional story (v. 12). This is certainly clumsy, but should not lead us to disregard the theological point which is being made by use of these different "crowds". In the Johannine sections "the crowd" comes to believe in Jesus (vv. 9-12). Some have seen him raise Lazarus from the dead (v. 17), while others are attracted to Jesus because they have heard of the miracle (v. 9). Many of these also come to believe in Jesus (v. 11). This is also the reason why "a crowd" goes out to meet Jesus (v. 18), and they bear witness to him (v. 17). The traditional passage has "a crowd" in Jerusalem (vv. 12-15), preparing to meet Jesus. This crowd is used as a mouthpiece for a proclamation of their messianic expectations. It is the belief, the witness and the proclamation which should occupy the interpreter's attention.[27]

The relationship of the Johannine account of the anointing at Bethany (vv. 1-8) and the triumphant entry into Jerusalem (vv. 12-15) to the Synoptic accounts of the same incidents (Mk. 14,3-9; Matt. 26,6-13; Lk. 7,36-50; Mk. 11,1-11; Matt. 21,1-11; Lk. 19,28-40) is too complicated to be discussed at length here. There seem to be many points of contact. Both John and Mark use the term νάρδου πιστικῆς (see Jn. 12,3; Mk. 14,3),[28] yet in the same verse John refers to the wiping of Jesus' feet with the woman's hair (12,3) which seems to be related to Lk. 7,38. In the account of the triumphal entry all the Synoptics quote from Ps. 118, 25-26 (see Mk. 11,10; Matt. 21,9; Lk. 19,38). It could be suggested that John has followed them in this, adding a reference to Jesus as the King of Israel (12,13), which may be his version

---

[25] See, A. Rasco, "Christus, granum frumenti (Jo. 12,24)", *VD* 37 (1959) 12-21 for a detailed discussion of the various rearrangement theories, and a defence of the unity of the passage.

[26] See C. H. Dodd, *Interpretation*, p. 369; R. E. Brown, *John*, pp. 459. 463-464.

[27] See R. E. Brown, *John*, pp. 456. 460. Brown links the crowd in v. 12 with that of v. 18 as "those who have heard about the miracle". This is not stated in v. 12, and we would prefer to keep v. 12 distinct from the crowds mentioned in the more Johannine passages. R. Schnackenburg, *Johannesevangelium* II, p. 473, commenting on v. 17 points out that this is John at work and concludes: "und darum sind Ueberlegungen zur Situation und zu den verschiedenen ὄχλοι überflüssig".

[28] Found only here in the New Testament. B. Lindars, *John*, pp. 415-416 suggests that this has come about by a copyist's assimilation of the Johannine text into Mark.

of the Marcan addition: "Blessed is the kingdom of our father David that is coming" (Mk. 11,10). Another Marcan contact could be found in the use of "Hosanna" (Jn. 12,13; Mk. 11,9 par Matt. 21,9).

While all scholars admit that John is using traditional material in his own particular way, many have argued for a direct dependence upon one or all of the Synoptics.[29] Lagrange, followed by Lemmonyer, holds that John's account of the anointing is a combination of the Synoptic stories,[30] while Loisy suggests that it is a compromise account.[31] The difficulty arises from the fact that there are close contacts with both the Marcan and the Lucan accounts, which seem to have their origins, in turn, in quite different traditions. Bernard has suggested that there were two events, one of which is reported in Luke 7, and another reported in Mk. 14.[32] Freed has argued that the use of the Old Testament in the account of the entry into Jerusalem (12,13-15) clearly indicates that John has used the Synoptics to strengthen his own particular theme of Jesus' kingship.[33]

In the light of this baffling mixture of Synoptic contacts and other material, recent scholarship has suggested that John is dependent upon a tradition differing from the Synoptics, but which has contacts with it. This tradition may well have been linked at a pre-literary stage;[34] in this way one

---

[29] C. K. Barrett, *St. John*, pp. 341. 346; W. Bauer, *Johannesevangelium*, pp. 158-160; J. H. Bernard, *St. John*, pp. 409-410; E. D. Freed, "The entry into Jerusalem in the Gospel of John", *JBL* 80 (1961) 329-338; E. C. Hoskyns, *Fourth Gospel*, p. 451; W. F. Howard, "St. John", p. 653; M.-J. Lagrange, *St. Jean*, pp. 320-321; A. Lemmonyer, "L'onction de Béthanie. Notes d'exégèse sur Jean 12,1-8", *RecSR* 18 (1928) 105-117; A. Loisy, *Quatrième Évangile*, p. 326; G. H. C. Macgregor, *John*, p. 258; J. Marsh, *St. John,* pp. 452-453. 460; L. Morris, *John*, pp. 371-374; A. Richardson, *St. John*, pp. 146-149; W. Temple, *Readings*, p. 188; B. Vawter, "John", p. 448; L. von Sybel, "Die Salbungen. Mt. 26,6-13; Mk. 14,3-9; Lk. 7,36-50; Joh. 12,1-8", *ZNW* 23 (1924) 184-193; T. Zahn, *Johannes*, pp. 488-490; T. W. Bevan, "The Four Anointings (Matt. 26,6-13; Mark 14,3-9; Luke 7,36-50; John 12,1-11)", *ET* 39 (1927-28) 137-139.

[30] M.-J. Lagrange, *St. Jean*, pp. 320-321; A. Lemmonyer, "L'onction de Béthanie...", pp. 110-111.

[31] A. Loisy, *Quatrième Évangile*, p. 362.

[32] J. H. Bernard, *St. John*, pp. 409-410.

[33] E. D. Freed, "The Entry into Jerusalem ...", pp. 329-338.

[34] See R. E. Brown, *John*, pp. 449-452. 459-461; L. Morris, *Studies in the Fourth Gospel*, (Exeter, Paternoster Press, 1969) pp. 31-36; R. Bultmann, *John*, p. 417; C. H. Dodd, *Tradition*, pp. 152-156. 162-173. Dodd has also argued that this is the case for 12,25, which has Synoptic parallels (see Mk. 8,35; Lk. 9,24; Mt. 10,39; Lk. 17,33). See "Some Johannine 'Herrnworte' with Parallels in the Synoptic Gospels", *NTS* 2 (1955-56) 78-81; R. Fortna, *The Gospel of Signs*, pp. 149-152; E. Haenchen, "Johanneische Probleme", p. 50, note 3; A. Legault, "An Application of the Form-Critique Method to the Anointings in Galilee (Lk. 7,36-50) and Bethany (Mt. 26,6-13; Mk. 14,3-9; Jn. 12,1-8)", *CBQ* 16 (1954) 131-145; W. A. Meeks, *The Prophet-King*, pp. 85-86; B. Lindars, *John*, p. 413; B. Noack, *Zur johanneischen Tradition*, pp. 109-113; J. Sanders, *St. John*, pp. 285-286; D. M. Smith, "Jn. 12,12ff and the Question of John's Use of the Synoptics", *JBL* 82

can understand how John can seem to be in touch with both Mark and Luke in 12,3. D. M. Smith has argued convincingly against Freed, to show that this is the case with John's use of the Old Testament in the scene of the triumphal entry.[35] While Dodd argues that there is only one basic incident behind the anointing scene,[36] Legault and Brown, like Bernard, argue for two different incidents.[37] Whatever the solution to this particular problem may be, it is more satisfactory to explain both the scenes which open chapter 12 as Johannine. They are based on traditional material, but it is a Johannine tradition. Its contacts with the Synoptics warn us against too rapid an isolation of the Fourth Gospel's historical and theological value.

Although the logical sequence of the chapter is at times difficult to follow, it seems to be divided into clear sections. Having decided that the chapter must be considered as it is found in the traditional text, it must be asked whether the argument starts at 12,1 or at 11,55. Many scholars see 11,55-57 as a conclusion to chapter 11, and thus commence their consideration of chapter 12 at verse 1.[38] However, there seem to be hints which point to 11,55-57 as an introduction to chapter 12.[39] The most important point of contact is the Passover, mentioned in 11,55. This seems to point forward to 12,1. Secondly, there is the desire of the crowd to find Jesus, which is taken up by 12,9.12.18, where the crowds go to meet him. It is also possible that John's mention of the traditional rituals before the Passover is ironic:[40] the Passover which is about to be celebrated in Jerusalem will bring something

(1963) 58-64; R. H. Strachan, *Fourth Gospel,* pp. 246-247; R. Schnackenburg, *Johannes-evangelium* II, pp. 464-466. Schnackenburg had earlier argued for a knowledge of Mark. See "Der johanneische Bericht von der Salbung in Bethanien (Jo. 12,1-8)" *MüTZ* 1 (1950) 48-52.

[35] D. M. Smith, "Jn. 12,12ff and the Question of John's Use of the Synoptics", pp. 58-64.

[36] C. H. Dodd, *Tradition,* pp. 162-173.

[37] A. Legault, "An Application of the Form-Critique Method...", pp. 131-145; R. E. Brown, *John,* pp. 450-452.

[38] W. Bauer, *Johannesevangelium,* p. 158; J. H. Bernard, *St. John,* p. 414; F.-M. Braun, "St. Jean", p. 419; R. E. Brown, *John,* p. 419; I. de la Potterie, "L'exaltation du Fils de l'homme...", p. 460; W. F. Howard, *St. John,* p. 653; J. Jeremias, *Johannes,* p 325; M.-J. Lagrange, *St. Jean,* p. 319; R. H. Lightfoot, *St. John,* p. 233; J. Marsh, *St. John,* p. 571; A. Richardson, *St. John,* p. 146; B. Vawter, "John", p. 448; B. F. Westcott, *St. John,* p. 176; T. Zahn, *Johannes,* p. 490.

[39] See C. K. Barrett, *John,* p. 340; R. Bultmann, *John,* p. 412; C. H. Dodd, *Interpretation,* pp. 368-369; J. C. Fenton, *John,* p. 217; B. Lindars, *John,* p. 411; D. Mollat, "St. Jean", p. 140; J. Sanders, *St. John,* p. 281; R. Schnackenburg, *Johannesevangelium* II, p. 456; F. Spitta, *Johannes,* p. 260; H. Strathmann, *Johannes,* p. 181; A. Wikenhauser, *Johannes,* p. 184. E. C. Hoskyns, *Fourth Gospel,* pp. 408-417 and R. H. Strachan, *Fourth Gospel,* p. 242, go further back into chapter 11 to find the introduction to chapter 12. For Hoskyns the first section is 11, 47-12, 11, while Strachan sees 11,45-57 as the introduction to chapter 12.

[40] See C. K. Barrett, *St. John,* p. 342; E. C. Hoskyns, *Fourth Gospel,* pp. 412-413; R. H. Lightfoot, *St. John,* p. 234.

entirely new; it is here that the Son of Man will be 'lifted up' for them to see and believe (see 12,23.32; see also 3,13-14; 8,28; 19,37), but John shows them busy about their ritual purifications, entirely ignorant of all that Jesus has come to bring. The questions they ask are idle curiosity — whether or not he will come to the Feast. For John the questions which should be asked are "Who is he?", "Where does he come from?". Thus the reaction of the Jews (11,55-56) and of their leaders (11,57) is a direct preparation for John's final word to them in 12,37-43. The section is not, of course, entirely separated from chapter 11,1-54. It continues the theme of the unbelief and opposition which the Lazarus miracle has caused (11,46-54). The mention of the Passover (11,55) links 11,55-57 more closely to chapter 12, but in many ways it joins what has gone before in chapter 11 with what is about to follow.

The rest of the chapter falls into clearly defined sections.[41]

12, 1-8 :   The anointing at Bethany.

9-19:   The triumphal entry, introduced (vv. 9-11) and concluded (vv. 16-19) by Johannine reflections.

20-36:   The request of the Greeks and the subsequent discourse.

37-43:   A Johannine reflection on the incredulity of the Jews.

44-50:   The conclusion of the public ministry.

The only point of discussion in this division is whether the discourse which follows the question of the Greeks concludes at v. 36a with the words of Jesus,[42] or in v. 36b with John's comment.[43] While this may not appear to be a very important issue, it is of interest to us in so far as v. 36b either marks the conclusion of Jesus' discourse which contains three references to the Son of Man, or it is the start of a Johannine reflection on the incredulity of the Jews. It appears more satisfactory to make v. 36b a concluding stament. What

---

[41] With the exception of some difference of opinion concerning v. 36, this division is followed by the vast majority of scholars. Some divide the material into larger blocks. For example, A. Richardson, *St. John*, p. 146, divides it into 12,1-11; 12-19; 20-50. J. Sanders, *St. John*, pp. 281-302 divides it: 11,55-12,19 and 12,20-50.

[42] The following divide the verse in the course of their rearrangements: J. H. Bernard, *St. John*, p. 455; R. Bultmann, *John*, p. 357; J. G. Gourbillon, "La parabole du serpent d'airain...", pp. 221-222; G. H. C. Macgregor, *John*, pp. 268-269. Other scholars do not rearrange but still see a break. See J. C. Fenton, *John*, pp. 137-138; W. F. Howard, "St. John", p. 667; B. Lindars, *John*, pp. 436-437; J. Marsh, *John*, p. 468; L. Morris, *John*, pp. 600-601; R. H. Strachan, *Fourth Gospel*, p. 258; W. Temple, *Readings*, p. 201; B. F. Westcott, *St. John*, p. 184; *The Greek New Testament*; RSV.

[43] See C. K. Barrett, *St. John*, p. 358; W. Bauer, *Johannesevangelium*, p. 163; J. Blank, *Krisis*, p. 296; R. E. Brown, *John*, pp. 479-480; I. de la Potterie, "L'exaltation du Fils de l'homme...", p. 460; C. H. Dodd, *Interpretation*, p. 397; E. C. Hoskyns, *Fourth Gospel*, pp. 426-427; M.-J. Lagrange, *St. Jean*, p. 336; R. Schnackenburg, *Johannesevangelium* II, p. 497; H. Strathmann, *Johannes*, p. 184; H. van den Bussche, *Jean*, p. 363; B. Vawter, "John", p. 450; J. Wellhausen, *Johannis*, p. 55; A. Wikenhauser, *Johannes*, p. 192; NEB.

happens in v. 36b is the result of the Jews' inability to accept him as the Son of Man, the bearer of God's revelation, the light. This has been his final word to them. They have refused it, so he hides himself from them. This leaves vv. 37-43 as a literary unit, free from any close link with the events which immediately precede.[44] It can be understood as a Johannine reflection, not only upon the events of chapter 12, but upon the steady increase of opposition to Jesus which has been growing throughout the Gospel. Thus the public ministry is concluded, not with one reflection upon the ministry of Jesus (vv. 44-50), but with two. Firstly, John gives his solution to the incredulity of the Jews: "For they loved the praise of men more than the praise of God" (v. 43), and he then places a final discourse in the mouth of Jesus which summarises the public ministry.[45]

The whole section, 11,55-12,36, the last act in the public ministry of Jesus, is purposely set in the context of his last Passover.[46] In this way the reader is informed that the end is drawing near, and that the events of the chapter should be understood in the light of Jesus' passion. In 11,55 John tells his readers: "Now the Passover of the Jews was at hand". Later he is more precise: "Six days before the Passover" (12,1). As if in explanation of these references, he announces in 13,1: "Now before the feast of the Passover, when Jesus knew that his hour had come to depart out of this world to the Father..." (see also 18,28.30; 19,14). As the Jews are preparing for this all-important Passover by fulfilling their ritual duty and asking pointless questions about Jesus (11,55-57), he comes to Bethany (12,1).

Although the anointing at Bethany reflects the traditional story found in the Synoptic Gospels,[47] its significance is closely linked to the present Johannine context. The mention of the Passover (v. 1), the presence of Lazarus, whose raising had led to the decision "that one man should die for the people"

---

[44] This solves the problem of the "though he had done so many signs before them" (v. 37). There are no signs or miracles in chapter 12. The reference is to all the public activity of Jesus, which is now concluded. See R. Schnackenburg, "Joh 12,39-41. Zur christologischen Schriftauslegung des vierten Evangeliums", in *Neues Testament und Geschichte,* p. 167, n. 1.

[45] This discourse, although put on the lips of Jesus, is the result of Johannine theologising, and has, perhaps, passed through some redactional stages. See above pp. 163-164. It is quite separate from the drama of chapter 12, but closely linked to the role of Jesus as God's revealer and the place of judgment, themes which we have found present throughout Jesus' discourses and closely linked to Jesus as the Son of Man. See on this A. Feuillet, "La composition littéraire de Jo. 9-12", in *Mélanges Bibliques rédigés en l'honneur de André Robert,* (Paris, Bloud & Gay, 1957), pp. 492-493; C. H. Dodd, *Interpretation,* pp. 380-381; D. Mollat, "St. Jean", p. 148; I. de la Potterie, "L'exaltation du Fils de l'homme...", pp. 460-461; H. van den Bussche, "La structure de Jean 1-13", in *L'Évangile de Jean. Études et problèmes,* Recherches Bibliques 3, (Bruges, Desclée de Brouwer, 1958), pp. 106-107.

[46] See C. K. Barrett, *St. John,* p. 342; H. Strathmann, *Johannes,* p. 184.

[47] See above pp. 164-166.

(11,50), the anointing, the presence of Judas the betrayer (v. 4), the prophecy of the burial (v. 7) and the announcement that they would not always have him (v. 8)[48] all indicate that this scene looks forward to the death of Jesus. While there are certainly other minor themes which come into play — the contrast between Mary and Judas,[49] the love and gratitude of Mary [50] — these do not appear to be the main issues. There is little trace in the text that this scene is one of repentance and forgiveness, as in the Lucan version,[51] or that the act is Mary's way of expressing gratitude for the restoration of her brother Lazarus.[52] Barrett has suggested that it is a symbolic anointing of Jesus as a royal figure.[53] While quite in accord with John's version of the passion, there is no evidence for this interpretation in the account. One would expect the head to be anointed for such symbolism, but it is not mentioned. The first suggestion of royalty appears in the scene of the triumphal entry (vv. 13-15), but we will suggest below that the royal acclamations are not a satisfactory confession of the royalty of Jesus.

Some scholars, following the Fathers,[54] see v. 3 as the Johannine version of Mk. 14,9. The spreading of the odour is a symbol of the spread of the message of the Gospel throughout the Gentile world.[55] Loisy has taken this even further and understands the whole incident as a symbol of the Gentile Church receiving the Gospel message at the feet of Jesus. The nard is the Gospel.[56] This is to read too much into the story as the odour of the perfume probably refers to the extravagance of this act of love.[57] Mary is in no way connected with the Gentile church. She administers the anointing, she does not receive it.

The point of the anointing scene is found in the extremely difficult v. 7.[58] There has been considerable discussion over the sense of ἵνα ... τηρήσῃ αὐτό. The Greek should be translated: "So that she might ,keep it for the day of the

---

[48] Against Bultmann (*John*, p. 415) who regards v. 8 as a marginal gloss which misses the point.
[49] See B. Lindars, *John*, p. 414; B. F. Westcott, *St. John*, p. 177; A. Wikenhauser, *Johannes*, p. 185.
[50] T. W. Bevan, "The Four Anointings...", p. 138.
[51] Against J. H. Bernard, *St. John*, pp. 417-418.
[52] Against W. F. Howard, "St. John", p. 658.
[53] C. K. Barrett, *St. John*, p. 341. See the further suggestions of J. E. Bruns, "A Note on Jn. 12,3", *CBQ* 28 (1966) 219-222.
[54] See Clement of Alexandria, *Paedagogus*, II,8.
[55] See W. Bauer, *Johannesevangelium*, p. 159; E. C. Hoskyns, *Fourth Gospel*, p. 415; R. H. Strachan, *Fourth Gospel*, p. 248.
[56] A. Loisy, *Quatrième Évangile*, pp. 362-363.
[57] See B. Lindars, *John*, p. 417; J. H. Bernard, *St. John*, p. 418; J. Sanders, *St. John*, p. 248; R. Schnackenburg, *Johannesevangelium* II, p. 460.
[58] See C. H. Dodd, *Interpretation*, p. 370: "It seems clear that for John's purpose the significant point of the story comes in 12,7 with its reference to the burial of Jesus".

preparation for my burial".[59]   If this is what is meant, then Mary is to keep some of the ointment for the anointing of Jesus after his death.[60]   In Mk. 14,3 the jar was broken and thus none of the ointment remained, but this is not mentioned in John. However, it is difficult to understand the text in this way. Why was Judas able to complain about the loss of the ointment (v. 5)? It is also difficult to see what the remnant of this jar of ointment would add to the extraordinary "hundred pounds" of spices which Nicodemus brings for the anointing of Jesus' body (see 19,39).

Although more difficult grammatically, it seems better to understand v. 7, in the light of v. 5, as the justification of the loss of the costly ointment.[61]   In this interpretation, one makes a major break after ἄφες αὐτήν. Following Brown, we translate ἵνα as "The purpose was that...".[62]   Thus we have: "Let her alone. The purpose was that she might keep this for the day of the preparation for my burial". This solution brings its own difficulties, but it seems to suit the context better, as that day of preparation for burial is symbolically fulfilled at Bethany.[63]   It is important, however, to insist that whatever translation one chooses for this verse,[64] the passion is in view, and the anointing is seen as a prophetic preparation for Jesus' death.[65]   In the context, the symbol is clear. Like Caiaphas (see 11,50), Mary has done more than she realised,[66] but, unlike Caiaphas, she has done it in recognition of Jesus.[67]

---

[59] The word ἐνταφιασμός does not mean "burial", but "laying out for burial". See H. G. Liddell-R. Scott, *A Greek-English Lexicon*, p. 575; J. H. Moulton-G. Milligan, *The Vocabulary of the Greek Testament*, p. 217. See the NEB, as against the RSV.

[60] See W. Bauer, *Johannesevangelium*, p. 159; A. Feuillet, "La composition littéraire de Jo. 9-12", p. 489; W. F. Howard, "St. John", p. 655; M.-J. Lagrange, *St. Jean*, p. 321; G. H. C. Macgregor, *John*, pp. 259-260; A. Richardson, *St. John*, p. 148; A. Schlatter, *Johannes*, p. 265; R. H. Strachan, *Fourth Gospel*, p. 248; W. Temple, *Readings*, pp. 189-191; B. F. Westcott, *St. John*, p. 178; A. Wikenhauser, *Johannes*, p. 185.

[61] See R. Schnackenburg, *Johannesevangelium* II, p. 462; B. Lindars, *John*, p. 414; B. F. Westcott, *St. John*, p. 177; E. C. Hoskyns, *Fourth Gospel*, pp. 415-416.

[62] R. E. Brown, *John*, p. 449.

[63] See H. Strathmann, *Johannes*, p. 186; R. Schnackenburg, *Johannesevangelium* II, p. 458; see also pp. 462-463; L. Morris, *John*, p. 470; J. Marsh, *St. John*, p. 454; B. Lindars, *John*, p. 419; R. E. Brown, *John*, pp. 447-449; M. Zerwick-M. Grosvenor, *A Grammatical Analysis of the Greek New Testament*, I, (Rome, Biblical Institute Press, 1974) pp. 323-324.

[64] What we have presented here are only two of several possibilities. For a fuller discussion of these possibilities, see W. Kühne, "Eine kritische Studie zu Joh. 12,7", *Theologische Studien und Kritiken*, 98-99 (1926), 476-477; J. A. Kleist, "A Note on the Greek Text of St. John 12,7", *Classical Journal* 21 (1925) 46-48; R. E. Brown, *John*, p. 449; R. Bultmann, *John*, p. 416, note 2; C. K. Barrett, *St. John*, pp. 345-346. Ultimately, one must agree with Barrett that, "It must however be admitted that no explanation of this difficult verse is entirely satisfactory" (p. 346).

[65] Against T. W. Bevan, "The Four Anointings ...", p. 138: "There is no reference to the anointings of the body before burial".

[66] See R. Bultmann, *John*, p. 416.

[67] See E. C. Hoskyns, *Fourth Gospel*, pp. 415-416.

Jesus is on his way to death: John introduces his version of the triumphal entry by reminding his readers of this fact, in an oblique way, in vv. 9-11. The Lazarus event had caused many people to seek him whom Jesus had raised from the dead. No longer is it important to remove only Jesus, but Lazarus,[68] a living witness to the power of Jesus, must also die. In this Johannine passage, the events of the previous chapter are cleverly linked to chapter 12. The main concern however, is not the death of Lazarus, but the death of Jesus.

After this introduction,[69] Jesus makes his last entry into Jerusalem, where he is met by a crowd of enthusiastic supporters. For the authors of the Synoptic Gospels the entry is the first time Jesus has come to the city of Jerusalem (see Mk. 11,1-11; Matt. 21,1-11; Lk. 19,28-40). They all seem to use the occasion for the proclamation of Jesus as a Messianic king. In all the Synoptic Gospels the cleansing of the Temple follows (see Mk. 11,15-17; Matt. 21,12-13; Lk. 19,45-46): Jesus comes as a Messianic king to claim his Temple.[70] John has a very different point to make.

Jesus is greeted by a crowd which comes out to meet him (εἰς ὑπάντησιν αὐτῷ)[71] with the waving of palm fronds and the acclamation of Ps. 118,25-26. As yet, Jesus has taken no initiative; there is no planning before this entry, as in the Synoptics (Mk. 14,12-16; Matt. 26,17-19; Lk. 22,7-13); it happens because the people have heard that he is coming to Jerusalem (v. 12; see 11,56). The use of the palm fronds has caused some scholars to see a link with the feast of Tabernacles, where palms were used.[72] This does not seem to be the point at issue. The only use of τὰ βαΐα in the LXX is found in I Macc. 13,51, where the Jews take possession of the Temple after Simon has conquered the Jerusalem citadel in 142 B.C. The palm also appears on coins from 140 B. C. to 70 A. D. bearing the inscription "For the Redemption of Zion".[73] Farmer has shown

---

[68] The use of καί meaning "also" in v. 10, shows the reader that the death of Jesus is already taken for granted.

[69] That vv. 9-11 are a Johannine introduction is clear. V. 10 is a reworking of 11,53, while v. 11 reflects the Johannine situation of church-Synagogue conflict. See on Jn. 9, p. 149, note 42. It must also be admitted that John's editorial work here is rather clumsy. See R. E. Brown, *John*, p. 459; B. Lindars, *John*, p. 419.

[70] See V. Taylor, *The Gospel According to Mark*, (London, Macmillan, 1966), pp. 451-452 for various interpretations of this sequence. See also H. Patsch, "Der Einzug Jesu in Jerusalem. Ein historischer Versuch", *ZTK* 68 (1971) 1-26.

[71] The terminology suggests that the crowd has gone to meet a king or an exalted person. See E. Peterson, "Die Einholung des Kyrios", *ZSyTh* 7 (1930) 682-702; R. Schnackenburg, *Johannesevangelium* II, pp. 469-470; R. Bultmann, *John*, pp. 417-418.

[72] See *Sukka* III,1; Strack-Billerbeck, *Kommentar* II, p. 789 ff; A. Schlatter, *Johannes*, p. 265; A. Wikenhauser, *Johannes*, p. 186.

[73] See W. R. Farmer, "The Palm Branches in John 12,13", *JTS* 3 (1952) 63; L. Morris, *John*, p. 584, note 39.

convincingly that this gesture is closely associated with Maccabean nationalism.[74] The crowds are acclaiming a national, political Messiah. John adds "The King of Israel" to his quotation from Ps. 118 to show what sort of king the crowds were expecting. This time Jesus does not flee from their acclamations, as he did in 6,15, but enters on an ass. Now he faces their acclamations, but sets about correcting them in the light of the text from Zechariah.[75] The "hour" has come for Jesus to affirm his kingly role (see v. 23). He will determine the nature of his kingship;[76] it will not be in the way expected by the crowds and by his disciples (v. 16).[77] Although the Johannine addition (vv. 16-19) is clumsy, it explains what the entry into Jerusalem means for John.[78] The kingship of Jesus is to be worked out through his elevation and glorification upon the cross (v. 16); now he is going to face this moment and yet the Jews still look for something in Jesus which is only half way to the truth. They seek him because he has worked a sign (vv. 17-18), and yet they do come to some sort of belief in him (v. 18) and, in transition to the request from the Gentile world to "see" Jesus, the Pharisees complain that "the world has gone after him" (v. 19).

As if to show the truth of the Pharisees' concern in v. 19, some Greeks come to "see" Jesus (vv. 20-21). They seek an audience with him through the services of Philip and Andrew (v. 22). On hearing of the advent of these representatives of the Gentile world, Jesus solemnly announces that the hour has come when the Son of Man must be lifted up (v. 23). What is meant by this is spelt out in the discourse which follows (vv. 24-32). Jesus refers continually to his death: the grain of wheat must die (v. 24); he who wants eternal life must hate his life in this world (v. 25), and anyone who wishes to follow Jesus must walk the same path of service.[79]

---

[74] W. R. Farmer, *art. cit.*, pp. 62-66. W. Bauer, *Johannesevangelium*, p. 160, suggests that the mention of palm fronds has come into the text from Christian liturgical practice (see Rev. 7,9). See also R. H. Strachan, *Fourth Gospel*, pp. 249-250.

[75] B. Lindars, *John*, pp. 420. 423, is probably correct when he argues that for John Jesus is not the fulfilment of the Zechariah text, which has come to John in the tradition. John uses the text over against the acclamations of the crowd to correct their false ideas.

[76] See W. Temple, *Readings*, pp. 192-193.

[77] With varying nuances, this is the interpretation of most current scholarship. See esp. R. E. Brown, *John*, 461-464; E. C. Hoskyns, *Fourth Gospel*, pp. 419-422; R. Schnackenburg, *Johannesevangelium* II, pp. 467-476; Idem, "Die Messiasfrage in Johannesevangelium", pp. 253-254; H. Patsch, "Der Einzug Jesu in Jerusalem", pp. 13-14. Some, however, see this as Jesus' acceptance of a Messianic role. For example, see G. H. C. Macgregor, *John*, p. 262.

[78] C. K. Barrett, *St. John*, p. 349 seems to overlook this when he complains of the historical impossibility of v. 16. If the disciples did not understand, neither would the crowds. In fact neither understood: the scene takes place because of a misunderstanding.

[79] See A. Rasco, "Christus, granum frumenti...", pp. 65-77; E. Käsemann, "Johannes 12, 20-26" in *Exegetische Versuche und Besinnungen* I, (Göttingen, Vandenhoeck und Ruprecht, 1960), pp. 254-257. This has been further spelt out by H. T. Wrege, "Jesus-

Reflecting the Synoptic Gethsemane traditions, Jesus speaks of the "terror" of the hour that stands before him, only to submit himself to the will of his Father (v. 27) and to receive the assurance that his final glorification will come through the "hour" (v. 28). The misunderstanding of the crowd (vv. 29-30) leads Jesus to speak of the consequences of his glorification — saving revelation and final judgment (vv. 31-32). All this will come about through his death on the cross (v. 33). Again the crowd is baffled. They cannot understand this message: the Messiah they acclaimed in vv. 12-15 was not one who would be "lifted up from the earth". Who then is this Son of Man? Jesus' answer, as in several other Son of Man sayings, is to point to himself as the light — the place where God is revealed, and the place where man must ultimately decide his destiny (vv. 35-36).

As this discourse is concerned throughout with Jesus as the Son of Man, we will turn now to a more detailed consideration of its implications for our understanding of the Johannine use of the term "the Son of Man".

II - The Son of Man in John 12,23.34

The anointing at Bethany was a symbolic preparation for the death of Jesus (v. 7), and the entry into Jerusalem was an indication that the kingship of Jesus was not that of a political figure, but one which would come through his glorification (v. 16). What follows in vv. 20-36 is a further clarification of what this "glorification" means, and the effects which it will have.

Verses 20-22 must be seen as an introduction to Jesus' discourse. It is the event which triggers off the explanation of the hour of Jesus' glorification. The discourse unfolds in the following manner:[80]

1. *a*) First revelation (vv. 23-28a) — the glorification of the Son of Man, with an explanation given by a heavenly voice.

    b) The misunderstanding of the crowd (v. 29) is corrected by Jesus (v. 30).

2. *a*) Second revelation (vv. 31-33) — the judgment of the world and the lifting up of Jesus, with an explanation given by the Evangelist.

geschichte und Jüngergeschick nach Joh 12, 20-33 und Hebr 5, 7-10" in E. Lohse-C. Burchard-B. Schaller (eds.), "*Der Ruf Jesu und die Antwort der Gemeinde. Exegetische Untersuchungen Joachim Jeremias zum 70. Geburtstag gewidmet von seinen Schülern*", (Göttingen, Vandenhoeck und Ruprecht, 1970), pp. 259-288. Wrege attempts to show that John and Hebrews are carrying on what has already been said in the Synoptics about the destiny of the disciples being the same as that of Jesus himself. In John, however, the theme has the added speculation of Wisdom traditions (ascent-descent and a dualistic world view).

[80] Although this division differs from his understanding of vv. 35-36, it was largely suggested by I. de la Potterie, "L'exaltation du Fils de l'homme ...", pp. 461-462.

b) The misunderstanding of the crowd (v. 34) is corrected by Jesus (vv. 35-36a).

3.   The conclusion of the Evangelist — Jesus hid himself from them (v. 36b).

It can be observed from this division that there is a certain repetition of revelation - explanation - misunderstanding - correction involved in the structure of the discourse. De la Potterie and Léon-Dufour have both arranged the discourse further, setting it out as a chiasm:[81]

v. 23: ἐλήλυθεν - ὥρα

a) v.24 — falls into the earth   *a'*) v.32 — lifted up from earth
      — dies   v.33 — die

b) v.25 — this world   *b'*) v.31 — this world

c) v.26 — Father   *c'*) v.28 — Father
      — will honour him   — glorify
                                            — glorify

d) Centre of chiasm: v. 27:
ἦλθον - ὥραν

This chiastic structure is very suggestive.   After the theme is announced in v. 23, there is a downward progression of humiliation from vv. 24-26, until the central v. 27 is reached, when Jesus confidently prays to the Father: "Bring me safely through this hour. For this purpose I have come to this hour".[82]   Having arrived at this point an upward movement of glorification starts until v. 32, when Jesus announces that he will be lifted up and draw all men to himself.[83]   There are, however, difficulties involved in this structure. De la Potterie and Léon-Dufour use it to determine the meaning of the text but it depends too much on a mere similarity of words.   For example, a parallel is drawn between the πατήρ of vv. 26 and 28, but in v. 26 Jesus is speaking of "the Father", while in v. 28 Jesus is speaking *to* his Father.   There is little similarity between the use of τιμάω and δοξάζω in vv. 26 and 28.

[81] I. de la Potterie, *art. cit.*, p. 463; X. Léon-Dufour, "Trois chiasmes johanniques", pp. 249-251.
[82] For this interpretation see X. Léon-Dufour, "Père, fais-moi passer sain et sauf à travers cette heure! (Jean 12,27)", in H. Baltensweiler & Bo Reicke (eds.), *Neues Testament und Geschichte. Historisches Geschehen und Deutung im Neuen Testament: Oscar Cullmann zum 70. Geburtstag*, (Tübingen, J. C. B. Mohr, 1972) pp. 156-165.
[83] See X. Léon-Dufour, "Trois chiasmes johanniques", p. 250.

Similarly, v. 27 is made the centre of the chiasm, parallel to v. 23, but in some ways it is more closely linked with the ideas of vv. 24-25 than with v. 23. The glorification of the Son of Man (v. 23) is, of course, the death mentioned in vv. 24-25 and the "hour" of v. 27, but the rigid application of these chiastic structures can rob the text of many of the innuendos which are found when one keeps the whole context in view. In this case, it involves vv. 29-30, 35-36 as well as vv. 23-28.31-33. The most serious problem with this structure is the omission of vv. 29-30. De la Potterie argues that the chiasm is structured around two pieces of discourse (vv. 23-28a. 31-32).[84] Léon-Dufour explains the difficulty by claiming that vv. 29-30 is an interruption. Using his "misunderstanding" technique, John widens the audience, as it is no longer only the Greeks who are in question.[85] What we have in this discourse is the descending in humiliation and the rising to glorification which are, for John, one and the same thing.[86]

There is in fact no question of interruptions; John has deliberately used his "misunderstanding" technique to introduce the upward movement of this thought. However, it does not stop there. The same technique is used to introduce the short discourse on the light (vv. 35-36). This last piece of the discourse is not as loosely connected to the rest of the passage as de la Potterie would suggest.[87] He claims that v. 34 shows that the Jews will not understand, so Jesus merely makes a general statement which does not enter the thought of the chiastic section of the discourse. This is to minimise the importance of Jesus' statements about the light, so often found in the context of the Son of Man (see 3,19-21; 8,12; 9,5). The whole of chapter 9 is .concerned with the question of light.[88] What we have in vv. 23-37 is the explanation of the "hour" of the Son of Man, which is initiated by the arrival of the Greeks. With their advent Jesus' mission is completed. Now, in order to bring it to full fruition (see v. 24) he must die on the cross (see vv. 24-26). However, this death on the cross will prove to be his glorification, when he will be lifted up on the cross and draw all men to himself (see vv. 28-33), as the light

---

[84] I. de la Potterie, *art. cit.,* p. 462.

[85] X. Léon-Dufour, *art. cit.,* p. 251.

[86] The unification of the humiliation with the glorification is Johannine. See W. Thüsing, "Wenn ich von der Erde erhöht bin ... (Joh 12,32). Die Erhöhung Jesu nach dem Johannesevangelium", *BuK* 20 (1965) 40. The descent in humiliation and ascent to glory are found in Phil. 2,5-11. C. F. D. Moule, "Further Reflections on Philippians 2, 5-11", in W. W. Gasque-R. P. Martin (eds.), *Apostolic History and the Gospel: Biblical and Historical Essays presented to F. F. Bruce on his 60th Birthday,* (Exeter, Paternoster Press, 1970) pp. 264-276, has suggested that the process of descent to humiliation and ascent to glory are not separate movements in Phil. 2,5-11, but, as in John, Jesus is glorified in his incarnation and death. The Philippians are invited to follow him in this.

[87] I. de la Potterie, *art. cit.,* p. 462 argues that the "he said to them" of v. 35 is more detached than the "he answered" of vv. 23 and 30.

[88] See above pp. 145-149.

of the world (vv. 35-36).[89]   It is within this context that one must discuss John's use of "the Son of Man" in vv. 23 and 34.

1.   *The Son of Man in John 12,23*

Although Jesus' reply (ἀποκρίνεται αὐτοῖς) does appear at first sight to have little to do with the visit of the Greeks, there is an important connection.   Verse 23 can be understood as a direct answer to the Greeks who have come to "see"[90] Jesus.[91]   They will see him, but as the glorified Son of Man, lifted up on the cross, drawing *all men* to himself (v. 32).   It is as the glorified Son of Man that the Gentile world will come to "see" Jesus. It is not the task of the earthly Jesus to preach to the Gentiles (see Matt. 10,5-6), but in the glorified Son of Man on the cross they will have their chance to "see" Jesus and the revelation which he has come to bring (see 19,37).   As Westcott has said, the answer of Jesus is "the permanent interpretation of the incident"[92] and so with the arrival of the Greeks, Jesus can at last say that the "hour" has come.   Up till now the "hour" has not yet come (see 2,4; 7,6.30; 8,20), but now it has (see also 13,1; 17,1).   It is clear that the "hour" refers to the cross.   The steady build-up of tension towards this hour is not worked out until the τετέλεσται of 19,30, when Jesus bows his head and "hands over" the Spirit.   However, the hour is not merely the physical crucifixion.   Both 13,1 and 17,1 speak of this hour as the moment when Jesus returns to the glory which was his with the Father (see 1,1: πρὸς τὸν θεόν).   While Thüsing in his work on the elevation and glorification

---

[89] See I. de la Potterie, *art. cit.*, pp. 463-464, where he explains the meaning of the chiasm.   We would add, however, the section on the light.

[90] The verb may simply mean "to visit".   See W. Bauer-W. F. Arndt-F. W. Gingrich, *A Greek-English Lexicon*, p. 220; but in the thought of John it may well be a suggestion of "belief in".   See C. Traets, *Voir Jésus et le Père en lui*, pp. 68-71.

[91] See R. Schnackenburg, *Johannesevangelium* II, p. 479: "Die Antwort Jesu an die beiden Jünger enthält keinen Bescheid für die Griechen, aber eine theologische Deutung ihrer Präsenz".   This is obscured by some commentators.   See R. E. Brown, *John*, p. 467: "Jesus' response is a comment on the whole scene, rather than a response to either group".   M.-J. Lagrange, *St. Jean*, p. 330 misses the point entirely claiming that, "Ce n'est pas le temps des interviews".   See also J. Sanders, *St. John*, p. 292, who quotes Lagrange favourably.   See the study of H. B. Kossen, "Who were the Greeks of John 12,20?" in *Studies in John*, pp. 97-110, esp. pp. 108-110.   See also N. A. Dahl, "The Johannine Church and History", in *Current Issues in New Testament Interpretation*, pp. 126-127. Recently, W. E. Moore, " 'Sir, We Wish to See Jesus'.   Was This an Occasion of Temptation?" *ScotJT* 20 (1967) 75-93, has argued that the coming of the Greeks is not so much a sign of the universality of Jesus' mission as a cause of a serious dilemma in the life of Jesus.   In deep sympathy with their longing for God, he was tempted to do what he could to satisfy this and to sidestep the cross.

[92] B. F. Westcott, *St. John*, p. 180.

of Jesus, claims that the hour refers strictly to the event of the cross,[93] others argue that the resurrection and the ascension are involved.[94] Blank has shown convincingly that there can be no separation and that

> "Die 'Stunde' bezeichnet demnach nicht in erster Linie die historisch fixierbare Todesstunde Jesu, obwohl sie diese selbstverständlich einschliesst. Auch nicht die Todesstunde plus deren Bedeutsamkeit. Sondern sie bezeichnet in erster Linie *ein Geschehen, eine Ereignis-Ganzheit oder einen Ereignis-Zusammenhang*, das 'Hinübergehen', die Verherrlichung des Menschensohnes".[95]

Thüsing, in an appendix to the second edition of his work, has accepted this criticism.[96] However, the context must be taken into consideration; we have seen that the whole of the chapter is directed to the passion. The immediate context explains to us what John means here by his use of "hour"; vv. 24-25 undoubtedly refer to the death of Jesus and v. 27 identifies the "hour" with the ταραχή of Jesus. It is clear that the cross is uppermost in John's mind in his use of "hour" in v. 23.[97]

In going to his death the Son of Man will be glorified. This Johannine idea is a clear indication that the "glorification" involved here has nothing to do with the Son of Man found in Jewish apocalyptic traditions, which Schulz uses to explain the presence of the title.[98] The glorification of Jesus is something which has had various moments throughout the Gospel, up till now:[99] in the first and the last of his miracles (2,11; 11,4) his glory could be seen; from 11,4 and 17,4 we can also see that already in the earthly work of Jesus his glory could be seen. However, this can only be a preparatory moment of glory before the supreme manifestation of the δόξα, as we are told in 7,39

---

[93] W. Thüsing, *Erhöhung*, pp. 75-100, esp. pp. 99-100.

[94] See R. E. Brown, review of W. Thüsing, *Erhöhung*, in *TS* 21 (1960) 637-639; Idem, *John*, pp. 475. 517-518; M.-E. Boismard, review of W. Thüsing, *Erhöhung*, in *RB* 71 (1964) 628; R. Bultmann, *John*, p. 424.

[95] J. Blank, *Krisis*, p. 139; stress Blank's. See also pp. 134-143. See also R. Schnackenburg, "Zur Johanneischen Theologie", *BZ* 6 (1962) 292-296.

[96] See W. Thüsing, *op. cit.*, p. 306.

[97] In this, Thüsing's original contribution remains valid. See *op. cit.*, pp. 75-78. 101-107. See also, I. de la Potterie, *art. cit.*, p. 464. For a detailed study of the "hour" in this passage, see G. Ferraro, *L'"ora" di Cristo*, pp. 178-201. Ferraro shows the close link between the "hour", the cross and the glorification. He fails, however, to see the importance of the use of "the Son of Man", which he identifies with "the Son". For example, he concludes: "Il Figlio dell'Uomo è il 'Figlio' che si rivolge al 'Padre' come tale" (p. 201). However, Jesus is not presented as "the Son" anwhere in this chapter.

[98] S. Schulz, *Untersuchungen*, p. 119. He sees this verse as a reflection of I Enoch 51,3 which has been christianised. For criticism of this, see J. Blank, *Krisis*, p. 270., note 13; A. J. B. Higgins, *Son of Man*, p. 179.

[99] On "glorification", see esp., W. Thüsing, *Erhöhung*, pp. 41-192; G. Kittel, Art. "δόξα", in *TDNT* II, pp. 247-255; W. Grossouw, "La glorification du Christ", in *L'Évangile de Jean*, pp. 131-145; J. Blank, *Krisis*, pp. 271-272; J. T. Forestell, *The Word of the Cross*, pp. 65-74; T. Worden, "The Glory of God", pp. 85-94.

that "as yet the Spirit had not been given, because Jesus was not yet glorified". The hour of glorification and the giving of the Spirit are intimately linked. This will take place when Jesus bows his head on the cross and παρέδωκεν τὸ πνεῦμα (19,30). It is, therefore, on the cross that Jesus will be glorified, and it is as the Son of Man that he receives this glory (see 3,13-14; 8,28; 12,23.28; 13,31). However, the glorification does not stop with the event of the cross; once he has died, then the glorified Son of Man will begin to bear fruit (see v. 24). The glorification will continue after the cross (see 14,13; 15,8; 16,14; 17,10),[100] but it takes place because of the cross (12,24).

The task of Jesus is to reveal the Father: "I glorified thee on earth, having accomplished the work (τὸ ἔργον τελειώσας) which thou gavest me to do" (17,4). This work was to bring eternal life to men — "And this is eternal life, to know thee the only true God, and Jesus Christ whom thou hast sent" (17,3). Jesus has glorified the Father in the performance of this task and thus, in the revelation of the Father to men, to bring them eternal life, Jesus is glorified.[101] The accomplishment (τελειώσας) of τὸ ἔργον comes about when Jesus, the Son of Man, is lifted up on the cross. There is a direct link between the τελειώσας of 17,4, the τελειωθῇ of 19,28 and the τετέλεσται of 19,30, when this work will be brought to its conclusion.[102]

The revelation of God which is accomplished by Jesus during his earthly life, and consummated on the cross, is the work of the Son of Man (see 3,13-14; 6,27.53; 8,28; 12,23. 28; 13,31). The continuation of that revelation, when the consummation of death bears its fruit (see 14,13; 15,8; 16,14; 17,10) no longer refers to Jesus as the Son of Man.[103] In the prologue John describes the incarnation: "The word became flesh and dwelt among us, full of grace and truth; we have beheld his glory, glory as of the only Son from the Father" (1,14). This glory as of (ὡς) the only Son is what is revealed in the incarnate Logos, the Son of Man. The incarnation is the fact upon which the revelation of the glory rests, but John uses "the Son of Man" only during his account of the earthly ministry of Jesus, with the exception of 13,31, which looks

---

[100] See on this W. Thüsing, *op. cit.*, pp. 107-123.

[101] R. H. Strachan, *Fourth Gospel*, p. 253.

[102] There are of course two different verbs involved, τελειόω and τελέω but they are both derived from τέλος (see 13,1). See W. Bauer-W. F. Arndt-F. W. Gingrich, *A Greek-English Lexicon*, pp. 817-820.

[103] Thüsing has shown that there is a period of *Hinübersteigen* which is the earthly work of Jesus, culminating in the hour of his death (12,23.24; 13,1; 13,31). This period during which Jesus glorifies the Father through the obedient performance of his will is marked by the use of the term "the Son of Man". Thüsing does not comment on this fact; his "second stage", the *Beim Vater sein* has the use of "Son" (see 14,13) but "the Son of Man" is never found. There is no reference to Jesus' return to the Father in 12,23, as is claimed by S. Schulz, *Johannes*, p. 166.

back over what has gone before and looks forward to what is about to happen in the passion.[104] In the heart of the passion narrative, Pilate may well proclaim Jesus as the Son of Man in his ἰδοὺ ὁ ἄνθρωπος (19,5).[105]

The use of the Son of Man in 12,23 is consistent with what has been said of that figure throughout the rest of the Gospel. The advent of the Greeks causes Jesus to announce that the supreme moment of revelation has arrived, when the Son of Man will be fully glorified in the full revelation of the Father, when he will be lifted up on the cross. "It is in conquering death by laying down His life that Christ both glorifies God and reveals the true glory which comes from God, though this is as yet far from explicit".[106]

The saying is Johannine in its expression; its reference to the passion as the place of Jesus' glorification as the Son of Man is consistent with other parts of the Gospel which refer to the cross (see 3,14; 6,53; 8,28).[107] This may well be a use of the title which has come to John through the tradition (see Mk. 8,31),[108] but the addition of the "glorification-revelation" theme is something new.[109]

Borsch and Smalley have both attempted to link 12,23 with traditional material.[110] Borsch suggests that the kingly Man and the Servant figure of Ps. 8,5; Is. 49,3; 52,13 and Ps. 21,5 stand behind the use of "the Son of Man" here.[111] In the Synoptic tradition he finds "some manner of association" between John 12,23; 13,31 and Mk. 8,31-38; 14,21.41.[112] The link seems to be very tenuous, and his speculation about the Kingly Man of Ps. 8,5 etc., has little to do with the figure of Jesus as the Son of Man in John 12,23, as we have come to understand it. There is, however, every possibility that

---

[104] Against A. J. B. Higgins, *Son of Man*, p. 155, where he claims that the title is scattered haphazardly throughout the first thirteen chapters of the Gospel. Its use is far from haphazard, as we hope we have shown.

[105] See below, pp. 202-206.

[106] C. H. Dodd, *Interpretation*, p. 374. See also W. F. Howard, "St. John", p. 661; H. van den Bussche, "Si le grain de blé ne tombe en terre ... (Jen 12,20-39)", *BibVChr* 5 (1954) 54-57.

[107] See J. H. Bernard, *St. John*, p. 433; J. Marsh, *St. John*, p. 463.

[108] See J. C. Fenton, *John*, p. 130.

[109] J. Blank, *Krisis*, p. 271 has attempted to show that John may have come to this position through such traditional passages as Lk. 24,26 and Acts 7,55-56. He also thinks that the Servant figure of Is. 52,13-53,12 has played a role in the development of this idea. D. Hill, "The Request of Zebedee's Sons and the Johannine δόξα Theme", *NTS* 13 (1966-67) 281-285 makes a similar link with Mk. 10,35-45.

[110] F. H. Borsch, *The Son of Man*, pp. 306-309; S. S. Smalley, "The Johannine Son of Man Sayings", p. 296.

[111] F. H. Borsch, *op. cit.*, p. 306.

[112] Smalley also sees Mk. 14,41 as a Synoptic parallel to Jn. 12,23 (*art. cit.*, p. 296). Borsch, p. 309, note 2, suggests that the whole passage of Mk. 8,28-9,1 is reflected in Jn. 12,23-34.

the lifting up and the glorification of the Servant in Is. 52,13 played some role in John's use of these same terms for his Son of Man.

Bultmann, who generally relegates the title to the hand of an ecclesiastical redactor, allows that here the title comes from the Gnostic revelatory discourse.[113] Originally the myth spoke of the glorification of the Son of Man as the moment of his ascent into heaven, which brought about a catastrophe for the cosmos, which up till that moment had been in the clutches of the demons. Now, with the return of the Son of Man to glory, the period of slavery is over.[114] When this is taken into the Christian tradition as evolved in the Fourth Gospel, it means that, "It is the hour when the Messenger will return to heavenly glory".[115] Because of his presuppositions concerning a Gnostic source and his rearrangement of the Gospel, Bultmann's suggestions are of little help in our attempt to understand John's use of the term "the Son of Man".

Lindars claims that the idea behind the glorification of Jesus as the Son of Man is, ultimately, the same as the vindication of the Son of Man in Dan. 7.[116] This may well be the case; there is every possibility that one of the influences which caused John to use the title "the Son of Man" was the traditional use of the title for Jesus, who was to be vindicated, like the Danielic Son of Man.[117] However, John has shifted the stress somewhat. No longer does the glory come in Jesus' future role as the Son of Man, but in his 'elevation' on the cross. As this is so, although the details of the scene in Dan. 7 probably have little bearing on the interpretation of Jn. 12,23, John may well have expressed the central idea.

Some scholars have suggested that the title is used here and elsewhere, to speak of Jesus' humanity.[118] This appears to be a valid suggestion, which is born out by the fact that the fulness of this revelation takes place in the very human event of death, which is so much to the fore in our present context.

> "Der Hinweis auf den Gekreuzigten besagt dann aber auch, dass schon der menschgewordene Logos, der in die Welt gesandte Sohn, der als Mensch gekreuzigt werden konnte, für Johannes der Menschensohn ist".[119]

The important fact remains, however, that this "man" once dwelt πρὸς τὸν θεόν (1,1). Because he has descended in the incarnation and become the

---

[113] R. Bultmann, *John*, p. 422.

[114] *ibid.*, p. 422.

[115] *ibid.*, p. 424.

[116] B. Lindars, *John*, p. 427.

[117] See on this M. D. Hooker, *The Son of Man in Mark*, pp. 182-198. See esp. p. 197

[118] See J. Jeremias, *Johannes*, p. 244; B. F. Westcott, *St. John*, p. 181; T. Zahn *Johannes*, pp. 505-506; T. Torrence, "We Would See Jesus (John 12,21)", *EvQu* 23 (1951) 171-172; R. Beauvery, "Jésus élevé attire les hommes à lui (Jean 12,20-33)", *EsprVie* 80 (1970) 118-119.

[119] J. Blank, *Krisis*, p. 288.

Son of Man (3,13), his death can be the hour for this Son of Man to reveal God, and to draw all men to himself (12,23.32).

It is interesting to note that the title has been used in a context immediately preceded by a misunderstanding of the nature and role of Jesus. As we have shown above,[120] the crowds have come to meet Jesus inspired by the hope of a political messianic king. They have greeted him with the titles ὁ ἐρχόμενος and "The King of Israel". These titles are not wrong; they are wrongly understood. Jesus has come, as the Son of Man, to do his Father's will: to die on the cross and to reveal the Father in this death. This is the true meaning of his kingship, and to correct false impressions, John has again used the title "the Son of Man".[121]

2. *The Son of Man in John 12,34.*

John's continual use of the title "the Son of Man" in a context which corrects or qualifies other notions concerning Jesus' person and role now receives its fullest expression. The crowd know all that is to be known about the Messiah; they have it from the Old Testament. Although the verb "to know" is not used here, the attitude adopted by the crowd is the same as that of the Pharisees in chapter 9. There they refused to listen to the evidence of the man born blind, and thus refused Jesus, because they "knew" that God had spoken to Moses. They needed to know of nothing else (see 9,24. 29.31).[122] In 12,34 the same stance is taken. Who is this man who would dare throw their knowledge into question? Their question is full of arrogance: "How can *you* say that the Son of Man must be lifted up? Who is *this* Son of man?" (12,34b). This is made clear by the deliberate use of λέγεις σύ and the derogatory sense of the οὗτος.,[123]

There appears to be an identification of the Son of Man with the Messiah here. This, however, need not necessarily be the case. It is important to understand v. 34 within the whole context of chapter 12. The scene of the

---

[120] See above pp. 171-172.
[121] Against W. A. Meeks, *The Prophet-King*, p. 87. Meeks argues that "there is no rejection of or protest against their acclamation in verse 15". He likens the crowd to Nathanael. We have attempted to show above that the acclamation of 1,49 is further qualified by the response of Jesus, in terms of "the Son of Man", in 1,51. See above on 1,51, pp. 33-37. This pattern has been found in almost every Son of Man saying.
[122] See above pp. 148-149.
[123] See F. Tillmann, *Der Menschensohn. Jesu Selbstzeugnis für seine messianische Würde*, (Bonn, P. Hauptmann, 1905) p. 51, note 1. H. van den Bussche, "Si le grain de blé...", p. 67.

entry into Jerusalem is still the background for the question of the crowd.[124] They have welcomed Jesus into Jerusalem as ὁ ἐρχόμενος [125] and as the King of Israel (v. 13), waving palm fronds in their expectation of a new political restoration.[126] The question from the Greeks (vv. 21-22), however, has given Jesus cause to correct this misinterpretation, in terms of the Son of Man whose hour of glory will come through his death (vv. 23-32). In the likelihood that the "lifting up" of this Son of Man be further misunderstood, John adds his own clarification in v. 33: "He said this to show by what death he was to die".[127] Indeed the crowd, understanding the "lifting up" to refer to crucifixion, has realised that Jesus is talking about death, and their complaint arises from the conviction that the Messiah would not die.[128] Again they are wrong; they have an understanding of the χριστός which Jesus has been correcting throughout the discourse, especially in vv. 23 and 32.

It is difficult to determine precisely what part of the Old Testament the crowd has in mind. Many passages have been suggested: Jer. 24,6; 33,17.22; Ez. 37,25; Ps. 110,4; Is. 9,6 from the Old Testament itself, and I Enoch 49,1; 62,14; Ps. Sol. 17,4; Orac. Sibyll. 3,49-50.766 from later Jewish literature. W. C. van Unnik has pointed out that none of these texts is satisfactory,[129] as the reference to the Old Testament is limited to the words εἰς τὸν αἰῶνα.[130] The key to the crowd's objection, however, is to be found in the idea of μένειν. All the above texts have a messianic context and speak of an eternal reign. This is not quite what the crowd says. They claim that the Messiah will *remain* for ever, and not die. A more precise parallel is found in LXX Ps. 88,37, where the Davidic line is promised that it will εἰς τὸν αἰῶνα μένει. In this reference we have a specific text and not a vague contact. As in the other uses of ὁ νόμος (10,34 and 15,25)

---

[124] See M.-J. Lagrange, *St. Jean,* p. 335: "On voit que la foule est encore sous l'impression de ses acclamations. Elle vient de saluer le roi d'Israël, estimant que Jésus se donnait comme tel."; See also R. H. Lightfoot, *St. John,* p. 243; R. Schnackenburg, *Johannesevangelium* II, p. 495.

[125] On the messianic use of this title, see J. Schneider, Art. "ἔρχομαι", *TDNT* II, p. 670; V. Taylor, *The Names of Jesus,* pp. 78-79; C. K. Barrett, *St. John,* p. 348, see, however, p. 349; J. H. Bernard, *St. John,* p. 424; R. E. Brown, *John,* p. 457; B. Lindars, *John,* p. 423; A. Schlatter, *Johannes,* p. 265: "Der im Namen Gottes kommende König is der Sieger".

[126] See above pp. 171-172.

[127] Against H. J. Flowers, "Interpolations in the Fourth Gospel", pp. 155-156, who sees v. 33 as an interpolation which has misunderstood what Jesus was saying.

[128] Again the use of ὑψωθῆναι has nothing to do with the ascension.

[129] W. C. van Unnik, "The Quotation from the Old Testament in John 12,34", pp. 174-179.

[130] These words appear in heavy print in both the Nestle-Aland and the Kilpatrick editions of the Greek New Testament.

a psalm is used, and the messianic reference to a specific seed of David is far better than the generalities of the other possible sources.[131]

The reason for the crowd's difficulty is that the Son of Man will die when he is lifted up. Many scholars object that the introduction of the Son of Man here is difficult to understand, as the title has not been mentioned in the immediate context.[132] For some, this has been the basis for rearrangements.[133] The Son of Man has, however, been mentioned in v. 23. As the discourse is a tightly linked whole,[134] it is this same Son of Man who comes into question when Jesus says: "I, when I am lifted up from the earth, will draw all men to myself" (v. 32). This should be clear to the readers, as all the other "lifting up" sayings in the Gospel (3,14; 8,28) speak of the Son of Man. Now, as John becomes more explicit at the end of the public ministry of Jesus, the Son of Man is identified with Jesus himself in the "I" saying of v. 32. The crowd has no difficulty in understanding this, and the use of "the Son of Man" here flows logically from the whole context of the discussion.[135]

Behind this question from the crowd lies a problem faced by the Johannine Church. The "crowd" clearly refers to the Jews, as they seek their answer in the Old Testament. They want to know, not the identity of Jesus, but the status and function which he claims.[136] Ultimately the Johannine Church would have to answer the question: does the Son of Man mean something other than the Messiah?[137] The Messiah welcomed by the Jews in v. 13 did not fulfil the role which Jesus had played. He was a Messiah who glorified the Father and was glorified himself by revealing the Father through his being "lifted up" on the cross. It was through his being lifted up on the cross that he would draw all men to himself (see 8,28; 12,32), not by a show of political power. This was an extraordinary message for those whose hopes were placed in a political Messiah, and it was one of the major difficulties

---

[131] See W. C. van Unnik, *art. cit.*, p. 179. The conclusions of van Unnik have been supported by G. Reim, *Studien zum alttestamentlichen Hintergrund*, pp. 32-34. E. D. Freed, *Old Testament Quotations in the Gospel of John*, does not discuss 12,34.

[132] See L. Morris, *John*, p. 599; S. S. Smalley, "The Johannine Son of Man Sayings", p. 296; B. F. Westcott, *St. John*, p. 183.

[133] See above pp. 160-162.

[134] See above pp. 166-168.

[135] See W. Thüsing, " 'Wenn ich von der Erde erhöht bin...' ", pp. 40-43; R. E. Brown, *John*, p. 478; R. Schnackenburg, *Johannesevangelium* II, p. 495; F. H. Borsch, *Son of Man*, p. 310.

[136] See J. Sanders, *St. John*, p. 296; M. de Jonge, "Jewish Expectations about the 'Messiah' ", p. 261.

[137] See F. H. Borsch, *Son of Man*, p. 312, note 1; B. Vawter, "John", p. 450. S. Sabugal, *Christos*, pp. 354-360, has seen this; however, he maintains (pp. 360-362) that on a redactional level, John wants to identify the Christ with the Son of Man who must suffer.

faced by the early Church (see I Cor. 1,18-25), but it was the message imposed upon the Church by the events of history.[138]

The words of Jesus which follow (vv. 35-36) are to be understood as a continuation of vv. 23-34. Throughout the Gospel the Son of Man has been presented as the place where men could find the revelation of God. Very often this has been further clarified by placing the Son of Man sayings in a context where Jesus is presented as the light (see 3,19-21; 8,12; chapter 9). The refusal to accept Jesus as the Son of Man, implied in v. 34, leads to a final proclamation of the same theme. The misunderstanding involved in v. 34 would not have been possible for people who were prepared to accept the revelation brought by the crucified Son of Man. Now Jesus states this fact again. He has come to bring the light. If they are to be saved they must follow this light. If they do not, then they will be taken up by darkness (v. 35). It is belief in the light — the revelation of the Son of Man — that will make them sons of light. It is implicit that a refusal of the light will make them sons of darkness.[139]

Again we find the Son of Man in a context of judgment. In v. 31 we were told that "Now is the judgment of this world, now shall the ruler of the world be cast out". In vv. 35-36 it is implicit that their acceptance or refusal of the Son of Man — the light of the world — shall determine the judgment of men.[140] Having made this final appeal, "he departed and hid himself from them" (v. 36b). The next time he will appear in public, it will be for the realisation of the lifting up of the Son of Man.

John 12 contains no reference to Jesus as the Son. The whole of the chapter, therefore, should be considered in the light of the use of "the Son of Man". Although we have shown that here, as elsewhere, what is implied in the use of this title is the presentation of Jesus as the unique revealer of God and consequently as the place where men will judge themselves, the stress throughout the chapter is on the passion. The hints that have been given throughout the Gospel that the supreme moment of revelation will take place on the cross (see 1,51; 3,13-14; 6,27.53; 8,28), have now been made fully explicit. Now is the hour for the glorification of the Son of Man (v. 23), when he will be lifted up on the cross to draw all men to himself (v. 32). This is also the moment of the final judgment of the world (v. 33). However,

---

[138] See R. Schnackenburg, *Johannesevangelium* II, p. 496; R. E. Brown, *John*, p. 479; M. de Jonge, "Jewish Expectations...", p. 261; B. Lindars, *John*, p. 434.

[139] See R. E. Brown, *John*, pp. 479-480. Brown points out that the Son of Man was closely connected with the theme of light in chapter 9. We would suggest that this is also important in chapters 3 and 8; E. C. Hoskyns, *Fourth Gospel*, B. Lindars, *John*, p. 436; R. H. Lightfoot, *St. John*, p. 245; R. Schnackenburg, *Johannesevangelium* II, pp. 496-497; H. Strathmann, *Johannes*, pp. 188-191.

[140] See C. F. D. Moule, *Phenomenon*, p. 92.

the Jews continue to insist that they have the answers in their knowledge of the Christ, ὁ ἐρχόμενος and the King of Israel (see vv. 13.34). Throughout the Gospel John has used the title "the Son of Man" to correct or complement false or only partially correct views of the nature and role of Jesus. The Son of Man is the pre-existent Logos who has become man (1,14); he has descended from the Father and, as such, can reveal that Father with unique authority (see 3,13; 6,62), but the Jews understand none of this. They continue to be satisfied by answers which they themselves can determine by their own understanding of their human traditions. Because of this John can explain their unbelief by saying: "For they valued their reputation with men rather than the honour which comes from God" (12,43, NEB).

CHAPTER NINE

NOW IS THE SON OF MAN GLORIFIED:
John 13,31; 19,5

I - General Structure and Meaning of John 13

The first section of the "Book of Glory", John 13, can be divided into three major sections:

vv. 1-20:   The footwashing
vv. 21-30: Prediction of the betrayal
vv. 31-38: Introduction to the last discourse.[1]

Some scholars prefer to examine the material of the last discourse in larger blocks. For example, R. H. Lightfoot and A. Schlatter both see chs. 13-14 as concerned with the theme of the Lord's departure and return.[2] Their commentaries, however, tend to follow the divisions given above.[3]

Rudolf Bultmann has worked out an elaborate rearrangement for the whole of the last discourse. The description of the last supper (13,1a.2-30)

---

[1] R. E. Brown, *John*, p. 545; J. C. Fenton, *John*, pp. 139-149; J. Marsh, *St. John*, pp. 482-498; C. H. Dodd, *Interpretation*, pp. 401-403; E. C. Hoskyns, *Fourth Gospel*, pp. 432-433; C. K. Barrett, *St. John*, pp. 363-378; W. Temple, *Readings*, pp. 207-229; M.-J. Lagrange, *St. Jean*, pp. 348-371; B. F. Westcott *St. John*, pp. 188-189; R. H. Strachan, *Fourth Gospel*, pp. 265-279; A. Loisy, *Quatrième Évangile*, pp. 382-403; A. Wikenhauser, *Johannes*, pp. 204-209; B. Vawter, "John", pp. 451-452; H. van den Bussche, *Jean*, pp. 385-386; W. Bauer, *Johannesevangelium*, pp. 167-177; T. Zahn, *Johannes*, pp. 522-566; P. Corssen, Die Abschiedsreden Jesu im vierten Evangelium", *ZNW* 8 (1907) 127; P. Gächter, "Der formale Aufbau der Abschiedsreden Jesu", *ZKT* 58 (1934) 160-165; S. Schulz, *Johannes*, pp. 170-182; A. Durand, "Le discours de la cène (Saint Jean 13,31-17,26)", *RecSR* 1 (1910) 121-122; G.-M. Behler, *The Last Discourse of Jesus*, (Baltimore, Helicon, 1966) p. 13; F.-M. Braun, "St. Jean", pp. 418-425.

[2] R. H. Lightfoot, *St. John*, p. 255; A. Schlatter, *Johannes*, pp. 278-326. Schlatter studies the whole discourse (13,1-17,26) without dividing it into sections.

[3] See, for example, R. H. Lightfoot, *St. John*, pp. 263-268. See R. E. Brown, *John*, pp. 608-609 for a convincing argument that 13,31-38, although an introduction to the last discourse, stands by itself. It already contains most of the elements which will be developed in the discourse. In a similar vein see J. Schneider, "Die Abschriedsreden Jesu. Ein Beitrag zur Frage der Komposition von Joh 13,31-17,26", in *Gott und die Götter. Festgabe für Erich Fascher zum 60. Geburtstag*, (Berlin, Evangelische Verlagsanstalt, 1958) pp. 105-106.

is seen as an introduction: "The Founding of the Community and its Law".[4] Verses 31-38 are assigned to various other parts of the discourse. Chapter 15 fits in after 13,35, as 15,1-17 is a commentary on the command of love (see 13,34-35); 13,36-38 follow 16,33. In this way Bultmann claims that he has restored the traditional order of the prophecies of the disciples' flight and of Peter's denial (see Mk. and Matt.).[5] Chapter 17 follows immediately after 13,30 and in the Johannine scheme it takes the place of the Synoptic last supper.[6] Thus the section is constructed in the following fashion:[7]

13,1bcd:	Introduction to the farewell prayer
17,1-26:	The farewell prayer
13,31-32:	Repetition of 17,1-8 when the hour of farewell is spelt out as the hour of glory
13,33:	This farewell and glory involve separation and distress
13,34-35:	The solution of this problem — love
15,1-17:	Further indications concerning how distress is overcome
15,18-16,11:	The Community in the world
16,12-33:	The believer's future as the eschatological situation
13,36-14,31:	Conclusion: The believer's fellowship with the Son and the Father.

This rearrangement has points in its favour as the section 14,25-31 does lead logically into the passion, concluding with the words: "Rise, let us go hence". The removal of chapter 17 to the beginning of the discourse, however, presents many difficulties. Bultmann has completely reworked 13,1, leaving the indications of time at the beginning of the footwashing scene[8] and re-organising what is left of the verse in such a way that it becomes a theological introduction to ch. 17.[9] This appears to be entirely unwarranted. The love of Jesus for his own εἰς τέλος makes admirable sense in its present position. It is both an introduction to the footwashing scene and to the whole of the

---

[4] R. Bultmann, *John*, p. 461. See pp. 461-479 where Bultmann assigns these verses, during his commentary, to the various stages of the redaction.

[5] *ibid.*, p. 460.

[6] *ibid.*, p. 461.

[7] *ibid.*, pp. 486-631. For a concise presentation of this rearrangement and the motives, both theological and linguistic, which inspire it, see D. M. Smith, *The Composition and Order of the Fourth Gospel*, pp. 168-172. For the rearranged text, see pp. 201-207.

[8] *op. cit.*, pp. 463-465. See also H. Thyen, "Johannes 13 und die kirchliche Redaktion des vierten Evangeliums" in *Tradition und Glaube: Das frühe Christentum in seiner Umwelt: Festgabe für Karl Georg Kuhn zum 65. Geburtstag*, (Göttingen, Vandenhoeck und Ruprecht, 1971), pp. 346-347. He sees vv. 1-3 as the work of an editor who corrected the Gnostic tendencies of the original Gospel.

[9] R. Bultmann, *op. cit.*, pp. 486-489.

book of glory, when Jesus "would depart out of this world to the Father".[10] Chapter 17 can also be understood in its present position.   There are literary difficulties involved in the traditional order, but these should be explained by a use of sources.   It is logical that at the end of the last discourse Jesus can say: "I glorified thee on earth, having accomplished (τελειώσας) the work which thou gavest me to do" (17,4).   Jesus has promised throughout that he would be finally glorified.   It is only fitting that when he has prayed to the Father: "Now Father, glorify thou me ..." (17,5), Jesus turns immediately to the cross.[11]

The literary difficulties have led other scholars to rearrange the material. J. H. Bernard suggests: 13,1-31a; ch. 15; ch. 16; 13,31b-38; ch. 14 and ch. 17.[12]   G. H. C. Macgregor sees the original text as 13,1-35; chs. 15,16,14, 17;[13] verses 36-38 are regarded as a later addition by a redactor.[14]   Other scholars attempt to establish an original *Grundschrift*.   F. Spitta sees it as 13,31a, chs. 15 and 16,[15] while E. Hirsch reconstructs the discourse from an amazing collection of various parts: 13,31-33; 16,4b-6; 14,1.2.3c-7a; 14,8-10; 12,16; 17; 16,5-7; 15,4-6 etc...[16]   H. Becker, constructing a supposed Gnostic source for the Johannine discourses, concludes that 13,31-38 may contain traces of the source but is, on the whole, the composition of the Evangelist.[17]

The variety of these suggestions[18] and the presuppositions of the scholars who make them cast doubt on the validity of this approach.   It is ironic to note that the only place in the Fourth Gospel where manuscript evidence gives support for a rearrangement (the Syriac version of 18,12-27[19]) is corrected by Bultmann as a later attempt to make the account more coherent by shuffling

[10] See G.-M. Behler, *The Last Discourse*, p. 19; F.-M. Braun, "St. Jean", p. 418; R. E. Brown, *John*, pp. 562-563; C. H. Dodd, *Interpretation*, pp. 401-402; E. C. Hoskyns, *Fourth Gospel*, p. 437; M.-J. Lagrange, *St. Jean*, p. 349; A. Schlatter, *Johannes*, p. 278.

[11] For further criticism of Bultmann's rearrangements, see D. M. Smith, *op. cit.*, pp. 172-175.

[12] J. H. Bernard, *St. John*, pp. 454-477. 522-530.

[13] G. H. C. Macgregor, *John*, pp. 281-282.

[14] *ibid.*, p. 282.

[15] F. Spitta, *Johannes*, pp. 297-301.   See also p. 328.

[16] E. Hirsch, *Studien zum vierten Evangelium*, pp. 106-108.

[17] H. Becker, *Die Reden des Johannesevangeliums*, p. 94.   See also J. Wellhausen, *Johannis*, pp. 61-62.

[18] For a further summary of other rearrangement theories, see W. F. Howard-C. K. Barrett, *The Fourth Gospel in Recent Criticism and Interpretation*, (London, Epworth Press, 1955) p. 303.

[19] Verse 24 is found immediately after v. 13 and vv. 16-18 follow v. 23 in the Sinaitic Syriac version.   See W. G. Kümmel, *Introduction to the New Testament*, (London, SCM Press, 1966) pp. 146. 371.   (English translation of *Einleitung in das Neue Testament*, [Heidelberg, Quelle und Meyer, 1965]); J. Schneider, "Zur Komposition von Joh 18,12-27, Kaiaphas und Hannas", *ZNW* 48 (1957) 11-19.

the verses.[20] If this is so, then it is not only the Sinaitic Syriac translator who has fallen into this trap. There are difficulties in the text, but these are best explained by the inelegant juxtaposition of various pieces of material,[21] and it is the task of the interpreter to attempt an explanation of the text as the early Church gave it to us.[22] It appears that John 13 is coherent in its traditional order.

Two sections of the chapter are closely linked to the meal. Verses 1-20 report the footwashing, while verses 21-30 are concerned with the betrayal of Judas. The last discourse begins in vv. 31-38. It runs, broken only by the interruptions of the misunderstandings of the disciples, of which vv. 36-38 are a typical example, until 17,26. But when did the last supper take place? Was it a Passover meal? What is the relationship between the Johannine and the Synoptic accounts of the meal? What is the meaning of the foot-washing scene? Is there any connection between the footwashing scene and the discourse which follows? Not all of these problems can be discussed here,[23] but a correct interpretation of the meaning of the footwashing and Judas' betrayal, along with the connection which these narratives have with the beginning of the discourse in 13,31-32, must precede any discussion of the use of "the Son of Man" in 13,31.

Throughout the Fourth Gospel the Evangelist has used narrative to set the scene for a discourse (see 3,1-10; 4,1-15; 5,1-18; 6,1-24; 9,1-41). It is often remarked that the Book of Glory works in the opposite direction. The discourse of chs. 13-17 precedes and explains the meaning of the events of the passion and glorification.[24] This is so because it is hardly possible for the Evangelist to write a Gospel which has the passion as its mid-point, followed by a lengthy discourse. However, a great deal of the last discourse is written as if the glorification has already taken place, and in this way it explains the passion and glorification of Jesus, who is giving the discourse.[25]

Yet it is not entirely true to claim that John's process of narrative followed by discourse is completely reversed, as the last discourse does begin with a

[20] R. Bultmann, *John*, pp. 643-644.
[21] After a detailed examination of all the various displacement theories, H. M. Teeple, *The Literary Origin of the Gospel of John*, (Evanston, Religion and Ethics Institute, 1974) p. 116 concludes: "The arguments against the displacement theories are so strong that most New Testament scholars rightly reject them. We must look in other directions if we are to find the solution to the puzzle of the literary origin of John".
[22] See esp. J. Schneider, "Die Abschiedsreden ...", pp. 103-112.
[23] See the commentaries, and esp. R. E. Brown, *John*, pp. 555-562 for a full discussion of these questions. For an exhaustive discussion of the history of the exegesis of this passage, see G. Richter, *Die Fusswaschung im Johannesevangelium*, Biblische Untersuchungen 1, (Regensburg, Pustet, 1967).
[24] C. K. Barrett, *St. John*, p. 363.
[25] R. E. Brown, *John*, pp. 581-582.

narrative. The story of the last supper, the footwashing and the betrayal of Judas are not loosely attached to the discourse, but they are to be understood as "a symbolic narrative ... which prefigures the crucifixion itself, and in doing so points the way to the interpretation of the crucifixion".[26]

The narrative is introduced by vv. 1-3. What is about to be enacted, first in the footwashing and then on the cross, is explained in v. 1.[27] The meal is set in the context of the Passover, when the sacrificial lamb of God was slain (see 1,29; 1,36; see also Rev. 7,14; 12,11; 17,14 et passim).[28] What this means for John is that the "hour" has come for another kind of "passing over", when Jesus would go back to his Father.[29] Jesus has performed the task which was given to him. He has loved his own and this love will be expressed in its most perfect way in its consummation upon the cross.[30] Jesus' death is seen as an act of love (see 13,34; 15,9.13; 17,23; I John 3,16); it is also the moment of his being "lifted up" (see 3,14; 8,28; 12,32), the moment when he will draw all men to himself (12,32). Because of this there is probably a further meaning involved in the use of εἰς τέλος in v. 1. It is in the moment of elevation on the cross that the fulness of revelation will come and, in this way, John has drawn back into the life of Jesus what was, in the Synoptics, a future eschatological end time.[31]

The use of the aorist ἠγάπησεν has led some scholars to restrict the meaning of this verse to the scene which immediately follows.[32] If one has to decide a single action which is referred to by this use of the aorist then it must refer to the cross. The εἰς τέλος should not be restricted to the footwashing, as it clearly refers to the moment of climax, of which the footwashing is only a sign (see 19,30 — τετέλεσται).[33]

---

[26] C. K. Barrett, *St. John*, p. 363.

[27] See above pp. 187-188 and especially W. Grossouw, "A Note on John 13,1-3", *NT* 8 (1966) 124-131.

[28] See on this J. Jeremias, *The Eucharistic Words of Jesus*, pp. 82-83.

[29] See above on John 12,23, pp. 176-178.

[30] That this dual interpretation is meant by the use of τέλος is admitted by most commentators. See C. K. Barrett, *St. John*, p. 365; W. Bauer, *Johannesevangelium*, p. 167; G.-M. Behler, *The Last Discourse*, p. 19; F.-M. Braun, "St. Jean", p. 418; R. E. Brown, *John*, p. 563; R. Bultmann, *John*, p. 465-466; E. C. Hoskyns, *Fourth Gospel*, p. 437; M.-J. Lagrange, *St. Jean*, p. 349; B. Lindars, *John*, p. 448; A. Schlatter, *Johannes*, p. 278; H. Strathmann, *Johannes*, pp. 195-196; See F. Blass-A. Debrunner-R. W. Funk, *A Greek Grammar*, para. 268,3.

[31] See C. K. Barrett, *St. John*, p. 365; B. Lindars, *John*, p. 448; J. N. Sanders, *St. John*, p. 304.

[32] See J. H. Bernard, *St. John*, p. 458.

[33] J. Marsh, *St. John*, p. 483; J. D. G. Dunn, "The Washing of the Disciples' Feet in John, 13,1-20", *ZNW* 61 (1970) 248. It is tempting to see this aorist as "inceptive": with the action which is about to start, the perfect love of Jesus will be manifested throughout. See F. Blass-A. Debrunner-R. W. Funk, *A Greek Grammar*, para. 331; M.

In vv. 2-3 John shifts from his general introduction to the event which prefigures the climax. It takes place δείπνου γινομένου ,[34] during supper. The betrayal is also referred to, anticipating vv. 21-30. Yet Jesus, "knowing" all this,[35] puts aside his garments and prepares himself to wash the feet of his disciples. The account of the footwashing is difficult. There seems to be a contradiction between v. 7 where Jesus tells Peter that he will only understand the meaning of the action afterwards, and vv. 12 and 17 where the disciples are asked if they know what he has done (v. 12) and they are promised a blessing if they will carry on what they have been taught by the action (v. 17). There is also a change between vv. 4-11 where the action of the footwashing and the discussion with Peter takes place, and vv. 12-20, which is a short discourse of Jesus.

Various attempts have been made to clarify these difficulties. Some show that this is the result of editing.[36] Boismard suggests that we are dealing with two completely different accounts, originally:[37]

  i. A moralising account: vv. 1-2; 12-15; 17; 18-19.
  ii. A sacramental account: vv. 3; 4-5; 6-11; 21-30.

This division of the material is somewhat of a *tour de force*. He excludes the Synoptic sounding vv. 16 and 20 as redactional, and thus smooths the way for the application of a systematic division of the material.[38] There do appear to be two interpretations of the footwashing involved, and they may have come from different sources; it is also probable that the hand of the editor will show as he attempts to put the two interpretations together.[39]

Zerwick, *Biblical Greek,* para. 250. It is not usual, however, to find ἀγαπάω used in this way.

[34] That this is the best reading is generally accepted, although there is good textual evidence for γενομένου See B. M. Metzger, *A Textual Commentary,* p. 239; R. E. Brown, *John,* p. 551.

[35] The "knowledge" which Jesus has of all that is to follow is common in John. In the passion narrative this foreknowledge makes Jesus the master of the situation (see 18,4; 19,28). There is no need to resort to the theory of a Gnostic revealer, as does R. Bultmann, *John,* pp. 465-466.

[36] R. Bultmann, *John,* pp. 462-464, thinks that originally the author had a written source containing vv. 4-5; 12-20. The Evangelist later added vv. 7-11. G. Richter, *Die Fusswaschung,* p. 309, suggests that vv. 10b-11 were added later in imitation of vv. 18-19; H. Thyen, "Johannes 13 und die kirchliche Redaktion..." pp. 349-351, claims that vv. 12-17 are the product of an ecclesiastical redactor, who added them to counteract the Gnostic "Weltloses Semeion" involved in vv. 4-10a, by attaching it to time and space.

[37] M.-E. Boismard, "Le Lavement des pieds (Jn. 13,1-17)", *RB* 71 (1964) 5-24.

[38] For a full criticism of Boismard's suggestions, see R. E. Brown, *John,* pp. 560-561.

[39] See G. Richter, *Die Fusswaschung im Johannesevangelium,* pp. 249-320 for a recent discussion of this.

What is important for our purposes, however, is to understand what he was trying to say by putting them together.[40]

Although vv. 1-3 introduce the action, there is no break between vv. 3 and 4. Knowing that all these things have been given into his charge, and that his time among "his own" is drawing to a close as he will be shortly going to his Father, he prepares himself for the washing, and begins to wash the feet of the disciples (vv. 3-5). The meaning of this symbolic washing has been indicated by vv. 1-3. Now it is further clarified by the discussion with Peter. It will be understood μετὰ ταῦτα. In the light of vv. 1-3 this is clearly a reference to the passion.[41] Peter's refusal leads to Jesus' affirmation of a basic Christian principle: "If I do not wash you — if you are not prepared to share the cross with me — you have no part in me" (v. 8). Peter's eventual over-enthusiastic acceptance of the washing leads to the difficult v. 10.

There are several textual variants here, but the most serious concerns the inclusion or exclusion of εἰ μὴ τοὺς πόδας.[42] The textual support is finely balanced and whatever reading one chooses still leaves the verse somewhat obscure. The saying must be understood in its context, where Peter has foolishly misunderstood the footwashing, supposing that a more extensive washing will give him a greater union with Jesus. In v. 10 Jesus replies, pointing out that once one has entered into the death of Christ, one is entirely clean; further washings are pointless.[43] If this is the case, then why should an exception be made for the washing of the feet? It would appear that the early Church has linked this saying with Baptism, and in the light of the practice of forgiving post-Baptismal sins, has added the phrase. Augustine and some recent scholars have argued for this penitential interpretation of the passage as original,[44] but in the light of the context it appears to be a scribal

---

[40] See N. Lazure, "Le Lavement des pieds", *AssSeign* 38 (1967) 40-51, who admits editions but studies the final product. In defence of the unity of the scene, see E. Lohmeyer, "Die Fusswaschung", *ZNW* 38 (1939) 74-94; A. Weiser, "John 13,12-20 — Zufügung eines späteren Herausgebers?", *BZ* 12 (1968) 252-257.

[41] See R. Bultmann, *John*, p. 467; B. Lindars, *John*, p. 450.

[42] Included by Vaticanus, Ephraem Rescript, Freer Gospels, Armenian version, Origen (in a minority of citations) and Augustine. Excluded by Sinaiticus, 2 versions of the Old Latin, Vulgate, Tertullian and Origen (in the majority of cases).

[43] See C. K. Barrett, *St. John*, p. 368; R. Bultmann, *John*, p. 471.

[44] See P. Grelot, "L'interprétation pénitentielle du lavement des pieds", in *L'homme devant Dieu, Mélanges H. de Lubac*, (Paris, Aubier, 1963), Vol. I, pp. 75-91; W. L. Knox, "John 13,1-30", *HTR* 43 (1950) 161-163. Most scholars who accept the longer reading explain it sacramentally. See G. H. C. Macgregor, *John*, p. 276; L. Morris, *John*, p. 618, note 5; B. Vawter, "John", p. 451; B. F. Westcott, *St. John*, pp. 191-192. See for a study of the sacramental interpretation of this verse in the Fathers: N. M. Haring, "Historical Notes on the Interpretation of John, 13,10", *CBQ* 13 (1951) 355-380.

addition.[45] It is possible that there are secondary references to Baptism in the footwashing scene,[46] but its primary purpose is to prefigure the passion.[47] If there is a reference to Baptism it comes through the intimate link which exists between the Sacrament and the Lord's death, into which converts are baptised (see Rom. 6,3).[48] Jesus' reply to Peter leads on to v. 11: the one who has no part in Jesus, who is not clean, will betray him. John continually recalls the betrayal that will lead to the cross (see v. 2; vv. 10-11; v. 18; vv. 21-30).

The section which follows in vv. 12-20, often regarded as a second interpretation, in no way excludes what has been explained by word and action in vv. 1-11. It is a further explanation of how the disciples will participate in the suffering of their Lord and Teacher (see vv. 13-14). This much they should be able to understand (vv. 12.17). The complete understanding of the significance of Jesus' humiliation will only come when the "lifting up" to glorification takes place;[49] then they will know who he is (v. 19; see 8,28).[50] They, like their master, must follow along the way of humiliation, for in so doing they too will be uniting themselves with the Father who has sent his Son to perform this task (see 3,16-17; 13,16.20).[51]

---

[45] Following C. K. Barrett, *St. John*, p. 368; R. E. Brown, *John*, pp. 567-568; E. C. Hoskyns, *Fourth Gospel*, pp. 438-439; G.-M. Behler, *The Last Discourse*, pp. 38-39; F.-M. Braun, "St. Jean", p. 420; N. Lazure, "Le Lavement des pieds", pp. 45-46; G. Richter, *Die Fusswaschung im Johannesevangelium*, p. 320; J. D. G. Dunn, "The Washing of the Disciples' Feet", pp. 251-252; J. Huby, *Le discours de Jésus après la cène*, Verbum Salutis, (Paris, Beauchesne, 1942) pp. 16-17; W. Grossouw, "A Note on John 13,1-3", pp. 129-131; M.-J. Lagrange, *St. Jean*, pp. 353-355; B. Lindars, *John,* p. 451; J. Marsh, *St. John*, p. 489; R. H. Strachan, *Fourth Gospel*, p. 266.

[46] See C. K. Barrett, *St. John*, p. 364; R. E. Brown, *John*, pp. 566-568. Some scholars claim that the only lesson to be drawn from the scene is one of humility. See M.-J. Lagrange, *St. Jean*, pp. 348-361, see esp. p. 349; J. H. Bernard, *St. John*, pp. 458-469; J. Michl, "Der Sinn der Fusswaschung", *Biblica* 40 (1954) 697-708; J. Huby, *Le Discours de Jésus...* pp. 13-24.

[47] See esp. E. C. Hoskyns, *Fourth Gospel*, pp. 436-437; G. Richter, "Die Fusswaschung. Joh. 13,1-20", *MüTZ* 16 (1965) 13-26; H. Strathmann, *Johannes*, p. 197. Strathmann claims that either reading means the same thing — the cleaning activity of the passion; W. Cadman, *The Open Heaven*, p. 133; J. D. G. Dunn, "The Washing of the Disciples' Feet", pp. 251-252; F. Stagg, "The Farewell Discourse, John 13-17", *Review and Expositor* 62 (1965) 460-463.

[48] See C. K. Barrett, *St. John*, p. 367; C. H. Dodd, *Interpretation*, pp. 400-402; H. von Campenhausen, "Zur Auslegung von Joh 13,6-10", *ZNW* 33 (1934) 259-271; N. Lazure, "Le Lavement des pieds", pp. 43-49.

[49] This is what is meant by v. 7. Verses 12 and 17 in no way contradict this. See W. Cadman, *The Open Heaven*, pp. 133-135.

[50] See R. E. Brown, *John*, p. 571.

[51] While vv. 16 and 20 do reflect Synoptic words of Jesus (see Mt. 10,34, par. Lk. 6,40; Mt. 10,40, par. Lk. 10,16), they are not to be regarded as secondary in their Johannine context. See on this C. H. Dodd, *Tradition*, pp. 335-338. 343-347. G. Snyder,

"The purity which Jesus effects consists in an active and serviceable humility. Those who have been cleansed by him do in fact love and serve one another, and there is no other test of their having been cleansed than this (v. 35; cf. I John 3.16f,23; 4,11 et al.). The death of Christ is at once the means by which men are cleansed from sin, and the example of the new life which they must henceforth follow".[52]

In the final scene in the supper room the knowledge of Jesus and the fact that ultimately he himself is responsible for the initiation of the passion are the key ideas (see vv. 21.26.27).[53] The statement of the fact of the betrayal (v. 21), the puzzlement of those who, unlike Jesus, do not "know", and the subsequent interrogation (vv. 22-25) lead finally to Jesus' giving his commission to Judas, telling him to go about his task with speed (vv. 26-27). The rest of the disciples remain oblivious of what has happened (vv. 28-29), but Judas goes on his way, and John concludes the narrative introduction to the last discourse with his ominous "And it was night", a phrase which is laden with theological, as well as chronological significance.[54]

John 13,1-30 is concerned with the passion of Jesus. Throughout John indicates what the passion meant for Jesus and what it must mean for his disciples, and he continually recalls the fact that one of his disciples will set the action of the passion into motion (see vv. 2.10-11.18.21-30).[55] Finally that motion commences, as Judas goes on his way, only to reappear at Gethsemane (see 18,2-3.5). Now that the scene is set and the passion is on its course, Jesus can turn to "his own" and speak clearly of the meaning of all that is to follow. It is in this context that we find our final Son of Man saying in 13,31.

II - The Son of Man in John 13,31

Macgregor wrote of Jn. 13,31-32: "These two verses sound like a shout of triumph from the heart of Jesus at seeing the traitor depart in the dark-

"John 13,16 and the Anti-Petrinism of the Johannine Tradition", *BRes* 16 (1971) 5-15 argues that 13,16 is evidence of the dispute over apostolic authority at the end of the first century. See also, J. D. G. Dunn, "The Washing of the Disciples' Feet", pp. 248-249. Both he and Snyder see the scene as a Johannine version of Mk. 10,32-45.

[52] C. K. Barrett, *St. John*, p. 369. See also J. A. T. Robinson, "The Significance of the Foot-washing", in *Neotestamentica et Patristica: in Honour of O. Cullmann*, SNT 6 (Leiden, E. J. Brill, 1962) pp. 144-147.

[53] See G.-M. Behler, *The Last Discourse*, p. 51; W. Cadman, *The Open Heaven*, p. 136; C. H. Dodd, *Interpretation*, p. 402. For Bultmann, *John*, p. 487, this knowledge shows Jesus to be "the perfected Gnostic".

[54] See R. E. Brown, *John*, p. 579.

[55] See G. Richter, "Die Deutung des Kreuzestodes Jesu in der Leidensgeschichte des Johannesevangeliums (Jo. 13-19)", *BuL* 9 (1968) 21-36.

ness".[56] The words ὅτε οὖν ἐξῆλθεν link what has gone before, particularly the beginning of the movement towards the passion which has taken place in vv. 21-30, with. what is to follow in vv. 31-38. Not only does v. 31 mention the departure of Judas, but John uses his favourite link-word οὖν to indicate that what is to follow is closely connected with what has immediately preceded.[57] This means that vv. 31-38 are to be considered in the light of the passion, which has dominated the thought of vv. 1-30.[58] There are clear indications that this is the case: in v. 33 Jesus tells his disciples, "Yet a little while I am with you... Where I am going you cannot come", and in vv. 36-38 Peter's future denial of Jesus is spoken of in terms of the laying down of one's life. Yet Macgregor is correct when he speaks of "triumph": for John, the cross is a moment of triumph.

Because of this context, the νῦν refers to the event of the cross, the lifting up of the Son of Man (see 3,14; 8,28; 12,23.32). The use of νῦν is to be closely linked with the theological use of ὥρα in the Fourth Gospel.[59] During the public life of Jesus, the "hour" was not yet at hand (see 2,4; 7,6.30; 8,20), but now it has ·arrived (see 12,23; 13,1) and the Son of Man is glorified. The problem of time is an acute one here. The νῦν is immediately followed by a two-fold use of an aorist passive ἐδοξάσθη. The whole of the passion and elevation to glory of the Son of Man must be regarded as a single event. The washing of the feet and the departure of Judas have already explained the meaning of the passion and put the event into motion.[60] Because, according to John, we are already in the midst of the passion, Jesus can say — "Now is the Son of man glorified".[61] Recently G. B. Caird has shown that the aorist passive use of δοξάζειν was a common way used by

[56] G. H. C. Macgregor, *John*, p. 283. He claims to quote Godet at this point, but in fact Godet speaks not of "triumph" but of "relief". See F. Godet, *Commentaire sur l'Evangile de Saint Jean*, III (Neuchatel, J. Attinger, 1902) p. 256: "Ces deux versets sont comme un cri de soulagement qui s'échappe du coeur de Jésus à la vue du traitre qui s'éloigne". See H. van den Bussche, *Jean*, p. 387; Idem, "Nu is de Mensenzoon verheelijkt (Jo. 13,31-38)", *CollGand* 36 (1953) 99-101; Idem, *Le discours d'adieu de Jésus*, (Tournai, Casterman, 1959) pp. 51-54; J. Huby, *Le discours de Jésus*, p. 30.

[57] See F. Blass-A. Debrunner-R. W. Funk, *A, Greek Grammar*, para. 551,1; E. A. Abbott, *Johannine Grammar*, (London A. & C. Black, 1906), nos. 2191-2200; F. Zorell, *Lexicon Graecum Novi Testamenti*, s.v. οὖν, no. 2a; I. de la Potterie, *Exegesis IVⁱ Evangelii. De Narratione Passionis et Mortis Christi. Joh 18-19*, (Rome, Biblical Institute, 1970-71) pp. 43-44.

[58] Against J. N. Sanders, *St. John*, p. 315. He claims that v. 31 refers only to the washing of the feet.

[59] See W. Thüsing, *Erhöhung*, p. 234; A. Durand, "Le discours de la cène", p. 121; A. Richardson, *St. John*, p. 160.

[60] See C. K. Barrett, *St. John*, p. 375; C. H. Dodd, *Interpretation*, p. 403; J. Marsh, *St. John*, pp. 495-496; R. H. Strachan, *Fourth Gospel*, p. 277.

[61] S. Schulz, *Johannes*, p. 179. See W. Thüsing, *Erhöhung*, p. 234; J. Blank, *Krisis*, p. 136.

the LXX to translate the MT's use of the Hebrew niphal *nikbad* to render the passive, intransitive sense, "to be glorified".[62] Caird explains:

> "It therefore seems reasonable ... to suppose that a Jew, searching for a Greek word to express the display of splendid activity by man or God, which in his native Hebrew could be expressed by the niphal *nikbad* might have felt justified in adapting the verb δοξάζεσθαι to this use, with every expectation that his Greek neighbour would correctly discern his meaning".[63]

Caird's study is concerned with v. 31c, but the same principles would apply to the use of the verb in v. 31b.[64]

In the passion the Son of Man is glorified and in him God is glorified. Jesus has completed the task entrusted to him by the Father. He has revealed the Father to men, and in this has glorified the Father (17,4).[65] In 17,5 he will ask the Father to glorify him in the Father's own presence with the glory which he had before the creation of the world. In 13,31, however, Jesus claims that he is already glorified. This is not a contradiction. In 17,5 Jesus refers to the pre-existent glory of the Word that he had before time and which will once again be his. In 13,31 Jesus affirms that now is the high point of his task as the revealer of his Father *on earth*. It is already in progress, and in the performance of this task the Son of Man is glorified (17,4 ἐδόξασα).[66] The glory of the Son of Man lies in the fact that by his act of loving obedience on the cross, already explained in the washing of the feet, he has fully revealed the Father.[67]

As this is the case, the second part of the saying, "and in him God is glorified" merely repeats what has been said about the Son of Man. Caird has claimed that this saying can only mean "God has revealed his glory in Jesus".[68] The glory of God involves the visible manifestation of God's activity [69] and as Jesus has been the embodiment of this activity among men,

[62] G.B. Caird, "The Glory of God in the Fourth Gospel: An Exercise in Biblical Semantics", *NTS* 15 (1968-69) 273-277.

[63] *ibid.*, p. 277. The LXX evidence is examined on pp. 273-275.

[64] See also W. Cadman, *The Open Heaven*, p. 137. Thüsing, *op. cit.*, p. 234 speaks of the verb as a complexive aorist, while Bernard, *St. John*, pp. 524-525, followed by Lindars, *John*, p. 462, speaks of a Hebrew prophetic perfect of certainty. H. van den Bussche, "Nu is de Mensenzoon verheelijkt..." pp. 100-101, also speaks of a prophetic oracle.

[65] See above on 12,23, pp. 177-178.

[66] Despite J. Blank, *Krisis*, p. 136, note 66 and A. Dauer, *Die Passionsgeschichte*, p. 239, n. 151. p. 240, W. Thüsing, *Erhöhung*, pp. 234-239 has correctly pointed out that there is a development in the Johannine presentation of the glorification of Jesus.

[67] See A. Dauer, *Die Passionsgeschichte*, pp. 278-294.

[68] G. B. Caird, *art. cit.*, pp. 270-273.

[69] See Exodus 16,7-19; 24,17. See R. E. Brown, *John*, pp. 503-504. 606; T. Worden, "The Glory of God", pp. 85-94.

throughout the public ministry he has glorified God through his works (see 7,18; 8,50.54; 11,4.40; 14,13; 15,8) and his miraculous signs (see 2,11; 11,40; 17,4).[70] Often, as we have seen when speaking of the revelation of God among men, John has used the title "the Son of Man" (see 1,51; 3, 13-14; 6,27.53.62; 8,28; 9,35; 12,23), but in several of these sayings a promise has been made of a greater moment in the future when the Son of Man would be lifted up and draw all men to himself in a final moment of revelation and judgment (see 1,51; 3,13-14; 5,27; 8,28; 12,23.32). With this saying, placed at the beginning of the last discourse, we are told conclusively that now, at the hour of the passion, all this is taking place. The Son of Man is being lifted up to reveal the glory of the Father, and in this he is reaching the supreme moment of his own glory.[71]

The use of the future tense in v. 32 is difficult. Jesus has just opened the discourse by claiming that now the passion is in motion, the Son of Man is glorified and the Father is glorified in him. Immediately, however, a rhetorical condition is made: "If God is glorified in him",[72] a fact which is, after v. 31, certain, then God will glorify him in himself at once. The aorists of v. 31 referred to the whole of the passion-elevation, the "hour" of the revelation of the Son of Man upon earth which is already understood as taking place. The future tense in v. 32 refers to the return to the glory which belonged to the Word before the world was made (17,5).[73] There are two moments in the glorification of Jesus: one is his being lifted up before men as the fulness of God's revelation, referred to throughout the Gospel as the lifting up of the Son of Man (see 3,14; 8,28; 12,32; 13,31), the other

[70] On the revelation of God in Jesus' "works" and "words" see J.T. Forestell, *The Word of the Cross*, pp. 44-57; J.M. Boice, *Witness and Revelation in the Gospel of John*, pp. 88-100.
[71] See W. Bauer, *Johannesevangelium*, p. 175; G.-M. Behler, *The Last Discourse*, p. 62; A. Dauer, *Die Passionsgeschichte*, pp. 238-239.
[72] Following R.E. Brown, *John*, p. 606; W. Bauer, *Johannesevangelium*, p. 176; J.H. Bernard, *St. John*, p. 525; R. Bultmann, *John*, p. 523, note 3; W.F. Howard, "St. John", p. 693; M.-J. Lagrange, *St. Jean*, p. 365; B. Lindars, *John*, p. 462; A. Loisy, *Quatrième Évangile*, p. 399; W. Thüsing, *Erhöhung*, pp. 235-236; *The Greek New Testament*. These scholars include v. 32a. It is missing in P66, Sinaiticus, Vaticanus, Ephraem Rescript, Bezae, Freer Gospels and several other very good witnesses. However, its exclusion is best explained as the result of a homeoteleuton. See, however, for a contrary opinion, C.K. Barrett, *St. John*, p. 326; J.C. Fenton, *John*, p. 147; G.H.C. Macgregor, *John*, p. 283; H. van den Bussche, *Jean*, p. 389; B.F. Westcott, *St. John*, p. 197.
[73] See above, pp. 194-196. See also W. Thüsing, *Erhöhung*, pp. 235-237; R.E. Brown, *John*, p. 610; S. Schulz, *Johannes*, p. 179; J.H. Bernard, *St. John*, p. 525; A. Durand, "Le discours de la cène", p. 123; H. van den Bussche, *Jean*, p. 387; R.H. Lightfoot, *St. John*, p. 267; E.C. Hoskyns, *Fourth Gospel*, pp. 449-450.

is the return of the Son to the Father, to have again his pre-existent glory (see 17,1-5; 13,32).[74]

This is further indicated in v. 32 when Jesus claims that the future glorification will be in God.[75] As God has been glorified in the humble obedience of Jesus, who has revealed the truth and the light and who has displayed the glory of the unique revealer upon the cross, so will God glorify him in himself, with the glory which belonged to the pre-existent Word. It is clear that there are two aspects of Jesus' glorification being referred to in these verses. There is the glory of the Son of Man, which comes from his revelation of the Father on the cross, then there is the glory which will be given to the Son "in the Father".[76]

Jesus announces that this latter glory will come about εὐθύς. There will be no need for a lengthy waiting for a second coming before this can be understood (contrast the time lag implied in Mk. 8,38).[77] For John, as for Luke, the Church was full of the glory of Christ. How this came to be will be explained in the chapters that follow, where Jesus tells his disciples that once he has risen and gone to his Father in his glory, then he will send the Paraclete to continue his abiding presence among his own (see 14,16; 14,25-27; 15,26; 16,7).[78] That this is what is meant by v. 32 is further indicated by vv. 33-35. The glorification of the Son of Man will call for his being lifted up on a cross (v. 31). Jesus' upward movement will start on a cross and finish when he is "in God", sending the Paraclete to continue his presence among them (v. 32; see 16,7). There will necessarily be a physical separation, but his presence among them — "All men will know that you

---

[74] Against R. G. Hamerton-Kelly, *Pre-Existence*, p. 234, who sees v. 31 as a reference to Jesus' pre-existent glory.

[75] The majority of scholars accept this meaning for ἐν αὐτῷ. See G. B. Caird, "The Glory of God...", p. 271; W. Thüsing, *op. cit.*, p. 236; R. E. Brown, *John*, p. 606; C. K. Barrett, *St. John*, p. 376; J. H. Bernard, *St. John*, p. 525; R. Bultmann, *John*, pp. 523-524; W. Cadman, *The Open Heaven*, p. 138; R. H. Strachan, *Fourth Gospel*, p. 277; B. F. Westcott, *St. John*, pp. 196-197. Some, however, argue that it means "in Jesus himself". See G.-M. Behler, *The Last Discourse*, p. 64; M.-J. Lagrange, *St. Jean*, p. 366; A. Wikenhauser, *Johannes*, p. 215.

[76] See W. Thüsing, *op. cit.*, p. 236: "Wie Gott in seine Offenbarer Jesus verherrlicht ist, so wird Jesus 'in Gott' d.h. in der Liebeseinheit des 'Beim-Vater-Seins' verherrlicht werden". See also J. T. Forestell, *The Word of the Cross*, p. 81; C. K. Barrett, *St. John*, p. 376; R. Bultmann, *John*, pp. 523-524; J. H. Bernard, *St. John*, p. 525; H. van den Bussche, *Jean*, p. 387.

[77] See R. Bultmann, *John*, p. 524. Bultmann, however (p. 524, note 4), regards v. 32c as excessive and added by the Evangelist to relate the whole passage to the passion.

[78] Thus C. K. Barrett, *St. John*, p. 376; B. Vawter, "St. John", p. 452; W. Thüsing, *op. cit.*, p. 237; A. Durand, *art. cit.*, p. 123; W. F. Howard, "St. John", p. 693; M.-J. Lagrange, *St. Jean*, pp. 367-368. Many scholars see this "at once" as a reference to the passion. See R. E. Brown, *John*, p. 606; G.-M. Behler, *The Last Discourse*, p. 64; J. H. Bernard, *St. John*, p. 525; R. Bultmann, *John*, p. 524; S. Schulz, *Johannes*, p. 179.

are *my* disciples" (v. 35) — will only be a reality if they truly love one another.[79]

In vv. 31-32 Jesus has proclaimed the whole purpose of his passion and glorification. In vv. 33-35 he has given his followers the basic law of their discipleship. John concludes his introduction to the last discourse by recalling the events of the passion itself. He reports the prophecy of Peter's denial. The whole passage, from v. 1 to v. 38, has never strayed far from the "hour" of the Son of Man.

Several times during this chapter Jesus is called "Lord" (vv. 6,9,13,14, 16,25,36,37). Jesus himself uses the title in vv. 13-14, but even here its meaning is probably an earthly "Master". The only other title used is "Teacher", also on the lips of Jesus in vv. 13-14. In the contexts in which they are found here the titles show nothing more than Jesus' authoritative position among his immediate disciples. This cannot be claimed for the other title found in the chapter — "the Son of Man" (v. 31).

Many scholars merely refer to "the Son" and his glorification when they comment on this passage.[80] Others claim that there is no distinction between the titles. They hold that in the Fourth Gospel the terms "the Son" and "the Son of Man" are interchangeable.[81] These scholars are often led to their conclusion by seeing 17,1 as a parallel to 13,31 [82] but, despite first appearances, these verses differ considerably. The sayings are framed differently: while 13,31 is written in the detached third person singular, 17,1 is a personal prayer from Jesus to his Father. A more important difference is that the glorification of God which Jesus had to perform has already been accomplished, according to 17,4. This is the glorification referred to in 13,31. The glorification of the Son prayed for in 17,1 is a glorification "in God's presence" (17,5). This has already been referred to in the future tense of the verb

---

[79] See L. Cerfaux, "La charité fraternelle et le retour du Christ (Jo. 13,33-38)", *ETL* 24 (1948) 321-322; R. E. Brown, *John*, pp. 608-616; against J. Becker, "Die Abschiedsreden Jesu im Johannesevangelium", *ZNW* 61 (1970) 220: "Mahnung zur gegenseitigen Liebe hat im Kontext 13,31-38 keinen Platz". These verses may have another source, see G. Richter, *Die Fusswaschung*, p. 311, note 2, but they certainly have a place in the present context. See for example, F. Mussner, *ZΩH*, pp. 158-164; C. Charlier, "La présence dans l'absence (Jo 13,31-14,31)", *BibVChr* 2 (1953) 66-75; J. M. Reese, "Literary Structure of John 13,31-14,31; 16,5-6; 16,16-33", *CBQ* 34 (1972) 323-324, and the literature mentioned in note 73.

[80] See W. Bauer, *Johannesevangelium*, p. 175; J. C. Fenton, *John*, p. 147; W. F. Howard, "St. John", pp. 691-692; B. Vawter, "John", p. 452.

[81] See R. E. Brown, *John*, pp. 610-611; H.-M. Dion, "Quelques traits originaux...", pp. 49-65; C. Colpe, *TDNT* VIII, pp. 467-468. E. D. Freed, "The Son of Man in the Fourth Gospel", pp. 407-408 admits that the title in 13,31 seems to mean the incarnate humanity of Jesus. For Freed the titles "Son", "Son of God", "Son of Man" are merely variables, without distinctive theological content, used to speak of "Jesus".

[82] See R. E. Brown, *John*, p. 611.

and the "in himself" of 13,32.[83] This distinction must be seen and kept, because it is precisely here that an important difference between John's use of "the Son of Man" and "the Son" is to be found. Consistent with the rest of the Gospel, the "hour" in 17,1 refers to the passion, and, in close proximity to the glorification of "the Son", should warn us against too sharp a distinction between the event of the cross and the glorification of the Son. Passion, death, resurrection and glorification all seem to be one in the Fourth Gospel. There still remains, however, a distinction between the glorification of the Son of Man, lifted up on the cross for all to gaze upon (see 8,28; 13,31; 19,37), and the glorification of the Son, who, through the cross, returns to his pre-existent glory with the Father (1,1-2; 13,32; 17,1.5).

R. Bultmann, who hesitatingly accepts that the title here belongs to the source,[84] explains it in terms of his Gnostic redeemer myth. The Gnostic revealer returns to his former glory. R. G. Hamerton-Kelly and others, although not using a Gnostic theory, claim that v. 31 refers to the return of Christ to his pre-existent unity with God.[85] These scholars, failing to make the distinction just mentioned, do not appreciate the link which the title "the Son of Man" has with the historical figure of Jesus Christ, and the fact that on the cross this figure is lifted up to glory.

Various attempts have been made to establish the origins of this Son of Man saying. For Schulz the passage vv. 31-32 is a pre-Johannine Son of Man hymn with a parallel in I Enoch 51,3. He suggests, therefore, that the use of the title here had its origins in Jewish apocalyptic traditions, and that it has gone through a Jewish Christian re-interpretation. The passage is now a hymn in honour of the enthronement of the Son of Man.[86] F. H. Borsch has also suggested that it had its origins in an enthronement hymn, but this time it is a "King-Man" who is enthroned. Borsch claims, with hesitation, that the saying is based on pre-resurrection traditions.[87] S. Smalley finds references to several Old Testament figures: the Suffering Servant, the Danielic Son of man and the Righteous Sufferer of Wisdom 2,12-20. Added to this is the Son of man in I Enoch. Thus in Jn. 13,31 the present, suffering and future figures of the Son of Man are all combined.[88] C. K. Barrett has also

[83] See above, p. 198 and note 75. See also W. Thüsing, *op. cit.*, pp. 236-237.

[84] See R. Bultmann, *John*, p. 149, note 4, where he accepts the originality of the title. However, on p. 523, note 4, he suggests that it may have originally only been "the Son". See also H. Becker, *Die Reden des Johannesevangeliums*, p. 92, note 5. He claims that the title here is the addition of the Evangelist. So also does A. J. B. Higgins, *The Son of Man*, p. 181.

[85] R. G. Hamerton-Kelly, *Pre-Existence*, pp. 234-235. See also W. Cadman, *The Open Heaven*, pp. 137-139; G. B. Caird, "The Glory of God...", pp. 269-270.

[86] S. Schulz, *Untersuchungen*, pp. 120-122.

[87] F. H. Borsch, *The Son of Man*, pp. 312-313.

[88] S. S. Smalley, "The Johannine Son of Man Sayings", p. 297.

pointed out that the glorious Son of man found in I Enoch and Dan. 7,13 and the suffering Son of man, found in Mark, are here combined.[89] While various elements from the Old Testament, I Enoch and the Synoptic Gospels may be present in Jn. 13,31, it is by looking to the Johannine context that one will best discover what is meant by the use of the title.[90]

It is clear from the context that John is presenting Jesus as the Son of Man who will be lifted up on the cross. In this he will be glorified and consequently, God will be glorified in him. The glorification comes about because Jesus has accomplished the task which he was given (17,3-4). He has revealed the Father among men, and the high point of that revelation has taken place on the cross (see 19,37).[91] The task of revealing God among men has been the task of the Son of Man. All of this activity belongs to the human figure of Jesus, the incarnate Logos. Jesus, as the Son of Man, is the man who has revealed God among men; in glorifying God by his loving obedience, he has achieved his own glorification. The title is used to speak of the human figure, Jesus of Nazareth.[92] The glorification of the Son of Man reaches its high point in the very human event of the crucifixion; and this explains why, throughout the Gospel, the verb ὑψοῦν could only be applied to "the Son of Man", (see 3,14; 8,28; 12,32), and never to the "Logos" or "the Son (of God)". The title is used throughout the public ministry when the man Jesus manifests the glory of God. As Jesus himself will later pray: "I glorified thee on earth, having accomplished the work which thou gavest me to do" (17,4).

After the conclusion of the public ministry the passion of Jesus starts with the betrayal of Judas, and Jesus can make his final utterance concerning the Son of Man. The task is done; the passion is in progress: "Now is the Son of man glorified, and in him God is glorified" (13,31). The title seems to be strictly limited to the historical life and death of Jesus. When John speaks about the glory which will come to Jesus when he returns through the "hour" of the cross (17,1), to his pre-existent state, he uses the title "the

---

[89] C.K. Barrett, *St. John*, p. 375.

[90] Schulz's pre-Johannine Son of man hymn is extremely speculative, as also is Borsch's hymn to the enthronement of the King-Man. We do not have sufficient parallels to make these claims in any way conclusive. The suggestion of J. Jeremias, *Johannes*, pp. 258-259 and R.P. Brown, "Ἐντολὴ καινή (St. John 13,34)", *TLond* 26 (1933) 188, that the Eucharist is taken for granted and referred to in vv. 31-32 appears far-fetched.

[91] See E.C. Hoskyns, *Fourth Gospel*. p. 49.

[92] See G.-M. Behler, *The Last Discourse*, p. 62; A. Durand, *art. cit.*, p. 122; J. Huby, *Le Discours de Jésus*, pp. 30-31; E.C. Hoskyns, *Fourth Gospel*, p. 449; M.-J. Lagrange, *St. Jean*, p. 365; A. Loisy, *Quatrième Évangile*, p. 399; J. Marsh, *St. John*, pp. 495-496; H.L. Pass, *The Glory of the Father. A Study of St. John 13-17*, (London, Mowbray, 1935), p. 52; A. Schlatter, *Johannes*, p. 287; W. Temple, *Readings*, pp. 221-222; B.F. Westcott, *St. John*, p. 196; E.D. Freed, *art. cit.*, pp. 407-408.

Son" (see 17,1-5), but "the Son of Man" is used only in contexts which refer to the historical appearance of Jesus, the revelation of God among men.[93]

III - Behold the Man: John 19,5

Throughout this study we have found "the Son of Man" used by Jesus in contexts which spoke of him as the authentic revelation of God (1,51; 3,13-14; 6,27.53; 8,28; 9,35; 12,23) because he was the only man ever to come down from God to perform this task (3,13; 6,62). Subsequently, he is presented as judge, or rather, as the place where men would judge them-selves according to their acceptance or refusal of this revelation (see esp. 5,27; 8,28; 9,35-39; 12,34-36). However, there has been a continual sugges-tion that, despite the revelation brought by Jesus' words and deeds during the physical presence of his public life (2,11; 11,40; 17,4),[94] the high point of this revelation will take place at some future moment (1,51; 6,27). As the Gospel proceeds, it is made clear that this moment will be the "lifting up" of the Son of Man upon the cross (3,13-14; 6,53; 8,28; 12,23.32). As the passion starts, with the betrayal of Judas, Jesus announces: "Now is the Son of man glorified" (13,31). The passion has been set in motion, and thus the high point of the revelation and glorification of God in the Son of Man has arrived.

The use of the title "the Son of Man" disappears with the announcement of 13,31. The cross has been indicated throughout as the place where the Son of Man would be "lifted up" and "exalted", but the passion account (18,1-19,30) makes no reference to Jesus as the Son of Man. There is only the enigmatic proclamation of Pilate: ἰδοὺ ὁ ἄνθρωπος (19,5).

B. F. Westcott suggested in 1880 that this use of ὁ ἄνθρωπος was a reference to the Son of Man.[95] The claim was repeated by J. Grill in 1902.[96] Since then a number of commentators have seen this possibility.[97] Recently J. Blank has argued that the term is used to speak of the Son of Man in

---

[93] Against H. van de Bussche, *Jean*, p. 388, who claims that v. 31 indicates that the glorification of the Son in death establishes Jesus as the Judge at the end of time — the Son of Man.

[94] On this aspect of the revelation of God in Jesus, see J. T. Forestell, *The Word of the Cross*, pp. 44-57; J. M. Boice, *Witness and Revelation in the Gospel of John*, pp. 88-100.

[95] B. F. Westcott, *St. John*, p. 269.

[96] J. Grill, *Untersuchung über die Entstehung des vierten Evangeliums I*, (Tübingen-Leipzig, J. C. B. Mohr, 1902), pp. 49-50, n. 1.

[97] A. Loisy, *Quatrième Évangile*, p. 474; R. H. Lighfoot, *St. John*, pp. 312-313; C. H. Dodd, *Interpretation*, pp. 436-437; C. K. Barrett, *St. John*, p. 450; M.-J. Lagrange, *St. Jean*, p. 481; G. H. C. Macgregor, *John*, p. 339; E. M. Sidebottom, *The Christ of the Fourth Gospel*, p. 96; H. van den Bussche, *Jean*, pp. 503-504; A. Dauer, *Die Passionsgeschichte*

the context of an ironic "Königsepiphanie".[98] W. A. Meeks has found background from LXX Zech. 6,12 and LXX Num. 24,17 for a messianic understanding of ὁ ἄνθρωπος.[99] There is no need to see the term as in any way linked with "the Son of man"; it was sufficiently messianic in its own right.[100] Many scholars refuse to see any connection with a messianic title. Some understand it as an effort on Pilate's part to excite pity,[101] and A. Bajsic has suggested that it was a formula of contempt to goad the crowd into freeing Jesus.[102] Schlatter has claimed that it may have been part of the Roman 'philanthropia',[103] while several commentators see the phrase as a reference to Jesus' abject state after the flogging; Pilate uses the phrase to show them that this man could not possibly be a political threat.[104] R. Bultmann continues this line of thought by suggesting that this terrible humiliation is but the ultimate consequence of the Word's becoming flesh.[105]

It is generally admitted that the Johannine passion narrative is a theological presentation of the traditional account.[106] It is also well structured.[107] A reading of the text shows three clear divisions:

im Johannesevangelium, p. 109; J. Sanders, *St. John,* p. 400; L. Morris, *John,* p. 793, n. 10; I. de la Potterie, *Exegesis Quarti Evangelii,* pp. 112-113; idem., "Jésus roi et juge d'après Jn. 19,13 Ἐκάθισεν ἐπὶ βήματος", *Biblica* 41 (1960) 239; M. Balagué, "La hora de Jésus", *RBiCalz* 31 (1969) 84-85; G. Sevenster, "Remarks on the Humanity of Jesus in the Gospel and Letters of John", in *Studies in John,* pp. 185-193.

[98] J. Blank, "Die Verhandlung vor Pilatus Joh 18,28-19,16 im Lichte johanneischer Theologie", *BZ* 3 (1959) 75-77.

[99] W. A. Meeks, *The Prophet-King,* pp. 69-72.

[100] He is followed by R. E. Brown, *John,* p. 876.

[101] F. Godet, *St. Jean,* p. 422; E. C. Hoskyns, *Fourth Gospel,* p. 523; W. Temple, *Readings,* p. 359.

[102] A. Bajsic, "Pilatus, Jesus und Barabbas", *Biblica* 48 (1967) 25.

[103] A. Schlatter, *Johannes,* p. 344. See also, H. Schlier, "Jesus und Pilatus nach dem Johannesevangelium", in *Die Zeit der Kirche. Exegetische Aufsätze und Vorträge,* (Freiburg, Herder, 1956) p. 68.

[104] R. H. Strachan, *Fourth Gospel,* p. 316; J. H. Bernard, *St. John,* p. 616; W. F. Howard, "St. John", p. 771; A. Wikenhauser, *Johannes,* p. 270; S. Schulz, *Johannes,* pp. 230-231; H. Strathmann, *Johannes,* p. 245; E. Haenchen, "Historie und Geschichte", p. 200.

[105] R. Bultmann, *John,* p. 659. See also W. Thüsing, *Erhöhung,* p. 30; F.-M. Braun, "St. Jean", p. 464; F. Hahn, "Der Prozess Jesu...", p. 44.

[106] Against C. H. Dodd, *Tradition,* pp. 21-151. See R. T. Fortna, *The Gospel of Signs,* pp. 113-144; E. Haenchen, "Jesus vor Pilatus (Joh 18,28-19,15)", in *Gott und Mensch. Gesammelte Aufsätze,* (Tübingen, J. C. B. Mohr, 1965) pp. 144-156; Ibid., "Historie und Geschichte", pp. 182-207; F. Hahn, "Der Prozess Jesu..." pp. 23-96; A. Dauer, *Die Passionsgeschichte,* pp. 231-338; M. de Jonge, "Jesus as Prophet and King", pp. 175-177; I. de la Potterie, *Exegesis Quarti Evangelii;* J. Blank, "Die Verhandlung vor Pilatus", pp. 60-65; H. Schlier, "Jesus und Pilatus...", pp. 56-74; J. T. Forestell, *The Word of the Cross,* pp. 82-92; W. A. Meeks, *The Prophet-King,* pp. 61-81.

[107] See, for example, R. E. Brown, *John,* pp. 785-786. 802-803; A. Dauer, *Die Passionsgeschichte,* pp. 100-112.

i. The arrest and interrogation of Jesus (18,1-27)

ii. His encounter with Pilate and the Jews (18,28-19,16a)

iii. The crucifixion and burial of Jesus (19,16b-42).

The central section of this division is a dramatic presentation of the encounter between Jesus, Pilate and the Jews. In the drama Jesus manifests himself, ironically through his suffering, as the revealer of truth. The kingship of Jesus lies in his having come into the world to bear witness to the truth (see esp. 18,36-38).[108] The continual use of verbs of motion (ἄγουσιν, εἰσῆλθεν, ἐξῆλθεν, etc.) divides the drama into seven scenes,[109] which develop in the following fashion:[110]

1. *Outside* (18,28-32)
Jews demand death.

2. *Inside* (18,33-38a)
Pilate questions Jesus about
kingship.

3. *Outside* (18,38b-40)
Jesus not guilty. Jews ask for
Barabbas instead of "King of the
Jews".

7. *Outside* (19,12-16a)
Jews obtain death.

6. *Inside* (19,9-11)
Pilate questions Jesus about
power.

5. *Outside* (19,4-8)
Jesus not guilty.
"Behold the Man"
"Crucify him!"

4. *Inside* (19,1-3)
Scourging. Jesus is clothed and
crowned as a king.

If the whole encounter with Pilate is ironically concerned with the nature of Jesus' kingship,[111] what role does 19,5 play in this context? From the scheme presented above, one can see that the fourth and central scene is

---

[108] The scene is not concerned with Jesus' encounter with the State, as is maintained by R. Bultmann, *John*, p. 633 and H. Schlier, "Jesus und Pilatus...", pp. 56-59 et passim. See instead, J. Blank, "Die Verhandlung vor Pilatus..." p. 63; E. Haenchen, "Jesus vor Pilatus...", pp. 149-150; F. Hahn, "Der Prozess Jesu...", pp. 46-47; E. Peterson, "Zeuge der Wahrheit", in *Theologische Traktate*, (München, Kösel, 1956), pp. 172.178-179.187-189; J. T. Forestell, *The Word of the Cross*, pp. 84-85; I. de la Potterie, *Exegesis Quarti Evangelii*, pp. 86-88.

[109] This was pointed out by B. F. Westcott, *St. John*, p. 258 and is now generally followed. See, for example, R. Bultmann, *John*, pp. 648-666; H. Schlier, "Jesus und Pilatus...", pp. 66-74; I. de la Potterie, *Exegesis Quarti Evangelii*, pp. 81-88; A. Wikenhauser, *Johannes*, pp. 266-273; H. van den Bussche, *Jean*, pp. 490-511; R. H. Strachan, *Fourth Gospel*, p. 310; R. E. Brown, *John*, pp. 857-858; H. Windisch, "Die johanneische Erzählungsstil", pp. 202-205; J.M. Thomson, "An Experiment in Translation", pp. 123-125; F. Hahn, "Der Prozess Jesu...," pp. 30-32; M. de Jonge, "Jesus as Prophet and King...", p. 175, n. 59; A. Janssens de Varebeke, "La structure des scènes du récit de la passion en Joh. 18-19", *ETL* 38 (1962) 506-509; A. Dauer, *Die Passionsgeschichte*, pp. 101-102.

[110] See R. E. Brown, *John*, pp. 858-859; A. Dauer, *Die Passionsgeschichte*, p. 102.

[111] See G. W. Macrae, "Theology and Irony in the Fourth Gospel", pp. 89-92.

concerned with the ironic investiture and coronation of Jesus. Framing this central scene we have two proclamations of the truth by Pilate, both of which are refused by the crowd. In v. 39 Pilate presents Jesus as ὁ βασιλεὺς τῶν Ἰουδαίων, and the Jews ask for Barabbas, who was a λῃστής[112] and in 19,5, Pilate presents Jesus before the crowd saying, ἰδοὺ ὁ ἄνθρωπος, and· they reply in 19,6 with "Crucify him! Crucify him!". In the passage from 18, 38b-19,8 we are at the centre of the central scene of John's dramatic presentation of the kingship and glorification of Jesus. It seems improbable that, in this context, the ἰδοὺ ὁ ἄνθρωπος would be without some particular significance.

There are other indications of this in v. 5 itself. "Jesus came out,[113] wearing[114] the crown of thorns and the purple robe" (v. 5a): he is still dressed as a king. These royal insignia are never explicitly taken from Jesus until the crucifixion, but there the robe that is mentioned is apparently his own (see 19,23-24). Earlier Pilate has referred to Jesus as ὁ ἄνθρωπος οὗτος (18,29), but here the use of the term ὁ ἄνθρωπος is in no way modified. Looking further into the encounter with Pilate and the Jews, v. 5 has a parallel in the identical final scene, where Pilate again presents Jesus to the Jews proclaiming: ἴδε ὁ βασιλεὺς ὑμῶν (v. 14).[115] The term in v. 5 is clearly a title of honour which the Jews refuse to accept.[116]

Some scholars see the Hebrew *ben 'ādām* or the Aramaic *bar nāshā'* behind the term, as the semitic expressions were ambiguous and could mean "Man" and "Son of Man" at the same time,[117] while Barrett and Meeks see a reference to Jewish and Hellenistic Anthropos mythology.[118] Restricting oneself to the immediate context one must conclude that none of this is certain; however, if one turns to the use of the term "the Son of Man" in the rest of the Gospel, some interesting similarities appear.

In 8,28, Jesus announced that the Jews would "lift up" the Son of Man. In 12,33, another Son of Man context (see 12,23.34), an explanatory note is

[112] See K. H. Rengstorf, Art. "λῃστής", *TDNT* IV, p. 258. Rengstorf observes that in Josephus the term "is constantly used for the Zealots". For this use of the term in Josephus, see M. Hengel, *Die Zeloten*, AGSU 1, (Leiden, E. J. Brill, 1961), pp. 25-47. The Jews choose a false messianic possibility.
[113] Note that he is not "led out". He is in command of his own situation.
[114] Not "clothed", but actively "wearing" (φορῶν) the crown and the robe.
[115] See H. van den Bussche, *Jean*, pp. 503-504; G. Sevenster, "Remarks on the Humanity of Jesus...", p. 186; I. de la Potterie, *Exegesis Quarti Evangelii*, p. 112; B. F. Westcott, *St. John*, p. 269; J. T. Forestell, *The Word of the Cross*, p. 85.
[116] There are, of course, two levels here. Pilate is not proclaiming Jesus as the Messiah ... John is.
[117] See J. Sanders, *St. John*, p. 400; A. Richardson, *St. John*, p. 192; B. Vawter, "John", p. 460.
[118] C. K. Barrett, *St. John*, p. 450; W. A. Meeks, *The Prophet-King*, pp. 69-72. See also R. E. Brown, *John*, p. 876.

added to the text in order to clarify what was meant by 12,32: "When I am lifted up from the earth" — "He said this to show by what death he was to die" (12,33). There is a direct link between the lifting up and the cross, between ὑψόω and σταυρόω. In 19,5, Jesus is presented as ὁ ἄνθρωπος and the Jews reject him with their cry: σταύρωσον σταύρωσον. It appears that the promise of 1,51; 3,14; 6,27.53 and 8,28 becomes fact when Pilate presents "the Man" and the Jews demand that he be crucified. The Jews are about to lift Jesus up from the earth, to be seen as the revelation of God by all who look upon him. In this way, the use of "the Man" in 19,5 seems to be linked with the use of "the Son of Man" in the rest of the Gospel.

In 19,5 there again appears to be a progression in the titles applied to Jesus. In 18,33.39; 19,3 he is called "King of the Jews". Jewish messianic terms such as this have continually been modified throughout Jesus' life by his own use of the title "the Son of Man". They are insufficient, and he answers in more satisfactory terms (see 1,51; 3,13; 6,27; 9,35; 12,23.34). In 19,5, "the Man" and in 19,7 "the Son of God" are used. If John is following the pattern he has used throughout the Gospel, these are to be understood as correct Johannine messianic terms.[119] At the end of his career, the Jews will not accept Jesus as a Jewish Messiah (18,33.39; 19,3), as "the Man" (19,5), or as the Son of God (19,7). All possibilities have now been exhausted. Meeks has argued that there is no progression to "Son of God" in v. 7; the scene proceeds to v. 14 where Jesus is presented as "your king": "If anything", he claims, "it is 'King of the Jews' that supersedes 'Anthropos', not *vice versa!*"[120] In fact, v. 14 does not call Jesus "King of the Jews". From 18,33 to 19,7, there is a use of clearly messianic terms, concluding with "the Son of God" in v. 7. This cannot be claimed for the use of "your king" in verse 14.[121] The Jews understand v. 14 in a secular way, as in v. 15 they reply that their king is Caesar. There is a parallelism between v. 5 and v. 14: "your king" is "the Man". We are not dealing with an eschatological figure in the traditional sense, but with a man who has appeared in time and space to reveal God to men. Jesus is king, according to the Johannine passion narrative, in his giving witness by his revelation of the truth (see especially 18,33-38).[122] What is said in v. 14 is true — Jesus is their king, but as the

[119]. J. Blank, "Die Verhandlung vor Pilatus ...", pp. 62-63. 75-77. See p. 75: "Ein höherer Titel als der Messias-Titel könnte zunächst nur der Menschensohn-Titel sein". R. Schnackenburg, *St. John* I, p. 532, refuses to accept any reference to an Anthropos myth, but carefully concludes: "At most, one could find in the 'ecce homo' an allusion to the 'Son of Man', in so far as this title also designates the Messiah in the Johannine sense (cf. 12,34)".

[120] W. A. Meeks, *The Prophet-King*, p. 70, n. 6.

[121] In the Johannine context, the messianic King is often referred to as "King of the Jews" or "of Israel" (see 1,50; 12,13; 18,33.39; 19,3.19.21).

[122] See A. Dauer, *Die Passionsgeschichte*, pp. 252-262.

Man who came to reveal the truth, not as the "King of the Jews" expected by current messianic hope. The correction of the messianic titles concludes at v. 7. What is said in v. 14 clarifies what is meant by v. 5.[123] Again it appears that there is a close link between "the Man" in 19,5 and such passages as 1,51; 3,13; 6,27; 9,35; 12,23.34, where "the Son of Man" was used over against current messianic titles.

The theme of judgment is central to the Johannine passion account.

"In the presence of this revelation the powers of evil finally declare themselves by their rejection of the light; and in so declaring themselves condemn themselves to extirpation".[124]

The rejection takes place in 19,5-6 when Jesus is presented to the Jews as "the Man", and they demand that he be crucified. The theme of judgment has been predominant throughout the whole of the Fourth Gospel's use of the title "the Son of Man". The consequence of the revelation of the Son of Man is the judgment which men will bring upon themselves by their accepting or rejecting that revelation. It is possible that in 19,5-6 we find the dramatic acting out of what has been promised in the earlier part of the Gospel, when speaking of "the Son of Man" (3,19-21; 5,27; 9,35-39; 12,34-36)[125] but here instead of "the Son of Man" we find "the Man".

Seen in the context of the whole Gospel, and John's use of "the Son of Man", it seems very probable that the title is implied here.[126] It appears that the theme of revelation and consequent judgment, the use of the title as a progression upon a Jewish messianic title, and the indication that it is in the "man" Jesus that all this takes place, are now gathered together in this terse scene. Throughout the Gospel the reader has been directed to look forward; in 13,31 he has been told: "Now is the Son of man glorified" and finally, in the ironic coronation and investiture of Jesus, it is Pilate who announces: "Here he is — the Son of Man!"[127] The absurd glorification through humiliation has reached its high point.[128]

---

[123] See I. de la Potterie, "Jésus roi et juge d'après Jn 19,13...", pp. 217-247.

[124] C. H. Dodd, *Interpretation*, p. 211. See also R. Bultmann, *John*, p. 350: "At the very moment when they think that they are passing judgement on him, he becomes their judge".

[125] I. de la Potterie, *Exegesis IV^i Evangelii*, p. 113, attempts to link this saying through 5,27 to Dan. 7,13. He claims that as in Dan. 7,13, the Son of Man in 19,5 has a "transcendent authority". There may be a link with Dan. 7,13, but it is probably more a question of vindication through suffering than of transcendent authority.

[126] See A. Dauer, *Die Passionsgeschichte*, p. 109 and J. Grill, *Untersuchung...* pp. 49-50, n. 1, who see the title here as a reflection of what has already been said of the Son of Man throughout the Gospel, especially in 8,28.

[127] The fact that it is Pilate who proclaims Jesus as "the Son of Man" would make this unique in the New Testament. One of the reasons why we do not have a clearer reference to the title in 19,5 may arise from John's respect for the title, which was traditionally used only by Jesus to speak of himself.

[128] See G. Sevenster, "Remarks on the Humanity of Jesus...", p. 193.

CHAPTER TEN

THE JOHANNINE SON OF MAN

It is often suggested that the meaning of the Johannine use of "the Son of Man" is determined by the more frequent use of "Son" or "Son of God". John has retained the title because of a certain respect for the tradition (Braun, de Beus, Jeremias, Bousset etc.); because it once formed part of a now lost christology which expressed all the major beliefs of the early Church in terms of the Son of Man (Higgins); because of the continuing influence of late Jewish apocalyptic (Schulz), or for various other reasons.[1]

The use of "the Son" is certainly one of the most outstanding characteristics of the Fourth Gospel.[2] The absolute use of the term appears only three times in the Synoptic Gospels (Matt. 11,27, par. Lk. 10,22; Mk. 13,32, par. Matt. 24,36; Matt. 28,19); once in Paul (I Cor. 15,28) and five times in Hebrews (Heb. 1,2.8; 3,6; 5,8; 7,28). In John, Jesus speaks of his sonship twenty times (3,16.17.18; 5,18 [twice]. 20.21.22.23 [twice]. 25.26; 6,40; 8,35-36; 10,36; 11,4; 14,13; 17,1 [twice]); four times it is a Johannine comment (3,35.36 [twice][3]; 20,31); it appears once in the prologue (1,18) and four times on the lips of others (1,34 — John the Baptist; 1,49 — Nathanael; 11, 27 — Martha; 19,7 — the "Jews").[4] This material comparison with the other parts of the New Testament is already sufficient testimony of the importance of the term in the Fourth Gospel. There are, beside the sayings which explicitly mention Jesus' Sonship, a series of further sayings in which Jesus refers to God as his Father. As well as repeating many of the notions also found in the Son sayings, they add further dimensions to our understanding of the relationship of Jesus with God, whom he calls his Father.[5] It is beyond

---

[1] For a survey of the various suggestions, see above, pp. 1-22.

[2] See R. Schnackenburg, *Johannesevangelium* II, pp. 150-151. See his excellent excursus " 'Der Sohn' als Selbstbezeichnung Jesu im Joh-Ev." (pp. 150-168).

[3] See above on 3,13-14, pp. 50-51.

[4] For an analysis of these sayings, see R. Schnackenburg, *Johannesevangelium* II, pp. 152-154. For the textual problems of 1,18.34, see B. Metzger, *A Textual Commentary*, pp. 198.200.

[5] For an analysis of these sayings, see R. Schnackenburg, *Johannesevangelium* II, pp. 154-157.

the scope of this work to study these sayings in detail[6] but the main lines of the use of "the Son" can be rapidly sketched.

These sayings nearly always express a direct relationship between God and Jesus (1,18.34; 3,16.18.35; 5,19-26; 6,40; 10,36; 11,4; 14,13; 17,1; 19,7 [negatively]). If Jesus is to call God his Father, then his Sonship will be expressed in terms of that relationship. The relationship is not expressed as a static privilege, as the Son was sent by the Father to bring salvation to all those who would believe in him.[7] This is made very clear in the two places in the Gospel where there is a heavy concentration upon Jesus' Sonship: 3,16-21 and 5,19-26.

In 3,16-21 and the parallel 3,34-36[8] the purpose of Jesus' mission is explained in terms of God's having so loved the world that he sent his only Son (v. 16) in order that the world may have the opportunity of accepting or refusing the light and truth (vv. 19-21.35-36) which is to be found in him (vv. 18 and 36), and thus come to salvation or condemnation (vv. 17 and 36). In 5,19-26 there is a greater concentration on the nature of the union between the Father and the Son. It is one of total dependence of the Son upon the Father (vv. 19-22.26), but it is a dependence which leads to a certain equality, where the honour which is due to the Father is due also to the Son (v. 23). The passage is mainly concerned with Jesus' authority, which has been questioned by the Pharisees (v. 18), so he must turn back to the Father, who gives purpose to his existence. However, it is not allowed to rest there, as Jesus speaks clearly of the consequences of his oneness with the Father: he who is open to the revelation (the word) brought by the Son already has eternal life (vv. 24-25).

Other sayings, spread throughout the Gospel, make the same claims for Jesus. John the Baptist, whose role in the Gospel is to point to the true meaning and purpose of Jesus' person and mission,[9] announces that "this is the Son of God" (1,34), and at the centre of the discourse on the Bread of Life, Jesus himself points out what this means: "For this is the will of my

[6] See ·R. Schnackenburg, *Johannesevangelium* II, pp. 151-152, note 2, for bibliography to which should be added: J.P. Miranda, *Der Vater der mich gesandt hat: religions-geschichtliche Untersuchungen zu den johanneischen Sendungsformeln; zugleich ein Beitrag zur johanneischen Christologie und Ekklesiologie*, European University Papers 23/7, (Bern, Herbert Lang, 1972); H. Schneider, " 'The Word was made Flesh'. An Analysis of the Theology of Revelation in the Fourth Gospel", *CBQ* 31 (1969) 344-356; F.J. Moloney, "The Johannine Son of God", *Salesianum* 38 (1976) 71-86.
[7] See R. Schnackenburg, *Johannesevangelium* II, p. 167: "Die joh Sohn-Christologie ist wesentlich Heilslehre für die Glaubenden, also nicht isolierte Lehre über Jesus Christus selbst, sondern im Hinblick auf die Menschen entworfene Lehre von ihm als Gottes Gesandten, der das Heil offenbart und vermittelt".
[8] See above, on 3,13-14, pp. 46-51. 65-66.
[9] See above, pp. 48-49 and p. 49, note 41.

Father, that everyone who sees the Son and believes in him should have eternal life" (6,40). True freedom could come to the Jews if they would but accept the revelation ('my words', 10,37) brought by the Son from his Father (8,34-38).[10] However, they will never admit that Jesus is the Son of God; instead they accuse him of blasphemy because of this claim (10,36) and finally they reject him totally and crucify him "because he has made himself the Son of God" (19,7).

On three occasions Jesus speaks of the glory of the Son of God (11,4; 14,13; 17,1). In 14,13 and 17,1, it is clear that Jesus is speaking of that glory which will be his when he returns to the presence of the Father — the glory which was his before the world was made (see 17,5). In 11,4, however, there is the immediate context of the raising of Lazarus. When Martha questions Jesus he speaks only of the glory of God: "Did I not tell you that if you would believe you would see the glory of God?" (11,40). Verse 4 must be interpreted in view of v. 40.[11] What is being revealed in the miracle is the glory of God (v. 4b), as is normal in the Fourth Gospel (see 1,14; 2,11; 17,4). The whole account of the miracle, however, is closely linked with the passion (see 11,45-53), and this is referred to in v. 4c. There are, therefore, two points being made by 11,4 — the glory of God is revealed in the sign of the miracle, and glory will come to the Son as a consequence of the miracle, i.e. through the passion. The glory spoken of in 11,4 is the glory which the Son will have when he returns to the presence of his Father (as in 14,13 and 17,1) but this glory will only be his as a result of the event of the cross.

Twice Jesus is called the Son of God by people who profess faith in him. In 1,49 Nathanael calls him Rabbi, Son of God and King of Israel. He is answered in terms of "greater things" which he would "see" — the Son of Man. Nathanael's profession of faith in Jesus is to be understood in the light of Jewish messianic expectations (see 2 Sam. 7,7.14; Ps. 2,7), and it is modified by Jesus' reply.[12] In 11,27, Martha professes faith in Jesus as "the Christ, the Son of God, he who is coming into the world". Again we are dealing with Jewish messianic hopes.[13] Jesus was the Christ, the Son of God and ὁ ἐρχόμενος, but the whole context of lack of faith shows that, for John, she has not understood what that meant. This is betrayed in v. 28 when, immediately after her confession, she says to her sister, "The Teacher is here", recalling the term used by Nicodemus (3,2), which was also corrected by Jesus' use of the title "the Son of Man" (3,13-14).[14]

---

[10] The christological meaning of "the Son" in 10,36 is sometimes questioned. For a discussion of this problem and a defence of its full theological meaning, see R. Schnackenburg, *Johannesevangelium* II, p. 153.

[11] See W. Thüsing, *Erhöhung*, pp. 229-232.

[12] See above, pp. 35-37.

[13] See G. Segalla, "Cinque schemi cristologici...", pp. 8-10.

[14] See above, pp. 51-53. R. Schnackenburg, "Die Messiasfrage im Johannesevangelium",

The exalted claims of Jesus, that he is the Son of God and that because of his Sonship he has authority to reveal what he has seen with his Father and thus bring eternal life to those who believe in him, is a strange message. It can only be understood in the light of the prologue, where the readers are given the key to the whole mystery.[15] They have already been told: "No one has ever seen God; the only Son who is in the bosom of the Father, he has made him known" (1,18). To do this, the pre-existent Son, whom John has called the "Word", became flesh and dwelt among us, revealing the truth, and displaying a glory in his human state "as of" (ὡς) the only Son from the Father (see 1,14). John has written a Gospel so that people may come to believe in this revelation, confess Jesus as the Son and thus come to eternal life (see 20,31).

The dominant themes of the Fourth Gospel are the revelation of the truth in Jesus Christ and the salvation which can come from the acceptance of this revelation.[16] These fundamental themes are found throughout the Gospel, whether Jesus is presented as the Son (of God) or as the Son of Man. However, the use of the different titles shows a careful distinction between the different roles of Christ. From our analysis of the Son of Man sayings and from the above sketch of Jesus as the Son of God, the following scheme shows how the two titles both refer to Jesus as the revealer and as revelation itself, but in very different ways.

The Son of Man	*The Son of God*
The title is always used in the detached 3rd person. It is never associated with "I". That it refers to Jesus is made clear by the use of "I" with ὑψοῦν in 12,32.	There is sometimes a clear identification between Jesus and the Son, see 1,49; 5,30 in the light of 5,19. See 5,23-25; 10,36-38; 11,27; 14,13-14; 17,1-5; 19,7; 20,31.
It is used of the human Jesus. He has pre-existed and we know this from 3,13 and 6,62. However, the title is used only of Jesus in his human state.	It is sometimes used to refer to the pre-existent Christ (1,18; 17,1.5).

p. 244, n. 15, sees the use of Son of God here as a correction of Martha's use of "the Christ", and thus a fully Johannine confession. See also, S. Sabugal, '*Christos*', pp. 341-351. They neglect the use of ὁ διδάσκαλος in v. 28. See the similar hopes of the Samaritan woman in 4,25; the Jews in 6,14; 7,41-42; 12,13.

[15] See above, p. 36, note 66.
[16] See R. Schnackenburg, "Offenbarung und Glaube", pp. 165-180; J. M. Boice, *Witness and Revelation in the Gospel of John*, pp. 39-74.

The title is never used in relation to the Father, except in 6,27 where his revelation is "sealed" by the Father. This does not refer to a Father-Son of Man relationship.

The title is nearly always used in close relation with the Father, in the sense of a Father-Son relationship.

The Son of Man is the unique revealer of God because he is the only one who has come down from heaven (3,13; 6,62). The stress is on the incarnation.

The Son is the unique revealer of God because of his union with the Father (passim, but esp. 3,16-21. 34-36; 5, 19-26).

He is a judge (5,27, see 1,51; 8,28; 9,35-41; 13,31-36; 19,5).

The Son has not come into the world to judge (3,17; 8,15; 12,47). However, his "being in the world" necessarily brings judgment (see 3,17-21), and this judging role of the incarnate Son is generally spoken of in terms of "the Son of Man" (see 5,27: κρίσιν ποιεῖν).

The title is applied throughout the earthly career of Jesus, starting with the promise of 1,51 and ending in glory on the cross (8.28; 12,23; 13, 31; 19,5-6).

The title is applied to the pre-existent (1,18; 17,1-5), human (esp. 3,16, but passim) and glorified (8,35; 17,1) Christ. The Father-Son relationship is first mentioned "in the bosom of the Father" (1,18) and it concludes in the Father's presence (17,5).

The Son of Man is lifted up on the cross in the ambiguous sense implied by the use of the verb ὑψοῦν (3,13; 8,28; 12,23.32.34). The Son of Man, being human, can be crucified.

The verb ὑψοῦν is never used of the Son (of God). John never speaks of the crucifixion of the Son (of God).

He is glorified on the cross (12,23; 13,31; 19,5).

He is glorified, through the cross (11, 4; 17,1) in his return to the Father's presence (13,32; 14,13; 17.1.5).

The high point of his revelation is built up to by the use of the "hour" which is not yet come until it is reached in the passion and death of Jesus: 1,51; 3,14; 6,27; 8,28 — all

The Son is never linked with the movement towards the passion. The revelation of the Father in the Son is a permanent fact, even if not believed in.

speak of some event in the future
when the Son of Man will be "seen",
"lifted up", "given", "eaten".   In
12,23.34; 13,31; 19,5, the hour has
arrived as Jesus goes to the cross.

There is a concentration on the human figure of Jesus in the use of the
title "the Son of Man".   It is a title which is entirely dependent upon the
incarnation.   The Son of Man reveals the truth to men because he is man
— because of the incarnation.   O. Cullmann and C. Colpe may not be far
from the truth when they suggest that 1,14 is a possible reference to the Son
of Man.[17]   F.-M. Braun has done well to explain the link which exists between
the Logos and the Son of Man.[18]   When the Word became flesh, it became the
Son of Man.   The glory which is seen in the incarnate Logos is not identified
with that of the Son, but "as of" (ὡς) the only Son of the Father (1,14).
The Son of Man revealed God to men and brought judgment to men through
his presence, as a man, among them.   The high point of this revelation and
judgment took place on the cross.   After the glorification of the Son of Man
on the cross, the title no longer has any meaning for John.[19]   There is a very
important distinction between this idea and John's use of "the Son (of God)".[20]
The latter speaks of the basis of Jesus' existence and purpose — his union with
the Father before, during and after the incarnation.[21]

The consequences of failure to distinguish between John's use of "the
Son (of God)" and "the Son of Man" can be found in the influential work
of Ernst Käsemann, who has recently argued that Johannine christology can
be described as a "naïve docetism".[22]   For Käsemann, the prologue portrays
Jesus as the Logos coming from eternity into time, while in the prayer of
John 17 he returns to eternity.   At no stage of the Johannine Gospel is
Jesus presented as a human figure; the Christ is on a journey from pre-existence,
through time, back to eternity.[23]   To fit this scheme Käsemann claims that
"apart from a few remarks that point ahead to it, the passion comes into

---

[17] O. Cullmann, *Christology*, p. 187; C. Colpe, *TDNT* VIII, p. 470.   See above, p. 7.
[18] F.-M. Braun, "Messie, Logos et Fils de l'homme", pp. 133-147.   See above, pp. 8-9.
[19] Against G. Segalla, "Cinque schemi cristologici...", pp. 13-21, who tries to fit the
title into a scheme involving pre-existence, human activity and a returning to judge.
[20] See R. Schnackenburg, *Johannesevangelium* II, pp. 166-167.
[21] See W. F. Lofthouse, "Vater und Sohn im Johannesevangelium", *TB* 11 (1932)
col. 298: "Er war vor allen Dingen der Sohn, wie Gott der Vater war, und all sein Tun
konnte nur durch seine Beziehung zu Gott verstanden werden".   See also cols. 299-300.
[22] E. Käsemann, *The Testament of Jesus*, pp. 26. 66. 70 etc.
[23] This is the thesis of the whole of Käsemann's essay on John 17 (*ibid.*).   See also
R. Bultmann, *John*, p. 13.

view in John only at the very end. One is tempted to regard it as being a mere postscript which had to be included because John could not ignore this tradition nor yet could he fit it organically into his work"[24] We hope that we have shown that this is to do violence to the evidence of the Gospel itself. The use of "the hour", "lifting up" and "the Son of Man" — themes which are closely linked throughout John 1-13 — points to a christology in which the human Jesus is glorified in his being "lifted up" upon the cross as the revelation of God to men (see esp. 12,23; 13,31, but also 3,14; 6,27; 8,28; 19,5). Because of the revelation which took place in the *human* event of the cross, *men* can be judged by their reaction to it (see esp. 5,27, but also 1,51; 3,13-14; 6,27.53; 8,28; 9,35-41; 19,5).

Why has John chosen to speak of the incarnate Logos in terms of the Son of Man? The first indication of a solution to this question may be found in the traditional use of the title in 5,27, where we have a direct reference to Dan. 7,13.[25] In Mk. 14,62 (Matt. 26,64; Lk. 21,27) Jesus promises that the Son of Man will come as a judge, in fulfilment of the Danielic prophecy. In Jn. 5,27 he is already the judge. This is merely a johannisation of a traditional motif, and it depends upon the same Old Testament text. "The old eschatological concept of the Son of Man as judge is merged into the Johannine theology".[26] This is not the only point of contact which we have found with earlier tradition. Almost every saying is a concluding statement, on the lips of Jesus, resolving a series of questions or insufficient confessions about the nature of Jesus (1,51; 3,13-14; 6,27; 8,28; 9,35; 12,23.34; 19,5). This repeats a traditional "pattern", where Jesus replied to his interlocutors — who had suggested their own answers concerning his person and role — in terms of the Son of Man (see Mk. 8,27-9,1, parr. Matt. 16,13-28; Lk. 9,18-27; Mk. 14,61-62, parr. Matt. 26,63-64; Lk. 22,67-71). Throughout the Fourth Gospel the Jews and even the disciples grapple with the problem of the heavenly origin of Jesus. The reader knows the answer because he has read the prologue, but the actors in the drama of the life of Jesus do not know it, and they have to come to it through an act of faith in his signs and words. "The Son of Man" appears to be used to give the correct answer to the question: "Who is Jesus?" In the Synoptic Gospels Jesus himself asks the disciples, "Who do men say that I am?" The answers he receives are not sufficient — not even the confession of Peter. Jesus gives the answer himself, in terms of the Son of Man (see Mk. 8,27-29; parr. Matt. 16,13-15; Lk. 9, 18-20). John repeats this in his own way.

---

[24] E. Käsemann, *op. cit.*, p. 7.

[25] See C. F. D. Moule, *Phenomenon*, p. 92; R. Schnackenburg, *St. John* I, p. 535. See above, pp. 81-82.

[26] R. Schnackenburg, *St. John* I, p. 532.

"Soweit und in welchem Sinne ich mich als 'den Messias' bezeugen konnte, habe ich es getan; aber diese meine Selbstoffenbarung ist euch unzugänglich, weil ihr nicht glaubt... In der Distanzierung Jesu vom Messias-Prädikat im jüdischen Sinn geht der vierte Evangelist mit Markus einig".[27]

The movement to correct faith in Jesus grows until it finally arrives at a confession in Jesus as the Son of Man. This is presented dramatically in John's account of the man born blind (ch. 9). The man slowly comes to understand who Jesus is (see vv. 11.17.33) concluding with a confession in Jesus as the Son of Man (v. 35). The identical process is described in Mk. 8,22-26, where the blind man comes to correct sight in stages. This man is a model of what is to follow. Peter's confession of Jesus as the Christ is answered by Jesus in terms of the Son of Man (Mk. 8,29-31). The latter is the perfect sight which the disciples have not yet attained.

Twice in the Fourth Gospel we are told that the Son of Man must (δεῖ) be lifted up (3,14; 12,34) and once it is announced that the Jews will lift Jesus up (8,28). There is a close link here with the threefold passion predictions of the Synoptic tradition (Mk. 8,31, parr. Mt. 16,21; Lk. 9,22; Mk. 9,31, parr. Matt. 17,22-23; Lk. 9,44; Mk. 10,33-34, parr. Matt. 20,18-19; Lk. 18,31-33). The Johannine crucifixion is at once a "lifting up" on a cross and an "exaltation", but behind the Johannine sayings which forecast this glorious "lifting up" of the Son of Man stand the traditional predictions of the suffering Son of Man.[28]

The Johannine Son of Man has always referred to the historical presence of Jesus. The Synoptic tradition also speaks of Jesus as a human figure at work among men, who must suffer (Mk. 2,10.27-28; 8,31; 9,9; 9,31; 10,33.45; 14,21.41; Matt. 13,37; 16,13; 26,2; Lk. 6,22; 7,34; 9,58; 11,30; 12,10; 17, 24-26; 19,10; 22,48; 24,6-7).[29] In this it is akin to the Johannine use of the term. The Synoptic tradition, however, also speaks of the Son of Man as a future figure, who will come at the end of time to judge all men (Mk. 8,38; 13,26; 14,62; Matt. 13,41; 16,28; 19,28; 24,29-30.39; 25,31; Lk. 11,30; 12, 8; 12,40; 17,22.24.26.30; 18,8; 21,36). For John, judgment takes place already in the person of Jesus Christ, the Son of Man, and thus he draws the Synoptic use of the term back into history (5,27; 8,28; 9,35-39; 12,34-36; 19,5). Again we are dealing with a johannisation of a traditional theme. It

---

[27] R. Schnackenburg, "Die Messiasfrage im Johannesevangelium", pp. 255-256. See also C.H. Dodd, *Interpretation*, pp. 91-93; N.A. Dahl, "The Johannine Church and History", pp. 128-130.

[28] See R. Schnackenburg, *St. John* I, pp. 535-536; E. Ruckstuhl, "Die johanneische Menschensohnforschung ...", p. 277; G. Iber, *Untersuchungen*, pp. 149-151.

[29] Most of these sayings have parallels. For a useful arrangement of the Synoptic sayings, see P.C. Hodgson, "The Son of Man and the Problem of Historical Knowledge", *JR* 41 (1961) 104-106.

should be noticed, however, that a future judgment is not totally excluded in the Fourth Gospel,[30] and in the place where this is made most clear (5,28-29) we find "the Son of Man" in the immediate context (5,27).

There appears to be little necessity to look beyond early Christian traditions to find a source for the Johannine use of "the Son of Man".[31] The presence of so many traditional traits should not, however, distract us from the central meaning of the Johannine Son of Man — the incarnate Logos who is at once the revealer and the revelation of God among men, the one who came to bring light and life to those who would believe in him. This is the essentially Johannine characteristic which has been added to the traditional figure of the Son of Man. Even here, however, we possibly have a development of the traditional idea of the Son of Man.[32] M. D. Hooker and C. F. D. Moule have argued that the Synoptic Son of Man is a reinterpretation of Dan. 7,13.[33] The figure of the Son of Man in the famous vision represents or symbolises the faithful Israelites during the persecutions of Antiochus IV. What is promised in the vision is that these faithful ones will be finally vindicated. Through obedience to the will of God and humble acceptance of the suffering which this obedience must bring with it, the Son of Man will be ultimately vindicated in the court of heaven. Because of the Jewish idea of "corporate personality", this term can oscillate between the people as a whole and a single figure who represents the people as "perfect humanity". The certainty of his final vindication gives the Son of Man his authority; he is the one who will have the last word.[34] From this understanding of Dan. 7,

[30] See above, pp. 78-81.

[31] Bultmann and others who claim a Gnostic source for the Johannine Son of Man, obscure this very important link between the Johannine and the Synoptic traditions. Most recently, H. M. Teeple, *The Literary Origins of the Gospel of John,* has assigned all the Son of Man sayings with the exception of 12,34 and 13,31 which come from an editor, to a "collection of documents expounding a theology of Hellenistic, semi-Gnostic mysticism" (see pp. 147-152). See on this, E. Ruckstuhl, "Die Johanneische Menschensohnforschung ...", pp. 277-282.

[32] It is important to note that it is different from the traditional idea, even though it has developed directly from that idea. It is not sufficient to claim "St. John clarifies the doctrine and re-states it in his own individual way, but he neither adds nor subtracts from it" (A. Richardson, *An Introduction to the Theology of the New Testament,* [London, SCM Press, 1958] p. 141).

[33] M. D. Hooker, *The Son of Man in Mark*; see C. F. D. Moule, "Neglected Features in the Problem of 'the Son of Man' ", pp. 413-428. Programmatic for both of these works was the earlier essay from Moule, "From Defendent to Judge — and Deliverer: An Inquiry into the Use and Limitations of the Theme of Vindication in the New Testament", in *Phenomenon,* pp. 82-99. This article originally appeared in *Bulletin of the Studiorum Novi Testamenti Societas* III (1952) 40-53.

[34] See M. D. Hooker, *op. cit.,* pp. 11-30; C. F. D. Moule, *art. cit.,* pp. 413-422; see also S. S. Smalley, "The Johannine Son of Man Sayings", pp. 281-287, where he adopts this interpretation. The individualisation of the figure results from Jewish Adam speculation,

one can see the Son of Man sayings in the Synoptic Gospels as Jesus' application of this idea to himself, as he has perfectly fulfilled the pattern of humble obedience, suffering and vindication in the resurrection.[35] It is, then, in the acceptance or refusal of the authority of the Son of Man — which implies a sharing or a refusal to share in the same suffering — that men can either gain or lose their own ultimate vindication.[36]

In the Fourth Gospel this vindication is drawn back into history. In the Synoptic tradition the cross was the lowest point of Jesus' suffering. In John it becomes the place of his elevation and glorification, two concepts which are continually linked with "the Son of Man" (3,14; 8,28; 12,23.32.34; 13,31, see 19,5). The glorification no longer belongs to the future, as we find that again John has drawn the traditional eschatological theme of glorification back into history. Because Jesus has come down from heaven (3,13; 6,62) and has become man (1,14), he can speak of God with ultimate authority. The Synoptic tradition placed the reason for Jesus' authority at the end of his human existence in the resurrection, but John has placed it at the beginning: Jesus has his authority because of the incarnation. Again we are dealing with the extraordinary Johannine development of the christology of the early Church. In the Marcan tradition it is the acceptance or refusal of the authority of Jesus, vindicated in the resurrection, which results in the gaining or losing of a share in Jesus' vindication; in John it is the acceptance or refusal of the authoritative revelation of the Son of Man, who comes from heaven, which brings life or death.[37] What Hooker has written of the Marcan Son of Man could, *mutatis mutandis*, well be said of the Johannine Son of Man:

> "Jesus used the term 'Son of man' of himself not as a convenient 'messianic' term, or as a claim to supernatural powers, but as an expression of the basis and meaning of his person and destiny: it expresses his position in the world, a position founded upon his relationship with God, for it is his relationship with God ... which explains his relationship with men".[38]

The Johannine Son of Man is not a convenient messianic term, and it does explain why he is in the world — to reveal God. The role of the Son of Man

---

reflected in Gen. 1-3, Ps. 8, Ezekiel and I Enoch. This does not mean that there is a direct literary link between all these texts. There is what Moule (*Phenomenon*, p. 83) calls, "a common fund of thoughts behind them". On the possibility of an individual reinterpretation of Ps. 8, see F. J. Moloney, "The Targum on Ps. 8 and the New Testament", *Salesianum* 37 (1975) 326-336.

[35] See M. D. Hooker, *op. cit.*, pp. 178-182; C. F. D. Moule, *art. cit.*, pp. 419-422. Moule points out that this process is indicated by the use of the definite article — *the* Son of Man.

[36] See M. D. Hooker, *op. cit.*, pp. 193-194.

[37] See J. T. Forestell, *The Word of the Cross*, pp. 61-65; F. Mussner, ZΩH, pp. 86-93.

[38] M. D. Hooker, *op. cit.*, p. 192. See also S. S. Smalley, "The Johannine Son of Man Sayings", p. 299.

can only be understood when one understands his relationship with God — he
has come from God, and thus can reveal him with ultimate authority.

S. Smalley and F. H. Borsch have also attempted to show that the
Johannine Son of Man is a product of the traditional use of the term.[39] Smalley
has followed the suggestions of Hooker and Moule which stand behind our
own conclusions.[40] He attempts to show that the Johannine use of the term
is much closer to the historical Jesus than is commonly admitted. Borsch has
turned to a wide selection of sources which, in his opinion, stand behind the
Son of Man traditions throughout the New Testament. From these common
sources, both the Johannine and Synoptic sayings have their origin. In this
way he is able to trace every Johannine saying back to one or more of the
Synoptic sayings.[41] All of this work is helpful and there may be a great deal
of truth in some of the suggestions which these scholars make, but they both
fail to appreciate the all-important Johannine aspect of revelation/judgment
which is central to the use of the term in the Fourth Gospel.

R. Schnackenburg has argued that there is a close link between the
Johannine and the Synoptic use of the term.[42] He sees 5,27 as an immediate
link with the Synoptic traditions. The three sayings which refer to the lifting
up of the Son of Man are also the result of Johannine speculation on the
Synoptic passion predictions — or rather, on the traditions which stand behind
them.[43] He is convinced, however, that the Johannine Son of Man came down
from heaven to give life and to judge, and then to ascend again. He understands 3,13 and 6,62 as a reference to the ascension of the Son of Man,
and he concludes that the glorification of the Son of Man is to take place as
a result of this ascension. Because of this, Schnackenburg claims that there
is no link between the earthly Son of Man in the Synoptic tradition (see Mk.
2,10.28; Lk. 9,58) and the Johannine Son of Man. When speaking of the
glorification of the Son of Man, Schnackenburg sees a reference to Mk. 8,38,
parr.; 13,26; Matt. 25,31, which refer to the Son of Man who will come in
glory at the end of time. All this has been 'realised' in John, but for Schnackenburg, the exaltation and glorification refer to the Son of Man who has ascended
to the Father.[44] There is no reference to the ascension in 3,13 and 6,62 as
both texts are concerned with Jesus' origin, not with what will happen to him
after his death.[45] The notion of the ascension in the Lucan sense, plays no

[39] S. S. Smalley, *art. cit.*, pp. 278-301; F. H. Borsch, *The Son of Man*, pp. 232-313.

[40] S. S. Smalley, *art. cit.*, pp. 281-287.

[41] This, however, leads Borsch to reject some evident and important parallels with
the Synoptic tradition. For example, he refuses to see any link between Dan. 7 and
Jn. 5,27, (*op. cit.*, p. 249).

[42] R. Schnackenburg, *St. John* I, pp. 535-538.

[43] *ibid.*, p. 535.

[44] *ibid.*, pp. 535-538.

[45] See above, pp. 53-58; 120-123.

part in the Johannine theology because the elevation and glorification of the Son of Man take place on the cross. This is a human event, as only a human being can be nailed to a cross, but it is in this event that paradoxically the Son of Man is glorified as he fulfills the task given to him — to reveal God to men (12,23; 13,31; 8,28; 19,5; see 17,4). It is because of the revelatory nature of the Johannine cross that the Son of Man has authority (see Mk. 2,10.28) and, in the strange Johannine paradox, it is the Son of Man who is utterly abandoned on the cross (see Lk. 9,58), who is lifted up to his glorification.

> "The cross is an elevation of the Son of Man as a sign of salvation for those who view it with faith, like the brazen serpent in the desert. It is also the hour of Jesus' glorification whereby he in turn glorifies the Father. *This glorification is a visible manifestation of the power and presence of God among men*".[46]

Schnackenburg has not admitted this johannisation of a traditional theme of ultimate vindication and authority, and thus has not appreciated the possible link between all the Johannine Son of Man sayings (whose unity of idea he stoutly defends[47]) and the traditional theology of the Son of Man found in Daniel 7 and in the Synoptic Gospels.

John has taken the term "the Son of Man" from Christian tradition. He has used this term in a way which betrays his own theological stance in every instance, even in 5,27,[48] but the Johannine Son of Man is the continuation of a dynamic, growing interpretation of Dan. 7,13, which can be found in the Synoptic Gospels, I Enoch, IV Esdras, the Fourth Gospel and which even extends into the writings of the early Fathers.[49] It is not precise enough to say that the Fathers only used the term "the Son of Man" to speak of the humanity of Jesus. Justin Martyr and Cyril of Jerusalem use it in the context of Dan. 7,13 in a way similar to the New Testament (Justin, *Dial.* 31,1; 76,1; Cyril, *Catech.* 10,4). Even when it is applied to the human Jesus, it often refers to him as the representative and perfect man, because of the incarnation. Irenaeus uses these categories both in describing heresies (*Adv. Haer.* I,6,3;

---

[46] J. T. Forestell, *The Word of the Cross*, p. 101. Stress mine. See his whole chapter: "The Johannine Treatment of the Cross", pp. 58-102. Further bibliography on this question is indicated there. See, most recently, T. Worden, "The Glory of God", pp. 85-94.

[47] See R. Schnackenburg, *St. John* I, pp. 530-532.

[48] See C. H. Dodd, "The Portrait of Jesus in John and the Synoptics", pp. 183-198.

[49] It is not true to claim that the idea disappears rapidly in the early Church. We hope that we have shown that it is very important for John. It is not found as a title in the letters (but see Acts 7,56; Heb. 2,6 and Rev. 1,13; 14,14) but this may be because of its pride of place in the tradition on the lips of Jesus. It does not mean that a Son of Man christology is not found in Paul. The Fathers were the first to break with the tradition by using the title to speak of Jesus.

I,8,14) and in combating them (III, 19,1; V,14,1-2; V,21,1).[50] However, between the earlier use of "the Son of Man" who would come at the end of time as judge and the Fathers' use of the term to speak of Jesus (see also Ignatius, *Ephes.* 20,2; Barnabas 12,10; Hippolytus, *Contra Noetum* 2,15) there is certainly a change of interest; the humanity of Jesus is now their primary concern, even if other elements are still found there.[51] Perhaps John's use of the title provides the link. The Johannine Son of Man is the human Jesus, the incarnate Logos; he has come to reveal God with a unique and ultimate authority and in the acceptance or refusal of this revelation the world judges itself. It seems possible that John's link with the traditional Son of Man on the one hand, and his accentuation of the human figure on the other, could well place him at the cross-roads between the New Testament and the Fathers of the early Church. It is beyond our scope to investigate this possibility, but Irenaeus sounds very Johannine when he writes of the Son of Man:

"Verbum Dei quod habitavit in homine, et Filius
hominis factus est, ut assuesceret hominem
percipere Deum, et assuesceret Deum habitare
in homine, secundum placitum Patris".

(Adv. Haer. III,21,2)

---

[50] See L. Bouyer, "La notion christologique du Fils de l'homme a-t-elle disparu dans la patristique grecque?" in *Mélanges bibliques rédigés en l'honneur de André Robert,* (Paris, Bloud et Gay, 1957) pp. 519-530.

[51] See T. E. Pollard, *Johannine Christology and the Early Church,* pp. 32-33. 52-58. Another 'post-Johannine' use of the title can be found in the Gnostic literature (see above, p. 56, note 76). The theme of the revelation of God in the human figure of Jesus, the Son of Man, is also found there. See, for example, Irenaeus, *Adv. Haer.,* I,12,3; 15,3; 30,1.6; Hippolytus, *Ref.* V,26.30; VIII,13,1-4. The Nag Hammadi material generally uses the title, in obvious speculations on the New Testament, in contexts which show little contact with the Johannine idea. See, for example, *Letter of Eugnostus,* 81, 84, 85; *Treatise on the Resurrection,* 44,23.31; 46,15; *Gospel of Philip,* 54, 102, 120. All of these texts are found in English in W. Foerster-R. McL. Wilson, *Gnosis. A Selection of Gnostic Texts.* However, the recently translated Codex XIII provides an interesting parallel in 49,10-25. For the text, French translation and a commentary, see Y. Janssens, "Le Codex XIII de Nag Hammadi", *Le Muséon* 87 (1974) 341-413. See pp. 388-389 for the passage cited. For an assessment of the relationship between this document and the Fourth Gospel, see C. Colpe, "Heidnische, jüdische und christliche Ueberlieferung in den Schriften aus Nag Hammadi III", *Jahrbuch für Antike und Christentum* 17 (1974) 119-125.

THE JOHANNINE SON OF MAN 1976-1977 [1]

Although the first edition of this book left my desk in late 1975, it would now take a further volume of similar dimensions to discuss fully all the publications which have in some way touched upon the Fourth Gospel's use of the title "the Son of Man" since that time.[2] My reading of this literature, in the light of the critical remarks of my reviewers, has led me to conclude that there are two major areas which need further attention:

1. The background to John's use of the title.

2. The place of the Johannine understanding of Jesus as "the Son of Man" within the developing christology of the community which eventually produced the Fourth Gospel.

Closely associated with the first area is my refusal to accept the pre-existence, ascension and post-existence of the Son of Man in 3,13 and 6,62, and I will discuss that problem under the first heading.[3]

---

[1] As the original work was largely written in England, and this appendix is being written in Rome, I have often had difficulty in obtaining English translations of European books. Whenever possible I will refer to English translations, but often (e.g. the first volume R. Schnackenburg's commentary) I will have to refer to the original work, even though an English translation is available, and has been referred to in the first edition.

[2] See B. Lindars, *Behind the Fourth Gospel,* Studies in Creative Criticism 3 (London, SPCK, 1971) p. 11: "The literature on it (the Fourth Gospel) is immense, and even a scholar who devotes all his time to the study of the New Testament cannot hope to keep. up with it". I have already published a full discussion of R. Pesch-R. Schnackenburg-O. Kaiser (eds.), *Jesus und der Menschensohn: Für Anton Vögtle* (Freiburg, Herder, 1975) in "A Johannine Son of Man Discussion?", *Salesianum* 39 (1977) 93-102. I will not repeat that survey here.

[3] Some reviewers object to points of exegesis without giving reasons. See, for example, J. Schlosser, "Chronique d'exégèse du Nouveau Testament", *RSR* 52 (1978) 40 where he objects to my explanation of 6,53; G. Testa in *DThom* 80 (1977) 313 and J. Coppens in *ETL* 52 (1976) 393 on 19,5. On the other hand, G. Segalla in *StPat* 24 (1977) 100 and J. Painter in *ABR* 25 (1977) 43 raise serious objections to my understanding of 3,13 and 6,62. See also M. de Jonge in *NedTTs* 31 (1977) 253-254 who approves my understanding of 3,13 but regards the explanation of 6,62 as unlikely.

1. The Background to John's Use of "the Son of Man"[4]

There is a growing consensus of opinion that the Fourth Gospel was born, developed and came to maturity in some sort of sectarian Jewish group where early Gnosticism may have been present in some form, but where the contact with mainstream (synagogue) Judaism was still strongly present in a negative sense, i.e. the Johannine community had been "put out of the Synagogue" (see 9,22; 12,42; 16,2).[5] This group's theological point of view was not only

---

[4] This question was only treated in passing (see above, p. 56 note 76 and pp. 213-220) as I deliberately limited my attention to the specifically Johannine theological point of view which stands behind the Fourth Evangelist's use of the title. Most reviewers have appreciated (even if they have not all approved) this decision. A few, e.g. H. Wansbrough in *New Blackfriars* 58 (1977) 153 and A. E. Harvey in *JTS* 28 (1977) 553, insist that a study of the background to the Johannine Son of Man is the only way to come to a correct understanding of it.   The major reason for the strict limitation of my theme was a practical one. The Faculty of Theology at Oxford University has a wise rule that a D. Phil. thesis must not exceed 100,000 words, including footnotes. For the wisdom of this regulation, see the *shortened* version of the (excellent) Münster thesis of S. Pancaro, *The Law in the Fourth Gospel. The Torah and the Gospel. Moses and Jesus, Judaism and Christianity according to John*, SNT 42 (Leiden, E. J. Brill, 1975), which runs to 571 tightly printed pages.

[5] See, for an excellent survey and further bibliography, D. M. Smith, "Johannine Christianity: Some Reflections on its Character and Delineation", *NTS* 21 (1974-75) 222-248, esp. pp. 238-248.   There is an ever-growing interest in the question, especially in the United States (highlighted by scholars at Duke University). Some of these studies will be given detailed consideration at a later stage, but I will indicate the relevant bibliography here. D. M. Smith, "The Milieu of the Johannine Miracle Source: A Proposal", in R. Hamerton-Kelly - R. Scroggs (eds.), *Jews Greeks and Christians. Religious Cultures in Late Antiquity: Essays in Honor of William David Davies*, SJLA 21 (Leiden, E. J. Brill, 1976) pp. 164-180; Idem, "The Setting and Shape of a Johannine Narrative Source", *JBL* 95 (1976) 231-241; R. E. Brown, "Johannine Ecclesiology - The Community's Origins", *Interp* 31 (1977) 379-393; J. L. Martyn, "Source Criticism and Religionsgeschichte in the Fourth Gospel", in *Jesus and Man's Hope* (Pittsburgh, Pittsburgh Theological Seminary, 1971) Vol. I, pp. 247-273; Idem, "Glimpses into the History of the Johannine Community From its Origin through the Period of its Life in Which the Fourth Gospel Was Composed", in M. de Jonge (ed.), *L'Évangile de Jean. Sources, rédaction, théologie*, BETL 44 (Gembloux, Duculot, 1977) pp. 149-174; Idem, "We Have Found Elijah", in *Jews, Greeks and Christians*, pp. 181-219. Martyn has a further study, "Clementine Recognitions 1, 33-71, Jewish Christianity and the Fourth Gospel", in J. Jervell-W.A. Meeks (eds.), *Festschrift N. A. Dahl* (Oslo, 1976), but it was not available to me. W. A. Meeks, " 'Am I a Jew?' - Johannine Christianity and Judaism", in J. Neusner (ed.), *Christianity, Judaism and Other Greco-Roman Cults: Studies for Morton Smith at Sixty*, SJLA 12 (Leiden, E. J. Brill, 1975) Vol. I, pp. 163-186. As well as this very significant contribution from American scholars, particularly important is the work of Georg Richter, whose recent premature death in August 1975 has cut short a very original contribution to Johannine studies. His most important contribution to this discussion was: "Präsentische und futurische Eschatologie im 4. Evangelium", in P. Fiedler - D. Zeller (eds.), *Gegenwart und kommendes Reich: Schülergabe Anton Vögtle zum 65. Geburtstag* (Stuttgart, Katholisches Bibelwerk, 1975) pp. 117-152. There is an excellent summary and assessment of Richter's work in A. J. Mattill, "Johannine Communities Behind the Fourth Gospel", *TS* 38 (1977) 294-315. Similar attempts, with different results, have been made in recent years by J. Becker,

the result of a linear development of Christian traditions but it was forged, through various crises, in a unique socio-cultural situation as the community struggled to find its feet and express its understanding of Jesus their Christ,[6] in a foreign world, cut off from their native Judaism.[7] The Johannine community and its Gospel cannot be comfortably filed under "Jewish", "Gnostic", "Hellenistic" or any other single classification. A community forced out of the synagogue because of its heterodox beliefs can no longer be called Jewish in the strict sense of that word, but on the other hand, a community with its ethnic and religious roots in Judaism, struggling to adapt its life-style, thought patterns and religious practice to the maelstrom of late first century syncretism cannot justly be called Hellenistic or Gnostic.[8]   J. M. Robinson has stated the situation succinctly when he wrote of the "Johannine trajectory".[9]

The second section of this appendix will be devoted to an attempt to locate my earlier discussion of the Johannine concept of the Son of Man within the developing christological consciousness of the Johannine Church.[10]

"J 3,1-21 als Reflex johanneischer Schuldiskussion", in H. Balz-S. Schulz (eds.), *Das Wort und die Wörter. Festschrift Gerhard Friedrich zum 65. Geburtstag* (Stuttgart, Kohlhammer, 1973) pp. 85-95; Idem, "Wunder und Christologie.   Zum literarkritischen und christologischen Problem der Wunder im Johannesevengelium", *NTS* 16 (1969-70) 130-148; Idem, "Die Abschiedsreden im Johannesevangelium", *ZNW* 61 (1970) 215-246; Idem, "Beobachtungen zum Dualismus im Johannesevangelium", *ZNW* 65 (1974) 71-87 and U. B. Müller, *Die Geschichte der Christologie in der johanneischen Gemeinde,* SBS (Stuttgart, Katholisches Bibelwerk, 1975).   Another German scholar whose interest is moving in this direction is R. Schnackenburg. See especially his "Entwicklung und Stand der Johanneischen Forschung seit 1955", in M. de Jonge (ed.), *L'Evangile de Jean,* pp. 19-44.   From England, C. K. Barrett already pointed in this direction in his Franz Delitzsch-Vorlesungen in 1967.   See C. K. Barrett, *Das Johannesevangelium und das Judentum* (Stuttgart, Kohlhammer, 1970) esp. pp. 43-75.

  [6] Precisely because he was their Christ they were put out of the synagogue.   See, above all, J. L. Martyn, *History and Theology in the Fourth Gospel* (New York, Harper and Row, 1968), and, most recently, S. Pancaro, *The Law in the Fourth Gospel,* pp. 247-253; 494-497; 510-514.   See also, F. J. Moloney, "The Fourth Gospel's Presentation of Jesus as 'the Christ' and J. A. T. Robinson's 'Redating' ", *The Downside Review* 95 (1977) 239-253.

  [7] Important in this regard was the earlier article of W. A. Meeks, "The Man from Heaven in Johannine Sectarianism", *JBL* 91 (1972) 327-351.

  [8] D. M. Smith, "Johannine Christianity ...", pp. 238-244 sees the material of the Gospel as the product of such varied influences as: eye-witnesses, miracle traditions, a passion narrative, the controversy with the synagogue, incipient Gnosticism or quasi-Gnosticism and charismatic prophecy.

  [9] J. M. Robinson - H. Koester, *Trajectories through Early Christianity* (Philadelphia, Fortress Press, 1971) pp. 232-268.   Although I will continue to use the word, "trajectory" gives the impression of a pre-determined pattern of movement, and this was certainly not the case for any of the communities of the early Church.   The German title of this book has the much more satisfactory "Entwicklungslinien".

  [10] As requested by the encouraging review of D. M. Smith in *CBQ* 39 (1977) 441 and also by J. Coppens in *ETL* 52 (1976) 394, although Coppens speaks of a "strate littéraire", which I think is a little ambitious.

Here I will consider two recent suggestions concerning the origin and background of the use of this title in the Fourth Gospel:

— the myth of a descending-ascending redeemer
— Jewish and early Christian "agent" speculation.

As both of these suggestions lean heavily upon a certain interpretation of Jn. 3,13 and 6,62, I will discuss those passages within this context.

The Myth of a Descending-Ascending Redeemer

Since the discovery and publication of the Nag-Hammadi material there have been a series of attempts to link the Johannine Gospel with the Gnostic systems,[11] but there has been no return to R. Bultmann's suggestion that the Johannine use of the term "the Son of Man" comes directly from the myth of a Gnostic redeemer figure.[12] Nevertheless, in his review of my work

---

[11] See the most recent summary of K. Rudoph, *Die Gnosis. Wesen und Geschichte einer spätantiken Religion* (Göttingen, Vandenhoeck und Ruprecht, 1977) pp. 173-174; 324-325, and the list of recent works linking John with Gnostic thought on pp. 411-412 note 134. Rudolph, following E. Käsemann, concludes: "Der uns unbekannte Autor ... ist ein christlicher Gnostiker, der die geradezu unvorstellbare Kühnheit besetzt, ein Evangelium des von ihm erfahrenen, in die Welt der Gnosis hineinsprechenden Christus zu schreiben" (p. 327). There remains, in German scholarship (which often pays little attention to work outside German-speaking circles) two different approaches to John's use of his Gnostic sources. For Käsemann (whom Rudolph follows), the Evangelist is an incipient Gnostic whose Gospel has been accepted into the Canon through what can be called "theologisch gesehen, ein glücklicher Irrtum" (*Jesu letzter Wille*, p. 157). The other view, following Bultmann, is that John christianised and historicised the Gnostic myth. Most recently in this line is P. Vielhauer, *Geschichte der urchristlichen Literatur. Einleitung in das Neue Testament, die Apokryphen und die Apostolischen Väter* (Berlin/New York, Walter de Gruyter, 1975) pp. 445-450. See, on this discussion, K. M. Fischer, "Der johanneische Christus und der gnostische Erlöser. Ueberlegungen auf Grund von Joh 10", in K.-W. Tröger (ed.), *Gnosis und Neues Testament. Studien aus Religionswissenschaft und Theologie* (Gütersloh, Gerd Mohn, 1973) pp. 245-250. This study of Jn. 10 (running from pp. 245-266) finds that Gnostic categories are central to John's argument, but that the Evangelist (although not Ireneus or Hippolytus) is anti-Gnostic. A similar conclusion in reached, in a wider survey of the Gospel, by K.-W. Tröger, "Ja oder Nein zur Welt. War der Evangelist Johannes Christ oder Gnostiker?", *Theologische Versuche* 7 (1976) 61-80. See esp. p. 76 where he takes issue with Käsemann: "Das Christuszeugnis des Johannes steht als völlig zu Recht im Kanon und hat zudem für die spätere Auseinandersetzung der Kirche mit der Gnosis eine wichtige und fruchtbare Vorarbeit geleistet". See also, J. Giblet, "Développements dans la théologie johannique", in M. de Jonge (ed.), *L'Évangile de Jean. Sources rédaction, théologie*, BETL 44 (Gembloux, Duculot, 1977) pp. 45-72, esp. pp. 55-72 on recent Gnostic interpretations (Bultmannian tradition, Käsemann and Schottroff).

[12] See above, p. 56 note 76, and futher, C. Colpe, "New Testament and Gnostic Christology", in J. Neusner (ed.), *Religions in Antiquity: Essays in Memory of Erwin Ramsdell Goodenough*, Studies in the History of Religions 14 (Leiden, E. J. Brill, 1968)

H. Wansbrough wrote: "There is one special factor which seems to me to spring to attention about the Johannine use of the expression which Dr. Moloney does not sufficiently evaluate, and that is (with the possible exception of 5,27) each of the passages is concerned with vertical movement, either coming down from heaven or being glorified to heaven. This is such a salient feature that it must surely be an important clue in any investigation, though its significance is not immediately obvious".[13]   Wansbrough hints that there must be some special Johannine background for this "vertical movement" of the Son of Man.[14]   This means that we should return to the sources which speak of the

pp. 227-243.   The most comprehensive recent Gnostic reading of John, L. Schottroff, *Der Glaubende und die feindliche Welt. Beobachtungen zum gnostischen Dualismus und seiner Bedeutung für Paulus und das Johannesevangelium*, WMANT 37 (Neukirchen, Neukirchener Verlag, 1970) makes no mention of Bultmann's suggestions. See p. 292 note 3 where she accepts that the descent-ascent motif is not necessarily Gnostic. The most recent refusal of the bultmannian position is Jan-A. Bühner, *Der Gesandte und sein Weg im 4. Evangelium. Die kultur- und religionsgeschichtlichen Grundlagen der johanneischen Sendungschristologie sowie ihre traditionsgeschichtliche Entwicklung*, WUNT 2. Reihe 2 (Tübingen, J. C. B. Mohr, 1977) pp. 24-47. Still fundamental in this discussion is C. Colpe, *Die Religionsgeschichtliche Schule. Darstellung und Kritik ihres Bildes von gnostischen Erlösermythus*, FRLANT 60 (Göttingen, Vandenhoeck und Ruprecht, 1961).

    [13]   *New Blackfriars* 58 (1977) 153.

    [14]   Although not mentioned in the review, I suspect that Wansbrough's general stance on the Son of Man question enters here. See H. Wansbrough, "The Mission of Jesus III: Jesus and his Future", *The Clergy Review* 57 (1972) 923-933; Idem, "Jesus of Galilee: Who did he think he was?", *The Clergy Review* 60 (1975) 647-657; Idem, "Jesus of Galilee: The Son of Man", *The Clergy Review* 60 (1975) 760-766. See also his favourable report on G. Vermes' Oxford paper (see below) in *The Tablet*, April 29th, 1978, p. 402. Wansbrough accepts the argument of G. Vermes, that "the son of man" in late Judaism was merely a circumlocution for the first person singular, and he argues that Jesus deliberately used this form of speech so that all attention would be directed to God, his Father. For Vermes' position, see G. Vermes, "The Use of *br nsh/br nsh'* in Jewish Aramaic", in M. Black, *An Aramaic Approach to the Gospels and Acts* (Oxford, Clarendon Press, 1967) pp. 310-328 and *Jesus the Jew. A Historian's Reading of the Gospel* (London, Collins, 1973) pp. 160-191. He recently repeated the same arguments in a paper entitled "The Present State of the Son of Man Debate" at the Sixth International Congress on Biblical Studies (Oxford, 3-7 April 1978). This paper is, as yet, unpublished. An acceptance of Vermes' position leads to a situation recently summed up by M. Casey, "The Use of Term (sic) 'Son of Man' in the Similitudes of Enoch", *JSJ* 7 (1976) 29: "The way is left open for us to deny the existence of a special 'Son of Man' concept in Judaism. We can then go ahead and use the evidence collected by Vermes to attack the supposedly insoluble problem of the use of the term 'son of man' in the New Testament". I do not believe that the question can be resolved so simply. Vermes has certainly produced evidence which should ease the search for a messianic significance behind every occurrence of "Son of Man", but there are two areas which, in my opinion, Vermes' work still leaves uncovered.

1.   When the Gospel of Mark uses an "I-saying" and Matthew and/or Luke change it to a "Son of Man saying" (e.g. Mk. 8,27 = Matt. 16,13) or when a Q passage is an "I-saying" in Matthew or Luke, but a "Son of Man saying" in the parallel (e.g. Matt. 5,11 = Lk. 6,22), I have every reason to suppose that "the Son of Man" meant something which was not conveyed by "I". As these authors were writing in Greek, it is

descent and ascent of a redeemer, although Wansbrough does not explicitly say this.[15]

I remain convinced that to search the descending-ascending redeemer myths for background is to look in the wrong place, as the Johannine Son of Man is *not* concerned with vertical movement. A survey of the thirteen sayings, in the light of my earlier study, shows that:

— In 1,51 the angels, but not the Son of Man, ascend and descend.[16]

— I refuse to accept that 3,13 is about descent and ascent, although this is certainly the most common understanding of the passage. I have argued that it is concerned only with the descent involved in the incarnation.[17]

— The only movement in 3,14 is the lifting up of Jesus on the Cross. The verb ὑψόω refers to crucifixion, not to the ascension.[18]

— 5,27 is allowed as not being concerned with vertical movement.

— In 6,27 Jesus speaks of the food which will be given by the Son of Man. There is no immediate concern with vertical movement.

— The same can be said of 6,53 where Jesus speaks of the necessity to eat the flesh and drink the blood of the Son of Man.

not good enough to say (as did Vermes in his Oxford lecture) that this is further proof for the argument that "son of man" = "I". On the contrary! "The Son of Man" meant something more than "I", and whole passages were re-written to present Jesus as "the Son of Man" where an earlier version of the saying had "I". Why did they change "I-sayings" into "Son of Man sayings"? This was also raised by B. Lindars, "Re-Enter the Apocalyptic Son of Man", *NTS* 22 (1975-76) 53-54; 65-66, but Vermes has never given a satisfactory solution. I would suggest that the term meant more to the early Church than just "I", and that they received from contemporary Judaism and from Jesus himself a term that was in some way titular.

2. Wansbrough and Casey (among others) believe that Vermes has put an end to the search for a messianic use of the term in non-Christian Jewish sources. It appears to me that there is such a use of the term "the Son of Man" in the Targum on Psalms which may at least hint at what "the Son of Man" meant in first century Judaism, and which Vermes has not considered. See F. J. Moloney, "The Targum on Ps. 8 and the New Testament", *Salesianum* 37 (1975) 326-336 (not mentioned by Vermes in his 1978 lecture) and Idem, "The Use of the Old Testament in the New: Psalm VIII, a Test Case", to be published shortly in *NTS*.

[15] Naturally, this would take us back to re-examine the material which Bultmann had at his disposal, and any further evidence coming to us from the newly-found Gnostic documents. However, I am deliberately avoiding the use of the term Gnostic Redeemer myth because this was only one (certainly the most famous) of the descending-ascending redeemer figures in the ancient world. See, on this, the excellent survey of C. H. Talbert, "The Myth of a Descending-Ascending Redeemer in Mediterranean Antiquity", *NTS* 22 (1975-76) 418-440. On the Fourth Gospel's use of this widespread descent-ascent myth, see pp. 438-440.

[16] I pointed this out above on p. 38 note 76.

[17] See above, pp. 54-59.

[18] See below, pp. 227-230.

— I refuse to accept that 6,62 refers to Jesus' ascension, although again this is the most widely accepted interpretation. I have argued that Jesus *refuses* to ascend.[19]

— As in 3,14, the verb ὑψόω is used in 8,28 to refer to the Cross, not the ascension.

— There is not the slightest hint of vertical movement in 9,35 where Jesus asks the man born blind if he believes in the Son of Man.

— The use of the verbs δοξάζω and ὑψόω in 12,23.34 both refer to the crucifixion.

— As in 12,23 the aorist tense δοξάζειν is a reference to the Cross in 13,31 and must be understood as a moment separated from the future glorification of 13,32.[20]

We must be careful not to be so fascinated by a few outstanding passages (3,13 and 6,62) that we are led to determine the whole of the Johannine· Son of Man christology by them. Once under the fascination of a supposed descent-ascent motif in 3,13 and 6,62 everything (eleven further sayings!) is often interpreted in that light.

My last statement could be demonstrated by a careful scrutiny of Bultmann's original suggestions, but it is seen again in Wansbrough's claim that the Johannine Son of Man is "glorified to heaven".[21] This is *never* said of the Son of Man in the Fourth Gospel, and it is obvious that the verbs δοξάζω and ὑψόω are being read entirely in the light of the supposed vertical movement in 3,13 and 6,62.

It need not be repeated at great length here that central to Johannine christology is the application of the Old Testament theme of the kᵉbôd Jahweh to Jesus. The Old Testament idea of an external, physical and visible manifestation of God among his people is personalised in Jesus of Nazareth. A random selection of texts from all over the Old Testament (see, for example, Exod. 16,7-10; 24,16-17; Lev. 9,6.23; Num. 14,21; II Chron. 5,14; Is. 35,2; Ps. 19,2; Is. 40,5) shows that the kᵉbôd Jahweh is always *seen* and *experienced*. This obviously technical and theologically significant term is regularly translated in the LXX as δόξα τοῦ θεοῦ.[22] John makes it clear in his programmatic

---

[19] See above, pp. 120-123.

[20] See below, note 28.

[21] *New Blackfriars* 58 (1977) 153.

[22] It has often been pointed out that the choice of the noun δόξα to translate *kabôd* is very surprising. The Greek word means "notion, opinion, esteem, repute" etc. See H. G. Liddell - R. Scott, *A Greek-English Lexicon*, s.v. See also W. Grossouw, "La glorification du Christ dans le quatrième Evangile", in *L'Evangile de Jean. Etudes et problèmes*, Recherches Bibliques III (Bruges, Desclée de Brouwer, 1958) pp. 131-133. This fact indicates that John knows and deliberately chooses the Old Testament expression to speak of Jesus as ἡ δόξα.

statement in 1,14 (ἐθεασάμεθα τὴν δόξαν αὐτοῦ) that he uses the term δόξα in the same way. This cannot refer to Jesus' glorification into heaven (which men and women — "we" — could not "see"); it must be a reference to the human experience of "seeing" something in history, just as the people of old "saw" the k^eb̂ôd Jahweh. It is clear from 2,11 and 11,4.40 that the miraculous activity of Jesus was understood as a reflection of the δόξα τοῦ θεοῦ, but especially important are 5,41-44; 7,18 and 12,43 where John has a play on words between the secular and the biblical meaning of δόξα, indicating that some were more interested in a reputation (δόξα) which they could measure by worldly standards, rather than the unique opportunity offered by the inbreak of God's visible presence among them (δόξα τοῦ θεοῦ) in the person of Jesus (see especially 12,43 where this observation closes John's reflection on the Jewish failure to accept Jesus). All of this is limited to time and history, within the experience of men and women.

If the historical presence of Jesus is the visible revelation of God among men, then the Cross (for the Fourth Evangelist) becomes the moment *par excellence* for that revelation. In that event a God who is love (I Jn 4,8.16) and who sent his Son because of his love for the world (Jn 3,16-17) is revealed by means of a supreme act of love (see 15,13). To make this point John employs several techniques,[23] but closely associated with the Son of Man theme is his use of the verb ὑψόω, "to lift up" and "to exalt" (3,14; 8,28; 12,32.34).[24] Again there is the danger that even this verb be understood as a reference to the beginning of some sort of journey "upwards", especially in 3,14 where it is so close to the use of ἀναβαίνειν in v. 13. The text must be read carefully. Jesus announces:

Just as (καθώς) Moses lifted up (ὕψωσεν) the serpent in the desert
So also (οὕτως) must the Son of Man be lifted up (ὑψωθῆναι).

The sense of the "just as ... so also" must be preserved: the Son of Man must be lifted up on a stake and hang there, so that men and women can gaze upon him (see 19,37).[25] The same point is made in 12,32-33:

---

[23] The theme of "the hour of Jesus", the use of τέλος and related verbs, the description of Jesus life and death as an ἔργον etc. See above, pp. 177-179 and the bibliography given there.

[24] For a discussion of this word and a more detailed explanation of what follows, see above, pp. 59-64. To the bibliography in note 106 one should add R. E. Brown, "The Passion according to John: chapters 18-19", *Worship* 40 (1975) 126-134.

[25] This is lost in the position of J. Coppens, "Le Fils de l'homme dans l'évangile johannique", *ETL* 52 (1976) 48: "Partout cependant le terme ὑψοῦν connote la glorification". The texts (3,14; 8,28; 12,32-34) do not indicate this. In his review of my book Coppens (*ETL* 52 [1976] 393-394) states that our conclusions are very similar. This surprises me, as both in method and in conclusions we differ considerably. Some elements of Coppens' treatment are puzzling. On pp. 30-31, 39 and 57 he writes of 12,34 being a word of Jesus addressed to the crowd. There are many points of interpretation where we differ radically. 1,51 is described as a promised heavenly moment (p. 45); both 3,13 and

"And I, when I am lifted up (ὑψωθῶ) from the earth, will draw all men to myself" (v. 32).

The redactional note which follows in v. 33 should end all discussion about what the final editor of the Gospel meant by his use of ὑψόω:

"He said this to show *by what death he was to die*".[26]

There can be no "ascent" motif, and the Evangelist himself insists that ὑψωθῆναι = to be crucified.

The use of δοξάζω and ὑψόω in close association to speak of the "glorification" and the "lifting up" of the Son of Man must be linked with the human event of the Cross.[27] I would insist that the Johannine Son of Man is never involved in a descent-ascent scheme. On one occasion (3,13) Jesus claims that the Son of Man, the unique revealer has descended, but that no one has gone up on high to become a revealer, and on another occasion he refuses to submit to current schemes of ascending revealer-figures (6,62). Descended in the incarnation, his only ascent as the Son of Man is in the human event of the Cross, so that he may be seen by all, that they may find life in him (3,15). According to the Fourth Gospel, Jesus brings his earthly ἔργον to its consummation on the Cross (see 17,4; 19,30) and thus Jesus can claim to have revealed (glorified) God (13,31; 17,4). It is within this very "earthly" and human sphere that the Gospel speaks of Jesus as the Son of Man.

While 3,13 and 6,62 still pose problems the Son of Man is not "glorified to heaven" in 12,23.34 or 13,31,[28] and the rest of the sayings have nothing

6,62 refer to the ascension (pp. 47 and 53) and 8,28 is understood as meaning "I am the Son of Man" (pp. 54 and 69 note 138). The reader will be aware that I have refused to accept all these interpretations. Coppens does not appear to have recognised the centrality of my insistence that the title is used by John to speak *exclusively* of the human activity of Jesus. On p. 71 of his study he refuses to accept this position because it is contrary to his understanding of the Son of Man in Dan. 7, whom he understands as a heavenly being, an angel. See on this J. Coppens, "Le Fils d'homme daniélique et les relectures du Dan vii, 13, dans les apocryphes et les écrits du Nouveau Testament", *ETL* 37 (1961) 5-19; Idem, "La vision daniélique du Fils d'homme", *VT* 19 (1969) 171-182. On this, see below, notes 49, 66 and 72. On John's use of καθώς, see O. de Dinechin, "Kathōs. La similitude dans l'evangile de saint Jean", *RecSR* 58 (1970) 195-236. On 3,14 see pp. 224-225.

[26] It could be argued that 12,33 has been added by a redactor with anti-docetic purposes. See R. Bultmann, *Johannes*, p. 331 note 5. Bultman claims that v. 32 originally referred to the return of the redeemer in the Gnostic myth, but this is corrected in v. 33. Even if the language had its origin in these myths (which would still have to be proved), the overall Johannine presentation of the Son of Man was never connected with an "ascent".

[27] There is, of course, a very important use of δοξάζειν, quite separate from the Son of Man and ὑψοῦν which clearly refers to the glorification of the Son "with the Father" (e.g. 13,32 and 17,5).

[28] Against J. Coppens, "Le Fils de l'homme...", pp. 57-59. Coppens studies 13,31-32 as if both. uses of δοξάζειν referred to the Son of Man title. The passage, with its change from an aorist in v. 31 to a future in v. 32 refers to two moments in the glorification of Jesus.

to do with vertical movement. The significance of this title for the Fourth Gospel seems to be intimately linked to the earthly task of the man, Jesus of Nazareth, and I believe that the background to John's use of the title will not be found in literature which speaks of a descending and ascending redeemer, simply because the Johannine Son of Man does not descend and ascend.[29]

Jewish and early Christian "agent" speculation

In a collection of studies commemorating E. R. Goodenough in 1968, Peder Borgen contributed a most original article entitled "God's Agent in the Fourth Gospel".[30] He brought forward considerable evidence to show that there were striking parallels between the Jewish halakhic principles of agency and the presentation of Jesus in the Fourth Gospel: [31]

— a unity between the agent and the sender

— the agent always remains subordinate

1. In v. 31 the νῦν of "the hour" of Jesus (see 13,1) is said to be accomplished, and thus is the Son of Man glorified (see 17,4).

2. Given the performance of the task (13,32a), then the future glorification of Jesus "in the Father" will certainly take place (see 17,5).
In v. 32 there is no use of the *title*, but αὐτόν is found. For the Fourth Evangelist Jesus pre-existed as the Logos, was a historical person, and also returned to the Father. I am convinced, however, that the Evangelist carefully chose his titles to refer to the different stages of activity for the same person. For a full discussion of this question see F. J. Moloney, *The Word Became Flesh: a Study of Jesus in the Fourth Gospel* (Cork, Mercier Press, 1978) In the Press.

[29] Because of this conclusion I see no point in tediously investigating various descending and ascending Man — Primal Man — Son of Man — Angel figures in mediterranean antiquity, as I do not think that they are relevant. The material is, however, well surveyed by C. H. Talbert, "The Myth of a Descending-Ascending Redeemer...", pp. 418-440. Talbert himself (pp: 439-440) accepts the classification of the Johannine Son of Man sayings proposed by A. J. B. Higgins, *Jesus and the Son of Man* (London, Lutterworth, 1964) pp. 153-157, that 3,13; 6,27.53.62; 12,23 and 13,31-32 are about a Son of Man who descends and ascends, and claims that John is using a common pattern alongside a series of more synoptic-like Son of Man sayings. In doing this John associates the descent and ascent with Jesus, and thus attempts to *separate* the descent-ascent motifs from angel speculation, widely found in Hellenistic Judaism (see below). Even if one admits that the Johannine Son of Man descends and ascends, the search for background material for such a scheme has generally led to negative results. See, for example, C. Colpe, "New Testament and Gnostic Christology", pp. 227-243 and R. Schnackenburg, *Johannes-evangelium* I, pp. 420-423; 433-447. Most recently, see Jan-A. Bühner, *Der Gesandte und sein Weg*, pp. 24-47. Bühner concludes: "*Den* gnostischen Mythos gibt es in frühchristlicher Zeit noch nicht, vielmehr ist religionsgeschichtlich eine Vielzahl von Motiven gegeben, die sich erst allmählich auf einen Grundbestand reduziert" (p. 46).

[30] P. Borgen, "God's Agent in the Fourth Gospel", in J. Neusner (ed.), *Religions in Antiquity*, pp. 137-148.

[31] See *ibid.*, pp. 138-144 where the Jewish material and numerous Johannine parallels are given.

— he is always obedient to the will of the sender

— he must return and report to the sender

— before he returns he can appoint other agents as an extension of his own mission.

However, it would be a mistake if we read this evidence as proof that the Fourth Gospel could be easily fitted into mainstream Judaism. Jesus, for the Fourth Gospel "is not just a human and earthly agent but a divine and heavenly agent who has come down among men".[32]

According to Borgen, if we are to find a background for this extraordinary point of view we must find a stream of Jewish thought which has a combination of halakah, heavenly figures, and agents from the heavenly world. Borgen suggests that this background is to be found in an early form of Jewish Merkabah speculations.[33] Through two passages (*Conf.* 146 and *Leg. All.* I,43) from Philo, who is known to be influenced by early Merkabah mysticism,[34] Borgen concludes that John and Philo have in common the idea of a heavenly figure who sees God, and they both associate this figure with the ideal "Israel" (e.g., 1,51 is to be understood as a presentation of the Son of Man as the heavenly model of Jacob/Israel[35]) The descent-ascent motif behind the Son of Man sayings (especially 3,3-13), however, shows that John has reversed the general pattern. For Philo (*Quae. Ex.* II,46) Moses ascended into heaven to see God, was there changed from an earthly to a heavenly man in a "rebirth", and thus was a great revealer. For John it is a heavenly man who descends to bring about a rebirth (3,3-13). John seems to be opposing the view presented by the Jewish traditions behind Philo.[36]

In a very recent paper, delivered at the *Journées Bibliques* at Louvain in 1975, Borgen took this last reflection further.[37] He argues: "Since the ascent in Jn 3,13-14 is denied to Moses, but applied to Jesus, the point of departure is not that of a human, but of a divine being. Thus the concept of the Sinaitic ascent and descent is turned upside down, and is changed into the idea of descent and ascent".[38] The difficulty of the perfect tense of the

---

[32] *ibid.*, p. 144.

[33] *ibid.*, p. 144. See, on the Merkabah mysticism, G. Scholem, *Major Trends in Jewish Mysticism* (London, Thames and Hudson, 1955) pp. 40-79; Idem, *Gnosticism, Merkabah Mysticism and Talmudic Tradition* (New York, Jewish Theological Seminary of America, 1965²) pp. 9-30.

[34] More parallels are needed. The work of Philo is so vast, at times obscure, and covers so many areas, that I sometimes suspect that Philonic parallels could be found for almost any position!

[35] A position defended recently by J. Painter. See below, note 53.

[36] See P. Borgen, "God's Agent...", pp. 144-147.

[37] P. Borgen, "Some Jewish Exegetical Traditions as Background for the Son of Man Sayings in John's Gospel (Jn 3,13-14 and context)", in M. de Jonge (ed.), *L'Évangile de Jean*, pp. 243-258.

[38] *ibid.*, p. 246. The denial that anyone (especially Moses) has ever ascended is also

ἀναβέβηκεν remains. Nobody *has ascended* except the descended one. Is there an ascension *previous* to the descent? Borgen argues that there is. The use of ἀναβαίνειν in 3,13 a does not refer to Jesus' ascension at the end of his human career, but to "a pre-existent installing in office".[39] Thus, according to Borgen, one can trace three stages in John's presentation of Jesus:

1. His pre-existent installation (17,2 taking up the theme of Dan. 7,14).
2. The commissioning of Jesus for his earthly task (8,42; 12,49; 3,34; 7,16; 8,26; 14,24; 17,6. Here the "agent" scheme is involved).
3. The glorification (17,5).

All of these moments can be found in Jn. 17: installation (17,2), descent to perform his task (17,4) and the return to glory (17,5). "Against this background the ascent of the Son of Man in 6,62 means his re-ascent to the place of office originally bestowed at the pre-existent ascent 3,13".[40] This is what is denied to Moses and the other saints of Israel whom some traditions claimed had ascended to "see God".[41] The idea of an ascent to a throne of a heavenly being is found in the Old Testament (I Sam. 2,10 f.; Pss. 47,6; 68,19) and also in some Jewish material (*Num. R.* 12-11).

Given this background to 3,13, Borgen then proceeds to show how John arrived at his use of the title "the Son of Man".[42] The word ὑψωθῆναι a key expression in Is. 52,13, was applied to the passion and death of Jesus. As in the synoptic tradition (see esp. Mk. 9,31 and Lk. 9,22) John also uses δεῖ τὸν υἱὸν τοῦ ἀνθρώπου... to speak of Jesus' death (3,14 and 12,34). However, as this expression was linked to the verb ὑψωθῆναι, it was open to another meaning, as the verb also means "to exalt". Thus a link was made, via "the Son of Man", to Dan. 7,13 which was understood as an installation in a royal office. That this was the case can be seen from the close verbal links which exist between Jn. 3,13; 17,2 and Dan. 7,13-14.

Borgen paraphrases the whole of 3,13-14 as follows: "Only he who descended from heaven to execute his office, the divine being, the Son of Man, has ascended to heaven for the installing in office prior to his descent. The subsequent return of the Son of Man to his place of glory (Jn 6,46; 17,5.24) must take place as an exaltation through the death on the Cross, to mediate life to those who believe".[43]

central to my understanding of 3,13. For further background (overlooked in the first edition) see W. A. Meeks, "Moses as God and King", in J. Neusner (ed.) *Religions in Antiquity*, pp. 354-371. Meeks shows, from Jewish and Samaritan sources, that Moses was sometimes thought to have ascended, and to have been transformed into a divine being in heaven.

[39] P. Borgen, "Some Jewish Exegetical Traditions...", p. 249.
[40] *ibid.*, p. 251.
[41] See above, pp. 54-57.
[42] P. Borgen, *art. cit.*, pp. 252-254.
[43] *ibid.*, p. 254.

This is an impressive case, but I believe that there are three areas which Borgen still leaves uncovered.

1. He has lost the whole point of the denial of an ascent to Moses, which he himself claims is behind John's argument here.[44] The point of the Jewish speculations on the ascent of Moses is that he sets off *from earth,* ascends the mountain of Sinai, and is eventually carried on high, where he sees God and is transformed through a rebirth. According to Borgen the "No one has ascended into heaven" refuses that claim by insisting that there was only one ascension, and that was the pre-existent ascension to a throne of glory of a kingly and heavenly Son of Man. One can imagine a Jewish audience replying to this argument that this claim has nothing to do with their claim. If they were Christians they may be quite content with a pre-existent enthronement of a heavenly Son of Man. This figure pre-existed, and ascended to his throne in his pre-existence to receive all authority so that he could eventually descend to perform his task. The argument for Moses is quite different. Moses was one of mankind, and his ascent has nothing to do with a pre-existent heavenly enthronement of a divine king. I would insist that the denial of an ascent *from earth* must be maintained. The Moses speculation would be in no way contradicted by reference to a pre-existent ascent to a heavenly throne, as such a discussion would be irrelevant to such speculation.

2. What are we to make of the Prologue to the Gospel in the light of this theory that at some stage of his pre-existence the Son of Man was exalted and enthroned to receive authority to perform his task among men? The Prologue may well have existed separately from the Gospel at some stage of its development, but as we have it now the story of the Gospel spell out the theology of the Prologue, and the theology of the Prologue illuminates the story of the Gospel.[45] There is not the slightest hint of any enthronement and commissioning in 1,1-18. In fact, given 1,1-5, it would almost have been blasphemous to think that such a process would be needed before the Word could become flesh and reveal the δόξα τοῦ θεοῦ among men, so that all who accepted him might become children of God (1,13-14). Although John's presentation of Jesus as the Son of Man does not dominate his thought in the same way as his Son of God christology,[46] it is nevertheless a product of its own particular background, Dan. 7, Jesus and Christian tradition. In the explicitly "Son of Man" passages, there is never a reference (apart from Borgen's interpretation of 3,13) to his being commissioned to perform his task among men. Thus, in neither the Logos material nor the Son of Man

[44] See *ibid.*, pp. 243-246; "God's Agent...", pp. 144-147.
[45] See C. K. Barrett, *New Testament Essays* (London, SPCK, 1972) pp. 27-48. See esp. p. 48: "The Prologue is necessary to the Gospel, as the Gospel is necessary to the Prologue. The history explicates the theology, and the theology interprets the history".
[46] See F. J. Moloney, "The Johannine Son of God", *Salesianum* 38 (1976) 71-86.

passages does this pre-existent commissioning seem to play a role. However, there are numerous references to such a commissioning in material which is closely associated with Jesus' relation to God as his Father, and his speaking of himself as Son (of God). A careful reading of 3,34; 7,16; 8,26.42; 12,49; 14,24 and 17,2.6 shows that all of these sayings are "Father — Son" or "Father — I" sayings. I would suggest that Borgen has uncovered a probable background for this pattern in the Jewish "agent" speculation. It is not to be found, in my opinion, in Dan. 7. It certainly does not appear in the only place in the Gospel where John deals systematically with the "pre-existence" question, 1,1-18 which, in my opinion, reflects yet another influence upon Johannine thought: Wisdom speculation. Johannine christology is a blending of various strands, all of which have been somehow united into a more or less coherent whole (there are, of course, aporia) within the context of a struggling Christian Church, forced out of the synagogue over the last half of the first century. It is important to recognise these "strands", as any attempt to explain the background of one of them (e.g. the Son of Man) by reference to the other (e.g. the Father — Son) only leads to confusion.

3. This leads me to a critique of Borgen's understanding of Dan. 7,13 which is central to his discussion of John's use of "the Son of Man". He explains John's use of the Daniel passage as follows: "It is probable that Jn 3,13 presupposes the idea in Dan 7,13 that one like a son of man came, with/on the clouds of heaven *to* God's throne: 'with ... the clouds of heaven there came... ... to the Ancient of Days' ", and he refers back to Dan. 7,9 where "thrones were placed and one that was ancient of days took his seat".[47] Thus, for Borgen, John understood the "one like a son of man" in Dan. 7,13 as some sort of heavenly pre-existent figure who was enthroned. I do not think that this was the case. As I have already mentioned, John himself indicates (see 3,14 and 12,33) that ὑψωθῆναι = to be crucified. He also uses the traditional δεῖ τὸν υἱὸν τοῦ ἀνθρώπου in close connection with ὑψωθῆναι. The exaltation of the Johannine Son of Man happens on the Cross, and does not continue into heaven. There is no link between ὑψωθῆναι and a heavenly enthronement anywhere in the Gospel. For John, the Son of Man is a crucified figure.[48] Where does John get this idea from? As far as background is

---

[47] P. Borgen, "Some Jewish Exegetical Traditions...", p. 253. See also the recent study of M. Black, "The Throne-Theophany Prophetic Commission and the 'Son of Man': A Study in Tradition-History", in R. Hamerton-Kelly - R. Scroggs (eds.), *Jews, Greeks and Christians*, pp. 57-73. Black argues that even though the Similitudes of Enoch may be post-Christian, both Dan. 7,13 and Enoch reflect a growing Jewish tradition, based on the theophanic enthronement of Ez. 1, of the enthronement and prophetic commissioning of a divine-human Israel figure.
[48] I insist that this is vital to the Johannine understanding of the Son of Man. John *never* writes of the crucifixion of the Logos (!) or of the Son of God, but δεῖ ὑψωθῆναι is *always* used in association with the Son of Man (3,14; 12,34).

concerned, it matters little that this Gospel makes the event of the crucifixion the moment of glory in the human activity of Jesus. The fact remains that the Son of Man idea is intimately linked with the Cross. John's background for this idea comes from an interpretation of "one like a son of man" = the Saints of the Most High in Dan. 7. The figure of the one like a son of man is the nation Israel, suffering under the fourth beast, but promised that there would eventually be a restoration of the nation.

> "The Son of man clearly represents in some way the Saints of the Most High, and there can be no doubt that they suffered. There is, it is true, only one brief reference to their experiences in the vision — in v. 7 — but this ᐱwas sufficient to make the author's meaning clear. There was no need for him to elaborate the theme or to emphasize the severity of their sufferings, for they were only too much in evidence, and were indeed the very cause of the book's existence. The Son of man may symbolize the victory of the Saints and not their suffering, but unless we detach him from them and regard him as a separate figure with independent experiences we cannot dissociate him from what happens to them".[49]

[49] M. D. Hooker, *The Son of Man in Mark. A Study of the background of the term "Son of Man" and its use in St. Mark's Gospel* (London, SPCK, 1967) pp. 27-28. Here I am taking a position in a never-ending discussion over the identity of the "one like a son of man" in Dan 7,13 and "the Saints of the Most High" with whom (at least at the level of the last redaction of Daniel) the former figure was identified (see Dan. 7,18.21. 22.25). This matter will come under further discussion below, but in identifying the "one like a son of man" and "the Saints of the Most High"' with what A. A. Di Lella has described as the "faithful Israel responsive to the demands of God even in the face of their present humiliation and suffering, (who) will come into the divine presence in order to receive everlasting dominion in holiness, nobility, and grandeur, and so will replace the depraved, brutal and vile kingdoms of the pagan world which were opposed to the reign of God and to his holy people" ("The One in Human Likeness and the Holy Ones of the Most High in Daniel 7", *CBQ* 39 [1977] 19) I am refusing to accept that "the one like a son of man" is a glorious heavenly eschatological king, nor the angelic hosts, nor their representatives, Michael or Gabriel (see below, notes 66, 72-73). See, for my position, A. A. Di Lella, "The One in Human Likeness ...", pp. 1-19; S. R. Driver, *The Book of Daniel* (Cambridge, University Press, 1900) pp. 107-108; J. A. Montgomery, *A Critical and Exegetical Commentary on the Book of Daniel*, ICC (Edinburgh, T. & T. Clark, 1927) pp. 317-324; G. Rinaldi, *Daniele*, La Sacra Bibbia (Torino, Marietti, 1962⁴) pp. 106-113; D. S. Russell, *The Method and Message of Jewish Apocalyptic* (London, SCM Press, 1964) pp. 326-327; N. W. Porteous, *Das Danielbuch*, ATD (Göttingen, Vandenhoeck und Ruprecht, 1962) pp. 88-91; M. D. Hooker, *Son of Man*, pp. 11-30; M. Delcor, *Le livre de Daniel*, Sources Bibliques (Paris, Gabalda, 1971) pp. 154-156; 162-167; G. Bernini, *Daniele*, Nuovissima Versione della Bibbia 28 (Rome, Edizioni Paoline, 1975) pp. 74-76; C. H. W. Brekelmans, "The Saints of the Most High and their Kingdom", *OTS* 14 (1965) 305-329; R. Hanhart, "Die ᐱHeiligen des Höchsten", in *Hebräische Wortforschung: Festschrift zum 80. Geburtstag von Walter Baumgartner*, VTS 16 (Leiden, E. J. Brill, 1967) pp. 90-101; A.-M. Dubarle, Art. "Prophètes d'Israel: Daniel", *DBS* 6 (1972) 743-747; A. Lenglet, "La structure littéraire de Daniel 2-7", *Biblica* 53 (1972) 175-179; G. F. Hasel, "The Identity of 'The Saints of the Most High' in Daniel 7", *Biblica* 56 (1975) 173-192; A. Deissler, "Der 'Menschensohn' und 'das Volk der Heiligen des Höchsten' in Dan 7", in R. Pesch - R. Schnackenburg - O. Kaiser (eds.), *Jesus und der Menschensohn*, pp. 81-91; V. S. Poythress, "The Holy Ones of the Most High in Daniel VII", *VT* 26

With the disappearance of I Enoch 37-71 and IV Esdras 13 as evidence of a pre-Christian use of "the Son of Man" as a gloriously enthroned eschatological figure, there is little evidence to show that the figure was ever detached from the sufferings of the Saints of the Most High.[50] If it did take place, despite our lack of evidence, it seemed to have little influence on the Gospel tradition which, in its earliest moment looked back (I suggest) to Dan. 7 and said that it is "written of the Son of Man, that he should suffer many things and be treated with contempt" (Mk. 9,12).[51] Borgen argues that John came to his use of the term "the Son of Man" via the following process: [52]

— the Cross of history.

— a traditional expression is used to explain that event: δεῖ τὸν υἱὸν τοῦ ἀνθρώπου.

— John applies the word ὑψωθῆναι from Is. 52,13 to this formula.

— the double meaning allows the theme of "exaltation" to enter, and thus Dan. 7,13, understood as a heavenly enthronement, comes into play.

My query to this line of thought is: why did the tradition use "the Son of Man" in immediate association with the Cross in the first place?   Answering this query I would suggest that the development of the tradition went along the following lines:

— the Cross of history

— explained through the application of Dan. 7,13 where one like a son of man is a figure who comes to authority through his suffering.

(1976) 208-213. I am well aware that this sheer weight of bibliography (and more could be added) proves nothing. I am indicating this cross-section of scholarship to show that my position is well supported by contemporary (and more classical) scholarship.

[50] There is no need to repeat here the discussions over the Similitudes of Enoch. See especially J. T. Milik - M. Black (ed.), *The Books of Enoch. Aramaic Fragments of Qumrân Cave 4* (Oxford, Clarendon Press, 1976) esp. pp. 89-98. See also J. A. Fitzmyer, "Implications of the New Enoch Literature from Qumran", *TS* 38 (1977) 332-345. My belief (see above, note 14) that late Judaism did change the term from "one like a son of man" in Dan. 7,13 into "the Son of Man" does not change my argument. The Targums on Pss. 8 and 80 refer to the *God-given* authority of a kingly Son of Man, not to his *pre-existent* enthronement.

[51] See M. D. Hooker, *Son of Man*, p. 30. See on Mk. 9,12, P. Benoit - M.-E. Boismard, *Synopse des Quatre Évangiles en Français* (Paris, Editions de Cerf, 1972) Vol. II, p. 255: "Dans Daniel, le Fils d'homme représente avant tout le peuple de Dieu, les 'saints du Très-Haut' (7,18) dont il est dit: 'cette corne (=Antiochus Épiphane) faisait la guerre aux Saints et l'emportait sur eux' (v. 21); ou encore: '(le dixième roi) mettra à l'épreuve les Saints du Très-Haut' (v. 25). L'idée de 'beaucoup souffrir' est donc intimement liée à la figure du Fils de l'homme de Daniel, bien que l'expression littéraire soit différente. Précisons que, dans de logion sur la Passion, le titre 'Fils de l'homme' n'est plus pris au sens collectif, mais au sens personnel".

[52] P. Borgen, "Some Jewish Exegetical Traditions ...", pp. 252-253.

— this is spelt out in a traditional formula: δεῖ τὸν υἱὸν τοῦ ἀνθρώπου

— using Is. 52,13, John uses ὑψωθῆναι to deliberately indicate the double meaning of the Cross. It is at once a physical "lifting up" and the "exaltation" of Jesus.

Ultimately, it is here that Borgen's understanding of the Johannine use of the term "the Son of Man" differs radically from mine. While he sees John taking over the title to refer to a gloriously enthroned heavenly Son of Man, I understand the figure — both in Dan. 7 and in the tradition taken over by John — as a figure who will come to his glory only through suffering.[53]

It is most important to notice that both in our acceptance of Borgen's "agent" theory, and our refusal to accept his collocation of the background to the Son of Man within that same line of speculation, we are certainly moving within the area of *Randjudentum* which recent scholarship sees, with increasing unanimity, as the cultural and religious background of the Fourth Gospel.[54] A most important recent monograph by Jan-A. Bühner has carried Borgen's discussion further, and placed a part of it upon a very firm footing.[55] Bühner sets his argument within the current discussions of "the sent one",[56] and he is particularly critical of Bultmann's suggestion that this peculiarly Johannine theme comes from the Gnostic myth.[57]

---

[53] Very close to Borgen is J. Painter, *John: Witness and Theologian* (London, SPCK, 1975) pp. 53-57. I would query almost every element in his brief analysis of the background material on p. 54 which concludes: "For John, the Son of Man is the supernatural heavenly king, revealer of heavenly secrets" (p. 55). In a more recent article: "Christ and the Church in John 1,45-51", in M. de Jonge (ed.) *L'Évangile de Jean*, pp. 359-362, Painter argues the same case for Jn. 1,51. He very soundly points out that the title "Son of Man" in John *corrects* all the previous confessions, especially the "Kingly" confession of Nathanael in v. 49 (see pp. 360-361. See also above, pp. 33-38), but he claims that authentic faith will be possible only when the disciples see the Son of Man ·exalted to his place in heaven as king, by way of the Cross (p. 361). He complains that the idea of a promise that the disciples would see the communication of the heavenly in the human Jesus is never fulfilled in the rest of the Gospel (see *John: Witness and Theologian*, pp. 55-56). This astonishes me, as the whole of the Gospel fulfills that promise. I would claim, rather, that the *vision* of the heavenly, enthroned Son of Man is, never fulfilled in this Gospel. See on this S. Smalley, "Johannes 1,51 und die Einleitung zum vierten Evangelium", in *Jesus und der Menschensohn*, pp. 300-313. Painter, among others, sees the movement of the angels in 1,51 as "towards" the enthroned heavenly Son of Man. This is to force the Greek, which reads ἀναβαίνοντας καὶ καταβαίνοντας ἐπί: "ascending and *coming down upon*".

[54] See above, pp. 222-223 and note 5.

[55] Jan-A. Bühner, *Der Gesandte und sein Weg im 4. Evangelium*.

[56] On pp. 8-115 he critically assesses the suggestions that this concept reflects a Gnostic background, "divine man" speculations, Hellenistic religious thought, early Christian enthusiastic streams and Wisdom speculation. He concludes that none of these theories provides *the* solution to the problem.

[57] See esp. *ibid.*, pp. 24-47. However, the whole book is a continual *Auseinandersetzung* with Bultmann's positions.

He then sets out to provide an alternative suggestion. He first studies the ancient East's concept of a "messenger", intimately linked to the sender, entrusted with a task, after which he is required to return to where he belongs. There is a very familiar pattern of "commission — performance of a task — return".[58] This pattern finds many parallels in the Johannine presentation of Jesus as "the sent one". Bühner then traces another close link between the Jewish "messenger" teaching and the Johannine Gospel in the messenger's use of ἦλθον + a task and the ἐγώ εἰμι + a predicate to justify his presence while he is performing his task.[59] Once this platform has been laid, Bühner carefully examines how the Johannine concept of Jesus as "the sent one" takes over and christianises what was the official Rabbinic halakah on agency. From this he is able to locate the Johannine community in a cultural setting. It was mainly a Jewish group, well capable of using the categories and systems of official Judaism, but which used them for its own specifically *Christian* purposes, in open conflict with Rabbinic Judaism.[60]

The final part of the work investigates the ascending and descending messengers of God in Judaism as a background to Johannine christology.[61] Bühner shows that the Rabbis used the "messenger" scheme in their own particular way to speak of a prophet as a heavenly messenger. Fundamental to this notion was that the prophet (especially the first and greatest "prophet", Moses) "went up" so that he might see the heavenly. While he was there he was transformed into an "angel", and eventually came down as an authentic revealer. Ultimately, the prophet is understood as an angel who has seen the heavenly by means of an ascent, has been transformed, and who then descends to perform his task as a "messenger" of God.[62]

Into this scheme Bühner places Johannine christology.[63] John presents Jesus as an "anabatisch-visionärer Prophet".[64] The christology of the Fourth Gospel depends upon the scheme of "above" and "below", the "heavenly" and the "earthly", and thus the importance of the scheme ἀναβαίνειν-καταβαίνειν. This language is exclusively associated with "the Son of Man" in John's Gospel, and this indication leads Bühner (via Jn. 5,27) to see John's oldest

---

[58] *ibid.*, pp. 118-137. Bühner's terms are: "Beauftragung - Durchführung - Rückkehr".

[59] *ibid.*, pp. 138-179.

[60] *ibid.*, pp. 181-267. Thus far I find the work most enlightening. Bühner has produced a massive amount of Rabbinic material which leaves no doubt that the "messenger-scheme" was a part of their thought. However, the perrenial problem remains: can we use this generally much later material in such a discussion? The close parallel with John's presentation of Jesus and the conflict with official Judaism which is evident from other parts of the Gospel (e.g. the use of the term "the Jews", and the background to 9,22; 12,42 and 16,2) indicate that Bühner (and Borgen) may well be correct, despite the lateness of the rabbinic material.

[61] *ibid.*, pp. 270-373.

[62] See esp. *ibid.*, pp. 341-373.

[63] *ibid.*, pp. 374-433.

[64] See *ibid.*, pp. 392-393, and passim.

christology as coming from apocalyptic visionary circles.[65] Dan. 7,13 and Enoch show that these circles used the term "the Son of Man" to speak of a human figure enthroned as the protecting angel of Israel, having authority over all other authorities.[66] This identification of Son of Man = Angel is the all important link between Jesus as a visionary prophet and Jesus as the Son of Man.

Using 3,13, Bühner argues that John's christology is based on Jesus' being the only one who has ever ascended to become the Son of Man — Angel, and that he comes down as the unique prophet, able to reveal what he has seen. However — and here Bühner runs parallel to Borgen's most recent suggestions — the ἀναβέβηκεν of 3,13a does not refer to an earth-heaven ascension, but to a pre-existent heavenly enthronement as the Son of Man. Nobody else has ever had such an enthronement, as. *all* other prophets (including Moses) came "from below". Thus, the birthplace of this strata of Johannine christology can clearly be seen as a peripheral group of Jews, in conflict with the Rabbis who had expelled them from their midst. The Rabbis had their theories of "visionary prophets" (especially with reference to Moses) but the Johannine community, using the same schemes, presented Jesus as the unique angel — messenger — revealer. He is the only one who has gone up to be enthroned as the angel-prophet, the heavenly Son of Man on earth.

The rest of the Son of Man sayings have to be understood in this light. The presence of the angels in 1,51 is the assurance that he is a heavenly figure.[68] The use of ὑψωθῆναι and δοξασθῆναι in close association with the Son of Man also shows that he is an exalted and glorified figure, as in Dan. 7 where he is exalted above all other creatures. This is also clear in 12,28-33 where his "lifting up" is also the "casting out" of the "ruler of this world".[69]

---

[65] Bühner correctly looks at words here which are linked with the Son of Man concept. My complaint is that he misinterprets that linguistic context.

[66] Bühner adopts the position that Son of Man = the protecting Angel of Israel in Dan. 7,13 on *ibid.*, pp. 386-387. In his notes he cites C. Colpe, Art. " ὁ υἱὸς τοῦ ἀνθρώπου " *TDNT* VIII (1972) 419-420, but one must read Colpe's statement about "the Son of Man" = an angel within the context of the whole article. Colpe sees two moments in the development of the passage in Dan 7. The angel idea comes from Colpe's hypothesis of a Canaanite myth. When he comes to examine the second and final stage in the composition of Dan. 7 (pp. 420-423) he points out that from v. 21 onwards the Son of Man is interpreted as the Saints of the Most High who are "that portion of the Jewish people who remained loyal to the ancient traditions of Israel in the days of the Maccabees" (p. 423). He also cites U. B. Müller, *Messias und Menschensohn in jüdischen Apokalypsen und in der Offenbarung des Johannes* StNT 6 (Gütersloch, Gerd Mohn, 1972) pp. 27ff., 32, 34. Müller deals with the whole discussion on pp. 19-36. Bühner's other authority in K. Berger, *Die Auferstehung des Phropheten und die Erhöhung des Menschensohnes. Traditionsgeschichtliche Untersuchungen zur Deutung des Geschickes Jesu in frühchristlichen Texten*, SUNT 13 Göttingen, Vandenhoeck und Ruprecht, 1976) pp. 412-413.

[67] Jan-A. Bühner, *Der Gesandte und sein Weg*, pp. 385-391.

[68] *ibid.*, pp. 391-392.

[69] *ibid.*, pp. 395-396.

John takes his notion of Jesus as the Son of Man entirely from this heavenly background, and then is able to present the *historical* Jesus as the heavenly Son of Man (the angel — prophet — sent one) on earth. As in 11QMelch, a heavenly scheme has been transferred to earth, and John makes the Cross "nicht Zwischenstation auf dem Weg Jesu ... sondern Zielpunkt des Menschensohn— (und Gesandten—) Weges".[70] This has to be understood according to a scheme of *Urbild* and *Abbild.* From the Johannine point of view, the heavenly enthronement and the elevation above the powers of this world (*Urbild*) works itself out in the earthly mission and death of the heavenly Son of Man (*Abbild*), and the vertical "lifting up" of the Son of Man on the Cross is the point where the *Abbild* and the *Urbild* meet.

Bühner's analysis of the Johannine Son of Man is not convincing, and I would like to raise two major objections to his basic theory, and then raise some further allied difficulties.

1. So much is made of the "ascent-descent". In fact, Bühner's whole thesis depends upon the link that he makes between the prophet-angel and the angel-Son of Man through the common denominator "angel" who ascends and descends. Yet, as I have already insisted, there are only two uses of these words *together* in the whole of the Gospel. In 1,51 it is the angels who go up and down upon the Son of Man. The Son of Man does not move, so this saying is disqualified as evidence of an ascending and descending angel-Son of Man. In 3,13 I believe that Jesus refuses the possibility of other revealers who have ascended to see the heavenly. The authentic reavealer in the Son of Man, the incarnate one. It strikes me that to claim that the ἀναβαίνειν-καταβαίνειν language is closely linked with Johannine Son of Man christology,[71] and to then proceed to understand the background for the whole of John's use of the title from the vertical motion which these verbs imply, is to abuse the evidence. As I said above, 1,51; 3,14; 5,27; 6,27.53; 8,28; 9.35; 12,23.34; 13,31 and 19,5 are in no way concerned with the ἀναβαίνειν-καταβαίνειν scheme. Even if we were to accept that 3,13 and 6,62 *were* concerned with vertical motion (which I do not), would it be methodologically sound to explain the background for thirteen saying on the basis of the language of two of them? I rather think not.

2. As long as Bühner argues the case that there was a "messenger scheme" in Rabbinic Judaism, and that this scheme was further developed to speak of a prophet as a messenger-angel who went up to heaven and returned, his work is convincing. However, his step from there to the thesis that the prophet-angel scheme was taken over by the Johannine community through

---

[70] *ibid.,* p. 397.
[71] *ibid.,* p. 386.

the medium of Jewish apocalyptic, and especially through the Son of Man — Angel figure, is much less convincing. He begins to move from one hypothesis to another. The most important of these hypotheses (although he simply presents it and accepts it within a few paragraphs) is that the Danielic Son of Man was understood as an angel. This thesis is hotly disputed,[72] and I continue to maintain that the figure, identified with the Saints of the Most High, stands for Israel, faithful to the demands of Jahweh under the persecution of Antiochus IV.[73] G. F. Hasel has most recently described the figure of the Saints of the Most High as "His chosen ones, set apart from the rest of the nations, persecuted by the power opposing God, but keeping covenant faith and maintaining their trust in God from whom they finally receive an everlasting kingdom".[74] I concur with this interpretation, and once the link prophet — Angel — Son of Man is removed from Bühner's hypothesis, then his presentation of the Johannine Son of Man must fall.

3. Further problems remain:

a. Bühner, like Borgen, has shown us that the Johannine concept of Jesus as "the sent one" comes from Judaism, and not from the Gnostic myth. His movement from here to the Son of Man is not justified, as there is no link between Jesus as the Sent One and Jesus as the Son of Man. The verb πέμπειν is never used of the latter, while it is always associated with Jesus as the Son or, at least, in passages where Jesus speaks of his relationship with the Father, who sent him (see 4,34; 5.23.24.30.37; 6,38.39.44; 7,16 etc.). Bühner himself has shown in his analysis of the Jewish "agent" material that when the agent is a *ben bayith*, "a son of the house", there are very close

---

[72] See the works mentioned above in note 49. A full indication of the positions taken in this discussion, with the relevant bibliography, is found in G. F. Hasel, "The Identity of 'The Saints of the Most High'...", pp. 173-176.

[73] As A. Di Lella "The One in Human Likeness ...", pp. 7-8 has pointed out, if "the one like a son of man", i.e. "the Saints of the Most High" represent the angelic hosts or Michael or Gabriel, then:

1. Dan. 7 would have meant little to the people for whom it was written, i.e. the Jews being persecuted by Antiochus IV, the small horn which sprouted up (see Dan. 7,8.11.20-21.24).

2. The writer responsible for the final form of Dan. 7 was guilty of a deplorable use of symbolism. It is generally agreed that the four beasts = the four pagan empires and the Ancient of Days = the God of Israel. These symbols have a one-to-one relationship with the reality which they symbolise. Di Lella, coining a term, writes of "unireferential symbols" (p. 8). So must it also be with the one like a son of man. He does not represent Michael or Gabriel or the heavenly hosts, as he "must be a unireferential symbol of only 'the holy ones of the Most High', i.e. the historically recognizable Jews who suffered and died rather than apostatize" (p. 8). See further, G. F. Hasel, "The Identity of 'The Saints of the Most High'...", pp. 176-188.

[74] G. F. Hasel, *art. cit.,* p. 192.

parallels with Johannine "Son" material.[75]   These two titles for Jesus, "the Son (of God)" and "the Son of Man", and the study of their background, must be kept separate.   Although together they form an impressive section of John's overall christological point of view, they say different things about Jesus, and must be distinguished.[76]

b.   At the end of his treatment of the Son of Man material Bühner resolves the nagging difficulty that none of the Johannine Son of Man sayings refers to a figure who is "in heaven" by recourse to a scheme of *Urbild* and *Abbild,* offering   only 11QMelch as a contemporary parallel.   To convince me of this subtlety he would have to prove that it was a recognisable Johannine technique.   This particular step in his whole study runs very close to being pure speculation.

As a conclusion to this rather critical presentation of the work of both P. Borgen and Jan-A. Bühner I would like to stress that I find their work on the Jewish "agency" material, and the close links which they make with the Fourth Gospel, quite convincing.   I regard this as a major contribution to our understanding of the historical, cultural and religious background of the Johannine community, and more immediately, as background to John's unique Son (of God) christology.   However, when they turn to examine Son of Man material (under the perennial fascination of his supposed "vertical motion") I feel that their conclusions come under the censure issued by F. H. Borsch in another context: "Altogether it is so long a step from the Son of man with whom (they) begin to (their) view of the Fourth Gospel's version of the tradition that one must wonder if there are not more credible starting points".[77]

It appears to me that the process was much simpler.   It began with Dan. 7,13 where one like a son of man [78] represented the suffering people who would eventually be given authority by God himself, to a use, witnessed by the Targums on Pss. 8 and 80 of "the Son of Man" as a kingly Messiah to whom, in fact, God has given authority among men.   Jesus referred to himself as "the Son of Man", but very much in the line of Dan. 7,13: he believed that he would come to a God-given authority through suffering. Here there was probably a double use of the term "the son of man" at work.

[75] For example, Jan-A. Bühner, *Der Gesandte und sein Weg,* pp. 195-198.

[76] See above, pp. 208-214.   For an excellent survey of John's "Sent One" christology, closely linking it with "prophetic agency" theories, but *not* with the Son of Man, see J. P. Miranda, *Die Sendung Jesu im vierten Evangelium. Religions- und theologiegeschichtliche Untersuchungen zu den Sendungsformeln,* SBS 87 (Stuttgart, Katholisches Bibelwerk, 1977).

[77] F. H. Borsch, *The Son of Man in Myth and History* (London, SCM Press, 1967) p. 261.   Borsch's criticism was aimed at S. Schulz.   See above, p. 6.

[78] The Danielic figure, of course, is linked with the whole of the Old Testament and Jewish "man" ideas.   See esp. M. D. Hooker, *Son of Man,* pp. 3-22 and A. A. Di Lella, "The One in Human Likeness ...", pp. 14-18.

It is quite possible that Jesus used the term in the sense defended by G. Vermes and applied most recently to the New Testament by B. Lindars and M. Casey,[79] but this must not eliminate a reference back to the "one like a son of man" = the Saints of the Most High in Dan. 7,13. Jesus took upon himself the role of the Saints of the Most High, and used "the Son of Man" to indicate this.[80] This shift to a titular use was already present, in my opinion, in contemporary Judaism, and is found in the Aramaic versions of Pss. 8 and 80. Only in this way can the importance of the title for all four Evangelists be satisfactorily explained.

The Gospel traditions went their own way in their use of "the Son of Man". Some patterns, however, remain strongly present in all four Gospels. One of these is the continued use of "the Son of Man" to indicate that Jesus *must* suffer (see Mk. 8,31; 9,31; 10,33-34 parrs.). This is found in the Johannine use of δεῖ ὑψωθῆναι in 3,14 and 12,34 (see also 8,28, where the idea is conveyed, but in an active rather than passive sense). Another pattern found in the synoptic tradition is the use of "the Son of Man" on the lips of Jesus to correct false messianic hopes (see Mk. 8,31; 14,61-62 parrs.). This same pattern is found in almost every Johannine Son of Man saying.[81] The uniquely Johannine contribution to this traditional title comes from the particular view of the Cross which is found in this Gospel. Already in the synoptic tradition (directly from Jesus?) it is the Son of Man who must suffer, but for John the Cross is Jesus' ὕψωσις. Thus, through Is. 52,13, John had no hesitation in speaking of the Son of Man who must be "lifted up" and "glorified". Given the centrality of this point of view in Johannine thought, it was natural that the whole of the Johannine Son of Man christology eventually presented Jesus as the unique revealer and the revelation of God who had to be lifted up so that men and women could gaze upon him and judge themselves in their acceptance or refusal of the enigmatic revelation which comes from a pierced one (see 3,14-15; 8,28; 19,37). There is little need to look beyond

[79] B. Lindars, "Re-Enter the Apocalyptic Son of Man", pp. 52-72; P. M. Casey, "The Son of Man Problem", ZNW 67 (1976) 147-154. Casey understands the authentic sayings (found in Mark and Q only) to have the double sense of "man" and Jesus' reference to himself as "I". The translation into Greek eventually leads to a misunderstanding and a titular application, especially in Matthew and John.

[80] In this regard, see the important article of M. Casey, "The Corporate Interpretation of 'One Like a Son of Man' (Dan. 7,13) at the Time of Jesus", NT 18 (1976) 167-180. Casey, who refuses to see any titular use of the title (see previous note, and note 14 above) also refuses the "angelic" interpretation of the one like a son of man (see esp. p. 167 note 2). He argues from Midrash on Ps. 21,5 and Tanchuma Toledoth 20 that the idea of "one like a son of man" was used as a corporate figure at the time of Jesus to represent Israel.

[81] See above, pp. 33-37 (on 1,51); 51-53 (on 3,13-14); 108-109 (on 6,27); 139-140 (on 8,28); 157 (on 9,35); 181 (on 12,23); 181-182 (on 12,34); 206 (on 19,5). See also pp. 214-215.

Christian tradition to find the background for the Johannine use of the term
"the Son of Man".[82]

Pre-existence, Ascension and Post-Existence in Jn 3,13 and 6,62

The position which I adopted on these two Son of Man passages in the
first edition of this work remains unchanged. There is no point in repeating
here the explanation which I have already given.[83] Opinions on these finer
points of exegesis will necessarily differ,[84] but I would like to take up a point

---

[82] See above, p. 216.   See also my treatment of the contact with the synoptic
tradition on pp. 214-219. For a position on the synoptic use of the title similar to my
own, see J. D. G. Dunn, *Unity and Diversity in the New Testament. An Inquiry into
the Character of Earliest Christianity* (London, SCM Press, 1977) pp. 35-50. Most
recently M. L. Appold, *The Oneness Motif in the Fourth Gospel. Motif Analysis and
Exegetical Probe into the Theology of John,* WUNT 2. Reihe 1 (Tübingen, J. C. B. Mohr,
1976) pp. 48-55 has argued that John's Son of Man christology is totally determined by
"the community's reflection on and conviction of Jesus' oneness with God" (p. 55). As
such, the central role which I give to the Cross as the uniquely *human* event, reserved for
the *human* Son of Man, is denied. Appold argues that the use of ὑψωθῆναι and δοξασθῆναι
indicate that "the cross must also be viewed accordingly not as an intervening break
but as the point of return for the exalted Son of Man" (pp. 32-33).   His treatment
does not *prove* the oneness motif behind John's use of "the Son of Man", but *presupposes*
it. His criticism of Dodd's recourse to Is. 52,13 for a contact with ὑψωθῆναι and δοξασθῆναι
as eisegesis (pp. 52-53 note 5) is quite unjustified.   He refuses any contact with the
synoptic tradition (p. 48). He claims that the Johannine Son of Man is "God manifest
in the human sphere". Docetism is close at hand. On the contrary, I argue that God
is revealed through the eminently *human* event of the crucifixion.
[83] See above, pp. 51-59 (on 3,13) and 120-123 (on 6,62).
[84] It is interesting to see how opinions vary. In the two most recent commentaries
on this Gospel we find varying positions. S. A. Panimolle, *Lettura Pastorale del Vangelo
di Giovanni,* Lettura pastorale della Bibbia (Bologna, Dehoniane, 1978) pp. 267; 288-289;
302-303 accepts my position, that the εἰ μή has the sense of excluding any possible ascension
to become a revealer. He writes: "Il quarto evangelista perciò in Gv 3,13 non intende
sottolineare il fatto dell'ascensione di Gesù, ma la realtà della sua origine celeste, che
autentica la sua rivelazione" (p. 288).   On the other hand, G. Segalla, *Giovanni,* Nuovissima versione della Bibbia 36 (Roma, Edizioni Paoline, 1976) p. 179 sees the problem
and states that "per l'ascesa al cielo non si trova nessun vero parallelo". He refuses to
accept a Gnostic solution, and claims that it must come from the early Church's
experience of the resurrection-ascension, as in 6,62 and 20,17.   In an article devoted
entirely to 3,13-14, E. Ruckstuhl, "Abstieg und Erhöhung des johanneischen Menschensohns",
in *Jesus und der Menschensohn,* pp. 314-341, comes to a position identical with mine.
He paraphrases 3,13 as follows (p. 325):

> "Und keiner ist zum Himmel aufgestiegen
> (und hat die himmlischen Dinge gesehen)
> Nur der vom Himmel Herabgestiegene, der Menschensohn
> (hat sie gesehen).

Most recently my case has received support from A. Serra, *Contributi dell'antica letteratura
Giudaica per l'esegesi di Giovanni 2,1-12 e 19,25-27,* Scripta Pontificiae Facultatis Theologicae
"Marianum" 31, Nova Series 3 (Roma, Herder, 1977) pp. 296-297. John Painter, in his

made by G. Segalla who insists that, even granting my exegesis of 3,13 and 6,62, we are dealing with a pre-existent Son of Man.[85] If, as I have maintained, the Son of Man has come from heaven, then he must be allowed as a pre-existent figure. My contention is that John is most careful in his use of christological titles. It is always Jesus who is spoken of, whether as the Logos, the Christ, the Son of Man, the Son of God, the Lamb of God etc. However, each of these titles indicates a different aspect and function of Jesus within John's overall christological plan.[86] Certainly, Jesus came from "above", from God, where he pre-existed as the Logos (1,1). However, once the Logos became flesh (1,14) the *title* "Logos" never again appears. It is not sufficient to say that this happened because John took over a Logos-hymn, and once he was finished with the source which spoke of "Logos" he needed the title no longer. He may well have used a Christian Logos-hymn, but his decision never to use the title again was his, and he would not have been such a slave to his sources that he could not use a title except in the context in which his source gave it to him. Only as "the Son" is Jesus presented as a pre-existent, a

review of my work in the *ABR* 25 (1977) 43, argues that my position is grammatically impossible. All one can do is refer to specialists who take my side. As well as Ruckstuhl, a leading authority on Johannine language and style, I should mention the distinguished humanist and classical scholar, Ronald Knox, who translates 3,13 as follows: "No man has ever gone up into heaven, but there is one who has come down from heaven, the Son of Man", and he notes, "The same Hebrew idiom occurs in Apoc 21,27, and many other passages (*The Bible. A Translation from the Latin Vulgate in the Light of the Hebrew and Greek Originals* [New York, Sheed and Ward, 1956] p. 88). He fills this out in his *A New Testament Commentary For English Readers* (London, Burns, Oates and Washbourne, 1955) Vol. I, p. 209: "Verse 13 runs literally 'No one has ever gone up to heaven except he who came down from heaven', but this is an eccentricity of Hebrew idiom". He then cites in full Matt. 20,23; 26,42 and Apoc. 21,27 and concludes with the translation as given above, suggesting that there may be reference to Deut. 30,12. The outstanding grammarian, P. Joüon, *L'évangile de Notre-Seigneur Jésus-Christ. Traduction et commentaire du texte original grec, compte tenu du substrat sémitique*, Verbum Salutis V (Paris, Beauchesne, 1930) p. 473 translates 3,13 as follows: "Personne n'est monté au ciel, mais quelqu'un est descendu du ciel, le Fils de l'homme". The Greek is difficult. However, even if one was forced to accept that the verse did refer to the ascension in 13a (and I insist that the only ascension involved is the ascension of visionaries), then I would still insist further that it is the human figure of Jesus referred to as the Son of Man in v. 13b. I would explain the verse as follows:

    i. No one has ascended = a polemic against ascending revealers .
    ii. Except Jesus who is the one who came down as the incarnate one.
    iii. That incarnate one is called "the Son of Man".

If the ascended one *must* be identified with the descended one (as Painter insists), the term "the Son of Man" must be understood as in apposition to ὁ καταβάς. It would not be scientifically correct to take *one* saying and interpret *twelve* others in the light of that isolated saying. The process must be reversed. Thus, even if "the descended one" has ascended (which I do not think is necessary for a correct interpretation of 3,13), it is only as the one descended in the incarnation that Jesus is called "the Son of Man".

[85] In *StPat* 24 (1977) 99-102. See esp. p. 101.
[86] This is my thesis in *The Word Became Flesh*.

historical and a glorified figure, especially in the summary of 17,1-5 where all three "stages" are involved in Jesus' prayer to his Father. There can be no doubt about John's mind on pre-existence, historical presence and post-existence, but I would still maintain that both 3,13 and 6,62 use the title "the Son of Man" to speak of his specifically *human* presence. The Son of Man is the only authentic revealer, as he has come down from above. However, only as the incarnate historical revealer (this is the sense of ὁ καταβάς) is he called "the Son of Man" (3,13).[87]

Similarly (and in conflict with the same Jewish speculations [88]) in reply to the scandal which Jesus' discourse from 6,25-59 has caused (6,61) he warns them that he will not succumb to their demands; he will not fulfill their preconceived idea of what an authentic revealer must do. He will not ascend to heaven — he has come from there; he was there before (6,62). This is the meaning of ἡ σάρξ οὐκ ὠφελεῖ οὐδέν in 6,63. His listeners are scandalised because Jesus, the Son of Man, is speaking to them in such an extraordinary way. How can he speak like this unless he has had some special sort of revelation ... unless he has first ascended? In other words, they will not accept Jesus' words because they are judging κατὰ τὴν σάρκα as they did in 8,15 (see also the κατ' ὄψιν of 7,24); they are unable to go beyond a merely external experience because they stop at the "fleshly" Jesus.[89] This evaluation of Jesus "is of no avail". They must believe the *words* which he has spoken (the verb λελάληκα is in the perfect, and refers to the discourse just concluded), i.e. the revelation which takes place between the man Jesus (the Son of Man) and the men and women with whom he has communicated in the usual human fashion — through *words*. However, the word of Jesus, the Son of Man, is not an ambiguous human word, but an authentic revelation to men, because one who has come from above has spoken them. This has been the insistence of the opening part of the discourse, especially vv. 35-50. As such, they are spirit and life, but he will not ascend as other revealers have claimed to have done. He has come from above. The passage has nothing to do with an ascension and a promised post-existence. Although he has his authoritative word because he has pre-existed, it is the historical, visible, speaking, revealing Jesus who is referred to as "the Son of Man".

[87] See note 84 above, where I argue that this would remain as the meaning of the term "the Son of Man" in 3,13b, even if I accepted the link with the ascension in v. 13a.

[88] The great value of the work of Borgen and Bühner is that they have established that ascension speculation played a prominent part in Rabbinic thought. Thus 3,13 and 6,62 are clear evidence of the Johannine community's conflict with a well developed Rabbinic Judaism.

[89] See above, p. 129. See also the excellent article on this, W. Stenger, " 'Der Geist ist es, der lebendig macht, das Fleisch nützt nichts' (Joh 6,63)", *TrierTZ* 85 (1976) 116-122. There is no contradiction between 6,51-58 and 6,63 as the significance of the word σάρξ is different in each case, yet each significance has its parallels in the rest of the Gospel.

My position in this matter has been accurately understood and summarized by M.-V. Leroy:

> "Certes celui-ci préexiste à son Incarnation (3,13; 6,62) le Fils de l'homme vient du ciel, mais il est toujours evisagé dans sa condition humaine terrestre, jamais dans sa préexistence divine ou sa glorification post-pascale".[89a]

2. The Place of the Johannine Understanding of Jesus as "the Son of Man" within the Johannine Community

In the contemporary search for the identity and character of the Johannine community,[90] the names of J. L. Martyn, G. Richter and R. E. Brown must be associated with a recent and precise attempt to locate the historical, cultural and religious situation behind the group of christians in the early Church which eventually produced our Fourth Gospel.[90a]

In 1971 J. L. Martyn advanced a theory of at least three theological moments in the development of the christology of the Fourth Gospel.[91] Accepting, as a working hypothesis, R. T. Fortna's Signs Source,[92] he attempts to show that this source presented Jesus as an Elijah-like, Elisha-like, Moses-like, prophetic "divine man".[93] This position, however, caused difficulties for the community, as the Jewish opponents identified themselves as the followers of Moses himself, who had ascended into heaven from Sinai to receive the heavenly secrets. Thus the Signs Source is corrected, especially in terms of the Son of Man, to adjust it "in the face of inadequacies in it which have been revealed in the course of Jewish opposition to it".[94] Thus we can see John's community as an anti-Moses group which claims that *no-one* has ever

---

[89a] M.-V. Leroy, in *RThom* 76 (1976) 511.

[90] See above, pp. 222-223 and notes 5-9.

[90a] See above, note 5 for full bibliographical details. It is impossible here to survey all the theories of pre-Gospel editions, sources etc. For an excellent survey see R. Kysar, *The Fourth Evangelist and His Gospel. An examination of contemporary scholarship* (Minneapolis, Augsburg, 1975) pp. 13-54. R. E. Brown, "Johannine Ecclesiology...", as well as presenting his own view, is a most helpful discussion of the recent positions of J. L. Martyn and G. Richter. I will make use of Brown's excellent synthesis (pp. 381-384) in what follows. For a full-scale treatment of Richter's position, see A. J. Mattill, "Johannine Communities Behind the Fourth Gospel: Georg Richter's Analysis", *TS* 38 (1977) 294-315.

[91] J. L. Martyn, "Source Criticism and Religionsgeschichte...", pp. 247-273.

[92] See R. T. Fortna, *The Gospel of Signs. A Reconstruction of the Narrative Source underlying the Fourth Gospel*, SNTS Monograph Series 11 (Cambridge, University Press, 1970).

[93] J. L. Martyn, "Source Criticism and Religionsgeschichte...", p. 255.

[94] *ibid.*, p. 258. It is important to notice that Fortna himself, in several articles, refuses to accept that the Evangelist has corrected his Signs Source. See, for example, R. T. Fortna, "From Christology to Soteriology. A Redaction Critical Study of Salvation in the Fourth Gospel", *Interp* 27 (1973) 31-47; Idem, "Christology in the Fourth Gospel: Redactional Critical Perspectives", *NTS* 21 (1974-75) 489-504.

seen God (1,18) except the Son and anyone who has truly seen the Son (14, 8-9), and that *no-one* has ascended to heaven, except the Son of Man (3,13) — not even Moses. All this shows that the group had close contacts with Judaism, but there are other elements in the second level which must be explained as Gnostic: the idea of pre-existence and the 'use of ἀναβαίνειν-καταβαίνειν, neither of which is 'at home' either in Jewish apocalyptic or in Jewish mysticism.

This thesis was spelt out in greater detail in a paper which Martyn delivered at the *Journées Bibliques* at Louvain in 1975.[95] He described three major periods in the growth of the Gospel.

1. *The Early Period*.[96] This period covers the years before 70, until the 80's. Using 1,35-49 as a test case, Martyn claims that the Gospel began with a series of homilies which attempted to present Jesus to the Jews as the Messiah. In other words, Jesus is shown as the fulfillment of the messianic hopes of Israel, and thus could be given all the traditional Jewish messianic titles. Any convert to this group would have had little difficulty in living his new faith within his life of Torah and synagogue. Martyn calls this group *Christian Jews*. These homilies were eventually gathered, and roughly formed what is today identified as the Signs Source.

2. *The Middle Period*.[97] This period is marked by two traumas within the community's life. Firstly, the synagogue becomes suspicious, demands discussion and midrashic debate over the claims of Jesus, and eventually issues the *Birkat ha-Minim* to force confessing christians out of their midst. This process of midrash, confession and expulsion is dramatically acted out in Jn. 9. Some of the Christian Jews remain within the synagogue, hiding their real identity, but those who remain firm, and are excluded from the synagogue can now be called *Jewish Christians*. The second trauma was caused by the threat of physical persecution and death, as is seen in such passages as 10,28-29; 15,18 and 1,11. In this situation the community sees itself as "not of this world", hated by the world.[98]

---

[95] J. L. Martyn, "Glimpses into the History of the Johannine Community...", pp. 149-174.

[96] *ibid.*, pp. 151-160.

[97] *ibid.*, pp. 160-164.

[98] This is the situation which, according to W. A. Meeks, "The Man from Heaven in Johannine Sectarianism", pp. 44-72, caused the development of John's unique christology of a heavenly revealer, a christology assuring a persecuted and ostracised group that only they had the ultimate answer, because it had been revealed "from heaven". See also H. Leroy, *Rätsel und Missverständnis. Ein Beitrag zur Formgeschichte des Johannesevangeliums*, Bonner Biblische Beiträge 30 (Bonn, Hanstein, 1968) who argues (see esp. pp. 81-82 and 132) that the technique of "enigma" and "misunderstanding" was used by a group which, over against the synagogue, claimed that only they had true Judaism. They looked upon themselves as a privileged group whose language remained unintelligible to outsiders.

3. *The Late Period.*[99]   This period is made up of a complex situation in
which the Johannine community, finding its legs and growing in confidence,
related itself to the Christian Jews who remained in the synagogue, telling
them that there was no middle way.   The community also addressed itself
to the other Jewish Christians who had been scattered because of the persecution.
These were referred to as the "other sheep" (see 10,16) and they were promised
that there would eventually be one flock under one Good Shepherd.

Martyn thus attempts to show the growth of a Gospel through a series
of social, historical and religious crises of a community.[100]   It could be claimed
that he shows how the Gospel grew within a continuously developing situation.
G. Richter's analysis works from a different premise.[101]   He posits a *Grundschrift*
which has then been reworked by variant groups, with differing christologies.
Each of these groups has left its traces in the Gospel as we have it now.
Thus the Gospel is a result, not so much of a chronological movement from
period to period, but of the interraction of variant christologies *within* the
group.   Richter saw the Gospel's development along the following lines:

1. *The Mosaic-prophet Christians.*[102]   This group saw Jesus as the fulfillment
of Deut. 18,15-18.   This christology can be found in 1,29-34.45; 6,14; 7,31.
Jesus is not a Davidic messiah, but the Prophet like Moses.   He was chosen
from among men to be Messiah.   This group produced the *Grundschrift* after

---

[99] J. L. Martyn, « Glimpses into the History...", pp. 164-174.

[100] The 1971 study appeared to accept Fortna's Signs Source, and then proceed, by way
of the redactional critical method, to show how later use of the source changed its theological
point of view.   The weakness of this approach was the hypothetical nature of the signs
source.   There is a growing consensus that such a source stands behind the Gospel. See the
over-sanguine remarks of R. Kysar, "The Source Analysis of the Fourth Gospel. A Growing
Consensus?", NT 15 (1973) 134-152.   If we can identify this source, then we are clearly in a
position to practise the redactional critical method. See on this, J. M. Robinson, *Trajectories*,
pp. 235-252.   However, W. A. Meeks, " 'Am I a Jew?'...", pp. 184-185 rightly remarks that
Martyn's weakest point was his point of departure, Fortna's Signs Source. This defect has,
in my opinion, been considerably rectified in Martyn's 1975 paper, where his departure point
is 9,22: the expulsion of the Johannine community from the synagogue.   His hypothesis
works backwards and forwards from that point. See J. L. Martyn, "Glimpses into the
History...", p. 151, note 6.

[101] I will refer to G. Richter, "Präsentische und futurische Eschatologie im 4. Evangelium", where his theory is most clearly set out (see esp. pp. 126-131). Also important in
this regard is his essay "Zum gemeindebildenden Element in den johanneischen Schriften",
in J. Hainz (ed.), *Kirche im Werden. Studien zum Thema Amt und Gemeinde im Neuen
Testament*, In Zusammenarbeit mit dem Collegium Biblicum München, (München, Schöningh,
1976) pp. 253-292.   See my review of this work in *Salesianum* 38 (1976) 968-969.   His
theories about the "communities inside the community" stand behind all his most recent work.
See the full bibliography in A. J. Mattill, "Johannine Communities...", p. 294 note 2, and the
essays collected posthumously by the Collegium Biblicum München in G. Richter, *Studien
zum Johannesevangelium* (Leiden, E. J. Brill, 1976).

[102] Idem, "Präsentische und futurische Eschatologie...", pp. 126-127.

they were put out of the synagogues in the diaspora of Northern Palestine, Syria and Transjordan.

2. *The Son of God Christians.*[103]   A part of the earliest community reworked the *Grundschrift* as they began to establish themselves in a non-Jewish world. Jesus was now spoken of as a Son of God, a man from heaven who brings eschatological salvation *now*. Not all the community followed this development, and thus they split. This second group rewrote the *Grundschrift* in the light of their Son of God christology (see 1,1-13; 8,27-28; 12,16; 13,7; 14,20.26). The writer of this revised *Grundschrift* can be called the Evangelist.

3. *The Docetic Christians.*[104]   This group carried the Son of God christology of the Evangelist to its extreme, and claimed that Jesus was not really human. They have made no direct contribution to the Gospel, but we know of their existence from the evidence of the last stage in the Gospel's growth. Also this group broke off from the community to follow its own particular christological development.

4. *The anti-Docetic Redaction.*[105]   The Gospel was revised in an attempt to play down any elements which provided fuel for a docetic interpretation. See especially the additions in 1,14-18; 19,34-35. This same attitude is reflected in I Jn. 4,2-3 and II Jn. 7. The resultant christology lies somewhere between the Mosaic prophet of the *Grundschrift* and the Son of God idea of the Evangelist, as the anti-docetic redaction drew back behind the position taken by the Evangelist.

R. E. Brown has proposed another scheme, but limits himself, for the present, to a discussion of the development of thought within the Johannine community *before* the writing of the Gospel as we have it now. He proposes three identifiable stages:

1. In general agreement with Martyn and Richter, Brown sees the earliest stage of the Gospel in a group of Jewish Christians who identified Jesus with their messianic expectations. This is especially clear in 1,35-51.[106] The Beloved Disciple, ignored by Martyn and Richter, played a vital role here. Brown, like R. Schnackenburg, defended an identification between the Beloved Disciple

---

[103] *ibid.*, pp. 127-128.
[104] *ibid.*, pp. 128-129.
[105] *ibid.*, pp. 129-130.
[106] R. E. Brown, "Johannine Ecclesiology..", pp. 384-385. Brown agrees with Martyn, against Richter that Jesus fulfilled Jewish messianic hopes for this earliest group. Richter is more specific, as he limits the expectations of the group to the Mosaic prophet. They refused to identify Jesus with a Davidic Messiah, according to Richter. Brown claims that this is contradicted by 1,35-51.

and the Son of Zebedee in his commentary,[107] also follows Schnackenburg in now arguing that he must have been an outsider to the group of best known disciples, but that he was still an ex-disciple of the Baptist who went to Jesus of Nazareth. This is the person who provides the community with their contact with the living Jesus.[108]

2. The second stage, which sees the introduction of a christology beyond the identification of Jesus with the Jewish Messiah, leads the community to a heterodox position which eventually caused the *Birkat ha-Minim*. Brown suggests that this development comes from the introduction of the Samaritans to the community. They introduce a Moses centred messianism, an opposition to the Temple and a generally hostile attitude to official Judaism. They also bring with them a new way of understanding Jesus, whom they confess as "the Saviour of the world" (4,42).[109]

3. The final moment must do justice to the presence of the Gentiles in the Gospel, so often ignored by scholarship. Brown sees 7,35 and 12,20-23 as indications that the Gentile presence in the Johannine community is already (before the writing of the Gospel) an accepted fact. This explains the universality of the Gospel which hails "Jesus as the stranger from above".[110]

This is not the place for a detailed criticism of these suggestions. I offer them here as a background to my own reflections of the place John's Son of Man christology occupied within his community. Each of the above scholars would readily admit that their suggestions must remain as hypotheses until the whole of the Gospel is successfully analysed in the light of one or other of these suggested "trajectories".[111] They obviously cannot *all* be correct in every detail, but there are two very significant agreements. Firstly, all three

---

[107] R. E. Brown, *John*, pp. xcii-xcviii. See R. Schnackenburg, *Johannesevangelium* I, pp. 60-88.

[108] R. E. Brown, "Johannine Ecclesiology...", pp. 386-388; R. Schnackenburg, "Der Jünger, den Jesus liebte", in *EKK* 2 (1970) 97-117; Idem, "On the Origin of the Fourth Gospel", in *Jesus and Man's Hope*, Vol. I, pp. 234-243.

[109] R. E. Brown, "Johannine Ecclesiology...", pp. 388-391. The reader will notice that the Moses-centred christology which belonged to Richter's *Grundschrift* has now been placed in the second stage.

[110] *ibid.*, pp. 391-393. For the quotation, pp. 391.

[111] Some sample case-studies have been done. For Richter, as well as the article on present and future eschatology, already mentioned, see esp. "Die Fleischwerdung des Logos im Johannesevangelium", *NT* 13 (1971) 81-126; 14 (1972) 257-276; "Der Vater und Gott Jesu und seiner Brüder in Joh 20,17: Ein Beitrag zur Christologie des Johannesevangelium", *MüTZ* 24 (1973) 95-114; 25 (1974) 64-73; "Zu der Taufererzählungen Mk 1,9-11 und Joh 1,32-34", *ZNW* 65 (1974) 43-56; "Zum sogennanten Taufetext Joh 3,5", *MüTZ* 26 (1975) 101-152. For Martyn, see "We Have Found Elijah", in *Jews, Greeks and Christians*, pp. 181-219. Unfortunately not available to me is his further study, "Clementine Recognitions 1,33-71, Jewish Christianity and the Fourth Gospel".

scholars claim that the earliest stage of the Johannine Gospel came from Christian Jews who saw Jesus as the fulfillment of their Jewish messianic expectations. Although Brown does not mention any conflict situations, both Martyn and Richter see the higher Johannine christological point of view as a development which arose out of a conflict on two fronts: with the synagogue on the one hand, and with the Christian Jews who would not abandon their lower christology on the other.

Both of these suggestions sound a remarkably consistent chord with the results of my investigation of the strictly Johannine use of the term "the Son of Man". Although he appreciates the value of the results of my study, Robert Kysar claims that "tradition analysis promises more success than does the method of Moloney".[113] I wonder. The historico-critical analysis of the New Testament is a complicated task, and I believe that various aspects are best attempted in turn. At times different scholars, looking at the same material in different ways, will produce results which run parallel. As in any scientific pursuit, this type of result adds strength to the general hypothesis being tested.

One of the features which I noticed in my study of the Johannine use of the term "the Son of Man" was that the title was continually used to *correct* other Jewish messianic titles.[114] In the light of that discovery, it is interesting to read Martyn's earlier remarks: "I am inclined to think that John's introduction and shaping of the Son of Man tradition, wholly absent from SG,[115] and his — so I think — creation of two-level dramas [116] are also to be listed here, i.e. as adjustments of SG in the face of inadequacies in it which have been revealed in the course of Jewish opposition to it".[117]

It strikes me as more than probable that the Johannine use of the term "the Son of Man" made a specific contribution to the development of the christology of the Johannine community. The fact (often pointed out, and frequently given an exaggerated importance) that the terms ἀναβαίνειν, καταβαίνειν, ὑψωθῆναι and δοξασθῆναι are used together *only* with this title does show that the term had a special meaning for the community which used it.[118] Its continual use to correct other messianic titles is yet a further

---

[112] See R. E. Brown, "Johannine Ecclesiology...", p. 384.
[113] R. Kysar, "Community and Gospel: Vectors in Fourth Gospel Criticism", *Interp* 31 (1977) 361-362. The article runs from pp. 355-366, and the quote is found on p. 362.
[114] For references to the first edition, see above, note 81.
[115] Martyn's abbreviation for "the Signs Gospel".
[116] For Martyn's theory of a "two-level drama", see above, pp. 19-21.
[117] J. L. Martyn, "Source Criticism and Religionsgeschichte...", p. 258.
[118] J. Coppens, "Le Fils de l'homme...", pp. 59-65 attempts to identify a literary strata. I believe that this is to attempt too much. He then seeks to find the theological position of the strata, and ask why it was inserted into the Gospel. On p. 72 he notes that one of the reasons for this strata's presence in the Johannine community was to free Jesus from any association with Davidic messianic expectations.

indication in this direction.[119]   Was there a tendency, at some stage in the growth of the Johannine community, to settle for the expectations of Judaism? A comfortable existence within the synagogue in the pre-Birkat ha-Minim period would certainly lead to this position.   It could be argued, of course, that this regular pattern is entirely the work of the hand that wrote the final edition of the Gospel. He used this contrast, it could be argued, as a literary technique to show the uniqueness of Jesus. This interpretation of the contrast is correct, but when one notices that the same contrast is found throughout the Gospel tradition it is rash to claim that its presence in the Fourth Gospel is due entirely to the originality of the Fourth Evangelist.

That this pattern is the result of a *growing* literary tradition is most obvious in 1,35-51. The series of confessions reaches its peak in 1,49. John has assembled almost every important Jewish messianic title in these verses. He then adds v. 50 to introduce the theme of "correction", and the true nature of Jesus' role is presented in 1,51 in terms of the Son of Man.[120] 1,35-49 represents the hopes of a community who saw in Jesus the expected Jewish messiah, but v. 51 corrects that hope in terms of "greater things" (v. 50). Is it possible to locate the development and use of this Johannine Son of Man christology?   I have already indicated that the term comes to John from Christian tradition and that even the pattern of "correction" was a part of the traditional use of this strange title.   However, John does not merely repeat tradition. He insists on the unique revelation which takes place in the human figure of Jesus. There seem to be two sides of the question, a correction of purely Jewish hopes, and an insistence on the human figure of Jesus.

Martyn and Richter understand John's use of the Son of Man as a recourse to an ascending-descending figure,[121] but I have insisted that this is to misinterpret the evidence. I suspect that the term played a most important

[119] This has now been indicated by other scholars.   On 1,51 see J. Painter, "Christ and the Church in John 1,45-51", pp. 360-361, and his general insistence in his *John: Witness and Theologian,* p. 53 that John's use of "the Son of Man" determines what John meant by Jesus' kingship. Unfortunately Painter only sees the correction in the light of false "kingly" expectations. On 3,13 see G. Richter, "Zum sogennanten Taufetext Joh 3,5", pp. 113-114. However, many still miss this point, especially for 1,51 where, to my mind, it is programmatic. See, for example, S. Pancaro, "The Relationship of the Church to Israel in the Gospel of St. John", *NTS* 21 (1974-75) 398-399 and R. H. Fuller, "The Incarnation in Historical Perspective", *ATR* Supplementary Series 7 (1976) pp. 60-61.

[120] R. E. Brown, "Johannine Ecclesiology...", pp. 384-385 uses 1,35-51 to show that the earliest section of the community accepted Jesus as a traditional Jewish Messiah. He also seems to miss the point that this is the case for 1,35-49, but not for vv. 50-51, which correct the traditional hopes in terms of "something greater".

[121] See esp. J. L. Martyn, "We Have Found Elijah", pp. 217-218; "Source Criticism and Religionsgeschichte...", p. 267; G. Richter, "Zum sogennanten Taufetext Joh 3,5", pp. 113-114.

role over a long period of time in the community's development. If the use of the title in the Fourth Gospel comes from the tradition, then there must have been a close contact with that tradition (Brown's Beloved Disciple? [122]). If, on the other hand, it moves away from the tradition to stress the revelation which takes place in Jesus' humanity, it has been used by the community to face two problems. Not only does the Gospel use the title to go beyond any Jewish expectation, in the days in which the struggle between the community and the synagogue was intense, but it also holds back any tendency to lift Jesus out of the human sphere into a "divine man" figure by insisting that the heavenly was revealed in and through a man who was hung upon a Cross. Then there is the use of ἀναβαίνειν-καταβαίνειν. I have insisted that we must not start from these verbs to explain the Johannine Son of Man christology, yet a problem remains. As Talbert has shown recently, the idea of descending and ascending figures was found in Mediterranean antiquity both before and after the New Testament era, from pre-Christian Jewish angel figures to the saving figures of classical mythology.[123] The language is certainly found in Jewish Wisdom speculation (see, for example, LXX Prov. 24,27; 25,7; Qoh. 3,21; Sir. 50,20)[124] but it was also a part of other syncretistic systems, including the Gnostic systems. The all important point, however, is that the Johannine Son of Man *does not* ascend and descend. He descends in the incarnation (3,13), but he refuses to ascend (6,62). Yet, the all too familiar *words* are used. I would suggest that here John is using a *language* which would have been familiar to the syncretistic world in which this community had to suddenly find its way (and this does not mean that the words do not come from the Wisdom background). That language, however, totally conditioned by John's view of Jesus of Nazareth, is given a new *content* which was entirely dependent upon Christian tradition.

Where and when can one situate this development and use of the traditional term "the Son of Man"? We have traced a community which uses this term of Jesus:

1. To correct the identification of Jesus with the traditional Jewish Messiah.

2. To insist on the unique revelation of God in the man Jesus, and especially in the human event of the Cross.

3. To present Jesus in a *language* that would be familiar to late first-century syncretism, but with a *content* that betrayed nothing from early Christian tradition.

[122] R. E. Brown, "Johannine Ecclesiology...", pp. 386-388.
[123] C. H. Talbert, "The Myth of a Descending-Ascending Redeemer...", pp. 421-430.
[124] Although the words are not present, the concepts are important in the Wisdom traditions. See, for example, Sir. 24; Bar. 3,23-4,4; Wisd. 9,10; II Bar. 48,36.

We seem to have our feet in many camps, and this is already a warning against clear cut distinctions between various moments in the development of the Johannine community. The Johannine use of the term "the Son of Man":

1. Somehow retains a great deal of its traditional sense, and even some of the patterns in which it was used from earliest times.

2. Places the community in a period after the *Birkat ha-Minim,* or at least during the conflict which led to that situation, as there is on the one hand a refusal of traditional Jewish categories, and the other an openness to new language and thought.

3. Is still, nevertheless, being worked out in a largely Jewish community as it develops its special use of the title around Jewish discussions, and with the help of Is. 52,13.

4. Is used in close association with (but never identified with) the all-important Johannine Son of God christology. It is pointedly directed towards the human Jesus, probably as a warning against any exaggerated misunderstanding of the community's Son of God christology.

There is too much consistent theological thinking behind the Gospel's use of this title for all this to be mere chance. If the earliest christology of this community was made up of an identity between Jesus and Jewish messianic hopes, then it does not belong in this strata. However, from that point onwards, and in correction of that point of view (as a starting point) it seems to play an important role in the gradual evolution of Johannine christology, through all its crises. I would suggest that behind this movement from crisis to crisis there was a figure who, by his authority and genius, held the community and its christology together. The seemingly insoluble problem of the Beloved Disciple is not just a curiosity for academic ingenuity.[125] Behind this Gospel's use of the Son of Man title stands a key to a correct understanding of the Johannine trajectory. I do not believe that we can slot this christology into a comfortable point somewhere along that trajectory, as it was one of the major contributions which this enigmatic character made to the life and thought of the community. Because of this fact we find sayings which could well be as old as any Son of Man saying in the New Testament (5,27) and others which are puzzling in their originality (9,35; 12,23.34). This can best be explained by the presence of some individual who had a close contact with the oldest tradition but who was prepared to use that tradition freely to guide his community from a strictly Jewish world into the confusing world

---

[125] Unfortunately, this area is often used by scholars to exercise ingenuity. There were a number of papers on the question at the 1978 Oxford International Congress on Biblical Studies. He was shown to be a Jewish Priest, a Sadducee (D. E. H. Whitely) and a Samaritan (M. D. Goulder).

of late first century syncretism.   Behind the title stands the conviction, taken from Dan. 7, that the Son of Man must suffer many things.   This theme was first used to correct the strictly Jewish categories of an all-conquering Davidic Messiah, but at a later stage its connection with the Cross took it along the uniquely Johannine path of a Son of Man "lifted up" on a Cross to reveal God among men.   Thus the Son of Man is now the unique revealer of God among men, and the place where men can come to life or death in their acceptance or refusal of that revelation (3,14-15).   However, behind all this, in my opinion, stands a remarkable Evangelist who both inspired and directed this developing christology.   Although I am sympathetic to these attempts to understand the *Sitz im Leben* of the Johannine community so that we might come to a deeper understanding of the Gospel's christology, we must allow the *Gospel* to stand on its own.   The christology of this particular Gospel must be understood as a vigorous whole, and we must be careful not to reduce it to a series of differing christologies doing battle with one another, which somehow finally found themselves as bed-fellows!   It is immediately obvious that this would be to reduce the Fourth Gospel to something which it plainly is not — a hotch-potch of various opinions.   The evidence again, I believe, points to an authoritative and highly-respected Evangelist.   He is responsible for this remarkable unity.   As R. E. Brown has recently written: "In my judgment the fact that he (the Beloved Disciple) was a historical person and a companion of Jesus becomes all the more obvious in these new approaches to Johannine ecclesiology".[126]

---

[126] R. E. Brown, "Johannine Ecclesiology...", p. 386.   Brown (pp. 386-388) only considers the figure within the context of his first period, while I am suggesting that he had a longer influence on the group.   Most unfortunately, this appendix was already in a final proof stage before Brown's further development of his article reached me.   See R. E. Brown, " 'Other Sheep not of this Fold': The Johannine Perspective on Christian Diversity in the Late First Century" *JBL* 97 (1978) 5-22.   This most important article carries Brown's considerations from his earlier suggestions on the shape of the community *before* the Gospel to its *post*-Gospel stage.

THE JOHANNINE SON OF MAN REVISITED

I presented my doctoral dissertation, *The Johannine Son of Man*, at the University of Oxford in the Trinity Term of 1975[1]. From the beginning of critical New Testament scholarship, the Synoptic use of the expression "the Son of Man" has generated intense interest. It is virtually the only expression that the Jesus of the Gospels uses to speak of himself. It was hoped that analysis of this enigmatic expression would open up something of Jesus' self-understanding, of his preaching, or at least, of the earliest Palestinian Church's Christology[2]. Various schools of thought have emerged and gathered support, but the debate still rages[3]. Aware of that discussion, I was surprised to find, in the early 1970s, that the use of "the Son of Man" in the Gospel of John had aroused less scholarly interest. At that time, only S. Schulz had published a monograph on the question, and G. Iber's unpublished Heidelberg dissertation on the history of the Son of Man tradition contained a chapter on the Fourth Gospel[4]. Both of these studies, however, were more interested in the *Traditionsgeschichte* and the *Überlieferungs-*

---

1. The dissertation had been prepared under the supervision of Professor Morna D. Hooker. It was published as: F.J. MOLONEY, *The Johannine Son of Man* (Biblioteca di Scienze Religiose, 14), Rome, LAS, 1976. A second edition appeared, with the same publishers, in 1978. For a summary of the argument, cf. F.J. MOLONEY, *The Johannine Son of Man*, in *Biblical Theology Bulletin* 6 (1976) 177-189.

2. Cf. F. HAHN, *Christologische Hoheitstitel. Ihre Geschichte im frühen Christentum* (FRLANT, 83), Göttingen, Vandenhoeck & Ruprecht, ³1966, p. 13: "Von allen christologischen Titeln ist 'Menschensohn' am eingehendsten untersucht worden. Das hängt damit zusammen, dass man bei diesem Würdeprädikat hofft, unmittelbar zu der Verkündigung Jesu vorstossen zu können; ausserdem wird die Anschauung der frühen palästinischen Gemeinde über Person und Wirken Jesu in einem relativ geschlossenen Zusammenhang erkennbar". For an abbreviated English translation of this important book, cf. *The Titles of Jesus in Christology. Their History in Early Christianity*, trans. H. Knight – G. Ogg, London, Lutterworth Press, 1969.

3. For the "schools of thought," cf. the summary in F.J. MOLONEY, *The Gospel of Mark. A Commentary*, Peabody, MA, Hendrickson, 2002, pp. 212-213: "Excursus 1: The Son of Man Discussion". For a recent survey of the debate, cf. D.R. BURKETT, *The Son of Man Debate: A History and Evaluation* (SNTS MS, 107), Cambridge, Cambridge University Press, 2000.

4. S. SCHULZ, *Untersuchungen zur Menschensohn-Christologie im Johannesevangelium. Zugleich ein Beitrag zur Methodengeschichte der Auslegung des 4. Evangeliums*, Göttingen, Vandenhoeck & Ruprecht, 1957; G. IBER, *Überlieferungsgeschichtliche Untersuchungen zum Begriff des Menschensohn im Neuen Testament*, Unpublished Dissertation, Heidelberg, 1953.

geschichte of the Johannine use of ὁ υἱὸς τοῦ ἀνθρώπου[5]. However, despite the paucity of monographs, the issue had not been entirely ignored. There were some interesting and valuable scholarly articles that had either focused upon one or other of the Johannine Son of Man sayings, or surveyed the question as a whole[6].

It is now almost thirty years since the publication of my dissertation. It can no longer be claimed that there is scant interest in the Johannine Son of Man. A number of monographs[7], major sections in studies of the Son of Man in the New Testament[8], and a steady flow of scholarly articles[9], have generated what could now be called a "Johannine Son of

---

5. J. Ashton, *Understanding the Fourth Gospel*, Oxford, Clarendon Press, 1991, p. 341, is rightly critical of Schulz who attempts to distinguish the pre-Johannine from the Johannine use of the expression, without any "re-examination of the theme *in situ*". I am aware of an earlier PhD dissertation, P.D. Early, *The Conception of the Son of Man in the Fourth Gospel*, presented at the Southern Baptist Seminary in 1952. I have not had access to that work.

6. For a survey of this pre-1976 scholarship, cf. Moloney, *Son of Man* (n. 1), p. 122.

7. Cf., for example, C. Panackel, *ΙΔΟΥ Ο ΑΝΘΡΩΠΟΣ. An Exegetico-Theological Study of the Text in the Light of the Use of the Term ΑΝΘΡΩΠΟΣ Designating Jesus in the Fourth Gospel* (Analecta Gregoriana, 251), Rome, Editrice Pontificia Università Gregoriana, 1988; R. Rhea, *The Johannine Son of Man* (ATANT, 76), Zürich, Theologischer Verlag, 1991; D. Burkett, *The Son of Man in the Gospel of John* (JSNT SS, 56), Sheffield, Sheffield Academic Press, 1991; M.M. Pazdan, *The Son of Man. A Metaphor for Jesus in the Fourth Gospel*, Collegeville, MN, The Liturgical Press, 1991; M. Sasse, *Der Menschensohn im Evangelium nach Johannes* (TANZ, 35), Tübingen-Basel, Francke Verlag, 2000.

8. Cf., for example, the important studies of J.-A. Bühner, *Der Gesandte und sein Weg im 4. Evangelium. Die kultur- und religionsgeschichtlichen Grundlagen der johanneischen Sendungschristologie sowie ihre traditionsgeschichtliche Entwicklung* (WUNT, 2/2), Tübingen, Mohr (Paul Siebeck), 1977, pp. 374-399, 422-429; B. Lindars, *Jesus Son of Man. A Fresh Examination of the Son of Man Sayings in the Gospels*, London, SPCK, 1983, pp. 145-157; D.R.A. Hare, *The Son of Man Tradition*, Minneapolis, MN, Fortress Press, 1990, pp. 79-111; Ashton, *Understanding* (n. 5), pp. 337-373; W. Loader, *The Christology of the Fourth Gospel. Structure and Issues* (Beiträge zur biblischen Exegese und Theologie, 23), Frankfurt, Peter Lang, [2]1992, pp. 82-92, 107-121; J. Mateos – F. Camacho, *El Hijo del Hombre. Hacia la plenitud humana* (En los orígenes del Cristianismo, 9), Cordoba, Ediciones El Almendro, 1997, pp. 159-186, 203-209; R.E. Brown, *Introduction to the Gospel of John*, ed. F.J. Moloney (Anchor Bible Reference Library), New York, Doubleday, 2003, pp. 252-259.

9. Cf., for example, the following studies in R. Pesch – R. Schnackenburg – O. Kaiser (eds.), *Jesus und der Menschensohn: Für Anton Vögtle*, Freiburg, Herder, 1975: S. Smalley, *Johannes 1,51 und die Einleitung zum vierten Evangelium*, pp. 300-313; E. Ruckstuhl, *Abstieg und Erhöhung des johanneischen Menschensohns*, pp. 314-341; C.K. Barrett, *Das Fleisch des Menschensohnes (John 6:53)*, pp. 342-354; J. Riedl, *Wenn ihr den Menschensohn erhöht habt (Joh 8,28)*, pp. 355-370; R. Schnackenburg, *Die Ecce-homo-Szene und der Menschensohn*, pp. 371-386; P. Borgen, *Some Jewish Exegetical Traditions as Background for the Son of Man Sayings in John's Gospel*, in M. de Jonge (ed.), *L'Évangile de Jean, Sources, Rédaction, Théologie* (BETL, 44), Gembloux, Duculot, 1977, pp. 243-258; J. Coppens, *Le Fils de l'homme dans l'Évangile johannique*, in *ETL* 52 (1976) 21-81; J.P. Brown, *The Son of Man: "This Fellow"*, in

Man Debate"[10]. As the title of the present essay indicates, it is time for me to "revisit" *The Johannine Son of Man*. Given the limitations of this study, what follows will not pretend to be a *Forschungsbericht* of reflection upon the Johannine use of the expression "the Son of Man", but a re-statement of my own understanding of this aspect of Johannine Christology, if indeed, it is a part of the Johannine Christology[11]. Some of the literature that has appeared across the past thirty years will serve as my discussion partners. I will revisit the Johannine Son of Man under three headings. I will briefly restate those elements of my earlier understanding that call for some further clarification. Secondly, more detailed consideration will be given to the most troublesome element in my earlier work, my exegesis of 3,13 and 6,62. Finally, I will further develop elements that I regard as distinct within the Johannine Christology: "the Son (of God)" and "the Son of Man"[12].

Bib 58 (1977) 361-387; M. PAMMENT, *The Son of Man in the Fourth Gospel*, in *JTS* 36 (1985) 56-66; J. PAINTER, *The Enigmatic Johannine Son of Man*, in F. VAN SEGBROECK – C.M. TUCKETT – G. VAN BELLE – J. VERHEYDEN (eds.), *The Four Gospels 1992. Festschrift Frans Neirynck* (BETL, 100), 3 vols., Leuven, University Press – Peeters, 1992, vol. III, pp. 1868-1867; W. LOADER, *The Central Structure of Johannine Christology*, in *NTS* 30 (1984) 188-216; W. ROTH, *Jesus as the Son of Man: The Scriptural Identity of a Johannine Image*, in D.W. GROH – R. JEWETT (eds.), *The Living Text. Essays in Honor of Ernest W. Saunders*, Lanham, MD, University of America Press, 1985, pp. 11-26; C. HAM, *The Title 'Son of Man' in the Gospel of John*, in *Stone Campbell Journal* 1 (1998) 67-84; F. FERNANDEZ RAMOS, *El hijo del hombre en el cuarto evangelio*, in *Studium Legionense* 40 (1999) 45-92; W. WINK, *"The Son of Man" in the Gospel of John*, in R.T. FORTNA – T. THATCHER (eds.), *Jesus in the Johannine Tradition*, Louisville, KY, Westminster John Knox, 2001, pp. 117-123.

10. I am using this phrase in imitation of the widely used expression "the Son of Man Debate". For a report on the five studies dedicated to the Johannine Son of Man in the *Festschrift* for Anton Vögtle (cf. previous note), an indication of the increasing interest in the question, cf. F.J. MOLONEY, *A Johannine Son of Man Discussion?*, in *Salesianum* 39 (1977) 93-102.

11. One of the aims of the study of PAINTER, *Enigmatic* (n. 9), is to show that "there is no Son or Son of Man Christology in John but that motifs from these traditions contributed to John's Christology" (p. 1887; cf. also p. 1870).

12. PAINTER, *Enigmatic* (n. 9), pp. 1883-1887, argues that there is no distinction. BURKETT, *Son of Man* (n. 7), pp. 51-111, reconstructs Pr 30,1-4, reading *hagaber* (man) as *hagibbor* (the mighty one = God). On the basis of this unlikely reconstruction, he argues that for the Gospel of John "the Son of Man" = "the Son of God". Cf. my review of this book in *Pacifica* 6 (1993) 109-112. LOADER, *The Central Structure* (n. 9), pp. 188-216, and *Christology* (n. 8), pp. 82-92, 107-121, recognizes the primacy of the relationship between the Father and the Son, and the Son's revealing task (reflected especially in 3,31-36). This "central structure" is found throughout the Gospel. The Son of Man "cluster", basically limited to the ministry of Jesus (13,31 is the only exception) is related to Jesus' hour, glorification, ascension and "something greater". In the second half of the Gospel the Son of Man *title* disappears, but the *functions* (especially glorification, the return to the Father and the "greater things") are taken up by the Son. Thus, there is a *functional* unity between Jesus, Son, Son of Man, a figure both human and divine. PAZDAN, *The Son of Man* (n. 7), takes a different approach. She claims that it is misleading to separate the

I. THE HUMAN JESUS AND THE SON OF MAN

There is no such thing as an exegesis without presuppositions. Reading the debate over the Johannine use of ὁ υἱὸς τοῦ ἀνθρώπου that has emerged since 1976 indicates the truth of that claim. I have my presuppositions, and they are rejected by scholars who, on the basis of their justifiable presuppositions, come to different conclusions. Three issues divide us. In the first place, the unavoidable *diachronic* question: what is the origin of the Johannine use of "the Son of Man"? There is broad general consensus that several of the Johannine sayings (3,14; 8,28; 12,32-34) parallel the Synoptic passion predictions (cf. Mark 8,31; 9,31; 10,33-34, parrs.). A majority of scholars, fascinated by the ascent-descent motif associated with the Johannine use of ὁ υἱὸς τοῦ ἀνθρώπου, claim that the background to the Johannine Son of Man is some form of heavenly figure. From this perspective, the link with Jesus' death is a unique and surprising Johannine creation[13].

But this position is linked with a presupposition that "[a]mong the many puzzles presented by the Fourth Gospel one of the most intriguing is the paradoxical contrast between the titles "Son of God" and "Son of Man". "Son of God", originally at any rate, indicates a human being, the Messiah; whereas "Son of Man" points to a figure whose true home is in heaven"[14]. Behind this position lies a widespread (although nuanced) acceptance of Bultmann's claim, based upon a reading of Daniel 7 and other Jewish apocalyptic material, that the Synoptic use of "the Son of Man" had its origins in an eschatological figure. This figure, other than Jesus, was identified with Jesus in early Christian tradition, and eventually applied to his human experience, and to his suffering[15].

Johannine description of Jesus as Son and Son of Man, as these expressions are not primarily titles. She calls for "a recognition of the integral connection of Son and Son of man as two metaphors which invite the reader to reconsider the importance of the images and names used to describe Jesus as well as what they reveal about him as the incarnate Logos" (p. 85).

13. Cf., especially, BÜHNER, *Der Gesandte* (n. 8), pp. 374-379, 422-429, and ASHTON, *Understanding* (n. 5), pp. 368-373. These significant studies (Ashton is strongly influenced by Bühner) make an important contribution to the *diachronic* question, but in my opinion fail to do justice to the *synchronic* use of Johannine Son of Man sayings, both within their contexts and across the narrative as a whole. Cf., for example, BÜHNER, *Der Gesandte* (n. 8), pp. 385-399, who only considers 5,27 (to make the connection with the Danielic Son of Man as a heavenly figure), 1,51 and 3,13. What of 3,14; 6,27.53.62; 8,28; 9,35; 12,23; 13,31? This is not the case for PAINTER, *Enigmatic* (n. 9), who concludes that there is no Johannine Son of Man Christology, but the occasional presence of fragments from an older use of "the Son of Man".

14. ASHTON, *Understanding* (n. 5), p. 337.

15. Cf. especially R. BULTMANN, *Theology of the New Testament*, trans. K. Grobel, 2

However, a minority position, which I adopt, also starts from Daniel 7, but claims that already in that context, the "one like a son of man" in 7,13 is to be identified with the holy ones of the Most High of vv. 21-25. Their preparedness to experience suffering and even death at the hands of the enemies of Israel (and thus enemies of God) will lead to final vindication (cf. vv. 14, 27). The historical Jesus used an Aramaic expression that appeared in the Greek of the Gospels as ὁ υἱὸς τοῦ ἀνθρώπου to explain – perhaps to himself as well as to his listeners – his unswerving commitment to a life-style and a message that necessarily led to his rejection by both Jewish and Roman authorities. Personalizing the danielic "one like a son of man" as "the son of the man", he believed that, like "the one like a son of man" / "the holy ones of the most high", his openness to God, cost what it may, would lead to his vindication.

With this understanding, the tradition did not begin with an otherwordly eschatological "Son of Man", and develop in the tradition until it was applied to the suffering Son of Man. It developed in the other direction. It began with the suffering Son of Man (Dn 7 and Jesus) and was shaped – in both the Christian preaching and the Jewish apocalyptic material – into a heavenly, eschatological figure[16]. For the Christians, this was Jesus (cf. Mk 8,38; 13,24-27; 14,62), while in the Jewish apocalypses (especially 1 Enoch 37–71 and 4 Ez 13,1-58) it was a mysterious figure, variously identified[17]. Both the Synoptic and the Johannine Son of Man sayings have their origins in the association made by Jesus between the danielic "one like a son of man" and his suffering and death

volumes, London, SCM, 1952-55, vol. I, pp. 28-32; HAHN, *Christologische Hoheitstitel* (n. 2), pp. 13-53; H.E. TÖDT, *The Son of Man in the Synoptic Tradition*, trans. D.M. Barton, London, SCM, 1965.

16. Cf. C.F.D. MOULE, *Neglected Features in the Problem of 'the Son of Man'*, in J. GNILKA (ed.), *Neues Testament und Kirche: Festschrift für Rudolf Schnackenburg*, Freiburg, Herder, 1974, pp. 413-428; ID., *The Origin of Christology*, Cambridge, Cambridge University Press, 1977, pp. 11-22; M.D. HOOKER, *The Son of Man in Mark: A Study of the Background to the Term "the Son of Man" and Its Use in Mark's Gospel*, London, SPCK, 1967, pp. 174-98; ID., *Is the Son of Man Problem Really Insoluble?*, in E. BEST – R.MCL. WILSON (eds.), *Text and Interpretation: Studies in the New Testament Presented to Matthew Black*, Cambridge, Cambridge University Press, 1979, pp. 155-168; F.J. MOLONEY, *The End of the Son of Man?*, in *The Downside Review* 98 (1980) 280-290. Without the link with Dan 7, BROWN, *The Son of Man* (n. 9), pp. 361-387, also argues that the earliest (Galilean) tradition reaches back to the historical Jesus, and that the apocalyptic Son of Man sayings were a later development.

17. Daniel 7 continues to influence these apocalypses, as it continues to influence the developing Christian tradition. But the appearance of "the man" or "the son of man" becomes increasingly apocalyptic. It is beyond this article to take this issue further, but cf. HOOKER, *The Son of Man in Mark* (n. 16), pp. 33-74; M. CASEY, *Son of Man. The Interpretation and Influence of Daniel 7*, London, SPCK, 1979, pp. 99-141.

as "the son of the man"[18]. I would therefore claim, reversing Ashton's words, that "Son of Man" points to a figure whose true home is among suffering human beings[19].

The second major presupposition that determines differing explanations is located in the choice of synchrony over diachrony. This is a more complex matter, as scholarly objectivity is more difficult. We are dealing with hermeneutics, rather than the assessment of objective data[20]. There are two methodological issues that divide us. Interpreters, after a close analysis of the data, may decide that the roots of the Johannine use of "the Son of Man" are to be found in Jewish apocalyptic, the historical Jesus, the Gnostic heavenly man, the Philonic perfect man, an eschatological, divine, or some other form of "man" speculation that can be discovered in the ancient world. This background is then used to determine the meaning of the Johannine use of the expression. In this approach background determines meaning[21]. Secondly, a theory concerning the historical development of the Johannine text is adopted. For example, in his first contribution to reflection upon the Johannine Son of Man, Lindars espoused a two-edition history for the development of the Gospel, and located the Johannine Son of Man sayings within either the first or the second edition. He developed his understanding of the Johannine Son of Man Christology only on the basis of those sayings that belonged to the first edition[22]. Similarly, Painter has argued that the Son of Man passages in the Gospel of John were inserted into the Gospel at

18. Although nuanced differently, the dependence of the Johannine use of "the Son of Man" upon the Synoptic tradition has been argued by several scholars. Cf., for example, by A.J.B. HIGGINS, *Jesus and the Son of Man*, London, Lutterworth, 1964; R. MADDOX, *The Function of the Son of Man in the Gospel of John*, in R.J. BANKS (ed.), *Reconciliation and Hope: New Testament Essays on Atonement and Eschatology Presented to L.L. Morris on his 60th Birthday*, Exeter, Paternoster Press, 1974, pp. 186-204; R. SCHNACK-ENBURG, *Der Menschensohn im Johannesevangelium*, in *NTS* 11 (1964-65) 123-137; ID., *The Gospel According to St John* (HTCNT 4/1-3), 3 volumes, London, Burns & Oates; New York, Crossroad, 1968-82, vol. I, pp. 529-542. Cf. also MOLONEY, *Son of Man* (n. 1), pp. 214-20.

19. Cf. above, and n. 14.

20. It is important that this not be understood as a setting of the historical-critical method over against literary approaches to a text. Such a hermeneutical stance, although sometimes adopted, creates an unjustifiable opposition. Good literary approaches must ask historical questions of the text, and good historical-critical studies must also ask literary questions.

21. This approach is the feature of BÜHNER, *Der Gesandte* (n. 8), pp. 374-399, 422-429; ASHTON, *Understanding* (n. 5), pp. 337-373, and PAINTER, *Enigmatic* (n. 9), pp. 1869-1887.

22. B. LINDARS, *The Son of Man in the Johannine Christology*, in B. LINDARS – S.S. SMALLEY (eds.), *Christ and Spirit in the New Testament: Studies in Honour of Charles Francis Digby Moule*, Cambridge, Cambridge University Press, 1973, pp. 43-60.

a later stage in the development of the Gospel, in a period of conflict between the Johannine community and the post-War Synagogue. This polemic was one of the elements that generated a fragmentary use of an earlier Son of Man tradition[23]. In these approaches, the original "Sitz im Leben der Johanneischen Kirche" plays an important role in determining meaning[24].

I have no doubt that the Johannine text, as we have it now, was the product of a long history. I also agree that it is possible, and necessary, for the interpreter to devote attention to the tensions in the narrative that are best explained by the variety of religious and literary currents that played their part in generating the text. Nevertheless, the best interpreter of the Johannine text is the Johannine text. We must be clear about what we are doing as we approach a text. The archeological work required to unearth the background to a text, and the further critical work required to peel back the layers of tradition that have been placed side by side to form a complete narrative utterance, are essential elements of biblical scholarship. But equally "essential" is the interpretation of the text as we now have it, in terms of itself[25]. Not all will agree with this hermeneutical stance, and I respect that. Yet, it appears to me that that such a finely crafted text as the Gospel of John, although not without its literary tensions, the product of some seventy years of story-telling somewhere in the early Church, was presented as a finished story of Jesus so that it might be understood in terms of itself[26]. Was all the diachronic data, so painstakingly gathered by modern critics, in the minds and the imaginations of the first hearers/listeners to the Gospel of John? As R.E. Brown correctly affirms in his posthumous *Introduction to the Gospel of John*:

> Even though I think there was both an evangelist and a redactor, the duty of the commentator is not to decide what was composed by whom, or in what order it originally stood, nor whether these composers drew on a writ-

23. Cf. PAINTER, *Enigmatic* (n. 9), pp. 1869-1887.

24. This approach is also found in ASHTON, *Understanding* (n. 5). Cf., for example, his excursus on the structure of John 3, pp. 374-377.

25. In this, I agree with J. BLANK, *Krisis. Untersuchungen zur johanneischen Christologie und Eschatologie*, Freiburg, Lambertus Verlag, 1964, p. 26: "Denn der Text selbst hat darüber noch etwas zu sagen, was in den 'Traditionen' noch nicht enthalten ist. ... Die eigentliche Textauslegung beginnt doch erst, wenn die traditionsgeschichtlichen Bausteine beisammen sind". Cf. also HARE, *The Son of Man Tradition* (n. 8), p. 79.

26. For my attempt to read the Johannine text in this way, cf. F.J. MOLONEY, *Belief in the Word. Reading John 1–4*, Minneapolis, MN, Fortress, 1993; ID., *Signs and Shadows. Reading John 5–12*, Minneapolis, MN, Fortress, 1996; ID., *Glory not Dishonor. Reading John 13–21*, Minneapolis, MN, Fortress, 1998. Cf. also ID., *The Gospel of John* (Sacra Pagina, 4), Collegeville, MN, Liturgical Press, 1998.

ten source or an oral tradition. One should deal with the Gospel as it now
stands, for that is the only form that we are certain has ever existed[27].

Finally, one must recognize the interplay that goes on between the
text and the reader and the reader and the text[28]. It is only after acquir-
ing familiarity with a text that one comes to establish what can be
regarded as core arguments of a text, arguments that belong to the weave
and warp of the narrative. John struggled to maintain an almost impossible balancing act. He told a dangerous story about the revelation of God,
made visible in the *Logos*, Son of God, the one sent from heaven, whose
oneness with God was so intimate that what God was, the *Logos* also
was (cf. 1,1-2). But he also wished to insist upon the truth that the *Logos*
became fully human (1,14)[29]. The subsequent history of the reception of
the Gospel of John tells how dangerous it was to tell the story of Jesus
in this fashion. In antiquity it quickly became the favorite Gospel of the
Gnostic sects[30]. In modern scholarship the author has been understood as
either a Christian attempting to "baptize" Gnosticism, to draw it back
into Christian ranks[31], or as a Christian who is slipping off into naïve
Docetism[32]. Ashton rejects a number of scholarly attempts to argue that,
in John, the expression ὁ υἱὸς τοῦ ἀνθρώπου affirms Jesus' humanity.
He rightly points out that it is an "error to take the Christology of the
incarnate Logos as a kind of axiom *from which everything else
derives*"[33], but is it wrong to take "the Christology of the incarnate

27. BROWN, *Introduction* (n. 8), p. 111. These words recall the oft-attacked, but still
valid, remarks of C.H. DODD, *The Interpretation of the Fourth Gospel*, Cambridge, Cambridge University Press, 1953, that whoever may have been responsible for the text as we
have it "was not necessarily irresponsible or unintelligent" (p. 290). I have deliberately
chosen to refer to Dodd and Brown, who preceded the present interest in literary-critical
readings. For some reflections on a hermeneutic deriving from more recent studies, cf.
F.J. MOLONEY, *"A Hard Saying". The Gospel and Culture*, Collegeville, MN, The Liturgical Press, 2001, pp. 84-105 (*Narrative Criticism of the Gospels*), pp. 259-279 (*Adven-
ture with Nicodemus: An Exercise in Hermeneutics*).
28. This process, of course, is complex, and allows for a multiplicity of possible interpretations. It is beyond the scope of this article to develop the issue further. Cf., among
several, P. RICŒUR, *Interpretation Theory: Discourse and the Surplus of Meaning*, Fort
Worth, TX, Texas Christian University Press, 1976.
29. For more detail, cf. MOLONEY, *John* (n. 26), pp. 33-48.
30. On this reception, cf. R.E. BROWN, *The Epistles of John* (AncB, 30), Garden City,
NY, Doubleday, 1982, pp. 47-68. Cf. also F.J. MOLONEY, *Raymond Brown's New* Introduction to the Gospel of John*: A Presentation and Some Questions*, in *CBQ* 65 (2003)
18-20.
31. Cf., for example, R. BULTMANN, *Die Bedeutung der neuerschossenen mandäischen und manichäischen Quellen für das Verständnis des Johannesevangeliums*, in *ZNW*
24 (1925) 100-146.
32. Cf. E. KÄSEMANN, *The Testament of Jesus. A Study of John in the Light of Chapter 17*, trans. G. Krodel, London, SCM, 1965.
33. ASHTON, *Understanding* (n. 5), p. 340, n. 11 (stress mine). As well as my insis-

Logos as a kind of axiom"? Why is this exegetical stance wrong? The
Prologue (1,1-18) sets the agenda for the Gospel of John[34]. Although the
incarnation of the Logos should not be used as an axiom "from which
everything else derives", it is one of several *fundamental axioms* that
must be used for an understanding of the Johannine Christology. Does
the Johannine understanding of Jesus as the incarnation of the *Logos*
help to understand the Johannine use of the expression ὁ υἱὸς τοῦ
ἀνθρώπου?

A brief overview of the bulk of the thirteen Johannine Son of Man
sayings (1,51; 3,13.14; 5,27; 6,27.53.62; 8,28; 9,35; 12,23.34 [twice];
13,31) suggests that it does, but again certain presuppositions dominate
the debate. Three elements in the Johannine use of ὁ υἱὸς τοῦ ἀνθρώπου strongly influence scholarly discussion: its association with the
verbs ἀναβαίνω and καταβαίνω (1,51; 3,13; 6,62), ὑψόω (3,14; 8,28;
12,32-34) and δοξάζω (12,23; 13,31-32). It is too often *presupposed*
that the Johannine Son of Man is glorified (12,23; 13,31-32) by his
ascent into heaven (1,51; 3,13.14; 8,28; 12,32). The heavenly figure
returns to where he was before (6,62). Thus, the determining feature of
the Johannine Son of Man is his ascent into and his descent from
heaven. What he is able to do as a result of his descent to earth depends
upon the heavenly origins of the Son of Man[35]. But is this necessarily

tence on the use of "the Son of Man" to focus upon Jesus' humanity as the locus for the
revelation of God in history, he rejects the claims of DODD, *Interpretation* (n. 27), p. 244;
PAMMENT, *The Son of Man in the Fourth Gospel* (n. 9), pp. 56-66. Pamment does not
argue for a focus on Jesus' humanity as a locus of revelation. She claims that the Johannine use of "the Son of Man" is not titular, but "as representing not what everyone is, but
what man could and should be" (p. 58). Cf. also WINK, *"The Son of Man" in the Gospel
of John* (n. 9), pp. 117-123, and MATEOS – CAMACHO, *El Hijo del Hombre* (n. 8), pp. 159-
186, 203-205, who make a similar claim. Cf. also LINDARS, *Jesus Son of Man* (n. 8), pp.
145-157; HARE, *The Son of Man Tradition* (n. 8), pp. 79-111, RHEA, *Johannine Son of
Man* (n. 7), cf. esp. pp. 69-71, and HAM, *The Title 'Son of Man'* (n. 9), pp. 67-84. These
scholars are closer to my interpretation of the use of the expression to indicate the revelation of God in the human event of Jesus, rather than a presentation of a "perfect man".
Rhea, however, argues that the title links the Johannine Christology with "the messianic
expectation of the Mosaic-Prophet-Messiah, yet clearly distinguished from it" (*Johannine
Son of Man*, p. 48. Cf. esp. pp. 21-48).

34. Cf. especially C.K. BARRETT, *The Prologue of St John's Gospel*, in *New Testament Essays*, London, SPCK, 1972, pp. 27-48; M. THEOBALD, *Die Fleischwerdung des
Logos: Studien zum Verhältnis des Johannesprologs zum Corpus des Evangeliums und zu
1 Joh* (NTA n.s., 20), Münster, Aschendorff, 1988.

35. Cf., for example, the important work of BÜHNER, *Der Gesandte* (n. 8), pp. 385-
399, 422-429; PAINTER, *Enigmatic* (n. 9), pp. 1877-1880; LOADER, *Christology* (n. 8), pp.
82-92, 107-121; SASSE, *Der Menschensohn im Evangelium nach Johannes* (n. 7). Sasse
rightly claims that there is a coherent Son of Man Christology in the Fourth Gospel, but
insists, on the basis of the ascent-descent schema that "Der Menschensohn selbst ist ein
himmlischen Wesen" (p. 239 and passim). As such Jesus, the Son of Man, is a unique

the case? The only place where both ascent and descent (ἀναβαίνω – καταβαίνω) are associated with the Son of Man is in 3,13, and I will return to that problematic passage in the following section of this study[36]. Ascent is seen as more widespread when one takes the Johannine use of ὑψόω (3,14: ὑψωθῆναι δεῖ; 8,28: ὅταν ὑψώσητε; 12,32: κἀγὼ ἐὰν ὑψωθῶ ἐκ τῆς γῆς) as a reference to the ascension[37]. This is certainly behind the meaning of the expression in Phil 2,9 where, as a result of the κένωσις, Jesus is exalted by God. But the broader context of the Johannine understanding of the death of Jesus[38], and the immediate context of the ὑψόω-sayings themselves, indicate that John uses it differently.

The Johannine use of this verb is one of the several examples of words with "double-meanings" in this Gospel[39]. In this case, the word can mean a physical "lifting up" on a stake, as Moses did with the serpent in the wilderness (Jn 3,13a). But it can also mean "exaltation". For John, Jesus' crucifixion is his exaltation. It is there that he makes God known, reveals the δόξα of God, brings to perfection the task given him by the Father (4,34; 7,4; 19,13), and is himself glorified (13,31-32). For this reason, "they shall gaze upon him whom they have pierced" (19,37)[40]. Proleptically preparing the reader for his unique interpretation of the death of Jesus, John uses ὑψόω to mean a physical lifting up

giver of life. Cf. my review of this study in *JTS* 53 (2002) 210-215. BURKETT, *Son of Man* (n. 7), pp. 38-75, sees the ascent-descent scheme as the unanswered question in Johannine Son of Man debate. He resolves it by claiming that it comes from Pr 30,1-4. BROWN, *Introduction* (n. 8), p. 259, links the Son of man with Jewish Wisdom speculation (and possibly later Gnostic speculation, the Philonic and *Poimandes* portrayals [n. 90]). He summarizes the portrait as: "preexistence with God, coming from heaven into this world, communication of revelation or divine knowledge, offer of spiritual food, producing division or self-judgment when some people accept and other refuse".

36. The ascent-descent motif is also often associated with the Son of Man in 1,51. I will address that possibility below.

37. Cf., among many, PAINTER, *Enigmatic* (n. 9), pp. 1877-1880, 1883-1884; SASSE, *Der Menschensohn* (n. 7), pp. 79-156; BROWN, *Introduction* (n. 8), pp. 255-256.

38. On this, cf. F.J. MOLONEY, *Telling God's Story: The Fourth Gospel*, in A.A. DAS – F.J. MATERA (eds.), *The Forgotten God. Perspectives in Biblical Theology. Essays in Honor of Paul J. Achtemeier on the Occasion of his Seventy-Fifth Birthday*, Louisville, KY, Westminster John Knox Press, 2002, pp. 107-122.

39. On the significance of these "double meanings," cf. O. CULLMANN, *Der johanneische Gebrauch doppeldeutiger Ausdrücke als Schlüssel zum Verständnis des 4. Evangeliums*, in *TZ* 4 (1948) 360-372; R. BULTMANN, *The Gospel of John. A Commentary*, trans. G.R. Beasley-Murray, Oxford, Blackwell, 1971, p. 127 n. 1; R.A. CULPEPPER, *Anatomy of the Fourth Gospel. A Study in Literary Design* (Foundations and Facets: New Testament), Philadelphia, PA, Fortress, 1983, pp. 152-165.

40. For a full development of this interpretation of the Johannine passion narrative, cf. F.J. MOLONEY, *The Johannine Passion and the Christian Community*, in *Salesianum* 57 (1995) 25-61; ID., *Glory not Dishonor* (n. 21), pp. 127-152.

which is, at one and the same time, Jesus' moment of exaltation. Unlike Phil 2,9 where the ὕψωσις is the result (διὸ καί) of Jesus' death on the cross (v. 8c), for John, Jesus' ὕψωσις takes place on the cross. In 3,14 Jesus insists that just as (καθώς) Moses lifted up the serpent, so also (οὕτως) the Son of Man must be lifted up. There is no suggestion, either in Numbers 21,19 or in Jn 3,14, that the serpent detached itself from the stake and ascended into heaven. Interestingly, Gnostic reflection does have the snake ascend, but this is a fantastic speculation upon the Johannine text (!)[41]. The close parallel drawn in the text between the "lifting up" of the serpent on a spear, and the "lifting up" of the Son of Man must be respected. The final ὑψόω-text in the Johannine narrative appears in 12,32: "And I, when I am lifted up from the earth, I will draw everyone to myself". In a "footnote" to this passage, the Evangelist explains what he means by the use of "lifting up from the earth": "He said this to show by what death he was to die (ποίῳ θανάτῳ ἤμελλεν ἀποθνῄσκειν)". If the best interpreter of the Johannine text is the Johannine text itself, credence must be given to these "footnotes" added to the text by the author[42]. Jesus' being lifted up is explained as the means by which he was to die: crucifixion (cf. also 18,32)[43].

This leaves only 8,28: ὅταν ὑψώσητε τὸν υἱὸν τοῦ ἀνθρώπου, τότε γνώσεσθε ὅτι ἐγώ εἰμι. This passage occurs within the context of Jesus' bitter conflict with "the Jews" at the Feast of Tabernacles (7,1–10,21). Jesus tells "the Jews" that they are to "lift up" the Son of Man. Does this mean they will crucify him, or send him upwards in his ascent into heaven? It could be argued that Jesus is ironically informing them that they will be responsible for his ascension[44], but in the light of 3,14 and 12,32-33, and the context of anger and the desire of "the Jews" to eliminate Jesus (cf. 7,32.45; 8,20.59), Jesus is informing "the Jews" that his being "lifted up" in crucifixion will be a climactic revelation of God (τότε γνώσεσθε ὅτι ἐγώ εἰμι). The Johannine use of ὑψόω should not be associated with ascension. It is a crucial part of the Gospel's theolog-

---

41. Cf. Hippolytus, *Ref.* V.12,1-17,13, esp. V.12,6-12;16,4-6. These texts can be found in W. FOERSTER – R.MCL. WILSON (eds.), *Gnosis. A Selection of Gnostic Texts*, 2 volumes, Oxford, University Press, 1972, vol. I, pp. 284-292.

42. I am borrowing the expression "footnote" from M.C. TENNEY, *The Footnotes of John's Gospel*, in *Bibliotheca Sacra* 117 (1960) 350-364. Cf. also, the excellent survey of these "footnotes" by G. VAN BELLE, *Les parenthèses johanniques. Un premier bilan*, in VAN SEGBROECK – VAN BELLE – VERHEYDEN (eds.), *The Four Gospels 1992* (n. 9), vol. III, pp. 1901-1033.

43. Cf. also LINDARS, *Jesus Son of Man* (n. 8), pp. 145-147.

44. As is argued, for example, by PAINTER, *Enigmatic* (n. 9), pp. 1883-1884. I regard such readings as something of a desperate measure to defend the indefensible. They do not allow John to be John.

ical understanding of the death of Jesus as a physical "lifting up" that is also his "exaltation"[45].

The enigmatic promise made by Jesus to the first disciples in 1,51 is also drawn into the ascent-descent motif. As always, much depends upon one's presuppositions in the interpretation of this passage. It has long been regarded as a strange intrusion into a series of initial confessions of faith, climaxing in the words of Nathanael to Jesus in 1,49. The problem is resolved by claiming that vv. 50-51 do not belong to this context, and that originally Nathanael's confession led directly into 2,1-11[46]. More convincing, however, has been the synchronic reading of 1,19–2,11 as a Christian re-reading, on the basis of Ex 19,7-19 and the midrashic commentary on Exodus 19 in the Mekilta de Rabbi Ishmael, of the celebration of the Sinaitic gift of the δόξα of the Law at Pentecost. The four "days" of preparation (Jn 1,19-51) lead to the gift of the δόξα at Cana (2,11; cf. LXX Ex 19,11 [twice].15.16: τῇ ἡμέρᾳ τῇ τρίτῃ)[47]. This reading respects both the possible world behind the text that produced 1,19–2,11 (diachrony), and the present literary unity of the text as we have it, once the traditions have been placed side by side (synchrony)[48].

Once the overall context of revelation is established, via the link with the background of Pentecost and the gift of the δόξα at Sinai, 1,51 is a promise of the revelation of the heavenly. Following a Jewish tradition that shifted the ascent and the descent of the angels in Gn 28,12 from the ladder to Jacob[49], the apocalyptic opening of the heavens promises the revelation of God, and the ascent and descent of the angels upon (ἐπί)

45. This was conclusively argued many years ago by W. THÜSING, *Die Erhöhung und Verherrlichung Jesu im Johannesevangelium* (NTA, 21/1-2), Münster, Aschendorff, [2]1970. I have yet to see Thüsing's case systematically dismantled by those who argue that the "lifting up" means the ascension.

46. Cf., for example, M.-É. BOISMARD, *Du Baptême à Cana (Jean 1,19–2,11)*, Paris, Cerf, 1956, p. 105; R.E. BROWN, *The Gospel According to John* (AncB, 29.29a), 2 volumes, Garden City, NY, Doubleday, 1966-70, vol. I, p. 88; SCHNACKENBURG, *John* (n. 9), vol. I, p. 320; R.T. FORTNA, *The Gospel of Signs. A Reconstruction of the Narrative Source Underlying the Fourth Gospel* (SNTS MS, 11), Cambridge, Cambridge University Press, 1970, pp. 179-189. Most recently, cf. PAINTER, *Enigmatic* (n. 9), p. 1873.

47. Cf. J. POTIN, *La fête juive de la Pentecôte* (LD, 65), 2 volumes, Paris, Cerf, 1971, vol. I, pp. 46-70 (for the midrishic and other targumic texts, cf. vol. II, pp. 7-32); MOLONEY, *Belief in the Word* (n. 26), pp. 53-60.

48. Cf. BLANK, *Krisis* (n. 25), p. 26. This position, limiting the lifting up and glorification of the Son of Man to the human experience of Jesus, detaching it from his ascension and return to glory, is rejected by many. Cf. especially LOADER, *Central Structure* (n. 9), pp. 197-200; ID., *Christology* (n. 8), pp. 82-85, 107-121.

49. Very influential for this suggestion is the work of H. ODEBERG, *The Fourth Gospel: Interpreted in Its Relation to Contemporaneous Religious Currents in Palestine and the Hellenistic-Oriental World*, Uppsala, Almqvist, 1929, pp. 33-42. Cf. MOLONEY, *Son of Man* (n. 1), pp. 26-28.

the Son of Man indicates that this revelation will be seen (cf. v. 50: ὄψῃ v. 51: ὄψεσθε). The Son of Man is firmly upon earth, and the angels ascend and descend upon him, communicating the revelation of the heavenly[50]. It is thus not legitimate to claim 1,51 as a passage that associates the ascent-descent motif with the Son of Man.

Nor is it legitimate to associate the ὑψόω-sayings with that motif, via a reference to Jesus' ascension. Thus 1,51; 3,14; 8,28 and 12,32 should be removed from any discussion of the ascent-descent of the Son of Man. The following sayings do not call for a "heavenly" interpretation: 5,27 (the Son of Man as judge), 6,27 (the Son of Man who will give a food that will not perish), 6,53 (the gift of the Son of Man, his flesh and blood), 9,35 (belief in the Son of Man), and 12,34 (the query from the crowd concerning the death of the Son of Man)[51]. We must investigate the one saying that refers to the ascent and descent of the Son of Man (3,13), the further saying that asks about his possible ascent (6,62), and the sayings that speak of the glorification of the Son of Man (12,23;

50. Cf. also WINK, "The Son of Man" in the Gospel of John (n. 9), pp. 118-119. BÜHNER, Der Gesandte (n. 8), pp. 391-392, and PAINTER, Enigmatic (n. 9), pp. 1873-1877, reject this suggestion. Before Painter can do this, he makes some crucial diachronic decisions. In the first place, he disassociates 1,51 from its context, claiming that it is a fragment of a Son of Man Christology that never becomes a coherent whole within the Fourth Gospel. Secondly, he rejects the widely accepted link between the ascent and the descent of the angels upon the Son of Man with the parallel experience of Jacob in Gn 28,12, as interpreted in Jewish tradition. For Painter, 1,51 speaks of an enthroned heavenly Son of Man toward whom the angels move (cf. also BÜHNER, Der Gesandte [n. 8], p. 392). Painter argues that, against the Synagogue, this fragment from a Son of Man Christology affirms the heavenly origin of Jesus (cf. p. 1877). HARE, The Son of Man Tradition (n. 8), pp. 82-85, also questions Odeberg's use of Jewish midrashic interpretations, and asks what is meant by the ἐπί in this passage. However, he concludes: "This passage speaks of something that happens in connection with the earthly life of Jesus" (p. 84). PAINTER, Enigmatic (n. 9), p. 1873-1875, points to the lack of "fulfillment" for the promise of 1,51 in the earthly sphere. Although overstated (i.e. the Gospel is a midrash on 1,51), SMALLEY, Johannes 1,51 und die Einleitung zum vierten Evangelium (n. 9), pp. 300-313, correctly points to the life, teaching, death and resurrection as the fulfillment of 1,51. Cf. MOLONEY, A Johannine Son of Man Discussion? (n. 10), pp. 94-95.

51. In 12,34, the crowd rightly interprets Jesus' words on his being "lifted up" as a reference to his death, and object that this is impossible, as they know that the Messiah would live forever. On this, cf. W.C. VAN UNNIK, The Quotation from the Old Testament in John 12,34, in NT 3 (1959) 174-179, and the discussion in M.J.J. MENKEN, Old Testament Quotations in the Fourth Gospel. Studies in Textual Form (CBET, 15), Kampen, Kok Pharos, 1996, p. 17, n. 20. For RHEA, Johannine Son of Man (n. 7), pp. 11-48, the expression does not have any apocalyptic associations. The link between 5,27 and 5,28-29 make this hard to maintain. For another attempt to disassociate 5,27 from Dan 7,13, cf. HARE, The Son of Man Tradition (n. 8), pp. 90-96. Rhea and Hare are correct, however, in their attempt to free the Johannine Son of Man from an association with an apocalyptic figure who will come from heaven. However, for the danielic background to 5,27, cf., among many, MOLONEY, Son of Man (n. 1), pp. 77-86; ASHTON, Understanding (n. 5), pp. 357-363.

13,31-32). But at this stage of our revisiting the question of the Johannine Son of Man, it appears that 1,51; 3,14; 5,27; 6,27.53; 8,28; 9,35; and 12,34 (twice) refer to the human figure of Jesus. Nine of the thirteen Johannine Son of Man sayings can be interpreted as associated with the earthly activity of Jesus: the one in whom a lasting revelation takes place (1,51; 6,27), when he is lifted up on a cross (3,14; 6,53; 8,28; 12,34). Readers are summoned to belief in this revelation (9,35), and judgment flows from its acceptance or rejection (5,27)[52]. If this is the case, is it not helpful "to take the Christology of the incarnate Logos as a kind of axiom" in the interpretation of the Johannine Son of Man[53]? However, we must not rush to conclusions. The ascent and descent of the Son of Man in 3,13, the ascent of the Son of Man in 6,62, and the glorification of the Son of Man in 12,23 and 13,31 call for attention. Only when they have been located within a possible Johannine Son of Man Christology can one draw conclusions. One must evaluate all the data[54].

II. JOHN 3,13 AND 6,62

In 1976, arguing strenuously against any suggestion that the Johannine Son of Man was a heavenly figure, I read 3,13 (καὶ οὐδεὶς ἀναβέβηκεν εἰς τὸν οὐρανὸν εἰ μὴ ὁ ἐκ τοῦ οὐρανοῦ καταβάς, ὁ υἱὸς τοῦ ἀνθρώπου) as a strong negation of any ascent (οὐδείς), and an affirmation of the Son of Man's descent from heaven. I claimed that v. 13a was a polemic against Jewish speculation that revealers, from Moses onward, had ascended into heaven; not one of them had ascended into heaven. Rendering εἰ μή as "but", I claimed that v. 13b affirmed

---

52. I say "readers" because the Gospel was not written to tell of the experience of "the Jews" (5,27) or the man born blind (9,35). The positioning of the prologue (1,1-18) and the conclusion (20,30-31) indicate that the author tells his story for his readers. On this, cf. F.J. MOLONEY, *The Gospel of John and Evangelization*, in *Josephinum Journal of Theology* 10 (2003) 19-32.

53. Cf. ASHTON, *Understanding* (n. 5), p. 340, n. 11. In support of the use of Son of Man as a reflection of the Johannine incarnational theology, cf. HARE, *The Son of Man Tradition* (n. 8), pp. 79-82, 111.

54. The most serious weakness of SASSE, *Der Menschensohn* (n. 7), is his focus upon those texts that suit his argument, namely 3,13; 6,27 and 6,53. Cf. above, n. 13, where I level the same objection against the work of Bühner, whose focus was 1,51; 3,13 and 5,27. The same could also be said of Ashton, who depends upon Bühner, but bases his work on 1,51; 3,13; 5,27, and then surveys 3,14; 8,28 and 12,32 in the light of his conclusions concerning 1,51; 3,13 and 5,27. This is not the case for Painter, who argues that there is no Johannine Son of Man Christology, but surveys all the Johannine Son of Man sayings to show that they reflect a fragmentary use of older traditions.

that the only revealer was someone who had come down from heaven, the Son of Man. In sum, my interpretation of 3,13 produced the paraphrase: "There is no one who has ascended, but, contrary to the fact of the protasis, one has descended, the Son of Man"[55]. As has been often pointed out, in both reviews and discussions of my work, "this solution places an unbearable strain on the Greek"[56]. Caught up in intense focus generated by the exercise of writing a doctoral dissertation, I leant on the authority of some celebrated grammarians, translators and Johannine scholars who had made this case[57]. But indeed, this solution places an unbearable strain on the Greek[58].

One must look further into the story of the Gospel and the ancient world that produced this text for a more satisfactory explanation of the use of the ascent and descent theme in v. 13. The evidence pointing to a Jewish myth of the ascent of the great revealers, especially Moses but claimed for other important figures in Israel's relationship with God, remains the general background for v. 13a[59]. The link between ascent and descent into and from heaven is a *topos* found across the ancient world, clearly present in Dt 30,11-12 and Pr 30,4, possibly also forming intertext for Sir 1,3.8; Pr 25,2-3 and Wis 9,16-18[60]. "The main purpose

---

55. MOLONEY, *Son of Man* (n. 1), pp. 54-57. In the appendix added to the second edition of this work, I strongly defended my original position in the face of the rejection of this interpretation by many of my reviewers. Cf. *ibid.*, pp. 244-245.

56. ASHTON, *Understanding* (n. 5), p. 350.

57. For example, P. JOÜON, *L'évangile de Notre-Seigneur Jésus-Christ. Traduction et commentaire du texte original grec, compte tenu du substrat sémitique* (Verbum Salutis, 5), Paris, Beauchesne, 1930, p. 473; R. KNOX, *A New Testament Commentary for English Readers*, 2 volumes, London, Burns, Oates & Washbourne, 1955, vol. I, p. 209; RUCKSTUHL, *Abstieg und Erhöhung des johanneischen Menschensohns"* (n. 9), pp. 314-341, esp. p. 325.

58. I am not shifting from my original position easily, as it remains true that εἰ μή can mean "but", and not only "except". Cf., for example, Gal 1,19. Does Paul see none of the ἀπόστολοι, *but* (εἰ μή) James, the brother of the Lord (excluding James from the ἀπόστολοι)? Or does he see none of them *except* (εἰ μή) James (including James among the ἀπόστολοι)? Cf. *BDAG*, p. 278, s.v. εἰ, para. 6, i, α-β. In support of my original position, calling upon the authority of Moule and Sidebottom, as well as Ruckstuhl and myself, cf. HARE, *The Son of Man Tradition* (n. 8), pp. 85-88.

59. Cf. BORGEN, *Some Jewish Exegetical Traditions as Background for the Son of Man Sayings in John's Gospel* (n. 9), pp. 243-258; BÜHNER, *Der Gesandte* (n. 8), pp. 374-385. Cf. also ASHTON, *Understanding* (n. 5), pp. 349-354. Ashton concludes on pp. 353-354: "The belligerent assertion that no one has ascended to heaven except Jesus finds a satisfactory *Sitz-im-Leben*, then, in a polemic against counter claims of unique privilege made on behalf of Moses by more 'orthodox' or conservative groups within the synagogue". He refers to 9,28: "You are his disciples, we are disciples of Moses".

60. Cf. the extensive collection of this material from Mesopotamia, and various renditions of the Old Babylonian myths, in R.C. VAN LEEUWEN, *The Background to Proverbs 30:4a*, in M.L. BARRÉ (ed.), *Wisdom, You Are My Sister. Studies in Honor of Roland E. Murphy, O. Carm., on the Occasion of His Eightieth Birthday* (CBQ MS, 29), Washing-

of the *topos* is to reaffirm the great gulf that separates humans from the divine realm and the prerogatives of deity, such as immortality, super-human knowledge, wisdom, and power"[61]. For the author of the Fourth Gospel, Jesus of Nazareth is the unique revealer of God. No other figure in human history can claim to have ascended and descended to plumb the depths of the heavenly, but the Son of Man.

Jn 3,13 is not about pre-existence or post-existence. One does not have to worry about its relationship with the reference to Jesus' ascent to the Father in 20,17[62], because there is none. The words of Jesus use a widespread literary topos to insist upon his uniqueness as the revelation of the heavenly. The first person singular ("I") is replaced by the expression "the Son of Man", as in all Gospel traditions[63]. A promise, also using the expression "the Son of Man", was made to the first dis-ciples in 1,51. That promise has now been further articulated in a state-ment of the same truth in 3,13, utilizing a traditional topos to indicate the uniqueness of the Son of Man. Only Jesus, the Son of Man, can claim to have plumbed the mysteries of the heavenly and to have made them known. Of course, this claim can only make sense because, for the reader, he has come from heaven (1,1-18). The reader is aware of Jesus' "superhuman knowledge, wisdom, and power"[64]. What is perhaps more important for the Johannine Son of Man Christology, however, is the statement that follows immediately: "For just as Moses lifted up the serpent in the wilderness, so also must the Son of Man also be lifted up, so that whoever believes in him may have eternal life" (3,14-15). As we have already seen, this statement, following hard on the heels of v. 13,

ton, DC, The Catholic Biblical Association of America, 1997, pp. 102-121. As has been mentioned, for BURKETT, *Son of Man* (n. 7), the Johannine Son of Man, and its associa-tion with the ascent-descent myth, has its roots in Pr 30,1-4 (cf. above, n. 12). Burkett also suggests that this background might explain the historical Jesus' use of "the Son of Man" (pp. 177-178).

61. VAN LEEUWEN, *The Background* (n. 60), p. 121.

62. Cf. ASHTON, *Understanding* (n. 5), p. 356, with reference to Bultmann, Barrett, Schnackenburg and Brown.

63. On Jesus as the "speaker" in Jn 3,11-21, cf. the discussion in MOLONEY, *Son of Man* (n. 1), pp. 42-46.

64. VAN LEEUWEN, *The Background* (n. 60), p. 121. On the basis of my hermeneutic, there is no point insisting that one cannot use the teaching of 1,1-18 to explain Jesus' use of the Son of Man because it was formed later in the tradition (cf., for example, ASHTON, *Understanding* [n. 5], p. 353, n. 51; PAINTER, *Enigmatic* [n. 9], p. 1879, n. 46). The reader reads 1,1-18 *first*, and then arrives at 1,51, and subsequently 3,13-14. I am not question-ing the importance of the work of scholars who, like Bühner, Ashton and Painter, strive to locate the *history* of the traditions. I am attempting to perform another necessary task. However late or early these elements were formulated in the Johannine tradition is of no relevance in determining the Christology of the *Johannine narrative*.

insists that Jesus, the Son of Man, must be physically lifted up on a cross and there be exalted. Any one who believes that this moment of crucifixion/exaltation is the revelation of God will have eternal life. Together, vv. 13-14 make two closely related affirmations: Jesus is the unique revealer of the heavenly (v. 13; cf. 1,51), and that life-giving revelation takes place, enigmatically, on the cross (v. 14)[65]. Only a human being can be crucified, and the use of ὁ υἱὸς τοῦ ἀνθρώπου in both v. 13 and v. 14 insists that the human Jesus, who came from heaven (cf. 1,1-18), is the unique revelation of God among women and men, and that this revelation can be seen in the crucified one: "They shall gaze upon him (revelation) whom they have pierced (crucifixion)" (19,37)[66].

My interpretation of 6,62 has also generated agreement, disagreement and healthy criticism. This is a difficult verse, made so as it only offers the protasis of a rhetorical question: ἐὰν οὖν θεωρῆτε τὸν υἱὸν τοῦ ἀνθρώπου ἀναβαίνοντα ὅπου ἦν τὸ πρότερον; Typically, the suppression of the apodosis, as here, and not the protasis, amounts to an aposiopesis. This is the case with protases in the first, second or third class conditions[67]. Robertson writes, "Aposiopesis stands to itself since it is a conscious suppression of part of a sentence under the influence of strong emotion like anger, fear or pity"[68]. There is little unanimity among the commentators regarding what exactly is being communicated by this ellipsis. Some suggest that if the Son of Man were to ascend to where he was before, the difficulty of the disciples would increase. Others argue the opposite: the ascent of the Son of Man would remove the offense of his words[69]. I suggested in 1976 that if more attention were given to the immediate context, and the background provided by 3,13 and 1,18, further nuances emerge.

65. Cf. LINDARS, *Jesus Son of Man* (n. 8), pp. 147-150, 150-151; HARE, *The Son of Man Tradition* (n. 8), pp. 88-90.
66. Cf. also 8,28: "When you have lifted up (ὑψώσητε) the Son of Man (crucifixion), then you will know that I am he (γνώσεσθε ὅτι ἐγώ εἰμι: revelation). Cf. MOLONEY, *A Johannine Son of Man Discussion?* (n. 10), pp. 98-99.
67. In 6,62 we have a third class condition, which generally indicates a condition of uncertainty of fulfillment, but still likely. Cf. D.B. WALLACE, *Greek Grammar Beyond the Basics. An Exegetical Syntax of the New Testament*, Grand Rapids, MI, Zondervan, 1996, pp. 696-697.
68. A.T. ROBERTSON, *A Grammar of the Greek New Testament in the Light of Historical Research*, New York, Hodder & Stoughton, ⁴1923, p. 1203. Cf. also BDF, p. 255, par. 482: "Aposiopesis in the strict sense, i.e. a breaking off of speech due to strong emotion or to modesty is unknown in the NT. On the other hand, aposiopesis takes the form of the omission of the apodosis to a conditional subordinated clause (protasis)". Both Robertson and BDF give 6,62 as an example.
69. For a survey of the discussion, cf. MOLONEY, *Son of Man* (n. 1), pp. 120-121.

In the immediate context, disciples are finding the words of Jesus, the teaching of 6,25-58, a hard saying (v. 60: σκληρός ἐστιν ὁ λόγος οὗτος). Aware of this offense, Jesus asks the unfinished rhetorical question of v. 62. The words of Jesus in v. 63 pick up a central Johannine theme: judging in a "fleshly" way, i.e., by mere appearances (cf. 8,15: κατὰ τὴν σάρκα κρίνετε cf. also 7,24: μὴ κρίνετε κατ' ὄψιν), is of no avail. Jesus' words are spirit and life, and as such they give life. The background to the rhetorical question of 6,62 is the same as 3,13a[70]. Jesus' words in vv. 61-63 are something of a rebuke. He realizes that the disciples are complaining and offended by what he has said, and he sets about challenging their attitude. With some emotion (generated by the aposiopesis), he asks his disciples if they would like him to fulfill their expectations of a heavenly revealer. Would they be satisfied if the Son of Man, the human being who is with them, speaking these life-giving words, were to ascend into heaven, as Moses and other revealers had done, according to some traditions? "What if you saw the Son of Man ascend to where he was before? Would you still be offended by the things I am saying?" The suggestion is that an ascent would serve as a guarantee to them that the words they found hard to accept were the words of a revealer. I agree with those commentators who claim that the absent apodosis would suggest that the offense is removed[71]. But, at least for the reader, there is no reason for Jesus to respond to these unexpressed desires. He points this out to his disciples in his thinly veiled accusation in v. 63: they are too superficial. They are judging Jesus according to appearances, asking that he ascend to validate the authenticity of his words. They are thus not open to the words of vv. 25-58, words that are spirit and life[72].

The background to the difficult half-uttered rhetorical question is much the same as 3,13: the ascent and descent of a revealer. The point of Jesus' terse and perhaps emotional question, however, is contained in

70. In my opinion, it is also behind the strong negative Θεὸν οὐδεὶς ἑώρακεν πώποτε of 1,18. Cf. MOLONEY, John (n. 26), p. 46.

71. Cf., for example, W. BAUER, Das Johannesevangelium erklärt (HNT, 6), Tübingen, Mohr (Paul Siebeck), ³1933, p. 101; M.-J. LAGRANGE, Évangile selon Saint Jean (ÉB), Paris, Gabalda, 1936, p. 187; E.C. HOSKYNS, The Fourth Gospel, ed. F.N. DAVEY, London, Faber & Faber, 1947, p. 300; R.H. LIGHTFOOT, St John's Gospel, ed. C.F. EVANS, Oxford, University Press, 1956, p. 169.

72. This is not the place to enter into the issue, raised originally by G. BORNKAMM, Die eucharistische Rede im Johannesevangelium, in ZNW 47 (1956) 161-169, of the apparent contradiction between the positive use of σάρξ in 6,51c-58 and the negative use of the same word in v. 63. In the end, as the prologue makes clear (cf. v. 14), it depends upon whose σάρξ is being discussed. The σάρξ of Jesus is always positive (1,14; 6,51c-58), while any other σάρξ can lead to superficial judgment (6,63; 8,15; cf. 7,24).

his indication to the disciples that he comes from above. He asks them if they would like "the Son of Man" to ascend "to where he was before (ὅπου ἦν τὸ πρότερον)". For the Fourth Evangelist, there is no reason for Jesus to ascend, as other revealers are acclaimed as having done. He comes from above. He has been there before, and it is this that gives authority to his words as spirit and life (v. 63). Again, as with 3,13, the information provided for the reader in the prologue (1,1-18) lies behind the question that Jesus poses to the disciples. The question of 6,62 is not about the ascension of the Son of Man, but the rejection of any such possibility. The earthly Son of Man has no need to ascend into heaven; he has been there before, and he comes from there[73].

There can be no sidestepping the fact that 3,13 and 6,62 are very difficult texts, nor that my reading of those texts in 1976 and 1978 called for more nuance and care. However, in terms of the narrative Christology developed by John, they do not demand that the Johannine Son of Man be regarded as a heavenly figure who has come to earth, and who will return to heaven again. I am not suggesting that an interpretation of 3,13 along those lines is impossible. However, the impression created by the cumulative experience of the reading process, from 1,51 to 3,13, read side by side with 3,14 and its reference to the crucifixion, suggests that in 3,13 Jesus teaches that the Son of Man is the unique revelation the heavenly among women and men. If one adds the further cumulative reading experience of 6,27.53; 8,28; 9,35; 12,32-34, each within its own literary and narrative context, that impression is strengthened[74]. It is not entirely true that I am taking this position because I regard "the Christology of the incarnate Logos as a kind of axiom"[75]. The relationship between the prologue and the story is bi-directional. This relationship has been best expressed by C.K. Barrett: "[T]he Prologue is necessary

73. In a conversation at Cambridge, England, in 1978, C.F.D. Moule told me that he was supportive of my reading of the Johannine Son of Man, but wondered whether the οὖν in 6,62 could bear the adversative meaning that I was giving it. However, cf. the discussion of a possible "slightly adversarial sense" in *BDAG*, p. 737, s.v. οὖν, para. 4. I am grateful to my doctoral student, Christopher Skinner, with whom I have discussed this difficult verse. His comments, both written and oral, have been most helpful.

74. Cf. above, section I of this study. Given the limitations of this article, it is impossible to develop the consequences of the primary claim, that the Son of Man is used to express Johannine belief in the revelation of God in the human event of Jesus. Unlike the traditions of Moses, this revelation will provide a nourishment that will endure forever (6,27), in the event of the cross (6,53; 8,28; 12,32-34). The reader is called to believe in this revelation (9,35), and judgment flows from its acceptance or refusal (5,27). The associated themes of the revelation that takes place on the cross and the subsequent judgment is also present in the association of "the Son of Man" with the two ἐγώ εἰμι-sayings in 8,21-30 (cf. vv. 24, 28).

75. ASHTON, *Understanding* (n. 5), p. 340, n. 11.

to the Gospel as the Gospel is necessary to the Prologue. The history explicates the theology, and the theology interprets the history"[76]. Or, as the same scholar says elsewhere, commenting on Jn 1,1: "The deeds and words of Jesus are the deeds and words of God; if this be not true, the book is blasphemous"[77].

III. GLORY AND GLORIFICATION

Two Son of Man sayings are associated with glorification. On hearing of the arrival of the Greeks in 12,22, Jesus solemnly announces: ἐλήλυθεν ἡ ὥρα ἵνα δοξασθῇ ὁ υἱὸς τοῦ ἀνθρώπου (v. 23). As Judas leaves the upper room to betray Jesus, it was night (13,30). "When he had gone out (v. 31a: Ὅτε οὖν ἐξῆλθεν), Jesus announces: νῦν ἐδοξάσθη ὁ υἱὸς τοῦ ἀνθρώπου καὶ ὁ θεὸς ἐδοξάσθη ἐν αὐτῷ (v. 31bc). There is a similarity between these sayings. Do they refer to the final glorification of the Son, in his return to the place where he was before the world was made (cf. 17,1.5)? If there is no distinction between the Johannine use of "the Son of Man" and "the Son (of God)" language, then this is a logical and justifiable conclusion. However, the immediate contexts, and the broader context of the Gospel story itself, suggest that the glorification referred to in 12,23 and 13,31 points forward to Jesus' ὕψωσις on the cross.

On three earlier occasions in the narrative, an explanation from the narrator mentions Jesus' glorification[78]. In 2,22, after Jesus offers the sign of his death and resurrection as proof of his authority in the Temple (2,17-21), the narrator comments: "When therefore he was raised from the dead, his disciples remembered that he had said this" (v. 22). The death and resurrection of Jesus generate right memory and belief among the disciples. Another important text that looks forward to Jesus' glorification is a further comment from the narrator in 7,39. Explaining the gift of rivers of living water (7,37-38)[79], he adds: "Now this he said about the Spirit, which those who believed in him were to receive; for as yet

76. BARRETT, *The Prologue of St John's Gospel* (n. 9), p. 48.
77. C.K. BARRETT, *The Gospel According to St. John*, London, SPCK, ²1978, p. 156.
78. As in any narrative, the comments made by the storyteller to directly address the reader are the clearest indications of the storyteller's point of view. Here we have an insight into what John means by the "glorification" of Jesus.
79. Much scholarly discussion surrounds 7,37-38. The exegete must resolve serious textual problems associated with the punctuation of the passage, the "Scripture" referred to, as well as the interpretation. For a summary of the discussion, and my own view (the water flows from Jesus, not from the believer), cf. MOLONEY, *Signs and Shadows* (n. 21), pp. 84-88.

the Spirit had not yet been given, because Jesus was not yet glorified (οὐδέπω ἐδοξάσθη)" (7,39). There is to be a time in the future when Jesus will be glorified and the Spirit will be given. The theme of Jesus as king, important to the Johannine passion narrative (cf. esp. 18,28–19,16a; 19,16b-37), appears in the narrative in Jn 12,12-19, especially in the quotation of Zech 9,9 (12,15). But Jesus will exercise his kingship on the cross, and not in glorious acclamation. This is the point of Jesus' initiative in finding an ass and mounting it for his entry into Jerusalem[80]. The narrator enters the story, clarifying the actions of Jesus, and commenting upon the understanding of the disciples. He remarks: "His disciples did not understand this at first; but when Jesus was glorified (ὅτε ἐδοξάσθη), they remembered that this had been written of him, and had been done to him (καὶ ταῦτα ἐποίησαν αὐτῷ)". Something is "done" to Jesus that is to be identified with his glorification. We have already seen that Jesus' ὕψωσις takes place on the cross (3,14; 8,28; 12,32-33). Is it possible that these three indications from the narrator also look forward to the cross, when something will be "done" to Jesus (12,16)?

The solution to that question lies in the gift of the Spirit, linked with the glorification of Jesus in 7,39. This passage looks back to the right remembering and believing of the disciples in 2,22 after Jesus' death and resurrection, and forward to the same experience, after Jesus is glorified, in 12,16. The gift of the Spirit at Jesus' glorification will enable ignorant disciples to remember Jesus' words and understand the Scriptures. There is a link between the death and resurrection of Jesus and the glorification. Most scholars look to 20,22 as the fulfillment of 7,39. But an earlier gift of the Spirit is found in 19,30. On the cross Jesus has been declared as king (19,17-22), a symbol of his intimate possession that will not be torn apart has been offered (vv. 23-25a), and he has instituted a new family in the Beloved Disciple and his Mother (vv. 25b-27). Jesus knows that everything is now finished (v. 28a: πάντα τετέλεσται), the Scriptures have been fulfilled (v. 28b: τελειωθῇ). After receiving the vinegar (v. 29), he declares: τετέλεσται (v. 30a). The steady use of the related verbs τελειόω and τελέω make it clear that Jesus has brought to a perfect end the task that the Father gave him (cf. 4,34: τελειώσω αὐτοῦ τὸ ἔργον; 13,1: εἰς τέλος; 17,4: τὸ ἔργον τελειώσας)[81]. His

80. For more detail in support of this interpretation, cf. MOLONEY, *Signs and Shadows* (n. 21), pp. 184-185.

81. This is another example of John's tendency to use different verbs to say the same thing, for the sake of stylistic variety (e.g. ἀποστέλλω/πέμπω; ἀγαπάω/φιλέω). For an overview of this issue, and an argument that subtle distinctions are often present, cf. K.L.

final action is described in v. 30b: καὶ κλίνας τὴν κεφαλὴν παρέδωκεν τὸ πνεῦμα. Despite the widespread interpretation of these words as
a euphemism for death (e.g. "gave up his spirit" [RSV]), that is not what
the Greek says. The passage must be translated: "he gave down (παρέδωκεν) the Spirit (τὸ πνεῦμα)". For the Fourth Gospel, the gift of the
Spirit does not take place at Pentecost, but at the cross, at "the hour" of
Jesus (cf. v. 27: ἀπ᾽ ἐκείνης τῆς ὥρας). A consequence of Jesus' bringing to a perfect end all that the Father gave him to do is to pour the Spirit
down upon the infant Church, symbolized by the Beloved Disciple and
his Mother at the foot of the cross[82].

The death of Jesus is the moment of glorification anticipated by his
words in 12,23, announcing the hour of the glorification of the Son of
Man. It will be the time and the place where sheep not of this fold will
be gathered to the good shepherd (10,16), the scattered children of God
will be gathered (11,52), the grain of wheat will fall and die, so that it
might bear much fruit (12,24). On the cross the Son of Man will be lifted
up (3,14; 8,28), to gather everyone to himself (12,32). "The hour" of
Jesus, long described by Jesus and by the narrator as "not yet" (2,5;
7,30; 8,20), has now come. As "the Jews" complain, "The world has
gone after him" (11,19), Greeks come to Jesus, who is present in
Jerusalem at the time of the Passover (cf. 11,55; 12,1.12). He turns
toward his death and declares that "the hour has come" (ἐλήλυθεν ἡ
ὥρα) for the Son of Man to be glorified (v. 23).

The first words of 13,31, the continuation of v. 30 that dramatically
reports Judas' departure in to the night, are generally overlooked:
"When he had gone out" (v. 31a). This temporal link between the departure of the betrayer and Jesus words in v. 31 is a first hint that the glorification of the Son of Man (v. 31b) is to be associated with his death.
Reading 13,31-32 as part of the conclusion to the literary unit of
13,1-38, and not as the opening words of the first discourse (i.e.
13,31–14,31), heightens this association[83]. There can be no gainsaying

McKay, *Style and Significance in the Language of John 21:15-17*, in *NT* 27 (1985) 319-
333.

82. This interpretation of Jesus' death, although not universally accepted, has been
argued by others. For a detailed study of the passage, and full reference to the scholarly
discussions surrounding this moment in the Johannine narrative, cf. Moloney, *Glory not
Dishonor* (n. 21), pp. 142-150. On the two gifts of the Spirit, the first in 19,30 (founda-
tional) and the second in 20,22 (commission), unified by their taking place in "the hour"
of Jesus, cf. Moloney, *John* (n. 26), pp. 531-532.

83. Most scholars disassociate vv. 31-38 from 13,1-30, and read 13,31–14,31 as the
first (and probably oldest) section of the final discourse. But vv. 31-38 are not entirely
discourse. Closing a series of indications of betrayal, ignorance and denial, Peter's denials
are foretold in vv. 36-38. There is more. The gift of the new commandment (vv. 34-35)

the truth that the death of Jesus has been anticipated by his washing the
feet of the disciples (vv. 5-15), the gift of the morsel, even to Judas
(vv. 21-30). These gestures, with their accompanying teaching, demonstrate Jesus love for his own εἰς τέλος (v. 1), and ask that they follow
his example (v. 15), loving one another as he has loved them (vv. 34-
35). In the midst of prophecies of betrayal and denials (vv. 2, 10-11, 18,
21-30, 36-38) Jesus explains to his ignorant and failing disciples: "I tell
you this now before it takes place so that when it takes place you may
believe that I am he (ἵνα πιστεύσητε ὅταν γένηται ὅτι ἐγώ εἰμι).
Jesus both shows and tells the consummate perfection of his love for
them before the event of the cross. He does this so that when the hour of
the cross comes, they may recognize the revelation of God (ὅτι ἐγώ
εἰμι) in the crucified one (cf. also 3,13-14; 8,28). In 12,22-23 the arrival
of the Greeks led to Jesus' announcing that the hour of his glorification
on the cross had come. In a parallel fashion, as Judas departs to betray
him (v. 31a), Jesus announces that "now" the Son of Man is glorified.
The glorification of Jesus on the cross is at hand, and he will make God
known[84].

In all the earlier asides the narrator explained that Jesus was to be glorified (2,22; 7,39; 12,16). On two occasions, Jesus declares that "the
Son of Man" is glorified (12,23; 13,31). The narrator's commentary and
the words of Jesus indicate that Jesus of Nazareth will be glorified on the
cross, and on two occasions "the Son of Man" is associated with that
eminently human experience[85]. Other passages in the Fourth Gospel
speak of the glory and the glorification of the Son (cf. 1,14; 8,54; 11,4;
16,14; 17,1.5). These passages make clear the pre-existence (17,1.5), the
genuine incarnation (1,14; 8,54; 16,14), and the post-existence (11,4;
17,5) of Jesus, the Son (of God). The glorification of Jesus (2,22; 7,39;
12,22), the Son of Man (12,23; 13,31), focuses upon the consummate
human experience of Jesus of Nazareth, his death by crucifixion[86]. I sus-

is closely related to the gift of example (v. 15), and predictions of failure that dominate
vv. 1-30 continue. The Johannine double "amen" opens (v. 21) and closes (v. 31) this
narrative sub-section (vv. 21-38). For the above position, cf. Y. SIMOENS, *La gloire
d'aimer. Structures stylistiques et interprétatives dans le Discours de la Cène* (AnBib,
90), Rome, Biblical Institute Press, 1981, pp. 81-104; R.A. CULPEPPER, *The Johannine
hypodeigma: A Reading of John 13:1-38*, in *Semeia* 53 (1991) 133-152; F.J. MOLONEY,
A Sacramental Reading of John 13:1-38, in *CBQ* 53 (1991) 237-256.

84. On the cross Jesus is glorified (v. 31b), and God is made known, i.e. "glorified in
him" (v. 31c). This action depends totally upon God, and it will take place "at once"
(εὐθύς) (v. 32). For this interpretation of 13,1-38, cf. MOLONEY, *Glory not Dishonor*
(n. 21), pp. 1-28.

85. Against, among several, LOADER, *Christology* (n. 8), pp. 107-121.

86. As HARE, *The Son of Man Tradition* (n. 8), p. 110, rightly claims: "The glorifica-

pect that a reader would be surprised to find – as the story drew to its close – a prayer of Jesus that asked: "Father, the hour has come, glorify your Son of Man so that the Son of Man might glorify you. Glorify the Son of Man in your own presence with the glory that the Son of Man had before the world was made" (cf. 17,1.5)[87]. The Son of Man glorifies God, and is himself glorified in the crucifixion of Jesus of Nazareth (2,22; 3,14; 7,39; 8,28; 12,16.23.32-34; 13,31-32; 19,5?)[88].

CONCLUSION

I approached this task of "revisiting" the Johannine Son of Man after almost thirty years of teaching, writing, and reflection upon the Gospel of John. Although the important work carried out on the Johannine Son of Man in those years has not forced me to alter my position dramatically, it is clear where I differ from those who reject my limiting of the expression "the Son of Man" to the human Jesus. On the one hand, I cannot accept that either ὑψόω (3,14; 8,28; 12,32-33) or δοξάζω (when used in association with ὁ υἱὸς τοῦ ἀνθρώπου [12,23; 13,31]) refer to

tion of the Son of man is related to a historical event". For a contrary position, cf. PAINTER, *Enigmatic* (n. 9), pp. 1883-1884. For LOADER, *Christology* (n. 8), 107-121, it is both the cross and the return to glory by means of the ascension. I am continuing to reject the argument that there is no distinction between the use of "the Son of Man" and "the Son (of God)" in the Fourth Gospel. Cf. especially, BURKETT, *Son of Man* (n. 7), and the discussion in n. 12, above.

87. As in all four Gospels, "the Son of Man" replaces "I" in Jesus' speech, I have done so in v. 4, inserting "the Son of Man" where the Greek original identifies the "I" of Jesus with "the Son" of v. 1. If, for John, "the Son" = "the Son of Man," this would be a legitimate reading of 17,1.5. Cf. also, MOLONEY, *Raymond Brown's* New Introduction (n. 30), p. 9. This distinction has been suggestively resolved by LOADER, *Christology* (n. 8), pp. 107-121, 206-209 (cf. also his *Central Structure* [n. 9], 199-202). Loader argues that the Son of Man "cluster" (the lifting up and glorification of the Son of Man both on the cross and in his ascension) has been adopted by the "central structure" of the Johannine Christology in the second half of the Gospel. This thoughtful suggestion would be acceptable if (as with Loader) Jesus' being lifted up and glorified indicated *both* his crucifixion *and* his ascension into glory. The Johannine text (3,14; 8,28; 12,32-33) *explicitly* links the lifting up with the cross. In 1976, C.K. Barrett pointed out to me that the theological use of "the Son of Man", to speak of the revelation of the presence of God during the account of Jesus' physical *presence*, is taken over by the Paraclete in the time of his *absence*.

88. For simplicity's sake, I have not introduced the "Ecce homo" scene of 19,5 into the above discussion. It highlights my association of "the Son of Man" with the crucifixion (the origins of the Son of Man tradition?). Cf. MOLONEY, *Son of Man* (n. 1), pp. 202-207. For a survey of the discussion, and a respectful rejection of this identification between "the man" of 19,5 with the Son of Man sayings, cf. SCHNACKENBURG, *Die Ecce-homo-Szene und der Menschensohn* (n. 9), pp. 371-386. For a response, cf. MOLONEY, *A Johannine Son of Man Discussion?* (n. 10), pp. 99-101.

both the crucifixion and the return to heaven in glory by means of ascension or exaltation. On the other, I have become increasingly impressed by the narrative unity of the Johannine text and the subsequent need to interpret John in the light of John before asking diachronic questions.

The more I read the Fourth Gospel, the clearer it appears to me that its author could not have used the name "Jesus" to speak of the pre-existent Logos (1,1-2). Not until the Logos becomes flesh (v. 14) can John introduce the name "Jesus Christ" (v. 17). Similarly, he uses the term "the Son", and not "Jesus", to speak of the one who returns to the glory that was his before the world was made (17,1.5). The same must be said for the other expression used to speak of the human experience of "Jesus": "the Son of Man". Readers familiar with *The Johannine Son of Man* will be aware, however, of a change in hermeneutical stance. I now approach the text of the Fourth Gospel as a whole literary utterance that must be read from start to finish, allowing the cumulative impact of the reading experience to determine interpretation[89]. I hope that the above essay makes it clear, however, that I have not abandoned diachrony for synchrony. What is perhaps most important with this study is that a different approach to the Johannine text has produced the same results.

There are, of course, some necessary changes. My earlier work created the false impression that the Johannine Son (of God) and Son of Man Christologies were to be radically separated[90]. This position misunderstands the unity of the Johannine Christology that should not be broken into separate compartments. Jesus Christ is the Son of Man, and he is also the incarnate Logos, the pre-existent, present and post-existent Son (of God)[91]. Of course the Son of Man came from heaven, but only a human being can be crucified, and John never speaks of the crucifixion of the Son. Yet, on the other hand, John never speaks of the "sending" of the Son of Man. The Johannine use of the expression of "the Son of Man" came into the Fourth Gospel from the primitive tradition, and especially its association with the passion predictions (cf. Mk 8,31; 9,31; 10,32-34 and parrs)[92]. Its focus upon the human figure and experience of Jesus opens the door to the tendency, in both the Greek and the Latin Patristic traditions, to use the expression "Son of Man" to stress

89. This change of direction emerged in my three-volume narrative commentary on the Gospel of John. Cf. above, n. 26. For the theoretical basis of this change of direction, cf. MOLONEY, *Belief in the Word* (n. 26), pp. 1-22.

90. Cf. MOLONEY, *Son of Man* (n. 1), pp. 208-220. PAZDAN, *The Son of Man* (n. 7), p. 80, claimed that I maintained "an absolute distinction between the two titles". This was not intended, and needs correction.

91. On this, cf. PAZDAN, *The Son of Man* (n. 7), pp. 76-86.

92. Cf. LINDARS, *Jesus Son of Man* (n. 8), pp. 155-157.

Jesus' humanity, and the expression "Son of God" to stress his divinity[93]. This is not the Johannine understanding of the two expressions, but the Fathers correctly caught the link between the Johannine use of "the Son of Man" for the presentation of the revelation of God in the human event of Jesus Christ, especially in his being "lifted up" on a cross (cf. 3,14; 8,28; 12,32; 19,5?).

School of Theology and Religious Studies Francis J. MOLONEY
The Catholic University of America
Washington, DC 20064
U.S.A.

93. This distinction is already found in the Apostolic Fathers. Cf. IGNATIUS, *Ephesians*, 20.2; *Letter of Barnabas*, 12.10 (cf. K. LAKE, *The Apostolic Fathers* [Loeb Classical Library], 2 volumes, London, William Heinemann; Cambridge, MA, Harvard University Press, vol. I, p. 195 (Ignatius), vol. I, p. 387 (*Barnabas*). It becomes almost axiomatic in both Greek and Latin patristic writers. For MADDOX, *The Function of the Son of Man* (n. 18), p. 189, n. 2, this is regarded as a "distinct break". Perhaps it would be better to speak of "continuity/discontinuity". Cf. PAMMENT, *Son of Man* (n. 9), p. 56, n. 9.

BIBLIOGRAPHY

SOURCES

ALAND, K. (ed.), *Synopsis Quattuor Evangeliorum. Locis parallelis evangeliorum apocryphorum et patrum adhibitis,* (Stuttgart, Württembergische Bibelanstalt, 1969⁶).

ALAND, K.-BLACK, M.-MARTINI, C.M.-METZGER, B.M.-WIKGREN, A. (eds.), *The Greek New Testament,* (Stuttgart, United Bible Societies, 1973²).

The Catechetical Lectures of S. Cyril, Archbishop of Jerusalem, Library of the Fathers, (Oxford, OUP, 1839).

CHARLES, R. H. (ed.), *The Apocrypha and Pseudepigrapha of the Old Testament in English* (Oxford, OUP, 1913) 2 vols.

COLSON, F.H.-WHITAKER, G.H. (eds.), *Philo,* Loeb Classical Library, (London-Cambridge, Mass., W. Heinemann, 1949) 12 vols.

DANBY, H. (ed.), *The Mishnah, Translated from the Hebrew with Introduction and Brief Explanatory Notes,* (Oxford, OUP, 1933).

DIEZ MACHO, A. (ed.), *Neophyti 1. Targum Palestinense MS de la Biblioteca Vaticana,* (Madrid, Consejo Superior de investigaciones cientificas, 1968-). As yet four volumes have appeared: Genesis, Exodus, Leviticus and Numbers.

EPSTEIN, I. (ed.), *The Talmud,* (London, Soncino, 1948-1952) 35 vols.

ETHERIDGE, J.W. (ed.), *The Targum of Onkelos and Jonathan Ben Uzziel on the Pentateuch, with the Fragments of the Jerusalem Targum: From the Chaldee,* (London, Longman, Green, Longman and Roberts, 1862-65) 2 vols.

FOERSTER, W. (ed.), *Gnosis. A Selection of Gnostic Texts,* Vol. I: Patristic Evidence, (Oxford, OUP, 1972); Vol. II: Coptic and Mandean Sources, (Oxford, OUP, 1974). An English translation of *Die Gnosis,* (Zürich, Artemis, 1969-71), edited by R. McL. Wilson.

FRIEDMAN, H.-SIMON, M. (eds.), *Midrash Rabbah,* (London, Soncino, 1939) 10 vols.

GINSBURGER, M. (ed.), *Pseudo-Jonathan (Thargum Jonathan ben Usiël zum Pentateuch). Nach der Londoner Handschrift (Brit. Mus. add 27031),* (Berlin, S. Calvary, 1903).

HARVEY, W.W. (ed.), *Sancti Irenaei Episcopi Lugdunensis Libros Quinque Adversus Haereses,* (Cambridge, Typis Academicis, 1857) 2 vols.

HENNECKE, E.-SCHNEEMELCHER, W.-WILSON, R. McL. (eds.), *New Testament Apocrypha,* (London, Lutterworth, 1965) 2 vols.

The Holy Bible. Revised Standard Version Containing the Old and New Testaments, (New York, OUP, 1973).

The Works now extant of S. Justin the Martyr, Translated with Notes and Indices, Library of the Fathers, (Oxford, OUP, 1861).

KITTEL, R. (ed.), *Biblia Hebraica,* (Stuttgart, Württembergische Bibelanstalt, 1949⁴).

LAKE, K. (ed.), *The Apostolic Fathers, with an English Translation,* Loeb Classical Library, (London-Cambridge, Mass., W. Heinemann, 1912).

LAUTERBACH, J.Z. (ed.), *Mekilta de-Rabbi Ishmael. A Critical Edition on the Basis of the Manuscripts and Early Editions with an English Translation, Introduction and Notes,* The Schiff Library of Jewish Classics, (Philadelphia, The Jewish Publication Society of America, 1933) 3 vols.

LOHSE, E. (ed.), *Die Texte aus Qumran. Hebräisch und Deutsch,* (München, Kösel, 1971²)

The New English Bible with the Apocrypha, (Oxford and Cambridge, OUP and CUP, 1970).

PACK, R.A. (ed.), *Artemidori Daldiani Onirocriticon Libri V,* Bibliotheca Scriptorum Graecorum et Romanorum Teubneriana, (Lipsia, B. G. Teubner, 1963).

RAHLFS, A. (ed.), *Septuaginta,* (Stuttgart, Württembergische Bibelanstalt, 1965⁸).

SCHWAB, M. (ed.), *Le Talmud de Jérusalem,* (Paris, Maisonneuve et Cie., 1878-1890) 11 vols.

SPERBER, A. (ed.), *The Bible in Aramaic. Based on Old Manuscripts and Printed Texts,* (Leiden, E.J. Brill, 1959-73) 4 vols.

STRACK, H.L.-BILLERBECK, P., *Kommentar zum Neuen Testament aus Talmud und Midrasch,* (München, C. H. Beck, 1922-61) 6 vols.

The Testament of Abraham. The Greek Recensions, Translated by M. E. Stone, Texts and Translations 2. Pseudepigrapha Series, (Missoula, Society for Biblical Literature, 1972).

TISCHENDORF, C., *Novum Testamentum Graece,* Editio octava critica maior, (Leipzig, Geisecke und Devrient, 1869-1872) 2 vols.

VERMES, G., *The Dead Sea Scrolls in English,* (Harmondsworth, Penguin Books, 1968).

WALTON, B. (ed.), *Sanctissima Biblia Polyglotta,* (London, 1657), 7 vols.

REFERENCE WORKS

AA.VV., *Encyclopaedia Judaica,* (Jerusalem, Keter, 1971) 16 vols.

ABBOTT, E.A., *Johannine Grammar,* (London, A. and C. Black, 1906).

BAUER, W. - ARNDT, W.F. - GINGRICH, F.W., *A Greek-English Lexicon of the New Testament and Other Early Christian Literature,* (Chicago, University of Chicago Press, 1957).

BLASS, F. - DEBRUNNER, R. - FUNK, R.W., *A Greek Grammar of the New Testament and Other Early Christian Literature,* (Chicago, University of Chicago Press, 1967).

BROWN, F. - DRIVER, S.R. - BRIGGS, C.A. (eds.), *A Hebrew and English Lexicon of the Old Testament with an Appendix Containing the Biblical Aramaic,* (Oxford, Clarendon Press, 1907).

CROSS, F.L. - LIVINGSTONE, E.A. (eds.), *The Oxford Dictionary of the Christian Church,* (London, OUP, 1974).

HATCH, E. - REDPATH, H.A., *A Concordance to the Septuagint and Other Greek Versions of the Old Testament (Including the Apocryphal Books),* (Oxford, Clarendon Press, 1897).

The Interpreter's Dictionary of the Bible. An Illustrated Encyclopedia, (New York-Nashville, Abingdon Press, 1962) 4 vols.

JASTROW, M., *Dictionary of Talmud Babli, Yerushalmi, Midrashic Literature and Targumim,* (New York, Pardes, 1950) 2 vols.

JOÜON, P., *Grammaire de l'Hébreu Biblique,* (Rome, Pontifical Biblical Institute, 1923).

LAMPE, G.W.H., *A Patristic Greek Lexicon,* (Oxford, OUP, 1961).

LIDDELL, H.G. - SCOTT, R., *A Greek-English Lexicon,* (Oxford, OUP, 1940).

LISOWSKY, G., *Konkordanz zum Hebräischen Alten Testament,* (Stuttgart, Württembergische Bibelanstalt, 1958²).

METZGER, B., *A Textual Commentary on the Greek New Testament,* (London/New York, United Bible Societies, 1971). ·

MOULE, C.F.D., *An Idiom Book of New Testament Greek,* (Cambridge, CUP, 1959²).

MOULTON, J.H., *A Grammar of New Testament Greek,* Vol. I: Prolegomena (Edinburgh, T. & T. Clark, 1908).

MOULTON, J.H. - MILLIGAN, G., *The Vocabulary of the Greek Testament Illustrated from the Papyri and Other Non-Literary Sources,* (London, Hodder & Stoughton, 1930).

ZERWICK, M., *Biblical Greek,* (Rome, Biblical Institute Press, 1963).

ZERWICK, M. - GROSVENOR, M., *A Grammatical Analysis of the Greek New Testament,* (Rome, Biblical Institute Press, 1974), vol. I.

ZORELL, F., *Lexicon Graecum Novi Testamenti,* (Paris, Lethielleux, 1961).

COMMENTARIES

BARRETT, C.K., *The Gospel according to St. John*, (London, SPCK, 1954).
BAUER, W., *Das Johannesevangelium erklärt*, HZNT 6, (Tübingen, J. C. B. Mohr, 1935).
BERNARD, J.H., *A Critical and Exegetical Commentary on the Gospel of St. John*, ICC, 2 vols. (Edinburgh, T. and T. Clark, 1929).
BRAUN, F.-M., « Commentaire de l'Évangile selon Saint Jean », in L. Pirot-A. Clamer, (eds.), *La Sainte Bible*, Vol. 10, (Paris, Letouzey et Ané, 1935) pp. 295-487.
BROWN, R.E., *The Gospel according to John*, The Anchor Bible 29 and 29a (New York, Doubleday, 1966-1970).
BULTMANN, R., *The Gospel of John. A Commentary*, (Oxford, Basil Blackwell, 1971). English translation of *Das Evangelium des Johannes*, (Göttingen, Vandenhoeck und Ruprecht, 1964), including the supplement of 1966.
DODD, C.H., *The Interpretation of the Fourth Gospel*, (Cambridge, CUP, 1953).
FENTON, J.C., *The Gospel according to John*, NCB (Oxford, Clarendon Press, 1970).
GODET, F., *Commentaire sur l'Evangile de Saint Jean*, (Neuchatel, J. Attinger, 1902) 3 vols.
GRUNDMANN, W., *Das Evangelium nach Matthäus*, THNT 1, (Berlin, Evangelische Verlagsanstalt, 1971).
— *Das Evangelium nach Markus*, THNT 2, (Berlin, Evangelische Verlagsanstalt, 1973).
GUICHOU, P., *Evangile de Jean*, (Paris, Lethielleux, 1962).
HOSKYNS, E.C. - DAVEY, F.N. (ed.), *The Fourth Gospel*, (London, Faber and Faber, 1947²).
HOWARD, W.F. - GOSSIP, A.J., "The Gospel according to St. John", in *IB*, (New York/ Nashville, Abingdon, 1952), Vol. VIII, pp. 435-811.
JEREMIAS, J., *Das Evangelium nach Johannes. Eine Urchristliche Erklärung für die Gegenwart*, (Chemnitz, Müller, 1931).
JOHNSON, S.E., *A Commentary on the Gospel According to St. Mark*, Black's New Testament Commentaries, (London, A. & C. Black, 1972).
LAGRANGE, M.-J., *Évangile selon saint Jean*, Études Bibliques, (Paris, Gabalda, 1964). A reprint of 1936⁵.
— *Évangile selon Saint Marc*, (Paris, Gabalda, 1920).
LIGHTFOOT, R.H. - EVANS, C.F. (ed.), *St. John's Gospel. A Commentary with the Revised Version Text*, (Oxford, OUP, 1956).
LINDARS, B., *The Gospel of John*, New Century Bible, (London, Oliphants, 1972).
LOISY, A., *Le quatrième Évangile*, (Paris, Alphonse Picard et Fils, 1903).
— *Le quatrième Évangile*, (Paris, Emile Nourry, 1921).
MACGREGOR, G.H.C., *The Gospel of John, Moffatt Commentary*, (London, Hodder & Stoughton, 1928).
MARSH, J., *Saint John*, The Pelican New Testament Commentaries, (Harmondsworth, Penguin Books, 1968).
MOLLAT, D. - BRAUN, F.-M., "L'Évangile et les Épîtres de Saint Jean", in *La Sainte Bible*, (Paris, Éditions du Cerf, 1953).
MORRIS, L., *The Gospel according to John: The English Text with Introduction, Exposition and Notes*, The New International Commentary on the New Testament, (London, Marshall, Morgan and Scott, 1971).
NINEHAM, D.E., *Saint Mark*, Pelican Gospel Commentaries, (Harmondsworth, Penguin Books, 1963).
ODEBERG, H., *The Fourth Gospel. Interpreted in Relation to Contemporaneous Religious Currents in Palestine and the Hellenistic-Oriental World*, (Uppsala, Almqvist, 1929).
RICHARDSON, A., *The Gospel According to Saint John*, Torch Commentaries, (London, SCM Press, 1959).
SANDERS, J.N. - MASTIN, B.A., *A Commentary on the Gospel according to St. John*, Black's New Testament Commentaries, (London, A. & C. Black, 1968).
SCHLATTER, A., *Der Evangelist Johannes. Wie er spricht, denkt und glaubt. Ein Kommentar zum 4. Evangelium*, (Stuttgart, Calwer, 1948²).

SCHNACKENBURG, R., *The Gospel according to St. John,* Volume I, (London, Herder & Herder, 1968). English translation of *Das Johannesevangelium* I. Teil, HTKNT (Freiburg, Herder, 1965).

— *Das Johannesevangelium,* II. Teil, HTKNT, (Freiburg, Herder, 1971).

SCHULZ, S., *Das Evangelium nach Johannes,* NTD 4, (Göttingen, Vandenhoeck und Ruprecht, 1972).

SCHWANK, B., *Das Johannesevangelium,* Die Welt der Bibel, (Düsseldorf, Patmos, 1966-68) 2 vols.

SCHWEIZER, E., *The Good News according to Mark,* (London, SPCK, 1971). English translation of *Das Evangelium nach Markus,* (Göttingen, Vandenhoeck und Ruprecht, 1967).

STRACHAN, R.H., *The Fourth Gospel. Its Significance and Environment,* (London, SCM Press, 1941³).

STRATHMANN, H., *Das Evangelium des Johannes,* NTD 4, (Göttingen, Vandenhoeck und Ruprecht, 1963¹⁰).

TAYLOR, V., *The Gospel According to St. Mark. The Greek Text with Introduction, Notes and Indexes,* (London, Macmillan, 1966²).

TEMPLE, W., *Readings in St. John's Gospel. First and Second Series,* (London, Macmillan, 1945).

TILLMANN, F., *Das Johannesevangelium übersetzt und erklärt,* (Berlin, Hermann Walther, 1914).

VAN DEN BUSSCHE, H., *Jean. Commentaire de l'Évangile Spirituel,* (Bruges, Desclée de Brouwer, 1967).

VAWTER, B., "The Gospel according to John", in *JBC,* pp. 414-466.

WELLHAUSEN, J., *Das Evangelium Johannis,* (Berlin, Georg Reimer, 1908).

WESTCOTT, B.F., *The Gospel according to St. John,* (London, John Murray, 1908).

WIKENHAUSER, A., *Das Evangelium nach Johannes,* RNT, (Regensburg, Pustet, 1948).

ZAHN, T., *Das Evangelium des Johannes,* KNT, (Leipzig, A. Deichert, 1908).

OTHER WORKS QUOTED

AGNEW, F., "Vocatio primorum discipulorum in traditione synoptica", *VD* 46 (1968) 128-147.

ALETTI, J.-N., "Le discours sur le pain de vie. La Fonction des citations de l'Ancien Testament", *RecSR* 62 (1974) 169-197.

BAJSIC, A., "Pilatus, Jesus und Barabbas", *Biblica* 48 (1967) 7-28.

BALAGUÉ, M., "Diálogo con Nicodemo", *CuBíb* 16 (1959) 193-206.

— "La hora de Jesús", *RBíCalz* 31 (1969) 82-85.

— *Jesucristo Vida y Luz. Estudio de los doce primeros capitulos del Evangelio de S. Juan,* (Madrid, Studium, 1963).

— "Jesús y Nicodemo. Cataquesis bautismal (Jn. 3,1-21)", *RBíCalz* 21 (1959) 153-163.

BARON, M., "La progression des confessions de foi dans les dialogues de S. Jean", *BibVChr* 82 (1968) 32-44.

BARRETT, C.K., "John and the Synoptic Gospels", *ET* 85 (1973-74) 228-233.

— *New Testament Essays,* (London, SPCK, 1972).

BAUER, J.-B., "πῶς in der griechischen Bibel", *NT* 2 (1958) 81-91.

BEAUVERY, R., "Jésus élevé attire les hommes à lui (Jean 12,20-33)", *EsprVie* 80 (1970) 117-119.

BECKER, H., *Die Reden des Johannesevangeliums und der Stil der gnostischen Offenbarungsreden,* (Göttingen, Vandenhoeck und Ruprecht, 1956).

BECKER, J., "Die Abschiedsreden Jesu im Johannesevangelium", *ZNW* 61 (1970) 215-246.

BEEL, A., "Colloquium Jesu cum Nicodemo", *CollBrug* 39 (1939) 203-208. 273-278. 301-304.

— "Sermo Jesu post paralytici sanationem (Jo. 5,19-30)", *CollBrug* 39 (1939) 433-439.

BEHLER, G.-M., *The Last Discourse of Jesus*, (Baltimore, Helicon, 1966). English translation of *Les paroles d'adieux du Seigneur*, Lectio Divina 27 (Paris, Editions du Cerf, 1960).

BERGER, K., *Die Amen-Worte Jesu. Eine Untersuchung der Legitimation in Apokalyptischen Rede*, BZNW 39, (Berlin, Walter de Gruyter, 1970).

BERROUARD, M.-F., "La Multiplication des pains et le discours du pain de vie (Jean 6)", *LumVie* 18 (1969) 63-75.

BERTRAM, G., Art. "ὑψόω", *TDNT* VIII, pp. 602-620.

BEVAN, T.W., "The Four Anointings (Jn. 12,1-11 etc.)", *ET* 39 (1927-28) 137-139.

BLACK, M., *An Aramaic Approach to the Gospels and Acts*, (Oxford, OUP, 1967).

— "The 'Son of Man' Passion Sayings in the Gospel Traditions", *ZNW* 60 (1969) 1-8.

— "The Son of Man Problem in Recent Research and Debate", *BJRL* 45 (1963) 305-318.

BLANK, J., "Die johanneische Brotrede", *BuL* 7 (1966) 193-207; 255-270.

— *Krisis. Untersuchungen zur johanneischen Christologie und Eschatologie*, (Freiburg, Lambertus-Verlag, 1964).

— "Die Verhandlung vor Pilatus Joh 18,28-19,16 im Lichte johanneischer Theologie", *BZ* 3 (1959) 60-81.

BLIGH, J., "Four Studies in John I: The Man born Blind", *HeyJ* 7 (1966) 129-144.

— "Four Studies in John II: Nicodemus", *HeyJ* 8 (1967) 40-51.

— "Jesus in Galilee", *HeyJ* 5 (1964) 3-21.

— "Jesus in Jerusalem", *HeyJ* 4 (1963) 115-134.

BLINZLER, J., *Giovanni e i Sinottici. Rassegna informativa*, (Brescia, Paideia, 1969). Revised Italian translation of *Johannes und die Synoptiker. Ein Forschungsbericht*, (Stuttgart, Katholisches Bibelwerk, 1965).

BOCCALI, G., "Un 'mashal' evangelico e la sua applicazione: Gv 6,63", *BibOr* 10 (1968) 53-58.

BOICE, J.M., *Witness and Revelation in the Gospel of John*, (Grand Rapids, Eerdmans, 1970).

BOISMARD, M.-E., "Aenon, près de Salem (Jean 3,23)", *RB* 24 (1973) 218-229.

— *Du Baptême à Cana (Jean 1,19-2,11)*, (Paris, Editions du Cerf, 1956).

— "Le caractère adventice de Jn 12, 45-50", in J. Coppens et alii (eds.), *Sacra Pagina. Miscellanea Biblica. Congressus Internationalis Catholicus de Re Biblica*, (Gembloux, Duculot, 1959), Vol. II, pp. 189-192.

— "Les citations targumiques dans le quatrième Évangile", *RB* 66 (1959) 374-378.

— "L'évolution du thème eschatologique dans les traditions johanniques", *RB* 68 (1961) 514-518.

— "Le lavement des pieds (Jn. 13,1-17)", *RB* 71 (1964) 5-24.

— "La Royauté du Christ dans le quatrième évangile", *LumVie* 57 (1963) 43-63.

— "Les traditions johanniques concernant le Baptiste", *RB* 70 (1963) 5-42.

BORGEN, P., *Bread from Heaven. An Exegetical Study of the Conception of Manna in the Gospel of John and the Writings of Philo*, SNT 10, (Leiden, E.J. Brill, 1965).

— "God's Agent in the Fourth Gospel", in J. Neusner (ed.), *Religions in Antiquity, Essays in Memory of Erwin Ramsdell Goodenough*, Studies in the History of Religions XIV, (Leiden, E.J. Brill, 1968) pp. 137-148.

— "Observations on the Midrashic Character of John 6", *ZNW* 54 (1963) 232-240.

— "The Unity of the Discourse in John 6", *ZNW* 50 (1959) 277-278.

BORNKAMM, G., "Die eucharistische Rede im Johannes-Evangelium", *ZNW* 47 (1956) 161-169.

— "Die Heilung des Blindgeborenen. Johannes 9", in *Geschichte und Glaube II*, Beiträge zur EvTh 53, (München, Kaiser Verlag, 1971) pp. 65-72.

— "Der Paraklet im Johannesevangelium", in *Festschrift Rudolf Bultmann, zur 65. Geburtstag überreicht*, (Stuttgart, W. Kohlhammer, 1949) pp. 12-35.

— "Vorjohanneische Tradition oder nachjohanneische Bearbeitung in der eucharistische Rede Johannes 6", in *Geschichte und Glaube II*, Beitr. zur EvTh 53, (München, Kaiser Verlag, 1971) pp. 51-64.

BORSCH, F.H., *The Son of Man in Myth and History*, (London, SCM Press, 1967).

BOURKE, M.M., Review of BROWN, R.E., *The Gospel according to John, I-XII*, in *CBQ* 28 (1966) 342-345.

BOUSSET, W., *Kyrios Christos. A History of the Belief in Christ from the Beginnings of Christianity to Irenaeus*, (New York, Abingdon, 1970). Englis translation of *Kyrios Christos: Geschichte des Christusglaubens von den Anfängen des Christentums bis Irenaeus*, FRLANT 4, (Göttingen, Vandenhoeck und Ruprecht, 1926).

BOUYER, L., "La notion christologique du Fils de l'homme a-t-elle disparu dans la patristique grecque?", in *Mélanges bibliques rédigés en l'honneur de André Robert*, (Paris, Bloud et Gay, 1957) pp. 519-530.

BOWMAN, J., "The Identity and Date of the Unnamed Feast of John 5,1", in H. Goedicke (ed.), *Near Eastern Studies in Honor of William Foxwell Albright*, (Baltimore/London, Routledge and Kegan Paul, 1971) pp. 43-56.

BOYD, W.J.P., "Ascension according to John", *TLond* 70 (1967) 207-211.

BRAUN, F.-M., "L'eucharistie selon S. Jean", *RThom* 70 (1970) 5-29.

— *Jean le Théologien et son évangile dans l'église ancienne*, Etudes Bibliques, (Paris, Gabalda, 1959).

— *Jean le Théologien et les grandes traditions d'Israel et l'accord des écritures selon le quatrième évangile*, Etudes Bibliques, (Paris, Gabalda, 1964).

— *Jean le Théologien. Sa Théologie I: Le Mystère de Jésus Christ*, Etudes Bibliques, (Paris, Gabalda, 1966).

— *Jean le Théologien. Sa Théologie II: Le Christ, Notre Seigneur*, Etudes Bibliques, (Paris, Gabalda, 1972).

— "In Spiritu et Veritate", *RThom* 52 (1952) 245-274. 485-507.

— "Messie, Logos et Fils de l'homme", in E. Massaux (ed.), *La Venue du Messie*, Recherches Bibliques VI, (Bruges, Desclée de Brouwer, 1962), pp. 133-147.

— "La vie d'en haut (Jn. 3,1-15)", *RSPT* 40 (1956) 3-24.

BRAUN, H., *Qumran und das Neue Testament*, (Tübingen, J.C.B. Mohr, 1966), 2 Bände.

BROOKS, O.S., "The Johannine Eucharist", *JBL* 82 (1963) 293-300.

BROWN, R.E., "The Eucharist and Baptism in John" in *New Testament Essays,* (London, Geoffrey Chapman, 1967), pp. 77-95.

BROWN, R.P., " Εντολὴ καινή (St. John 13,34)", *TLond* 26 (1933) 184-193.

BRUN, L., "Jesus als Zeuge von irdischen und himmlischen Dingen. Jo. 3, 12-13", *SymbOs* 8 (1929) 57-77.

BRUNS, J.E., "A Note on Jn. 12,3", *CBQ* 8 (1966) 219-222.

BULTMANN, R., Art. "ἀλήθεια", *TDNT* I, pp. 238-251.

— "Die Bedeutung der neuerschlossenen mandäischen und manichäischen Quellen für das Verständnis des Johannesevangeliums", *ZNW* 24 (1925) 100-146.

— Art. " γινώσκω ", *TDNT* I, pp. 689-719.

— *Glauben und Verstehen* I, (Tübingen, J.C.B. Mohr, 1954).

— *The History of the Synoptic Tradition*, (Oxford, Basil Blackwell, 1968). English translation of *Die Geschichte der synoptischen Tradition*, (Göttingen, Vandenhoeck und Ruprecht, 1931).

— Art. "πιστεύω ", *TDNT* VI, pp. 197-228.

BURKITT, F.C., "On 'lifting up' and 'exalting' ", *JTS* 20 (1918-19) 336-338.

BURNEY, C.F., *The Aramaic Origin of the Fourth Gospel*, (Oxford, OUP, 1922).

CADMAN, W.H. - CAIRD, G.B., *The Open Heaven. The Revelation of God in the Johannine Sayings of Jesus*, (Oxford, Basil Blackwell, 1969).

CADOUX, C.J., "The Johannine Account of the Early Ministry of Jesus", *JTS* 20 (1919) 311-320.

CAIRD, G.B., "The Development of the Doctrine of Christ in the New Testament", in N. Pittenger (ed.), *Christ for Us Today*. Papers read at the Conference for Modern Churchmen, Somerville College, Oxford, July 1967, (London, SCM Press, 1968), pp. 66-80.

— "The Glory of God in the Fourth Gospel: An Exercise in Biblical Semantics", *NTS* 15 (1968-69) 265-277.

— "Judgment and Salvation. An Exposition of Jn 12,31-32", *CanadJT* 2 (1956) 231-237.

CARROLL, K.L., "The Fourth Gospel and the Exclusion of Christians from the Synagogues", *BJRL* 40 (1957) 19-32.

CERFAUX, L., "La charité fraternelle et le retour du Christ (Jn. xiii 33-38)", *ETL* 24 (1948) 321-332.

CHARLESWORTH, J.H. (ed.), *John and Qumran*, (London, Geoffrey Chapman, 1972«.

CHARLIER, C., "La présence dans l'absence (Jn. 12,31-14,31)", *BibVChr* 2 (1953) 61-75.

CHARLIER, J.-P., "L'exégèse johannique d'un précepte légal: Jean 8,17", *RB* 67 (1960) 503-515.

CIPRIANI, S., "La confessione di Pietro in Giov. 6, 69-71 e i suoi rapporti con quella dei sinottici (Mc. 8,27-33 e paralleli)", in *San Pietro* Atti della XIX settimana Biblica, (Brescia, Paideia, 1967) pp. 93-111.

CLAVIER, H., "Le problème du rite et du mythe dans le 4ᵉ Évangile", *RHPR* 31 (1951) 275-292.

COLPE, C., "Heidnische, jüdische und christliche Ueberlieferung in den Schriften aus Nag Hammadi III", *Jahrbuch für Antike und Christentum* 17 (1974) 109-125.

— *Die Religionsgeschichtliche Schule. Darstellung und Kritik ihres Bildes von gnostischen Erlösermythus*, FRLANT 60, (Göttingen, Vandenhoeck und Ruprecht, 1961).

— Art. "υἱὸς τοῦ ἀνθρώπου", *TDNT* VIII, pp. 403-481.

COLWELL, E.C., "A Definite Rule for the Use of the Article in the Greek New Testament", *JBL* 52 (1933) 12-31.

CONTI, M., *Il discorso del pane di vita nella tradizione sapienziale*, (Levanto, 1967).

CONZELMANN, H., Art. "Jesus Christus" in *RGG*, (Tübingen, J.C.B. Mohr, 1959³), III, cols. 619-653.

— *An Outline of the Theology of the New Testament*, (London, SCM Press, 1969). English translation of *Grundriss der Theologie des Neuen Testaments*, (Munich, Kaiser, 1968).

CORELL, A., *Consummatum est, Eschatology and Church in the Gospel of St. John*, (London, SPCK, 1958). English translation of *Consummatum est. Eskatologi och Kyrka i Johannesevangeliet*, (Stockholm, Svenska Kyrkans Diakonistyrelses Bokförlag, 1950).

CORSSEN, P., "Die Abschiedsreden Jesu im vierten Evangelium", *ZNW* 8 (1907) 125-142.

COUTTS, J., "The Messianic Secret in St. John's Gospel", *StEv* 3 (1964) 45-57.

CULLMANN, O., *The Christology of the New Testament*, (London, SCM Press, 1963). English translation of *Die Christologie des Neuen Testaments*, (Tübingen, J.C.B. Mohr, 1957).

— *Early Christian Worship*, SBT 10, (London, SCM Press, 1953). English translation of *Urchristentum und Gottesdienst*, (Zürich, Zwingli-Verlag, 1950) and *Les Sacrements dans l'Évangile johannique*, (Paris, Presses Universitaires de France, 1951).

— "Εἶδεν καὶ ἐπίστευσεν". La vie de Jésus, objet de la 'vue' et de la 'foi' d'après le quatrième évangile", in *Aux Sources de la Tradition chrétienne, Mélanges Goguel*, (Neuchâtel, Delachaux & Niestlé, 1950) pp. 52-61.

— *Salvation in History*, (London, SCM Press, 1967). English translation of *Heil als Geschichte: Heilsgeschichtliche Existenz im Neuen Testament*, (Tübingen, J.C.B. Mohr, 1965).

CROCETTI, G., "Le linee fondamentali del concetto di vita in Jo. 6,57", *RBibIt* 19 (1971) 375-394.

DAHL, N.A., "The Johannine Church and History", in W. Klassen-G.F. Snyder (eds.), *Current Issues in New Testament Interpretation*, (London, SCM Press, 1962), pp. 124-142.

DAUBE, D., *The New Testament and Rabbinic Judaism*, (London, Athlone Press, 1956).

DAUER, A., *Die Passionsgeschichte im Johannesevangelium. Eine traditionsgeschichtliche und theologische Untersuchung zu Joh 18,1-19,30,* Studien zum Álten und Neuen Testament, (München, Kösel, 1972).

DAVIES, W.D., *The Gospel and the Land. Early Christianity and Jewish Territorial Doctrine,* (Berkeley-Los Angeles-London, University of California Press, 1974).

DAVEY, J.E., *The Jesus of St. John,* (London, Lutterworth, 1958).

DE AUSEJO, S., "El concepto de 'carne' aplicado a Cristo en el IV Evangelio", in J. Coppens et alii (eds.), *Sacra Pagina,* Miscellanea Biblica Congressus Internationalis Catholici de Re Biblica, (Gembloux, Duculot, 1959), Vol. II, pp. 219-234.

DE BEUS, C., "Achtergrond en inhoud van de uitdrukking 'de Zoon des Mensen' in de synoptische evangeliën", *NedTTs* 9 (1954-55) 272-295.

— "Het gebruik en de betekenis de uitdrukking 'De Zoon des Mensen' en het Evangelie van Johannes", *NedTTs* 10 (1955-56) 237-251.

DEEKS, D., "The Structure of the Fourth Gospel", *NTS* 15 (1968-69) 107-129.

DE JONGE, M., "Jesus as Prophet and King in the Fourth Gospel", *ETL* 49 (1973) 160-179.

— "Jewish Expectations about the 'Messiah' according to the Fourth Gospel", *NTS* 19 (1973) 246-270.

— "Nicodemus and Jesus: Some observations on Misunderstanding and Understanding in the Fourth Gospel", *BJRL* 53 (1970) 337-359.

DE KRUIJF, T.C., "The Glory of the Only Son (John 1,14)", in *Studies in John, presented to Professor Dr. J.N. Sevenster on the occasion of his seventieth Birthady,* SNT 24, (Leiden, E.J. Brill, 1970) pp. 111-123.

DE LA POTTERIE, I., "Ad Dialogum Jesu cum Nicodemo (Jo. 2,23-3,21)", *VD* 46 (1969) 141-150.

— *Exegesis IVⁱ Evangelii. De Narratione Passionis et Mortis Christi. Joh 18-19,* (Rome, Pontifical Biblical Institute, 1970-71).

— "L'exaltation du Fils de l'homme (Jn. 12,31-36)", *Greg* 49 (1968) 460-478.

— "Jésus, roi et juge d'après Jn 19,13 " Ἐκάθισεν ἐπὶ βήματος ", *Biblica* 41 (1960) 217-247.

— *Gesù Verità,* (Torino, Marietti, 1973).

— "Jesus et Nicodemus: de necessitate generationis ex Spiritu (Jo. 3,1-10)", *VD* 47 (1969) 194-214.

— "Jesus et Nicodemus: de revelatione Jesu et vera fide in Eum (Jo. 3,11-21)", *VD* 47 (1969) 257-283.

— "Nascere dall'acqua e nascere dallo Spirito", in I. de la Potterie-S. Lyonnet, *La Vita secondo lo Spirito,* (Rome, Editrice Ave, 1967), pp. 35-74. Originally: "Naître de l'eau et naître de l'Esprit", *ScEccl* 14 (1962) 351-374.

— "La notion de témoignage dans Saint Jean", in *Sacra Pagina* II, pp. 193-208.

— "οἶδα et γινώσκω. Les deux modes de la connaissance dans le quatrième évangile", *Biblica* 40 (1959) 709-725.

— "Structura Primae Partis Evangelii Johannis (Capita III et IV)", *VD* 47 (1969) 130-140.

DERRETT, J.D.M., "Figtrees in the New Testament", *HeyJ* 14 (1973) 249-265.

— *Law in the New Testament,* (London, Darton, Longman & Todd, 1970).

DIBELIUS, M., *Die Formgeschichte des Evangeliums,* (Tübingen, J.C.B. Mohr, 1971⁶).

DIECKMANN, H., " ·Der Sohn des Menschen' im Johannesevangelium", *Schol* 2 (1927), 229-247.

DION, H.-M., "Quelques traits originaux de la conception johannique du Fils de l'Homme", *ScEccl* 19 (1967) 49-65.

DODD, C.H., "A l'arrière-plan d'un discours johannique", *RHPR* 37 (1957) 5-17.

— "Eternal Life", in *New Testament Studies,* (Manchester, MUP, 1953), pp. 161-173.

— "A Hidden Parable in the Fourth Gospel", in *More New Testament Studies,* (Manchester, MUP, 1968), pp. 30-40.

— *Historical Tradition in the Fourth Gospel,* (Cambridge, CUP, 1965).

— "The Portrait of Jesus in John and in the Synoptics", in W.R. Farmer-C.F.D. Moule-R.R. Niebuhr (eds.), *Christian History and Interpretation: Studies Presented to John*

Knox, (Cambridge, CUP, 1967) pp. 183-198.

— "Some Johannine 'Herrnworte' with parallels in the Synoptic Gospels", *NTS* 2 (1955-56) 75-86.

DUNN, J.D.G., "John VI — A Eucharistic Discourse?", *NTS* 17 (1970-71) 328-338.

— "The Washing of the Disciples' Feet in John 13,1-20", *ZNW* 61 (1970) 247-252.

DUPONT, J., *Essais sur la Christologie de Saint Jean,* (Bruges, Editions de l'Abbaye de Saint André, 1951).

DUPREZ, A., *Jésus et les dieux guérisseurs. A propos de Jean V,* CahRB 12, (Paris, Gabalda, 1970).

DURAND, A., "Le discours de la Cène (Saint Jean xiii 31-xvii 26)", *RecSR* 1 (1910) 97-131. 513-539; 2 (1911) 321-349. 521-545.

EARLY, P.D., *The Conception of the Son of Man in the Fourth Gospel,* (Unpublished Dissertation. Southern Baptist Seminary, 1952).

FARMER, W.R., "The Palm Branches in John 12,13", *JTS* 3 (1952) 62-66.

FASCHER, E., "Theologische Beobachtungen zu δεῖ ", in *Neutestamentliche Studien für Rudolf Bultmann,* BZNW 21, (Berlin, Alfred Töpelmann, 1957), pp. 228-254.

FERRARO, G., *L'"ora" di Cristo nel Quarto Vangelo,* Aloisiana 10 (Roma, Herder, 1974).

FEUILLET, A., "Les *Ego Eimi* christologiques du quatrième évangile", *RecSR* 54 (1966) 5-22. 213-240.

— "La composition littéraire de Jo. 9-12", in *Mélanges bibliques redigés en l'honneur de André Robert,* (Paris, Bloud et Gay, 1957), pp. 478-493.

— "Les thèmes bibliques majeurs du discours sur le pain de vie", in *Études Johanniques,* (Paris, Desclée de Brouwer, 1962) pp. 47-129.

FINKEL, A., *The Pharisees and the Teacher of Nazareth. A Sudy of their Background, their Halachic and Midrashic Teachings, the Similarities and Differences,* AGSU 4, (Leiden, E.J. Brill, 1964).

FLOWERS, H.J., "Interpolations in the Fourth Gospel (5,28-29; 6,39.40.54; 4,2; 2,21-22; 7,39; 12,33; 18,9; 19,35)", *JBL* 40 (1921) 146-158.

FORESTELL, J.T., *The Word of the Cross. Salvation as Revelation in the Fourth Gospel,* Analecta Biblica 57, (Rome, Pontifical Biblical Institute, 1974).

FORTNA, R., *The Gospel of Signs. A Reconstruction of the Narrative Source underlying the Fourth Gospel,* SNTS Monograph Series 11, (Cambridge, CUP, 1970).

FREED, E.D., "The Entry into Jerusalem in the Gospel of John", *JBL* 80 (1961) 329-338.

— *Old Testament Quotations in the Gospel of John,* SNT 11, (Leiden, E.J. Brill, 1965).

— "The Son of Man in the Fourth Gospel", *JBL* 86 (1967) 402-409.

FRITSCH, I., " '... videbitis ... angelos ascendentes et descendentes ...' (Io. 1,51)", *VD* 37 (1959) 1-11.

GÄCHTER, P., "Die Form der eucharistischen Rede Jesu", *ZKT* 59 (1935) 419-441.

— "Zur Form von Joh 5,19-30", in J. Blinzler-O. Kuss-F. Mussner (eds.), *Neutestamentliche Aufsätze,* (Regensburg, Pustet, 1963), pp. 65-68.

— "Der formale Aufbau der Abschiedsreden Jesu", *ZKT* 58 (1934) 155-207.

GÄRTNER, B., *John 6 and the Jewish Passover,* Coniectanea Neotestamentica 17, (Lund, Gleerup, 1959).

GAETA, G., *Il dialogo con Nicodemo,* Studi Biblici 26, (Brescia, Paideia, 1974).

GALBIATI, E., "Il Pane della Vita", *BibOr* 5 (1963) 101-110.

GAUGLER, E., "Das Christuszeugnis des Johannesevangeliums", in K.L. Schmidt (ed.), *Christus im Zeugnis der heiligen Schrift und der Kirche,* Beihefte zur EvTh 2, (München, Kaiser, 1936), pp. 34-69.

GHIBERTI, G., "Il c. 6 di Giovanni e la presenza dell'eucaristia nel 4° Vangelo", *Parole di Vita* 14 (1969) 105-125.

GIBLET, J., "L'Eucharistie dans l'évangile de Jean", *Concilium* 40 (1969) 55-62.

— "Jésus et 'le Père' dans le Quatrième Évangile", dans *L'Évangile de Jean,* Recherches Bibliques III, (Bruges, Desclée de Brouwer, 1958) pp. 111-130.

GLASSON, T.F., *Moses in the Fourth Gospel*, SBT 40 (London, SCM Press, 1963).

GNILKA, J., "Zur Theologie des Hörens nach den Aussagen des Neuen Testaments", *BuL* 2 (1961) 71-81.

— "Der historische Jesus als der gegenwärtige Christus im Johannesevangelium", in J. Sint (ed.), *Bibel und Zeitgemässer Glaube II: Neues Testament*, (Klosterneuberg, Klosterneuberger Verlagsanstalt, 1967), pp. 159-171.

GOGUEL, M., *Jean-Baptiste*, (Paris, Payot, 1928).

GOURBILLON, J.G., "La parabole du serpent d'airain et la 'lacune' du ch. III de l'Évangile selon S. Jean", *Vivre et Penser* 2 (1942) 213-226.

GRAF, J., "Nikodemus (Joh 3,1-21)", *TüTQ* 132 (1952) 62-86.

GRÄSSER, E, "Die antijüdische Polemik im Johannesevangelium", *NTS* 11 (1964-65) 74-90.

GRELOT, P., "L'interprétation pénitentielle du lavement des pieds", in *L'homme devant Dieu: Mélanges H. de Lubac*, (Paris, Aubier, 1963), Vol. I, pp. 75-91.

GRILL, J., *Untersuchung über die Entstehung des vierten Evangeliums*, (Tübingen-Leipzig, J.C.B. Mohr, 1902. 1923), 2 vols.

GROSHEIDE, F.W., "Υἱὸς τοῦ ἀνθρώπου en het Evangelium naar Johannes", *Theologische Studiën* 35 (1917) 242-248.

GROSSOUW, W., "La glorification du Christ", in *L'Évangile de Jean. Études et problèmes*, Recherches Bibliques III, (Bruges, Desclée de Brouwer, 1958), pp. 131-145.

— "A Note on John 13,1-3", *NT* 8 (1966) 124-131.

GRUNDMANN, W., "Matt. 11,27 und die johanneische 'der Vater und der Sohn' — Stellen", *NTS* 12 (1965-66) 42-49.

GUILDING, A., *The Fourth Gospel and Jewish Worship. A Study of the Relation of St. John's Gospel to the Ancient Jewish Lectionary System*, (Oxford, OUP, 1960).

HAENCHEN, E., "Historie und Geschichte in den johanneischen Passionsberichten", in *Die Bibel und Wir. Gesammelte Aufsätze II*, (Tübingen, J.C.B. Mohr, 1968) pp. 182-207.

— "Jesus vor Pilatus (Joh 18,28-19-15)", in *Gott und Mensch. Gesammelte Aufsätze*, (Tübingen, J.C.B. Mohr, 1965) pp. 144-156.

— "Johanneische Probleme", *ZKT* 56 (1959) 19-54.

— " 'Der Vater der mich gesandt hat' ", *NTS* 9 (1962-63) 208-216.

HAHN, F., "Die alttestamentlichen Motive der urchristlichen Abendmahls-Ueberlieferung" *EvTh* 27 (1967) 337-374.

— *Christologische Hoheitstitel. Ihre Geschichte im frühen Christentum*, FRLANT 83, (Göttingen, Vandenhoeck und Ruprecht, 1966³).

— "Die Jüngerberufung Joh 1,35-51", in J. Gnilka (ed.), *Neues Testament und Kirche: Für Rudolf Schnackenburg*, (Freibur, Herder, 1974) pp. 172-190.

— *Mission in the New Testament*, SBT 47, (London, SCM Press, 1965). English translation of *Das Verständnis der Mission im neuen Testament*, (Neukirchen-Vluyn, Neukirchener-Verlag, 1963).

— "Der Prozess Jesu nach dem Johannesevangelium", *EKK* 2 (1970) 23-96.

— "Sehen und Glauben im Johannesevangelium", in H. Baltensweiler-Bo Reicke (eds.), *Neues Testament und Geschichte. Historisches Geschehen und Deutung im Neuen Testament: Oscar Cullmann zum 70. Geburtstag*, (Tübingen, J.C.B. Mohr, 1972) pp. 125-141.

HAMERTON-KELLY, R.G., *Pre-Existence, Wisdom and the Son of Man: A Study of the Idea of Pre-Existence in the New Testament*, SNTS monograph series 21, (Cambridge, CUP, 1973).

HARING, N.M., "Historical Notes on the Interpretation of John 13,10", *CBQ* 13 (1951) 355-380.

HARNER, P.B., *The "I am" of the Fourth Gospel*, Facet Books, Biblical Series 26, (Philadelphia, Fortress Press, 1970).

— "Qualitative Anarthrous Predicate Nouns: Mark 15,39 and John 1,1", *JBL* 92 (1973) 75-87.

HAUCK, F., Art. "μένω", *TDNT* IV, pp. 574-588.

HENGEL, M., *Die Zeloten*, AGSU 1, (Leiden, E.J. Brill, 1961).

HÉRING, J., *Le Royaume de Dieu et sa venue*, (Neuchatel, Delachaux et Niestlé, 1959).

HIGGINS, A.J.B., *Jesus and the Son of Man*, (London, Lutterworth, 1964).

HILL, D., "The Request of Zebedee's Sons and the Johannine δόξα theme", *NTS* 13 (1966-67) 281-285.

HINDLEY, J.C., "Towards a Date for the Similitudes of Enoch", *NTS* 14 (1967-68) 551-565.

HIRSCH, E., *Studien zum vierten Evangelium*, Beiträge zur historischen Theologie 11, (Tübingen, J.C.B. Mohr, 1936).

HODGSON, P.C., "The Son of Man and the Problem of Historical Knowledge", *JR* 41 (1961) 91-108.

HOLZMEISTER, U., "Nathanael fuitne idem ac S. Bartholomaeus Apostolus?", *Biblica* 21 (1940) 28-39.

— "Grundgedanke und Gedankengang im Gespräche des Herrn mit Nikodemus", *ZKT* 45 (1921) 527-548.

HOOKER, M.D., "In his own Image?", in M.D. Hooker-C. Hickling (eds.), *What about the New Testament? Essays in Honour of Christopher Evans*, (London, SCM Press, 1975) pp. 28-44.

— *Jesus and the Servant*, (London, SPCK, 1959).

— "The Johannine Prologue and the Messianic Secret", *NTS* 21 (1974-75) 40-58.

— "John the Baptist and the Johannine Prologue", *NTS* 16 (1969-70) 354-358.

— *The Son of Man in Mark*, (London, SPCK, 1967).

HOSKYNS, E.C., "John 3,1-21", *TLond* 1 (1920) 83-89.

HOWARD, J.K., "Passover and Eucharist in the Fourth Gospel", *ScotJT* 20 (1967) 329-337.

HOWARD, W.F., *Christianity according to St. John*, (London, Duckworth, 1943).

HOWARD, W.F. - BARRETT, C.K., *The Fourth Gospel in Recent Criticism and Interpretation*, (London, Epworth, 1955).

HSIA CH'I LUNG, "Lun Jowang fuyin chung ti 'jentzu' " (The "Son of Man" in John's Gospel), *Collectanea Theologica Universitatis Fujen* 10 (1971), pp. 467-502.

HUBY, J., *Le discours de Jésus après la Cène*, (Paris, Beauchesne, Verbum Salutis, 1942²).

IBER, G., *Ueberlieferungsgeschichtliche Untersuchungen zum Begriff des Menschensohn im Neuen Testament*, (Unpublished Dissertation, Heidelberg, 1953).

JANOT, E., "Le Pain de Vie", *Greg* 11 (1930) 161-170.

JANSSENS, Y., "Le Codex XIII de Nag Hammadi", *Le Muséon* 87 (1974) 341-413.

JANSSENS DE VAREBEKE, A., "La structure des scènes du récit de la passion en Jn. 18-19", *ETL* 38 (1962) 504-522.

JEREMIAS, J., "Die älteste Schichte der Menschensohn-Logien", *ZNW* 58 (1967) 159-172.

— "Die Berufung des Nathanael", *Angelos* 3 (1928) 2-5.

— *The Eucharistic Words of Jesus*, (London, SCM Press, 1966). English translation of *Die Abendmahlsworte Jesu*, (Göttingen, Vandenhoeck und Ruprecht, 1960).

— *Jesus' Promise to the Nations*, SBT 24, (London, SCM Press, 1967²). English translation of *Jesu Verheissung für die Völker*, (Stuttgart, Kohlhammer, 1959).

— "Joh 6,51c-58 — redaktionell?", *ZNW* 44 (1952-53) 256-257.

— "Johanneische Literarkritik", *TB* 20 (1941) 33-46.

— *New Testament Theology*, Vol. I: "The Proclamation of Jesus", (London, SCM Press, 1971). English translation of *Neutestamentliche Theologie* I. Teil: Die Verkündigung Jesu, (Gütersloh, Gerd Mohn, 1971).

— "Zum nicht-responsorischen Amen", *ZNW* 64 (1973) 122-123.

JOCZ, J., "Die Juden im Johannesevangelium", *Judaica* 9 (1953) 129-142.

JOHNSON, S.E., "King Parables in the Synoptic Gospels", *JBL* 74 (1955) 37-39.

JOHNSTON, E.D., "The Johannine Version of the Feeding of the Five Thousand — an Independent Tradition?", *NTS* 8 (1961-62) 151-154.

KÄSEMANN, E., "Johannes 12,20-26", in *Exegetische Versuche und Besinnungen* I, (Göttingen, Vandenhoeck und Ruprecht, 1960), pp. 254-257.

— "The Prologue to John's Gospel", in *New Testament Questions of Today*, (London, SCM Press, 1969), pp. 138-167. English translation of *Exegetische Versuche und Besinnungen* II, (Göttingen, Vandenhoeck und Ruprecht, 1965).

— *The Testament of Jesus*, (London, SCM Press, 1968). English translation of *Jesu letzter Wille nach Johannes 17*, (Tübingen, J.C.B. Mohr, 1966).

KERN, W., "Die symmetrische Gesamtaufbau von Joh. 8,12-58", *ZKT* 78 (1956) 451-454.

KIEFFER, R., *Au delà des recensions? L'évolution textuelle dans Jean VI, 52-71*, Coniectanea Biblica. New Testament Series 3, (Lund, Gleerup, 1968).

KILMARTIN, E.J., "The Formation of the Bread of Life Discourse (John 6)", *Script* 12 (1960) 75-78.

— "Liturgical Influence on John 6", *CBQ* 22 (1960) 183-191.

KINNIBURGH, E., "The Johannine Son of Man", *StEv* 4 (1968) 64-71.

KITTEL, G., Art. ἀκολουθέω, in *TDNT* I, pp. 210-216.

— "'izdᵉqēph = ὑψωθῆναι = Gekreuzigtwerden", *ZNW* 35 (1936) 282-285.

KITTEL, G. - VON RAD, G., Art. "δόξα" in *TDNT* II pp. 232-255.

KLEIST, J.A., "A Note on the Greek Text of St. John 12,7", *Classical Journal* 21 (1925) 46-48.

KLOS, H., *Die Sakramente im Johannesevangelium*, (Stuttgart, Katholisches Bibelwerk, 1970).

KNOX, W.L., "John 13,1-30", *HTR* 43 (1950) 161-163.

KOSSEN, H.B., "Who were the Greeks of John 12,20?", in *Studies in John*, pp. 97-110.

KÜHNE, W., "Eine kritische Studie zu Joh. 12,7", *Theologische Studien und Kritiken* 98-99 (1926) 476-477.

KÜMMEL, W.G., "Die Eschatologie der Evangelien", *TB* 15 (1936) 225-241.

— *Introduction to the New Testament*, (London, SCM Press, 1966). English translation of *Einleitung in das Neue Testament*, (Heidelberg, Quelle und Meyer, 1965).

— *The New Testament. The History of the Investigation of its Problems*, (London, SCM Press, 1973). English translation of *Das Neue Testament: Geschichte der Erforschung seiner Probleme*, (Freiburg, Karl Alber, 1970).

— *The Theology of the New Testament According to its Major Witnesses: Jesus — Paul — John*, (London, SCM Press, 1974). English translation of *Die Theologie des Neuen Testaments nach seinen Hauptzeugen*, (Göttingen, Vandenhoeck und Ruprecht, 1972).

LAZURE, N., "Le lavement des pieds", *AssSeign* 38 (1967) 40-51.

LE DÉAUT, R., "Targumic Literature and New Testament Interpretation", *BTB* 4 (1974) 243-289.

— "Une aggadah targumique et les murmures de Jean 6", *Biblica* 51 (1970) 80-83.

LEE, E.K., "St. Mark and the Fourth Gospel", *NTS* (1956-57) 50-58.

— *The Religious Thought of St. John*, (London, SPCK, 1962).

LEENHARDT, F.J., "La structure du chapitre 6 de l'évangile de Jean", *RHPR* 39 (1959) 1-13.

LEGAULT, A., "An Application of the Form-Critique Method to the Anointings in Galilee (Lk. 7,36-50) and Bethany (Mt. 26,6-13; Mk. 14,3-9; Jn. 12,1-8)", *CBQ* 16 (1954) 131-145.

LEIVESTAD, R., "Der apokalyptische Menschensohn ein theologisches Phantom", in *Annual of the Swedish Theological Institute* VI (1960) pp. 49-105.

— "Exit the Apocalyptic Son of Man", *NTS* 18 (1971-72) 234-267.

LEMONNYER, A., "L'onction de Béthanie. Notes d'exégèse sur Jean 12,1-8", *RecSR* 18 (1928) 105-117.

LENTZEN-DEIS, F.L., "Das Motiv der 'Himmelsöffnung' in verschiedenen Gattungen der Umweltliteratur des N.T.", *Biblica* 50 (1968) 315-327.

— *Die Taufe Jesu nach den Synoptikern. Literarkritische und Gattungsgeschichtliche Untersuchungen*, Theologische Studien 4, (Frankfurt, Josef Knecht, 1970).

LÉON-DUFOUR, X., "Le mystère du Pain de Vie (Jean VI)", *RecSR* 46 (1958) 481-523.

— " 'Père, fais-moi passer sain et sauf à travers cette heure!' (Jn. 12,27)", in H. Baltensweiler-Bo Reicke (eds.), *Neues Testament und Geschichte. Historisches Geschehen und Deutung im Neuen Testament: Oscar Cullmann sum 70. Geburtstag*, (Tübingen,

J.C.B. Mohr, 1972), pp. 156-165.
— "Trois chiasmes johanniques", *NTS* 7 (1960-61) 253-255.
LEROY, H., "Das johanneische Missverständnis als literarische Form", *BuL* 9 (1968) 196-207.
— *Rätsel und Missverständnis. Ein Beitrag zur Formgeschichte des Johannesevangeliums,* Bonner Biblischer Beiträge 30, (Bonn, Hanstein, 1968).
LIGHTFOOT, R.H., *History and Interpretation in the Gospels,* (London, Hodder & Stoughton, 1935).
LILLY, J.L., "The Eucharistic Discourse of John 6", *CBQ* 12 (1950) 48-51.
LINDARS, B., *Behind the Fourth Gospel,* Studies in Creative Criticism 3, (London, SPCK, 1971).
— "The Son of Man in the Johannine Christology ", in B. Lindars-S.S. Smalley (eds.), *Christ and Spirit in the New Testament: Studies in Honour of Charles Francis Digby Moule,* (Cambridge, CUP, 1973), pp. 43-60.
— "Two Parables in John", *NTS* 16 (1970) 318-329.
LOFTHOUSE, W.F., "Vater und Sohn im Johannes-Evangelium", *TB* 11 (1932) 289-300.
LOHMEYER, E., "Die Fusswaschung", *ZNW* 38 (1939) 74-94.
LOHSE, E., "Miracles in the Fourth Gospel", in M.D. Hooker-C. Hickling (eds.), *What about the New Testament? Essays in Honour of Christopher Evans,* (London, SCM Press, 1975), pp. 64-75.
— "Wort und Sakrament im Johannesevangelium", *NTS* 7 (1960-61) 110-125.
McELENEY, N.J., Review of J.L. Martyn, *History and Theology in the Fourth Gospel,* in *The Seminary Journal* 21 (1968) 38-39.
MACGREGOR, G.H.C., "The Eucharist in the Fourth Gospel", *NTS* 9 (1962-63) 111-119.
— "A Suggested Rearrangement of the Johannine Text (Ioh. 3,14-36; 12, 30-36)", *ET* 35 (1923-24) 476-477.
McNAMARA, M., "The Ascension and the Exaltation of Christ in the Fourth Gospel", *Script* 19 (1967) 65-73.
McPOLIN, J., "Bultmanni theoria letteraria et Jo. 6, 51c-58c", *VD* 44 (1966) 248-258.
— *The "Name" of the Father and of the Son in the Johannine Writings,* Excerpt from Doctoral Dissertation, (Rome, Pontifical Biblical Institute, 1972).
MACRAE, G., "The Fourth Gospel and 'Religionsgeschichte' ", *CBQ* 32 (1970) 13-24.
— "Theology and Irony in the Fourth Gospel", in R.J. Clifford-G.W. Macrae (eds.), *The Word in the World: Essays in Honor of Frederick L. Moriarty, S.J.,* (Cambridge, Mass., Weston College Press, 1973) pp. 83-96.
MADDOX, R., "The Function of the Son of Man in the Gospel of John", in R.J. Banks (ed.), *Reconciliation and Hope: New Testament Essays on Atonement and Eschatology Presented to L.L. Morris on his 60th Birthday,* (Exeter, Paternoster Press, 1974) pp. 186-204.
MALATESTA, E., *St. John's Gospel 1920-1965. A Cumulative and Classified Bibliography of Books and Periodical Literature on the Fourth Gospel,* Analecta Biblica 32, (Rome, Biblical Institute Press, 1967).
MALDONADO, J., *De Exaltation Filii Hominis apud S. Johannem,* (Dissertation, Studium Biblicum Franciscanum, Jerusalem, 1964).
MALINA, B.J., *The Palestinian Manna-Tradition,* (Leiden, E.J. Brill, 1968).
MANSON, T.W., "The Argument from Prophecy", *JTS* 46 (1945) 129-136.
MARSHALL, I.H., "The Son of Man in Contemporary Debate", *EvQu* 42 (1970) 67-87.
— "The Synoptic Son of Man Sayings in Recent Discussion", *NTS* 12 (1965-66) 327-351.
MARTYN, J.L., *History and Theology in the Fourth Gospel,* (New York, Harper & Row, 1968).
MEEKS, W.A., "The Man from Heaven in Johannine Sectarianism", *JBL* 91 (1972) 44-72.
— *The Prophet-King. Moses Traditions and the Johannine Christology,* SNT 14, (Leiden, E.J. Brill, 1967).
MEES, M., "Erhöhung und Verherrlichung Jesu im Johannesevangelium nach dem Zeugnis neutestamentliche Papyri", *BZ* 18 (1974) 32-44.
— "Lectio brevior im Johannesevangelium und ihre Beziehung zum Urtext", *BZ* 12

296 *Bibliography*

(1968) 111-119.

— "Sinn und Bedeutung westlicher Textvarianten in Jo 6,31-58", *BZ* 13 (1969) 244-255.

MENDNER, S., "Nikodemus", *JBL* 77 (1958) 293-323.

— "Zum Problem 'Johannes und die Synoptiker' ", *NTS* 4 (1957-58) 282-307.

MENOUD, P.-H., "L'originalité de la pensée johannique", *RThPh* 28 (1940) 233-261.

MICHAELIS, W., "John 1,51, Gen 28,12 und das Menschensohn-Problem", *TLZ* 85 (1960) 561-578.

MICHAELS, J.R., "Nathanael under the Fig Tree", *ET* 78 (1966) 182-183.

MICHEL, O., "Der Menschensohn", *TZ* 27 (1971) 81-104.

MICHL, J., "Der Sinn der Fusswaschung", *Biblica* 40 (1954) 697-708.

MILIK, J.T., "Problèmes de la littérature hénochique à la lumière des fragments araméens de Qumran", *HTR* 64 (1971) 338-378.

— "Turfan et Qumran: livre des géants juif et manichéen", in *Tradition und Glaube. Das frühe Christentum in seiner Umwelt: Festgabe für Karl Georg Kuhn zum 65. Geburtstag*, (Göttingen, Vandenhoeck und Ruprecht, 1971) pp. 117-127.

MIRANDA, J.P., *Der Vater der mich gesandt hat: Religionsgeschichtliche Untersuchungen zu den johanneischen Sendungsformeln, zugleich ein Beitrag zur johanneischen Christologie und Ekklesiologie*, European University Papers 23/7, (Bern, Herbert Lang, 1972).

MOLLAT, D., "Le chapitre VIᵉ de Saint Jean", *LumVie* 31 (1957) 107-119.

— "La guérison de l'aveugle-né", *BibVChr* 23 (1958) 22-31.

— Art. "Jugement", *DBS* IV, cols. 1344-1394.

MOLONEY, F.J., "John 6 and the Celebration of the Eucharist", *The Downside Review* 93 (1975) 243-251.

— "The Johannine Son of God", *Salesianum* 38 (1976) 71-86.

— "The Targum on Ps. 8 and the New Testament", *Salesianum* 37 (1975) 326-336.

MOORE, F.J., "Eating the Flesh and Drinking the Blood: A Reconsideration", *ATR* 48 (1966) 70-75.

MOORE, W.E., "Sir, We Wish to See Jesus — Was This an Occasion of Temptation?", *ScotJT* 20 (1967) 75-93.

MORETON, M.J., "Feast, Sign and Discourse in John 5", *StEv* 4 (1968) 209-213.

MORRIS, L., *The New Testament and the Jewish Lectionaries*, (London, Tyndale Press, 1964).

— *Studies in the Fourth Gospel*, (Exeter, Paternoster Press, 1969).

MOULE, C.F.D., *The Birth of the New Testament*, Black's New Testament Commentaries, Companion Volume 1, (London, A. & C. Black, 1966).

— "Further Reflexions on Philippians 2,5-11", in W.W. Gasque-R.P. Martin (eds.), *Apostolic History and the Gospel: Biblical and Historical Essays presented to F.F. Bruce on his 60th Birthday*, (Exeter, Paternoster Press, 1970) pp. 264-276.

— "A Neglected Factor in the Interpretation of Johannine Eschatology", in *Studies in John: Presented to Professor Dr. J.N. Sevenster on the Occasion of his Seventieth Birthday*, SNT 24, (Leiden, E.J. Brill, 1970) pp. 155-160.

MOULE, C.F.D., "Neglected Features in the Problem of 'the Son of Man' ", in J. Gnilka (ed.), *Neues Testament und Kirche: Für Rudolf Schnackenburg*, (Freiburg, Herder, 1974) pp. 413-428.

— *The Phenomenon of the New Testament*, SBT second series 1, (London, SCM Press, 1967).

MÜLLER, K., "Joh 9,7 und das jüdische Verständnis des Siloh-Spruches", *BZ* 13 (1969) 251-256.

MÜLLER, T., *Das Heilsgeschehen im Johannesevangelium*, (Zürich, Gotthelf-Verlag, no date).

MURRAY, J.O.F., *Jesus according to St. John*, (London, Logmans, 1936).

MUSSNER, F., ZΩH. *Die Anschauung vom "Leben" im vierten Evangelium unter Berücksichtigung der Johannesbriefe*, Münchener Theologische Studien. Historische Abteilung 5, (München, Zink, 1952).

NOACK, B., *Zur johanneischen Tradition. Beiträge zur Kritik an der literarkritischen Analyse des vierten Evangeliums*, (Copenhagen, Rosenkilde, 1954).

OTTO, R., *The Kingdom of God and The Son of Man*, (London, Lutterworth, 1938). Revised English translation of *Reichgottes und Menschensohn. Ein religionsgeschichtlicher Versuch*, (München, C.H. Beck, 1934).

PASS, H.L., *The Glory of the Father. A Study of St. John 13-17*, (London, Mowbray, 1935).

PATSCH, H., "Der Einzug Jesu in Jerusalem, ein historischer Versuch", *ZTK* 68 (1971) 1-26.

PERCORARA, G., "De verbo 'manere' apud Joannem", *DThom* 14 (1937) 157-171.

PERRIN, N., *Rediscovering the Teaching of Jesus*, (London, SCM Press, 1967).

PETERSON, E., "Die Einholung des Kyrios", *ZSyTh* 7 (1930) 682-702.

— "Zeuge der Wahrheit" in *Theologische Traktate*, (München, Kösel, 1956) pp. 165-224.

POLLARD, T.E., *Johannine Christology and the Early Church*, SNTS Monograph Series 13, (Cambridge, CUP, 1970).

PORTER, C.L., "John IX. 38,39a: A Liturgical Addition to the Text", *NTS* 13 (1966-67) 387-394.

PREISKER, H., "Jüdische Apokalyptik und hellenistischer Synkretismus im Johannes-Evangelium, dargelegt an dem Begriff 'Licht' ", *TLZ* 77 (1952) 673-678.

PREISS, T., "Étude sur le ch. 6 de l'Évangile de Jean", *EThRel* 46 (1971) 143-167.

— "Le Fils de l'Homme dans le IVe Évangile", *EThRel* 28 (1953) 7-61.

— *Life in Christ*, SBT 13, (London, SCM Press, 1954). English translation of selected chapters from *La Vie en Christ*, (Neuchâtel, Delachaux et Niestlé, 1952).

PRIBNOW, H., *Die johanneische Anschauung vom "Leben". Eine biblisch-theologische Untersuchung in religionsgeschichtlicher Beleuchtung*, in Greifswalder Theologische Forschungen 4, (Greifswald, Bamberg, 1934).

QUISPEL, G., "Nathanael und der Menschensohn (Joh 1,51)", *ZNW* 47 (1956) 281-283.

QUELL, G., Art. ἀλήθεια, *TDNT* 1, pp. 232-237.

RACETTE, J., "L'unité du discours sur le pain de vie", *ScEccl* 9 (1957) 82-85.

RASCO, A., "Christus, granum frumenti (Jo 12,24)", *VD* 37 (1959) 12-25. 65-77.

REESE, J.M., "Literary Structure of John 13,31-14,31; 16,5-6; 16,16-33", *CBQ* 34 (1972) 321-331.

REIM, G., *Studien zum alttestamentlichen Hintergrund des Johannesevangeliums*, SNTS Monograph Series 22, (Cambridge, CUP, 1974).

REISER, W.E., "The Case of the Tidy Tomb: The Place of the Napkins of John 11,44 and 20,7", *HeyJ* 14 (1973) 47-57.

RENGSTORF, K.H., Art. ληστής *TDNT* IV, pp. 257-262.

RIAUD, J., "La gloire et la royauté de Jésus dans la passion selon saint Jean", *BibVChr* 56 (1964) 28-44.

RICCA, P., *Die Eschatologie des vierten Evangeliums*, (Zürich, Gotthelf Verlag. 1966).

RICHARDSON, A., *An Introduction to the Theology of the New Testament*, (London, SCM Press, 1958).

RICHTER, G., "Die alttestamentliche Zitate in der Rede vom Himmelsbrot, Joh. 6,26-51a", in J. Ernst (ed.), *Schriftauslesung*, Beiträge zur Hermeneutik des Neuen Testaments und im Neuen Testament, in Zusammenarbeit mit dem Colloquium Biblicum München, (Münster in Westfallen, Schöninghaus, 1972) pp. 193-279.

— "Die Deutung des Kreuzestodes Jesu in der Leidensgeschichte des Johannesevangeliums (Jo. 13-19)", *BuL* 9 (1968) 21-36.

— "Zur Formgeschichte und literarischen Einheit von Joh 6,31-58", *ZNW* 60 (1969) 21-55.

— *Die Fusswaschung im Johannesevangelium*, Biblische Untersuchungen 1, (Regensburg, Pustet, 1967).

— "Die Fusswaschung Joh 13,1-20", *MüTZ* 16 (1965) 13-26.

RIGG, W.H., "St. John 3,13", *TLond* 20 (1930) 98-99.

ROBINSON, J.A.T., "The Significance of the Foot-washing", in *Neotestamentica et Patristica: in Honour of O. Cullmann*, SNT 6, (Leiden, E.J. Brill, 1962), pp. 144-147.

ROBINSON, J.M., "Recent Research in the Fourth Gospel", *JBL* 78 (1959) 242-252.

RUCKSTUHL, E., "Die johanneische Menschensohnforschung 1957-1969", in J. Pfammatter-F. Furger (eds.), *Theologische Berichte* I, (Einsiedeln, Benziger, 1972) 171-284.

— *Die literarische Einheit des Johannesevangeliums, der gegenwärtige Stand der einschlägigen Forschungen,* Studia Friburgensia, n.f. 3, (Freiburg in der Schweiz, Ed. S. Paul, 1951).

— "Literarkritik am Johannesevangelium und eucharistische Rede (Jo. 6,51c-58)", *DivThom* 23 (1945) 153-190; 301-333.

— "Wesen und Kraft der Eucharistie in der Sicht des Johannesevangeliums", in *Das Opfer der Kirche. Exegetische, dogmatische und pastoraltheologische Studien zum Verständnis der Messe,* (Luzern, Rex-Verlag, 1954) pp. 47-90.

SABUGAL, S., *'CHRISTOS'. Investigación exegética sobre la cristología joannea,* (Barcelona, Herder, 1972).

SALMON, V., *Quatrième Évangile. Histoire de la tradition textuelle de l'original grec,* (Paris, Letouzey, 1969).

SCHELKLE, K.H., *Die Passion Jesu in der Verkündingung des Neuen Testaments,* (Heidelberg, F.H. Kerle, 1949).

SCHENKE, H.-M., *Der Gott "Mensch" in der Gnosis. Ein religionsgeschichtliche Beitrag zur Diskussion über der paulinische Anschauung von der Kirche als Leib Christi,* (Göttingen, Vandenhoeck und Ruprecht, 1962).

SCHLIER, H., "Jesus und Pilatus nach dem Johannesevangelium" in *Die Zeit der Kirche. Exegetische Aufsätze und Vorträge,* (Freiburg, Herder, 1956) pp. 56-74.

— "Joh 6 und das joh Verständnis der Eucharistie", in J. Sint (ed.), *Bibel und Zeitgemässer Glaube,* (Klosterneuburg, Klosterneuberger Verlag, 1967) Vol. 11, pp. 69-95.

SCHNACKENBURG, R., "Das Brot des Lebens", in *Tradition und Glaube. Das frühe Christentum in seiner Umwelt: Festgabe für Karl Georg Kuhn zum 65. Geburtstag,* (Göttingen, Vandenhoeck und Ruprecht, 1971) pp. 328-342.

— *Das erste Wunder Jesu (Joh 2,1-11),* (Freiburg, Herder, 1951).

— "Zur Herkunft des Johannesevangeliums", *BZ* 14 (1970) 1-23.

— "Joh 12, 39-41. Zur christologischen Schriftauslegung des vierten Evangeliums", in *Neues Testament und Geschichte,* pp. 167-177.

— "Der johanneische Bericht von der Salbung in Bethanien (Jo 12,1-8)", *MüTZ* 1 (1950) 48-52.

— "Zur johanneischen Theologie", *BZ* 6 (1962) 289-299.

— "Der Menschensohn im Johannesevangelium", *NTS* 11 (1964-65) 123-137.

— "Die Messiasfrage im Johannesevangelium", in J. Blinzler-O. Kuss-F. Mussner (eds.), *Neutestamentliche Aufsätze: Festschrift J. Schmid zum 70. Geburtstag,* (Regensburg, Pustet, 1963) pp. 240-264.

— "Zur Rede vom Brot aus dem Himmel: eine Beobachtung zu Joh 6,52", *BZ* 12 (1968) 248-252.

— "Offenbarung und Glaube im Johannesevangelium", *BuL* 7 (1966) 165-180.

— "Die situationsgelösten Redestücke in Joh 3", *ZNW* 49 (1958) 88-99.

— "Die Sakramente im Johannesevangelium", in Coppens-A. Deschamps-E. Massaux (eds.), *Sacra Pagina,* Miscellanea Biblica Congressus Internationalis Catholici de Re Biblica, (Gembloux, Duculot, 1959), Vol. II, pp. 235-254.

— "Das Schriftzitat in Joh 19,37", in J. Schreiner (ed.), *Wort, Lied und Gottesspruch: Beiträge zu Psalmen und Propheten: Feitschrift für Joseph Ziegler,* Forschung zur Bibel 2, (Würzburg, Echter, 1972) pp. 239-245.

SCHNEIDER, H., " 'The Word was Made Flesh'. An Analysis of the Theology of Revelation in the Fourth Gospel", *CBQ* 31 (1969) 344-356.

SCHNEIDER, J., "Die Abschiedsreden Jesu. Ein Beitrag zur Frage der Komposition von Joh 13,31-17,26", in *Gott und die Götter: Festgabe E. Fascher zum 60. Geburtstag,* (Berlin, Evangelische Verlagsanstalt, 1958) pp. 103-112.

— Art. ἔρχομαι, *TDNT* II, pp. 666-684.

— "Zur Frage der Komposition von Joh. 6,27-58 (59) — Die Himmelsbrotrede", in W. Schmauch (ed.), *In Memoriam Ernst Lohmeyer,* (Stuttgart, Evang. Verlagswerk, 1951) pp. 132-142.

— "Zur Komposition von Joh 18, 12-17, Kaiaphas und Hannas", *ZNW* 48 (1957) 11-19.
SCHOLEM, G.G., *Major Trends in Jewish Mysticism*, (London, Thames and Hudson, 1955).
SCHULZ, S., *Komposition und Herkunft der Johanneischen Reden*, (Stuttgart, Kohlhammer, 1960).
— *Die Stunde der Botschaft. Einführung in die Theologie der vier Evangelisten*, (Hamburg, Furche, 1967).
— *Untersuchungen zur Menschensohn-Christologie im Johannesevangelium. Zugleich ein Beitrag zur Methodengeschichte der Auslegung des 4 Evangeliums*, (Göttingen, Vandenhoeck und Ruprecht, 1957).
SCHÜRMANN, H., "Joh 6,51c — ein Schlüssel zur grossen johanneischen Brotrede", *BZ* 2 (1958) 244-262.
— "Die Eucharistie als Representation und Applikation des Heilsgeschehens nach Joh 6, 53-58", *TrTZ* 68 (1959) 30-45. 108-118.
SCHWARTZ, E., "Aporien im vierten Evangelium", *Nachrichten von der königlichen Gesellschaft der Wissenschaften zu Göttingen*, (1907), pp. 342-372; (1908), pp. 115-148. 149-188. 497-560.
SCHWEIZER, E., *Ego Eimi ... Die Religionsgeschichtliche Herkunft und theologische Bedeutung der johanneischen Bildreden, zugleich ein Beitrag zur Quellenfrage des vierten Evangeliums*, FRLANT 38, (Göttingen, Vandenhoeck und Ruprecht, 1939).
— *Erniedrigung und Erhöhung bei Jesus und seinen Nachfolgern*, ATANT 28, (Zürich, Zwingli-Verlag, 1955).
— "Das johanneischen Zeugnis vom Herrenmahl", *EvTh* 12 (1952-53) 341-363.
— "Die Kirche als Leib Christi in den paulinischen Homologumena", *TLZ* 86 (1961), 161-174.
— "Der Menschensohn", *ZNW* 50 (1959) 185-209.
— Art. σάρξ *TDNT* VII, pp. 124-151.
— Art. υἱός, *TDNT* VIII, pp. 363-392.
SEGALLA, G., "Cinque schemi cristologici in Giovanni", *StPat* 20 (1973) 5-53.
— "L'esperienza cristiana in Giovanni", *StPat* 18 (1971) 299-342.
— "La struttura circolare-chiasmatica di Gv 6,26-58 e il suo significato teologico", *BibOr* 13 (1971) 191-198.
— "Preesistenza, Incarnazione e Divinità di Cristo in Giovanni", *RBibIt* 22 (1974) 155-181.
— "Rassegna di Cristologia Giovannea", *StPat* 18 (1971) 693-732.
SERRA, A., "Le tradizioni della teofania Sinaitica nel Targum del pseudo-Jonathan Es. 19.24 e in Giov. 1,19-2,12", *Marianum* 33 (1971) 1-39.
SEVENSTER, G., "Remarks on the Humanity of Jesus in the Gospel and Letters of John", in *Studies in John*, pp. 185-193.
SHORTER, M., "The Position of Chapter VI in the Fourth Gospel", *ET* 84 (1973) 181-183.
SIDEBOTTOM, E.M., "The Ascent and Descent of the Son of Man in the Gospel of St. John", *ATR* 2 (1957) 115-122.
— *The Christ of the Fourth Gospel in the Light of the First Century Thought*, (London, SPCK, 1961).
— "The Son of Man as Man in the Fourth Gospel", *ET* 68 (1956-57) 231-235. 280-283.
SKRINJAR, J., "De terminologia sacrificali in Jo 6,51-56", *DThom* 74 (1971) 189-197.
SMALLEY, S.S., "Diversity and Development in John", *NTS* 17 (1970-71) 276-292.
— "The Johannine Son of Man Sayings", *NTS* 15 (1968-69) 278-301.
— "Liturgy and Sacrament in the Fourth Gospel", *EvQu* 29 (1957) 159-170.
— "New Light on the Fourth Gospel", *TynBull* 17 (1966) 34-62.
SMITH, D.M., *The Composition and Order of the Fourth Gospel. Bultmann's Literary Theory*, (New Haven, Yale University Press, 1965).
— "Johannine Christianity: Some Reflections on its Character and Delineation", *NTS* 21 (1974-75) 222-248.
— "Jn. 12,12ff and the Question of John's Use of the Synoptics", *JBL* 82 (1963) 58-64.
SMITH, M., "Observations on *Hekhalot Rabbati*", in A. Altmann (ed.), *Biblical and*

Other Studies, Lown Institute, *Studies and Texts,* Vol. 1., (Harvard, Harvard University Press, 1963), pp. 142-160.

SNYDER, G., "John 13,16 and the Anti-Petrinism of the Johannine Tradition", *BRes* 16 (1971) 5-15.

SPITTA, F., *Das Johannes-Evangelium als Quelle der Geschichte Jesu,* (Göttingen, Vandenhoeck und Ruprecht, 1910).

SPRINGER, E., "Die Einheit der Rede von Kaphernaum (Jo 6)", *BZ* 15 (1918-21) 319-334.

STÄHLIN, G., "Zum Problem der johanneischen Eschatologie", *ZNW* 33 (1934) 225-259.

STAGG, F., "The Farewell Discourses: John 13-17", *Review and Expositor* 62 (1965) 459-472.

STEMBERGER, G., *La symbolique du bien et du mal selon Saint Jean,* (Paris, Editions du Seuil, 1970).

STRAUSS, D.F., *The Life of Jesus Critically Examined,* Translated from the German *Das Leben Jesu kritisch bearbeitet,* under the editorship of P.C. Hodgson, (London, SCM Press, 1973).

SUNDBERG, A.C., "*Isos To Theo* Christology in John 5, 17-30", *BibRes* 15 (1970) 19-31.

TAYLOR, V., *The Names of Jesus,* (London, Macmillan, 1953).

— *The Person of Christ in New Testament Teaching,* (London, Macmillan, 1958).

TEEPLE, H.M., *The Literary Origin of the Gospel of John,* (Evanston, Religion and Ethics Institute, 1974).

TEMPLE, S., "A Key to the Composition of the Fourth Gospel", *JBL* 80 (1961) 220-232.

THOMSON, J.M., "An Experiment in Translation", *The Expositor,* 8th. Series, Vol. 16, (1918) pp. 117-125.

THÜSING, W., *Die Erhöhung und Verherrlichung Jesu im Johannesevangelium,* Neutestamentliche Abhandlungen 21,1, (Münster, Aschendorff, 1970²).

— " 'Wenn ich von der Erde erhöht bin ...' (Joh 12,32). Die Erhöhung nach dem Jo-Ev", *Bibel und Kirche* 20, 2 (1965) 40-42.

THYEN, H., "Aus der Literatur zum Johannesevangelium", *TR* 39 (1974) 1-69. 222-252.

— "Johannes 13 und die kirchliche Redaktion des vierten Evangeliums", in *Tradition und Glaube: Das frühe Christentum in seiner Umwelt: Festgabe für Karl Georg Kuhn zum 65. Geburtstag,* (Göttingen, Vandenhoeck und Ruprecht, 1971) pp. 343-356.

TILLMANN, F., "Jesus, der Menschensohn", *Biblische Zeitfragen* 1 (1908) 3-29.

— *Der Menschensohn. Jesu Selbstzeugnis für seine messianische Würde,* (Bonn, P. Hauptmann, 1905).

TÖDT, H.E., *The Son of Man in the Synoptic Tradition,* (London, SCM Press, 1965). English translation of *Der Menschensohn in der synoptischen Ueberlieferung,* (Gütersloh, Gerd Mohn, 1963).

TOPEL, L.J., "A Note on the Methodology of Structural Analysis in Jn. 2,23-3,21", *CBQ* 33 (1971) 211-20.

TORRENCE, T., "We would See Jesus (Jn 12,21)", *EvQu* 23 (1951) 171-182.

TORREY, C.C., " 'When I am lifted up from the earth'. John 12,32", *JBL* 51 (1932) 320-322.

TRAETS, C., *Voir Jésus et le Père en Lui selon l'Évangile de Saint Jean,* Analecta Gregoriana 159, (Rome, Gregorian University Press, 1967).

TREMEL, Y.B., "Le fils de l'homme selon S. Jean", *LumVie* 12 (1963) 65-92.

URICCHIO, N., "Le teorie delle trasposizioni nel Vangelo di S. Giovanni", *Biblica* 31 (1950) 129-163.

VAN DEN BUSSCHE, H., "L'attente de la grande Révélation dans le 4ᵉ évangile", *NRT* 75 (1953) 1009-1019.

— *Le discours d'adieux de Jésus,* (Tournai, Casterman, 1959).

— "Nu is de Mensenzoon verheelijkt (Jo 13,31-38)", *CollGand* 36 (1953) 97-105.

— "Si le grain de blé ne tombe en terre (Jn 12,20-39)", *BibVChr* 5 (1954) 53-67.

— "La Structure de Jean 1-13", in *L'Évangile de Jean. Études et problèmes,* Recherches Bibliques III, (Bruges, Desclée de Brouwer, 1968), pp. 61-109.

VAN HARTINGSVELD, L., *Die Eschatologie des Johannesevangeliums. Eine Auseinandersetzung mit Rudolf Bultmann,* (Assen, Van Gorcum, 1962).

VANHOYE, A., "La composition de Jn. 5,18-30", in A. Descamps-A. Halleux (eds.), *Mélanges Bibliques en hommage au R. P. Béda Rigaux,* (Gembloux, Duculot, 1970) pp. 259-274.
— "Interrogation johannique et exégèse de Cana (Jn. 2,4)", *Biblica* 55 (1974) 157-167.
VANNESTE, A., "Le pain de vie descendu du ciel", *AssSeign* 54 (1966) 41-53.
VAN UNNIK, W.C., "The Quotation from the Old Testament in John 12,34", *NT* 3 (1959) 174-179.
VAWTER, B., "Ezekiel and John", *CBQ* 26 (1964) 450-458.
— "The Johannine Sacramentary", *TS* 17 (1956) 151-166.
— "Some Recent Developments in Johannine Theology", *BTB* 1 (1971) 30-58.
VERGOTE, A., "L'Exaltation du Christ en Croix selon le quatrième évangile", *ETL* 28 (1952) 5-23.
VERMES, G., "He is the Bread: Targum Neofiti Exodus 16,15", in E.E. Ellis-M. Wilcox (eds.), *Neotestamentica et Semitica: Studies in Honour of Matthew Black,* (Edinburgh, T. & T. Clark, 1969) pp. 256-263.
VON CAMPENHAUSEN, H., "Zur Auslegung von Joh 13,6-10", *ZNW* 33 (1934) 259-271.
VON SYBEL, L., "Die Salbungen. Mt. 26,6-13; Mk. 14,3-9; Lk. 7,36-50; Joh 12,1-8", *ZNW* 23 (1924) 184-193.
WALKER, W.O., "The Origin of the Son of Man Concept as Applied to Jesus", *JBL* 91 (1972) 482-490.
WEAD, D.W., *The Literary Devices in John's Gospel,* Theologische Dissertationen IV, (Basel, Kommissionsverlag F. Reinhart, 1970).
WEISER, A., "Joh 13,12-20 — Zufüng eines späteren Herausgebers?", *BZ* 12 (1968) 252-257.
WENDLAND, H.-D., *Die Eschatologie des Reiches Gottes bei Jesus. Eine Studie über den Zusammenhang von Eschatologie, Ethik und Kirchenproblem,* (Gütersloh, Bertelsmann, 1931).
WETTER, G.P., *"Der Sohn Gottes": Eine Untersuchung über den Charakter und die Tendenz des Johannes-Evangeliums,* (Göttingen, Vandenhoeck und Ruprecht, 1916).
WILCKENS, U., "Der eucharistische Abschnitt der johanneischen Rede vom Lebensbrot (Joh 6,51c-58)", in *Neues Testament und Kirche,* pp. 220-248.
WILKENS, W., "Das Abendmahlzeugnis im vierten Evangelium", *EvTh* 18 (1958) 354-370.
— "Evangelist und Tradition im Johannesevangelium", *TZ* 16 (1960) 81-90.
WILSON, W.G., "The Original Text of the Fourth Gospel: Some objective evidence against the theory of page displacements", *JTS* 50 (1949) 59-60.
WINDISCH, H., "Angelophanien um den Menschensohn auf Erden. Ein Kommentar zu Joh. 1,51", *ZNW* 30 (1931) 215-233.
— "Joh 1,51 und die Auferstehung Jesu", *ZNW* 31 (1932) 199-204.
— "Der johanneische Erzählungsstil", in *'EUCHARISTERION'. Studien zur Religion und Literatur des Alten und Neuen Testaments Hermann Gunkel zum 60. Geburtstag dargebracht von seinen Schülern und Freunden,* FRLANT 19, (Göttingen, Vandenhoeck und Ruprecht, 1923) Vol. II, pp. 174-213.
WORDEN, T., "The Glory of God", *The Clergy Review* 60 (1975) 85-94.
— "The Holy Eucharist in St. John", *Script* 15 (1963) 97-106; 16 (1964) 5-16.
WREGE, H.T., "Jesusgeschichte und Jüngergeschick nach Joh 12,20-33 und Hebr 5,7-10", in E. Lohse-C. Burchard-B. Schaller (eds.), *Der Ruf Jesu und die Antwort der Gemeinde. Exegetische Untersuchungen Joachim Jeremias zum 70. Geburtstag gewidmet von seinen Schülern,* (Göttingen, Vandenhoeck und Ruprecht, 1970) pp. 259-288.
WRIGHT, C.J., "Jesus, the Revelation of God. His Mission and Message according to St. John", in H.D.A. Major-T.W. Manson-C.J. Wright, *The Mission and Message of Jesus. An Exposition of the Gospels in the Light of Modern Research,* (London, Ivor Nicholson and Watson, 1937) pp. 643-958.

YOUNG, A., "A Study of the Relation of Isaiah to the Fourth Gospel", *ZNW* 46 (1955) 215-223.

ZIENER, G., "Johannesevangelium und urchristliche Passafeier", *BZ* 2 (1958) 263-274.

ZIMMERLI, W., "Ich bin Jahwe", in *Geschichte und Altes Testament: Albrecht Alt zum 70. Geburtstag,* Beiträge zur historischen Theologie 16, (Tübingen, J.C.B. Mohr, 1953) pp. 179-209.

ZIMMERMAN, H., "Das absolute ᾿Εγώ ἐìμι als neutestamentliche Offenbarungsformel", *BZ* 4 (1960) 54-69. 266-276.

— *Neutestamentliche Methodenlehre. Darstellung der historisch-kritischen Methode,* (Stuttgart, Katholisches Bibelwerk, 1968).

BIBLIOGRAPHY TO THE SECOND EDITION

Further abbreviations

ABR	The Australian Biblical Review
ATD	Das Alte Testament Deutsch
JSJ	Journal for the Study of Judaism
OTD	Oudtestamentische Studiën
RSR	Revue des Sciences Religieuses
SJLA	Studies in Judaism in Late Antiquity
StNT	Studien zum Neuen Testament
SUNT	Studien zum Umwelt des Neuen Testament
VT	Vetus Testamentum
VTS	Vetus Testamentum Supplements
WMANT	Wissenschaftliche Monographien zum Alten und Neuen Testament
WMUNT	Wissenschaftliche Monographien zum Umwelt des Neuen Testaments
WUNT	Wissenschaftliche Untersuchungen zum Neuen Testament

Reviews of **The Johannine Son of Man**

R. F. COLLINS in *The Downside Review* 94 (1977) 76-77.
J. COPPENS in *ETL* 52 (1976) 392-394.
M. DE JONGE in *NedTTs* 31 (1977) 253-254.
TH. C. DE KRUIJF in *Bijdragen* 38 (1977) 99.
R. T. FORTNA in *Interp* 31 (1977) 429.
R. H. FULLER in *Religious Studies Review* 4 (1978) 63.
A. E. HARVEY in *JTS* 28 (1977) 552-553.
R. LEIVESTAD in *Norsk teologisk tidsskrift* 78 (1977) 111-112.
M.-V. LEROY in *RThom* 76 (1976) 510-511.
G. MENESTRINA in *BibOr* 19 (1978) 230.
J. RAMSEY MICHAELS in *JBL* 97 (1978) 149-150.·
E.L. MILLER in *TZ* 34 (1978) 109.
D. J. MURPHY in *TS* 38 (1977) 198.
J. PAINTER in *ABR* 25 (1977) 43-44.
G. RAVASI in *La Scuola Cattolica* 105 (1977) 269-270.
J. SCHLOSSER, "Chronique d'exégèse du Nouveau Testament", *RSR* 52 (1978) 39-41.
G. SEGALLA in *StPat* 24 (1977) 99-102.
A. SEGOVIA in *Archivo Teológico Granadino* 40 (1977) 273-274.
S. S. SMALLEY in *ET* 88 (1977) 183.
D. M. SMITH in *CBQ* 39 (1977) 440-441.
E. STOCKTON in *The Australasian Catholic Record* 54 (1977) 290-291.
G. TESTA in *DThom* 80 (1977) 313-314.
SJ. VAN TILBORG in *Tijdschrift voor Theologie* 17 (1977) 193.
H. WANSROUGH in *New Blackfriars* 58 (1977) 153.

Books and Articles

APPOLD, M. L., *The Oneness Motif in the Fourth Gospel. Motif Analysis and Exegetical Probe into the Theology of John*, WUNT 2. Reihe 1 (Tübingen, J. C. B. Mohr, 1976).

BARRETT, C. K., *Das Johannesevangelium und das Judentum*, Franz Delitzch-Vorlesungen 1967 (Stuttgart, Kohlhammer, 1970).

BECKER, J., "*Beobachtungen zum Dualismus im Johannesevangelium*", ZNW 65 (1974) 71-87.

— "J3,1-21 als Reflex johanneischer Schuldiskussion", in H. BALZ - S. SCHULZ (eds.), *Das Wort und die Wörter. Festschrift Gerhard Friedrich zum 65. Geburtstag* (Stuttgart, Kohlhammer, 1973) pp. 85-95.

— "Wunder und Christologie. Zum literarkritischen und christologischen Problem der Wunder im Johannesevangelium", NTS 16 (1970) 130-148.

BENOIT, P. - BOISMARD, M.-E., *Synopse des Quatre Evangiles en Français* (Paris, Editions du Cerf, 1965-1977) 3 Vols.

BERGER K., *Die Auferstehung des Propheten und die Erhöhung des Menschensohnes. Traditionsgeschichtliche Untersuchungen zur Deutung des Geschickes Jesu in frühchristlichen Texten*, SUNT 13 (Göttingen, Vandenhoeck und Ruprecht, 1976).

BERNARD, J., "La guérison de Bethesda. Harmoniques judéo-hellénistiques d'un récit de miracle un jour de sabbat", *Mélanges de science religieuse* 33 (1976) 3-34; 34 (1977) 13-44.

BERNINI, G., *Daniele*, Nuovissima Versione della Bibbia 28 (Roma, Edizioni Paoline, 1975).

BLACK, M., "Die Apotheose Israels: eine neue Interpretation des danielischen 'Menschensohns' ", in R. PESCH - R. SCHNACKENBURG - O. KAISER (eds.), *Jesus und der Menschensohn: Für Anton Vögtle* (Freiburg, Herder, 1975) pp. 92-99.

BORGEN, P., "Some Jewish Exegetical Traditions as Background for Son of Man Sayings in John's Gospel (3,13-14 and context)", in M. DE JONGE (ed.), *L'Évangile de Jean. Sources, rédaction, théologie*, BETL 44 (Gembloux, Duculot, 1977) pp. 243-258.

BREKELMANS, C. H. W., "The Saints of the Most High and their Kingdom", OTS 14 (1965) 305-329.

BROWN, R. E., "Johannine Ecclesiology — The Community's Origins", Interp 31 (1977) 379-393.

— "The Passion according to John: chapters 18 and 19", *Worship* 40 (1975) 126-134.

BÜHNER, JAN-A., *Der Gesandte und sein Weg im 4. Evangelium. Die kultur— und religionsgeschichtlichen Grundlangen der johanneischen Sendungschristologie sowie ihre traditionsgeschichtliche Entwicklung*, WUNT 2. Reihe 2 (Tübingen, J. C. B. Mohr, 1977).

CASEY, M., "The Corporate Interpretation of 'One Like a Son of Man' (Dan VII 13) at the Time of Jesus", NT 18 (1976) 167-180.

— "The Son of Man Problem", ZNW 67 (1976) 147-154.

— "The Use of Term 'Son of Man' in the Similitudes of Enoch", JSJ 7 (1976) 11-29.

COLLINS, R. F., "The Representative Figures of the Fourth Gospel", *The Downside Review* 94 (1976) 26-46; 118-132.

COLPE, C., "New Testament and Gnostic Christology", in J. NEUSNER (ed.), *Religions in Antiquity: Essays in Memory of Erwin Ramsdell Goodenough*, Studies in the History of Religions 14 (Leiden, E. J. Brill, 1968) pp. 227-243.

COPPENS, J., "Le Fils d'homme daniélique et les relectures du Dan vii,13, dans les apocryphes et les écrits du Nouveau Testament", ETL 37 (1961) 5-19.

— "Le Fils de l'homme dans l'évangile johannique", ETL 52 (1976) 28-81.

— "Le logia johannique du Fils de l'homme", in M. DE JONGE (ed.), *L'Évangile de Jean. Sources, Rédaction, théologie*, BETL 44 (Gembloux, Duculot, 1977) pp. 311-315.

— "La vision daniélique du Fils d'homme", VT 19 (1969) 171-182.

CROATTO, J. S., "Rilleture dell'Esodo nel cap. 6 di S. Giovanni", BibOr 17 (1975) 11-20.

DE DINECHIN, O., "Kathôs. La Similitude dans l'évangile de saint Jean", RechSR 58 (1970) 195-236.

DEISSLER, A., "Der 'Menschensohn' und 'das Volk der Heiligen des Höchsten' in Dan 7", in R. PESCH - R. SCHNACKENBURG - O. KAISER (eds.), *Jesus und das Menschensohn: Für Anton Vögtle* (Freiburg, Herder, 1975) pp. 81-91.

DELCOR, M., *Le Livre de Daniel*, Sources Bibliques (Paris, Gabalda, 1971).

DI LELLA, A. A., "The One in Human Likeness and the Holy Ones of the Most High in Daniel 7", *CBQ* 39 (1977) 1-19.

DRIVER, S. R., *The Book of Daniel* (Cambridge, University Press, 1900).

DUBARLE, A.-M., Art. "Prophètes d'Israel: Daniel", *DBS* 8 (1972) 735-758.

DUNN, J. D. G., *Unity and Diversity in the New Testament. An Inquiry into the Character of Earliest Christianity* (London, SCM Press, 1977).

FISCHER, K.M., "Der johanneische Christus und der gnostische Erlöser. Ueberlegungen auf Grund von Joh 10", in K. W. TRÖGER (ed.), *Gnosis und Neues Testament. Studien aus Religionswissenschaft und Theologie* (Gütersloh, Gerd Mohn, 1973) pp. 245-266.

FORTNA, R. T., "From Christology to Soteriology. A Redaction Critical Study of Salvation in the Fourth Gospel", *Interp* 27 (1973) 31-47.

— "Christology in the Fourth Gospel: Redaction Critical Perspectives", *NTS* 21 (1974-75) 489-504.

GIBLET, J., "Développements dans la théologie johannique", in M. DE JONGE (ed.), L'Évangile de Jean. *Sources, rédaction, théologie*, BETL 44 (Grembloux, Duculot, 1977) pp. 45-72.

HAACKER, K., *Die Stiftung des Heils. Untersuchungen zur Struktur der johanneischen Theologie*, Arbeiten zur Theologie (Stuttgart, Calwer, 1972).

HANHART, R., "Die Heiligen des Höchsten", in *Hebräische Wortforschung: Festschrift zum 80. Geburtstag von Walter Baumgartner*, VTS 16 (Leiden, E. J. Brill, 1976) pp. 99-101.

JAUBERT, A., *Approches de l'Evangile de Jean* (Paris, Editions du Cerf, 1976).

JOÜON, P., *L'évangile de Notre-Seigneur Jésus-Christ. Traduction et commentaire du texte original grec, compte tenu du substrat sémitique*, Verbum Salutis 5 (Paris, Beauchesne, 1930).

KYSAR, R., "Community and Gospel: Vectors in Fourth Gospel Criticism", *Interp* 31 (1977) 355-366.

— *The Fourth Evangelist and His Gospel. An examination of contemporary scholarship* (Minneapolis, Augsburg, 1975).

— "The Source Analysis of the Fourth Gospel — A Growing Consensus?", *NT* 15 (1973) 134-152.

LENGLET, A., "La structure littéraire de Daniel 2-7", *Biblica* 53 (1972) 169-190.

LINDARS, B., "Re-Enter the Apocalyptic Son of Man", *NTS* 22 (1975-76) 52-72.

— "Word and Sacrament in the Fourth Gospel", *SJT* 29 (1976) 49-63.

MARTYN, J. L., "Clementine Recognitions 1,33-71, Jewish Christianity, and the Fourth Gospel", in J. JERVELL - W. A. MEEKS (eds.), *Festschrift for N. A. Dahl* (Oslo, 1976).

— "Glimpses into the History of the Johannine Community. From its Origin through the Period of Its Life in Which The Fourth Gospel was Composed", in M. DE JONGE (ed.), *L'Évangile de Jean. Sources, rédaction, théologie*, BETL 44 (Gembloux, Duculot, 1977) pp. 149-175.

— "Source Criticism and Religionsgeschichte in the Fourth Gospel", in *Jesus and Man's Hope* (Pittsburgh, Pittsburgh Theological Seminary, 1971) Vol. I, pp. 247-273.

— "We Have Found Elijah"; in R. HAMERTON-KELLY - R. SCROGGS (eds.), *Jews, Greeks and Christians. Religious Cultures in Late Antiquity: Essays in Honor of William David Davies*, SJLA 21 (Leiden, E. J. Brill, 1976) pp. 180-219.

MASTIN, B. A., "A Neglected Feature of the Christology of the Fourth Gospel", *NTS* 22 (1975-76) 32-51.

MATTILL, A. J., "Johannine Communities Behind the Fourth Gospel: Georg Richter's Analysis", *TS* 38 (1977) 294-315.

MEEKS, W. A., " 'Am I a Jew?' Johannine Christianity and Judaism", in J. NEUSNER (ed.),

Christianity, Judaism and Other Greco-Roman Cults: Studies for Morton Smith at Sixty, SJLA 12 (Leiden, E. J. Brill, 1975) Vol. I, pp. 163-186.

— "Moses as God and King", in J. NEUSNER (ed.), *Religions in Antiquity: Essays in Memory of Erwin Ramsdell Goodenough,* Studies in the History of Religions 14 (Leiden, E. J. Brill, 1968) pp. 354-371.

MICHEL, O., "Die Botenlehre des vierten Evangeliums", *Theologische Beiträge* 7 (1976) 56-60.

MICHON, E., "Znaczenie i teologiczna interpretacja logionu J1,51", *Studia Warminskie* 10 (1973) 133-191; 11 (1974) 249-307.

MILIK, J. T. - BLACK, M. (ed.), *The Books of Enoch. Fragments of Qumrân Cave 4* (Oxford, Clarendon Press, 1976).

MIRANDA, J. P., *Die Sendung Jesu im vierten Evangelium. Religion und theologiegeschichtliche Untersuchungen zu den Sendungsformeln,* SBS 87 (Stuttgart, Katholisches Bibelwerk, 1977).

MOLONEY, F. J., "The Fourth Gospel's Presentation of Jesus as 'the Christ' and J. A. T. Robinson's 'Redating'", *The Downside Review* 95 (1977) 239-253.

— "A Johannine Son of Man Discussion?", *Salesianum* 39 (1977) 93-102.

— "The Use of the Old Testament in the New: Psalm VIII, a Test Case", *NTS.* To be published.

— *The Word Became Flesh: A Study of Jesus in the Fourth Gospel* (Cork, Mercier Press, 1978). In the Press.

MONTGOMERY, J. A., *A Critical and Exegetical Commentary on the Book of Daniel,* ICC (Edinburgh, T. & T. Clark, 1927).

MÜLLER, U. B., *Die Geschichte der Christologie in der johanneischen Gemeinde,* SBS 77 (Stuttgart, Katholisches Bibelwerk, 1975).

— *Messias und Menschensohn in jüdischen Apokalypsen und in der Offenbarung des Johannes,* StNT 6 (Gütersloh, Germ Mohn, 1972).

NEWMAN, B. M., "Some Observations Regarding the Argument, Structure and Literary Character of the Gospel of John", *The Bible Translator* 26 (1975) 234-239.

O'GRADY, J. F., *Individual and Community in John,* Excerpta ex dissertatione ad Doctoratum (Rome, Pontifical Biblical Institute, 1978).

PAINTER, J., "Christ and the Church in John 1,45-51", in M. DE JONGE (ed.), *L'Évangile de Jean. Sources, rédaction, théologie,* BETL 44 (Gembloux, Duculot, 1977) pp. 359-362.

— *John: Witness and Theologian* (London, SPCK, 1975).

PANCARO, S., *The Law in the Fourth Gospel. The Torah. Moses and Jesus, Judaism and Christianity according to John,* SNT 42 (Leiden, E. J. Brill, 1975).

— "The Relationship of the Church to Israel in the Gospel of St John", *NTS* 21 (1975-76) 396-405.

PANIMOLLE, S. A., *Lettura Pastorale del Vangelo di Giovanni,* Lettura pastorale della Bibbia (Bologna, Dehoniane, 1978) Vol. I: Gv 1-4.

PORTEOUS, N. W., *Das Danielbuch,* ATD 37 (Göttingen, Vandenhoeck und Ruprecht, 1962).

POYTHRESS, V. S., "The Holy Ones of the Most High in Daniel VII", *VT* 26 (1976) 208-213.

RICHTER, G., "Die Fleischwerdung des Logos im Johannesevangelium", *NT* 13 (1971) 81-126; 14 (1972) 257-276.

— "Zum gemeindebildenden Element in den johanneischen Schriften", in J. HAINZ (ed.), *Kirche im Werden. Studien zum Thema Amt und Gemeinde im Neuen Testament,* In Zusammenarbeit mit dem Collegium Biblicum München (München, Schöningh, 1976) pp. 253-292.

— "Präsentische und futurische Eschatologie im 4. Evangelium", in P. FIEDLER - D. ZELLER (eds.), *Gegenwart und kommendes Reich: Schülergabe Anton Vögtle zum 65. Geburtstag* (Stuttgart, Katholisches Bibelwerk, 1975) pp. 117-152.

— *Studien zum Johannesevangelium* (Leiden, E. J. Brill, 1976).

— "Zu der Taufererzählung Mk 1,9-11 und Joh 1,32-34", *ZNW* 65 (1974) 43-56.

— "Zum sogennanten Taufetext Joh 3,5", *MüTZ* 26 (1975) 101-125.
— "Der Vater und Gott Jesu und seiner Brüder in Joh 20,17: Ein Beitrag zur Christologie des Johannesevangeliums", *MüTZ* 24 (1973) 95-114; 25 (1974) 64-73.
RINALDI, G., *Daniele*, La Sacra Bibbia (Torino, Marietti, 1962⁴).
ROBINSON, J. M. - KOESTER, H., *Trajectories through Early Christianity* (Philadelphia, Fortress Press, 1971).
RUDOLPH, K., *Die Gnosis. Wesen und Geschichte einer spätantiken Religion* (Göttingen, Vandenhoeck und Ruprecht, 1977).
RUSSELL, D. S., *The Method and Message of Jewish Apocalyptic* (London, SCM Press, 1964).
SCHLOSSER, J., "Chronique d'exégèse du Nouveau Testament", *RSR* 52 (1978) 29-49.
SCHNACKENBURG, R., "Entwicklung und Stand der johanneischen Forschung seit 1955", in M. DE JONGE (ed.), *L'Évangile de Jean. Sources, Rédaction, théologie*, BETL 44 (Gembloux, Duculot, 1977) pp. 19-44.
— "Die johanneische Gemeinde und ihre Geistererfahrung", in R. SCHNACKENBURG - J. ERNST - J. WANKE (eds.), *Die Kirche des Anfangs. Festschrift Hein Schürmann zuum 65. Geburtstag* (Leipzig, St. Benno-Verlag, 1977) pp. 277-306.
— "On the Origin of the Fourth Gospel", in *Jesus and Man's Hope* (Pittburgh, Pittsburgh Theological Seminary, 1970) pp. 223-246.
SCHOTTROFF, L., *Der Glaubende und die feindliche Welt. Beobachtungen zum gnostischen Dualismus und seiner Bedeutung für Paulus und das Johannesevangelium*, WMANT 37 (Neukirchen, Neukirchener Verlag, 1970).
SEGALLA, G., *Gesù Pane del Cielo per la Vita del Mondo. Cristologia ed Eucaristia in Giovanni*, Conoscere il Vangelo 6 (Padova, Edizioni Messaggero, 1976).
— *Giovanni*, Nuovissima Versione della Bibbia 36 (Roma, Edizioni Paoline, 1976).
SERRA, A., *Contributi dell'antica letteratura Giudaica per l'esegesi di Giovanni 2,12 e 19,25-27*, Scripta Pontificiae Facultatis Theologicae "Marianum" 31, Nova Series 3 (Roma, Herder, 1977).
SMALLEY, S. S., "Johannes 1,51 und die Einleitung zum vierten Evangelium", in R. PESCH - R. SCHNACKENBURG - O. KAISER (eds.), *Jesus und der Menschensohn: Für Anton Vögtle* (Freiburg, Herder, 1975).
SMITH, D. M., "Johannine Christianity: Some Reflections on its Character and Delineation", *NTS* 21 (1975-76) 222-248.
— "The Milieu of the Johannine Miracle Source: A Proposal", in R. HAMERTON-KELLY - R. SCROGGS (eds.), *Jews, Greeks and Christians. Religious Cultures in Late Antiquity: Essays in Honor of William David Davies*, SJLA 21 (Leiden, E. J. Brill, 1976) pp. 164-180.
— "The Setting and Shape of a Johannine Narrative Source», *JBL* 95 (1976) 231-241.
SMITH, T. C., "The Christology of the Fourth Gospel", *Review and Expositor* 71 (1974) 19-30.
STENGER, W. " 'Der Geist ist es, der lebendig macht, das Fleisch nützt nichts' (Joh 6,63)", *TrierTZ* 85 (1976) 116-122.
SUNDBERG, A. C., "Christology in the Fourth Gospel", *BRes* 21 (1976) 29-37.
TALBERT, C. H., "The Myth of a Descending-Ascending Redeemer in Mediterranean Antiquity" *NTS* 22 (1975-76) 418-440.
TRÖGER, K. W., "Ja oder Nein zur Welt. War der Evangelist Johannes Christ oder Gnostiker?", *Theologische Versuche* 7 (1976) 61-80.
TSUCHIDO, K., "The Composition of the Nicodemus Episode, Jo 2,23-3,21", *Annual of the Japanese Biblical Institute* 1 (1975) 91-103.
VERMES, G., *Jesus the Jew. A Historian's Reading of the Gospel* (London, Collins, 1973).
— "The Use of *br nsh/br nsh'* in Jewish Aramaic", in M. BLACK, *An Aramaic Approach to the Gospels and Acts* (Oxford, Clarendon Press, 1967) pp. 310-328.
VIELHAUER, P., *Geschichte der urchristlichen Literatur. Einleitung in das Neue Testament, die Apokryphen und Apostolischen Väter* (Berlin/New York, Walter de Gruyter, 1975).
VON ROHDEN, W., "Die Handlungslehre nach Jo 13", *Theologische Versuche* 7 (1976) 81-89.

WALTER, L., *L'incroyance des croyants selon ·saint Jean*, Lire la Bible 43 (Paris, Editions du Cerf, 1976).

— "Jean 3,1-21: selon la foi et l'incredulité", *Esprit et Vie* 87 (1977) 369-378; 385-390.

WANSBROUGH, H., "Jesus of Galilee: Who did He think He was?", *The Clergy Review* 60 (1975) 647-657.

— "Jesus of Galilee: The Son of Man", *The Clergy Review* 60 (1975) 760-766.

— "The Mission of Jesus III: Jesus and his Future", *The Clergy Review* 57 (1972) 923-933.

ZIMMERMANN, H., "Die christliche Taufe nach Joh. 3. Ein Beitrag zur Logoschristologie des vierten Evangeliums", *Catholica* 30 (1976) 81-93.

INDICES

INDEX OF PASSAGES CITED

OLD TESTAMENT

NEW TESTAMENT

JEWISH LITERATURE

PHILO

NAG HAMMADI

FATHERS OF THE CHURCH

GREEK LITERATURE

INDEX OF AUTHORS